INFORMATION TECHNOLOGY LAW

Information Technology Law

The law and society

Andrew Murray

OXFORD
UNIVERSITY PRESS

OXFORD
UNIVERSITY PRESS

Great Clarendon Street, Oxford OX2 6DP

Oxford University Press is a department of the University of Oxford.
It furthers the University's objective of excellence in research, scholarship,
and education by publishing worldwide in

Oxford New York

Auckland Cape Town Dar es Salaam Hong Kong Karachi
Kuala Lumpur Madrid Melbourne Mexico City Nairobi
New Delhi Shanghai Taipei Toronto

With offices in

Argentina Austria Brazil Chile Czech Republic France Greece
Guatemala Hungary Italy Japan Poland Portugal Singapore
South Korea Switzerland Thailand Turkey Ukraine Vietnam

Oxford is a registered trade mark of Oxford University Press
in the UK and in certain other countries

Published in the United States
by Oxford University Press Inc., New York

British Library Cataloguing in Publication Data
Data available

Library of Congress Cataloging in Publication Data
Data available

Typeset by MPS Limited, A Macmillan Company
Printed in Great Britain on acid-free paper by
Ashford Colour Press Limited, Gosport, Hampshire

ISBN 978-0-19-954842-2

10 9 8 7 5 6 4 3 2

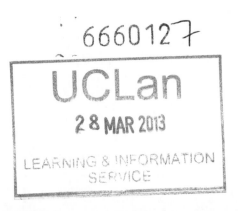

To my parents Andrew & Sarah Murray
May you enjoy your retirement

To Rachel
This book is as much yours as mine

PREFACE

The study of Information Technology Law is often seen by students as complex and technical. This is often because students perceive the subject as being one driven by technology with complex buzzwords and concepts such as Web 2.0, Virtual Environments and Augmented Reality driving the subject. In truth the subject is like any study of law, a study of people and relationships and how the law interacts with them and regulates their activity.

The subject is still, especially at undergraduate level, in its infancy: as are the textbooks which explain and develop our understanding of it. The first book which looks like an information technology law textbook was Colin Tapper's book *Computer Law* published in 1978. Since then a number of great academics have published a series of textbooks, many with OUP, including Ian Lloyd's bestselling *Information Technology Law* series, David Bainbridge's *Introduction to Computer Law* series and Chris Reed and John Angel's *Computer Law* series. It is the aim of this book to add and to build upon this illustrious series of books. The title of this book is slightly different to those which have gone before. It is *Information Technology Law: The Law and Society*. The key is the social element of the study of information technology law employed throughout. Unlike previous texts this book does not place the technology of the information society at its heart. All too often when one discusses Information Technology the emphasis is placed on the technology aspect with discussions of computers, MP3 players, Smartphones or internet connections. This book places the emphasis on the information aspect of the phrase. We live in the Information Society with value in Informational Products, yet there is little focus on the law of information, in particular digital information. This book sets out to remedy this.

The book is divided into seven parts: (I) Information and Society; (II) Governance in the Information Society; (III) Digital Content and Intellectual Property Rights; (IV) Criminal Activity in the Information Society; (V) Ecommerce; (VI) Privacy in the Information Society and (VII) Future Challenges for Information Law. It is designed to be read consecutively, that is if you read the book from page one of Chapter 1 to the final page of Chapter 22 you will have a complete understanding of the issues, challenges, threats and opportunities of the information society for lawyers, lawmakers and students of the law as I understand them. Equally though each chapter is designed as a 'stand-alone' essay on the subject in question. As such the chapters may be read in any order to meet the structural needs of whichever course of study the reader is following. Pedagogically the chapters have a series of boxed content bringing key examples and topics to the fore: there are Highlight boxes, used to highlight key issues; Case Study Boxes used to highlight examples and issues drawn from the real world; and Example Boxes used for imagined examples. Each chapter closes with a short list of proposed further readings. In addition a number of diagrams and tables explain and illustrate key concepts.

The nature of this subject is that it is fast-moving and always developing. The law in the text is up-to-date as of 30 October 2009. Even as I write this introduction though developments continue with Lord Mandelson announcing a 'three-strike' policy for

UK file sharers on 28 October 2009. That development arrived too late to be added to Chapter 10, instead it will no doubt become one of many developments that will be discussed in the Online Resource Centre: a vital responsive tool for any book attempting to crystallise the law in such a fast-moving subject.

This leaves me to fulfil that most pleasurable of experiences offered to an author: the chance to thank in print those who have assisted me. Foremost these thanks go to all the students of Information Technology Law and Internet Law at the LSE. These are the students of LL.210: Information Technology Law between 2000–2010; the students of LL.420: Legal Regulation of Information Technology between 2002–2010; the students of LL.421: New Media Regulation between 2003–2010; and finally the students of LL.4B5: Internet and New Media Law between 2005–2010. This book is born out of all the discussions and debates I have had with all of you over the years: it is the distillation of all our experiences and knowledge and I thank you all. From among the students I have taught it seems unfair to excerpt a few for special thanks. I must though thank in particular my doctoral students Net Le, Jiabo Liu, Emily Laidlaw and Paul Bernal, especially to Emily and Paul who have more recently become co-teachers on some of my courses.

This brings me neatly on to colleagues who have provided support and encouragement. I should thank Professors Chris Reed and Roger Brownsword for general support and advice. My thanks also to Dr Carlisle George who provided useful advice and support as well as providing essential teaching cover to allow me to take leave to complete this mammoth task on time. Finally particular thanks to Dr Mathias Klang who is as always a guiding light on much of my thinking.

I must also thank all those at OUP who got me to this stage. In particular thanks to Paula Harris who did an exemplary job of managing the writing and reviewing process and to Tom Young and his team of production and marketing staff.

Finally most importantly one person read this book in a number of drafts giving tireless feedback as well as proof-reading the entire text. This person is my wife Rachel. She deserves praise and thanks for her patience, attention to detail and encouragement throughout the writing process. She has probably read this book in its entirety in at least four forms. I hope she is pleased with the end product, as I hope are all readers of this book.

Andrew Murray, London, 30 October 2009.

CONTENTS

GUIDE TO THE BOOK   xvii
GUIDE TO THE ONLINE RESOURCE CENTRE   xviii
TABLE OF CASES   xix
TABLE OF STATUTES   xxv

PART I INFORMATION AND SOCIETY   1

---

1 The world of bits   3
  1.1 An introduction to bits   5
        1.1.1 The process of digitisation   7
  1.2 Moving from atoms to bits   9
        1.2.1 Music goes digital   10
        1.2.2 Digital goods and society   11
  1.3 Rivalrous and nonrivalrous goods   12
  1.4 The legal challenge of the information society   13

---

2 The network of networks   16
  2.1 Introducing the internet (history)   17
        2.1.1 Building the ARPANET   18
        2.1.2 Building the internet   19
  2.2 How the modern internet functions   23
        2.2.1 Net neutrality   27
  2.3 Higher level protocols   30

---

3 Digitisation and society   35
  3.1 The digitisation of information   36
        3.1.1 Information collection, aggregation and exploitation 38
        3.1.2 Information disintermediation   39
        3.1.3 Information management   43
  3.2 Digital convergence   44
  3.3 The cross-border challenge of information law   47
  3.4 Digitisation and law   50

PART II GOVERNANCE IN THE INFORMATION SOCIETY   53

---

4 Regulating the digital environment   55
  4.1 Can we regulate the digital environment?   56
        4.1.1 Cyberlibertarianism   56
        4.1.2 Cyberpaternalism   60

4.2   Lawrence Lessig's modalities of regulation   62
4.3   Network communitarianism   66
4.4   Regulators in cyberspace: private regulators   70
4.5   Regulators in cyberspace: states and supranational regulation   73
        4.5.1   WSIS and the IGF   75
4.6   Conclusion   80

5   Digital ownership   83
5.1   Digital property   84
        5.1.1   Information as property   85
        5.1.2   Statutory intellectual property rights   86
        5.1.3   Confidential information   88
5.2   Digital trespass   89
        5.2.1   Trespass to servers   90
        5.2.2   Indexing and scraping   91
        5.2.3   Intel v Hamidi   93
        5.2.4   Digital trespass at UK law   93
        5.2.5   Adware and spyware   95
5.3   Virtual property   96
        5.3.1   Virtual theft   97
        5.3.2   Misappropriation of virtual goods   99
5.4   Conclusions   101

6   Cyber-speech   103
6.1   Introduction   103
6.2   From web 1.0 to web 2.0   104
        6.2.1   Web 1.0: internet fora   105
        6.2.2   Web 1.0: personal websites   106
        6.2.3   Web 1.0: law and society   107
        6.2.4   Web 2.0   107
6.3   Freedom of expression and social responsibility   110
        6.3.1   Freedom of expression: the 'First Amendment' approach   110
        6.3.2   Freedom of expression: the European approach   111
        6.3.3   Freedom of expression: the approaches compared   112
        6.3.4   Licra et UEJF v Yahoo! Inc. and Yahoo! France   113
        6.3.5   Cross-border speech   114
        6.3.6   Yahoo! Inc. v LICRA   116
        6.3.7   Free expression online   118
6.4   Political speech   119
        6.4.1   Political speech: economics and media   120
        6.4.2   Online political speech   122
6.5   Hate speech   124
        6.5.1   Hate speech and society   125
        6.5.2   Inter-state speech   126

6.6   Commercial speech   127
       6.6.1 Commercial speech and the First Amendment   127
       6.6.2 Commercial speech and the information society   128
       6.6.3 Regulating spam in Europe   129
       6.6.4 Regulating spam in the US   131

6.7   Conclusion: cyber-speech and free expression   133

7 Defamation   **135**

7.1   The tort of defamation   136
       7.1.1 Statements, publication, and defences   137

7.2   Digital defamation: publication and republication   141
       7.2.1 Dow Jones v Gutnick   142
       7.2.2 Loutchansky v Times newspapers: republication and limitation   145
       7.2.3 King v Lewis   147
       7.2.4 Dow Jones v Jameel   148
       7.2.5 Online defamation post Jameel   150
       7.2.6 The ministry of justice consultation paper   151

7.3   Intermediary liability   152
       7.3.1 Early cases: ISPs as publishers   153
       7.3.2 CDA §230: safe harbour   155
       7.3.3 ISP publisher liability in the UK   156

7.4   Digital defamation and UGC   160
       7.4.1 Facebook libel   162
       7.4.2 Libel in the blogosphere   164

7.5   Conclusion   165

PART III DIGITAL CONTENT AND INTELLECTUAL PROPERTY RIGHTS   **169**

8 Intellectual property rights and the information society   **171**

8.1   An introduction to IPRs   172
       8.1.1 Copyright   173
       8.1.2 Patents   175
       8.1.3 Trade marks   177
       8.1.4 The database right   179

8.2   IPRs and digitisation   180

9 Software   **183**

9.1   Protecting software: history   183

9.2   Copyright in computer software   186
       9.2.1 Obtaining copyright protection   186
       9.2.2 The scope of copyright protection   189

9.3   Copyright infringement and software: literal copying   191
       9.3.1 Offline piracy   192
       9.3.2 Online piracy   193
       9.3.3 Employee piracy   194

9.4 Copyright infringement and software: non-literal copying   196
    9.4.1 Introducing look and feel infringement   197
    9.4.2 Look and feel infringement: Computer Associates v Altai   199
    9.4.3 Look and feel infringement: Lotus v Borland   201
    9.4.4 Look and feel before the UK courts   202
    9.4.5 Look and feel: Navitaire v easyJet   205
    9.4.6 Look and feel in the UK after navitaire   207

9.5 Copyright infringement and software: permitted acts   209

9.6 Patent protection for computer software   212
    9.6.1 VICOM/computer-related invention   214
    9.6.2 The effect of State Street Bank   215
    9.6.3 De facto software patents under the european patent convention   217
    9.6.4 Aerotel Ltd v Telco and Macrossan's Application   218

9.7 Conclusion   220

10 Copyright in the digital environment   **222**

10.1 Linking, caching, and aggregating   223
    10.1.1 Web-linking   224
    10.1.2 Google Inc. v Copiepresse SCRL   228

10.2 Peer-to-peer networks   233
    10.2.1 Early cases   234
    10.2.2 A&M records, Inc. v Napster, Inc.   236
    10.2.3 Post Napster: MGM Studios, Inc. v Grokster, Ltd   241
    10.2.4 Peer-to-peer litigation outwith the US   246
    10.2.5 Sweden v Neij et al. (The pirate bay case)   250
    10.2.6 Other methods to prevent illegal file sharing: technical measures 254
    10.2.7 Other methods to prevent illegal file sharing: volume litigation 258

10.3 Information and the public domain   260
    10.3.1 Creative commons   261

10.4 Conclusion   265

11 Databases   **267**

11.1 Copyright and the database right   268
    11.1.1 The listings cases   269
    11.1.2 The database directive   271

11.2 The database right   274
    11.2.1 The fixtures marketing cases   276
    11.2.2 British Horseracing Board Ltd v William Hill   279
    11.2.3 After *BHB*   284

11.3 Databases and the information society   286

12 Branding and trade marks in the information society   **289**

12.1 Trade marks and branding   289

12.2   Trade marks in the global business environment   291
 12.2.1   Registered and unregistered trade marks   291
 12.2.2   Trade mark characteristics   293

12.3   Domain names as badges of identity   294
 12.3.1   Sex.com   296

12.4   Trade mark/domain name disputes   298
 12.4.1   Early disputes in the US   298
 12.4.2   Early disputes in the UK   301
 12.4.3   Cybersquatting before the UK courts   303
 12.4.4   Phones4u Ltd v Phone4u.co.uk   305

12.5   The ICANN UDRP   307

12.6   The nominet DRS   312
 12.6.1   Reviewing the nominet DRS   316

12.7   Brand identities, search engines and secondary markets   316
 12.7.1   Secondary markets   317
 12.7.2   Search engines   320

12.8   Conclusion   322

PART IV   CRIMINAL ACTIVITY IN THE INFORMATION SOCIETY   **325**

13   Computer misuse   **327**

13.1   Hacking   330
 13.1.1   Employee hackers   332
 13.1.2   External hackers   337
 13.1.3   The McKinnon case   340

13.2   Viruses, criminal damage, and mailbombing   342
 13.2.1   Early cases: the Mad Hacker and the Black Baron   342
 13.2.2   Later cases: web defacement and mailbombing   345

13.3   Denial of service and supply of devices   346
 13.3.1   Section 3A   350

14   Pornography and obscenity in the information society   **353**

14.1   Obscenity   354
 14.1.1   The Hicklin principle   355
 14.1.2   The obscene publications acts   356

14.2   Pornography   357
 14.2.1   The UK standard   358
 14.2.2   A global standard?   361
 14.2.3   US statutory interventions   363
 14.2.4   The decision heard 'round the world'   367

14.3   Child abuse images and pseudo images   369
 14.3.1   Policing pseudo-images in the UK   371
 14.3.2   Policing pseudo-images internationally   375

14.4   Age play   377
14.5   Extreme pornography   379
14.6   Private regulation of pornographic imagery   383
14.7   Conclusions   386

15   Crime and law enforcement in the information society   387
15.1   Fraud and identity theft   388
   15.1.1   Fraud   388
   15.1.2   Identity theft and identity fraud   392
15.2   Grooming, harassment, and cyberstalking   395
   15.2.1   Grooming   395
   15.2.2   Harassment and stalking   397
15.3   Cyberterrorism   398
15.4   Bandwidth theft   403
15.5   The convention on cybercrime   405
15.6   Conclusion   408

PART V ECOMMERCE   411

16   Electronic contracts   413
16.1   Contracting informally   413
   16.1.1   Contract formation   414
16.2   Regulating offer and acceptance   416
   16.2.1   Articles 9–11 of the electronic commerce directive   416
   16.2.2   Communicating acceptance   418
16.3   Contractual terms   420
   16.3.1   Express terms   421
   16.3.2   Terms incorporated by reference   421
   16.3.3   Implied terms   422
   16.3.4   Enforcing terms: consumer protection laws   423
16.4   Formal contracts   424
16.5   Electronic signatures   427
   16.5.1   Formalising electronic signatures   429
   16.5.2   Advanced electronic signatures   430
16.6   Conclusion   434

17   Electronic payments and taxation   436
17.1   A history of international payments methods   436
17.2   Electronic payments   439
   17.2.1   Token payments   439
   17.2.2   Alternative payment systems   440
   17.2.3   Early e-money   441

17.3 The electronic money directive   444
    17.3.1 E-money issuers   444
    17.3.2 Commission review of the e-money directive
         and the 2009 e-money directive   448
17.4 Ecommerce taxation   452
17.5 Conclusions   457

PART VI **PRIVACY IN THE INFORMATION SOCIETY**   **461**

18 Data protection   **463**
18.1 Digitisation, personal data, and the data industry   464
18.2 Data protection act 1998: background and structure   465
    18.2.1 The data protection act 1984   466
    18.2.2 The data protection directive   467
18.3 The data protection act 1998   468
    18.3.1 Forms of data   468
    18.3.2 Processing and use of data   470
    18.3.3 Personnel of the data protection act   473
18.4 The data protection principles, processing, and fairness   474
    18.4.1 Processing data: Bodil Lindqvist   475
    18.4.2 Processing data: Johnson v Medical Defence Union   477
18.5 Conditions for processing of personal data   479
    18.5.1 Consent   480
    18.5.2 Processing sensitive personal data   483
18.6 Supervision of data controllers: data subject rights   484
    18.6.1 Subject access: Durant v the Financial Services Authority 485
    18.6.2 Correcting and managing data   490
18.7 State supervision of data controllers   491
    18.7.1 The information commissioner as regulator   492
18.8 Conclusion   494

19 Data and personal privacy   **496**
19.1 Enhanced CCTV   496
    19.1.1 Pattern recognition: ANPR   498
    19.1.2 Pattern recognition: biometrics   499
    19.1.3 Regulating CCTV: the code of practice   502
19.2 RFID tracking   507
    19.2.1 Regulating RFID   509
    19.2.2 The EU action plan   512
19.3 Data retention and identity   514
    19.3.1 The regulation of investigatory powers act   516
    19.3.2 Data retention   517
19.4 Conclusions   521

PART VII **FUTURE CHALLENGES FOR INFORMATION LAW**   **523**

20 The digital public sphere   **525**

   20.1 E-government   527
         20.1.1 UK e-government   528
         20.1.2 The ministerial declaration and transformational government   533

   20.2 The digital divide   538
         20.2.1 The global divide   538
         20.2.2 The social divide   539
         20.2.3 The social divide: opening competition in products and services   541

   20.3 The democratic divide   544
         20.3.1 The democratic divide and the blogosphere 545
         20.3.2 Anonymity and free speech   549
         20.3.3 The democratic divide and social networking   551

   20.4 Conclusion   553

21 Virtual environments   **556**

   21.1 Virtual worlds, virtual people   557

   21.2 The virtual gods   559

   21.3 The game versus the law   560
         21.3.1 Virtual property disputes   562

   21.4 Conclusion: when worlds collide   565

22 What way next?   **569**

   22.1 Future developments   570
         22.1.1 Greater connectivity, greater control   570
         22.1.2 Greater connectivity, greater freedom   572
         22.1.3 Developing technologies and legal responses   573

   22.2 Web 3.0   574

   22.3 Law 2.0   576

INDEX   581

GUIDE TO THE BOOK

Information Technology Law: The law and society contains a range of useful features, which have been designed to enhance your understanding of the subject.

→ **Highlight** Thomas Jefferson's Letter to Isaac

If nature has made any one thing less susceptible than all other action of the thinking power called an idea, which an individual as he keeps it to himself; but the moment it is divulged, it forc every one, and the receiver cannot dispossess himself of it. Its no one possesses the less, because every other possesses the w idea from me, receives instruction himself without lessening mir mine, receives light without darkening mine.

Highlights

Featuring definitions of crucial concepts, ideas and principles, the highlight boxes give you an insight into the debates that surround the relationship between law and the information society. They may be a quotation from a leading figure, an outline of a legal term or procedure, or an extract from a case. In every instance they will help you to focus on and understand the key elements of the topic under discussion.

✱ **Example** Contempt of Court

In 2007 two men attempted to blackmail a member of the UK granted under the Contempt of Court Act 1981 meaning it was the person involved (it still is). Despite this it is extremely easy for of the person involved with a quick Google search as the name several overseas news organisations and gossip sites which are al even be possible for a UK resident to publish this person's name,

Examples

How do the legal rules developed to meet the challenges of the information society operate in practice? The example boxes use short fictional examples to demonstrate the application of the law clearly and concisely.

✎ **Case Study** Napster

Everyone knows at least part of the story of Napster. In June 199 Boston's Northeastern University, released his 'Napster' protocol
  Fanning created Napster out of frustration: he, like many colle fan who was strapped for cash. He was frustrated for several search for digital music files but the only option available at the engines which would search the entirety of a library with no spe

Case studies

From Napster to the economics behind recent US Presidential elections, the case study boxes illustrate the real-life examples that have shaped the development of information technology law.

▮ **FURTHER READING**

Books

F.H. Cate, *Privacy in the Information Age* (1997)
I. de Sola Pool, *The Technologies of Freedom* (1983)
H. Jenkins, *Convergence Culture: Where Old and New Media C*

Chapters and Articles

Further reading

Select and seek out titles from the further reading sources at the end of each chapter in order to broaden your knowledge of the individual topics covered.

GUIDE TO THE ONLINE RESOURCE CENTRE

This book is accompanied by an **Online Resource Centre** – a website providing free and easy-to-use resources which complement and support the textbook.

http://www.oxfordtextbooks.co.uk/orc/murray/

Audio updates

Regular audio updates from the author cover the latest developments in IT law which have occurred since publication of the book.

Web links

A list of useful websites enables you to click straight through to reliable sources of online information, and efficiently direct your online study.

Flashcard glossary of key terms

Test your knowledge and understanding of the specialised terminology used in information technology law, using this useful revision tool which can be downloaded to iPods and other portable devices.

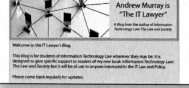

A link to an IT law blog

Keep up to date with the latest developments in the subject by following an information technology law blog, which is written by Andrew Murray.

TABLE OF CASES

44 Liquormart Inc. v Rhode Island (1996) ... 127

A&M Records v Napster Inc. (2000) ... 10, 42, 63, 236, 238, 244

ACLU v Reno (1996) ... 366

ACLU v Reno (1996a) ... 367

Aerotel Ltd v Telco and Macrossan's Application (2006) ... 218, 219

Al Amoudi v Brisard & Anor (2006) ... 150

Alexander v North Eastern Railway (1865) ... 140

Amazon.com Inc. v Barnesandnoble.com Inc. (2001) ... 87

America Online Inc. v IMS (1998) ... 91

America Online Inc. v LCGM (1998) ... 91

America Online Inc. v National Health Care Discount Inc. (2000) ... 91

American Airlines Inc. v Farechase Inc. (2003) ... 92, 93

American Libraries Association et al. v Pataki (1997) ... 363, 364

American Standard v Toeppen (1996) ... 300

Anheuser-Busch v Budejovicky Budvar (1984) ... 293

Applause Store Productions Ltd & Anor v Raphael (2008) ... 119, 162, 164, 165, 166, 548, 558

Apple Computers, Inc. v Computer Edge Pty Ltd (1984) ... 186

Ashcroft v ACLU (2004) ... 367

Ashcroft v Free Speech Coalition (2002) ... 375

Atkins v Director of Public Prosecutions (2000) ... 57

Attorney General's Reference No.1 of 1991 (1991) ... 331

Attorney General's Reference (Nos 85, 86 and 87 of 2007) (2007) ... 400

Author of a Blog v Times Newspapers Ltd (2009) ... 550

Bachchan v India Abroad Publications Inc. (1992) ... 115, 145

Baigent & Anor v The Random House Group Ltd (The Da Vinci Code) (2006) ... 190, 196

Barrett v Rosenthal (2006) ... 156, 161

Blue Nile Inc. v Ice.com and Odimo, Inc. (2007) ... 202

Blumenthal v Drudge (1998) ... 155

Bodil Lindqvist (2004) ... 475, 476

Brady v Norman (2008) ... 150

Bragg v Linden & Rosedale (2007) ... 99, 100, 563, 564

Brinkibon Ltd v Stahag Stahl und Stahlwarenhandels-Gesellschaft (1983) ... 419

British Horseracing Board Ltd & Ors v William Hill Organization Ltd (2001a) ... 280

British Horseracing Board Ltd & Ors v William Hill Organization Ltd (2001) ... 280

British Horseracing Board Ltd & Ors v William Hill Organization Ltd (2005a) ... 284

British Horseracing Board Ltd v William Hill Organization Ltd (2005) ... 279

British Leyland v Armstrong (1986) ... 212

British Telecommunications plc. and Ors v One in a Million Ltd and Ors (1998) ... 303, 305

Buchhaltungsprogram (1993) ... 188

BUMA & STEMRA v Kazaa (2001) ... 247, 248

Bunt v Tilley & Ors (2006) ... 159

Caesars World Inc. v Caesars-Palace.com (2000) ... 298

Cantor Fitzgerald International v Tradition (UK) Ltd (2000) ... 195, 196, 205

Carlill v Carbolic Smokeball Company (1893) ... 415, 416

Carmarthen Developments Ltd v Pennington (2008) ... 419

Carrie v Tolkien (2009) ... 165

CBS Songs Ltd v Amstrad Consumer Electronics plc (1988) ... 238, 319

Chapelton v Barry UDC (1940) ... 422

Chaplinsky v New Hampshire (1941) ... 112

Chelsea Man v Chelsea Girl (1987) ... 306

Cheney Brothers v Doris Silk Corporation (1929) ... 86

Chicago Lawyers' Committee for Civil Rights under Law, Inc. v Craigslist, Inc. (2008) ... 119, 156

Coco v AN Clarke (Engineers) Ltd (1969) ... 886

Collett v Smith & Anor (2008) ... 101

Commission of the EU v Microsoft Corporation (2004) ... 543

Commission of the EU v Microsoft Corporation (2008) ... 543

CompuServe Inc. v Cyber Promotions Inc. (1997) ... 90, 93

Conagra Inc. v McCain Frozen Foods (Aust) Pty (1991) ... 293

Conegate Ltd v HM Customs & Excise (1987) ... 49, 360

Consumer Advocates Rights Enforcement Society v 180Solutions Inc. (2005) ... 95

Cubby Inc. v CompuServe Inc. (1991) ... 153

Cyber Promotions Inc. v America Online Inc. (1996) ... 90

Derbyshire County Council v Times Newspapers (1993) ... 120, 136

Director General of Fair Trading v First National Bank Plc (2002) ... 423

Doe v America Online, Inc. (1998) ... 155

Doe v GTE (2003) ... 155

Doe v MySpace (2007) ... 119

Donoghue v Stevenson (1932) ... 83

Dow Jones v Gutnick (2002) ... 139, 142

DPP v Bignell (1998) ... 332

DPP v Lennon (2006) ... 345

DPP v Ray (1974) ... 388

Durant v Financial Services Authority (2004) ... 485, 486, 487, 488

eBay Inc. v Bidder's Edge Inc. (2000) ... 91

EETPU v Times Newspapers Ltd (1980) ... 136

Eli Lilly & Company v Clayton (2001) ... 312

Ellis v DPP (No.1) (2001) ... 338

Entores Ltd v Miles Far East Corporation (1955) ... 418

Eros LLC v Leatherwood et al (2008) ... 100, 564

Eros LLC v Simon et al (2007) ... 100, 561, 564

Erven Warnink BV v J Townend & Sons (1979) ... 178, 292

Exxon Corp. v Exxon Insurance Consultants International Ltd (1982) ... 206

Facebook, Inc. v Adam Guerbuez and Atlantis Blue Capital (2008) ... 132

Farina v Silverlock (1855) ... 304

Fisher v Bell (1961) ... 415

Fixtures Marketing Ltd v Organismos Prognostikon Agonon Podosfairou (OPAP) (2005) ... 276

Fixtures Marketing Ltd v Oy Veikkaus AB (2005) ... 276

Fixtures Marketing Ltd v Svenska Spel AB (2005) ... 276

Fortnum & Mason plc v Fortnum Ltd (1994) ... 294

Fraser v Evans (1969) ... 88

Fujitsu Ltd's Application (1997) ... 215

Gale's Application (1991) ... 213, 215

Genentech Inc.'s Patent (1989) ... 215

Gevers' Application (1969) ... 213

Glaxo Plc v Glaxowellcome Ltd (1996) ... 304

Godfrey v Demon Internet Service (1999) ... 107, 156

Goldsmith v Boyrul (1997) ... 136

Goodland v DPP (2000) ... 374

Google Inc. v Copiepresse SCRL (2007) ... 228, 229, 231, 232, 268, 286

Gottschalk, Commissioner of Patents v Benson et al. (1972) ... 183

Gutnick v Dow Jones & Co. Inc. (2001) ... 143

Harrods Ltd v UK Network Services Ltd (1996) ... 303

Hasbro v Internet Entertainment Group (1996) ... 300

Havas Numerique et Cadre On Line v Keljob (2000) ... 226, 286

HITACHI/Auction method (2004) ... 217

Home A/S v Ofir (2006) ... 228, 233, 286, 287

Hotmail Corp. v Van$ Money Pie Inc. (1998) ... 91

IBCOS Computers Ltd v Barclays Mercantile Highland Finance Ltd (1994) ... 194, 204

IBM's Application (1999) ... 215

In re Bernard L. Bilski and Rand (2008) ... 215, 220

Independent Television Publications Ltd v Time Out Ltd (1984) ... 179

Intel Corp. v Hamidi (2003) ... 93

Intermatic, Inc. v Toeppen (1996) ... 300

International News Service v Associated Press (1918) ... 85

Inwood Laboratories v Ives Laboratories (1982) ... 318

J F Home Improvements Ltd v Giddy (2005) ... 313

Jameel v Dow Jones (2005) ... 139, 148

Jameel v Wall Street Journal (2007) ... 136

Jenkins v Georgia (1974) ... 362

Jersild v Denmark (1995) ... 125

John Richardson Computers Ltd v Flanders (No.2) (1993) ... 202, 204, 268

John Walker & Sons Ltd v Henry Ost & Co Ltd (1970) ... 304

Johnson v Medical Defence Union Ltd (2007) ... 477

Johnson v The Medical Defence Union Ltd [2006] ... 477

Johnston v Orr-Ewing (1879) ... 307

Keith-Smith v Williams (2006) ... 161

Kerrins v Intermix Media Inc. (2006) ... 95

King v Lewis (2004) ... 147

Kremen v Cohen (2003) ... 296, 297

L'Oreal v eBay (2009) ... 318

Ladbroke (Football) Ltd v William Hill (Football) Ltd (1964) ... 179, 187

Lehideux & Isorni v France (2000) ... 126

Licra et UEJF v Yahoo! Inc. and Yahoo! France (2000) ... 112, 126, 145

Lightbody's Trustees v Hutchison (1886) ... 422

Linguaphone Institute v Data Protection Registrar (1994) ... 482

LiveUniverse, Inc. v MySpace, Inc. (2007) ... 552

London Artists v Littler (1969) ... 140

London Founders Association Ltd and Palmer v Clarke (1888) ... 422

Lotus Development Corp. v Borland International Inc. (1995) ... 201

Loutchansky v Times Newspapers Ltd (2002) ... 145, 548

Lunney v Prodigy Services Company (1999) ... 155

Lyme Valley Squash Club Ltd v Newcastle under Lyme BC (1985) ... 422

Mars UK Ltd v Teknowledge Ltd (1999) ... 212

McIntosh v Alam (1997) ... 419

McKinnon v Government of the United States of America and another (2008) ... 341

McKinnon v Government of the USA and Secretary of State for the Home Department (2007) ... 340, 341

McKinnon v Secretary of State for the Home Department (2009) ... 341

Merrill Lynch's Application (1989) ... 214, 218

Meteodata v Bernegger Bau (2002) ... 227

MGM Studios Inc. v Grokster Ltd (2005) ... 63, 236, 241, 243

Michaeli v eXact Advertising (2005) ... 95

MICROSOFT/Clipboard formats I (2006) ... 218

MICROSOFT/Clipboard formats II (2006) ... 218

Miller v California (1973) ... 112, 361, 364

Minsky v Linden Research, Inc. (2009) ... 564

Mosley v News Group Newspapers Ltd (2008) ... 548

M'Pherson v Daniels (1829) ... 140

MySpace Inc. v Wallace et al. (2008) ... 132

Navitaire Inc. v easyJet Airline Co. & Anor (2004) ... 205, 272

New York Times v Sullivan (1964) ... 147

New York v Ferber (1982) ... 368, 375

Nova Productions Ltd v Mazooma Games Ltd (2007) ... 208

NVM Estate Agents v ZAH (2006) ... 286

NVM v Zoekallehuizen.nl (2006) ... 287

Ohralik v Ohio State Bar Association (1978) ... 127

Online Partners.com Inc. v Atlanticnet Media Corp. (2000) ... 298

Osborne v Ohio (1990) ... 375

Oyster Software Inc. v Forms Processing Inc. (2001) ... 91

Panavision International v Toeppen (1998) ... 299

Parker v Flook (1976) ... 184, 213

Partridge v Crittenden (1968) ... 415, 416

PBS Partnership/Controlling pension benefits systems (2002) ... 216

PCM v Kranten.com (2002) ... 227

Pennwell Publishing (UK) Ltd v Ornstien & Ors (2007) ... 273

Perry v Truefitt (1842) ... 177

Pharmaceutical Society of Great Britain v Boots Cash Chemists (Southern) Ltd (1953) ... 414

Phones4u Ltd v Phones4u.co.uk (2006) ... 305

Pitman Training Ltd v Nominet UK (1997) ... 301

Planned Parenthood Federation of America v Richard Bucci (1997) ... 299

Plant v Service Direct (UK) (2006) ... 94

Pope v Illinois (1987) . . . 362

President's Reference/Computer Program Exclusion (2009) . . . 220

Prince plc. v Prince Sportswear Group Inc. (1998) . . . 301

Princeton Review. v Stanley H. Kaplan Educational Center Ltd (1994) . . . 298, 577

PSINet v Chapman (2004) . . . 363

R. (on the application of ProLife Alliance) v BBC (2004) . . . 75, 120

R. v Barry Philip Halloren (2004) . . . 49, 357

R. v Bedworth (1993) . . . 337

R. v Bennett (1991) . . . 332

R. v Bonnett (1995) . . . 332

R. v Bow Street Magistrates Court and Allison, Ex Parte Government of the United States of America (1999) . . . 335

R. v Bowden (2001) . . . 57

R. v Bowden (2001) . . . 345, 374

R. v Brown (1996) . . . 333, 470

R. v Byrne (2006) . . . 345

R. v Cropp (1991) . . . 331

R. v Culbert (2000) . . . 337

R. v Cuthbert (2005) . . . 338

R. v Fellows & Arnold (1997) . . . 57, 373

R. v Feltis (1996) . . . 344

R. v Forbes (2002) . . . 49, 360

R. v Gold and Schifreen (1987) . . . 329

R. v Gold and Schifreen (1988) . . . 328

R. v Goulden (1992) . . . 337

R. v Hardy (1992) . . . 344

R. v James (2000) . . . 49, 357

R. v Jayson (2002) . . . 57

R. v M (2007) . . . 399, 400

R. v M (No 2) (2007) . . . 402

R. v Mansfield (2005) . . . 396

R. v Morris and Airlie (1997) . . . 345

R. v Pile (1995) . . . 344

R. v Pointon (1997) . . . 376

R. v Rahman and Mohammed (2008) . . . 402

R. v Ross Andrew McKinnon (2004) . . . 49, 357

R. v Sharpe (2001) . . . 376

R. v Stephane Laurent Perrin (2002) . . . 49, 357

R. v Strickland, R. v Woods (1993) . . . 338

R. v Uxbridge Justices ex parte David Webb (1994) . . . 356

R. v Vallor (2003) . . . 345

R. v Video Appeals Committee of British Board of Film Classification (ex parte British Board of Film Classification) (2000) . . . 359

R. v Wellman (2007) . . . 393

R. v Whitely (1991) . . . 343

R. v Whittaker (1993) . . . 344

R. v Zafar (2008) . . . 402

Ralph Lauren v eBay (2009) . . . 322

RCA Manufacturing Co. v Whiteman (1940) . . . 86

Re AT&T Knowledge Ventures LP (2009) . . . 219

Reckitt & Colman Products Ltd v Borden Inc. (1990) . . . 178, 292

Register.com Inc. v Verio Inc. (2000) . . . 92, 93

Reno v ACLU (1997) . . . 59, 113, 126, 154

Rex v Ensor (1887) . . . 136

Reynolds v Times Newspapers Ltd and Others (1999) . . . 136, 140

Rolls Razor Ltd v Rolls (Lighters) Ltd (1949) . . . 294

Roth v United States (1957) . . . 361

Ryanair Limited v Michael Coulston (2006) . . . 315

Saltman Engineering v Campbell (1948) . . . 88

SARL Stepstone France v SARL Ofir France (2000) . . . 226

Sega Enterprises v Richards (1983) . . . 185

Seiko UK Ltd v Designer Time/Wanderweb (2002) . . . 313

Sheffield Wednesday Football Club & Ors. v Hargreaves (2007) . . . 162

Shetland Times Ltd v Wills (1997) . . . 93, 101, 136, 224

Simios v 180Solutions Inc. (2005) . . . 95

Smith v ADVFN Plc & Ors (2008) . . . 164

Sony Corp of America v Universal City Studios (1984) . . . 42, 234

Sotelo v DirectRevenue LLC (2005) . . . 95

Spiliada Maritime Corp v Cansulex Ltd (1987) . . . 139

Spurling v Bradshaw (1956) . . . 422

State Street Bank & Trust Co. v Signature Financial Group (1998) . . . 215

Steel v State Line Steamship Co. (1877) . . . 422

Stepstone v Ofir (2001) . . . 226, 286

Stoneygate 48 Ltd v Rooney (2006) . . . 313

Stratton Oakmont Inc. v Prodigy Services Co (1995) . . . 153

Sudwestdeutsche Inkasso KG v Bappert and Burker Computer GmbH (1985) ... 188

Symbian Ltd v Comptroller General of Patents (2008) ... 220

Taser International v Linden Research (2009) ... 564

Taylor v Glasgow Corporation (1952) ... 422

Telnikoff v Matusevitch (1997) ... 115, 145

The Moorcock (1889) ... 422

Thornton v Shoe Lane Parking Ltd (1971) ... 415, 421, 434

Thrifty-Tel, Inc. v Bezenek (1996) ... 90

Ticketmaster v Tickets.com (2003) ... 92

Tiffany v eBay (2008) ... 318

Total Information Processing Systems Ltd v Daman Ltd (1992) ... 195

UMG Recordings v MP3.Com (2000) ... 234

Unilever plc v Gillette (UK) Ltd (1989) ... 319

Union Des Association Europeenes De Football & Ors. v Briscomb & Ors (2006) ... 233

United States of America v Microsoft Corporation (1999) ... 542, 543

United States of America v Microsoft Corporation (2002) ... 543

United States v Beddow (1992) ... 363

United States v Thomas (1996) ... 362

United States v Williams (1986) ... 363

Universal Music Australia Pty Ltd v Sharman License Holdings Ltd (2005) ... 236

University of London Press Ltd v University Tutorial Press Ltd (1916) ... 187, 269

Valentine v Chrestensen (1942) ... 127

Verlagsgruppe Handelsblatt GmbH v Paperboy (2005) ... 199, 227, 287

Viacom International v YouTube (2007) ... 109

VICOM/Computer-related Invention (1987) ... 214

Victoria Park Racing & Recreation Grounds Co. Ltd v Taylor (1937) ... 86

Wang Laboratories Inc.'s Application (1991) ... 215

Waterlow Directories Ltd v Reed Information Services Ltd (1992) ... 270

Waterlow Publishers Ltd v Rose (1995) ... 269

Watson v McEwan (1905) ... 141

Whelan Associates Inc. v Jaslow Dental Laboratory Inc. (1986) ... 197, 268

Wilson v Yahoo! (2008) ... 321

World Wrestling Federation Entertainment Inc. v Michael Bosman (1999) ... 209

Yahoo Inc. v LICRA (2001) ... 112, 115, 127

Yahoo Inc. v LICRA (2004) ... 112, 116

Yahoo Inc. v LICRA (2006) ... 112, 116, 117

Zeran v America Online, Inc. (1997) ... 107

TABLE OF STATUTES

UK Legislation

Bill of Rights 1689 ... 141

Broadcasting Act 1990, s.36 ... 121

s.107 ... 121

s.177 ... 116

Civic Government (Scotland) Act 1982 ... 380

Communications Act 2003, s.125 ... 404

s.319(2)(g) ... 121

s.333 ... 121

s.45 ... 29

Computer Misuse Act 1990, s.1 ... 398, 404

s.2 ... 331, 341, 404

s.3 ... 339, 341

s.3(3) ... 404

s.3A ... 339

s.17(5) ... 331

Consumer Credit Act 1974, s.6 ... 424

s.75 ... 442

Copyright Designs and Patents
Act 1988, s.1 ... 87

s.1(1) ... 177

s.1(3) ... 177

s.3(1)(a) ... 268

s.3(1)(b) ... 177, 187

s.3(2) ... 40, 187, 188

s.3A(2) ... 179, 273

s.11(2) ... 175

s.16 ... 175

s.17 ... 62, 225

s.17(2) ... 46, 190

s.17(6) ... 188

s.18 ... 191

s.20 ... 225, 233

s.21(3)(ab) ... 190

s.23(c) ... 250

s.24(2) ... 250

s.29 ... 209

s.30 ... 210, 231

s.30(2) ... 227

s.44A ... 261

s.50A ... 46, 210, 570

s.50B ... 210, 570

s.70(1) ... 174

s.70(2) ... 174

s.107 ... 190, 251

s.153 ... 189

s.154(1)(c) ... 268

s.155(3) ... 189

s.178 ... 188

Ch.2 ... 87

Criminal Damage Act 1971, s.1(1) ... 343

s.10(1) ... 343

s.10(5) ... 344

Criminal Justice
Act 1988, s.160 ... 71, 355, 369, 372, 378

Criminal Justice and Immigration
Act 2008, s.63 ... 50, 69, 71, 355

s.63(3) ... 354

s.63(7) ... 381

s.63(7)(a) ... 382

Sch.16 ... 125

Criminal Justice and Public
Order Act 1994, s.84 ... 372

Currency and Bank Notes
Act 1954, s.2 ... 438

Customs and Excise Management
Act 1979 ... 380

Customs Consolidation Act 1876 ... 380

s.42 ... 48, 58, 355, 360

Data Protection Act 1984
(Repealed), s.1(2) ... 466

s.1(7) ... 470

s.4 ... 466

s.5 ... 466

s.10 ... 466

s.11 ... 466

Sch. 1 ... 466

Data Protection Act 1998, s.1(1) ... 468, 469, 475

s.2 ... 469

s.4(4) ... 467, 474

s.6 ... 473

s.7 ... 505

s.10 ... 482, 490

s.11 ... 467, 482, 490

s.12 ... 490

s.13 ... 477

s.14 ... 491

s.16 ... 473

s.17 ... 469, 473, 491

s.21 ... 491

s.28 ... 492

s.29 ... 492

s.31 ... 492

s.32 ... 492, 493

s.33 ... 492

s.36 ... 492, 493

s.40 ... 493

s.42 ... 492

s.43 ... 492

s.44 ... 492

s.45 ... 493

s.46 ... 493

s.47 ... 492

s.48 ... 492

s.51 ... 474, 492

s.52 ... 474, 492

s.55 ... 472, 473

s.60 ... 494

Sch 9 ... 492

Sch.1 ... 467, 474

Sch.2 ... 482

Defamation Act 1952, s.1 ... 136

Defamation Act 1996, s.1 ... 137

s.13 ... 141

s.14 ... 141

sch.1 ... 141

Electronic Communications Act 2000, s.7 ... 426

s.7(1) ... 426

s.8 ... 425, 426

Employment Rights Act 1996, s.43B ... 549

s.43G ... 549

ss.43C-F ... 549

Extradition Act 2003 ... 340

Forgery and Counterfeiting
   Act 1981, s.1 ... 328

s.8 ... 328

Fraud Act 2006 ... 388

s.2 ... 388

s.2(5) ... 388

s.3 ... 388

s.4 ... 388

s.5(2) ... 388

Human Rights Act 1998 ... 111, 503, 517, 520

s.1 ... 547

s.12 ... 551

Identity Cards Act 2006, s.1 ... 521

s.2(1) ... 521

s.2(4) ... 521

Interpretation Act 1978, Sch. 1 ... 425

Land Registration Act 2002, Part 8 ... 426

Legal Deposit Libraries Act 2003, s.14 ... 261

Limitation Act 1980, s.4A ... 145, 151

Malicious Communications Act 1988 ... 395

s.1 ... 397

Obscene Publications Act 1959 ... 356

s.1(1) ... 48, 354, 355, 358

s.2 ... 48, 71, 355, 360, 378

Patents Act 1949 ... 213

Patents Act 1977, s.1 ... 86

s.1(1) ... 176

s.1(2)(b) ... 177

s.1(2)(c) ... 87, 177, 212, 213

s.14(2)(b) ... 40

s.125(1) ... 176

Political Parties, Elections and
   Referendums Act 2000, s.146 ... 122

Sch.9 ... 121

Prevention of Terrorism (Temporary
   Provisions) Act 1989, Sch.1 ... 399

Protection from Harassment
   Act 1997 ... 395

s.1(1) ... 397

s.1(2) ... 397

s.2 ... 397

s.5 ... 397

Protection of Children
   Act 1978, s.1 ... 55, 369, 372

s.1A ... 370

s.7(6) ... 370

s.7(7) ... 71

Protection of Children and Prevention of
   Sexual Offences (Scotland) Act 2005 ... 370

Public Interest Disclosure Act 1998 ... 549

Public Order Act 1986, Part IIIa ... 71
s.17 ... 111, 125
s.18 ... 71
s.19 ... 71
s.20 ... 71
s.21 ... 71
s.22 ... 71
s.23 ... 71, 111
s.29B ... 125
s.29C ... 125
s.29JA ... 125

Race Relations Act 1965, s 6(1) ... 111
Racial and Religious Hatred
    Act 2006 ... 125
Regulation of Investigatory Powers
    Act 2000, s.1 ... 516
s.3 ... 516
s.7 ... 516
s.26(2) ... 516
s.28 ... 516
Representation of the People
    Act 1983, s.76(2)(a) ... 121
s.93 ... 121

Sex Offenders Act 1997, Sch II ... 56
Sexual Offences Act 2003, s.15 ... 396
s.45(2) ... 355
Statute of Anne, 1710 ... 174
Statute of Monopolies 1624, s.6 ... 176

Terrorism Act 2006, s.1(2) ... 401
s.2 ... 401
s.3(2) ... 402
s.3(3)(a) ... 401
s.3(3)(b) ... 401
s.3(3)(c) ... 402
s.3(3)(d) ... 402
s.4 ... 401
s.57 ... 399
s.58 ... 399
s.59 ... 400
s.121 ... 399
The Police and Justice
Act 2006, ss35-38 ... 348, 398
Theft Act 1968, s.1 ... 13, 84, 55, 566
s.4(1) ... 566

Torts (Interference with Goods)
    Act 1977, s.14(1) ... 94
Trade Marks Act 1994, s.1 ... 289
s.9(1) ... 292, 293
s.9(3) ... 292
s.10 ... 292
s.10(1) ... 292
s.10(2) ... 292
s.10(3) ... 292
s.10(4) ... 292
s.11(2)(a) ... 292
s.11(2)(b) ... 292
s.11(2)(c) ... 292
s.21 ... 302
s.32 ... 291
s.32(2)(d) ... 40
s.40(1) ... 178
s.42 ... 178
s.42(1) ... 292
s.42(2) ... 292
s.43 ... 178
s.63 ... 291
Trade Marks Registration Act 1875 ... 178
Trespass (Scotland) Act 1865 ... 95

Unfair Contract Terms Act 1977, s.2 ... 423
s.3 ... 423
s.5 ... 423

Video Recordings Act 1984, s.12 ... 355

USA Legislation

Child Online Protection Act 1998 ... 367
Child Pornography Prevention Act 1996 ... 375
Child Protection and Obscenity Enforcement
    Act 1988 ... 371
Communications Decency Act 1996 ... 364
s230(c)(1) ... 154

Internet Tax Nondiscrimination
    Act 2004 ... 455

Prosecutorial Remedies and Other Tools to
    end the Exploitation of Children Today
    (PROTECT) Act 2003 ... 376

Telecommunications Act 1996 ... 577
The Internet Tax Freedom Act 1998 ... 455

PART I

Information and society

How the World around us has changed as information has become the key
to economic success.

1 **The world of bits**

    1.1 An introduction to bits

    1.2 Moving from atoms to bits

    1.3 Rivalrous and nonrivalrous goods

    1.4 The legal challenge of the information society

2 **The network of networks**

    2.1 Introducing the internet (history)

    2.2 How the modern internet functions

    2.3 Higher level protocols

3 **Digitisation and society**

    3.1 The digitisation of information

    3.2 Digital convergence

    3.3 The cross-border challenge of information law

    3.4 Digitisation and law

The world of bits

In reading this book you will be asked to think about the world around you slightly differently. While the question at the heart of most legal textbooks is: 'how does the rule of law affect individuals within the environment over which this law is effective', the question at the heart of this book is: 'how does the environment over which the law seeks to be effective affect the rule of law'. The reason for this distinctive approach is the distinctive subject which this book examines. This is the first book to look in detail at the relationship between established legal settlements and the rise of the information society.[1] While you may consider digital information, the internet, and applications such as such as YouTube or social networking tools like Bebo, MySpace, or Facebook, to be simply part of the fabric of everyday life,[2] the British legal system, which can trace its roots through at least seven hundred years of Common Law tradition,[3] finds these developments to be extremely disruptive. These disruptive effects, once the preserve of the interested academic commentator,[4] have become of critical importance to politicians, economists, lawyers, and in turn to us all, as developed economies move from the traditional economic question of 'what can we produce?' to 'what can we control?'.

This change in economic language reflects a wider change in modern developed economies. The traditional measure of an economic superpower was their output. Economies were measured by their ability to support communities. Agrarian economies measured how efficiently the land could be managed and farmed to support the surrounding

---

[1] While many books such as Ian Lloyd's *Information Technology Law* (5th ed., 2008), Chris Reed and John Angel's *Computer Law* (6th ed., 2007) and David Bainbridge's *Introduction to Information Technology Law* (6th ed., 2007) examine the effect of 'computerisation' on the law, they take a technology-centred approach and focus on the narrow application of the law to computer systems, computer programmes and technology related legal issues such as data protection. This book will take a wider approach looking at the interaction of the law and the information society.

[2] This may be determined by your age. If you are 18, you were born when the World Wide Web was released and have never known a world without it. You were probably active on social networking sites before you were a teenager and find a mobile telephone more useful as an SMS device than as a telephone. Older readers though may remember the excitement of their first internet connection and signing their first mobile phone contract.

[3] For a discussion of the Common Law tradition of the English Legal System see S.F.C. Milson, *Historical Foundations of the Common Law* (2nd ed., 1981). For a discussion of the different legal tradition of Scotland see H. MacQueen and A.K.R. Kiralfy (eds), *New Perspectives in Scottish Legal History* (1984).

[4] See L. Lessig, *Code and Other Laws of Cyberspace* (1999); N. Negroponte, *Being Digital* (1995); M. Castells, *The Internet Galaxy* (2001); F. Webster, *Theories of the Information Society* (2000); R. Mansell, *Inside the Communication Revolution: Evolving Patterns of Social and Technical Interaction* (2002).

community; freeing members of that community from the soil to allow them to carry out more specialised roles such as fletcher, blacksmith, or cooper. Such economies were though conspicuously inefficient, as demonstrated by Adam Smith in his famous text *The Wealth of Nations*.[5] In this, Smith demonstrated how specialisation could improve individual output, a process which led eventually to the development of the factory, the production line and, with the introduction of steam power to the equation, the industrial revolution.[6]

The industrial economic model became the dominant economic model of the nineteenth and early twentieth centuries. The industrial economy was driven by economies of scale and by mechanisation. No longer was economic success measured at a local level, it was now measured by output at a national level.[7] It led industrialised nations such as the UK to seek to extend empires across the globe to secure the raw materials which could be turned into textiles, iron, or later aluminium or steel. Industrial economies made money by making things: ships, weapons, clothing, railway tracks, and later aircraft. Industrialists grew wealthy but the workers did not: a few grew exceedingly wealthy while exploiting the human capital of the many.[8] Following the economic downturn of the 1920s, the effects of worker revolt such as the General Strike and the terrible impact of two world wars on the industrial capital of European states a new economic model began to appear in post war Europe. It is this new model of post-industrial economics that gives us our first insight into the importance and value of this subject, and therefore this book.

Post-industrial economics emerged in the UK immediately after World War II. With the cost of production of traditional industrial products such as shipbuilding and steel production being cheaper offshore, the UK's industrial capital began to move to places such as India, Malaysia, and Hong Kong. The UK economy started the painful transition from industrial values of 'what can we produce?' to the newly developing service sector and the question 'what can we provide?' With a massive growth in professional services such as banking, insurance, legal services, education, and media, the UK became the archetypal post-industrial, or service, economy. We no longer made money from making things, we made money from providing services. In the 1980s the last vestiges of our old industrial economy were swept aside. We closed car plants, coal mines, shipyards, and steelworks. The UK was going to be the world's leading service economy, but then something happened and it is that something which is at the core of this book. The post-industrial, or service, economy was itself overtaken only forty years or so after it was first developed. The new economic model is known as the 'information economy' while its correspondent theory in social sciences is the 'information society'. While the UK had invested in banking, insurance, and financial support services, the US, or at least parts of it, had developed an economy built upon the systems that allowed information to be collected, stored, and processed. In so doing they created a new generation of super-rich industrialists who far surpassed the wealth of the nineteenth century

---

[5] A. Smith, *An Inquiry into the Nature and Causes of the Wealth of Nations* (1776, new ed., 1982).
[6] *ibid*. Book 1 Ch. 1.
[7] Gross Domestic Product became the touchstone of economic success.
[8] This of course had been explored by Karl Marx in his famous text *Das Kapital* (1867).

industrialists. These were people like Steve Jobs, Larry Ellison, and most famously Bill Gates who recognised the value wasn't in the information itself; it was in what you could enable people to do with it. They started to ask the question which is at the heart of this book: 'what can we control?'[9] This question is the thesis which underpins both the information society and the knowledge economy. It represents a shift from ownership or control of things to ownership of or control over information.[10] It represents the maturity of information technology and most importantly signals a change in economic value from owning things, or in physical terms *atoms,* to owning information which in the digital environment means *bits*. This transition from the world which saw economic value in atoms to a world which values information in *bits* will form the focus of the remainder of this chapter.

1.1 **An introduction to bits**

The move from economic value being sited within physical goods, to economic value being sited within information, is referred to by Nicholas Negroponte, Director of the Media Laboratory at MIT, as the move from atoms to bits.[11] Negroponte, and others,[12] believe that in time this move from atomic value to value in bits may prove to be as important to social scientists and economists as the discovery of quantum physics was to physical scientists.[13] Before we embark on the deeper impact of the move from atoms to bits we need to answer the basic question what is a 'bit'? We all know what atoms are, or at least I assume we do. If you do need to have a basic seminar on atoms and their role in the physical world I suggest you read Chapter 9 of Bill Bryson's excellent book *A Short History of Nearly Everything*.[14] On the assumption we know the role and position of atoms in the physical world, what then is a bit, and what is its role in the information society?

> **Highlight** What is a Bit?
>
> At its simplest 'bit' is a truncation of the term 'binary digit'. To expand, a binary digit is simply either a 0 or a 1.

[9] To gain an insight into the thought process of Bill Gates during the early stages of what he calls the 'information age' read: B. Gates, *The Road Ahead* (1995), Ch. 2.

[10] The post-industrial economic model may be seen as a step along this road being about ownership of or control over knowledge.   [11] N. Negroponte, *Being Digital* (1995), 4.

[12] See M. Lemley, 'Place and Cyberspace' 91 *California Law Review* 521 (2003); L. Lessig, *Code and Other Laws of Cyberspace*, above n. 4; H. Jenkins, *Convergence Culture: Where Old and New Media Collide* (2006).

[13] For more on this read A. Murray, *The Regulation of Cyberspace: Control in the Online Environment* (2007), Ch. 9.   [14] B. Bryson, *A Short History of Nearly Everything* (2003).

The answer to what is a bit therefore doesn't get us any closer to the questions at the heart of this book 'why are bits economically valuable?', 'how do bits effect social interaction?', and most importantly for a legal textbook, 'why does the law have to take account of the effect of bits?' To answer these questions we must look, not narrowly at what a bit is, but more widely at what a bit does.

At the most basic level therefore a bit is simply a 0 or a 1, but like atoms, which on their own are not very impressive either, it is how bits can be used to construct larger, more complex systems that give them their economic value and social importance. In the world of computer systems a bit represents a single instruction to the computer. This instruction is either to do (1) or not to do (0) a particular function. The instruction is read by the brain of the computer, the Microprocessor or Central Processing Unit (CPU).[15] The CPU may be thought of as a superfast calculator which works in binary. Bits of information are fed to the CPU from the computer memory, the CPU does a calculation and based upon the result the personal computer (or PC) carries out a predetermined function. The process that is followed is called von Neumann architecture after mathematician and computer pioneer Jon von Neumann.[16]

Von Neumann architecture is a four step system that turns bits into computer operations or data. The first step is *fetch*, which involves the CPU retrieving an instruction (represented by bits) from program memory. These are instructions preloaded into the memory of the computer by a piece of software such as Microsoft Windows or Word. The second step is *decode*. In this step the single instruction is broken up by the CPU in separate instructions which require the CPU to do different operations. Thus a single instruction will usually contain an operational instruction telling the CPU what to do and a series of informational instructions giving the CPU the data it needs to fulfil the operational instruction. Step three is the *execute* step. In this step the CPU will carry out the operational instruction contained in the fetched data. This may be a purely internal process such as an autosave function managed completely by the software instructions fetched from the program memory or it may involve a user input where the actions of the user of the computer cause a particular event to happen (more will be said on this below). The execute step is a series of calculations using binary notation which gives a series of results managed by the CPU and carried out by a series of units on the microprocessor.[17] The final step is *writeback*. Here the CPU 'writes back' the result of its operational process to memory. This may be either the CPU memory (if it is about to carry out a further operation based on this result) or to the main memory if the operational process is complete for now. After writeback the whole process begins again with the cycle being repeated billions of times per second. At its most basic level therefore a computer CPU is simply a rather unimpressive calculator. It can add and subtract or multiply and divide but only in binary. It can do this billions of times per second and therefore is very powerful but as we are only dealing in 1s and 0s how does the manipulation of bits affect the established legal order? The answer is in the flexibility of the bit.

---

[15] This is the computer part that is advertised as 'Intel Core' or 'AMD Phenom' or similar in promotional material.

[16] For more on von Neumann see N. Macrae, *John Von Neumann: The Scientific Genius Who Pioneered the Modern Computer, Game Theory, Nuclear Deterrence, and Much More* (2000).

[17] For more on this see Gates, above n. 9, Ch. 2 which gives an exceedingly lucid description of this complex subject.

1.1.1 **The process of digitisation**

Much as atoms can be used in the physical world to construct everything from the human liver to an Airbus A380, bits are the basic building blocks of the information society. In his book *The Road Ahead* Microsoft co-founder Bill Gates explains the difference between the analogue world of atoms and the digital world of bits though a simple example.[18] He asks his readers to imagine a 250 watt light bulb attached to a dimmer switch. Using the dimmer the user may select graduated illumination from complete darkness (0) to full illumination (250). By turning the switch halfway you will get something around 125 watts of light and at one quarter distance about 63 watts. But as Gates points out exact replication of the level of illumination achieved in such an analogue set up is difficult. If I find one night that about one quarter turn is the perfect level of illumination to have a romantic dinner I could make a mark on the dimmer switch and use this as a level for future reference, but if I want to tell my friend in Seattle this I need to try to communicate to him exactly where on the switch I made my mark (usually descriptively by telephone). If he then passes this information on to his friend in Gothenburg he repeats the process, but as anyone who has played Chinese Whispers knows the message will over time change and deteriorate: this is known as analogue drop off and affects all analogue transmissions as anyone who has made a copy of a copy of a friend's mix tape knows.[19] If we replace the one 250 watt bulb with eight bulbs of differing output, each double the output of the previous, we create an analogy for a digital system. We now have eight switches, one for each bulb as seen below in Figure 1.1.

We can still control the level of lighting in the room from darkness (by switching all lights off) to full illumination (by switching them all on). But now instead of representing this as an analogue value between 0 and 250 we represent it using binary notation from 00000000 to 11111111 where 0 is 'off' and 1 is 'on'. Now if I find that the perfect level of lighting for a romantic meal is 93 watts I can set my switches as 'off' 'on' 'off' 'on' 'on' 'on' 'off' 'on' or in binary notation 01011101. Now if I want my friend in Seattle to be able to replicate the **exact** level of lighting I had I simply

Figure 1.1 A 'digital lighting' system

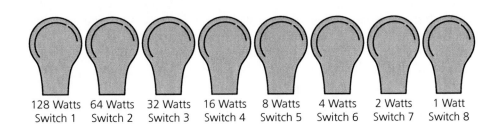

128 Watts   64 Watts   32 Watts   16 Watts   8 Watts   4 Watts   2 Watts   1 Watt
Switch 1   Switch 2   Switch 3   Switch 4   Switch 5   Switch 6   Switch 7   Switch 8

---

[18] What follows is based upon Gates' example contained at 26–28 of Gates, *ibid*.

[19] If you are too young to know what a mix tape is ask your parents.

send him this code. He may then send this code to his friend in Gothenburg who can exactly replicate what I did without ever speaking to me. Thus digital transmissions are less likely to suffer drop off as the message sent is short and precise, unlike analogue transmissions.

If we can represent levels of lighting in digital notation, what else can it be used to represent? The answer is almost anything. Gates gives the traditional example of ASCII or the American Standard Code for Information Interchange.[20] ASCII is the common system used by all computers to encode all the letters and punctuation of the English Language. ASCII gives each character a value between 0 and 255, 255 being the maximum number which can be created by an eight character byte of bits.[21] Capitals A–Z are given values 65–90 while lower case a–z are given values 97–122, while a space is valued at 32. Thus in ASCII the message 'Long live the Queen' is given as:

```
01001100   01101111   01101110   01100111   00100000   01101100
01101001   01110110   01100101   00100000   01110100   01101000
01100101   00100000   01010001   01110101   01100101   01100101
01101110
```

Of course it is not just text that may be represented in this way. As Negroponte points out we have been able over the years to represent more and more information in binary digits. Music has been distributed digitally since the early 1980s. It is digitally encoded by taking constant samples of the audio waveform (sound pressure measured as voltage): a numerical value which may then be encoded as bits. In digital photography each colour and shade is allocated a numerical value which allows for perfect replication and display of the encoded data on an output such as a computer monitor or digital photo frame. Digital video may be seen as a meshing of these two techniques. Here a constant stream of data replicating moving imagery is encoded on a DVD or HDD. The applications of bits are seemingly endless, with some physicists even believing that bits may eventually lead to the creation of a Star Trek style matter transporter.[22] As Negroponte points out: 'the emergence of continuity in [individual bits] is analogous to a similar phenomenon in the familiar world of matter. Matter is made of atoms. If you could look at a smoothly polished metal surface at a subatomic scale, you would see mostly holes. It appears smooth and solid because the discrete pieces are so small. Likewise digital output.'[23]

In the information society we see a shift from encoding information in atoms (such as writing it on the page) to encoding it in bits (such as word processing it). But this move is not limited to the written word: it may be sounds, images, or electrical outputs. Almost anything which may be recorded may be digitised. As digital information is cheaper to store, cheaper to distribute, and cheaper to encode there has been a widely publicised migration from analogue technologies to digital technologies and with it a shift in economic values of information.

---

[20] For more on ASCII visit http://www.asciitable.com/ where you can find the digital notation of all characters used on the keyboard.

[21] In case you wondered what the difference between a bit and a byte was, this is it. A bit is a single binary digit; a byte is a collection of eight bits used to create a single instruction to a CPU. Despite my earlier description of how a CPU works information is always sent in bytes not bits to the CPU. I left this out of the description at the earlier stage to avoid confusion.

[22] See D. Darling, *Teleportation: The Impossible Leap* (2005).

[23] Negroponte, above n. 11, 15.

1.2 **Moving from atoms to bits**

The economic driver of the move from atoms to bits is clear from the final paragraph of the preceding section. During the 1980s the computer moved out of the research laboratory and the workplace into the home environment. The home computer of the 1980s, devices such as the Sinclair Spectrum and the Commodore C64, were the trailblazers for the home PC or personal computer.[24] As the PC became a fixture of homes across North America, Europe, Australasia and the Pacific Rim, computerisation of media became the cutting edge technology. The first entertainment media to be digitised were children's games (although now they were often played by adults). The games console was the breakthrough technology of the 1970s. Although the first home games console, the Magnavox Odyssey released in 1972 was a failure, in 1977 games company Atari released the now legendary Atari 2600 games system which sold over thirty million units in its lifetime making it the iPod of the home video games industry, an industry which remains at the cutting edge of home electronics through products such as the Nintendo Wii, the Xbox 360, and the PS3.[25]

Most people though became aware of the digital revolution in the 1980s. Music was the first traditional mainstream media industry to go digital. With the advent of the Compact Disc digital distribution became the norm. Why did the music industry move over? It was because of perceived benefits in music production, where digitisation allowed for greater control over post-production cleanup and mixing and because the traditional analogue distribution systems for music (Compact Audio Tape and Vinyl Disc) were perceived to be of low quality. CD was more durable, offered better sound quality, and most importantly gave greater flexibility in post-production. I wonder since if the music industry has ever regretted being in the vanguard of digitisation. The story of the digitisation of the music industry is the most turbulent of all. While the first process of digitisation in the 1980s was evolutionary rather than revolutionary the second process which took place in the 1990s was set to cause a revolution in the music industry.

The introduction of the CD (as with its sister product the DVD some fifteen years later) was not to cause a digital revolution. The industry was in control of this evolution from the outset and the only discernable change to the consumer was a change in carrier media and in media player. Music was still carried on a disc, although now small and shiny rather than large and black, and was still played on some form of turntable device, although now read with a laser beam. Most importantly both the CD and DVD retained the traditional distribution models of their predecessors the tape/vinyl disc and the videocassette. You still visited your local HMV, Virgin, or Woolworths to purchase them. They were still carried by road haulage and they still were 'pressed' and packaged in a far off production line. This is why both CDs and DVDs

[24] Now many homes have several PC devices such as laptops and desktops which often share a wireless network creating a local area network or LAN which allows music, video, or other files to be streamed wirelessly between them.

[25] At this point I feel I should take a line or two of text to defend my decision to begin the story of digitisation of the entertainment market with a short discussion of the early success of Atari. Too often academic commentators dismiss the home video game market as unimportant, yet gamers spent $9.5bn on home video games in 2007 in the US, which compares favourably with the $16bn spent on DVD purchases and $2.9bn spent on music downloads.

are evolutionary: they are simply a better way to replicate what was already being done. But, as Negroponte points out one of the key values of digitisation is that it allows us to discard much of the baggage of the atomic world.[26]

1.2.1 Music goes digital

This occurred with respect to the music industry in 1994 when the release of the MP3 sound compression technique allowed us to reduce the size of music files down to between 6–8 Megabytes on average.[27] MP3, like all compression techniques, allows us to remove information not required for reproduction of the recorded data. With MP3 much of what is removed is information which refers to sounds recorded but outside normal levels of human hearing. There is a drop off in quality compared with high bitrate recordings such as full CD quality, but for the purposes of most consumers the MP3 quality is 'good enough'. The smaller file size allowed by MP3 allowed for distribution of music in a completely revolutionary way. Instead of pressing discs and distributing them via traditional routes such as high street stores with all the accompanying overheads these carry, some enterprising individuals demonstrated that music could be carried directly from computer to computer cutting out all the middle men.

One such service was offered by MP3.com an internet start up who offered consumers the opportunity to 'space shift' their music collection.[28] The concept was simple. You demonstrated you owned a particular album or single by placing your copy of the CD in your computer's CD drive. Once the MP3.com software confirmed the authenticity of the CD it allowed the music content of the CD to be added to your online library. Then wherever you were in the world, as long as you had internet access, you could access your entire music library via the MP3.com website. There were obvious problems with this system. Firstly MP3.com never established ownership of the CD placed in the computer: there was nothing to stop you borrowing your neighbour's CD collection and adding it to your library. Secondly MP3.com never had the permission of the rights holder to allow you remote access in this fashion.

As a result a copyright infringement case followed, the outcome of which we'll see in Chapter 10. Also in Chapter 10 we'll discuss the case which changed the music industry forever: *A&M Records Inc v Napster Inc*.[29] Napster is a vitally important legal decision and the legal impact of Napster will be discussed in depth in Chapter 10, but that is not the aspect of the Napster litigation I am interested in here. Napster was also of significant socio-economic impact. People not only learned the 'bad' lesson that they could get music for free, such free riding if left unchecked would have undermined the economic effectiveness of the entertainment industry as a whole not just the music industry, they also learned the 'good' lesson that music could be streamed directly to their computer, no leaving the house, no middlemen, no wasted costs on packaging, transport, etc. This lesson was the revolutionary application of MP3 technology that has changed the music distribution model, probably permanently. Following the success of Napster,[30]

---

[26] See Negroponte, above n. 11, 35–36.
[27] Allowing for up to 100 tracks to be put on a single CD.
[28] The concept of space-shifting is discussed in greater depth in Ch. 10.
[29] 114 F Supp 2d 896 (ND Cal 2000).
[30] Before legal action forced it to shut down it had in excess of 16 million customers.

industry players such as Apple have perfected the online music delivery model though systems such as iTunes/iPod to the point now where devices such as the iPhone and the iPod Touch no longer need a computer to download music, both being capable of downloading music directly through their WiFi connectivity.

1.2.2 Digital goods and society

The success of the iPod and its family of products including the iPhone heralds the digital future. Music is once again at the vanguard, but not far behind is a similar model for digital video. BitTorrent may be seen as the TV and film industry's Napster moment and the success of video streaming sites such as YouTube and the many thousands of imitators it has spawned point to a future model. A colleague has informed me that his fifteen year old daughter watches mainstream television programmes such as Lost in fifteen minute segments on video sharing sites rather than through the traditional broadcast model.[31] I'm sure this model will grow. Equally book publishers shouldn't imagine they are exempt. The success of Google Books and the launch of the Amazon Kindle and the Sony Reader suggest that the digitisation of books is near to hand. Thus anything we consume which is in nature information carried on a carrier media is ripe to go through a similar revolution to the one experienced by the music industry in the 1990s.

The experience of the music industry answers to some extent the questions 'why are bits economically valuable?' and 'how do bits effect social interaction?' Although there is much more to explore in relation to both these questions we can open by saying bits are economically valuable because they represent new and revolutionary models to market and deliver those products or services, which are by nature informational products and which are traditionally embedded in or attached to a separate carrier media. The music industry has already felt the full impact of this but other industries which may soon, or may already be feeling the impact of digital delivery include film and television production and broadcasting, telephone service providers, mail service providers, educational providers, publishing, advertising, print media, and even the legal profession.[32] Further, bits effect social interaction as they provide new avenues for communication, exchange of ideas, and for challenge to traditional orthodoxy. The reason the music industry was forced to change was because of Napster. Although there is no doubt the vast majority of Napster users were driven by economic desire to free ride (for which read get free music), once Napster was gone people realised they also valued the convenience of Napster and for some the feeling of belonging to the 'Napster community'. Although legal download sites such as iTunes replaced the convenience, these corporate sites do not have the same community spirit. I believe this led indirectly to the development of social networking sites, and in particular MySpace which is heavily influenced by popular culture and music culture. MySpace has in return influenced popular music through the promotion of bands and singers such as the Arctic Monkeys

---

[31] This anecdotal evidence is confirmed by columnist Jeremy Clarkson in his *Sunday Times* Column of 7 October 2007 'The Kids are all right with lousy TV' where he notes 'Now my daughter only really watches YouTube.'

[32] For a discussion of some of the challenges the legal profession may face see R. Susskind, *The End of Lawyers* (2008).

and Lily Allan. Whereas in the 1970s and 1980s groups of teenagers would meet in their local record shop to discuss music, now they do it on MySpace, mostly because iTunes and others do not support social networking (a rare missed trick from Steve Jobs). What remains though is the most important question for a legal textbook, 'why does the law have to take account of the effect of bits?'

1.3 **Rivalrous and nonrivalrous goods**

Rivalrous and nonrivalrous are terms of economic art. Rivalrous goods are goods whose consumption by one consumer prevents simultaneous consumption by other consumers. This generally is true of any 'atomic' good, for, notwithstanding some recent developments in quantum mechanics, it is generally accepted that no two atoms may occupy the same space simultaneously.[33] Thus should I borrow my wife's umbrella because it is raining, she cannot use it during the period it is in my possession: my possession is rivalrous to her possession. Atomic goods may be either durable or nondurable, but in general both are rivalrous goods. The umbrella example is an example of a durable rivalrous good. My use of the umbrella presents a barrier to others who desire to use that umbrella at the same time. However, my use of the umbrella does not 'use up' the umbrella, meaning that it, as with other durable rivalrous goods, can still be shared through time. By contrast nondurable rivalrous goods are destroyed by their use (consumption) and cannot be shared. A concert ticket is a nondurable rivalrous good: if I 'borrow' my wife's ticket to see a concert by her favourite band, the fact that I can return the ticket to her afterwards does not disguise the fact that I have 'consumed' the economic value of that ticket leaving her with a worthless piece of paper. Thus nondurable rivalrous goods cannot be shared through time. By contrast, nonrivalrous goods may be consumed by several consumers simultaneously. Nonrivalrous goods are usually intangible. The most famous example is probably that of an idea as presented by the eighteenth/nineteenth century scientist, philosopher and politician Thomas Jefferson.

➔ Highlight Thomas Jefferson's Letter to Isaac McPherson

If nature has made any one thing less susceptible than all other so exclusive property, it is the action of the thinking power called an idea, which an individual may exclusively possess as long as he keeps it to himself; but the moment it is divulged, it forces itself into the possession of every one, and the receiver cannot dispossess himself of it. Its peculiar character, too, is that no one possesses the less, because every other possesses the whole of it. He who receives an idea from me, receives instruction himself without lessening mine; as he who lights his taper at mine, receives light without darkening mine.

---

[33] This is an application of the 'Pauli exclusion principle'. To read more on the Pauli exclusion principle visit: http://hyperphysics.phy-astr.gsu.edu/Hbase/pauli.html.

Here Jefferson captures the key elements of nonrivalrous goods. By taking from the original owner you do not deny them of their possession and enjoyment of the goods, nor do you deny anyone else the opportunity to consume, simultaneously, the same good. In the modern world technology has enabled us to increase the number of non-rivalrous goods available to us. Television broadcasts are an example of a nonrivalrous good: if I turn on my TV set to watch a broadcast of 'Boston Legal' this does not prevent my next door neighbour, or anyone else, from watching the same show. Goods that are nonrivalrous are therefore goods that can be enjoyed simultaneously by an unlimited number of consumers.

If we list nonrivalrous goods we find an interesting commonality between them. Nonrivalrous goods include ideas, radiocommunications broadcasts (TV and Radio), visual light (think of a beautiful view or a sunset), digital media (you can 'give away' MP3 music while retaining the original), and sound (a speaker at Speaker's Corner may be heard by one person or one thousand without affecting the enjoyment of others). The commonality is that they are all 'informational goods'. All are about transmitting information from one source to another. To return to the earlier language of Negroponte they are all susceptible to be encoded as binary digital information (bits) to be stored or shared: thus ideas may be written on a document file (as I am currently doing), radiocommunications broadcasts are being replaced by digital broadcasts, digital pho-tography and video is capturing that beautiful view, and as we have seen, MP3's encode sound. Thus the move from the world of atoms to the world of bits, or the move from the industrial to informational society, can be similarly defined as a move from rival-rousness to nonrivalrousness.

1.4 **The legal challenge of the information society**

What does this all mean to lawyers and to lawmakers? Well we have now identified three effects of the move from the industrial to the informational society:

1. It represents a shift from ownership or control of things to ownership of or control over information;
2. It represents a new and revolutionary model to market and deliver products or services; and
3. It represents a move from rivalrousness to nonrivalrousness.

All three of these pose serious challenges to traditional legal values and traditional legal rules. All traditional legal systems, including the common law system found in the UK and the civilian tradition found on continental Europe, have a basic distinction between tangible and intangible goods. Tangible goods represent goods of economic value and are protected. Thus s. 1 of the Theft Act 1968, expects tangibility: 'A person is guilty of theft if they dishonestly appropriate property belonging to another with the intention to permanently deprive the other of it.' The key phrase is 'intention to permanently deprive' as this makes clear that to commit the offence of theft you must take something which is physical and rivalrous. Thus 'copying' an MP3 without the permission of the owner is not theft. Neither is intercepting a transmission without permission.[34] Both of these things are regulated elsewhere,[35] but neither is theft in the true sense of the word. This may not seem important: you may believe this is simply a matter of language, or you may believe it is simply a choice by lawmakers to distinguish between theft proper (the taking of a 'thing') and misappropriation of information. But this simple example reveals a greater tension between traditional legal values and the new economic values of the information society.

Traditional property theory examines how scarce resources ought to be put to use but in the world of bits scarcity loses its immediate impact. Although there are still limits which apply over storage space and bandwidth, the average user sees bits as almost limitless as they are infinitely scalable: want the new REM album but can't afford it?: someone will make it available for free, not by giving you access to their copy but by creating a brand new copy for you. Bits never run out and because bits never run out we can keep creating, the only limit is on how many bits we can store.

The traditional law of atomic property, and with it atomic values of wealth through owning and retaining things, is fundamentally altered by the scalability of bits, meaning those things which appear to be of economic value (information) seem perversely to be of no value because anyone can replicate it at any time at almost no outlay.[36]

> **Highlight** The Informational Paradox
>
> Information is valuable. It is also (almost) infinitely scalable, nonrivalrous, and intangible.

Our traditional legal values are predicated on an environment where valuable goods are either physical, tangible, and rivalrous or where intangible goods (as protected by intellectual property laws) are fixed to some form of tangible carrier: books, vinyl or compact discs, compact music cassettes, videocassettes, patent specifications, or attached as 'badges' to products. But as John Perry Barlow demonstrated in his famous polemic: *Economy of Ideas: Selling Wine Without Bottles on the Global Net*: 'with the advent of digitization, it is now possible to replace all previous information storage forms with complex and highly liquid patterns of ones and zeros.'[37] In Barlow's parlance the valuable content (the nonrivalrous good) is being separated from the traditional carrier (which was rivalrous). Not only is the move from atoms to bits affecting traditional property values, it also undermines our traditional models for enforcing intangible, intellectual property rights.

---

[34] Think here of erecting a satellite dish and installing an illegal decoder thus taking the economic benefit of the broadcast from the broadcaster without making payment.

[35] The copying without permission by the Copyright, Designs and Patents Act 1988, the broadcast example would be regulated by the Communications Act 1990 and/or the Regulation of Investigatory Powers Act 2000.

[36] This was recognised early on by Bill Gates who records in *The Road Ahead* 'It seemed to me that too many people were accepting, at face value, uncritically the idea that information was becoming the most valuable commodity. Information was at the library. Anybody could check it out for nothing. Didn't that accessibility undermine its value?', above n. 9, 22.

[37] 'The Economy of Ideas: Selling Wine Without Bottles on the Global Net', *Wired 2.03*, March 1994. This paper is discussed further in Ch. 3.

The question of how we protect the value of information in an age where it is instantly replicable, transmissible, and is almost infinitely scalable is the challenge lawyers face today. It is also the core value of this book and it represents the thread that draws together the chapters which follow on disparate subjects such as cyber-speech and defamation, databases, copyright in the information age, and computer crime. The common theme which will emerge is that attempts to broker a piecemeal settlement: here a Database Directive, there a Convention on Cybercrime are wrong-headed and will eventually lead to a fragmented approach which will fracture not just along jurisdictional lines but also along lines of technology and types of information. This would be the informational age equivalent of fragmented responses to different types of physical things in traditional legal settlements: thus instead of a law of property and chattels we have a law of the steam engine, a law of the gramophone, and a law of the pocket-watch. This is exactly what we are doing now in the world of bits by producing specific regulations to deal with copyright infringement, indecency, computer crime such as hacking, and informational products such as databases. This book will, in the traditional style examine the extant and proposed legal-regulatory framework of each of these (and many others), but it will also encourage you, the reader, to question whether it is time to take a more comprehensive approach to the legal regulation of digital information rather than attempting to fit the square peg of the world of bits into the round hole of a legal system designed for a world of atoms.

FURTHER READING

Books

N. Negroponte, *Being Digital* (1995)

M. Castells, *The Internet Galaxy* (2001)

B. Gates, *The Road Ahead* (1995)

D. Tapscott & A. Williams, *Wikinomics* (2008)

Chapters and Articles

M. Lemley, 'Place and Cyberspace' 91 *California Law Review* 521 (2003)

D. Hunter, 'Cyberspace as Place and the Tragedy of the Digital Anticommons'
    91 *California Law Review* 442 (2003)

M. O'Rourke, 'Property Rights and Competition on the Internet: In Search of an Appropriate
    Analogy' 16 *Berkeley Technology Law Journal* 561 (2001)

The network of networks

People use the term 'internet' every day without thinking what it actually means. It is in fact a compound word made up of 'inter' + 'net'. Inter is from the Latin root meaning between or among, while net is short for network.[1] In short the internet is not a single computer network as you may have previously imagined; it is a system that connects together many individual computer networks allowing for the transfer of digital data, or bits, across networks. The internet is basically a telecommunications system for computer networks: this is why it is sometimes called the network of networks.

The idea for the first computer network was put forward by a group of computer visionaries in the 1960s. The original idea can probably be traced to the eminent experimental psychologist J.C.R. Licklider. Licklider was a professor at the Massachusetts Institute of Technology (MIT). There he worked on the SAGE project as an expert on the interaction between humans and technology,[2] work which helped convince him of the great potential for human/computer interfaces. This led Licklider to write one of the most important papers in computer science, the 1960 paper, 'Man-Computer Symbiosis'[3] in which he stated:

> It seems reasonable to envision, for a time 10 or 15 years hence, a 'thinking center' that will incorporate the functions of present-day libraries together with anticipated advances in information storage and retrieval ... *The picture readily enlarges itself into a network of such centers, connected to one another by wide-band communication lines and to individual users by leased-wire services.* In such a system, the speed of the computers would be balanced, and the cost of the gigantic memories and the sophisticated programs would be divided by the number of users.[4]

Licklider was particularly interested in the idea of using wires to tie expensive mainframe computers together. He went on to develop this idea with a colleague, Wes Clark, who at that time worked at MIT's Lincoln Lab and who had several years earlier taught Licklider how to program the TX-2 mainframe computer. Together they wrote another

---

[1] All definitions in this section are drawn from the Oxford English Dictionary.

[2] The Semi-Automatic Ground Environment (SAGE) system was the first major real-time, computer-based command and control system. It was designed as a new air defence system to protect the US from long-range bombers and other weapons. The SAGE system sent information from geographically dispersed radars over telephone lines and gathered it at a central location for processing by a newly designed, large-scale digital computer. For more information about SAGE see: http://www.mitre.org/about/sage.html.

[3] J.C.R. Licklider, 'Man-Computer Symbiosis', *IRE Transactions on Human Factors in Electronics*, March 1960, Vol. HFE-14. A digital reprint of the paper may be accessed at: http://memex.org/licklider.pdf.   [4] *ibid*, 11 (emphasis added).

groundbreaking paper, 'On-Line Man Computer Communication', published in August 1962. In this they described a 'Galactic Network' which 'encompasses distributed social interactions through computer networks'.[5]

These papers and the visionary ideas contained therein may, like many other great ideas, have been destined to remain only an untested thought experiment, but fate was about to intervene. On 4 October 1957 the Soviet Union had launched the first man-made object into space, the satellite Sputnik I. This had not been predicted by analysts in the West and it caused immense shock and surprise to the US military and scientific establishment. President Eisenhower determined that the US would never again be taken by surprise on a technological frontier. In response he created a new research agency tied directly to the Office of the President and funded from the Department of Defense budget. This new agency would oversee cutting edge research of value to both the civilian and military establishments. It was to be called the Advanced Research Projects Agency or ARPA.[6]

As fortune would have it one of the first problems for ARPA was how to deal with the inefficient use of expensive scientific equipment. One particular problem was that at that time computers were expensive pieces of equipment which were underutilised. They used batch processing techniques which meant that hours or days could be spent inputting data on punch cards before the program could be run, and then the slightest error in data entry would invalidate all this work. Between time computers often lay idle. By the early 1960s every computer scientist wanted his own computer but the cost of providing this was prohibitive. The answer was clear: the users had to share the resources available more efficiently. This meant two things. Firstly, the development of time-sharing mainframe resources, an idea first put forward by researchers at MIT's Lincoln Lab in the 1950s,[7] and secondly a network of machines which would allow researchers in different parts of the country to share results and resources easily. ARPA decided to appoint Licklider to deal with these problems and so in October 1962, only two months after the publication of 'On-Line Man Computer Communication', Licklider found himself appointed as the first Project Director of ARPA's Information Processing Techniques Office or IPTO. Once in post he surrounded himself with a group of like-minded men. This group included his co-author of 'On-Line Man Computer Communication' Wes Clark, Bob Taylor of NASA, and Larry Roberts and Leonard Kleinrock, both outstanding PhD students at the Lincoln Lab. Together these men set out to build a communications system for computers: it would be called the Advanced Research Projects Agency Network or ARPANET.

2.1 **Introducing the internet (history)**

The number of histories of the internet which have been published, both on-line and off-line are too great to list. I do not intend to examine the history of the internet in detail. Those who wish to learn in detail about the development of this fascinating

---

[5] The paper was originally published as an ARPA memo, one of a series by Licklider on this subject in 1962. Reprinted in Proceedings of the IEEE, Special Issue on Packet Communications Networks, Vol. 66 No. 11, November 1978.

[6] ARPA came into existence on 7 February 1958: http://www.arpa.mil/body/arpa_darpa.html.

[7] K. Hafner & M. Lyon, *Where Wizards Stay Up Late: The Origins of the Internet* (1996), 25.

place should either read the excellent *Where Wizards Stay Up Late* by Katie Hafner and Matthew Lyon[8] or the Internet Society's *A Brief History of the Internet* [9] which is without doubt the best on-line history of Cyberspace. Much of the following is drawn from these two sources.

2.1.1 Building the ARPANET

Immediately following his appointment, Licklider and his team set to work in developing a network technology which would give effect to his vision. Led by Bob Taylor, they started work on making a shared computer network a reality. One of the key players in this was Leonard Kleinrock, who in 1961 had published one of the first papers on packet switching theory.[10] Packet switching was a radical new system being developed by Paul Baran of the RAND Corporation for military voice communications. In packet switching messages are broken up into small packets before they are sent. Each packet is transmitted individually across the network. The packets may even follow different routes to the destination. At the destination the packets are reassembled into the original message.[11] Baran was working on packet switching as a method to ensure military voice communications could withstand a nuclear first strike,[12] Kleinrock was looking for a way to connect computers without tying up expensive leased lines. Kleinrock convinced Taylor that the best way to connect computers on a network was by using packet switching rather than conventional circuit switching.[13] With the packet switching model adopted by ARPA they began work on the network. One of the first problems faced by the fledgling ARPANET was how to make all computers on the network compatible with one another. In the 1960s there was no standard operating system such as Windows: each computer used a different programming language and operating system. Just to get the individual machines to interface, or 'talk', with each other was going to consume vast amounts of the ARPANET project's time and resources. At a meeting for Principal Investigators for the project at Ann Arbour, Michigan in April 1967, Wes Clark offered a solution. Instead of connecting each machine directly to the network they could install a minicomputer called an 'interface message processor' or IMP at each site. The IMP would handle the interface between the host computer and the ARPANET network. This meant each site would only have to write one interface: that between that host and the IMP and, as all the IMPs used the same programming

---

[8] *ibid.*   [9] http://www.isoc.org/internet/history/brief.shtml.
[10] L. Kleinrock, 'Information Flow in Large Communication Nets', *RLE Quarterly Progress Report*, July 1961.   [11] A fuller explanation of packet switching will be given below.
[12] For an explanation as to how this would work see P. Baran, *On Distributed Communications* (1964): http://rand.org/about/history/baran.list.html.
[13] Circuit switching occurs when a dedicated channel (or circuit) is established for the duration of a transmission. All information is transmitted along this one dedicated link. The most ubiquitous circuit-switching network is the telephone system, which links together wire segments to create a single unbroken line for each telephone call. Conversely, packet switching, using Baran's model, would allow messages to be divided into segments (or packets) before being sent. Each packet is then transmitted individually and each can follow a different route to its destination. Once all the packets forming a message arrive at the destination, they are recompiled to form the original message. Packet switching is generally seen as more efficient as there is no 'silent time' between sections of the message as there is with circuit switching.

language; the network of IMPs would handle the rest.[14] With all the principles of the ARPANET network now in places: it would be a 'layered' design with the IMPs supporting the host computers and it would use packet switching in place of traditional circuit switching Larry Roberts, with engineering partners at Bolt, Beranek & Newman, a small computer company in Cambridge, Massachusetts, started building the network. Finally on 29 October 1969, the ARPANET vision became reality when Charlie Kline, an undergraduate at UCLA, successfully logged in to the SDS 940 host at the Stanford Research Institute through the Sigma 7 host at UCLA.[15] Further hosts were added at the University of California at Santa Barbara and at the University of Utah, and by December 1969 the original four node network was in place.

ARPANET may have been the first successful computer network, and it may also have been the forerunner of the modern internet, but it was quite dissimilar to the internet as we know it today. Modern definitions of the internet describe it as a 'vast collection of inter-connected networks'.[16] ARPANET was a single network. Furthermore ARPANET was what today would be described as a 'closed network': you could only gain access to the ARPANET network if you had a correctly configured IMP which had to be supplied by Bolt, Beranek & Newman. Thus the foundations of the modern internet architecture are not to be found in this part of the network's history. What happened next though was something quite special.

2.1.2 **Building the internet**

The ARPANET success was an exciting moment for network engineers. The design team had demonstrated that functioning computer networks could be constructed. As a result the early 1970s were a time of intense experimentation with computer networking and other applications of packet switching. One of the first experiments was in the carrier medium. ARPANET used the existing AT&T telecoms system to carry its messages but this was less efficient in areas where there was a lack good of telecoms coverage: areas such as inter-island communications in Hawaii. In 1969 the IPTO awarded funding to Professor Norm Abramson at the University of Hawaii to develop a wireless network. Abramson used this money to construct a simple network of seven computers across the islands using radios similar to those used by taxis to transmit and receive data. This network, called ALOHANET, used a different transmission system to ARPANET. In ARPANET communications the IMPs would manage data transmission and reception ensuring data was properly sent and received without interference. In ALOHANET the terminals were allowed to transmit whenever they wanted to; if the transmission was impeded by other traffic the recipient computer would ask for it to be resent, the sending computer

---

[14] This is recorded by Hafner & Lyon, above n. 7, 73.

[15] Commentators, including Leonard Kleinrock, recall that the first attempt by Klein to log in failed when the network crashed half-way through the procedure—see L. Kleinrock, *The Birth of the Internet* (1996): http://www.lk.cs.ucla.edu/LK/Inet/birth.html. Later that same day though Klein succeeded. The actual log entry recording the successful connection may be seen at: http://www.computerhistory.org/internet_history/full_size_images/imp_log.jpg.

[16] This definition is taken from Google, but it reflects the generally accepted view stated elsewhere.

would keep sending the message at random intervals until it got an 'ok' message from the recipient. ALOHANET received a lot of attention, not least from the military who recognised the advantages of a wireless network. The problem was though that the range of the network was limited and to build larger transmitters would centralise the network leaving it open to attack. An alternative was to use satellites which were becoming more common at the time. Although slower than ARPANET due to transmission lag a satellite network would allow for international transmissions.[17] To this end the US, UK, and Norway collaborated on the development of a satellite network: SATNET. Concurrently, local fixed-line networks were being developed in the UK and in France.[18]

With the development of several independent networks interest in linking these resources grew. Bob Kahn, who had helped design the IMPs at Bolt, Beranek & Newman, was working on a packet-radio project at the time.[19] He wanted to connect his network to the ARPANET computer network but at the time this was impossible as they were radically different networks. Kahn and others sought to end their frustration. What they wanted was a network of networks: an inter-network. They formed a group called the International Network Working Group and appointed Vint Cerf to be its chair.[20] That same year, 1972, Kahn was invited by Larry Roberts to join the IPTO to work on a net project: The Internetting Project. Kahn accepted and immediately started developing designs to connect together all the independent networks which had sprung up since 1969. Kahn realised the solution to the problem was in open architecture networking. Open architecture allows for each individual network to retain its unique network architecture, while connections between networks take place at a higher 'Internetworking Architecture Layer' as seen in Figure 2.1.[21] In an open architecture network, the individual networks may be separately designed and developed and each may have its own unique interface which it may offer to users and/or other providers. Each network can be designed in accordance with the specific environment and user requirements of that network. There are generally no constraints on the types of network that can be included or on their geographic scope.

Figure 2.1 Simplified open architecture network

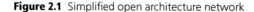

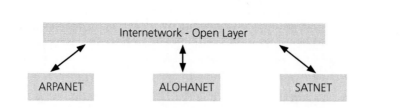

[17] At the time the fixed-line, or undersea, network, which was constructed of copper-wire, lacked the necessary capacity between the US and Europe to allow for effective network transmission between the two. This was remedied soon after when the telecoms companies laid high-speed fibre-optic cable in its place.

[18] All this is discussed in Hafner & Lyon, above n. 7, Ch. 8.

[19] Kahn was a Professor of Electrical Engineering at MIT who joined Bolt, Beranek & Newman to help them overcome communications errors in data transmission.

[20] Vinton 'Vint' Cerf is the man most commonly called 'the father of the internet'. In 1972 he was an assistant professor at Stanford University.

[21] Set out more fully in *A Brief History of the Internet*, above n. 9.

Designing this network was similar to designing the ARPANET. Like ARPANET the problem was that each host (in this case host network) used its own language, what was needed was a version of the IMP system which had bridged this gap on the ARPANET. Unfortunately the IMPs were also one of Kahn's major obstacles. The language of ARPANET, the Network Control Protocol (NCP), did not have the ability to interface with networks or machines further downstream than a destination IMP on the ARPANET.[22] Thus Kahn would need to re-write the NCP protocol.

Kahn set about designing a new, open architecture, protocol. In doing so he set out four ground rules for his new Internetwork Protocol:

→ Highlight Khan's Four Ground Rules for Internet Protocols

1. Each distinct network would have to stand on its own and no internal changes could be required to any such network to connect it to the internet;

2. Communications would be on a best effort basis. If a packet didn't make it to the final destination, it would shortly be retransmitted from the source;

3. Black boxes would be used to connect the networks (these would later be called gateways and routers). There would be no information retained by the black boxes about the individual flows of packets passing through them, thereby keeping them simple and avoiding complicated adaptation and recovery from various failure modes; and

4. There would be no global control at the operations level.

Kahn began working on his new protocol with Vint Cerf who joined in his role as Chair of the International Network Working Group. According to Cerf, Kahn introduced the problem to him by saying: 'Look my problem is how I get a computer that's on a satellite net and a computer on a radio net and a computer on the ARPANET to communicate uniformly with each other without realising what's going on in between.'[23] Cerf was fascinated by the problem and along with Kahn he worked on developing the new protocol which would allow transmission across networks. Each of these networks had its own set of rules though. They used different interfaces, different transmission rates and each allowed for differently sized packets of information to be carried. How could they write a protocol which could be used uniformly across networks? Throughout 1973 Cerf and Kahn continued to work on these problems. Finally in September 1973 Cerf presented his and Kahn's ideas at the International Network Working Group meeting at the University of Sussex. Their idea later refined and published as the seminal

---

[22] The reason for this short-sightedness was that in designing NCP control over packets of data, and therefore network reliability was given to the IMPs. This is because this was simpler and cheaper and at the time ARPANET was the only network envisaged by the designers.

[23] Hafner & Lyon, above n. 7, 223.

paper, *A Protocol for Packet Network Intercommunication*[24] was deceptively simple. Cerf realised that carriers often carried packets without ever knowing what was in them. A transport container has a standard size and shape, yet it may be carrying anything from televisions to chocolate bars. Due to the common size of the container it can be carried by road, sea, or rail and neither the ship's captain nor the truck or train driver need know what he is carrying. The only people who need know are the shipper and the recipient. Cerf applied this to digital data. He designed a new protocol: Transmission Control Protocol, or TCP, which would 'box up' the information and address it. Each message fragment, known as a datagram, would be the same size and could be handled by any of the networks. Once sent into the network packets could take any route to their destination; they were not all destined to follow each other across busy networks. This design would work, and allowed for transmission of data across networks, but by removing the IMPs from the process, there remained the problem of missing or damaged datagrams.

In ARPANET the IMPs were responsible for sending and reassembling all message packets. They worked to ensure message integrity by checking the message at every stage of its journey, so called hop-by-hop transmission. Cerf and Kahn changed all this in designing TCP. They returned to Norm Abramson's work on ALOHANET: to overcome the problem of interference or data corruption he placed the responsibility for data integrity on the sending and receiving computers, so called end-to-end reliability. In Cerf and Kahn's TCP design when packets of information were sent they carried with them a request for acknowledgement. If safely received the recipient host would signal the transmission host of success. If the packet failed to arrive or was corrupted in transmission the recipient would not signal. If no acknowledgement was received the transmission host would retransmit the packet at random intervals until a successful acknowledgement was received. By placing all these responsibilities with the hosts, the network itself could be significantly simplified. Like the container transports of the real world, only the sender and recipient need know the details of the contents, all the network needed to know was where to send them.

TCP was not quite an instant success. Although it did lead to the development of the first internet, a network which between 1973 and 1975 grew at a rate of about one new network node per month, the protocol itself was redrafted and redeveloped continually over the next few years. The most important of these occurred in January 1978 when Vint Cerf and Jon Postel posted 'TCP Version 3 Specification', which suggested the splitting of TCP into a dual protocol Transmission Control Protocol/Internet Protocol or TCP/IP. TCP had always been a multi-functional protocol but by splitting it into the dual layer TCP/IP these functions could now be clearly seen. The release of the TCP/IP protocol is now seen by most network historians as the day the modern internet came into being and is therefore the logical place to end our short excurses into the history of the network.

---

[24] V. Cerf & R. Kahn, 'A Protocol for Packet Network Interconnection', *IEEE Trans on Comms*, Vol. Com-22, No. 5, 627, May 1974.

2.2 **How the modern internet functions**

The modern internet still functions using the TCP/IP protocol. The TCP element of the protocol breaks the data into packets ready for transmission and recombines them on the receiving end. The IP element handles the addressing and routing of the data and makes sure it gets sent to the proper destination. The easiest way to imagine this working is to think in terms of traditional postal communications.

✳ Example Sending TCP/IP communications

Alistair wants to send a message to Barbara. In the real world he may write his message on a piece of paper and then place it inside an envelope before sealing the envelope and addressing it. He then places the envelope in the care of the Royal Mail who carries the envelope to Barbara. She then opens the envelope and reads the message.

TCP/IP works in a similar fashion, except in place of a single envelope the message is split into many 'packets' before being sent. If we were to use TCP/IP technology to send the simple message 'Meet me at 2pm' from Alistair to Barbara, the following operations would take place.

1. TCP would split the message into packets and numbers each packet [Meet]$_1$ [me at]$_2$ [2pm]$_3$.

2. Each packet is placed into a digital envelope before passing these envelopes on to the IP protocol.

3. IP would then address the envelopes with Barbara's IP address before sending them out across the network.

4. The network acts like the Royal Mail and carries these envelopes to their destination.

5. Upon arrival TCP opens the envelopes, checks all packets have been delivered safely and reassembles the message.

Let us take as an example the delivery of a file from one computer to another. This is a common internet operation and may occur where your operating system undertakes an automatic update, or it may be a requested download such as a music file from iTunes. We begin operations with two computers the Host (that is the computer on which the file is held) and the Recipient. The first thing to be aware of is that every digital device connected to the internet[25] must have a unique identification or address. The internet is a vast network of communications networks. Like all communications networks it relies upon the ability to deliver content to another party. Thus the telephone network functions because each telephone connected to the network has a unique identifier, or telephone number. In internet terms a similar system is managed by the IP protocol,

---

[25] Note all digital devices which are network enabled must have an IP address, not just computers. So when online mobile phones have such addresses as do, wi-fi enabled music players such as the iPod Touch and many other devices.

currently this may be a version known as IPv4 or IPv6. As internet communications are communications between computers the need for a linguistic addressing tool seemed minimal when the addressing protocol for the internet was developed. The primary addressing tool is therefore a numerical identifier called an Internet Protocol, or IP, address. As with a telephone number this number must be unique to allow for the smooth flow of information within the network. IP addresses are used when browsing the web to enable the transmission of communications between the user's web browser and server hosting the website. They are also used in the header of email messages and, in fact, are required for all programs that use the TCP/IP protocol.

Version 4 of the Internet Protocol (IPv4), which is still in use, uses an IP address consisting of 32 bits, usually shown as a 'dotted quad': four octets of binary numbers represented in decimal form in the range 0–255. For example, the IP address of the computer I am currently using is 158.143.112.199 but as computers do not work in decimal notation this will be converted by the network servers and routers into binary notation and be read by them as 10011110.10001111.1110000.11000111. As though it is easier for humans to remember decimals than it is to remember binary numbers we use decimal notation to represent IP addresses when describing them. The address space of the IPv4 protocol (the number of available unique identifiers allowed) is 2^{32} or 4,294,967,296 unique host interface addresses. At the time it was adopted this seemed to be an almost limitless supply of addresses, but as the network has developed the strain on this resource has become quite heavy. For this reason a new version of the IP protocol IPv6 has been adopted. In IPv6, addresses are 128 bits rather than 32 bits. This will allow 2^{128}, or about 3.403×10^{38}, unique host interface addresses: a mind-boggling availability of unique identifiers. An IPv6 address is written as eight four-digit hexadecimal numbers separated by colons. Thus to the human eye it looks something like: 3FFE:FFFF:0100:F101:0210:A4FF:FDE3:9566. Computers, including hosts and routers, will continue to read this as binary notation, but space prevents me from reproducing the binary equivalent of a hexadecimal IPv6 address. Both IPv4 and IPv6 addresses are descending unique identifiers like telephone numbers. You read them from left to right with the first two sets of quads being used to identify the network location of your computer. For example, all computers on the London School of Economics network are allocated an IPv4 address which begins 158.143, while King's College, London operates from the 137.73 address space while University of Oxford IP addresses all begin 163.1.[26] This information is of course double-edged. Not only is it essential for the functioning of the network it also allows data transmissions to be tracked to an end-user. The privacy implications of this will be discussed in chapter nineteen.

With both computers in our transaction allocated an IP address the transaction between computers can now take place. Our host computer will have the file to be transferred and the IP address of the recipient. The TCP protocol now takes the file and breaks it up into smaller packets as outlined above and prepares to send them. It places each packet into its electronic envelope and then attaches a header to that file. The header is basically all the information that is needed to deliver the packet and to reassemble the file. Thus it will contain the IP address of the recipient and basic information

---

[26] For more on the operation of IP addresses, including who regulates and assigns them see A. Murray, *The Regulation of Cyberspace: Control in the Online Environment* (2007), Ch. 4.

about the information contained in the packet to ensure that if it becomes damaged (corrupted) en route, the recipient is aware of this and can ask for the data to be resent if necessary.[27] These packets are all then sent into the physical infrastructure of the network which is made up of the wired network of telephone cables (both copper and fibre optic), wireless carriers such as Wireless Local Area Networks such as those provided in your local Starbucks or Wireless Wide Area Networks such as those operated across metropolitan areas such as *The Cloud* network across the City of London.[28] How this physical layer carries this information from the host to the recipient is a result of all these early technology designs such as packet switching and network layering. If the host is a major website like iTunes it will have a permanent network connection through a leased line, if it is a casual user, like your brother sending you a file by email, the connection will be temporarily created by using the modem in the user's machine to connect to their Internet Service Provider (ISP). In whichever form the initial connection is made the ISP will transfer the packets to the Internet Backbone. This is made up of many large networks which interconnect with each other. These large networks are known as Network Service Providers.[29] These Network Service Providers connect to each other to exchange packet traffic through a series of internet exchanges known as Network Access Points. These allow data packets to flow freely across the internet backbone. The management of the data flow across the backbone and thorough Network Access Points is controlled by a specialist piece of computer hardware known as a router. Routers are specially designed to manage the informational flow of the internet. When a data packet arrives at a router, the router examines the IP address put there by the IP protocol layer on the host. The router checks its records to see if it knows where the recipient is based. If the network containing the IP address is found, the packet is sent to that network. If the network containing the IP address is not found, then the router sends the packet on a default route, usually up the backbone hierarchy to the next router. Hopefully the next router will know where to send the packet. If it does not, again the packet is routed upwards until it reaches one of the core routers actually on the backbone. These core routers hold the largest records and here the packet will be routed to the correct backbone, where it will begin its journey downward through smaller and smaller networks until it finds its destination.[30]

There are some key operative parameters of the internet which may be gleaned from this short explanation of how TCP/IP works. Among these are that TCP works on a best effort basis.[31] Routers do not usually attempt to repair damaged packets. If the IP address cannot be found, or if there is a network failure which makes it impossible for packets to be forwarded they will be discarded. The recipient computer may request missing or

---

[27] For a more technically detailed description of the TCP Protocol see Information Sciences Institute, *Transmission Control Protocol: DARPA Internet Program Protocol Specification* (RFC 793, 1981). http://www.netfor2.com/rfc793.txt.

[28] To learn more on The Cloud: http://www.thecloud.net/About-us/.

[29] In the UK the largest NSPs are British Telecommunications (BT) and Virgin Media. Worldwide the major NSPs are Verizon, AT&T, Sprint, and NTT.

[30] For a technical discussion of how Internet Routers function see S. Halabi, *Internet Routing Architectures* (2nd ed., 2000). For a more general discussion of internet architecture see P. Gralla, *How the Internet Works* (8th ed., 2006).

[31] This is the second of Khan's four 'ground rules' for TCP discussed above.

damaged packets be resent, the router will not. Secondly, the route taken by discrete packets may differ from that taken by other packets. Thus there is no reason to assume that if a file is transmitted from a computer in Glasgow to one in London that all will follow the same route, or even that they will take the most direct route. Routers will send packets by the most efficient route in terms of network capacity, not in terms of network geography. Thus if the network between Glasgow and London is extremely congested one packet may go via Stockholm, another via Amsterdam and another via Detroit. As the fibre optic cables which make up the backbone all carry data at the speed of light it should be completely unnoticeable to the end user that one packet of data has travelled 1,000 miles while another has travelled 12,000 miles.[32] Thirdly, traditionally the network treated all data packets equally. Because the routers did not know what they were carrying they could not distinguish high value data (perhaps a streaming video or a VoIP call) from low value data (such as a SPAM email). This is the effect of two early network initiatives which are in many ways the opposite sides of the same coin: network neutrality and end-to-end architecture.

End-to-end architecture is a unique feature of distributed computing, as most famously employed in the current incarnation of the TCP protocol. The idea of end-to-end communications was first promulgated by Jerome Saltzer, David Reed, and David D. Clark in 1984 in their paper *End-to-end arguments in system design*.[33] The authors examined the developing internet, which at that time was beginning to play host to a variety of different end-user systems such as email, file transfers, online booking systems, and others, and concluded that: 'The function in question can completely and correctly be implemented only with the knowledge and help of the application standing at the end points of the communication system. Therefore, providing that questioned function as a feature of the communication system itself is not possible.'[34] In other words only the host who originated the file and the recipient of the file knew enough about the file to manage its transmission. The intelligence of the network was therefore in its applications held at each end of the communication rather than in the network architecture itself. This made the internet almost unique among communications media. Traditional media were centrally managed: think of the telephone exchange or the television broadcast facility, with dumb terminals at the ends. In fact the only other media of communication which used end-to-end principles was the mail delivery system. But as our discussion of the process of digitisation in chapter one has demonstrated, the internet offered many more and exciting opportunities than traditional mail carriers. The network would be developed to carry a variety of digital products from simple text-based emails to MP3 files to flash games to streaming MP4 and MPEG videos and on to VoIP telephone calls. The development of these new technologies, especially VoIP and streaming video which are both bandwidth intense and which require for low latency are challenging the continuing applicability of the end-to-end principle and its allied concept of network neutrality.[35]

---

[32] At the speed of light it takes approx 0.06 seconds to travel 11,000 miles.
[33] Vol. 2.4 *ACM Transactions on Computer Systems* 277 (1984).   [34] *ibid*, 278.
[35] Latency is the time delay between the moment something is initiated, and the moment one of its effects begins or becomes detectable. In streaming video and voice communications high latency render the system ineffective due to lag.

2.2.1 **Net neutrality**

Network neutrality, or more commonly net neutrality, is highly prized by many inter-net pioneers including Professor Sir Tim Berners-Lee creator of the World Wide Web.[36]

> ### Highlight Net Neutrality Defined
>
> Net neutrality is the principle that data packets on the internet should be moved impartially, without regard to content, destination or source. It is sometimes referred to as 'The First Amendment of the Internet'.

This previously widely accepted concept is currently though under review, some may even say challenge.[37] New routers from companies such as Cisco and IBM allow net-work carriers to prioritise certain traffic over others. Network providers argue this is a positive development as it allows them to prioritise traffic with a low latency threshold such as VoIP and streaming media over traffic with a higher latency threshold such as web browsing or a music download.[38] Network providers argue that in this way they can make a more efficient use of the limited resources available to them with everyone receiving the best service possible.[39] Critics argue that it also allows them to discriminate against certain applications or data types.[40] There are concerns that service providers may seek to deteriorate the quality of service of applications which compete with their products. Thus there are concerns that an ISP such as BT which provides both telephone and internet access may degrade the quality of service of a competitor product such as Skype or that an ISP like Virgin Media which provides video on demand services may degrade the quality of service of video sharing sites such as YouTube.[41] In addition they may place a restrictively low upload speed on your service making it difficult to upload

---

[36] T. Berners-Lee, *Net Neutrality: This is serious.* http://dig.csail.mit.edu/breadcrumbs/node/144.

[37] See, e.g. Berners-Lee, *ibid*; L. Lessig, 'Public must fight to maintain net neutrality', *San Francisco Chronicle*, April 17, 2008 http://www.sfgate.com/cgi-bin/article.cgi?f=/c/a/2008/04/16/EDM11064UL.DTL.

[38] High Tech Broadband Coalition, *Appropriate Framework for Broadband Access to the Internet over Wireline Facilities* (CC Docket No. 96-45 (2002)); High Tech Broadband Coalition, *Appropriate Regulatory Treatment for Broadband Access to the Internet over Cable Facilities* (CC Docket No. 96-45 (2002)). For an excellent discussion of the issues see B. van Schewick, 'Towards an Economic Framework for Network Neutrality Regulation', 5 *Journal on Telecommunications and High Technology Law* 329 (2007). http://papers.ssrn.com/sol3/papers.cfm?abstract_id=812991.

[39] Reports record that in 2007 video sharing site YouTube used as much bandwidth as the entire internet did in 2000, see S. Lohr, 'Video Road Hogs Stir Fear of Internet Traffic Jam', *New York Times*, March 13 2008: http://www.nytimes.com/2008/03/13/technology/13net.html and that up to ten hours of video are uploaded on YouTube every minute (http://www.internetnews.com/ec-news/article.php/3741691/Economic+Woes+Not+an+Issue+For+Google.htm).

[40] See High Tech Broadband Coalition *Ex Parte Letter*, June 17, 2002, III (C): http://gullfoss2.fcc.gov/prod/ecfs/retrieve.cgi?native_or_pdf=pdf&id_document=6513198353; T. Wu, 'Network Neutrality, Broadband Discrimination', 2 *Journal of Telecommunications and High Technology Law* 141 (2003).   [41] See the discussion in L. Lessig, *The Future of Ideas* (2001), Ch. 10.

content to file sharing sites such as Flikr or YouTube,[42] or as was discovered by Professor Tim Wu when he surveyed ISPs' service contracts, you may simply be contractually barred from certain activities by your ISP.[43]

Against this backdrop a campaign has begun in the US to enshrine the principle of net neutrality, that all data should be treated equally, into federal law. This campaign has high profile backers including Professor Lawrence Lessig, Professor Sir Tim Berners-Lee, Professor Tim Wu, and Craigslist founder Craig Newmark. In 2006, they met some degree of success when Senators Byron Dorgan and Olympia Snowe introduced the Internet Freedom Preservation Bill (or Dorgan-Snowe Bill) which sought to so enshrine the principle of net neutrality. The Bill though quickly became bogged down amid claims from the telecommunications industry that Dorgan-Snowe was disproportionate as there was no evidence that industry self-regulation was failing, that its effect would be to protect internet giants like Microsoft, Google, Yahoo!, and eBay rather than their customers and that the Bill would deter investment in high-speed-data networks. The original Bill fizzled out in summer 2006 when it failed to clear a congressional vote, but undeterred the campaigners for regulated net neutrality continued to press for action and recently have met with some degree of success. On 31 July 2009 five Democratic Congressmen introduced Bill HR 3458, The Internet Freedom Preservation Act of 2009, to the House. This is the latest in a long line of attempts to get Congress to enshrine net neutrality in US Law which began with the Dorgan-Snowe Bill, but this time the Bill has a realistic chance of becoming law having gained the backing of the chairman of the House Committee on Energy and Commerce, the committee which provides oversight for the Federal Communications Commission (FCC). At the time of writing the Bill is currently before the House Committee on Energy and Commerce, Subcommittee on Telecommunications and the Internet. Again telecommunications groups are campaigning against the legal enshrinement of the principle of net neutrality, and although it is too early to tell the outcome of this further attempt to gain Congressional intervention it seems popular support for the Bill is greater than for any previous net neutrality Bill. It is not only Congress though which is now moving to enshrine net neutrality in US Law. On 21 September 2009 the Chairman of the US telecommunications regulator, the FCC, stated that 'the free and open Internet faces emerging and substantial challenges', challenges which threaten the ability of the network to continue to evolve and innovate.[44] In response Chairman Genachowski states that 'the FCC must be a smart cop on the beat preserving a free and open Internet' and to that end he proposes two new principles to be added to the pre-existing four internet principles that the FCC apply in their day-to-day enforcement of communications law in the US.

[42] Again this is discussed by both Lessig and Wu.
[43] Wu, above n. 40, found that among the activities restricted were: Any commercial or business use of facilities; operating a server; overusing bandwidth; and in some cases even setting up a home network or wireless network (160–166).
[44] 'Preserving a Free and Open Internet: A Platform for Innovation, Opportunity, and Prosperity'. Speech by Chairman Julius Genachowski at The Brookings Institution, Washington DC, 21 September 2009: http://openinternet.gov/read-speech.html.

→ Highlight FCC Net Neutrality Principles

The fifth principle is one of non-discrimination—stating that broadband providers cannot discriminate against particular internet content or applications.

The sixth principle is a transparency principle—stating that providers of broadband internet access must be transparent about their network management practices.

The effect of these additional principles, if adopted, would be to enshrine net neutrality into the regulatory principles of the FCC. In effect it creates a net neutrality law in the US by the back door. Unsurprisingly these proposals have attracted a large number of negative responses with one Senator noting that 'these new regulatory mandates and restrictions could stifle investment incentives'.[45] There is a generally widely held concern that enshrined network neutrality could be particularly problematic for mobile communications operators who could find their systems overwhelmed by a large demand for mobile video applications and that large scale file sharers could 'hog' network resources leaving little for others to use unless telecommunications companies invest large amounts in network upgrades. It seems that this debate will continue to rage in the US, but with the current Obama administration strongly in favour of enshrined net neutrality and with Chairman Genachowsk a strong supporter of net neutrality it seems likely that some form of net neutrality regulation will soon be adopted in the US.

This issue has also been examined by Ofcom, the UK telecommunications regulator. At the Westminster eForum on net neutrality on 20 March 2007, Ofcom's Director of Policy Development, Dougal Scott, stated that a mixture of market regulation and competition law would be sufficient to protect UK customers against discrimination.[46] Scott noted that '[if] an ISP blocked, or severely degraded VoIP traffic on its network so that you couldn't use that application. [That] makes the ISP a less attractive proposition to consumers, because you can't use VoIP. So if consumers know that, and so long as they can switch easily, competition limits the ISPs' ability to do that'.[47] Further he notes that the provisions of the Communications Act 2003 protect customers from ISPs who have the ability to influence the market due to their market power, such as BT.[48] As Scott observed: 'The European Regulatory Framework allows us to deal with any particular problems that do arise. The Framework, which is transposed into our Communications Act, has a concept called Significant Market Power (SMP), which is close to concept of dominance, and which is the trigger for ex ante remedies. If a network operator with SMP was charging for prioritisation, or blocking of or degrading traffic, in ways which we considered anti-competitive, the current European Framework gives us the tools to put in place the necessary remedies.

---

[45] Senator Kay Bailey Hutchison cited in T. Bradley, 'Battle Lines Drawn in FCC Net Neutrality Fight' *PC World* 22 September 22, 2009. http://www.pcworld.com/businesscenter/article/172391/battle_lines_drawn_in_fcc_net_neutrality_fight.html.

[46] Speech: http://www.ofcom.org.uk/media/speeches/2007/03/regulate.   [47] *ibid.*

[48] The relevant provisions may be found in s. 45.

If a network operator without SMP was charging for prioritisation, or blocking or degrading traffic, then because of the operator's lack of SMP, this activity would be unlikely to be anti-competitive, and would not therefore need to be regulated.'[49] Why then does Scott feel the UK is in a position to allow ISPs to self-regulate, whereas in the US there is a strong and growing campaign for lawmakers to legally enshrine the principle of net neutrality? The difference is in the internet access market in the two countries. In the US broadband access is most commonly achieved through cable access using a cable modem. This means that for many subscribers they have a limited choice of perhaps only two or three (or even one) internet access provider. In the UK most people get their internet access over the phone line by using DSL modems. This means that the average UK consumer has a choice of several hundred internet access providers which they can change simply by getting a Migration Authorisation Code which ISPs are required to provide free of charge.[50] The theory of Ofcom therefore is that with greater competition in the internet access market, and with the regulatory authority to intervene should one of the behemoths of the internet access market in the UK such as BT, who control 29.5% of the UK internet access market,[51] decide to intervene in the quality of service of its customers there is no need for proscriptive regulatory intervention. Only time will tell who is right, but for the moment it is suggested the Ofcom approach is the right one, at least for the UK.

2.3 **Higher level protocols**

In Figure 2.1 I outlined how TCP/IP created an open layer built over or on top of the closed networks of the ARPANET, the ALOHANET and the SATNET. In this last section of this chapter I will introduce and explain the third network layer, the applications layer where higher level protocols such as Hypertext Transfer Protocol allow us to carry out operations such as web surfing. To explain how the modern internet lays higher level functionality such as web surfing or video streaming on top of the basic networking functionality of TCP/IP we start by looking at the environmental layering of the modern network.

Stratification or layering may be identified in any informational environment. Both network engineers and communications theorists recognise the vital function played by environmental layers in communications networks. In his book *Weaving the Web*,[52] the architect of the World Wide Web, Tim Berners-Lee, identifies four layers within the architecture of the internet: the transmission layer; the computer layer; the software layer; and the content layer.[53] This may be seen as a simplified version of the seven layer Open Systems Interconnection Reference Model (OSI Model) used by network engineers. This model divides the functions of a protocol into a series of layers. Each layer has the property that it only uses the functions of the layer below, and only exports functionality to the layer above. Typically, the lower layers are implemented in hardware, with the

---

[49] Scott, above n. 46.
[50] See Ofcom, *Switching Broadband Provider*, 13 December 2006, http://www.ofcom.org.uk/media/news/2006/12/nr_20061213.
[51] Figures calculated from http://www.ispreview.co.uk/review/top10.php.
[52] T. Berners-Lee, *Weaving the Web: The Original Design and Ultimate Destiny of the World Wide Web by Its Inventor* (2000).   [53] *ibid*, 129–130.

higher layers being implemented in software.[54] Although both the OSI Model and the Berners-Lee model are network architecture models, designed to describe the purely functional aspects of the network, they can easily be adapted to illustrate the challenges faced by regulators. For lawyers and regulators this has been most successfully done by Yochai Benkler in his eloquent paper *From Consumers to Users*[55] and it is that model which will be employed here.

Benkler describes a three layer network which is similar to Berners-Lee's four layer environment. Benkler labels his layers (1) the physical infrastructure layer, (2) the logical infrastructure layer, and (3) the content layer. What Benkler does is to reduce the OSI/Berners-Lee model to the three key environmental layers found on the internet. The foundational layer is the physical infrastructure layer. The physical infrastructure layer is the link between the physical world and Cyberspace and is made up of wires, cables, spectrum, and hardware such as computers and routers. The second layer is the logical infrastructure layer. This encompasses the necessary software components to carry, store, and deliver content, software such as the TCP/IP protocol, operating systems and browsers. Finally, the content layer encompasses all materials stored, transmitted, and accessed using the software tools of the logical infrastructure layer. Benkler's model was adapted by Lawrence Lessig in his book *The Future of Ideas*.[56] Lessig rebranded the layers the Physical Layer, the Code Layer, and the Content Layer, this allowed him to discuss the particular effectiveness in using the Code Layer to regulate the Content Layer, a subject he had previously raised in *Code and Other Laws of Cyberspace*,[57] and to which he would return in his third book, *Free Culture*.[58] Thus the role of TCP/IP is to act as the 'glue' which connects the physical infrastructure of the communications networks to the higher level protocols which we use daily to read blogs, post Facebook updates, and send and receive emails. Among the everyday higher level protocols you may use such as SMTP—Simple Mail Transfer Protocol, used to send and receive emails; VoIP— Voice over IP, used for internet telephony such as Skype; and RTP—Real-time Transport Protocol, which streams audio and video content such as YouTube. One protocol

[54] The seven OSI layers are (1) Physical layer: The major functions and services performed by the physical layer are: establishment and termination of a connection to a communications medium and participation in the process whereby the communication resources are effectively shared among multiple users (2) Data link layer: The Data link layer provides the functional and procedural means to transfer data between network entities and to detect and possibly correct errors that may occur in the Physical layer (3) Network layer: The Network layer provides the functional and procedural means of transferring data sequences from a source to a destination via one or more networks while maintaining the quality of service requested by the Transport layer (4) Transport layer: The Transport layer provides transparent transfer of data between end users (5) Session layer: The Session layer provides the mechanism for managing the dialogue between end-user application processes. It establishes checkpointing, adjournment, termination, and restart procedures (6) Presentation layer: The Presentation layer relieves the Application layer of concern regarding syntactical differences in data representation within the end-user systems and (7) Application layer, the highest layer: This layer interfaces directly to and performs common application services for the application processes. See D. Comer, *Internetworking with TCP/IP: Principles, Protocols and Architecture* (2000).
[55] Y. Benkler 'From Consumers to Users: Shifting the Deeper Structures of Regulation Toward Sustainable Commons and User Access', 52 *Federal Communications Law Journal* 561 (2000).
[56] Above, n. 41.   [57] L. Lessig, *Code and Other Laws of Cyberspace* (1999).
[58] L. Lessig, *Free Culture: The Nature and Future of Creativity* (2005).

suite stands out: it is HTTP—Hypertext Transfer Protocol and its allied programming language HTML—Hypertext Markup Language, between them these protocols for the foundation of the World Wide Web, by far the most important higher level network to operate using TCP/IP.

The World Wide Web, or simply 'the web', is not synonymous with the internet. As we have seen the internet is the network of computer networks which function using TCP/IP. The web is a higher level network which uses the internet as its carrier medium. The invention of the web is usually credited to Sir Tim Berners-Lee. Berners-Lee is a physicist who graduated from the University of Oxford in 1976. Upon leaving university he began working with Plessey Telecommunications as a software engineer, where he worked for two years on distributed systems, message relays, and bar-coding. He then joined DG Nash, a small software company, where he developed a multi-tasking operating system and typesetting software for intelligent printers. During this time he also developed a hypertexting system called Enquire.[59] Hypertext was not new, the term had been coined by filmmaker and computer programmer Ted Nelson in 1963 and the concept of hyper-linking was at the core of Project Xanadu, his hypertext project which ran from 1960 and which he discussed at length in his 1981 book, *Literary Machines*.[60] While Nelson was experimenting with hypertext, the first functioning hypertext system, Douglas Englebert's NLS, or oN-Line System, was developed. Englebert developed his system independently of Nelson's work and did not use the term hypertext to describe his system, but there is no doubt it was the first hypertext network. Englebert had been hugely influenced by Vannevar Bush's 1945 paper *As We May Think*,[61] which described a mechanised library system, or memex, with embedded links between documents. In his attempts to build Bush's memex Englebert turned to the potential of digital computers. In 1962 he started work on Augment, a project to develop computer tools to augment human capabilities.[62] This was possibly the most important computer project of the time (arguably even more important than ARPANET) and it produced the first computer mouse, graphical user interface, and hypertext program. All these developments were demonstrated by Englebert at the Fall Joint Computer Conference in San Francisco in December 1968. Englebert received a standing ovation and in tribute to his work his NLS system, and as a result the SDS 940 computer he used for these applications was selected as the second ARPANET node. It took another twenty years though for Englebert's invention to find a popular use, and that was in Tim Berners-Lee's web design.

---

[59] Hypertext is the now familiar user interface used on the web. It is designed to overcome some of the limitations of fixed written text. Rather than remaining static like traditional text, hypertext makes possible a dynamic organisation of information through links and connections (called hyperlinks). Hypertext can be designed to perform various tasks; for instance when a user clicks on the link it will usually cause his browser to load a related web page of information or if he allows his mouse to hover over it, a bubble with a description of the linked file may appear.

[60] T. Nelson, *Literary Machines* (1981).

[61] V. Bush, 'As We May Think', *The Atlantic Monthly*, July 1945, 101.

[62] The Augmentation Research Center at Stanford Research Institute in Menlo Park, CA was the precursor to the internationally famous Xerox PARC facility.

After developing his Enquire system, Berners-Lee joined the European Particle Physics Laboratory (CERN)[63] as a consultant. During his time there he secured funding to develop a digital hypertext library of CERN research which could be accessed from any facility on the CERN network. By March 1989 Berners-Lee had completed his project design to allow researchers in the High Energy Physics Department to communicate information online. His design had two key features: (1) like TCP/IP his new protocol was to have an open architecture to allow researchers to connect any computer no matter what operating system it was using, and (2) information was to be distributed using the network itself. Berners-Lee was joined in his project by Robert Cailliau, a computer engineer from Belgium. Throughout 1990 Berners-Lee, assisted by Cailliau, developed the first web server, 'httpd', and the first client, 'WorldWideWeb' a hypertext browser/editor. This work was started in October 1990 and by Christmas Day 1990 Berners-Lee and Cailliau were conversing across the world's first web server at info.cern.ch. In August 1991, Berners-Lee posted a notice to the alt.hypertext newsgroup informing users where his web server and browser software could be downloaded. At this stage the web was still in its infancy, there was no certainty it would develop in the way we experienced in the 1990s, but on 30 April 1993 the future of the web was secured when CERN gave notification that they were not intending to take control of the technology developed by Berners-Lee and Cailliau. On that date CERN announced and certified that the WWW technology developed at CERN was to be put into the public domain 'to further compatibility, common practices, and standards in networking and computer supported collaboration'.[64] This allowed any interested party to use and improve the CERN software, assuring the future of the web.

With its freedom assured the web became the 'killer application' of the internet.[65] The number of internet users quickly increased[66] and today it is estimated that there are 1.7 billion people online.[67] Thus while it is important to bear in mind that the internet and the web are two different things, the importance of the web to the development and penetration of the internet cannot be underestimated. Throughout this book we will look at the challenges of both the internet and the web to governments, lawmakers, lawyers, and to regulators and users more generally. Much of the focus of this will be on the regulation of the web: issues such as the distribution of pornographic content across borders via the web, or the distribution of movies and music in breach of copyright via

[63] CERN is the contraction of the Laboratory's French name: Conseil Européen pour la Recherché Nucléaire.
[64] Original certificate at: http://info.web.cern.ch/info/Announcements/CERN/2003/04-30TenYearsWWW/Declaration/Page1.html.
[65] The term killer application refers to any computer program or application that is so necessary or desirable that it affords the core value of some larger technology, such as an operating system, or a piece of computer hardware. Simply put, a killer application is so compelling that someone will buy the hardware or software components necessary to run it.
[66] Unfortunately figures for 1993 are not reliable but estimates suggest there were about 1.3 million internet users in January 1993 mostly based in the US (see http://www.isc.org/index.pl?/ops/ds/host-count-history.php). However accurate figures are available from 1995 when IDC Research began their user survey. From this we know there were 16 million internet users in December 1995, 36 million in December 1996, 76 million in November 1997, 147 million in September 1998, 195 million in August 1999 and 369 million in August 2000. See G. Gromov, *History of Internet and WWW: The Roads and Crossroads*, http://www.netvalley.com/intvalstat.html.
[67] See *World Internet Users and Population Stats*, http://www.internetworldstats.com/stats.htm.

the web, but sometimes it is other aspects of the internet's unique communications media that are at the core of the problem, such as with BitTorrent a communications protocol which allows users to share large files between computers. BitTorrent is not a web protocol. Like HTTP it runs across TCP/IP and is therefore a question properly of internet governance. Thus this book will look at the regulation and governance of digital content wherever found. You need to be aware of the distinction between the internet and the web to allow you to distinguish whether we are talking about regulation of the logical infrastructure layer (internet regulation) or regulation at the content layer (usually regulation of web content). Where possible I will make this clear but on some occasions you will need to apply the distinction yourself.

FURTHER READING

Books

K. Hafner & M. Lyon, *Where Wizards Stay Up Late: The Origins of the Internet* (Touchstone, 1996)

J. Naughton, *A Brief History of the Future: Origins of the Internet* (Phoenix, 2000)

T. Berners-Lee, *Weaving the Web: The Original Design and Ultimate Destiny of the World Wide Web by Its Inventor* (HarperCollins, 2000)

Chapters and Articles

Y. Benkler, 'From Consumers to Users: Shifting the Deeper Structures of Regulation Toward Sustainable Commons and User Access', 52 *Federal Communications Law Journal* 561 (2000)

M. Lemley & L. Lessig, 'The End of End-to-End: Preserving the Architecture of the Internet in the Broadband Era' 2000 *Berkeley Law & Economics Working Papers* No.8

B. Owen, 'The Net Neutrality Debate: Twenty Five Years After US v. AT&T and 120 Years After the Act to Regulate Commerce' 2(11) *Perspectives from FSF Scholars* 2007

Digitisation and society

As we saw in Chapter 1 the move from atoms to bits represents a challenge to the traditional economics of bricks and mortar industries as well as to established legal models. Both law and economics have traditionally assumed value and control may be achieved through rivalrousness and exclusivity, both of which are side effects of the atomic model. As also outlined in that chapter, the information society did not emerge fully formed in the 1980s; it had been slowly developing as the post-industrial society which grew at the end of the second world war slowly moved the bulk of the GDP of post-industrial states such as the UK from primary industries such as mining and quarrying and secondary industries such as shipbuilding and car manufacture into the tertiary sector of banking and insurance, and later to the quaternary sector of information broking.

Given this slow economic and social development of the information society it is amazing that traditional economic and legal models have found it so difficult to adapt to the challenges of digitisation. Commentators will cite that the speed of growth of information technologies from the 1960s to the present day as one of the reasons we have been caught out,[1] but in truth it is simpler than that: it is simply the disruptive effect of the process of digitisation. As we touched upon in Chapter 1 a bit can be used as the building block of all types of digital information. It is the informational equal of the atom and can be used to represent, send, and store, text, images, or sound. The bit is the natural way to store textual data such as books or academic papers, music, images such as holiday snaps, or even movies. What has driven the adoption of digital technologies over recent years is threefold. Firstly the cost of storing bits has fallen dramatically over the last fifty years,[2] secondly the cost and speed of transmitting bits across computer networks has equally fallen,[3] and thirdly consumers have fuelled a demand for the incorporation of greater storage capacity and multi-platform support

[1] See, e.g. N. Negroponte, *Being Digital* (1995), 5–6; F. Webster, *Theories of the Information Society* (2002), 9–11.

[2] In 1956 it cost $50,000 to buy the world's first hard drive which stored 5MB of data. This is $10,000 per MB of storage. By 1980 a 26MB HDD was down to $5,000 (or $193 per MB). In 1987 a 40MB Iomega HDD was $1,799 (or $45 per MB). By 1995 the price had dropped all the way to 85¢ per MB with the release of the 2.9GB, $2,899 dollar Seagate HDD. Remarkably the price per MB of HDD storage currently stands at 0.02¢ per MB. Data supplied from *Historical Notes about the Cost of Hard Drive Storage Space:* http://www.alts.net/ns1625/winchest.html.

[3] In the late 1990s a connection speed of 28.8K (or 28 KBs) would cost about £30 per month (in addition to the cost of the modem). By the turn of the millennium 56.6K dialup cost about £25 per month. Now 8MB broadband is available for as little as £5.89 per month.

in all digital devices by continually demanding more from device manufacturers.[4] These three effects have brought about a massive change in the way we use, store, and transmit information. It has freed information from the restrictions of atomic carrier media such as CDs, DVDs, and bound texts and has at the same time made information more valuable and more malleable. These developments will form the focus of this chapter.

3.1 **The digitisation of information**

Before the widespread adoption of digital information management information was held in discrete and often poorly catalogued packets.[5] If we take as our example your NHS medical records we see the difference digitisation makes to the value and accessibility of informational products. Traditionally NHS medical records were held on a variety of manual filing systems. Your GP and each specialist medical provider you visited would each keep their own discrete set of patient records. Thus if you regularly attended three different hospitals for different treatments you would have at least four sets of medical records, one at each hospital and one held by your GP, meaning no one set was complete or definitive. In addition, as all the data on these records was manually recorded and indexed, searching your file was a time-consuming exercise, and as indexing was a skilled job, and therefore expensive, only key information would be indexed in any event. The development of information technology[6] allows for a single record which can be accessed by all carers contemporaneously and which may, instantly, be searched by any keyword.[7] This example, and the example of the iPod given in footnote five, illustrates the power of digital informational management and retrieval. This is developed further by Professor Fred Cate, in his book *Privacy in the Information Age.*[8]

---

[4] Look in your pocket, bag, whatever. Do you have a mobile phone? Does it play music? What about movies? Does it take pictures? What about videos? Can you access the internet on it? What about your email? Can you edit documents? Finally can you use it to call people? If you answered yes to most of these think what would you have been able to do with your mobile phone in 1999.

[5] Think for a moment about the difference between your CD collection and your iPod. Your CD collection was made up of hundreds of individual plastic discs which were held discretely and which you would manually search. Your iPod can hold thousands of tracks and can be searched using titles, artists or genre. You can 'shuffle' your iPod to play music in an unexpected order which can throw up unusual combinations such as Jean-Michel Jarre followed by Iron Maiden in a way not possible when your music was held on discrete packets or discs.

[6] The key aspect of IT or information technology is in its ability to harness the power of information. Too often commentators focus on what the technology can do, not what the information allows. This is a critique levelled by Richard Susskind in his book, *Transforming the Law: Essays on Technology, Justice and the Legal Marketplace* (2000).

[7] This is the theory. In the interests of transparency it should be admitted that the NHS computer system described above is yet to be delivered in practice and recent reports have suggested that the current NHS computer programme will fail to deliver this level of delivery. See '£20bn NHS computer system "doomed to fail"', *The Daily Telegraph*, 13 February 2007: http://www.telegraph.co.uk/news/main.jhtml?xml=/news/2007/02/13/ncomputer13.xml.

[8] F.H. Cate, *Privacy in the Information Age* (1997), 14–15.

→ Highlight Cate's Four Reasons for Data Growth

1. Information is easier to generate, manipulate, transmit and store.
2. The cost of collecting, manipulating, storing, and transmitting data is lowered.
3. Electronic information has developed an intrinsic value not found in analogue information due to its very nature.
4. The operating parameters of computer systems and networks generate additional digital information through back-up copies and cache copies.

Professor Cate describes four generic reasons for the growth of digital information and digital information management. The first, which may be clearly seen from the example above, is that it is easier to generate, manipulate, transmit, and store information. Individuals with simple database programs such as Microsoft Access can manage and manipulate more data on a simple home PC than a medium sized organisation such as a school or small business could do in the analogue era. Secondly, the cost of collecting, manipulating, storing, and transmitting data is lowered. Cheap storage media such as external hard disk drives and flash media, the advent of cheap internet access and the development of file sharing systems such as BitTorrent mean that for a few pence thousands of pages of data may be uploaded, downloaded, or stored. Thirdly, electronic information has developed an intrinsic value not found in analogue information due to its very nature. As digital information is cheaply processed and stored it attracts a premium in the marketplace. This market advantage encourages gatherers of information to favour collection of digital information over analogue information, leading to vast increases in the volume of digital information available. Finally, Cate notes that the operating parameters of computer systems and networks generate additional digital information through back-up copies and cache copies. Due to these four factors Cate records that 'we are witnessing an explosion in digital data.'[9] The effects of such an explosion are more apparent in 2010 than they were when Professor Cate made that observation in 1997. The economies of scale that digital information offers are now significantly enhanced with both the previously observed collapse in the cost of digital storage media and with increased processing capability including keyword cataloguing and the promise in the near future of a semantic web.[10]

---

[9] *ibid*, 16.

[10] The semantic web is one where content information is understandable by computers, allowing them to perform more of the tedious work involved in finding, sharing and combining information on the web. It was described by Sir Tim Berners-Lee as '[a] Web [in which computers] become capable of analyzing all the data on the Web—the content, links, and transactions between people and computers. A "Semantic Web", which should make this possible, has yet to emerge, but when it does, the day-to-day mechanisms of trade, bureaucracy and our daily lives will be handled by machines talking to machines. The "intelligent agents" people have touted for ages will finally materialize'. See T. Berners-Lee & M. Fischetti, *Weaving the Web: The Original Design and Ultimate Destiny of the World Wide Web* (2000), 169. A more detailed analysis of the semantic web may be found in L. Yu, *Introduction to Semantic Web and Semantic Web Services* (2007).

3.1.1 **Information collection, aggregation and exploitation**

As we observed in Chapter 1, the modern economies of leading industrialised nations are now built upon the processing, storage, and transmission of data. A massive data processing industry has grown up, with Google the prime example of how to turn information into profit. We all know Google and we all use Google. According to reports Google is variously the world's most valuable and profitable brand[11] and the largest advertiser in the UK.[12] How did Google achieve this in only 12 years? It has done so by the aggregation of vast amounts of data including search data, data held in Gmail accounts, and data held in the Google shared storage system.[13] This data is then searched for keywords which are then use to make targeted advertisements, or in Google parlance, sponsored links. This type of advertising is much more efficient than television or radio broadcasting which most of the time reaches the wrong audience: it is an advertising cruise missile compared to the old fashioned technique of pattern bombing.

Other companies have caught on: BT have considered the introduction of a service known as Phorm. Phorm allows ISPs to anonymously survey their customers surfing habits and then, in the words of the Phorm website: 'Phorm's proprietary ad serving technology uses anonymised ISP data to deliver the right ad to the right person at the right time—the right number of times'.[14] Of course not everyone believes Phorm is as anonymous as it is claimed and several pressure groups have sprung up including Bad Phorm and Dephormation.[15] These pressure groups focus upon the issue of individual online privacy and advocate campaigning against the gathering of individual data. They achieved a major success in July 2009 when BT chose not to implement Phorm technology in its new Webwise software.[16]

This is the rub of the business model which makes profits from informational processing. To make money you have to either charge for your service, which means you will be undercut by free services, or you have to offer advertisers a better return on their investment than your competitors, this means gathering data about your customers, a process which may generate bad publicity. There is nothing new with this approach; offline supermarkets have done it for years through loyalty cards as have airlines and hotels. Loyalty cards bring two returns: the obvious that the customer is more likely to use your service if he gets something in return, but also less obviously they aggregate and then sell on the data collected via your loyalty account to third parties, as well as using

[11] See Millward Brown, The Top 100 most powerful brands, 08, http://www.brandz.com/upload/BrandZ-2008-RankingReport.pdf.

[12] D. Sabbagh 'Internet outshines ITV in ads war', *The Times*, 30 October 2007: http://business.timesonline.co.uk/tol/business/industry_sectors/media/article2767086.ece.

[13] See http://www.google.co.uk/support/accounts/bin/topic.py?topic=14145. See also R. Blakely, 'Google aims to become world's biggest holder of digital data', *The Times*, 28 November 2007: http://business.timesonline.co.uk/tol/business/industry_sectors/technology/article2957326.ece.

[14] Taken from http://www.phorm.com/.

[15] You can find out about these groups at respectively http://www.badphorm.co.uk/ and http://www.dephormation.org.uk/.

[16] R. Wray, 'BT drops plan to use Phorm targeted ad service after outcry over privacy', *The Guardian*, 6 July 2009: http://www.guardian.co.uk/business/2009/jul/06/btgroup-privacy-and-the-net.

it themselves.[17] The problem with these schemes, if there is a problem, is the informational asymmetry involved. We as customers are willing to give away vast amounts of personal data to get a Gmail or Yahoo! Mail account or in return for a 1% discount on our weekly shop. We are not aware of the potential value of this data on the secondary market and as a result, arguably, data protection laws have not yet caught up with the benefits that modern information processing brings. We will examine in detail much of these effects in Part VI—Privacy in the Information Society.

3.1.2 Information disintermediation

While Professor Cate has caused us to stop and consider the possible downside of the digitisation of information as it effects individual privacy, there is, as far as the individual end user is concerned a very clear upside also. Freed from the restrictions of atomic carrier media informational products have forged a new distribution system through the internet. While the supply of informational products were traditionally tied to the standard distribution chain of manufacturer-carrier-shop (think of a CD which would be pressed, distributed then sold on the high street), the modern distribution system for informational products such as music, movies, and newspapers and magazines is by direct delivery from the producer of the product to the consumer by digital download. This is part of a process known as disintermediation where the middle-men in a supply chain are cut out and the financial benefits are split between the supplier and the purchaser. Now instead of buying your music at Virgin or HMV on a CD you are more likely to download it from iTunes or Napster. You may even take it one stage further and get your music direct from the band via their MySpace page, thus also disintermediating the record producer. Similarly whereas you once bought your copy of *The Guardian* at your local newsagent now you can read the paper online in full, and should you want to read the paper exactly as typeset you can subscribe to the digital edition of the paper. Again you have the option of bypassing the editors and publishers of the newspaper and going straight to the source of many news stories through the advent of so-called citizen journalism where individuals play an active role in the process of collecting, reporting, analysing, and disseminating news and information, usually through the blogosphere.[18] In both these examples disintermediation of the distribution network may be imprecisely called Web 1.0 distribution. This is the traditional model of digital distribution in which content producers developed websites and download tools which were strictly one-way 'push' media. The second examples, which use social networking tools such as MySpace and blogging tools such as Blogger, are Web 2.0 systems where digital networks are harnessed to facilitate creativity, sharing of information, and collaboration among users.[19] The challenge online collaborative endeavours brings to traditional informational products is already well-known among producers of such products.

[17] To read about Tesco's Crucible database, operated by its marketing subsidiary 'Dunnhumby' see H. Tomlinson & R. Evans, 'Tesco stocks up on inside knowledge of shoppers' lives', *The Guardian*, 20 September 2005: http://www.guardian.co.uk/business/2005/sep/20/freedomofinformation.supermarkets.
[18] S. Bowman & C. Willis, *We Media: How Audiences are Shaping the Future of News and Information*. (2003): http://www.hypergene.net/wemedia/download/we_media.pdf.
[19] T. O'Reilly, What is Web 2.0: Design Patterns and Business Models for the Next Generation of Software (2007) 1 *Communications & Strategies* 17. Web 2.0 will be discussed in depth in Chs 6 and 20.

In 1994 respected cyber-commentator John Perry Barlow wrote a prophetic paper about the effects of disintermediation and the economic impact it would come to have. This paper, entitled *The Economy of Ideas: Selling Wine Without Bottles on the Global Net*,[20] is widely available online[21] and outlined many of the challenges disintermediation would bring to traditional informational entertainment industries such as the music industry. He defines the challenge as: '[as] digital technology is detaching information from the physical plane, where property law of all sorts has always found definition ... [this] property can be infinitely reproduced and instantaneously distributed all over the planet without cost, without our knowledge, without its even leaving our possession, how can we protect it? How are we going to get paid for the work we do with our minds? And, if we can't get paid, what will assure the continued creation and distribution of such work?'[22]

Barlow, who has some experience of the creative industries having worked as a lyricist for the Grateful Dead, reminds us it is not the ideas that are protected by intellectual property laws, but rather the expression of the ideas.[23] Taken a step further Barlow reminds us it is how the expression of the ideas is recorded that is protected: thus patents are specified,[24] trademarks are registered,[25] and copyright material is fixed.[26] In Barlow's terms: 'throughout the history of copyrights and patents, the proprietary assertions of thinkers have been focussed not on their ideas but on the expression of those ideas. The ideas themselves, as well as facts about the phenomena of the world, were considered to be the collective property of humanity. One could claim franchise, in the case of copyright, on the precise turn of phrase used to convey a particular idea or the order in which facts were presented. The point at which this franchise was imposed was that moment when the 'word became flesh' by departing the mind of its originator and entering some physical object, whether book or widget. The subsequent arrival of other commercial media besides books didn't alter the legal importance of this moment. Law protected expression and, with few (and recent) exceptions, to express was to make physical ... For all practical purposes, the value was in the conveyance and not the thought conveyed.'[27] Barlow developed a useful shorthand for this process: 'the bottle was protected, not the wine'.[28] Of course the ability to send information as bits across the telecommunications network changes this. The wine can now be carried without the bottle and as such, Barlow argues that traditional models of property law, in particular traditional intellectual property laws, will be required to evolve if they are to remain useful.

---

[20] *Wired 2.03*, March 1994.

[21] At many sources including: http://homes.eff.org/~barlow/EconomyOfIdeas.html; http://www.virtualschool.edu/mon/ElectronicFrontier/WineWithoutBottles.html; and http://www.selenasol.com/selena/extropia/idea_economy_article.html.   [22] *ibid.*

[23] H. MacQueen, C. Waelde & G. Laurie, *Contemporary Intellectual Property: Law and Policy* (2007), Ch. 2.   [24] Patents Act 1977, s. 14(2)(b).   [25] TMA 1994, s. 32(2)(d).

[26] CDPA 1988, s. 3(2).   [27] Barlow, above n. 20.   [28] *ibid.*

> **Case Study** Napster
>
> Everyone knows at least part of the story of Napster. In June 1999 Shawn Fanning, a student at Boston's Northeastern University, released his 'Napster' protocol.
>
> Fanning created Napster out of frustration: he, like many college students, was an avid music fan who was strapped for cash. He was frustrated for several reasons. Firstly, he wanted to search for digital music files but the only option available at the time was to use crude search engines which would search the entirety of a library with no specific ability to search for music files. Secondly he wanted to swap interesting pieces of music with like-minded individuals but didn't have the tools to do so, and thirdly he was frustrated by the quality of music available and the cost of replacing older collections on vinyl with newer collections on CD.
>
> Fanning designed his Napster protocol to meet these needs. It was, in his mind at least, primarily a tool designed to create a community where people could meet and talk about music. He initially envisaged that any trading of music files would take place outside the Napster community by email or Internet Relay Chat but late in the development of Napster he added a revolutionary option: the ability to interface directly with the computer of another Napster user and to download from his or her PC music files in MP3 format.
>
> Napster was an instant success. It rapidly gathered members from around the globe and Napster fundamentally altered the market structure for online music distribution with, at the peak of Napster's popularity, almost three billion music files being traded amongst members each month.

In design Napster was much like eBay: a consumer-to-consumer (C2C) trading community, but Napster was designed specifically around a single product: digital music files. This difference drove the early success of Napster, but was ultimately to lead to its downfall. As Barlow had pointed out five years earlier, creative goods are quite distinct from physical goods and whereas eBay is a valuable C2C reselling community which allows individuals to sell on items at the value the market attaches to them, members of the Napster community were engaged in something quite different. Napster was a C2C trading community, that much is true, but with Napster the trading was in copies of music files meaning the 'seller' never relinquished their original file: this in turn meant that there was no need to charge for files and so all music in the Napster community was available at no cost. The result was a market which was built on a clearly illegal activity and which fundamentally undermined the market model for paid-for digital music downloads: why pay Apple 99¢ per track when you could download it for free from Napster? The Napster market model was about to undermine the entire exercise of designing paid-for music download models: from the point of view of the media distribution industries it had to be closed down, and quickly.[29]

The response from the music industry was exactly as has been predicted by Barlow; information had to be 'propertised' again. The music industry made a two-pronged

---

[29] Napster will be discussed in depth in Ch. 10 but a short discussion of the Napster case here is useful.

attack. Firstly they set out to close down the immediate threat of Napster. As the vast majority of music available on Napster was protected by copyright, a group of leading music studios, including A&M Records, Geffen Records, MCA, Motown, and Capitol Records raised a suit against Napster claiming contributory and vicarious copyright infringement.[30] Following a trial hearing the District Court found that the complainants had successfully established a *prima facie* case of direct copyright infringement on the part of Napster's users. According to the Court, 'virtually all Napster users engage in the unauthorised downloading or up-loading of copyrighted music'[31] and 'Napster users get for free something they would ordinarily have to buy [which] suggests that they reap economic advantages from Napster use.'[32] Further the Court held that the effect of the use upon the value of the work and potential markets for the work weighed against finding that use of Napster constituted fair use. As a result it rejected Napster's fair use defence, and distinguished the Supreme Court's decision in *Sony Corp of America v Universal City Studios*[33] In particular, the Trial Judge noted that unlike VCRs, in which users were initially invited to view the television broadcast for free, Napster users obtained permanent copies of songs that they would otherwise have had to purchase. Further, the majority of VCR users merely enjoyed the tapes at home, in contrast, 'a Napster user who downloads a copy of a song to her hard drive may make that song available to millions of other individuals ... facilitating unauthorized distribution at an exponential rate.'[34] The District Court, in short, concluded that the conduct of Napster users could not be considered fair use because it threatened the incentives created by copyright. With this finding, the music industry obtained judgements against Napster for both contributory infringement,[35] and vicarious infringement.[36] An appeal by Napster to the Ninth Circuit proved to be unsuccessful[37] and in February 2001 Napster was closed down.

---

[30] *A&M Records Inc v Napster Inc* 114 F Supp 2d 896 (N D Cal 2000), affd in part and revd in part, 239 F 3d 1004 (9th Cir 2001).   [31] *ibid*, 911.   [32] *ibid*.

[33] 464 US 417 (1984).   [34] *A&M Records v Napster*, above n. 30, 913.

[35] Contributory infringement requires both knowledge of the infringing activity and a material contribution (actual assistance or inducement) to the alleged primary infringement. The Court interpreted the knowledge requirement as not merely that the Napster system allowed an infringing use, but that Napster had actual notice of the infringement and then failed to remove the offending material. The Court concluded that Napster knew or had reason to know of its users' infringement of plaintiffs' copyrights, that Napster failed to remove the material, and that Napster materially contributed to the infringing activity by providing the site and facilities for direct infringement.

[36] Vicarious infringement results when there has been a direct infringement and the vicarious infringer is in a position to control the direct infringer, fails to do so and benefits financially from the infringement. The Court held that Napster was vicariously liable as they failed to exercise their right and ability to prevent the exchange of copyrighted material. Further, Napster had a direct financial interest in the downloading activities since their revenue was dependent on user increase which was driven by the infringing activities of users.

[37] In fact Napster's appeal was partly successful. The Court of Appeal noted that: 'contributory liability may potentially be imposed only to the extent that Napster: (1) receives reasonable knowledge of specific infringing files with copyrighted musical compositions and sound recordings; (2) knows or should know that such files are available on the Napster system; and (3) fails to act to prevent viral distribution of the works. The mere existence of the Napster system, absent actual notice and Napster's demonstrated failure to remove the offending material, is insufficient to impose contributory liability' (1014). This meant the plaintiffs had to give Napster written notice of all infringing files.

3.1.3 **Information management**

The music industry knew that litigation on its own was not going to deal with the problem of illegal trading in MP3 files. What was needed was to replace the 'bottle' which had been lost: the re-propertisation of digital content. The music industry had since the mid 1990s been developing cryptography tools such as Digital Rights Management (DRM) and Digital Watermarking. Again this had been predicted by Barlow. He had defined cryptography as 'the 'material' from which the walls, boundaries—and bottles—of Cyberspace will be fashioned.'[38] DRMs offer the media distribution industries the most tantalising opportunity: distribution of their products in a carrier medium which cannot be copied. As DRMs use an encryption key to control access to the media file, they prevent not only against illegal access but also copying—they are a bit like having a book printed on unco-pyable paper where the text only becomes visible when the authorised owner of that book is reading it.[39]

The problem with DRM encryption is that any digital technology which can be engi-neered can also be reverse engineered, in other words months or years spent designing your encryption protocol may be undone in minutes by a cracker.[40] To prevent wide-spread cracking of DRMs the entertainment industries sought to give legal support to DRM technology by propertising DRMs. This was achieved through Articles 11 and 12 of the World Intellectual Property Organization (WIPO) Copyright Treaty adopted in Geneva in December 1996.[41] Article 11 requires all WIPO states to 'provide adequate legal protection and effective legal remedies against the circumvention of effective technological measures that are used by authors in connection with the exercise of their rights', while Article 12 requires WIPO states to criminalise attempts to 'remove or alter any electronic rights management information without authority'; or to 'distribute, import for distribution, broadcast or communicate to the public, without authority, works or copies of works knowing that electronic rights management information has been removed or altered without authority.'

In Europe the 2001 Directive on Copyright and Related Rights in the Information Society[42] gives effect to these provisions. This restricts all acts of circumvention,[43] bans the importation, sale, rental, or possession for commercial purposes of all tools designed to allow circumvention of encryption systems,[44] and the distribution of con-tent from which a rights management system has been removed.[45] This would appear to be the end of this tale. Bottles have been recreated through the use of cryptography.

---

[38] Barlow, above n. 20.

[39] It should be noted that DRMs do not on the whole prevent the digital media file from being replicated, but what is replicated is the *encrypted* file not the plaintext file, meaning that simply copying the file is worthless unless you have a license from the copyright owner to access it.

[40] Software cracking is the modification of software to remove encoded copy prevention. Those who carry out this activity are crackers, not hackers. The resultant decrypted files are is known as Warez and are widely distributed.

[41] http://www.wipo.int/treaties/en/ip/wct/trtdocs_wo033.html.   [42] Dir.2001/29/EC.

[43] Art. 6(1).   [44] Art .6(2).   [45] Art. 7(1).

Any attempt to tamper with, remove, or damage such bottles is criminalised. The status quo, which was unbalanced by the disintermediation of content and carrier, is digitally restored. But, I am pleased to say that while the content industry may be thinking small: we, their customers are thinking big. Fed up of the iTunes/iPod technical symbiotic relationship,[46] customers continued to lobby for DRM free files from iTunes and eventually, on 2 April 2007 Apple announced it would make available DRM free content.[47] Since this announcement more and more music has become available DRM free including the distribution of DRM free music from Sony, Warner, and Universal on MySpace and with DRM free music now being distributed by among others Amazon and Tesco, the crypto-bottle appears to be shattered which is good news as we seek to carry our digital content on ever more intelligent devices which can multi-task.

3.2 **Digital convergence**[48]

I have an iPhone: the iPhone is a truly remarkable device. On it you can (among other things): listen to music, phone people, text people, watch videos, send and receive email, surf the web, manage your calendar, take pictures, store pictures, write text, check your stocks, and plan your journeys using Google maps. Think back twenty years (if you are old enough). To do all these things I would have needed to carry a Walkman, a mobile phone, a laptop computer, a journal or diary, a camera, and a road atlas. Now I have a hand-held device that weighs 133g. This change has been brought about by the fifth generic reason for the growth of digital information and digital information management which we can add to Cate's original four: digital convergence.

Convergence can be seen as another side effect of the freeing of content from the carrier. Whereas previously all content had a different carrier medium: photographs used photographic film or paper, music used magnetic tape, optical discs (CD) or vinyl disks, while text used paper; now freed from these restrictions all content is carried equally, as 0s and 1s. The concept of convergence came to media and communications theory from the mathematical disciplines where it was used to refer to the coming together of physical things such as beams of light or non-parallel lines. Media and communications commentators began to apply the term to the coming together of media platforms in the late 1970s or early 1980s, it being extremely difficult to determine exactly when,

---

[46] Apple Encrypted AAC files as downloaded from iTunes will only play on Apple approved products such as iPods and some mobile phones.

[47] Originally DRM free content, called iTunes plus was more expensive than DRM encoded content, but from October 2007 all content supplied from iTunes is DRM free if allowed by the music publisher.

[48] Digital Convergence or digital platform convergence or sometimes technological convergence should not be confused with the related but different phenomena of media convergence. Media convergence is an economic strategy in which communications companies seek financial benefit by making the various media properties they own work together. For a discussion of media convergence see H. Jenkins, *Convergence Culture: Where Old and New Media Collide* (2006).

and by whom, the term was first used in this context. What is clear though is that communications theorist Ithiel de Sola Pool adopted this contextual use of the term and popularised it among media and communications theorists. In his landmark 1983 book, *The Technologies of Freedom*,[49] Pool wrote of the 'convergence between historically separated modes of communication' and argued that 'electronic technology is bringing all modes of communications into one grand system'.[50]

Despite writing in 1983 it took close to twenty-five years for Pool's vision to become reality, why did it take so long? One obvious reason was the delay in developing a fully digital informational distribution chain. For complete digital convergence to become a reality we require technological innovations in every stage of the information infrastructure. Information needs to be gathered digitally. This is now becoming quite commonplace with reporters filing stories by email and the use of digital cameras to record news events and television broadcasts. Then information needs to be stored and delivered in digital form. Again this is now becoming true. Most media outlets now store information in digital form and deliver it digitally, whether as digital television, digital radio, or as an online newspaper. Secondly it required a new generation of portable devices that would multi-task. The arrival of devices such as the Apple iPhone, the Nokia N95, and the RIM Blackberry signal that perhaps twenty-five years after Pool predicted it we stand on the threshold of the golden age of convergence.

What legal challenges will convergence bring? As we saw above digitisation challenged both privacy and property laws. As information and content became cheaper to gather, cheaper to process, and cheaper to distribute, the intellectual connection between information or data and concepts such as personhood, privacy, autonomy, and respect for private property were initially swept aside in a rush to experiment with new technologies and to profit from new data mining and data gathering techniques. In comparison with digitisation digital platform convergence is still in its infancy. The earliest platform convergence came about in 2000 with the release in Japan of the Sharp J-SH04 which was the world's first commercially available camera phone.[51] Thus it is still too early to predict with certainty all of the issues that platform convergence will raise but some that we may predict will be vexing lawyers and judges in the next five to ten years.

The first which comes to mind is payments to authors and creators for multiple applications of content. Music phones allow you use an MP3 file or similar for use as a personalised ringtone. The iPhone takes it one step further by allowing you to tailor a piece of iTunes purchased music to be used as your ringtone. The issue for composers of music is that they want to ensure they are properly recompensed for their efforts. If I pay 79p to download a single music track to my music enabled phone the author will receive a payment of royalties. If I then decide to use that MP3 as my ringtone the author should receive a separate payment. With retail value of the UK's music ringtone

---

[49] I. de Sola Pool, *The Technologies of Freedom* (1983).   [50] *ibid*, 28.
[51] The author acknowledges that General Purpose Computers could before this date do many things required of a convergent device such as play music, organise data, send and receive email, etc. but argues that as they were by name General Purpose machines they were as such not properly convergent devices.

market estimated at being worth between £100–120m, compared to £30m for full track mobile downloads, the value of this market to composers and music publishers is all too clear.[52] The risk comes from so-called sideloading of content. This is where the user loads content to their music enabled phone, either from a download site or from a CD or other media and then converts that to be used as a ringtone or for some other use. Composers of music sold as downloaded ringtones have their royalties collected on their behalf by the Performing Rights Society, but they have recently admitted that with people sideloading content to music enabled phones they have been only been able to collect less than 5% of the royalty value in ringtones and in online music streaming.[53] As more and more devices become multi-platform this problem is set to increase.

The second problem is multiple file copies. When a music publisher sold a CD he sold, and therefore took a royalty for the composer, on the basis that this was one copy of the music sold. As the law currently stands if I take a CD and 'rip' it to my MP3 player this is an infringement of copyright.[54] There is currently in the UK no right to back-up a music file,[55] thus all of us, myself included, who transferred their CD collection to their iPod or other MP3 player did so in breach of the current law. This has recently been reviewed by the Gowers' Review of Intellectual Property, [56] where it was recommended that the Government 'introduce a limited private copying exception by 2008 for for-mat shifting for works published after the date that the law comes into effect. There should be no accompanying levies for consumers.'[57] This recommendation has since been taken forward in the Triesman consultation,[58] where it has been recommended that 'a new exception to copyright to allow consumers to make a copy of a work they legally own, so that they can make the work accessible in another format for playback on a device in their lawful possession' be created.[59]

You may note this says I may make **one** copy of the work in another format. What about multi-device homes? In our house we have a CD player, a desktop computer, a laptop, two iPods and two iPhones. That suggests we need to make six copies of the orig-inal. Triesman goes on to say 'It would only permit format shifting, i.e. the copying of legitimately owned works to different formats for use on different devices. It would not include the broader range of private uses, such as multiple copying of all types of work or copying for friends and family.'[60] This confuses matters somewhat as it says devices, plural, but does not allow copying for friends and family, does this mean my wife can't put my copy of Employment by the Kaiser Chiefs on her iPod? This is then further

---

[52] Figures taken from A. Webb, 'Hanging up on ringtones', *The Guardian*, 28 June 2007: http://www.guardian.co.uk/technology/2007/jun/28/mobilephones.guardianweeklytechnologysection.
[53] K. Allen, 'Boom in live music and video clips gives PRS license to print money', *The Guard-ian*, 21 April 2008. Available at: http://www.guardian.co.uk/business/2008/apr/21/mediabusiness.digitalmedia.   [54] CDPA 1988, s. 17(2).
[55] Although s. 50A allows for backup copies to be made of computer software this is not permis-sible for other media.
[56] A. Gowers, *Review of Intellectual Property* (2006): http://www.hm-treasury.gov.uk/media/6/E/pbr06_gowers_report_755.pdf.   [57] Recommendation 8.
[58] D. Triesman, 'Taking Forward the Gowers Review of Intellectual Property Proposed Changes to Copyright Exceptions' (2008): http://www.ipo.gov.uk/consult-copyrightexceptions.pdf.
[59] *ibid*, [85].   [60] *ibid*, [86].

'clarified': 'While users will be allowed to make only one copy of a work for use on a different device, users will be able to copy a work sequentially without restriction to allow for developing technology, for example where formats and playback devices become obsolete and consumers replace an old player with a newer version. Currently, users might wish to copy from CDs to MP3 players, but in the future they are likely to need to copy from their MP3 onto another device. It is proposed that a consumer should be permitted to repeatedly shift content for use on different devices they own, provided they still retain possession of their original (and legitimate) copy.'[61] So it appears I can only have a copy on my iPod if I don't have a copy on my iPhone (unless the iPod is obsolete).

This fudge is caused by a lack of appreciation of convergent technologies. As more and more devices offer multi-platform support individuals will store content in a variety of sources to make it easy to access wherever they are. They will have an MP3 jukebox in their car which is also their SatNav and when not on the move will be a digital TV receiver and MP4 player and it will function as their in-car mobile attaching to their mobile phone via Bluetooth. This will have one music library. They will have a DVR or PVR,[62] connected to their TV, with a library of music and video. They will have a music phone such as the iPhone for music on the move. They will have old fashioned iTunes libraries and they will probably retain specialist devices such as the iPod nano or shuffle for when exercising. Thus the new law is out of date before even being written because people will have a plethora of devices which can all act as MP3 libraries and players.

These are just two of the challenges of platform convergence. These will be discussed more fully in chapters eight and ten. Others include a re-evaluation of the expectation one has to privacy as we are all turned into potential news reporters by our camera phones and as we are allowed to be news broadcasters through YouTube and others,[63] and the overwhelming production of obscene and indecent material which digital convergence has allowed, including the alarming rise of obscenity and child abuse images.[64] The latter of which is aided by the final palpable effect digitisation has had on society: the failure of laws to adequately cross borders.

3.3 **The cross-border challenge of information law**

The cross-border effects of digital information transfers were first identified by Professors David Post and David Johnson in their groundbreaking paper *Law and Borders—The Rise of Law in Cyberspace*.[65] Here they laid for the first time a legal interpretation,

---

[61] *ibid*, [94].
[62] A Digital Video Recorder (DVR) or Personal Video Recorder (PVR) is a device which records video in a digital format to a Hard Disk Drive. Early examples included TiVo. Most people in the UK know them as Sky+.   [63] Discussed in Chs. 18 and 19.   [64] Discussed in Ch. 14.
[65] 48 *Stanford Law Review* 1367 (1996): http://www.cli.org/X0025_LBFIN.html.

known as classical Cyberlibertarianism, which contends that regulation founded upon traditional state sovereignty, based as it is upon notions of physical borders, cannot function effectively in Cyberspace as individuals may move seamlessly between zones governed by differing regulatory regimes in accordance with their personal preferences.[66] Simply put, they claimed the internet was unregulable as laws were confined to the jurisdiction in which they were promulgated while content hosted and carried on the internet, including obscene content, flowed seamlessly over these borders.

The overwhelming problem that lawmakers face in dealing with online pornography is which standard to apply. In the UK we use the Obscene Publication Act 1959 to determine whether an item is obscene (and therefore illegal) or merely indecent. This states: 'For the purposes of this Act an article shall be deemed to be obscene if its effect or (where the article comprises two or more distinct items) the effect of any one of its items is, if taken as a whole, such as to tend to deprave and corrupt persons who are likely, having regard to all relevant circumstances, to read, see or hear the matter contained or embodied in it.'[67] This standard is specifically designed to be flexible and to change over time as community standards change and over the fifty years it has been in force the UK standard of obscenity has changed quite dramatically.[68]

Internationally individual states are continually altering their obscenity standard to meet contemporary community standards. What is considered sexually explicit but not obscene in the UK may well be considered to be obscene in the Republic of Ireland, and almost certainly material considered obscene in the Islamic Republic of Iran or in the Kingdom of Saudi Arabia would not be felt to be noteworthy in the UK. Similarly material which would be considered to be obscene in the UK would probably not be censored in Germany, Spain, or Sweden where a more tolerant approach to erotica and pornographic material is taken. What we are seeing in these differences is a spectrum of community standards which range from extremely conservative to extremely liberal. In general this system has functioned quite effectively in the real world due to the existence of physical borders and border controls. The easiest way for a state to apply its legal standard of obscenity within its borders is to prevent the importation of materials which offend the standard of that state, while simultaneously criminalising the production of such materials within the state. In the UK, for example, it is an offence to import indecent or obscene prints, paintings, photographs, books, cards, lithographic or other engravings, or any other indecent or obscene articles under s. 42 of the Customs Consolidation Act 1876, while s. 2 of the Obscene Publications Act 1959 criminalises the publication, or possession with intent to publish, of an obscene article.

The Customs Consolidation Act allows the UK to apply effective border controls. It allows HM Revenue and Customs to seize obscene items, and where necessary to prosecute those involved in their importation. This control provision continues to apply

---

[66] The Cyberlibertarian School will be discussed in depth in Ch. 4.
[67] Obscene Publications Act 1959, s. 1(1).
[68] For a discussion on the evolution of the obscenity standard see Ch. 14. Also see A. Murray, *The Regulation of Cyberspace: Control in the Online Environment* (2007), 205–209.

despite the UK's membership of the European Union, with it being held on several occasions that this power subsists in relation to material deemed obscene under the Obscene Publications Act despite the effects of Articles 28 and 30 of the EC Treaty.[69] But these traditional measures are predicated upon the assumption that the items in question will be fixed in a physical medium, and that they will require physical carriage to enter the state. With the advent of the digital age both these assumptions have been rendered null. The development of a global informational network has dismantled these traditional borders. The result of this is all too apparent, especially to parents trying to control what their children are exposed to. HM Revenue and Customs, along with the Police, have given up all attempts to apply the provisions of the Customs Consolidation Act or the Obscene Publications Acts to content found on the internet. Instead they have decided to focus their limited resources on narrow areas which produce a sound return on their investment. Thus despite surveys which show more than 10 million UK adults visit pornographic websites,[70] and that 57% of British 9-19 year olds who go online at least once a week have come into contact with online pornography,[71] there have been no prosecutions in England and Wales under either the Customs Consolidation Act or the Obscene Publications Act 1959 for privately viewing obscene material using an internet connection.

The authorities have instead focussed their attention on the storing and distribution of child abuse images,[72] and prosecuting those who run pornographic websites from overseas servers but who are resident in the UK and profit from this activity.[73] With the removal of the physical border between the UK and the rest of the world internet users were afforded the opportunity to access and view pornography held overseas in the blink of an eye and with little opportunity for the authorities to intercept the content *en route*. This caused a huge upsurge in consumption and left the authorities with a difficult decision to make. They could either invest large sums to attempt to enforce the law in the digital environment,[74] or they could *de facto* deregulate adult obscenity and focus their attentions on more pressing problems such as child abuse images. The UK authorities recognising the limits of the law in relation to this subject chose to focus their resources on only the most harmful content.

This case study, which will be developed further in Chapter 14, demonstrates the difficulty lawmakers find in applying geographically based legal rules in an environment

---

[69] *Conegate Ltd v HM Customs & Excise* [1987] QB 254 (ECJ); *R. v Forbes* [2002] 2 AC 512 (HL).

[70] A. Barnes & S. Goodchild, 'Porn UK', *The Independent on Sunday*, 28 May 2006: http://www.independent.co.uk/news/uk/this-britain/porn-uk-480084.html.

[71] S. Livingstone & M. Bober, *UK Children Go Online* (LSE Department of Media & Communication, 2005): http://www.lse.ac.uk/collections/children-go-online/UKCGOfinalReport.pdf.

[72] See *R. v Barry Philip Halloren* [2004] 2 Cr App R (S) 57; *R. v Snelleman* [2001] EWCA Crim 1530 and *R. v James* [2000] 2 Cr App R (S) 258.

[73] See *R. v Ross Andrew McKinnon* [2004] 2 Cr App R (S) 46 and *R. v Stephane Laurent Perrin* [2002] EWCA Crim 747.

[74] This could either be achieved by the investment of these funds into additional law enforcement personnel or by using the funds to design a technological solution to the problem such as a national firewall or filtering system which would in effect rebuild the natural border in Cyberspace. See R. Deibert & N. Villeneuve, 'Firewalls and Power: An Overview of Global State Censorship of the Internet' in M. Klang & A. Murray (eds), *Human Rights in the Digital Age* (2005).

which effectively floats over borders. That is not to say that law is ineffective in dealing with these issues. Throughout this book we will see the courts take effective jurisdiction over online defamation, pornography and child abuse images, computer hacking, computer fraud and data theft, copyright infringement, and a variety of other issues. The law is effective in cyberspace. The difficulty is in identifying which court has effective jurisdiction and in identifying who is the relevant person to pursue.[75]

3.4 **Digitisation and law**

This chapter has outlined several of the challenges digitisation brings to lawmakers. By replacing old fashioned analogue data which was expensive to gather, expensive to store, and expensive to search, and which was subject to decay in quality over time and would decay each time it was copied,[76] with digital data which is cheap to gather, cheap to store and search and which is perfectly replicated every time we have unleashed a wave of data gathering and data mining which threatens to unbalance our expectation to privacy. In addition we have allowed an expectation to grow that one may share content and may obtain content for free or at little cost because we convince ourselves that no-one is harmed by this.

Digital convergence and multi-purpose 'smart' devices are leading us to expect media distinctions to become blurred and are allowing us to sideload content from one media to another without paying for the privilege. Also as media devices become more portable and multi-functional we will find once again barriers between the private and public space are broken down as 'citizen journalists' record events and post them to the web. Finally the internet has forced lawmakers and lawyers to accept that we are part of an international community and we can no longer expect that we can close our border to things we do not like. The response of the UK legal establishment to the problem of online obscenity is instructive in this. The law enforcement authorities accepted that the community had accepted that most 'mainstream' pornography was not damaging to society and chose not to prosecute those who viewed such material, while focussing on the more obscene material people found most offensive.[77] These challenges are just a few of the challenges of the process of digitisation and a move to the world of bits. The remainder of this book, starting with the next chapter, will outline how the law and lawmakers have responded to these challenges.

---

[75] This is discussed more fully in Ch. 15.
[76] This is analogue drop off, discussed in Ch. 1.
[77] In relation to this the UK Government has recently moved to outlaw the possession of 'extreme pornography' through s. 63 of the Criminal Justice and Immigration Act 2008. See A. Murray, 'The Reclassification of Extreme Pornographic Material' (2009) 72 *MLR* 73.

FURTHER READING

Books

F.H. Cate, *Privacy in the Information Age* (1997)

I. de Sola Pool, *The Technologies of Freedom* (1983)

H. Jenkins, *Convergence Culture: Where Old and New Media Collide* (2008)

Chapters and Articles

J.P. Barlow, 'The Economy of Ideas: Selling Wine Without Bottles on the Global Net', *Wired* 2.03, March 1994

R. Deibert & N. Villeneuve, 'Firewalls and Power: An Overview of Global State Censorship of the Internet' in M. Klang & A. Murray (eds) *Human Rights in the Digital Age* (2005)

N. Rose, 'An overview of the proposed introduction of a private copying exception into UK copyright law' [2008] *Entertainment Law Review* 75

D. Lichtman, 'Defusing DRM' *Olin Working Paper* No. 282 (2006)

PART II

Governance in the information society

How can lawyers, lawmakers and judges control the actions of individuals in the online and virtual environments? Can traditional laws such as property law and defamation survive in the digital environment?

4 **Regulating the digital environment**

    4.1 Can we regulate the digital environment?

    4.2 Lawrence Lessig's modalities of regulation

    4.3 Network communitarianism

    4.4 Regulators in cyberspace: private regulators

    4.5 Regulators in cyberspace: states and supranational regulation

    4.6 Conclusion

5 **Digital ownership**

    5.1 Digital property

    5.2 Digital trespass

    5.3 Virtual property

    5.4 Conclusions

6 **Cyber-speech**

    6.1 Introduction

    6.2 From web 1.0 to web 2.0

    6.3 Freedom of expression and social responsibility

    6.4 Political speech

    6.5 Hate speech

    6.6 Commercial speech

    6.7 Conclusion: cyber-speech and free expression

7 Defamation

7.1 The tort of defamation

7.2 Digital defamation: publication and republication

7.3 Intermediary liability

7.4 Digital defamation and UGC

7.5 Conclusion

4

Regulating the digital environment

As discussed in Chapter 3, the process of digitisation is proving to be a logistical challenge for lawmakers. In the real world we design laws to protect physical goods and to control the actions of corporeal individuals. Thus, as was discussed in Chapter 1, s. 1 of the Theft Act 1968, expects that stolen goods are tangible. Similarly, and as discussed in Chapter 3, Copyright Law, although a law designed to deal with intangible goods, makes use of the physical environment to assist in the regulation of copyright infringement, while personal data privacy was, prior to digitisation, protected in part by the environmental factors which made storage of, access to, and cross-referencing of information held in physical files expensive and time consuming. The societal move from value in atoms to value in bits therefore offers a major challenge to lawmakers as it suggests traditional legal rules require to be re-evaluated when we consider extending them into the digital environment. For example, should the provisions of real world laws such as the Theft Act 1968 apply to virtual universes where virtual property is acquired and sometimes stolen?[1] Similarly should the legal provision designed to prevent abuse of children in the production of child abuse images, found in s. 1 of the Protection of Children Act 1978, be extended to prevent the production and possession of pseudo-images; images which appear to portray the abuse of a child but which have been computer generated?[2] These challenges of digitisation, allied to the ability of internet communications to cross borders without being subjected to border controls, led some lawyers and academics to suggest that traditional legal rules, predicated on the dual foundations of physicality of goods and persons and jurisdictional boundaries, could not be extended to Cyberspace. They believed that the incorporeal and borderless nature of the digital environment would render traditional lawmakers powerless, and would empower the community within Cyberspace to elect its own lawmakers and to design its own laws tailored to that environment. Others disagreed, and for a period of time the argument was not about which laws should be applied in the digital environment: it was more simply could we regulate the actions of individuals in the digital environment at all?

---

[1] This question will be discussed in depth in Ch. 21.
[2] This question will be discussed in depth in Ch. 14.

4.1 **Can we regulate the digital environment?**

4.1.1 **Cyberlibertarianism**

On 8 February 1996 John Perry Barlow published his declaration that Cyberspace was a separate sovereign space where real world laws and real world governments were of little or no effect.[3] His *Declaration of Independence for Cyberspace* was a powerful challenge to lawmakers and law enforcement bodies.

 Highlight Barlow's Declaration of Independence for Cyberspace

> Weary giants of flesh and steel you are not welcome among us and have no sovereignty where we gather.... You have no moral right to rule us nor do you possess any methods of enforcement we have true reason to fear.

The final part of this sentence sets out one of the key supports utilised by the school of thought that was soon to become known as cyberlibertarianism. They believed that as traditional lawmakers may only enforce their laws within the confines of their legal jurisdiction, subject of course to a few specialised examples of extraterritorial effect,[4] when a citizen of a real world jurisdiction, such as England and Wales, enters Cyberspace they cross a virtual border to a new sovereign state where the laws of the old state they left are no longer legitimate or valid. Further because this person is in a virtual (digital) environment they have no corporeal body to imprison and any digital goods they own are in limitless supply meaning that the sequestration of goods is an impractical method of punishment. This led to the belief, as expressed by Barlow, that traditional lawmakers could not enforce their laws against citizens of Cyberspace.

There is an obvious weakness in this argument. When one visits Cyberspace one does not travel to that place. Unlike the imaginary worlds of childhood fantasy such as Narnia or Alice's Wonderland, Cyberspace is not somewhere to which we are physically transported. This means that if an individual were to engage in illegal or anti-social behaviour online their corporeal body (and all the assets owned by that individual) remains at all times subject to the direct regulation of the state in which they are resident at that time.[5] Thus a UK citizen who visits online paedophilic

---

[3] J.P. Barlow, *A Declaration of Independence for Cyberspace*: http://homes.eff.org/~barlow/Declaration-Final.html.

[4] For example Sch. II of the Sex Offenders Act 1997 gives courts in the UK jurisdiction to prosecute UK citizens and residents who commit sex offences against children abroad. This law applies to British citizens and residents and is applicable even where the person in question was not a British citizen or UK resident at the time of the offence but has subsequently become one.

[5] Or the state in which the assets are to be found.

communities to engage in the trading and viewing of child abuse images remains at risk of apprehension and prosecution in the UK as their corporeal body is at all times subject to the actions of UK Law enforcement authorities.[6] This belies Barlow's claim that traditional lawmaking and enforcement bodies 'do not possess any methods of enforcement we have true reason to fear' and led to a number of responses indicating that there is nothing about the nature of the digital environment which naturally protects individuals from the controls of real world lawmakers and law enforcement authorities. Professor Chris Reed calls this cyberlibertarian environmental argument 'the Cyberspace fallacy'[7] pointing out that: '[this] states that the Internet is a new jurisdiction, in which none of the existing rules and regulations apply. This jurisdiction has no physical existence; it is a virtual space which expands and contracts as the different networks and computers, which collectively make up the Internet, connect to and disconnect from each other ... A moment's thought reveals the fallacy. All the actors involved in an Internet transaction have a real-world existence, and are located in one or more legal jurisdictions ... It is inconceivable that a real-world jurisdiction would deny that its laws potentially applied to the transaction.'[8] As Reed goes on to demonstrate, wherever traditional law enforcement bodies have faced the challenge of cross-border trade or harm the ordinary rules of private international law, jurisdiction and choice of law, have proven effective in identifying the correct forum and legal rules to apply.

The lack of physicality found in the digital environment forms only part of the Cyberlibertarian school of thought. The other key support, alluded to in Professor Reed's response, is that real world law enforcement bodies lack legitimacy to interfere in the operations of 'Sovereign Cyberspace'. This is predicated upon the twin beliefs that there is a border between real space and Cyberspace, a border not dissimilar to that we find between jurisdictions in real space, and that once one crosses this border into Cyberspace, one may move freely about in 'Sovereign Cyberspace' without barrier or challenge. In other words the Cyberlibertarian School believed that Cyberspace was a separate state, although not physically.

This concept is most fully explored in the groundbreaking work of two US Law Professors, David Johnson and David Post who in May 1996 published their highly influential paper *Law and Borders—The Rise of Law in Cyberspace*.[9] In this paper they set out fully, and for the first time, a legal interpretation of the Cyberlibertarian contention that regulation founded upon traditional state sovereignty cannot function effectively in Cyberspace. They argued that as individuals in Cyberspace may move seamlessly between zones governed by differing regulatory regimes in accordance with their personal preferences it was impossible to effectively regulate the activities of these individuals.

---

[6] As has been demonstrated on many occasions: see, e.g. *R. v Fellows & Arnold* [1997] 2 All ER 548; *R. v Bowden (Jonathan)* [2001] QB 88; *Atkins v Director of Public Prosecutions* [2000] 1 WLR 1427 or *R. v Jayson* [2002] EWCA Crim 683.

[7] C. Reed, *Internet Law: Text and Materials* (2nd ed. 2004).   [8] *ibid*, 174–175.

[9] 48 *Stanford Law Review* 1367 (1996).

★ Example Obscenity

Leo is a UK resident who wishes to access and download pornographic images which are in breach of the Obscene Publications Acts. Although illegal in the UK these images may be legal in the US. Leo therefore may access material hosted in the US and view it on his computer in the UK.

★ Example Contempt of Court

In 2007 two men attempted to blackmail a member of the UK Royal Family. A s. 11 Order was granted under the Contempt of Court Act 1981 meaning it was illegal to publish the name of the person involved (it still is). Despite this it is extremely easy for a UK resident to find the name of the person involved with a quick Google search as the name has been published online by several overseas news organisations and gossip sites which are all accessible in the UK. It would even be possible for a UK resident to publish this person's name, in breach of the Contempt of Court Act overseas, but if identified they may face prosecution.

This meant that citizens of Cyberspace could engage in a practice known as regulatory arbitrage. This occurs when an individual or group may potentially be regulated by a number of alternate regulatory bodies and is offered the opportunity to choose which one to be regulated by. The individual then arbitrages (or plays off) these regulators against each other to seek the best regulatory settlement for the individual.[10] In our obscene publications example our UK resident in the real world is directly regulated by the UK border and police forces. There is no opportunity to arbitrage their regulation (in enforcing the Obscene Publications Acts) against anyone else without leaving the jurisdiction of the UK courts. But in Cyberspace he or she may seek the shelter of the US regulatory authorities by sourcing their pornographic content from US based web servers. Technically the UK resident remains in breach of s. 42 of the Customs Consolidation Act 1876 which makes it an offence to import indecent or obscene prints, paintings, photographs, books, cards, lithographic or other engravings, or any other indecent or obscene articles. But with surveys suggesting that 10 million UK adults visit pornographic websites,[11] it is clear the authorities simply do not have the resources to prosecute such a mass programme of disobedience. This is demonstrated by the fact that to date there have been no prosecutions in England and Wales under either the Customs Consolidation Act or the Obscene Publications Act 1959 for privately

---

[10] See A. M. Froomkin, 'The Internet as a Source of Regulatory Arbitrage' in B. Kahin & C. Nesson (eds), *Borders in Cyberspace* (1997).
[11] Anthony Barnes & Sophie Goodchild, 'Porn UK', *The Independent on Sunday*, 28 May 2006: http://www.independent.co.uk/news/uk/this-britain/porn-uk-480084.html.

viewing obscene material using an internet connection. Thus the UK resident can safely arbitrage the UK regulatory framework of the Obscene Publications Acts and the Customs Consolidation Act for the US regulatory framework which has protection from the US First Amendment.[12] This allows, at least in cyberlibertarian theory, the citizen of Cyberspace to choose a different regulatory regime from that which regulates his or her activities in real space, undermining the effectiveness of traditional lawmaking processes and law enforcement institutions. Accordingly, the only effective 'Law of Cyberspace' would largely be determined by a free market in regulation in which network users would be able to choose those rule sets they found most congenial. Johnson and Post maintained that the various dimensions of inter-networking could be governed by 'decentralised, emergent law' wherein customary and privately produced laws, or rules, would be produced by decentralised collective action leading to the emergence of common standards for mutual coordination.[13] In other words, they believed that the decentralised and incorporeal nature of Cyberspace meant that the only possible regulatory system was one which developed organically with the consent of the majority of the citizens of Cyberspace.[14]

Cyberlibertarianism is clearly attractive for internet users. It suggests the development of new internet only laws designed to reflect the values of the community of internet users and separate from the old world values of state based lawmakers. Thus we could imagine copyright evolving to allow a private use copying right which would allow individuals to make multiple copies of files for use on several devices (Home PC, Laptop, Smartphone, MP3 player, etc.) or as appears to be the *de facto* position a relaxation of indecency laws to allow for far greater distribution of adult content. There are though clearly problems with such an approach. The first is who makes up the community of internet users, and who is authorised to speak for them?

The problem that the cyberlibertarians had to address was there is no homogenous community of internet users; instead in Cyberspace there are a series of heterogeneous communities with few shared values. This problem was highlighted by Professor Cass Sunstein in his book *Republic.com* where he suggested that the nature of the internet was to isolate individuals behind filters and screens rather than to provide for community building and democratic discourse.[15] Sunstein suggested that while a well functioning system of deliberative democracy requires a certain degree of information so that citizens can engage in monitoring and deliberative tasks,[16] the ability to filter information offered by digital technologies interferes with the flow of this information in two ways. The first is that the user may simply choose not to receive some of this information by using filters to ensure they only receive information of interest to them. As such there is no homogeneity of information across the macro community of users of

---

[12] *Reno v ACLU* 521 US 844 (1997).

[13] This notion parallels the concept of polycentric or non-statist law. See T. Bell, 'Polycentric Law' 7(1) *Humane Studies Review* 4 (1991/2); T Bell, 'Polycentric Law in the New Millennium.' Paper presented at The Mont Pelerin Society: 1998 Golden Anniversary Meeting, at Alexandria Virginia: http://www.tomwbell.com/writings/FAH.html.

[14] Johnson & Post, above n. 9. See also D. Johnson & D. Post, 'The New "Civic Virtue" of the Internet: A Complex Systems Model for the Governance of Cyberspace' in C.M. Firestone (ed.), *The Emerging Internet* (1998 Annual Review of the Institute for Information Studies).

[15] C. Sunstein, *Republic.com* (2001). [16] *ibid*, 174.

the internet making truly deliberative democratic discourse impossible. Further Sunstein recognised that with the advent of internet communications it becomes easier to locate likeminded individuals whatever one's shared interests may be. This creates in Sunstein's words 'fringe communities that have a common ideology but are dispersed geographically'.[17] In turn this leads to community fragmentation. There are little in the way of common experiences and knowledge among the larger macro community of internet users. As Sunstein quickly demonstrated there can be no cyberlibertarian ideal of a 'decentralised, emergent law' as decentralised collective action is highly unlikely to lead to the emergence of common standards for mutual coordination in the highly decentred and filtered environment of Cyberspace.

If Sunstein was correct this meant that Cyberspace lacked the necessary homogeneity to achieve the necessary levels of internal democratic discourse needed for the creation of Cyberspace Law and as a result the internet could not be effectively regulated from within. But, as Post and Johnson had demonstrated, attempts to impose external regulatory settlements in Cyberspace would be equally ineffectual due to the effects of regulatory arbitrage and a lack of physical borders. This suggested an impasse. There had to be a legal framework which could be utilised in the online environment for it to flourish as a place to do business, further there had to be a way to regulate and eliminate antisocial and anti-market activities such as the trade in pornography and copyright infringing digital media files.[18] Fortunately Professor Sunstein was not the only theorist who had taken issue with the cyberlibertarian approach.

4.1.2 Cyberpaternalism

A new school of thought was developing, one which did not believe Cyberspace was immune from regulatory intervention by real world regulators. One of the strongest early critics of the cyberlibertarian position was Joel Reidenberg of Fordham Law School. Despite sympathising with the cyberlibertarian view that the internet leads to the disintegration of territorial borders as the foundation for regulatory governance, Reidenberg argued that new models and sources of rules were being created in their place. He identified two new regulatory borders arising from new rule-making processes involving States, the private sector, technical interests, and citizens. He believed the first set of these were made up of the contractual agreements among various Internet Service Providers. The second was to be found in the network architecture. The key to Reidenberg's analysis was this second border, the new geography of the internet which unlike the geography of the natural world was man-made and in our control.

---

[17] *ibid*, 58.
[18] Note: I have not forgotten Professor Reed's point that the corpus of the individual user of online services remains subject to the direct control of the state where the individual is resident. Directly harmful activities such as the trade in child pornography will be directly regulated in this fashion. What is in issue here is more generally harmful or antisocial behaviour which is being engaged upon by a large number of users of online services and for whom direct legal regulation through the courts would be impracticable due to the large numbers of persons involved.

Reidenberg claimed that technical standards could function like geographical borders as they establish default boundary rules that impose order in network environments. Using the network architecture as a proxy for regulatory architecture Reidenberg suggested a new way of looking at control and regulation in the online environment a conceptualisation he called 'Lex Informatica'.[19] This draws upon the principle of *Lex Mercatoria* and refers to the 'laws' imposed on network users by technological capabilities and system design choices. Reidenberg asserted that, whereas political governance processes usually establish the substantive laws of nation states, in *Lex Informatica* the primary sources of default rule making are the technology developer(s) and the social processes through which customary uses of the technology evolve.[20] To this end, he argued that, rather than being inherently unregulable due to its design or architecture, the internet is in fact closely regulated by its architecture.

Reidenberg contended that in the light of *Lex Informatica's* dependence on design choices, the attributes of public oversight associated with regulatory regimes, could be maintained by shifting the focus of government actions away from direct regulation of Cyberspace, toward influencing changes to its architecture. Reidenberg's concept of regulatory control being implemented through the control mechanisms already in place in the network architecture led to development of the new cyberpaternalist school. This new school viewed legal controls as merely part of the network of effective regulatory controls in the online environment and suggested that lawmakers seeking to control the online activities of their citizens would seek to indirectly control these activities by mandating changes to the network architecture, or by supporting self-regulatory activities of network designers. This idea was most fully developed and explained by Professor Lawrence Lessig in his classic essay *Code and Other Laws of Cyberspace*.[21] Lessig contends that there are four 'Modalities of Regulation' which may be used individually or collectively either directly or indirectly by regulators to control the actions of individuals offline or online.[22] Further, Lessig suggests that Johnson and Post were wrong to suggest that regulatory arbitrage must undermine any attempt to regulate the activities of individuals online as regulators draw their legitimacy from the community they represent (and regulate) and as individuals we are therefore tied to the regulator in a way which Johnson and Post fail to recognise. As Lessig says: 'Even if we could construct cyberspace on the model of the market there are strong reasons not to. As life moves online, and more and more citizens from states X, Y, and Z come to interact in cyberspaces A, B, and C, these cyberspaces may well need to develop the kind of responsibility and attention that develops (ideally) within a democracy. Or, put differently, if cyberspace wants to be considered its own legitimate sovereign, and thus deserving of some measure of independence and respect, it must become more clearly a citizen sovereignty'.[23]

---

[19] J. Reidenberg, 'Governing Networks and Rule-Making in Cyberspace' (1996) 45 *Emory Law Journal* 911; J. Reidenberg, 'Lex Informatica: The Formation of Information Policy Rules Through Technology' 76 *Texas Law Review* (1998), 553.

[20] On the role of software designers in default rule making see P. Quintas, 'Software by Design' in R. Mansell and R. Silverstone (eds), *Communication by Design: The Politics of Information and Communication Technologies* (1998).   [21] Basic Books (1999).   [22] *ibid*, 88ff.

[23] L. Lessig, *Code Version 2.0*, (2006), 290.

Thus Johnson and Post's position that regulatory arbitrage, coupled with a physical border between real space and Cyberspace must lead to the development of a distinct and separate body of law for Cyberspace is in Lessig's view tautologous. By attempting to reject real world regulation citizens within Cyberspace undermine the possibility of competing real world regulators recognising the independence of Cyberspace as a sovereign space meaning that attempts to develop a separate set of principles for Cyberspace will fail. For Lessig the key to regulating all activity, whether it happens to be in the online or the offline environment is to be found in his four modalities of regulation: (1) laws (2) markets (3) architecture and (4) norms. Lessig believes that regulators may by using carefully selected hybrids of the four to achieve whatever regulatory outcome they desire. If Lessig is correct there is no doubt that we can regulate the digital environment and the cyberlibertarians were mistaken in their claims to the contrary.

4.2 **Lawrence Lessig's modalities of regulation**

Lawrence Lessig asked us to reconsider how one is regulated on a day-to-day basis. Although the law may say it is illegal to steal it is not usually the legal imperative that prevents most of us from stealing, rather the majority of people do not steal because they do not want to steal in the first place. We do not steal, not because we fear imprisonment but because we have been morally conditioned to accept that theft is a morally reprehensible act. Lessig concluded that four factors, or modalities, control the activities of individuals and each of these modalities functions by acting as a constraint on the choices of actions that individuals have. Thus law constrains through the threat of punishment, social norms constrain through the application of societal sanctions such as criticism or ostracism, the market constrains through price and price-related signals, and architecture physically constrains (examples include the locked door and the concrete parking bollard). To demonstrate how these four modalities function collectively on the choice of actions an individual Lessig had us imagine a 'pathetic dot' which represents the individual and then graphically represented the four modalities as external forces which act upon that dot in control of its actions. This is seen in Figure 4.1.

Lessig demonstrated how these modalities function by using examples such as the regulation of smoking[24] or in the supply of illegal drugs[25] or the right of a woman to choose to have an abortion.[26] A further contemporary example, perfect for a discussion of digital property rights, may be found in regulating the illegal secondary market for copyright infringing MP3 music files. It is clear that in the UK anyone who makes a copy of a copyright protected MP3 music file without the consent of the copyright holder commits a infringement of that copyright.[27] Further anyone who makes a copy of an MP3 file with the intent to sell or hire that copy or distribute it in the course of business commits a criminal offence.[28] Thus the legal controls on copyright infringement are clear. The law states that one cannot make and/or distribute a copy of a protected work in the UK without facing civil, or possibly even criminal, sanctions. To use the language of Lawrence Lessig the modality of law has been employed to prevent this activity.

---

[24] *ibid* 122–123.　　[25] *ibid*, 131.　　[26] *ibid*, 132.
[27] CDPA 1998, s. 17.　　[28] *ibid*, s. 107.

Figure 4.1 Lessig's modalities in action

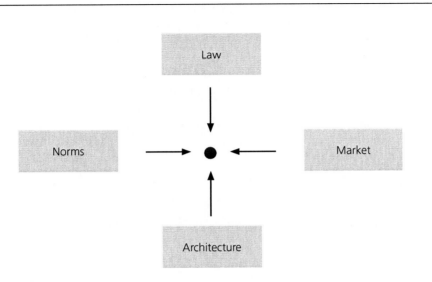

Source: Lawrence Lessig CC: BY: SA

Yet it appears that the application of the law in this area is of little impact as individuals continue to download and share music using illegal sources. This failure of the law to control individuals is the failure that was predicted by the cyberlibertarian movement. Individuals use the network to evade legal controls and do so by using tools such as BitTorrent.[29] But this does not mean that the MP3 market is not subject to control. For while the direct effects of the law may be failing the other modalities provide an alternative means of regulation.

The second of Lessig's modalities is markets and here the first successful regulatory intervention may be seen. With the success of technologies such as the iPod and its sister product iTunes Apple pioneered the technology for online MP3 sales. This market has now massively expanded with a variety of services offering the opportunity to legally buy an MP3 track or album, or offering subscription services which lease to you music on a monthly basis for payment of a fee.[30] As the costs of these services have fallen,[31] we saw for the first time in 2008 clear evidence that legal music downloads are

[29] While historically the copyright industries have had some success in litigating against file sharing technologies such as Napster (*A&M Records Inc. v Napster* 239 F.3d 1004 (9th Cir. 2001)) and Grokster/Kazaa (*MGM Studios, Inc. v Grokster, Ltd* 545 U.S. 913 (2005)), the completely decentralised nature of BitTorrent has proved a challenging proposition for real world laws. Despite the recent success of the copyright industry in the case of *Sweden v The Pirate Bay*, the Pirate Bay site remains in operation pending an appeal while other Torrent tracking sites remain in place should The Pirate Bay be closed down.

[30] For example, Napster's Hits Unlimited service costs £9.95 per month for unlimited access to the entire Napster catalogue.

[31] The price of Napster's unlimited service dropped from £14.95 to £9.95 in 2008, while the arrival of Amazon in the MP3 download market has seen a major provider offer single tracks for 59p and albums for £3 compared to Apple's 79p and £7.99.

growing faster than illegal file sharing in the UK.[32] Where the legal control failed to have impact we find that a market solution seems to be having effect. This is exactly as Lessig predicted. In the digital environment while the effect of direct legal controls is often diluted by a remoteness from the law enforcement authority and by a lack of border controls other modalities are strengthened including market modalities which benefit from greater transparency and speed of information.

The MP3 music market also demonstrates something else about the way Lessig's modalities function in the digital environment. It might be assumed that the most effective way to prevent illegal file sharing is to adjust the architecture of the digital files which carry the music to make illegal sharing of them impossible. This is the industry solution predicted by Lessig. Like Reidenberg he saw our ability to manipulate the network architecture as the most obvious development in Cyber-regulation. Where laws failed to have effect he believed industry would turn more to architectural or design-based modalities: 'We can build, or architect, or code cyberspace to protect values that we believe are fundamental. Or we can build, or architect, or code cyberspace to allow those values to disappear. There is no middle ground. There is no choice that does not include some kind of building'.[33]

In the case of MP3s the music industry did just as Lessig predicted. They began to design a suite of Digital Rights Management software (DRM) and began to place it on their digital music released on CD. Some of the more famous include Cactus Data Shield used by BMG and Universal Music, Sony Extended Copy Protection, and most famous of all Apple's FairPlay used on iTunes products. These systems were reinforced by strong legal provisions promulgated by the World Intellectual Property Organisation[34] and which once implemented in leading markets made it illegal to remove or reverse engineer the DRM protection in the US[35] and in the European Union.[36] What has happened

---

[32] See IFPI, *Digital Music Report 2008*: http://www.ifpi.org/content/library/DMR2008.pdf.

[33] Lessig, above n. 23, 6.

[34] Article 11 of the WIPO Copyright Treaty of 1996 requires that: '[States] shall provide adequate legal protection and effective legal remedies against the circumvention of effective technological measures that are used by authors in connection with the exercise of their rights under this Treaty or the Berne Convention and that restrict acts, in respect of their works, which are not authorized by the authors concerned or permitted by law'. In addition Article 18 of the WIPO Performances and Phonograms Treaty of 1996 requires that: '[States] shall provide adequate legal protection and effective legal remedies against the circumvention of effective technological measures that are used by performers or producers of phonograms in connection with the exercise of their rights under this Treaty and that restrict acts, in respect of their performances or phonograms, which are not authorized by the performers or the producers of phonograms concerned or permitted by law.'

[35] Section 103 of the Digital Millennium Copyright Act 1998 (17 U.S.C Sec. 1201(a)(1)) states that 'No person shall circumvent a technological measure that effectively controls access to a work protected under this title'. The penalty for so doing being the possibility for statutory damages of up to $2,500 for *each* violation in addition to actual damages should a civil case is brought. In criminal cases (where the accused is deemed to have acted wilfully and for purposes of commercial advantage or private financial gain (note this includes file sharing)) for a first offence you may be imprisoned for up to five years and fined up to $500,000. For subsequent offences you may be imprisoned for up to ten years and fined up to $1,000,000.

[36] Article 6 of the Directive on Harmonisation of Certain Aspects of Copyright and Related Rights in the Information Society (Dir. 2001/29/EC) requires states to 'provide adequate legal protection against the circumvention of any effective technological measures, which the person concerned carries out in the knowledge, or with reasonable grounds to know, that he or she is pursuing that objective'. In the UK this has been given effect in the Copyright and Related Rights Regulations 2003 (SI 2003/2498).

to all these DRM systems? Well, Cactus Data Shield became embroiled in controversy as discs containing the CDS software would not play on non Windows operating systems, nor on game systems such as the Xbox or the Playstation 2 or on older CD players which played protected discs with audible errors. As a result discs released with CDS often had to be reissued in a non-protected format rendering the DRM protection valueless. At the time of writing the author is unaware of any music releases still protected by CDS. The story of Sony's Extended Copy Protection (XCP) system is even more telling. In 2005 Sony released fifty-two titles with XCP protection. It quickly became apparent that the XCP system installed a rootkit, that is a piece of software installed without permission on the user's computer which can take control of hardware settings, and that due to a design flaw in this the software created security holes which could be exploited by malicious software such as worms or viruses. Within fifteen days of the flaw being discovered Sony BMG announced that it was backing out of its copy-protection software, recalling unsold CDs from all stores, and offering consumers to exchange their CDs with versions lacking the software.[37] Finally Apple FairPlay. It is by far the most enduring and successful DRM. It is designed to ensure people do not swap purchased music across Apple music devices. FairPlay encrypted audio tracks may be copied to any number of Apple portable music players, however, each player can only have tracks from a maximum of five different iTunes accounts, and in addition the track may only be played on up to five authorised computers simultaneously. Although it seems at first glance that the main beneficiary of FairPlay is Apple itself (it protects the iTunes market and makes the iPod/iTunes partnership irresistible) it appears Apple were forced into FairPlay by the music industry. Following a plea from Steve Jobs, CEO of Apple Inc., to the music industry,[38] it was announced on 6 April 2007 that Apple had reached agreement with EMI to make its music available DRM free, while on 6 January 2009 a further announcement made at the Macworld Conference and Expo revealed that from that date all music on iTunes would be DRM free.

All attempts to use design modalities to engineer music files which could not be copied have failed. Nearly all music available today, whether it be in MP3 format or encoded onto a CD comes free of DRM technology. The provisions of the WIPO treaties, the Digital Millennium Copyright Act and the Copyright and Related Rights in the Information Society Directive, look dated and irrelevant in the modern digital age, but why? Why if DRMs are the most effective and efficient way to protect against illegal file sharing have they failed to take effect? Surely if Lessig is right and we have to choose to either 'build, or architect, or code cyberspace to protect values that we believe are

---

[37] VNUnet.com, *Sony backs out of rootkit anti-piracy scheme*, 15 November 2005: http://www.vnunet.com/vnunet/news/2146053/sony-backs-root-kit-anti-piracy.

[38] On 6 February 2007, Steve Jobs, published an open letter entitled *Thoughts on Music* calling on the big four music companies to sell their music without DRM. According to Jobs, Apple does not want to use DRM but is forced by the four major musical labels with whom Apple negotiates contracts for iTunes. Jobs's main points were: (1) DRM has never and will never be perfect. Hackers will always find a method to break DRM. (2) DRM restrictions only hurt people using music legally. Illegal users aren't affected by DRM. (3) The restrictions of DRM encourage users to obtain unrestricted music which is usually only possible via illegal methods.

The vast majority of music is sold without DRM via CDs which has proven successful (see Steve Jobs, *Thoughts on Music*, 6 February 2007, http://www.apple.com/hotnews/thoughtsonmusic/).

fundamental. Or we can build, or architect, or code cyberspace to allow those values to disappear' we cannot end up with the scenario where all the built or architected changes are removed (or to stick to the building metaphor are demolished and the environment returned to open plain). Surely if we are all just pathetic dots the industry would have forced its DRM technology on us, after all as Lessig says 'Thus, four constraints regulate this pathetic dot-the law, social norms, the market, and architecture-and the "regulation" of this dot is the sum of these four constraints'.[39]

4.3 **Network communitarianism**

The reason for the failure of DRM systems in commercial music releases is explained by a new school of thought which has developed in the last few years. While cyberlibertarians believed the architecture of the network protected individuals from the attentions of real world regulators and cyberpaternalists believed rather the opposite, this new school of thought sees the relationship between the digital environment and the real world as a rather more fluid affair. This new school of thought is the network communitarian school.

Unlike cyberlibertarianism and cyberpaternalism this developed in Europe with much of the early work taking place in the UK. The main proponent of network communitarianism is Andrew Murray who in his book *The Regulation of Cyberspace* set out a model of network communitarian thought.[40] Murray believes that the cyberpaternalist model fails to account for the complexities of information flows found in a modern telecommunications/media system such as the internet. The main influences on network communitarianism are two European schools of thought which have yet to fully translate to the US, and which have therefore not influenced either cyberlibertarianism or cyberpaternalism. These are Actor Network Theory (ANT) developed in Paris in the 1980s by Michel Callon and Bruno Latour and Social Systems Theory (SST) developed in Germany by Niklaus Luhmann and Gunther Teubner.

ANT is a theory of social transactions which accepts a role for nonhuman actors in any social situation. Thus in a transaction between two individuals in a restaurant their transaction is also affected by the restaurant itself: one would expect a different transaction in a luxury Michelin starred restaurant than in a local café bar. The difference is not so much the surroundings themselves but the semiotic, or concepts, which the human actors have communicated to them through memory, experience, and surroundings.[41] A key concept of ANT is that social communications are made up of parallel transactions between the material (things) and semiotic (concepts) which together form a single network. This has the potential to be particularly powerful when applied to the internet. The internet is the largest person to person communication network yet designed. It allows individuals to move social transactions in space and time and

---

[39] Lessig, above n. 23, 123.
[40] A. Murray, *The Regulation of Cyberspace: Control in the Online Environment*, (2007).
[41] This is a woefully inadequate description of ANT which is extremely complex, rich, and valuable. Students interested in embarking on a study of ANT should start with B. Latour, *Reassembling the Social: An Introduction to Actor-network-theory* (2007).

it allows transactions between people with shared experiences who are geographically remote and between people with no common history who are geographically close.[42] The potential for new networks to form, dissolve, and reform on the internet is massive, leading one to reconceptualise the internet not merely as a communications/media tool but as a cultural/social tool.[43]

SST shares some roots with ANT but is quite distinct. SST attempts to explain and study the flow of information within increasingly complex systems of social communication. Luhmann attempts to explain how communications affect social transactions by defining social systems as systems of communication, and society as the most encompassing social system. A system is defined by a boundary between itself and its surrounding environment, dividing it from the infinitely complex, or chaotic, exterior.[44] The interior of the system is thus a zone of reduced complexity: Communication within a system operates by selecting only a limited amount of all information available outside. This process is also called reduction of complexity. The criterion according to which information is selected and processed is meaning.[45] Like ANT SST is an attempt to map and study the complex process of social interactions in the increasingly complex and connected environment of modern society. Whereas ANT is about the evolution and formation of networks, SST is about the filtering of information flows in the decision making process and the communication of ideas and concepts between systems.

Although these theories are quite distinct when taken together they can illuminate much of our understanding of communications and social interaction in a networked environment such as the internet with a variety of actors, both human and non-human.[46] This is what Murray attempts in *The Regulation of Cyberspace*. He re-examines the classical cyberpaternalist model discussed earlier in which a pathetic dot is found to reside among four regulatory modalities which act as a constraint on the choice of actions of that 'dot' and finds that in applying the principles of ANT and SST we can consider the 'dot' rather differently. The dot is in ANT terms a material node in the network, while in SST terms is part of a system. In either term the dot is not isolated, it forms part of a matrix of dots, or to put it another way the dot, which is designed to

---

[42] And obviously between people geographically remote and with no common history also.

[43] This is actually well worn ground in the field of communications and media studies although it seems quite alien to many lawyers and regulators. See, e.g. M. Castells, *The Internet Galaxy* (2001) or R. Mansell (ed.), *Inside the Communication Revolution: Evolving Patterns of Social and Technical Interaction* (2002).

[44] Thus a system may be the legal system where lawyers practice their trade and give advice against the background of the corpus of law. Lawyers may be asked 'is it legal to use offshore tax systems to process the profits of a particular transaction?' they will not be asked 'is it moral?' or is it 'socially harmful?' these are questions for respectively theologians (or philosophers) and politicians. Thus in the internal language of the legal profession the question is binary legal or illegal, rather than multifaceted in the wider system of society at large.

[45] As with ANT this is a woefully inadequate description of SST which is extremely complex, rich and valuable. Students interested in embarking on a study of SST should start with H. Moeller, *Luhmann Explained*, (2006). Law students may then be interested in N. Luhmann, *Law as a Social System* (2008).

[46] For a fascinating attempt to fuse the two together read G. Teubner, 'Rights of Non-humans? Electronic Agents and Animals as New Actors in Politics and Law' (2006) 33 *Journal of Law and Society* 497.

Figure 4.2 From the pathetic dot to the active dot matrix

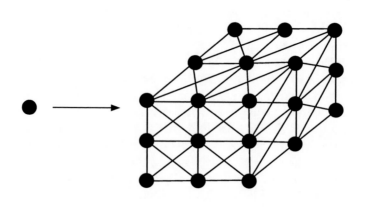

represent the individual, must always be considered to be part of the wider community and it is here that traditional cyberpaternalism runs into difficulty, for when one examines the modalities of regulation proposed by Lessig we find that of the four, three of them, Laws, Norms and Markets are in fact a proxy for community-based control. Laws are passed by lawmakers elected by the community,[47] markets are merely a reflection of value, demand, supply, and scarcity as reflected by the community in monetary terms and norms are merely the codification of community values. Murray recognised that these 'socially mediated modalities',[48] reflected an active role for the 'dot' in the regulatory process; far from being a 'pathetic dot' which was the subject of external regulatory forces the dot was in fact an 'active dot' taking part in the regulatory process.[49] For Murray there are two key distinctions between the classic cyberpaternalist model and the new network communitarian model. The first is to replace the isolated pathetic dot with a networked community (or matrix) of dots which share ideas, beliefs, ideals, and opinions (see Figure 4.2). The second is to recognise that the socially mediated modalities of law, norms, and markets draw their legitimacy from the community (or matrix of dots) meaning the regulatory process is in nature a dialogue not an externally imposed set of constraints, as illustrated in Figure 4.3.

What does this mean for our understanding of internet regulation? Firstly it suggests that regulation in the online environment is little different to regulation in the real world. Regulation is a process of discourse and dialogue between the individual and society. Sometimes society, either directly through the application of norms, or indirectly by distilling its opinions, norms, or standards down to laws wishes to force

---

[47] At least in democratic representative politics as found in the UK. In the UK we may view the rights of MPs (our representatives) to make laws as being power drawn from the community at large as part of our social contract between the state and citizen. See J. Rousseau, The *Social Contract* (1762, trans M. Cranston, 2004).   [48] Murray, above n. 40, 37.   [49] *ibid*, Ch. 8.

Figure 4.3 The regulatory discourse

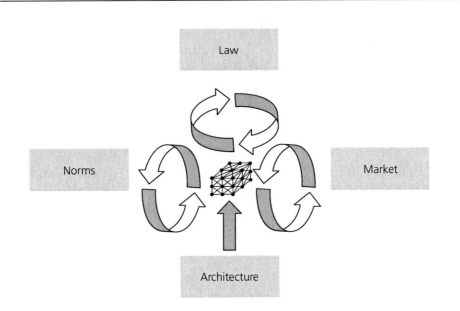

a change in behaviour of the individual.[50] But, sometimes it is the regulatory settlement itself which is challenged by society when there is no longer any support for it. This is most clearly illustrated by the fact that the UK enforcement authorities have declined to prosecute individuals under either the Customs Consolidation Act or the Obscene Publications Act 1959 for privately viewing obscene material using an internet connection. We, the community of dots, have collectively decided that the viewing of pornography by internet connection is no longer to be viewed as morally objectionable and have communicated this decision by both driving the market for material of this type and by communicating to our lawmakers where a line is to be drawn. We wish to sanction and criminalise those who possess or trade in images of child abuse (including pseudo images) and those who possess or trade in images of sexual violence, harm, bestiality, and necrophilia. Thus the regulatory settlement is not imposed upon us, if it were we would all avoid the viewing of obscene material for fear of prosecution under the Obscene Publications Acts, but is rather part of a dialogue in which the regulatory settlement evolves to reflect changes in society. This also explains why Digital Rights Management systems failed to have the desired effect. DRMs were viewed by the majority of music consumers to be an unreasonable, and sometimes damaging, restriction on their freedom to enjoy something they viewed,

---

[50] A good current example of such a change is s. 63 of the Criminal Justice and Immigration Act 2008 which makes it an offence to possess 'extreme pornographic images'. These are images of sexual violence, bestiality and necrophilia. This is society in the UK setting a limit on the free availability of pornographic images in the online environment. We cannot prevent pornography from entering the UK but we can criminalise the most offensive varieties of pornography to stifle demand, thus also allowing the market to make the production of such material less commercially attractive.

having paid to purchase it, as their property. When Cactus Data Shield prevented them from playing their new CD on their old CD player, or when Apple FairPlay restricted them to having five authorised computers (a problem in an extended family) or worst of all when Sony Extended Copy Protection was shown to leave their PCs vulnerable to attack, consumers reacted in the way one would expect: They collectively used their market power to respond. The industry could not force its DRM technology on us because we can withhold our market support for them. In network communitarian theory the power to determine the regulatory environment does not rest with the regulator alone.[51]

Whichever of the current schools of cyber-regulatory theory you subscribe to: cyberpaternalism or network communitarianism, one thing is clear. There is one key issue that both agree upon: that in the man-made environment of the digital sphere our ability to change the design of that place with a few well placed keystrokes means that the use of architecture as a modality of control (that is employed by one of the other modalities as a means of enforcing their values) is increasingly in evidence and is increasingly effective. For this reason the remainder of this chapter will look at who some of the key regulators in this environment are. Who are the people with the opportunity to amend the software code of the digital environment and on which basis do they exercise their power?

4.4 **Regulators in cyberspace: private regulators**

There are a number of private regulators at work in the digital environment with the ability to regulate certain activities directly by making design changes to the environment. The first line of private regulation most internet users encounter in the UK is their internet service provider (ISP). As it is impossible for individuals to gain access to the internet without employing the services of an ISP, ISPs can act as gatekeepers. The position of gatekeeper is a powerful one in regulatory theory as gatekeepers control access to and egress from a particular place or community. As a result of their role as internet gatekeeper ISPs have been tasked with ever increasing regulatory roles in the UK. The most high profile role for ISPs is their collective role in preventing access to child abuse images and other illegal content.

In an attempt to control the trade in illegal content the UK Government requires ISPs to block access to sites known to contain images of child abuse but which are domiciled outwith the UK, and which are therefore out of the direct control of UK laws. This is affected by a partnership between ISPs and an industry regulatory body known as the Internet Watch Foundation (IWF). The IWF operates the UK internet 'hotline' for the public to report potentially illegal online content (that is content portraying

---

[51] In this final analysis network communitarianism in the internet regulation context shares core values with decentred regulation in mainstream regulatory theory. See, J. Black, 'Decentring Regulation: Understanding the Role of Regulation and Self Regulation in a "Post-Regulatory" World' (2001) 54 *Current Legal Problems* 103; C. Scott, 'Regulation in the Age of Governance: The Rise of the Post Regulatory State' in J. Jordana and D. Levi-Faur (eds) *The Politics of Regulation: Institutions and Regulatory Reforms for the Age of Governance* (2004).

child abuse,[52] criminally obscene content hosted in the UK[53], content designed to incite racial or religious hatred content hosted in the UK,[54] and extreme pornography[55]). The IWF is a private industry body which is funded by industry partners and a European Union grant. It regulates content within its remit by creating a blacklist of sites which contain illegal content. This blacklist is then distributed to all UK ISPs who are expected to block access to all sites contained on the list. The blocking of access is therefore effected by private corporations (the ISPs) at the requirement of another private corporation (the IWF), but, it is a requirement of the UK Government that this private regulatory system be enforced.

This was illustrated in a Parliamentary written answer in 2006 when Home Office Minister Vernon Croaker noted that 'we are setting a target that by the end of 2007 all ISPs offering internet connectivity to the UK general public put in place technical measures that prevent their customers accessing websites containing illegal images of child abuse identified by the IWF.'[56] Failure to implement a private regulatory system would have led to legislation compelling ISPs to filter access. This requirement has subsequently been implemented, without the need for legislation, by all major UK commercial ISPs under a variety of names or systems. The best known of which is Cleanfeed developed by British Telecom and used by BT and most other major UK ISPs under licence. Cleanfeed works by filtering all user requests through an internet router which compares requests for pages against the IWF blacklist, if the requested page is blacklisted the Cleanfeed system will reroute this request to a BT proxy server which issues an error message to the customer. In theory Cleanfeed is extremely efficient. Unlike older forms of content blocking Cleanfeed does not black entire sites only blacklisted pages. Thus if one page on the MySpace site contained an indecent image Cleanfeed should only block access

---

[52] By s. 160 of the Criminal Justice Act 1988, as amended by the Criminal Justice and Public Order Act 1994, it is an offence for a person to have any indecent photograph or pseudo-photograph of a child in his possession. A pseudo-photograph is defined in s. 7(7) of the Protection of Children Act 1978 as 'an image, whether made by computer-graphics or otherwise howsoever, which appears to be a photograph'.

[53] By s. 2 of the Obscene Publications Act 1959 it is an offence to publish an obscene article in the UK. The definition of an obscene article is found in s. 1 and defines it as: '[where] its effect or (where the article comprises two or more distinct items) the effect of any one of its items is, if taken as a whole, such as to tend to deprave and corrupt persons who are likely, having regard to all relevant circumstances, to read, see or hear the matter contained or embodied in it'.

[54] Part 3 of the Public Order Act 1986 creates offences of use of words or behaviour or display of written material (s. 18), publishing or distributing written material (s. 19), public performance of a play (s. 20), distributing, showing, or playing a recording (s. 21), or broadcasting (s. 22), if the act is intended to stir up racial hatred, or possession of racially inflammatory material (s. 23). Part 3a was added by the Racial and Religious Hatred Act 2006 with the insertion of new sections 29A to 29N. This created mirror offences for acts intended to stir up religious hatred.

[55] By s. 63 of the Criminal Justice and Immigration Act 2008 it is an offence to possess an 'extreme pornographic image'. An extreme pornographic image is one which (1) is of such a nature that it must reasonably be assumed to have been produced solely or principally for the purpose of sexual arousal, (2) is grossly offensive, disgusting or otherwise of an obscene character, and (3) portrays, in an explicit and realistic way, any of the following: (a) an act which threatens a person's life, (b) an act which results, or is likely to result, in serious injury to a person's anus, breasts or genitals, (c) an act which involves sexual interference with a human corpse, or (d) a person performing an act of intercourse or oral sex with an animal (whether dead or alive).

[56] *Hansard*, 15 May 2006, Column 715W.

to that page not the entire MySpace network. The problem with ISP filtering of all types, including Cleanfeed, is that they simply block pages without explanation. The consumer simply receives an error message such as '404—page not found' or '403—forbidden'. There is no way for the consumer to differentiate between a page that you cannot see because the server is overloaded or has been relocated and one that has been blocked by the IWF.

Because of this, the practice of content filtering by the IWF and ISPs is not widely known or understood. Most UK internet users had probably not heard of the IWF at least that was the case until they became instantly famous in early December 2008.

Case Study Virgin Killer

In 1976 German band Scorpions released an album called Virgin Killer. The album has always been highly controversial as the cover art featured a naked prepubescent girl with a star of broken glass obscuring her genitals. The image has been widely circulated both offline and online for over thirty years, but sometime prior to 5 December 2008 it was reported to the IWF who determined that the image was illegal as being potentially in breach of the Protection of Children Act 1978. As a result on 5 December 2008, the IWF system started blacklisting a Wikipedia article and related image description page on the album. All major UK ISPs blocked access to the image and Wikipedia page.

This may have gone unnoticed as although popular, Scorpions remain a relatively obscure band in the UK, but for the peculiarities of the Wikipedia architecture. Wikipedia has a blacklist of its own which it uses to block individuals who have vandalised entries. As traffic to sites that are on IWF's blacklist is all channelled through Cleanfeed proxy servers it appeared to Wikipedia, once the page was blocked, that every visitor from the UK were coming from the same addresses. This block prevented UK users from amending Wikipedia pages, triggering an investigation by users and leading eventually to the discovery that this page had been blocked by the IWF/Cleanfeed. This immediately brought the IWF to public attention.

After Wikipedia instigated an appeal the IWF saw sense and on 9 December 2008 they removed the Wikipedia page and image from their blacklist stating that although 'the image in question is potentially in breach of the Protection of Children Act 1978 ... the IWF Board has today (9 December 2008) considered these findings and the contextual issues involved in this specific case and, in light of the length of time the image has existed and its wide availability, the decision has been taken to remove this webpage from our list.'

The Wikipedia controversy has, it appears, done little to change the day to day workings of the IWF or the functioning of Cleanfeed. End users are still not aware why access to a website has been blocked and as the media fire surrounding the Wikipedia affair died down the IWF went back to its day to day role. More controversially government proposals for the policing of illegal file sharing have suggested a greater use of the ISP gatekeeper function, perhaps even so far as requiring ISPs to block internet access for customers found to be repeat offenders.[57] This is a highly controversial proposal which would see ISPs tasked with the job of policing illegal file sharing. If adopted it would see a two-stage approach: the first stage is a simple notification procedure which would require ISPs to inform customers that data had been gathered on them indicating they were involved in illegal file sharing. This is relatively uncontroversial (except for the question of cost) as it merely removes the need for a Norwich Pharmaceutical order thereby reducing the strain on the courts and the costs involved. Much more controversial are the measures relating to 'serious infringers'. At paragraph 4.23 the consultation proposes that: 'Ofcom should have a power to require ISPs to take technical measures (which will be specified in the legislation) against serious repeat infringers aimed at preventing, deterring or reducing online copyright infringement, such as: Blocking (Site, IP, URL); Protocol blocking; Port blocking; Bandwidth capping (capping the speed of a subscriber's internet connection and/or capping the volume of data traffic which a subscriber can access); Bandwidth shaping (limiting the speed of a subscriber's access to selected protocols/services and/or capping the volume of data to selected protocols/services); and Content identification and filtering.' Although the media have widely reported that one option is disconnection of users this is in fact not the case as the proposal currently stands but paragraph 4.23 does indicate that future disconnection may be possible: 'It is entirely possible that the obligations on notification and collection of anonymised information on repeat infringers that may lead to legal actions taken by rights holders that we set out here will not, by themselves, deter some infringers. If that is established it is important that Ofcom should have the ability to take further steps to reduce copyright infringement significantly, in line with the long term objective'. This proposal is a half-way house between the stricter 'three-strike' laws seen in many countries which see an offender disconnected after two warnings and earlier UK proposals to have ISPs self-regulate. However it is packaged though it is clear that the gatekeeper function of the ISP is central to these proposals.

4.5 Regulators in cyberspace: states and supranational regulation

Of course it is not only private regulators who can utilise the architecture of the network to regulate end users. As Lawrence Lessig demonstrated states may use architecture-based modalities to control their citizens also. Most states use some form of filtering and/or content blocking. Australia is at the time of writing considering the mandatory installation of Cleanfeed filtering software,[58] while several other states use mandatory filtering or the operation of a State firewall to control access to content online. Probably the most famous example of this is the Chinese State firewall, colloquially known as 'The Great Firewall of China'. According to the Open Net Initiative 'China continues

[57] See Department of Business, Innovation and Skills, *Consultation on Legislation to Address Illicit Peer-to-Peer File Sharing*, 16 June 2009: http://www.berr.gov.uk/files/file51703.pdf.
[58] ABC News, *Conroy announces mandatory internet filters to protect children*, December 31 2007 http://www.abc.net.au/news/stories/2007/12/31/2129471.htm.

to expand on one of the largest and most sophisticated filtering systems in the world, despite the Government's occasional denial that it restricts any Internet content'.[59] The Great Firewall is kept constantly up to date and censors all types of comment with a particular focus on political and dissident speech. Major news organisations such as the BBC and Voice of America are blocked, along, not surprisingly, with the website of the *Epoch Times*.[60] The Ministry of Information Industry ensures the firewall remains secure by licensing a small number of ISPs, ten at the latest count, which for a country the size of China is an extremely small pool to police. These ISPs must ensure they comply with Ministry regulations, including new guidelines on video sharing sites issued immediately upon the widespread penetration of video sharing technology in China.[61] Underlying all regulation of the internet in China is an extensive list of proscribed content. Citizens are prohibited from disseminating between nine and eleven categories of content that appear consistently in most regulations;[62] all can be considered subversive and trigger fines, content removal, and criminal liability.[63] Because of the highly restrictive nature of state-based censorship in China much has been written about it[64] and systems and tools have been developed to subvert it.[65]

Despite this focus on China it is not the only State which uses filtering and blocking tools to control citizen access to the internet. Saudi Arabia for instance closely controls access. The authorities use a commercially available filtering tool allied to local government employees and reporting from ordinary citizens to aid the local implementation

---

[59] http://opennet.net/research/profiles/china.   [60] *ibid.*

[61] Xinhua News Agency, 'China to issue new regulations to censor online video programs', August 16, 2006.

[62] The nine types of content are: (1) violating the basic principles as they are confirmed in the Constitution; (2) endangering state security, divulging state secrets, subverting the national regime, or jeopardising the integrity of national unity; (3) harming national honour or interests; (4) inciting hatred against peoples, racism against peoples, or disrupting the solidarity of peoples; (5) disrupting national policies on religion, propagating evil cults and feudal superstitions; (6) spreading rumours, disturbing social order, or disrupting social stability; (7) spreading obscenity, pornography, gambling, violence, terror, or abetting the commission of a crime; (8) insulting or defaming third parties, infringing on legal rights and interests of third parties; and (9) other content prohibited by law and administrative regulations. Two categories of prohibited content were added in Art. 19 of the Provisions on the Administration of Internet News Information Services promulgated by the State Council Information Office and the Ministry of Information Industry on September 25, 2005. These two additional categories are (1) inciting illegal assemblies, associations, marches, demonstrations, or gatherings that disturb social order; and (2) conducting activities in the name of an illegal civil organisation. Translation at: http://www.cecc.gov/pages/virtualAcad/index.phpd?showsingle=24396.

[63] Z. Jianwen, *The Current Situation of Cybercrimes in China*, International Centre for Criminal Law Reform And Criminal Justice Policy, December 2006: http://www.icclr.law.ubc.ca/china_ccprcp/files/Presentations%20and%20Publications/47%20The%20Current%20Situation%20of%20Cybercrime%20in%20China_English.pdf.

[64] See, e.g. G. Walton, *China's Golden Shield: Corporations and the Development of Surveillance Technology in the People's Republic of China* (2001). R. Deibert, 'Dark Guests and Great Firewalls: The Internet and Chinese Security Policy' 58 *Journal of Social Issues* 143 (2002); A. Lin Neumann, *The Great Firewall: A CPJ Briefing:* http://planet.botany.uwc.ac.za/nisl/Scientific_methods/attachments/Great_Firewall.pdf.

[65] CBC News, *Software jumps China's firewall for news from Tibet*, March 20 2008: http://www.cbc.ca/arts/media/story/2008/03/20/tibet-firewall.html; P. Festa, 'Software rams great firewall of China', *cnet News* 16 April 2003: http://news.cnet.com/2100-1028-997101.html.

of the filtering regime. The Government makes no secret of its filtering, which is fully explained on a section of the ISU web site.[66] According to this, pornographic content is directly filtered by the State Information Services Unit, while other sites are blocked upon request from 'government security bodies'. The website also has forms through which internet users can request that certain sites be blocked or unblocked. In 2001 the Council of Ministers issued a resolution outlining content that internet users are prohibited from accessing and publishing. Among other things, it forbids content 'breaching public decency', material 'infringing the sanctity of Islam', and 'anything contrary to the state or its system'. The resolution also includes approval requirements for publishing on the internet and mechanical guidelines for service providers on recording and monitoring users' activities.[67] A new law, approved by the Saudi Shoura (Advisory) Council in October 2006, criminalises the use of the internet to defame or harm individuals and the development of websites that violate Saudi laws or Islamic values, or that serve terrorist organisations.[68] State based controls such as these are not unusual. The Open Net Initiative lists substantial filtering in a number of countries ranging from Bahrain to Yemen.[69]

4.5.1 WSIS and the IGF

With such a plurality of approaches and views on internet regulation and content regulation being displayed at national (state) level it is perhaps no surprise that until recently attempts to shape supra-national agreement on internet regulation were unsuccessful. Then in 1998 the International Telecommunications Union (ITU) recognised there was a need for supra-national cooperation on internet regulation. At their Plenipotentiary Conference in Minneapolis, that year they passed Resolution 73, which noted: that telecommunications were playing an increasingly decisive and driving role at the political, economic, social and cultural levels and called upon the United Nations: 'to ask the Secretary-General to coordinate with other international organizations and with the various partners concerned (Member States, Sector Members, etc.), with a view to holding a world summit on the information society'.[70] This request was heard at the ninetieth plenary meeting of the General Assembly of the United Nations in December 2001, where the General Assembly accepted and endorsed a proposal from the ITU that a World Summit on the Information Society

---

[66] http://www.isu.net.sa/saudi-internet/contenet-filtering/filtring.htm.

[67] Council of Ministers Resolution, Saudi Internet Rules, February 12, 2001: http://www.al-bab.com/media/docs/saudi.htm.

[68] Arab News, 'Shoura approves law to combat e-crimes', October 10, 2006: http://www.arabnews.com/?page=1&section=0&article=87941&d=10&m=10&y=2006.

[69] Substantial filtering is reported in Bahrain, Burma, China, Ethiopia, Iran, Libya, Oman, Pakistan, South Korea (in relation to security on the Korean peninsula), Saudi Arabia, Sudan, Syria, Thailand, Tunisia, UAE, Uzbekistan, Vietnam, and Yemen. They report no data on Cuba or North Korea but both are known to strictly control internet access.

[70] Resolution 73: http://www.itu.int/wsis/docs/background/resolutions/73.html. In effect what they were asking for was a UN Summit. Summits are designed to put long-term, complex problems like poverty and environmental degradation at the top of the global agenda. They are designed to provide leadership and to mould international opinion and to persuade world leaders to provide political support.

(WSIS) be convened, and instructed the Secretary-General of the UN to 'inform all heads of State and Government of the adoption of the present resolution'.[71] The WSIS was to take place in two phases, the first phase taking place in Geneva from 10–12 December 2003 and the second phase taking place in Tunis, from 16–18 November 2005. The objective of the Geneva phase was to develop and foster a clear statement of political will and take concrete steps to establish the foundations for an Information Society for all, reflecting all the different interests at stake. The objective of the second phase was to put the Geneva 'Plan of Action' into effect and to find solutions and reach agreements in the fields of internet governance, financing mechanisms, and follow-up and implementation of the Geneva and Tunis documents. WSIS invited Heads of State/Government, International NGOs, and Civil Society representatives[72] to contribute to a series of preparatory meetings (PrepComms) and to the Geneva and Tunis rounds on a series of issues ranging from the digital divide,[73] to freedom of expression, network security, unsolicited commercial communications (SPAM), and protection of children.[74] Central to the WSIS programme was though the issue of internet governance.

WSIS envisaged a 'people-centred, inclusive and development-orientated Information Society where everyone can create, access, utilise and share information and knowledge, enabling individuals, communities and peoples to achieve their full potential in promoting their sustainable development and improving their quality of life'.[75] Discussion as to how this was to be achieved began in the PrepComms. In these meetings numerous views were expressed about what was and was not 'internet governance', and the public policy involved. Some developing nations noted that they were unable to participate in many of the decision making processes central to management of the internet, such as management of the domain name system which was primarily in the hands of two American-based private regulators the Internet Corporation for Assigned Names and Numbers (ICANN) and the Internet Assigned Numbers Authority (IANA).[76] Others, predominantly the US, called for the principle of private sector involvement and investment to be enshrined. In the final PrepComm briefing on 3 December 2003 US Ambassador David Gross outlined what he called the 'three pillars' of the US position.

---

[71] Resolution adopted by the General Assembly [on the report of the Second Committee (A/56/558/Add.3)] 56/183. World Summit on the Information Society, 21 December 2001.

[72] In UN parlance, civil society encompasses all those who are not part of government, private enterprise, or intergovernmental organisations: in other words private individuals.

[73] The 'digital divide' reflects the technology gap which has opened up between technology rich Western States and technology poor African and Asian States, and on the growing divide within States between the professional classes with stable and fast internet access and the working class, in particular immigrant communities, where access may be unstable, slow and difficult to obtain. See P. Norris, *Digital Divide: Civic Engagement, Information Poverty and the Internet Worldwide* (2001); M. Warschauer, *Technology and Social Inclusion: Rethinking the Digital Divide* (2004).

[74] For a discussion of WSIS see M. Raboy & N. Landry, *Civil Society, Communication and Global Governance: Issues from the World Summit on the Information Society* (2004).

[75] WSIS, Declaration of Principles, Geneva 12 December 2003, Principle 1.

[76] Further discussion of the domain name system and the role in particular of ICANN takes place in Ch. 12.

> **→ Highlight** The US "Three Pillars" for ICT Regulation
>
> 1. As nations attempt to build a sustainable ICT sector, commitment to the private sector and rule of law must be emphasised so that countries can attract the necessary private investment to create the infrastructure;
>
> 2. The need for content creation and intellectual property rights protection in order to inspire ongoing content development; and
>
> 3. Nations must ensure security on the internet, in electronic communications and in electronic commerce.

Due to this divergence of views, when the Geneva Summit got under way the PrepComms had failed to produce agreement on the future development of internet governance. Although committed to a principle of multi-stakeholder agreement many developing nations, including China, Brazil, and most Arab States saw the US commitment to private sector initiatives as a barrier to progress while the US, and others including the EU, Japan, and Canada, feared that some governments wished to have a greater say in internet governance purely as a vehicle for censorship or content management. As a result agreement in Geneva proved impossible. Instead it was noted that: 'governance issues related to the internet are a complex challenge which needs a complex answer and which has to include all stakeholders—civil society, private industry and governments. No single body and no single stakeholder group alone is able to manage these challenges. This multi-stakeholder approach should be the guiding principle both for the technical coordination of the internet, as well as for broader public policy issues related to Cyberspace in general'.[77] To give effect to this recommendation, WSIS put together a Working Group on Internet Governance (WGIG) to report to the Tunis conference with recommendations. The group, chaired by Nitin Desai, Special Adviser to the Secretary-General for the WSIS, met four times between Geneva and Tunis, and published their final report on 18 July 2005.[78]

The group was asked to carry out their work under three broad heads: (1) to develop a working definition of internet governance; (2) to identify the public policy issues that are relevant to internet governance; and (3) to develop a common understanding of the respective roles and responsibilities of Governments, existing international organisations, and other forums, as well as the private sector and civil society in both developing and developed countries.[79] In dealing with the first the group suggested the following working definition: 'Internet governance is the development and application by Governments, the private sector and civil society, in their

---

[77] World Summit on the Information Society, *Visions in Process: Geneva 2003—Tunis 2005*, 41: http://www.worldsummit2003.de/download_de/Vision_in_process.pdf.

[78] Full details of WGIG may be found at http://www.wgig.org/.

[79] Taken from WGIG, *Report of the Working Group on Internet Governance*, Château de Bossey 18 June 2005, [5].

respective roles, of shared principles, norms, rules, decision-making procedures, and programmes that shape the evolution and use of the internet'.[80] From this base the group then moved on to its second head of study and listed thirteen public policy issues 'of the highest priority'.[81] With this achieved the group than made its critical recommendations on the respective roles and responsibilities of governments, existing international organisations, and other forums. It recommended that governments were to drive public policymaking and coordination and implementation, as appropriate, at the national level, and policy development and coordination at the regional and international levels.[82] This was to include development of best practices, capacity building, and promoting research and development. The private sector meanwhile was called upon to develop policy proposals, guidelines, and tools for policymakers and other stakeholders, this including industry self-regulation and arbitration and dispute resolution.[83] To manage the relationship between the public and private sector (and other stakeholders) WGIG recommended the creation of a new Internet Governance Forum (IGF) which would provide the opportunity for the free exchange of ideas between stakeholders and which would provide public policy guidance.[84] The mandate for the new forum is set out in paragraph 72 of the Tunis Agenda for the Information Society[85] which states:

→ Highlight IGF Mandate

The Forum is to:

a. Discuss public policy issues related to key elements of Internet governance in order to foster the sustainability, robustness, security, stability and development of the Internet.

b. Facilitate discourse between bodies dealing with different cross-cutting international public policies regarding the Internet and discuss issues that do not fall within the scope of any existing body.

c. Interface with appropriate intergovernmental organizations and other institutions on matters under their purview.

d. Facilitate the exchange of information and best practices, and in this regard make full use of the expertise of the academic, scientific and technical communities.

e. Advise all stakeholders in proposing ways and means to accelerate the availability and affordability of the Internet in the developing world.

→

---

[80] *ibid*, [10].

[81] These were: (1) Administration of the root zone files and system; (2) Interconnection costs; (3) Internet stability, security and cybercrime; (4) Spam; (5) Meaningful participation in global policy development; (6) Capacity-building; (7) Allocation of domain names; (8) IP addressing; (9) Intellectual Property Rights; (10) Freedom of expression; (11) Data protection and privacy rights; (12) Consumer rights; and (13) Multilingualism. Full discussion of these may be found at [15]–[27].

[82] *ibid*, [30].   [83] *ibid*, [31].   [84] *ibid*, [35]–[51].

[85] WSIS, *Tunis Agenda for the Information Society*, 18 November 2005: http://www.itu.int/wsis/docs2/tunis/off/6rev1.html.

> ➜
>
>   f. Strengthen and enhance the engagement of stakeholders in existing and/or future Internet governance mechanisms, particularly those from developing countries.
>
>   g. Identify emerging issues, bring them to the attention of the relevant bodies and the general public, and, where appropriate, make recommendations.
>
>   h. Contribute to capacity building for Internet governance in developing countries, drawing fully on local sources of knowledge and expertise.
>
>   i. Promote and assess, on an ongoing basis, the embodiment of WSIS principles in Internet governance processes.
>
>   j. Discuss, *inter alia*, issues relating to critical Internet resources.
>
>   k. Help to find solutions to the issues arising from the use and misuse of the Internet, of particular concern to everyday users.
>
>   l. Publish its proceedings.

At the date of writing the IGF has met on four occasions with little in the way of hard policy emerging from the meetings. At the most recent meeting in Sharm El Sheikh in November 2009 the event reports made for depressing reading. The meeting considered a synthesis paper, *On the desirability of the continuation of the Forum*.[86] Although this ultimately (and fortunately) concluded that: 'the General Assembly, when deliberating on the Forum's continuation, should decide on its continuation for another five-year period. Following that period, another review of the desirability of a further extension should take place in the process of an overall review of WSIS outcomes,'[87] the prior deliberation was not without the identification of clear failures of the IGF process. As the report noted: 'One commentator suggested that the Forum had a long way to go in fulfilling the real objective for which it was established—to assist in the democratic development of global public policies and, if necessary, new institutions, in the area of Internet governance, in the spirit of the Geneva Declaration of Principles,'[88] while another 'wrote that the IGF had only fulfilled its mandate selectively'[89] while a third 'felt that the Forum had only just begun to fulfil its mandate and that the first years' activities had clarified the breadth and scope of work to be undertaken.'[90] Many felt the Forum to be too reactive noting that the Forum should be proactive in encouraging institutions involved in internet governance to debate and discuss by providing an open space specifically for such activities at its annual meetings, and that the IGF should take an 'adaptive approach to its work' and extend its focus to other areas affected by internet

---

[86] IGF Secretariat, *On the desirability of the continuation of the Forum*, August 2009: http://www.intgovforum.org/cms/2009/synthesis_paper/K0952729.E.IGF.Synthesis.Paper.final.pdf.

[87] *ibid*, [99].   [88] *ibid*, [22].   [89] *ibid*, [23].   [90] *ibid*, [24].

policy and technology.[91] This chimes with earlier findings in the official publication reviewing the first two IGF meetings,[92] where Markus Kummer, eEnvoy of the Swiss Government, notes that: 'governments remain the decision makers'.[93]

The formation of the IGF is a step in the direction of cooperative supranational internet regulation, but the nature of the IGF as a forum to 'discuss public policy issues related to key elements of Internet governance' means it falls far short, currently, of playing a meaningful role in the regulation of the internet and digital content. Worse, the IGF though may never play a meaningful role in internet governance. The Prep-Comms provided an insight into why international cooperation at an operational level is unlikely to follow from discussion at IGF meetings. There is a digital divide between most developed and developing nations which means that there are different economic interests in play. Further, there appears to be a societal divide between the key states members of the IGF. The US in particular seems quite unshiftable on its twin positions of private sector investment and allowing the market to regulate. This is not acceptable to many nations including China, the other major states party at the IGF. Without agreement between these two digital superpowers the IGF will remain locked down and will prove to be merely a forum for discussion. This is not to belittle the potential contribution of the IGF which discusses open access, network standards, protection for freedom, and network stability and security, merely to say that the existence of the IGF does not change, and is unlikely to change, the established primacy of the nation state in internet governance.

4.6 **Conclusion**

What does all this mean for the study of cyber-regulation? The cyberpaternalists may argue that the effectiveness of filtering tools in countries such as China, Saudi Arabia, and Burma prove that by using legal controls to mandate changes the network architecture, either by filtering content or by restricting the ability of users to get online control may be effected in the digital environment. They may further point to the fact that when the IWF blacklisted the Wikipedia entry of *Virgin Killer* reports of the effectiveness of the Cleanfeed system ranged between 85–95% effective, demonstrating that even in democratic nations effective controls may be implemented at network architecture level. Cyber-libertarians may respond by citing that tools such as Peacefire.org's *Circumventor* software allow a large proportion of end-users in even the most regulated of states to circumvent state based controls.[94] The problem faced by cyberlibertarians is that it is impossible to deny that in each case the state *is* effectively controlling the online actions of their citizens, and that these controls may only be circumvented using specialist tools or with expert knowledge of computer networks.

---

[91] *ibid*, [87]–[88].

[92] A. Doria & W. Kleinwächter, *Internet Governance Forum (IGF) The First Two Years:* http://www.intgovforum.org/cms/hydera/IGFBook_the_first_two_years.pdf.   [93] *ibid*, 16.

[94] Festa, above n. 65; S. Olsen, 'Maxthon: China's hip browser' *cnet News*, 22 June 2006: http://news.cnet.com/2100-1032_3-6086632.html.

This is far removed from John Perry Barlow's claim that real world regulators 'do [not] possess any methods of enforcement we have true reason to fear'. The experience of the real world and the development of the Cyberpaternalist School seem to have consigned cyberlibertarianism to the pages of the history books. What of network communitarianism? Surely these real life examples of control implemented either at the network gatekeeper level or at state level undermine the network communitarian claim that 'regulation is a process of discourse and dialogue between the individual and society'? The network communitarian response would be that each of these real world examples can be perfectly rationalised with network communitarian thought. The UK *Virgin Killer* example is a perfect example of network communitarian regulation in action. Once the action of the IWF was brought into the public domain an extensive discourse took place and it only took four days for the block to be removed, this despite the assertion from the IWF that 'the image in question is potentially in breach of the Protection of Children Act 1978'. In other words the IWF still believe the image may be illegal to download and possess in the UK, but rather than fulfil their remit to 'minimise the availability of this (abusive) content' they chose to listen to the overwhelming view of British internet users that content of this type should not be blocked without consultation. This is network communitarianism in action. What about effectiveness of state level filtering though? Well if one looks at the lists of states which effectively filter at a state level we find that overwhelmingly they fall into one of two categories. The first are states where political discourse is routinely suppressed, states such as China, Burma, and Pakistan. The second are Islamic states where religious teachings forbid certain types of content, in particular anti-Islamic content or pornographic content. In each of these examples because political discourse is suppressed naturally in the real world we see a similar suppression of discourse in the online environment. Thus it appears one may choose to see the regulation in the digital environment in a similar fashion as regulation in the physical environment. It may either be centred, command and control regulation or it may be decentred and part of the democratic process. What is clear is that there is nothing particularly special about designing effective regulation in the digital environment.

FURTHER READING

Books

L. Lessig, *Code Version 2.0* (2006).

A. Murray, *The Regulation of Cyberspace: Control in the Online Environment* (2007)

J. Zittrain, *The Future of the Internet and How to Stop It* (2008)

J. Goldsmith & T. Wu, *Who controls the Internet?* (2006)

L. Bygrave & J. Bing, *Internet Governance: Infrastructure and Institutions* (2009)

Chapters and Articles

J. Reidenberg, 'Lex Informatica: The Formation of Information Policy Rules Through Technology' 76 *Texas Law Review* 553 (1998)

V. Mayer-Schönberger, 'Demystifying Lessig' [2008] *Wisconsin Law Review* 714

P. de Hert, S. Gutwirth., & L. de Sutter, 'The trouble with technology regulation from a legal perspective: Why Lessig's "optimal mix" will not work' in R. Brownsword & K. Yeung (eds), *Regulating Technologies: Legal Futures, Regulatory Frames and Technological Fixes* (2009)

Digital ownership

The law of property forms one of the central tenets of modern legal systems. The functioning of modern society, based upon principles of free markets and the ability to trade, requires that the legal system recognise rights in things as well as obligations between persons. Attempting to define property law, and property rights, is difficult in the physical world, but as we shall see is even more challenging in the digital environment where traditional values such as possession and rivalrousness are rendered ineffective by the limitless nature of bits.[1]

The starting point for any discussion of digital ownership is to examine how property law functions in the real world. Definitions of property differ but they all appear to have some elements in common. The first is that property defines a relationship between a person and a thing. Unlike obligations which normalise relations between persons, one tangent of the axis in a property relationship must be a thing. This is because property, and property law, regulate one's right to own, buy and sell, dispose, or destroy. These rights may only be exercised over things: it has been illegal to take rights such as these over persons in the UK for almost 200 years.[2] The second common theme of property law is that it is exclusive. The rights that property law confers upon the owner, or other rightsholder such as a lessee, are of the nature of rights *in rem* as opposed to rights *ad personam*. This means that the property rights holder has a right which may be exercised against any individual who attempts to interfere with his or her property right without the need for a prior relationship with that person. This may be contrasted with obligations which arise out of a prior relationship such as a contractual relationship or a relationship which establishes a duty of care in tort.[3] As James Penner explains in his book *The Idea of Property in Law*, the essential element of these rights is the right to exclude others from exercising competing rights over your property.[4]

We tend not to notice the monopolistic nature of property rights when we are dealing with everyday items such as cars, computers, or shoes as the monopoly one person exercises over *their car, their computer,* or *their shoes* cannot effect the wider market for shoes, cars, or computers, but when we are dealing with rare or unique items this becomes more apparent as with rare artworks such as L.S. Lowry's *A Fairground* which was kept

---

[1] Rivalrous and Nonrivalrous goods are discussed in Ch. 1, while at least some of the effects of digitisation and the limitless supply of bits are discussed in Ch. 3.
[2] Slavery Abolition Act 1833.   [3] See *Donoghue v Stevenson* [1932] AC 562.
[4] J. Penner, *The Idea of Property in Law* (1997), Ch. 4.

in a private collection and never exhibited for over fifty years,[5] or with intellectual property rights such as copyright where the property right may be used to prevent distribution or exhibition of the work.[6]

> ### ✳ **Example** Physical Products
>
> Eleanor has bought a new car. She may use her property rights in it to prevent anyone else from possessing the car or from dispossessing her of, or economically exploiting, the car.
>
> In addition as exclusive rights property rights create a natural monopoly over property. Although Eleanor's car may not be unique, she holds a monopoly over the use of **that** car: in other words she monopolises the rights in relation to that particular car. She may choose to sell or rent the car, she may choose to destroy it, or she may choose merely to enjoy it herself.

The final element of property law which is generally agreed upon by commentators on the subject is that property law, as opposed to property, represents a bundle of rights distinct from the thing itself. Thus by owning a car I have the most basic property right: ownership, but I also possess the right to take economic fruits from it by renting it to someone else, to destroy it (subject to environmental laws) and to securitise it (that it to use it as security for a loan), among other rights. Thus although we tend to think of property rights as ownership—'this is my car' there are a bundle of additional rights the property owner also possesses.

5.1 **Digital property**

As discussed in Chapter 1, the nature of digital goods is quite unlike physical goods and as a result the application of property law to digital goods is not clear cut. The problem is that traditional property values and principles assume that goods are rivalrous. Rivalrousness lends itself to the principle of exclusion. Among the many reasons I may have as to why I may wish to exclude others from economically exploiting my property is that in so doing they are likely to affect my enjoyment of my property. We can see this assumption of rivalrousness if we look to s. 1 of the Theft Act 1968 which states, 'A person is guilty of theft if they dishonestly appropriate property belonging to another with the intention to permanently deprive the other of it'. Rivalrousness in physical property means that traditional property laws are as much about the enjoyment of property as they are about exclusion of competing interests. Once we move into intangible properties this aspect of property is removed. In dealing with informational products a different rationale must apply.

---

[5] See M. Kennedy, 'Little-known Lowry painting up for auction' *The Guardian*, 23 August 2007.
[6] As with Stanley Kubrick's film version of *A Clockwork Orange* which Kubrick refused to allow to be exhibited in the UK from 1973 to his death in 1999. See A. Mullins and J. Robins, 'Kubrick considered "Clockwork Orange" re-release', *The Independent*, 3 December 1999.

> ⊛ **Example** Informational Products
>
> If I make and sell copies of Julian Barnes' novel *Arthur & George* this does not directly affect Mr. Barnes' enjoyment of his copyright; he may continue to produce copies or adaptations of the work or he may license a film adaptation or a translation. Thus my production of a competing version of his copyright material allows me to enjoy all the fruits of property ownership including the taking of economic rents without directly dispossessing Mr Barnes of his prior and better right.

There are two points which have to be made about this example. The first is that you may assume I have made a false assumption here: that the correct comparison is not between properties of a genus, but between property of a type. That is when I talk about not infringing Mr Barnes' rights in his text I'm making the mistake of equating copies of *Arthur & George* generally with specifically *his* copy of *Arthur & George*. Thus if someone produces exact copies of my car and sells them on the open market my interests in *my* car are unaffected: the same may be said here of Mr Barnes and *his* book. This though is not the case as copyright protects not the book itself but the intangible expression of an idea as recorded in the pages of a book. To make and sell copies of *Arthur & George* is to directly interfere with, or in copyright terms infringe, Mr Barnes' property right. Secondly, although Mr Barnes has not been dispossessed of his property right in the copyright of *Arthur & George*, it is clear my actions will have adversely affected his property interest as the available amount of property rents he may receive for his copyright has been reduced by my action. This, at least in part, explains why we protect certain intangible properties even though they are of a nonrivalrous nature.

5.1.1 Information as property

Traditionally property law does not define information as a good unless it is of a particular character. In the American case of *International News Service v Associated Press*,[7] the US Supreme Court did recognise a proprietary nature in news information. Following unfavourable reporting on British losses by William Randolph Hearst's INS, they were barred from using Allied telegraph lines to report news from the front. To remedy this they took information printed by AP on the US east coast and wired it to their west coast newspapers. This was then rewritten by journalists on these papers and published. As the information was rewritten there was no breach of copyright. AP claimed a quasi-proprietary right in their information and surprisingly the Supreme Court upheld their claim in unfair competition based upon this principle.

Recognising a proprietary interest in raw information is though potentially very damaging for competition as it creates an exclusionary effect of preventing third parties from using the information.[8] Because of this Justice Brandeis dissented vigorously in the case and subsequent attempts to apply the principle of quasi ownership in information have fallen foul of a narrow interpretation of the case. Thus in *Cheney*

---

[7] (1918) 248 US 215.   [8] See R. Smith, *Property Law* 6th ed. (2009), 5.

Brothers v Doris Silk Corporation[9] Judge Learned Hand confided to the other members of the panel that 'the Associated Press Case is somewhat of a stumbling block . . . I do not believe that the five justices who united in Pitney, J's opinion meant to lay down a general rule that a man is entitled to "property" in the form of whatever he makes with his labor and money, so as to prevent others from copying it. To do so would be to short-circuit the Patent Office and throw upon courts the winnowing out of all such designs that might be presented. While I agree that on principle it is hard to distinguish, and that the language applies, I cannot suppose that any principle of such far-reaching consequence was intended. It will make patent cases an exception; it will give to State courts jurisdiction over inventions; it will overthrow the practice of centuries'.[10] To circumvent this problem Hand concluded that INS had to be understood as a case that dealt with the narrow and peculiar problems of a news service. Thus the case could be restricted to its facts despite being a decision of the Supreme Court. This approach was confirmed in the later case of *RCA Manufacturing Co. v Whiteman*,[11] where Judge Clark settled that INS was to be so restricted and noted off the record to Judge Hand that 'In principle, this case is entirely indistinguishable from INS, and we might as well admit it. But we have conquered the News case before; it can be done again'[12] before going on to hold that using licenses to expand copyright was unconstitutional. With courts in the US striving to restrict INS to its facts it is not surprising that UK courts have conspicuously failed to find any type of property right in information of a general nature.[13]

5.1.2 **Statutory intellectual property rights**

This is not to say that ownership in information is impossible in the UK. The most obvious examples are the statutory intellectual property rights created over certain categories of information; perhaps the best known example of which is to be found in the law of patents. A patent is a statutory property right awarded following a process of application and review to an idea or process which is capable of industrial application.[14] The owner of a patent has, for a limited time,[15] the right to prevent others from developing competing products or services based upon the idea or process outlined in the patent. In other words a patent protects the use of the idea or process for the lifetime of the patent.

Patents, although valuable, are of little direct impact in digital property as the patent must be for a process or idea capable of industrial application, and further cannot be 'a scheme, rule or method for performing a mental act, playing a game or doing

---

[9] 35 F.2d 279 (2d Cir. 1929).

[10] Reported in D. Baird, 'Property, Natural Monopoly, and the Uneasy Legacy of INS v. APU' *Chicago Law & Economics, Olin Working Paper No. 246*. SSRN: http://ssrn.com/abstract=730024 or DOI: 10.2139/ssrn.730024, 29.

[11] 114 F.2d 86 (2d Cir. 1940).   [12] Again this is reported in Baird, above n. 10, 30.

[13] UK Courts have tended to follow the principle of 'no ownership in raw information' as espoused in the Australian case of *Victoria Park Racing & Recreation Grounds Co. Ltd v Taylor* (1937) 58 CLR 479.   [14] Patents Act 1977, s. 1.   [15] Up to 20 years: Patents Act 1977, s. 25.

business, or a program for a computer'.[16] With digital goods being basically a series of ones and zeros, operated on by a CPU it is extremely difficult for them to gain protection given this qualification. Some attempts have been made to protect computer software, despite the Act excluding protection for 'a program for a computer',[17] and also attempts have been made, mostly in the US, to protect methods of doing business in the digital environment.

The most famous patent application in the field of digital goods is probably the Amazon '1 click' patent. Amazon developed their '1 click' ordering system in the late 1990s and in September 1997 they sought a patent for a method of placing an order using one click of the computer mouse. The patent was awarded in September 1999 and Amazon subsequently used the system on their own website and licensed it to Apple for use on their iTunes site. The same year Barnes & Noble, a direct competitor of Amazon, attempted to install their own 1 click shopping system known as 'express lane'. This led Amazon to sue for infringement. Before the District Court they were awarded injunctive relief, but on appeal the US Court of Appeals for the Federal Circuit reversed this on the basis that Barnes & Noble had raised a substantial challenge to the validity of Amazon's patent on grounds of obviousness.[18] Following this decision the parties agreed a settlement in which it was reported that Barnes & Noble agreed to pay to licence the Amazon technology.[19] If this was the end of this tale it would suggest that patentability of digital products was a potential way to protect digital goods, but the story is much more complex than this. Firstly an attempt by Amazon to have their 1 click patent recognised in Europe failed after the European Patent Office indicated to Amazon that it were not patentable under European patent rules.[20] Further the US patent has recently been substantially narrowed in effect following a re-examination by the US Patents and Trademarks Office.[21] Patents are clearly not an effective way to protect the majority of digital goods. Another method of protection must be found.

Like a patent, a copyright is a statutory property right, this time awarded by the Copyright, Designs and Patents Act 1988. Unlike a patent a copyright arises automatically and is awarded to original literary, dramatic, musical or artistic works, sound recordings, films, broadcasts or cable programmes, and the typographical arrangement of published editions.[22] Copyright is a natural monopoly right which allows the author or creator of the work to control the distribution of their original work by restricting to them the right to make copies of the original. Copyright is quite unlike traditional property rights as the exclusive rights are to control the making and distribution of copies of the work, or the display or public performance of the work.[23] You cannot directly use your copyright to prevent an individual reading or viewing your work provided they do not have to make or obtain an illegal copy, or attend an unlawful public performance, to

---

[16] Patents Act 1977, s. 1(2)(c).   [17] Patent protection for computer software is analysed in Ch. 9.
[18] *Amazon.com Inc. v Barnesandnoble.com Inc.* (2001) 239 F 3d 1343.
[19] Tim Cook, *Amazon Patent Challenge*, http://www.it-analysis.com/content.php?cid=8546.
[20] See European Patent Office, *EPO revokes patent for 'electronic ordering system'*, http://www.epo.org/about-us/press/releases/archive/2007/20071207a.html.
[21] USPTO, Ex Parte Re-examination of Patent Number 5960411: http://www.out-law.com/PDF/Amazon_Patent_interview_summary.pdf.   [22] CDPA 1988, s. 1.
[23] CDPA 1988, Ch. 2 (ss. 16–27).

do so. Because the mere use of a copyright work without permission does not interfere with the copyright holder's ability to enjoy his work,[24] there is no concept in copyright which is akin to trespass in physical property. I cannot 'trespass' on the copyright of Julian Barnes by simply reading *Arthur & George* whereas I could trespass on his property rights by pitching a tent in his front garden or by moving in to his car.[25] Unlike a patent holder, a copyright holder cannot therefore prevent passive enjoyment of his copyright protected material. When discussing digital ownership and digital property this is a key concept as the use of copyright law to prevent someone from passively accessing a webpage, video blog, or other digital offering is not possible. If the owner/operator of a digital site wishes to prevent access they must seek to rely on traditional property law concepts not copyright law.

5.1.3 **Confidential information**

There is another potential body of law which may be used to protect digital goods distinct from the application of the statutory property rights. This is by the application of the law of confidential information. In truth, protecting informational products by the application of confidentiality is not application of property law principles, rather its roots are in the law of obligations. To qualify for protection the information must first be 'confidential': this has been defined by Lord Greene MR as to mean that the information is not public property and public knowledge.[26] This means the information does not have to be secret as such, just not readily available to the public. Secondly the information must have been disclosed in circumstances which give rise to an obligation of confidence. This generally means that in disclosing the information to the recipient the owner of the information did so for a limited and defined purpose. In *Saltman Engineering v Campbell* the claimants gave the defendants confidential designs for tools which the defendants were to manufacture solely for the claimants. The defendants went on to manufacture and market the tools themselves leading to a claim of breach of confidentiality. The court held the designs had been handed over for a limited purpose only and the defendants were not entitled to use them outwith that purpose.[27] The final quality of confidential information is that there must be an actual or anticipated unauthorised disclosure of the information.[28] As is clear from these requirements the status of confidentiality is usually conferred upon information as a result of a pre-existing contractual relationship between the parties.

Confidentiality is a form of protection offered by obligations not property principles. This has several effects. Firstly the right to enforce the obligation of confidentiality is a right *ad personam* not a right *in rem*. That is the rights, and reciprocal duties attach to the parties not the information itself. This can be seen in the case of *Fraser v Evans*.[29] Here the claimant wrote a confidential report for the Greek government. His contract

---

[24] As copyright works are nonrivalrous properties. See Ch. 1.

[25] Technically the second example, moving in to his car, is not trespass as trespass relates to Real Property (land). The second example would almost certainly be prosecuted as theft under the Theft Act 1968.

[26] Lord Greene MR in *Saltman Engineering v Campbell* (1948) 65 RPC 203.   [27] *ibid.*

[28] *Coco v AN Clarke (Engineers) Ltd.* [1969] RPC 41, per Megarry J.   [29] [1969] 1 QB 349.

stated that he was to keep confidential any information he gathered in compiling the report. There was though no reciprocal obligation on the Greek government to keep confidential any information Mr Fraser supplied to them. The report was later leaked by an unknown source in the Greek government to a newspaper. Mr Fraser sought to restrain publication of an article based on the document on grounds of breach of confidence. The court held that Mr Fraser was not due an obligation of confidentiality despite the information being described in his contract as confidential. Thus it is clear that information is not confidential itself it is rather the expectation placed upon the party which creates the circumstance of confidentiality.

What does this mean for the use of confidentiality as a proxy for property protection when dealing with digital information? There is clearly a restricted role for confidentiality where parties are in some form of relationship with each other. Examples would include using confidentiality to protect valuable software code shared between software developers or using confidentiality to protect private areas on websites which are password protected and to which access may only be achieved once one agrees to treat information contained therein as confidential. The problem with utilising confidentiality as a tool to protect digital property in the wider sense is the first nature of confidential information; that is that it is not public property and/or public knowledge. The very nature of most property is that it is to be seen in and accessed through the public domain. To draw a property law analogy with the use of confidentiality as a proxy for digital property instead of using the law of property to prevent anyone from stealing, occupying, or damaging my car, I instead lock my car in a garage and keep only a few keys for myself, my wife and my immediate family to enter. I forbid them from taking the car out and I forbid them from telling anyone about the car. It is clear when you discuss confidential information in this way that it cannot fulfil the roles of property law. Property law is about excluding others from access to your property by enshrining protection for its boundaries in a series of legal principles. Confidentiality is about excluding others from access to your property by removing it from public knowledge. Thus I can never drive my car in public if I rely upon the protection of confidentiality. Equally, returning to the sphere of digital goods we cannot use confidentiality to protect digital goods which are open to the public, observable in public, or which are accessible from a public place. This rules this out as a methodology of protecting software in which the source code is accessible, web pages and their allied content and digital media such as images, sounds and video accessible from any open network source.

5.2 **Digital trespass**

With the inability of traditional intangible property rights such as patents, copyright, and confidentiality to protect the vast majority of digital goods the owners and developers of digital property have turned to more inventive ways to protect their investment in digital properties.[30] One such approach has been to attempt to use traditional property

---

[30] It should be noted that we should treat computer software as a unique form of digital property as there is a separate and well established order of protecting software by both copyright law and patents. This will be discussed in full in ch. 9.

principles such as trespass in the digital, incorporeal environment. This idea, unsurprisingly, originates in the US and much of the case law on the concept of digital trespass is to be found there, particularly in the State of California.

5.2.1 **Trespass to servers**

The first case to examine the applicability of trespass to chattels to digital goods was a Californian case from 1996. In *Thrifty-Tel, Inc. v Bezenek*[31] two young hackers tried to gain access to free long distance calls by means of sending digital signals from their computer to the telephone exchange server. In attempting to gain access to the Thrifty-Tel carrier network Ryan Bezenek (one of the defendants) overburdened the Thrifty-Tel system, denying some subscribers access to phones lines. At this point Thrifty-Tel took action claiming attempted fraud and misappropriation. To determine whether harm was likely the court looked at whether the actions of the Bezenek brothers amounted to trespass to chattels. The Court of Appeal of California found that the boys' action of sending of electronic signals to the computers were sufficiently tangible to support a cause of action in trespass. This decision was highly controversial.[32] One commentary notes that *Thrifty-Tel* 'opened the floodgates to judicial adoption of cyberproperty' and that 'courts seized on *Thrifty-Tel* to punish such activity without even considering whether plaintiffs alleged damage to chattel'.[33]

The reason for the flood of cases referred to was that *Thrifty-Tel* offered a tantalising opportunity to network providers (such as telecoms companies and ISPs) to use principles of property law, and in particular trespass to chattels, to deal with 'spammers'—individuals who send vast amounts of unsolicited commercial communications across the email system—in a time when there was no legislative framework to protect them from their activities.[34] If, as the court had said in *Thrifty-Tel*, the sending of data down a telephone cable could amount to trespass to chattels then spammers who sent vast amounts of emails simultaneously could equally be found to be digitally trespassing. This was first tested in two cases against a SPAM organisation called Cyber Promotions.[35] The more controversial of the two Cyber Promotions cases was *CompuServe Inc. v Cyber Promotions Inc.*,[36] for in that case the District Court for the Southern District of Ohio found that trespass to chattels could be established without harm to

---

[31] 54 Cal. Rptr. 2d 468 (Ct. App. 1996).

[32] Critical commentaries include: L. Quilter, 'Cyberlaw: The Continuing Expansion of Cyberspace Trespass to Chattels' 17 *Berkeley Technology Law Journal* 421 (2002); C. Merrell, 'Trespass to Chattels in the Age of the Internet', 80 *Washington University Law Quarterly* 675 (2002); M. Bendotoff & E. Gosse, '"Stay Off My Cyberproperty!": Trespass to Chattels on the Internet'(2001), 6 *Intellectual Property. Law Bulletin* 12; E. Lee, 'Rules and Standards for Cyberspace', 77 *Notre Dame Law Review* 1275 (2002).

[33] M. Carrier & G. Lastowska, 'Against Cyberproperty' 22 *Berkeley Technology Law Journal* 1483 (2007), 1489.

[34] There is now a legislative framework to deal with SPAM in both the US (The Controlling the Assault of Non-Solicited Pornography and Marketing Act 2003 (CAN-SPAM Act), 15 USC 7701) and in Europe (Directive 2002/58/EC of the European Parliament and of the Council of 12 July 2002 Concerning the Processing of Personal Data and the Protection of Privacy in the Electronic Communications Sector (ePrivacy Directive), Art.13. SPAM regulation will be discussed in Ch. 6.

[35] *Cyber Promotions Inc. v America Online Inc.* 948 F. Supp 436 (1996); *CompuServe Inc. v Cyber Promotions Inc.* 962 F. Supp. 1015 (1997).   [36] *ibid.*

the computer network in question. The court found that there was sufficient tangibility to establish trespass to chattels in 'the electronic signals sent by computer',[37] and found that there was actual trespass (or harm) without damage as 'spam email demands the disk space and drains the processing power of computer equipment' it prevents these resources being available for paying customers.[38] The court concluded that even though the CompuServe network and its servers were not physically harmed by the defendants' actions the value of the equipment to CompuServe was diminished and found in their favour. The decision in CompuServe signalled a change in approach in digital trespass. Courts would no longer look for evidence of actual harm, as they had in *Thrifty-Tel*, they would now look for evidence of economic harm. A flurry of cases followed, mostly focussed on SPAM email,[39] but a few cases developed around a different practice which appears to be more closely aligned with the traditional practice of trespass in the real world.

5.2.2 Indexing and scraping

These cases surrounded the practices of indexing and scraping. These are the practices of accessing websites either for the purpose of gathering data from that website to place in an index (such as a search engine) or to gather data such as prices or availability of goods or services for a price comparison site or similar. The first case on scraping is the well known case of *eBay Inc. v Bidder's Edge Inc.*,[40] in which the defendants operated an 'auction aggregator' which captured eBay's auction data and supplied it to the public as a form of price comparison. eBay claimed trespass to chattels even though admitting that the actions of Bidder's Edge did not significantly affect the ability of its web servers to function normally. Instead eBay, following a more traditional property law rationale, claimed that as eBay had not authorised Bidder's Edge to access this information they were in fact trespassing. The District Court for the Northern District of California agreed and issued an injunction prohibiting Bidder's Edge from accessing eBay's web pages.[41] It seems the court was particularly concerned with potential rather than actual harm, for although eBay had conceded the actions of Bidder's Edge were not currently impairing the eBay network, the court was concerned that other companies may begin to aggregate eBay's auction data should eBay's claim fail, at which point actual harm may occur. Thus the decision in eBay may be characterised as being one of potential rather than actual harm.[42]

The US courts were though still willing to push the envelope of digital trespass a little further. In the following case, *Oyster Software Inc. v Forms Processing Inc.*,[43] the District Court for the Northern District of California found trespass to chattels not only where there was no actual damage, but where there was no likelihood of future damage either. In this case the defendant copied the plaintiff's meta tags from his website and placed these copies on his web site with the intent of redirecting

[37] *ibid*, 1021.   [38] *ibid*, 1022.
[39] Cases such as *Hotmail Corp. v Van$ Money Pie Inc.* 47 USPQ 2d 1020 (1998); *America Online Inc. v IMS* 24 F. Supp 2d 548 (1998); *America Online Inc. v LCGM* 46 F. Supp. 2d 444 (1998) and *America Online Inc. v National Health Care Discount Inc.* 121 F. Supp. 2d 1255 (2000).
[40] 100 F. Supp. 2d 1058 (2000).   [41] *ibid*, 1073.   [42] *ibid*, 1066.   [43] 2001 WL 1736382.

potential customers from the plaintiff's website to the defendant's. The plaintiff sued for trademark infringement and copyright infringement, but also claimed trespass to chattels by the defendant. The court took the view that the *eBay* decision had dispensed with the requirement of injury at Californian Law and found that the action of making entry to the plaintiff's computers without permission was a trespass to chattels.

Several cases followed, all American, which seemed to establish a general principle that unauthorised access to a computer connected to a public network was a trespass to chattels.[44] Over time though decisions emerged which departed from this orthodoxy. In *Ticketmaster v Tickets.com*,[45] the plaintiff sought to press a claim of trespass to chattels against a competitor who was using a spider to list on their website tickets for events sold on the Ticketmaster site.[46] If Tickets.com had no tickets available for an event they would use the information gathered by the spider to offer their customers a link to the relevant page on the Ticketmaster site. In this way they could continue to offer their customers a way to obtain tickets to an event they had no tickets available for and Ticketmaster would obtain a sale. It may sound like both parties won, but Ticketmaster saw things differently. If Tickets.com could offer tickets via Ticketmaster when their allocation of tickets ran out then customers would continue to use Tickets. com and would not transfer to Ticketmaster. Also it created in the customer a link or association between the two companies which was not in place. Ticketmaster claimed that the information Tickets.com obtained by the use of the spider was valuable, and that it spent time and money attempting to frustrate the spider. But the court found that neither of these claims showed damage to their computers or their operation. Distinguishing the *eBay* decision, they found that 'one must keep in mind that we are talking about the common law tort of trespass, not damage from breach of contract or copyright infringement. The tort claim may not succeed without proof of tort-type damage. Plaintiff Ticketmaster has the burden to show such damage. None is shown here. The motion for summary judgment is granted to eliminate the claim for trespass to chattels. This approach to the tort of trespass to chattels should hurt no one's policy feelings; after all, what is being attempted is to apply a medieval common law concept in an entirely new situation which should be disposed of by modern law designed to protect intellectual property interests'.[47] Ticketmaster at once offered a new approach from the Californian courts. This was a clear indication from the bench that cases such as *eBay* and *Oyster* had gone too far in finding trespass where there was no harm. As the decision in Ticketmaster said, no harm, no tort, and as trespass is a tortuous claim (in the US)[48] a claim for trespass should not be entertained without evidence of harm.

---

[44] See, e.g. *Register.com Inc. v Verio Inc.* 126 F. Supp. 2d 238 (2000); *American Airlines Inc. v Farechase Inc.* Case No. 067-194022-02 (DC Tx.) 8 March 2003: http://www.eff.org/files/filenode/AA_v_Farechase/20030310_prelim_inj.pdf.   [45] 2003 US Dist. LEXIS 6483.

[46] A spider (or web crawler) is a computer program that browses the Web in a methodical, automated manner gathering data. They are used extensively by search engines to catalogue the content of web sites.   [47] *ibid.*   [48] An examination of the UK position will follow.

5.2.3 **Intel v Hamidi**

This approach was confirmed later that year by the California Supreme Court in the case of *Intel Corp. v Hamidi*.[49] Ken Hamidi was a former employee of Intel who co-founded an organisation called FACE-Intel ('Former and Current Employees of Intel'), which was critical of the company's employment practices. Between 1996 and 1998, Hamidi, on behalf of the FACE-Intel, sent six separate emails critical of the company, each to more than thirty thousand Intel employees. Intel sued Hamidi, claiming that, even though its chattels were not damaged, it had suffered harm from lost employee productivity and the time it had spent trying to block his messages.[50] The District Court, in an action affirmed by the Court of Appeal, issued a permanent injunction that prohibited Mr Hamidi from 'sending unsolicited e-mail to addresses on Intel's computer systems', but the California Supreme Court reversed these orders finding by a four to three majority that actual damage or impairment to the chattel was a requirement for a trespass to chattels claim.[51] The majority were of the opinion that what Mr Hamidi was doing in sending these mass emails via the Intel mail server was using the server for what it had been designed for: the receipt and sending of email. Further, they suggested, Intel by allowing external access the mail server through an external internet connection must expect that external users will use that mail server to send email to Intel employees. The court, however, refused to overrule the *Thrifty-Tel/CompuServe* line of cases, explaining that the spamming activities in those cases 'overburdened the ISP's own computers and made the entire computer system harder to use for recipients'.[52] Thus the final fallout from a series of cases, mostly heard in California between 1996 and 2003 is that there is a recognised tort of trespass to chattels on digital communication networks in California, and probably by extension through cases such as *CompuServe*[53], *American Airlines*[54], and *Register.com*[55] the US as a whole, if the plaintiff can establish damage, or the likelihood of damage to the network. If there is no harm or no likelihood of harm then applying *Ticketmaster* and *Hamidi* the tort is not made out. The question for the reader of this book is though what effect will this have on the application of trespass principles in the UK?

5.2.4 **Digital trespass at UK law**

Firstly it has to be recognised that the reason this analysis has been preoccupied by American, and in particular Californian, case law on this subject is because there is no British case law to date on this subject. We have but two cases which tangentially deal with the issue of digital goods as property. The first is *Shetland Times Ltd v Wills*.[56] This is a case involving the practice of deep linking which is discussed in more depth in Chapter 10. Deep linking involves linking to content on another's website while

---

[49] 30 Cal. 4th 1342 (2003); 71 P.3d 296 (2003).   [50] 30 Cal. 4th 1342, 1348.
[51] *ibid*, 1347.   [52] *ibid*.
[53] *CompuServe Inc. v Cyber Promotions Inc.*, above n. 35: Decided in the Southern District of Ohio.   [54] *American Airlines Inc. v Farechase Inc.* above n. 44: Decided in Texas.
[55] *Register.com Inc. v Verio Inc.*, above n. 44: Decided in the Southern District of New York.
[56] 1997 SC 316. This case is discussed in greater depth in Ch. 10.

bypassing the front or home page of the site. The Shetland Times is an established newspaper publisher producing a local newspaper servicing the Shetland Isles. Prior to October 1996 they began publishing an online version of their newspaper on the expectation that once this became popular they would be able to sell advertising space on the front page of the site. Dr. Wills operates a web only news publication covering the Shetland Isles called The Shetland News. Rather than producing all original content for his Shetland News page he began to deep link to stories on the Shetland Times site. The Shetland Times sued, but unfortunately for our purposes here, they did not do so in property law, rather they claimed copyright infringement in the unauthorised reproduction of their content. At an interim hearing Lord Hamilton concluded that the pursuers had a *prima facia* case and made an interim order in their favour following which the parties agreed a settlement. This case which dates to 1996 predates nearly all the US case law on digital trespass. It is therefore perhaps unsurprising that counsel for The Shetland Times elected to follow the simpler approach of applying copyright law in the instant case. It is though, like all deep linking cases really about unauthorised access to one's private web space and therefore may be seen as the world's first digital trespass decision.

The second is *Plant v Service Direct (UK).*[57] This was an application for leave to appeal a decision of the Southampton County Court and was heard by Jacob LJ. Mr Plant had a contract with the defendant under which they made arrangements with a domain name registrar to allow him to operate the domain name, *nicholasplant.com*. Mr Plant became concerned about the service offered by the defendant and so he made arrangements to transfer the domain name to another host, but in so doing refused to pay an outstanding debt to the defendant. When the new host asked for the transfer of the domain name the defendant refused to release the registration until they were paid the outstanding amount due to them. Mr Plant claimed this amounted to 'wrongful interference with goods' as defined in the Torts (Interference with Goods) Act 1977. He argued that the domain name qualified for protection under the Act as s. 14(1) provides that '"goods" includes all chattels personal, other than things in action and money'. He claimed that by failing to allow him access to the domain name the defendant was denying him access to his property and he drew an analogy with an e-airline ticket or photographs held by a third party. Jacob LJ refused Mr Plant's application for leave to appeal. He stated that: 'copies of documents maintained in the register by the third party are not physically at any time the property of anybody other than the third party whose computer the documents are maintained on. They are copies of documents. Copies may exist elsewhere; they may not. But no right of property exists in the computer or its memory of the computer of the third party ... they are the third party's copies'.[58] This decision does not shed a great deal of light onto how the UK would deal with a case such as *CompuServe* or *Hamidi*; it is a rather narrow examination of whether the defendant was unreasonably interfering with the claimant's right to enjoy his domain name, not an example of the wider issue of trespass on digital networks as seen in the American cases.

---

[57] [2006] EWCA Civ 1259.   [58] *ibid*, [8].

Secondly, the issue which divided the judiciary in the US is not directly relevant in the UK. In the UK it is not necessary to prove that trespass has caused damage, rather the complainant must show that the interference with his property has 'gone beyond generally acceptable standards of conduct'.[59] Thus the question of damage is not directly at the heart of the question, 'has trespass occurred?'.

With a lack of case law in this area we can only speculate as to how British judges would apply trespass to chattels in the field of digital property. It may be assumed that in cases where there is repeated and harmful access as in the *Thrifty-Tel* and *CompuServe* cases a British judge would be open to an argument that trespass had taken place. In cases where there is repeated but not demonstrably harmful conduct, such as in the *eBay* and *Ticketmaster* cases it is again likely that a British judge would be open to an argument that trespass had taken place. Finally in cases where there is no 'abuse' as in *Hamidi* or *Oyster Software* it may be assumed that a British judge would be unlikely to find that trespass had occurred. This is of course conjecture: the English Law of Trespass is quite different to its American cousin,[60] while the Law of Trespass in Scotland is radically different again.[61] It may be though that a British Judge is asked to rule on this in the near future as Trespass to Digital Chattels has found a new lease of life in the US in dealing with the issue of adware and spyware.

5.2.5 **Adware and spyware**

Adware and spyware are terms often used interchangeably which describe software installed on an individual's computer and used to send back varying kinds of information to a commercial entity's server either for the purpose of sending targeted pop up advertisements, to report browsing habits, or for more disreputable purposes. Adware and spyware usually take the form of small software programs which require to be downloaded onto a consumer's hard drive at the same time as the requested content. This is usually contractually permitted by the user as the right to install the adware or spyware is somewhere in the small print of the licensing agreement for the piece of software they wanted to download. While it may be argued that the contractual relationship overrides the trespass issue the US Courts have decided on at least five occasions that the surreptitious installation of spyware or adware on a personal computer may amount to trespass to chattels.[62] The best known of these decisions is the case of *Sotelo v DirectRevenue*,[63] in which the District Court for the Northern District of Illinois held

---

[59] N. McCormick, 'Internet Trespass: Measuring and Controlling Internet-distributed Advertiser-funded Content', Intellectual Property Law Updates, April 2006: http://www.musiclawupdates.com/06Aprillawupdates.htm.

[60] Commentary on Trespass Law is thin on the ground. The most detailed is probably the practitioner text: *Unlawful Interference with Land: Nuisance, Trespass, Covenants and Statutes* 2nd Rev. ed. by D. Elvin and J. Karas (2002).

[61] For the Scots Law on trespass see the Trespass (Scotland) Act 1865.

[62] The five cases are: *Sotelo v DirectRevenue LLC*, No. 05 C 2562 (N.D. Ill. Aug. 29, 2005); *Kerrins v Intermix Media, Inc.*, No. 2:05-cv-05408-RGK-SS (C.D. Cal. Jan. 10, 2006); *Simios v. 180Solutions, Inc.*, No. 05C 5235 (N.D. Ill. complaint filed Sept. 13, 2005); *Michaeli v eXact Advertising*, No. 05 CV 8331 (SDNY complaint filed Sept. 27, 2005) and *Consumer Advocates Rights Enforcement Society v 180Solutions, Inc.*, No. 05 CV 027141 (E.D. Cal. Dec. 14, 2005). [63] *ibid*.

that 'the cause of action (trespass) may be asserted by an individual computer user who alleges unauthorized electronic contact with his computer system that causes harm, such as Spyware.'[64] This decision has been followed and applied in each of the following cases and may be applicable in the UK.

There is doubt over whether spyware and adware is outlawed by the Computer Misuse Act 1990, the UK's criminal law on unauthorised access to computers and data and unauthorised modification of data,[65] due to the fact that the customer 'consents' to its installation when they agree to the licence terms for the piece of software they do want. As a result it may be that a claim of trespass to chattels may be brought to the UK courts in an attempt to deal with harmful spyware or adware. On the basis of the prior analysis it is to be suggested that such a claim would stand a reasonable chance of success as the question of 'has there been an interference with his property which has "gone beyond generally acceptable standards of conduct"', would almost certainly be answered in the affirmative if the spyware or adware caused any interference with the usual operations of the computer system in question, which is often the case with such software often causing the system to slow down, 'hang', or even crash. Thus we should not dismiss the US case law on trespass to chattels just because we have not yet had to address this thorny issue in the UK. Claims based upon the principles found in cases such as *CompuServe*, *eBay*, and *Sotelo* may not be far off.

5.3 **Virtual property**

In recent years a new form of digital property and ownership has developed. This surrounds disputes over 'property' in virtual gaming environments such as *Second Life*, *World of Warcraft*, or *Entropia Universe*. These online gaming experiences known as MMORPGs (Massively Multiplayer Online Role Playing Games) attract millions of gamers every year.[66] There has always been an issue of ownership and property with materials and goods gathered in these MMORPG games, with sites such as *playerauctions.com* allowing players to buy and sell player accounts, valuable items such as swords or potions or just to trade 'gold' the online currency of most games for cash. These issues have been magnified of late with the development of 'real world currency' in MMORPGs such as Entropia Universe and Second Life. In both these games the in-game currency the Project Entropia Dollar (PED) and the Linden Dollar (L$) have a currency exchange system that allows for the exchange of in game currency with real world US$ allowing you to seamlessly transfer money between the real world and the virtual.[67]

---

[64] *ibid*, 19.

[65] The Computer Misuse Act will be discussed in Ch. 13. For another view on the legality (or otherwise) of spyware and adware under the Computer Misuse Act see S. Fafinsk, 'Computer Misuse: the Implications of the Police and Justice Act 2006' (2008) 72 *Journal of Criminal Law* 53.

[66] *Entropia Universe* reports 805,453 active players on 21 January 2009. On the same date *Second Life* reports 1,444,530 players who have logged in in the last 60 days. *World of Warcraft* doesn't give up to date statistics in the same way but in December 2008 Blizzard Entertainment, makers of *World of Warcraft* claimed to have 11.5 million paying subscribers.

[67] The PED, has a fixed exchange rate with the US dollar, where 10 PED = 1US$, the L$ has a floating exchange rate set on the in game LindX exchange.

With these developments speculation in virtual property has risen in recent years and with speculation comes property disputes and questions over property rights for virtual land and goods.

5.3.1 **Virtual theft**

Fantasy MMORPGs such as *World of Warcraft* and *Everquest* have proven to be particularly popular in China and the Pacific Rim. Some Chinese gamers in particular see games such as these as a way to make money and will play for hours at a time gathering items and gold to be sold on the open market in a process known as 'gold farming'. It is therefore no surprise that the earliest reported incidents of virtual property misappropriation were generated in China. Original case reports tend to be in Mandarin and are hard to find so to piece together the story of virtual property in China relies somewhat on media reports. The first of these to come to widespread attention was in 2003. Reuters reported that a Chinese court ordered an online video game company to return virtual property, including a stockpile of bio-chemical weapons, to a player whose game account was looted by a hacker.[68] It was reported that Li Hongchen had spent two years, and 10,000 Yuan playing *Hongyue*, (Red Moon) before weapons he had accumulated were stolen by a hacker in February 2003. Mr Li asked the company behind the game, Beijing Arctic Ice Technology, to identify the player who stole his virtual property, but it declined, saying it could not give out a player's private details. The police said they could not help so Mr Li took his case to court. The company argued that the value of the virtual property only existed in the game and was 'just piles of data to our operating companies', but the Beijing's Chaoyang District People's Court ruled that the firm should restore Mr Li's lost items, finding the company liable because of loopholes in the server programs that made it easy for hackers to break in. Following this case there have been many reports of virtual property disputes in China.

In a further case in 2005 an online gamer in Chengdu found his 'currency' and 'equipment' in the online computer game The Legend of Mir abruptly disappeared. The gamer, Mr Zhao, appears to be a gold farmer as it is reported that 'he hired a person to test the game around the clock for three months and paid him 1,500 Yuan each month.'[69] It is reported that Mr Zhao complained to the Consumers' Association of Sichuan Province. According to Law of the People's Republic of China on Protection of Consumer Rights and Interests, Article 44 'Business operators shall, if the commodities or services they supply have caused damage to the properties of consumers, bear civil liabilities by repair, remanufacture, replacement, return of goods, make-up for the short commodity, return of payment for goods and services, or compensation for losses and so on as demanded by consumers. If consumers and business operators have otherwise agreed upon, such agreements shall be fulfilled'. The Consumers' Association judged that Mr Zhao's rights should be so protected and the operators of the game should compensate Mr Zhao. It is not known though how much compensation was paid to Mr Zhao.[70]

---

[68] See CNN, *Online gamer in China wins virtual theft suit*, 20 December 2003: http://www.cnn.com/2003/TECH/fun.games/12/19/china.gamer.reut/.

[69] S. Xuan, Virtual Property in Greater China: http://www.hg.org/article.asp?id=5538.

[70] *ibid.*

The most dramatic case to come out of China is though the case of Qiu Chengwei. It was widely reported in 2005 that Mr Qiu stabbed a fellow gamer, Zhu Caoyuan, in the chest, killing him when he found out he had sold a virtual sword he had loaned to Mr Zhu. Mr Qiu was eventually sentenced to a suspended death sentence (life imprisonment) for the murder.[71] Following these cases the Chinese media have called for closer state regulation of virtual property,[72] and proposals have been developed to put virtual property on a sound legal footing.[73]

China is not the only country to face the issue of virtual theft. The Netherlands has twice had to deal with issues of virtual misappropriation. In 2007 it was reported that five teenagers had been arrested by police in Amsterdam for stealing virtual property known as 'furni' from the online social network site *Habbo*.[74] They had fraudulently obtained login details and passwords from other users and then had 'moved' nearly £3,000 worth of furni from the accounts of other users into their accounts. At the time a spokesperson for the Amsterdam Police stated that 'We are trying to bring charges of theft. It is a little difficult and new. There has not yet been a judgment in a case like this … The furniture may not be physical objects but because it represents a certain value we think theft is involved.'[75] It is unclear whether charges were ever brought as further reports of the case are not available, but what is clear is that in a separate case in Leeuwarden charges were brought against a fifteen year old and a fourteen year old who forced a thirteen year old to transfer a mask, an amulet, and some credits (virtual cash) to their account in the game *RuneScape*. From reports of the case on 6 September 2007 the two older boys attacked the victim kicking him and threatening him with a knife until he transferred the virtual goods and the credit. The attackers were convicted of 'violent theft' and sentenced to 200 hours community service (for the fifteen year old) and 160 hours community service (for the fourteen year old).[76] What is interesting is that they were found guilty not of assault but aggravated theft. The attack on the victim was clearly a common assault; it is the way the court dealt with the transfer of the virtual property which makes this a watershed decision. The court is reported to have said in a summary of its ruling that 'these virtual goods are goods (under Dutch law), so this is theft.'[77] This is the first time a court in Europe has made such a statement, but it may be expected that courts in the Netherlands and elsewhere in Europe may soon be asked frequently to rule on the nature of virtual property if the lead from the US in their area is followed here.

---

[71] BBC News, *Chinese gamer sentenced to life*, 8 June 2005: http://news.bbc.co.uk/1/hi/technology/4072704.stm.

[72] See e.g. China View, *Virtual sword theft is real theft*, 28 August 2007: http://news.xinhuanet.com/english/2007-08/28/content_6614685.htm.

[73] See L. Jeffery, 'QQ numbers: property under law?', *Virtual China*, 10 April 2007: http://www.virtual-china.org/2007/04/10/qq-numbers-property-under-law/.

[74] B. Waterfield, 'World's first arrests for "virtual theft"', *The Telegraph*, 15 November 2007.

[75] *ibid.*

[76] New Zealand Herald, *Teens convicted for virtual theft in RuneScape heist*, 22 October 2008: http://www.nzherald.co.nz/games/news/article.cfm?c_id=38&objectid=10538822.   [77] *ibid.*

5.3.2 **Misappropriation of virtual goods**

As with virtual trespass the US leads the development of virtual property law in the Western legal world. Although there have been no cases such as the Dutch *RuneScape* case where criminal charges have been brought for the 'theft' of virtual goods there have been several civil cases in the US for misappropriation of virtual goods. The first, and best known of these is *Bragg v Linden & Rosedale*.[78] The plaintiff Marc Bragg is a Pennsylvania attorney and was a *Second Life* land developer known as Marc Woebegone. The defendants were Linden Labs, creator and operator of *Second Life* and Philip Rosedale, CEO of Linden Labs. It was alleged that due to a bug in Linden's system Bragg gained an unfair advantage by accessing land auction pages for parcels of land that were not yet released for auction enabling him to acquire land in *Second Life* below Linden's cost for that land. In particular it was alleged he paid only $300 for an entire region known as 'Taessot'. Linden Labs suspended Bragg's account for investigation, and then closed the account for violation of the Terms of Service—dissolving his virtual assets. Bragg declared that this process caused him actual losses of between $4000 and $6000, and filed a civil suit against Linden Labs for breach of contract and unfair trade practices.[79] Linden Labs attempted to have the case struck out claiming that the court lacked personal jurisdiction over Mr Rosedale and argued that because of an arbitration clause in their player agreement, Mr Bragg was compelled to go to arbitration. The court refused all of Linden's motions. It found that a lack of mutuality meant that the arbitration cause should be struck out[80] and that it had jurisdiction over both Linden Labs and Mr Rosedale.[81] The court appeared to be swayed by the evidence laid before it by Mr Bragg that the defendants had promoted *Second Life's* unique properties of land ownership and preservation of property rights.[82] Having failed to have the case struck out Linden Labs then sought a settlement with Marc Bragg and on 4 October 2007 it was announced that a settlement had been reached. Although the terms of the settlement remain confidential it is worth noting that in Linden's press release they concede that 'Mr Bragg's "Marc Woebegone" account, privileges and responsibilities to the Second Life community have been restored'.[83] This suggests the 'winner' in the settlement was Mr Bragg.

This case is extremely interesting in that it is the first time a common law court has sat in judgement on a civil virtual property dispute. A note of caution though must be sounded. Despite being a case *about* virtual property it is not a case which *examines* virtual property. Instead this is a contractual case with elements of jurisdiction thrown in. Even the most cursory read through of the decision makes it clear that the two legal issues which preoccupy the judge are personal jurisdiction and mutuality; not the issue of ownership of bits. Thus, although textbooks will discuss this

---

[78] Case 2:06-cv-04925-ER (ED Pa) 30 May 2007: http://www.nylawyer.com/adgifs/decisions/101507robreno.pdf.

[79] The motion was initially lodged with the Court of Common Pleas of Chester County, Pennsylvania on 3 October 2006. This was moved to the Federal District Court for the Eastern District of Pennsylvania at the motion of the defendants.

[80] *ibid*, 32–34.   [81] *ibid*, 2–22.   [82] *ibid*, 3–5.

[83] Linden Labs, Resolution of Lawsuit, 4 October 2007: http://blog.secondlife.com/2007/10/04/resolution-of-lawsuit/.

case, including this one, and although students will continue to study it, it is not a true case of digital property or digital ownership.

Neither, unfortunately, are the other American cases which are often cited alongside *Bragg*. These are the sister cases of *Eros LLC v Simon et al.*[84] and *Eros LLC v Leatherwood et al.*[85] In both cases Eros LLC sued for copyright and trademark infringement. Eros are the producers of a *Second Life* sex aid, known as the SexGen Bed, a digital bed with built-in sex position animations which allow avaters to have virtual sex in *Second Life*. Their products are extremely popular and have been widely pirated. They identified Mr Simon and Mr Leatherwood as two of the pirates copying their goods and filed the lawsuits in New York and Florida respectively. In both cases a quick settlement followed with Mr Simon agreeing to pay $525 in damages to Eros and their co-complainants (that being the sum his illicit activites had earned him) and to agree to be enjoined from further unauthorised copying or advertising of goods in *Second Life*. In the case of Mr Leatherwood it appears no financial settlement was sought, instead he was merely enjoined from copying or displaying any of Eros's merchandise without permission. Again, though like the *Bragg* case these are cases *about* virtual property they do not *examine* virtual property. In both cases it was traditional intellectual property rights, copyright, and trademarks which were in issue. Also the cases quickly and easily reached settlement because the defendants were clearly involved in infringing activity. If anything is to be learned from the Eros cases it is not about virtual property, rather it is confirmation, if it were needed that traditional intellectual property rights apply in virtual environments and infringements which occur there may be pursued in real world courts.

Where does this leave the law in the UK? We still cannot say for certain whether a judge in the UK would find a property right in virtual property. To date the only direct engagement from the UK legal/regulatory establishment with virtual goods has been a warning from the Fraud Advisory Panel that the Government should legislate to prevent fraud, tax evasion, and money laundering in virtual environments.[86] There is no case law and no indication from the legislature as to how it intends to deal with this issue. The international case law is also far from instructive. The American cases of *Bragg* and *Eros* are not cases which examine or establish any precedent as to the propertisation of virtual goods and land: they are merely cases in which virtual property is the underlying subject matter of the dispute, not the legal principle in issue. The Chinese and Dutch cases more directly address the issue of property in virtual goods, but again a close examination of the Chinese cases show they are more directly cases of consumer protection law rather than out and out property cases. To date it appears the only country which has directly grappled with the concept of propertisation of virtual goods is the Netherlands. In both cases they have clearly treated the virtual goods in question as property, but a major note of caution must be sounded in that both are criminal cases of theft rather than civil cases of ownership and appropriation.

---

[84] Case: 1:07-cv-04447-SLT-JMA (DC ED NY): 3 December 2007: http://www.citmedialaw.org/sites/citmedialaw.org/files/2008-01-03-Judgment%20by%20Consent%20as%20to%20Simon.pdf.
[85] Case: 8:2007-cv-01158 (DC MD Fla.): 19 March 2008: http://media.tbo.com/pdf/032108erossettlement.pdf.
[86] Fraud Advisory Panel, *Government Should Extend Legislation into Virtual World*, 1 May 2007: http://www.fraudadvisorypanel.org/newsite/pdf_show.php?id=31.

What is clear is that people treat virtual goods like property. They accumulate virtual goods and trade in them. They attach value to them, sometimes massive values such as the $100,000USD that John 'Neverdie' Jacobs paid in 2005 for the Asteroid Space Resort (now known as Club NEVERDIE) in *Entropia Universe*,[87] and they develop and sell/rent virtual goods and land. With considerable financial investment in virtual goods and land there is a need for the law to protect investor confidence. Currently that is being maintained by the developers of these online environments: Mindark (*Entropia Universe*), Linden Labs (*Second Life*), Blizzard Entertainment (*World of Warcraft*), and Sulake (*Habbo*). Through their player agreements they contractually manage the relationships between inhabitants of their worlds. They act currently as a benevolent dictator, setting the 'rules of the game' prior to the participants taking part. But, as the trickle of cases thus far is showing, when players in the game believe they have been treated unfairly, or have been defrauded, duped, or the victim of a crime they will refer to the traditional courts. This is quite usual: we see the same in traditional games such as football where the Football Association (FA) is allowed by tradition, agreement, and law to arbitrate in most disputes which occur on the pitch. But when a player feels they have lost out and the FA is inadequate to offer the resolution they require they often revert to traditional courts of justice.[88] Based on previous experience of real world games and pastimes, and what we have seen from overseas it can only be a matter of time before a British judge is asked: are virtual goods property?

5.4 **Conclusions**

The shift in economic value from atomic goods to bits has already raised a number of legal questions, including is virtual space a form of property? Is virtual property to be equated to physical property and how should virtual property and virtual space be legally protected? These questions are likely to continue to be raised over the next few years as greater investment in virtual properties and web spaces cause more individuals to seek recourse to the law to protect their investments. In the UK we are in the very early stages of exploring these issues. Cases such as *Plant v Service Direct*[89] and the *Shetland Times v Wills*[90] are merely the tip of a potential number of cases involving both virtual property and online trespass. As we have seen the US has heard a number of such cases, while cases on virtual property are being heard in such diverse jurisdictions as the People's Republic of China and The Netherlands. The value of bits is greater than just in entertainment products such as music, movies and television shows. These cases from overseas show there is a demand for the propertisation of bits, not just for the application of traditional copyright principles. Soon UK courts may have to deal head on with these issues as their US and Dutch colleagues have done. This is an exciting and developing area of information law.

---

[87] See Virtual World News, *Entropia Sets Guinness Record for Most Expensive Virtual Object*, 18 September 2007: http://www.virtualworldsnews.com/2007/09/entropia-sets-g.html.
[88] See e.g. *Collett v Smith & Anor* [2008] EWHC 1962 (QB) (11 August 2008) in which former footballer Ben Collet sued Gary Smith and Middlesbrough Football Club over a tackle and injury which ended his career. See further Ch. 21.   [89] Above n. 57.   [90] Above n. 56.

FURTHER READING

Books

J. Penner, *The Idea of Property Law* (1997)

J. M. Balkin & B. Noveck (Eds), *The State of Play: Law, Games, and Virtual Worlds* (2006)

B. Duranske, *Virtual Law* (2008)

Chapters and Articles

L. Quilter, 'Cyberlaw: The Continuing Expansion of Cyberspace Trespass to Chattels' 17 *Berkeley Technology Law Journal* 421 (2002)

J. Fairfield, 'Virtual Property' 85 *Boston University Law Review* 1047 (2005)

M. Carrier & G. Lastowska, 'Against Cyberproperty' 22 *Berkeley Technology Law Journal* 1483 (2007)

Cyber-speech

6.1 Introduction

One of the most powerful developments of the digital society has been individual empowerment. By converging the functions of broadcast media and telecommunications systems the digital environment has subtly shifted the balance of power in modern society; empowering the individual, perhaps at a cost to society as a whole.

Historically the power over information and its mass distribution rested with a few media organisations. When an event happened, be it mundane, such as the passing of planning permission for a new school or world shattering such as the death of a major political or social figure, information about this occurrence could only be distributed via two discrete informational channels. Firstly, individuals who had possession of the information could pass the information on to others that were within their circle of communications. They could do this by face to face meeting where they would directly pass on the information to other parties, or they could use one of the telecommunications (communication at a distance) methods developed more recently such as a personal letter or a telephone call. These methods have become more efficient as technology has developed: the fax machine combines the two systems allowing for a letter to be sent instantaneously while mobile and satellite phones have made person to person voice calling more efficient and immediate. All these pre-digital personal communications systems though share the characteristic of narrowcasting: they may only be used to pass on information to one person or a small group of people at a time.[1]

To address a large group in the pre-digital era one had to have access to a form of broadcast or mass media. Broadcast and mass media are informational media that allow the transfer of information from one to many through a designated central broadcast point. Mass and broadcast media thus centralised the point of information control allowing for control of the information flow by an individual or a small group. Mass media tends to be the term applied to media with a mass reach with a centralised point of production but no centralised distribution point. This is newspapers and similar

---

[1] The largest group an ordinary individual would hope to address without some form of access to media would be a small public meeting in a town hall or at a designated venue such as Speaker's Corner in Hyde Park. A larger group would require considerable organisation and the obtaining of permits from the authorities. With the help of technology systems such as Citizen Band radio would allow a group to be addressed at a distance but only with the aid of costly and bulky equipment and specialist knowledge.

news media including magazines, films and newsreels, and books and periodicals. Broadcast media describes mass media which is distributed via a broadcast centre; this is predominantly radio and television. The fact that mass media/broadcast media were in centralised control made these media forms easy to regulate[2] and led many to assume conspiracies of silence would be struck between media providers and states.[3] Digitisation has interrupted the settled environment, both socially and legally with digital mass communications technology changing both the way people interact and the way regulators seek to control content. Nowhere is this more clearly demonstrated than in the development of Web 2.0: a term coined to describe this process of media/communications convergence which allows for enhanced creativity, communications, information sharing, collaboration, and functionality of the web.

This chapter will examine several aspects of this shift in power, and with it the responsibility to act with consideration to fellow citizens. It begins with a background discussion of the technologies involved: from web 1.0 systems such as web pages and internet fora to web 2.0 staples such as blogs, media sharing sites, syndication and ranking sites and social networking sites. In so doing it will look at the social implications of the shift in power from centralised media organisations to decentralised 'citizen journalism'. We will explore what responsibilities citizens owe to each other in this exciting new environment and ask how regulators may ensure social responsibility is met. We also ask and address the vital question: whose values predominate when regulating a global media tool which does not recognise traditional borders. From here we will examine three particular case-studies (1) Political Speech; (2) Hate Speech, and (3) Commercial Speech. These three are proving to be the most difficult issues currently as there are highly divergent regulatory values in play between in particular the US, which applies a first amendment principle, and the European Union which applies a slightly more restrictive 'tolerances' approach. By the end of the chapter the reader should be familiar with the key values, tensions, and current legal settlements in these areas.

6.2 **From web 1.0 to web 2.0**

Understanding how digital communications upset the established order of media and communications is essential to this chapter and our analysis of Cyber-speech. As we saw in Chapter 2 the internet has a longer history than most casual users are aware of. Dating from 1969 it is more than forty years old, but much of its life has been spent hidden away in universities and research labs. The internet only really came of age in the early 1990s when Berners-Lee and Cailliau's hypertext-based World Wide Web application was released to the general public through the NCSA Mosaic web browser. This development, which we may call web 1.0, gave consumers their first experience of

---

[2] In the UK the BBC were regulated by the BBC Board of Governors and the Broadcasting Standards Commission (BSC), independent television was regulated by the Independent Television Commission (ITC), newspapers were regulated, and still are, by the Press Complaints Commission while commercial radio was regulated by the Radio Authority (RA). Three of these, the BSC, the ITC, and the RA became part of the merged super-regulator Ofcom on 1 January 2004.

[3] So called conspiracy theories number the thousands. Among the more famous are the Kennedy Assassination, the death of Diana, Princess of Wales, and the Roswell cover up.

a converged media/communications tool. Now the average person could address large groups, as large as any media mogul could through their mass media outlet, and in addition they could address groups or individuals globally, not only locally, this is something that all but a few media barons such as Rupert Murdoch could only imagine.

6.2.1 Web 1.0: internet fora

For most web 1.0 consumers their first experience of this newly liberated power came through their first experience of internet fora. An internet forum, or message board, is an online media exchange system which allows members to post messages which may be read at a later date by other forum users and to exchange information on a series of related (or even unrelated) issues. Well known UK internet fora include The Leaky Cauldron,[4] Outpost Gallifrey,[5] and The Student Room.[6]

→ Highlight Internet Fora

Internationally the largest internet fora can have in excess of 5 million members, with the largest Gaia Online, an anime-themed discussion forum, having in excess of 16 million members.

Internet fora allowed an individual to address groups which could theoretically number in the millions, although which more likely would be measured in the tens of thousands. Nevertheless with nothing more specialist, or expensive, than a PC with an internet connection the individual for the first time could engage in a form of broadcasting. A posting on an internet forum could transcend space (and even time) and address audiences of a size previously only available to broadcasters. This has empowered the individual internet user: it is a technology which magnifies speech as previously only commercial print works and broadcast towers could.

Internet fora have proved to be extremely powerful tools with Harry Potter fan forum The Leaky Cauldron credited with breaking the story in 2007 that Albus Dumbledore, a leading character in the Harry Potter book series, was gay.[7] Internet fora also allowed special interest groups to form, groups that due to physical remoteness or simply a lack of social acceptance may never have formed in the real world. Among the more unusual internet fora formed are The Marmite Forum which brings together fans of a particular yeast extract, Worms Direct a forum on worm farming and Looner Fetish, a forum for individuals with a sexual fetish about balloons. The existence of these niche interest fora alongside the mass audience sites such as The Student Room may be evidence that predictions made by Nicholas Negroponte in the mid 1990s have come to pass.

---

[4] A Harry Potter themed internet forum.   [5] A Dr Who themed internet forum.
[6] A forum for students and young people.
[7] See http://www.the-leaky-cauldron.org/2007/10/20/j-k-rowling-at-carnegie-hall-reveals-dumbledore-is-gay-neville-marries-hannah-abbott-and-scores-more.

Negroponte predicted individualisation in delivery of informational content: this predicts that narrower common interests may support a community in the digital environment.[8] If you have a very narrow or specialised interest such as worm farming you will find it extremely difficult to find others who share your interests in the physical world. This is because there are few people who share this interest and they are likely to be physically remote from you. The likelihood of finding people who share a socially marginalising interest such as a sexual fetish about balloons is even less likely due to social pressures to conform. The introduction of internet fora changes all this. Negroponte cited two primary reasons for this: the first is that internet fora are 'places without space': that is they are places in which physical remoteness is unimportant. If an individual with a narrow interest such as worm farming is in a physically remote area, such as the Scottish Highlands then through an internet forum he may form a community with worm farmers in Boise, Idaho or Kendujhar in India. Thus digital communications shrink distances between people who share an interest. The second effect Negroponte cited was 'being asynchronous' this allows people to share a two way conversation across different time zones with each able to leave a message for the other to collect at a later time. Negroponte though also predicted that new media outlets such as internet fora would lead to a weakening of the social glue that holds society together. This was the negative effect of a multiplication of media and communication resources that he called the *Daily Me*.[9] Negroponte's *Daily Me* is a personalised news service which only carries news of interest to the reader.[10] The danger of such a development is that internet users may become insular in their views, and may seek social inclusion, even if they are seeking to normalise dangerous activities such as child abuse.

6.2.2 Web 1.0: personal websites

Around about the same time as internet fora began to flourish individuals also began to offer personal web sites. Personal web sites are quite different from fora in that they are not designed to offer an interactive function. They instead function more like a traditional newspaper in that they allow individuals to 'publish' their views on any subject and to address them to the world at large. Unlike traditional newspapers of course there was almost no start-up cost and no cost of production. Publication was instantaneous and unlike newspapers could stand as a (semi)permanent record without the need to archive. Also publication on the web was global. A personal webpage, like an internet forum, could reach a potential audience that all but the most powerful media mogul could only dream of. Personal web sites could reach a massive audience and like internet fora could make the news as well as react to it. Probably the most famous example of a personal web site reaching global acclaim was in January 1998 when Matt Drudge's Drudge Report published the story that President Bill Clinton was having an affair with Monica Lewinski, a White House intern.

---

[8] Discussed in N. Negroponte, *Being Digital* (1995), 164–171.
[9] The *Daily Me* has been discussed previously in Ch. 4.
[10] Negroponte, above n. 8, 152–154.

6.2.3 **Web 1.0: law and society**

Most discussions of internet fora and personal web sites focus on the positive aspects of the technologies. As we have seen, they shrink distances, allow individuals to address large audiences, and provide positive reinforcement. In addition they also allow individuals to develop new business models (though e-commerce), allow the sharing of personal content such as images, and allow people who have lost touch to find each other again. But there are also negative sides to these technological developments, and as is often the case it is the dark side of the web which first attracted the interest of lawmakers. Firstly these technologies may be used to service illegal as well as antisocial activities. Internet fora may positively reinforce the actions of child abusers and can be used to facilitate the trading of pornographic images of children;[11] in addition internet fora and web sites may be used for criminal activity such as the distribution of pornographic images, money laundering, or the support of terrorist activity.[12] A further issue with both fora and web sites is defamation, which will be examined fully in the following chapter. During the 1990s several defamation actions were raised both in the UK and the US surrounding issues such as falsely accusing an individual of selling items of clothing praising the Oklahoma City bomber[13] to false claims that an individual had made 'squalid and obscene' comments about Thailand.[14] The reason for the explosion in anti-social and illegal activity seen in the 1990s was that the web empowered individuals to address large groups internationally without the need for an intermediary. The same reason that gave rise to all the positive benefits also causes the negative effects as individuals feel they may act independently of state based regulation in a way that mass and broadcast media never would. Some do this for profit,[15] and may be seen as the negative side of ecommerce, others do it because they see it as their right to speak freely without state censor or license, often these individuals quote Article 10 of the European Convention on Human Rights, or if based in the US, the First Amendment to the US Constitution.

6.2.4 **Web 2.0**

The web has moved on from the pre-millennial explosion which led to among other things the dotcom bubble and the creation of the first internet celebrities such as Matt Drudge. Now as we are often told we have left behind the web of static web pages

---

[11] See M. Eneman, 'The New Face of Child Pornography' in Internet' in M. Klang & A. Murray (eds), *Human Rights in the Digital Age* (2005).

[12] In April 1997 the US Department of Justice noted that: 'Bombmaking information is literally at the fingertips of anyone with access to a home computer equipped with a modem. To demonstrate such availability, a member of the DOJ Committee accessed a single website on the World Wide Web and obtained the titles to over 110 different bombmaking texts, including "Calcium Carbide Bomb", "Jug Bomb", "How To Make a CO2 Bomb", "Cherry Bomb", "Mail Grenade" and "Chemical Fire Bottle".' Source: US Department of Justice, *1997 Report on the Availability of Bombmaking Information.* Available from: http://www.usdoj.gov/criminal/cybercrime/bombmakinginfo.html.

[13] *Zeran v America Online, Inc.* 129 F.3d 327 (1997).

[14] *Godfrey v Demon Internet Service* [1999] 4 All ER 342.

[15] Such as those supplying internet pornography.

and internet fora to move to a new environment where user generated content is king and where web pages must be dynamic and interactive.[16] In short we have left behind web 1.0 and moved to web 2.0. Although all experts agree that web 2.0 is the current model of the web, and although examples of web 2.0 successes may be identified such as social networking sites Facebook and MySpace, social messaging site Twitter, blogging site Blogger, and most spectacularly video sharing site YouTube, there is no agreed definition of web 2.0.

The term itself was first coined in 2005 by publisher and entrepreneur Tim O'Reilly who defined it rather loosely.

> **➡ Highlight** Tim O'Reilly Defines Web 2.0
>
> 'Web 2.0 doesn't have a hard boundary, but rather, a gravitational core. You can visualize web 2.0 as a set of principles and practices that tie together a veritable solar system of sites that demonstrate some or all of those principles, at a varying distance from that core'.

O'Reilly sees web 2.0 as a business concept rather than a technical one. It is basically a model where businesses seek to harness the inter-human connections and network effects of the internet to their business model rather than seeking to use the network as a platform for their model developed independently of the network. The key about this is that web 2.0 is not new: this definition includes sites include eBay (established 1995), Craigslist (established 1995), and Wikipedia (established 2001) as archetypical web 2.0 sites. This is rather different to the model most of us probably have of web 2.0 which more reflects the definition given by writer/comedian Steven Fry.

> **➡ Highlight** Steven Fry Defines Web 2.0
>
> 'Web 2.0 is an idea in people's heads rather than a reality. It's actually an idea that the reciprocity between the user and the provider is what is emphasised. In other words, genuine interactivity, if you like, simply because people can upload as well as download'.

This is the model we probably mostly have in mind: web 2.0 is about citizen journalism, user empowerment, and the creative power of the network: It is about video sharing sites such as YouTube and others such as Dailymotion and Metacafe; blogging tools such as Blogger; social networking sites such as MySpace, Facebook and Bebo and ranking and syndication sites such as Digg and Del.icio.us. What is common

---

[16] See, e.g. T. Funk, *Web 2.0 and Beyond* (2008); C. Anderson, *The Long Tail: How Endless Choice is Creating Unlimited Demand* (2007); G. Reynolds, *An Army of Davids: How Markets and Technology Empower Ordinary People to Beat Big Media, Big Government, and Other Goliaths* (2007).

among all the definitions is interactivity is at the heart of web 2.0. Whereas much of web 1.0 was unidirective: content was held on central servers and directed to users, web 2.0 is about interactivity. Web 1.0 may be seen to be an extension of traditional broadcast media with content being radiated out from a central source. Sites such as BBC News, university websites like *lse.ac.uk* and traditional e-commerce sites such as Amazon simply, in the view of O'Reilly, transported a traditional media/communications model to cyberspace. Web 2.0 sites such as eBay and Craigslist did not: they harnessed the network effects to create user interactivity on a previously unparalleled scale: this is, in part, why they survived the dotcom bust (and indeed flourished) while others did not.

There is a clear connection between Tim O'Reilly's view of web 2.0 as 'a business concept rather than a technical one' and the view given form by Stephen Fry that it is 'an idea that the reciprocity between the user and the provider is what is emphasised'. But the evolution from web 1.0 to web 2.0 like the original development of web 1.0 in the 1990s brings both opportunities and challenges. While as a society the development of social networking sites such as MySpace may be seen to be a positive development they carry risks. Several media organisations have reported an increase in social network stalking,[17] as well as identity theft[18] and bullying.[19] Video networking site YouTube while promoting the distribution of user generated content is the subject of a $1bn copyright infringement lawsuit,[20] while a flurry of pornographic imitators has sprung up. This expresses some of the web 2.0 challenge from a regulatory perspective. New media has always empowered a challenge to the traditional regulatory settlement but even web 1.0 with its traditional centralised distribution model was subject to effective regulation (to an extent). Web 2.0 though functions decentrally: there is no moderator or gatekeeper (on most) web 2.0 sites partly due to the prohibitive costs involved. Web 2.0 sites, if they are moderated are usually reactively moderated not proactively. They give unprecedented media distribution ability to those least able to manage it: children and young people. The costs of the printing press and the broadcast tower, originally replaced in the 1990s by the cost of the PC and internet connection have now been replaced by a free mobile phone with video capability and these days a free laptop: in other words the cost of broadcasting is negligible.

These developments are the classic double edged sword. Although there are a great number of positive effects to be felt from web 2.0, primarily in social networking, ease of access, and empowering individuals to distribute content there are also some potentially harmful negative effects. The remainder of this chapter will discuss these potentially harmful effects against the backdrop of free expression that web 2.0

---

[17] See, e.g. Stephanie Clifford, 'Teaching teenagers about harassment', *New York Times*, 26 January 2009. Available from: http://www.nytimes.com/2009/01/27/business/media/27adco.html?ref=technology.

[18] See, e.g. Josh Kowalkowski, '"Friend" phishing scam surfaces on Facebook', *The Baltimore Examiner*, 28 January 2009. Available from: http://www.baltimoreexaminer.com/local/crime/012809facebook.html.

[19] See *BBC News*, 'Fight Cyberbullies, Schools Told' 21 September 2007. Available from: http://news.bbc.co.uk/1/hi/education/7005389.stm.

[20] *Viacom International, Inc. et al. v YouTube, Inc. et al.* Case No. 1: 2007cv02103, Filed March 13, 2007.

technologies power. It shall ask where the line should be drawn between freedom of expression and protection for the individual and society given that speech may be psychologically harmful (as in bullying and hate speech), socially harmful (as in pornography), personally harmful (as in defamatory speech), and economically harmful (as in copyright infringement).

6.3 Freedom of expression and social responsibility

6.3.1 Freedom of expression: the 'First Amendment' approach

The 'right' of free expression is jealously guarded in western democratic culture. Many First Amendment scholars in the US argue that freedom of expression is vital for the functioning of a modern deliberative democracy: in a school of thought which mirrors the foundations of the adversarial system practiced at common law they argue that a 'free trade in ideas' advances the search for truth.[21]

→ Highlight The First Amendment to the US Constitution

'Congress shall make no law respecting an establishment of religion, or prohibiting the free exercise thereof; or abridging the freedom of speech, or of the press; or the right of the people peaceably to assemble, and to petition the Government for a redress of grievances'.

As explained by Douglas Vick this school of thought believes that 'When false ideas are expressed by some citizens, the best response is not sanction by the state but vigorous rebuttal by other citizens. Reliance on state regulation makes for an "inert people", the "greatest menace to freedom", but unimpeded public discussion allows the "power of reason" to triumph in the end'.[22] It is the belief of this 'marketplace of ideas' school that censorship or restriction of free speech is harmful as suppression of harmful speech may inadvertently boost its appeal. On the other hand, by allowing the unfettered expression of opinions despicable to the majority of citizens, the fundamental liberal value of tolerance should be promoted.[23]

The other primary school of thought in the US emphasises the need for free and unrestricted speech in the exercise of personal autonomy, arguing that free speech is a necessary precondition for individual autonomy, self-realisation and self-fulfilment.[24] This school believes that individuals not only have the right to receive information

---

[21] See F. Schauer, *Free Speech* (1982) 15–34; W. Marshall, 'In Defense of the Search for Truth as a First Amendment Justification' 30 *Georgia Law Review* 1 (1995).

[22] D. Vick, 'Regulating Hatred' in M. Klang & A. Murray (eds) *Human Rights in the Digital Age* (2005), 47.

[23] L. Bollinger, *The Tolerant Society*, (1986).

[24] See C. Wells, 'Reinvigorating Autonomy: Freedom and Responsibility in the Supreme Court's First Amendment Jurisprudence' 32 *Harvard Civil Rights-Civil Liberties Law Review* 159 (1997).

uncensored by the state, 'they have the right to form their own beliefs and express them to others ... state suppression of speech therefore violates the "sanctity of individual choice" and is an affront to the dignity of the individual'.[25]

6.3.2 **Freedom of expression: the European approach**

The European approach is slightly different. Although the philosophical foundations of free expression share certain common characteristics with the US, in particular John Stuart Mill's assertion that if we tolerate restrictions placed on speech this may restrict the ascertainment and publication of facts and valuable opinion,[26] we have different tolerances than those found in the US.

European values, perhaps shaped by our experiences of the first half of the twentieth century, particularly the powerful effect of the Nazi rhetoric which cost so many lives during the Reich and the Second World War, provides greater weighting to dignity when striking a balance between the interest of free expression and the (sometimes) conflicting value of respect for human dignity. Thus in Germany and France there are laws which restrict expression designed to deny the holocaust or offend the memory of the country.[27] But the experience of the harm speech can cause, as demonstrated in Nazi Germany, not only causes European scholars and legislatures to narrowly restrict Nazi speech. Seeing how Hitler turned public opinion against disenfranchised groups such as communists, Jews, and homosexuals we have taken steps to protect groups within society who could otherwise feel stigmatised by their distinction from the mainstream, causing them to withdraw rather than to participate in public discourse. For instance in the UK, racial unrest in the 1960s led to the banning of 'threatening, abusive, or insulting' public statements made with the intent to incite racial hatred.[28] In addition it is a criminal offence to possess with the intent to publish material or recordings which are likely to stir up racial hatred.[29]

It may be expected that laws such as those contained in the Public Order Act 1986 (as amended) which restrict speech on grounds of racial or religious hatred or found at the common law of blasphemy, which restricts speech harmful to Christianity,[30] would not survive the modern legal order where Article 10 of the European Convention on Human Rights is given effect in the UK through the Human Rights Act. But when one reads Article 10 in full it becomes clear that such restrictions on speech are justified. Article 10 states: '(1) Everyone has the right to respect for his private and family life, his home and his correspondence. (2) There shall be no interference by a public authority with the exercise of this right *except such as is in accordance with the law and is necessary*

---

[25] Vick, above n. 22. See also Schaur, above n. 21, 62, 68.

[26] Discussed in E. Barendt, *Freedom of Speech* 2nd ed. (2005), 7–13.

[27] For discussions of German law, see D. Kommers, *The Constitutional Jurisprudence of the Federal Republic of Germany*, 2nd ed. (1997). A discussion of the French position follows.

[28] Race Relations Act 1965, s. 6(1). The law, now found in the Public Order Act 1986, which defines 'racial hatred' as hatred against a group based on their 'colour, race, nationality (including citizenship) or ethnic or national origins', s. 17.   [29] Public Order Act 1986, s. 23.

[30] A discussion of the Common Law of Blasphemy may be found in Barendt, above n. 26, 186–188.

in a democratic society in the interests of national security, public safety or the economic well-being of the country, for the prevention of disorder or crime, for the protection of health or morals, or for the protection of the rights and freedoms of others' (emphasis added).

6.3.3 Freedom of expression: the approaches compared

The key distinction between the US First Amendment approach and the European Approach is in the exceptions. The right given in Article 10 is not absolute: in fact the exceptions found in Article 10(2) are extensive. This may be compared with the First Amendment to the US Constitution which states: 'Congress shall make no law respecting an establishment of religion, or prohibiting the free exercise thereof; or abridging the freedom of speech, or of the press; or the right of the people peaceably to assemble, and to petition the Government for a redress of grievances'. The first amendment is noticeable for its lack of exceptions. This does not mean there are no exceptions to the first amendment: obscene speech is still illegal,[31] as are words designed to incite imminent violence (so-called 'fighting words').[32]

Despite these limitations the First Amendment is little restricted whereas European restrictions on Article 10 are varied and extensive and include, the aforementioned restrictions on racial and religious hatred and Nazi/Holocaust denial speech as well as restrictions on obscenity, libel and slander and reporting of matters *sub judicae* as well as allowing advertising restrictions on products such as tobacco, all of which are much more restrictive than their US counterparts.

This distinction in approaches between the US and the EU/UK has in the past been of little import. Media outlets tended to be focussed on a particular state and would comply with the laws and practices of that state: individuals lacking the ability to be heard outside their home jurisdiction need only comply with the legal standard of that place. But as we have seen the development of web 1.0 and later web 2.0 have both changed the focal point for media organisations who may now address an international audience as easily as a domestic one, and for individuals who are empowered to reach a global mass audience. It was only a matter of time until the inherent tensions between the European approach to free expression and the US approach came to light. It was eventually, and starkly, highlighted in a series of hearings in Paris and in San José and San Francisco, California. In total across six years a series of six judgements were required in the related cases of *Licra et UEJF v Yahoo! Inc. and Yahoo! France,*[33] and *Yahoo! Inc. v LICRA*[34] an action described by one US commentator as 'a backlash response to the cultural and technological hegemony of the United States in the on-line world'.[35]

---

[31] *Miller v California* 413 US 15 (1973).   [32] *Chaplinsky v New Hampshire* 315 US 568 (1941).

[33] Tribunal de Grande Instance de Paris (Superior Court of Paris). There are three separate orders in this case. To make sense of the case you should read all three. Order of 22 May 2000—http://www.lapres.net/yahen.html; Order of 11 August 2000—http://www.lapres.net/yahen8.html; Order of 20 November 2000—http://www.lapres.net/yahen11.html.

[34] There were three hearings in California. A hearing before the District Court in which a decision was filed on 7 November 2001—*Yahoo Inc. v LICRA* 145 F. Supp. 2d 1168 (ND Cal. 2001) an appeal to the 9th Circuit in which a ruling was filed on 23 August 2004—*Yahoo Inc. v LICRA* 379 F. 3d 1120 (9th Cir. 2004) and an *en banc* rehearing before the 9th Circuit in which a ruling was filed on 12 January 2006—*Yahoo Inc. v LICRA* 433 F.3d 1199 (9th Cir. 2006).

[35] M. Fagin, 'Regulating Speech Across Borders: Technology vs Values' 9 *Michigan Telecommunications and Technology Law Review* 395, 421 (2003). Available at: http://www.mttlr.org/volnine/Fagin.pdf.

6.3.4 **Licra et UEJF v Yahoo! Inc. and Yahoo! France**

The cases began in Paris in May 2000 when the League Against Racism and Anti-semitism (LICRA) and the Union of French Jewish Students (UEJF) raised an action against Yahoo! Inc and Yahoo! France alleging that Yahoo! Inc (the American parent company) hosted an auction site which offered for sale many items of Nazi memorabilia and paraphernalia including copies of the book *Mein Kampf* by Adolph Hitler and that Yahoo! France provided links and access to this material via the Yahoo.com website.

On 22 May 2000 the Tribunal de Grande Instance de Paris held that access by French internet users to the auction site was an offence under French Law.[36] They ordered Yahoo! Inc. to 'take such measures as may be necessary to prevent the exhibition or sale on its Yahoo.com site of Nazi objects throughout the territory of France'. In addition Yahoo! France was ordered to warn all internet users of the risk of viewing sites which contravene French law.

Yahoo! Inc. argued that the Grande Instance de Paris was not competent to make a ruling in this case as the services offered (the auction website and the Yahoo.com site) and Yahoo! Inc. itself were all offered in or domiciled in the US. The Tribunal replied that as 'the harm is suffered in France; our jurisdiction is therefore competent over this matter pursuant to Article 46 of the New Code of Civil Procedure'. Yahoo! Inc. further argued that there were no technical means capable of allowing them to satisfy the order, and that even if such means were to exist their implementation would be at an undue cost to Yahoo! and would compromise the internet's character as a space of liberty and freedom. This they said was reflected in the application of the US Constitution which guaranteed freedom of opinion and expression to every US citizen which had been recognised as applying to internet speech in *Reno v ACLU*,[37] and further that as its services are directed primarily at internet users in the US and its servers are based in the US that the order of 22 May was 'a coercive measure [which] could have no application in the United States'.[38]

To answer the technical challenges that Yahoo! Inc had raised a panel of experts was convened and in August the Court ordered that the panel be appointed to review Yahoo!'s technical claims. The panel was formed of one French expert (François Wallon),[39] one American expert (Vinton Cerf)[40] and one independent European expert (Ben Laurie).[41] The experts reported to the Tribunal on 6 November 2000. They estimated that 'almost 70% of the IP addresses attributed to French internauts may be associated with certainty

---

[36] It is an offence under Article R.645-1 of the Penal Code to display or offer for sale any material which offends the collective memory of the country. Such materials include any uniforms insignia or emblems resembling those worn by the Nazis. See the Order of 22 May 2000—http://www.lapres.net/yahen.html.   [37] 521 US 844 (1997).

[38] For a discussion of this see D. Vick, 'The Internet and the First Amendment' 61 *MLR* 414 (1998).   [39] A lawyer with considerable computer law experience.

[40] Vinton (Vint) Cerf is known as the father of the internet and helped design the TCP/IP protocol. He is discussed in Ch. 2.

[41] A software designer who among other things wrote Apache-SSL which is used for secure data transmission on the internet.

to a French domiciliation of the access provider and be filtered'[42] In fact it was pointed out by the expert panel that 'Yahoo! carries out a posting of advertising banners targeting internauts which the company thinks are French and that it has available the technical means enabling it to identify them.'[43] Two of the consultants (Wallon and Laurie) suggested that in those cases where nationality was not clear from IP address identification Yahoo! Inc. could ask visitors to Yahoo! sites to make a declaration of nationality. By a combination of these two techniques it was estimated by M. Wallon and Mr Laurie that Yahoo! would achieve a filtering success rate approaching 90%. Vinton Cerf disagreed with points of the technical report. He was concerned about privacy issues if this approach went ahead: 'Some users consider such questions to be an invasion of privacy. While I am not completely acquainted with privacy provisions in the Europe Union, it might be considered a violation of the rights of privacy of European users, including French users to request this information. Of course if this information is required solely because of the French Court Order, one might wonder on what grounds all other users all over the world are required to comply'.[44] Despite these concerns Cerf approved the report of the two other experts.

On the basis of this report the Tribunal ordered that 'the combination of technical means available and of the initiatives which it can implement if only for the sake of elementary public morals therefore make it possible to satisfy the injunctions contained in the order of May 22, 2000: that is through filtering of access to the site auctioning Nazi [paraphernalia] and of any other site or service which contains an apology of Nazism' and that '[following] a period of three months which will be allowed for compliance with this order ... it [Yahoo! Inc.] shall be liable to pay F100,000 per day of delay until execution shall have been fully accomplished'.[45]

6.3.5 Cross-border speech

Following the order of the court of 22 May Yahoo! France had made steps to ensure compliance with the part of the order directed at them. This was 'to warn all internet users of the risk of viewing sites which contravene French law'. To comply with this order Yahoo! France by modifying its terms and conditions which could be accessed through the 'Find out about Yahoo!' link on the bottom of all Yahoo! web pages.[46] In addition Yahoo! France placed a warning when the user chose to search Yahoo.com from Yahoo.fr.[47] In the 20 November order the court noted that 'Yahoo! France has for

---

[42] Order of 20 November 2000—http://www.lapres.net/yahen11.html.   [43] *ibid.*
[44] *ibid.*   [45] *ibid.* At current values this is just over €15,000 per day.
[46] The new text read 'If in the context of a search conducted on www.yahoo.fr from a tree structure or keywords, the result of the search is to point to sites, pages or forums whose title and/or content contravenes French law, considering notably that Yahoo! France has no control over the content of those sites and external sources (including content referenced on other Yahoo! sites and services worldwide) you must desist from viewing the site concerned or you may be subject to the penalties provided in French law or legal action may be brought against you': *ibid.*
[47] This warning stated: 'If you continue this search on Yahoo! US, you could be invited to view revisionist sites of which the content contravenes French law and the viewing of which could lead to prosecution': *ibid.*

the most part fulfilled the letter and the spirit of the decision of May 22, 2000 which contains an injunction applicable to Yahoo! France'. As a result of this Yahoo! France were exempted from further enforcement actions.[48] Yahoo! Inc. claimed the order was incompetent but the court reinforced it.

Rather than continue to pursue the action in France Yahoo! Inc. retreated to the US. There Yahoo! raised a claim in the Federal District Court for the Northern District of California in San José. They sought a declaration that the French decisions were unenforceable in the US as they were in violation of the First Amendment.

Applying the precedents of earlier cases including *Telnikoff v Matusevitch*[49] and *Bachchan v India Abroad Publications Inc,*[50] the District Court found that the French judgments had violated basic precepts of US law, noting: 'Although France has the sovereign right to regulate what speech is permissible in France, this court may not enforce a foreign order that ... chills protected speech [occurring] simultaneously within our borders'.[51] In effect the District Court was stating publicly what had always been the issue in this series of hearings: the speech in question was, due to the borderless nature of internet communications, being broadcast simultaneously in both the US and in France (and in fact in every other state worldwide which had internet access). This is the pressure point where the freedom to express oneself and the duty to exercise that freedom responsibly meets. As George Bernard Shaw famously said 'Liberty means responsibility. That is why most men dread it'.[52]

With traditional broadcast and mass media we could entrust the publishers or broadcasters to act to protect wider social values. It did not matter if they agreed with those values or not, as they had made considerable financial investments in their distribution networks they were susceptible to state-based regulation. Further as the geographical reach of their media outlets was limited by the natural geography of the physical environment it was often the case that a single state regulator could effectively police the speech of a single broadcast outlet. Television capable of reception in the UK was generally broadcast from the UK and was regulated by the Broadcasting Standards Council and the Independent Television Commission.[53] Even the arrival of satellite television changes little. Most viewers in the UK get satellite television signals from two satellite providers Astra and Eurobird. These satellites site in a geostationary orbit close enough to each other to be picked up by the same fixed satellite dish. To get a signal from other satellites requires an expensive motorised dish. These satellites carry many hundreds of TV and Radio Channels, not all of which are licensed to broadcast to the UK but a second layer of regulation ensures that in most cases only channels licensed to be

---

[48] *ibid.*

[49] 702 A 2d 230 (Md 1997). In which case it was held that an attempt to enforce a libel judgment entered in England was contrary to the public policy of the State of Maryland as well as the First Amendment.

[50] 585 NYS 2d 661 (NY 1992). A similar case in which an attempt to enforce a libel judgment entered in England was contrary to the public policy of the State of New York as well as the First Amendment.   [51] *Yahoo Inc. v LICRA* 145 F. Supp. 2d 1168 (ND Cal. 2001), 1192.

[52] Source: *Oxford Dictionary of Quotations* 3rd ed. (1979).

[53] The one exception to this was that near to the border viewers in Northern Ireland may pick up television broadcasts from the Republic of Ireland.

broadcast within the UK are received here and that is in the satellite decoder. A satellite dish alone does not allow you to watch satellite television; you also need a decoder, and often a 'smartcard' as satellite transmissions are broadcast in an encrypted format. This allows states-based regulators to control satellite signals within their borders. You may not be able to prevent the signal itself from being broadcast across your borders but you can control the possibility of citizens decoding and viewing that signal.

This is the approach taken by successive UK governments. Under s. 177 of the Broadcasting Act 1990 the Independent Television Commission (now Ofcom) can recommend to the Secretary of State for Culture, Media and Sport that a foreign channel is made the subject of a proscription order if it is satisfied the channel repeatedly 'offends against good taste and decency'. A proscription order makes it a criminal offence in the UK to sell smartcards and decoders or subscriptions, to publish programme information, or to advertise designated services. In recent years a number of channels broadcasting hard-core pornography have been proscribed including most famously 'Red Hot Dutch'.[54]

What the Yahoo! case demonstrated at a stroke was that the internet was different. There is no need of specialist equipment to receive it: it was the first truly global media. Yahoo!'s sites were available both in the US and in France simultaneously. The pages were not simply published in the US, where the first amendment applied, they were also published in France where Article R.645-1 of the Penal Code applied. There were two competing regulators, each equally valid in their claim. In addition to this it should be remembered that this case was a web 1.0 case. The defendant was a major multinational company, a traditional media company if you will. In future cases regulators may be trying to control the actions of individuals who use a number of web 2.0 outlets making it extremely difficult to control harmful speech.

6.3.6 **Yahoo! Inc. v LICRA**

The Yahoo! case went on to have two appeals in California. In the first appeal,[55] LICRA and EUJF argued that the District Court erred in finding it had jurisdiction to hear the case. They argued that the District Court lacked personal jurisdiction, that the case was not ripe (because they have not yet sought to enforce the French judgment in the US), and that the abstention doctrine applied.[56] The majority (Judges Ferguson and Tashima) found that the District Court had erred in finding personal jurisdiction and reversed the decision.[57] Judge Brunetti wrote a strong dissenting judgement. He argued first that 'the case law in our circuit makes clear that, although wrongful conduct will satisfy the Supreme Court's constitutional standard for the exercise of in personam jurisdiction, it is not necessarily required in all cases; indeed, I believe that the Supreme Court's "express aiming" test may be met by a defendant's intentional targeting of his actions

---

[54] For a discussion of these actions see A. Harcourt, 'Institution-driven Competition: The Regulation of Cross-border Broadcasting in the EU', (2007) 27 *Journal of Public Policy* 293.

[55] *Yahoo Inc. v LICRA* 379 F. 3d 1120 (9th Cir. 2004).

[56] The abstention doctrine states that a court of law should (or in some cases must) refuse to hear a case, when hearing the case would potentially intrude upon the powers of another court (in this case the Tribunal de Grande Instance de Paris).   [57] They did not rule on the two other issues.

at the plaintiff in the forum state'.[58] Further, he argued that 'the record provides ample indication that LICRA and UEJF targeted Yahoo! in California by successfully moving the French court to issue an order requiring Yahoo!'s American website to comply with French law, serving Yahoo! with such order in the US, and thereby subjecting Yahoo! to significant and daily accruing fines if Yahoo! refuses to so comply; it is immaterial to the analysis that LICRA and UEJF have yet to enforce the monetary implications of Yahoo!'s refusal to acquiesce in the French court order'.[59]

With such a strong dissenting judgement it is no surprise that Yahoo! continued to press their case. They convinced the Court of Appeal to rehear the case and a rehearing *en banc* by a panel of eleven judges was approved. The judgement of the court was given on 12 January 2006 with a narrow majority of 6–5 electing to refuse the appeal and dismiss the case, but this fact does not convey the complexity of this decision.[60] Of the eleven members of the panel eight found that the court did hold personal jurisdiction over the respondents and could hear the case. Thus on personal jurisdiction the majority verdict would have been 8–3 in favour of allowing the appeal. But, the question of ripeness (argued by UEJF and LICRA in the first appeal) remained. On this ground there were five votes for ripeness, three votes against ripeness, and three members of the court who did not reach the question (the three who had dismissed the appeal on the personal jurisdiction claim). This strange set of affairs led to a very unusual and complex result: the court held that because a three-judge plurality concluded that the suit was not ripe, '[w]hen the votes of the three judges who conclude that the suit is unripe are combined with the votes of the three dissenting judges who conclude that there is no personal jurisdiction over LICRA and UEJF, there are six votes to dismiss Yahoo!'s suit'.[61]

This is a highly unusual decision caused by a large *en banc* panel. Technically there never was a majority to dismiss the appeal on either of the grounds of appeal. Three judges rejected the first ground (personal jurisdiction) and three (different) judges rejected the second ground (ripeness) but because three of the panel never examined that ground we will never know what their decision may have been. It is possible that eight judges may have found in favour of each of Yahoo!'s grounds of appeal but they could still have lost on the narrow 6–5 decision. It is not surprising that following this decision that Yahoo! applied to the Supreme Court to hear the case. Unfortunately *certiorari* was denied in May 2006, effectively ending the case unless LICRA decides to enforce the judgment against Yahoo! in the future which seems highly unlikely as Yahoo! Inc announced in January 2001 that it would no longer allow Nazi or Ku Klux Klan memorabilia to be displayed on its websites and that a new proactive filtering and monitoring system would be installed.[62] This means that since January 2001 Yahoo! Inc. has probably been in compliance with the orders of May 22 and November 20. The cases in California were in fact mostly moot, which is probably why the Supreme Court denied *certiorari*.

---

[58] *Yahoo!*, n. 55 above, 1127.   [59] *ibid.*
[60] *Yahoo Inc. v LICRA* 433 F.3d 1199 (9th Cir. 2006).   [61] *ibid*, 1248.
[62] M. Ward, 'Yahoo looks for hate', *BBC News* 3 January 2001. Available from: http://www.news.bbc.co.uk/1/hi/sci/tech/1098761.stm; D. Usborne, 'Yahoo! to ban trade in racist material on website', *The Independent*, 4 January 2001. Available from: http://www.independent.co.uk/news/business/news/yahoo-to-ban-trade-in-racist-material-on-website-705370.html.

6.3.7 **Free expression online**

This series of cases is in itself fascinating for the insight it provides into the difficulties national laws and state-based regulators are having, and will continue to have in enforcing national legal standards in the digital environment.[63] As predicted by David Post and David Johnson national laws conflict with each other in the borderless environment of the internet.[64] Yahoo! Inc. could not serve two masters. It had an equal duty to respect the wishes and values of the people and the nation of France in their desire to restrict expression harmful and distasteful to the national identity, memory, and history of France, and to the wishes and values of the people and the nation of the US which values the marketplace of speech and autonomy of expression most highly.

With the power of speech magnified by digital and network technologies the question of how to resolve this issue is pressing. Yahoo! Inc. was a major multinational company. The background of Yahoo! is not dissimilar to an international telecommunications or media company, yet still it fell afoul of different community and legal standards when it attempted to bridge the gap between the US and Europe.

The issues demonstrated in the Yahoo! case are likely to be substantially magnified in the web 2.0 environment where the person speaking is more likely to be an individual rather than a corporation. Whereas corporations have to fulfil standards of corporate social responsibility and must be sensitive to community values of all their customers wherever they are,[65] individuals have no such responsibility or sensitivities. Furthermore individuals need not necessarily even be aware of different community or legal standards elsewhere.

A real concern of web 2.0 is that it becomes a cacophony of speech rather than a marketplace for speech. Everyone feels they can say whatever they want, whenever they want and they feel it is their right not to be censored and to address the world: this is in breach of Shaw's principle.

> → **Highlight** Shaw's Principle Restated
>
> 'Liberty means Responsibility': to be allowed to speak in a public forum one must respect other members of that forum. The right to free expression should not be allowed to trump another individual's rights such as their privacy or their right to security or to a fair trial.

The problem with the information society in general and web 2.0 in particular is that it will be very difficult to protect the rights of others as there seems to be an assumption that speech must be protected to protect the 'core values' of internet civil society and further with the backbone of web 2.0 systems provided from the US the primacy of free expression is again to the fore.

---

[63] We will revisit this case in Ch. 16 when we examine jurisdictional issues.

[64] D. Johnson and D. Post, 'Law and Borders—The Rise of Law in Cyberspace' 48 *Stanford Law Review* 1367 (1996). Available from: http://www.cli.org/X0025_LBFIN.html.

[65] This may explain why Yahoo! voluntarily removed offensive material from its sites.

We are already seeing cases of harmful web 2.0 speech appearing in the media and in the courts. In early 2009 it was reported that a San Francisco chiropractor had settled out of court with a former patient who suggested in a review posted on the social network/review site, Yelp, that he may have been dishonest.[66] What is most noticeable about this case was that the defendant, Christopher Norberg, stated publicly that 'I chose to ignore Dr. Biegal's initial request to discuss my posting. In hindsight I should have remained open to his concerns ... We both encourage the internet community to act responsibly'.[67] More cases are being publicised daily involving postings and comments on web 2.0 sites including MySpace,[68] Craigslist,[69] and Facebook.[70] It is to be hoped that in time individuals will exercise social responsibility in their use of web 2.0 technologies. Until then we will have to examine how the current law deals with some of the more common issues which arise.

6.4 **Political speech**

When most commentators discuss the archetypal example of free expression they usually give political speech, or rather political debate and discourse, as the paradigm. The principle of free, that is unrestricted, speech in the political sphere is an extension of democracy itself. This is most clearly enunciated in the judgment of Justice Brandeis in the US Supreme Court case of *Whitney v California* in which he said: 'Those who won our independence believed that the final end of the State was to make men free to develop their faculties, and that, in its government, the deliberative forces should prevail over the arbitrary. They valued liberty both as an end, and as a means. They believed liberty to be the secret of happiness, and courage to be the secret of liberty. They believed that freedom to think as you will and to speak as you think are means indispensable to the discovery and spread of political truth; that, without free speech and assembly, discussion would be futile; that, with them, discussion affords ordinarily adequate protection against the dissemination of noxious doctrine; that the greatest menace to freedom is an inert people; that public discussion is a political duty, and that this should be a fundamental principle of the American government'.[71]

In the latter half of the twentieth century the greatest proponent of this principle of 'democratic speech' was the American scholar Alexander Meiklejohn who suggested that the primary purpose of the first amendment is to protect the right of all citizens to understand political issues and through this to participate in democracy.[72] Although

---

[66] W. Davis, Parties Settle Libel Lawsuit Over Yelp Review, *Online Media Daily*, 12 January 2009. Available from: http://www.mediapost.com/publications/?fa=Articles.showArticle&art_aid=98118.

[67] From http://standforspeech.com/.

[68] See *Doe v MySpace* 474 F.Supp.2d 843 (WD Tex. 2007).

[69] *Chicago Lawyers' Committee for Civil Rights under the Law, Inc. v Craigslist, Inc.* 461 F.Supp.2d 681, (ND Ill. 2006).

[70] *Applause Store Productions Ltd & Anor v Raphael* [2008] EWHC 1781 (QB).

[71] *Whitney v California* 274 US 357 (1927), 375–8.

[72] See A. Meiklejohn, *Political Freedom: The Constitutional Powers of the People* (1960); A. Meiklejohn, 'The First Amendment is an Absolute' [1961] *Supreme Court Review* 245.

Eric Barendt, writing from the UK point of view is suspicious of the Meiklejohn position he recognises that political speech is treated as a special case by courts.[73] He notes that two decisions in particular demonstrate that English courts are willing to give strong protection to political speech and perhaps even raise it above other forms of speech. In *Derbyshire County Council v Times Newspapers* the House of Lords held that it was contrary to public interest to allow any government authority to make a claim for libel as that would fetter free political discourse, with Lord Keith commenting that: 'it is vital that a democratically elected governmental body, or indeed any governmental body, should be open to uninhibited public criticism'.[74] Then in the later case of *R. (on the application of ProLife Alliance) v BBC*,[75] the Court of Appeal gave explicit protection to 'freedom of political debate' in holding that the refusal of the BBC to transmit a party election broadcast of the ProLife Alliance on the grounds that it offended good taste and decency was unlawful. Although the House of Lords later upheld an appeal from the BBC, as Eric Barendt notes, it did not in so doing question the value of political speech: its decision was solely based on the view that the BBC should not have to transmit any material which offended taste and decency.[76]

6.4.1 **Political speech: economics and media**

It is though another aspect of the democratic nature of free speech which draws the attention of lawyers in the information environment. If one accepts that political speech is a key component of democratic discourse one must face the challenge that potentially those individuals who have greatest access to media and other mass discourse tools have the potential to dominate political discourse, perhaps to the detriment of democracy.

The US famously does not restrict political advertising and promotional spend in election campaigns. This means there is an open avenue of criticism that money, not ideology buys the White House.

Case Study Economics of US Presidential Elections 2000–2008

In 2008 Barack Obama won the White House having spent $712m on campaigning, considerably more than his opponent John McCain's $326m. In 2004 Bush spent $268m to Kerry's $224m, while in 2000 although figures for the overall spend of candidates are difficult to source the figure for key television adverting spend shows that Bush spent $86m to Gore's $77m.

This pattern is not uncommon in US politics where it is quite usual for the candidate who spends most on campaigning to win the presidency. In his paper *Campaign Spending and Presidential Election Results*, David Nice notes that: 'Of the thirty-one presidential elections held from 1860 through 1980, the winner outspent the loser 22 out of 31 times. If we focus just on open races, those with no incumbent running,

---

[73] Barendt, above n. 26, 18–21, 154–155. [74] [1993] AC 534, 547.
[75] [2002] 2 All ER 756. [76] *R. (on the application of ProLife Alliance) v BBC* [2004] 1 AC 185.

the winner outspent the loser in 11 out of 12 races. By contrast, when an incumbent was running, a challenger who spent 41 percent or more of the two-party expenditure had a 50 per-cent chance of victory. All challengers who spent less than 41 percent of the two-party expenditure lost.[77] This suggests one is to be suspicious of unfettered free political speech at a time of election as the democratic process may be subverted by the candidate best able to get across his or her campaign rhetoric to the electorate.

To prevent the risk of subversion of the electorate in the UK we have strict campaign regulations. Under the Representation of the People Act 1983 (as amended) a candidate at a General Election may only spend £5,483 plus 4.6p for every registered voter (in a borough constituency) or 6.2p every registered voter (in a county constituency).[78] The reason for the distinction between the two types of constituency is to reflect the fact that electioneering in rural constituency costs more than in an urban one. As the average constituency size for Parliamentary elections is approximately 74,000 registered voters this limits local spending by candidates during General Elections to around £9,000. This does not, though, limit national spending by political parties which used to be unlimited. This money could only though be spent on newspaper or billboard advertising with the exception of Party Political and Party Election broadcasts, which are strictly regulated;[79] it is illegal to place political advertising on radio and television in the UK.[80]

Following the report of the Neill Committee into Standards in Public Life in 1999 even this provision was changed with new limits placed on national expenditure. By Schedule 9 of the Political Parties, Elections and Referendums Act 2000, a political party may only spend £30,000 multiplied by the number of constituencies contested by the party in that part of Great Britain or Northern Ireland; or if higher (a) in relation to England, £810,000; (b) in relation to Scotland, £120,000; and (c) in relation to Wales, £60,000. This means a party which campaigned in all 646 constituencies in the UK would have a maximum national campaign expenditure of £19,380,000.[81]

With political advertising strictly regulated political parties often seek media coverage of speeches and events. To combat an imbalance of coverage between mainstream and minor parties the Representation of the People Act 1983 requires broadcasters to draw up codes of good practice, which require to be reviewed by the Electoral Commission, to ensure fair and impartial coverage of political speech during elections.[82]

[77] 19 *Polity* 464 (1987), 468.   [78] Representation of the People Act 1983, s. 76(2)(a).

[79] See Communications Act 2003, s. 333; Broadcasting Act 1990, s. 36, s. 107.

[80] Communications Act 2003, s. 319(2)(g).

[81] In the 2005 General Election the Labour Party spent £17,939,617; the Conservatives spent £17,852,240 and the Liberal Democrats £4,300,000. Source: David Hencke, '£40m spree that bought groundhogs, gurus, makeup and Mr Spock outfits', *The Guardian*, 25 April 2006. Available from: http://www.guardian.co.uk/politics/2006/apr/25/uk.conservatives.

[82] Representation of the People Act 1983, s. 93.

6.4.2 **Online political speech**

The question is how does online speech affect these provisions? These laws are predicated upon the idea that communication between political parties and candidates and the general public will be transmitted through traditional media routes. Whereas the Communications Act and the Broadcasting Act regulate electoral media transmissions through radio and television channels they are silent as to new media channels such as SMS messaging, blogs, websites, and YouTube Channels.[83] Any expenditure by political parties on new media messaging will, of course, have to be accounted for in their election returns and will count towards maximum expenditure limits discussed above. In this sense new media advertising may be seen to be akin to traditional billboard or newspaper advertising.

This was the view of the Electoral Commission in their 2003 report *Online Election Campaigns*.[84] Following an extensive review of the use of campaign websites, SMS messaging, and email campaigning (the report predates YouTube and most social networking sites such as Facebook) the Electoral Commission concluded that they: 'value the level playing field and platform for free speech which the internet and other online communication technologies can provide.' As a result they reported that 'while we do not accept that online campaign activities should be entirely free from regulatory restrictions, any regulatory action should be limited to the minimum necessary to protect a fair campaign environment.'[85] As a result they made no proposals to specifically regulate online activities of political parties, except to recommend that s. 146 of the Political Parties, Elections and Referendums Act 2000, which requires the name and address of the promoter of political communications to appear on the communication, be extended to digital communications.

It may be suggested though that the Electoral Commission underestimated the potential impact of digital communications in the field of political speech. At the time of the report it may have seemed, with web 1.0 technologies dominant, that digital communications could be seen to be an incremental development of traditional mass media outlets such as newspapers or billboards. Even the use of SMS messaging suggested a 'broadcast' model with the information originating from a single source. It is therefore understandable that they focussed on online campaigning rather than online political discourse more generally.

With the advent of web 2.0 systems there are a number of new outlets for electioneering outwith the control (and direct funding) of the political parties themselves. These outlets are therefore not subject to expenditure limits, and as they are not traditional media outlets are not subject to the impartiality requirements of radio or television channels. These outlets include political YouTube channels such as James

---

[83] All the major political parties in the UK have YouTube Channels which are used extensively during electioneering. All three main parties also used SMS messaging in the 2005 General Election campaign.
[84] Electoral Commission, *Online Election Campaigns: Report and Recommendations*, April 2003. Available from: http://www.electoralcommission.org.uk/__data/assets/electoral_commission_pdf_file/0012/16050/Onlineelectioncampaignsfinalversion_8485-7286__E__N__S__W__.pdf.
[85] *ibid*, 4.

Alexander's *Time 4 Change* channel, social network sites such as Jason Brown's *Politics_UK* Twitter and bloggers such as Guido Fawkes. While these outlets, and the environment of online political speech in the UK remains quite benign, there have been warnings served up from the US that unregulated online political speech is not always positive.

The 2004 presidential election was a famously hard-fought and ill-tempered affair. Although the incumbent, President George Bush, always seemed to hold an advantage throughout the election campaign right-wing political commentators took little chances. Through the 'Blogs for Bush' campaign over 1,400 individual Blog sites which were supportive of the Bush election campaign were linked and ordered.[86] The collective power of these individual sites was brought to bear at two vital points in the election campaign.

Case Study Swift Boat Veterans for Truth

In summer 2004, with John Kerry doing well in the polls, bloggers supporting George Bush forced mainstream media outlets to revisit and re-evaluate the claims of a political group called 'Swift Boat Veterans for Truth'. The story had initially not been widely reported by mainstream media outlets, but following considerable development of the story among members of the 'Blogs for Bush' campaign, it was forced back into the mainstream media arena, a point which may have tipped the election in favour of George Bush.

In September 2004, right-wing Bloggers once again came to George Bush's aid. On 8 September, the 60 Minutes II news programme ran a story attacking President Bush's service in the Texas Air National Guard. Based upon memos purportedly written by the President's then commander, Lt Col Jerry Killian, reporter Dan Rather presented that President Bush had failed to fulfil the required standards of fitness for the U.S. Air Force and the National Guard, and that he failed to submit to a physical examination, and as a result of this failure he had been grounded by Lt Col Killian. A few hours after the release of the segment, a discussion began on Free Republic, a right-wing internet forum. This quickly spread to various Blogs, including Powerline[87] and Little Green Footballs.[88] One contributor on the Free Republic forum, known as Buckhead, immediately doubted the veracity of the documents.[89] A powerful campaign to debunk the documents arose almost immediately, much

---

[86] Although Blogs for Bush was officially independent of the Republican Party, there is no doubt that officials of the Party would have been keen to encourage site owner Matt Margolis in his actions. He has since become a well known right-wing commentator as can be seen for example in his interview in the USA Today newspaper on 1 February 2005 in a commentary entitled 'As Bush prepares address, Iraq sharpens national divide' by Chuck Raasch. On Election Day, 2 November 2004, 1,465 individual Blogs were linked to from Margolis's Blogs for Bush web page: http://www.blogsforbush.com/.

[87] http://www.powerlineblog.com/.

[88] http://www.littlegreenfootballs.com/weblog/weblog.php.

[89] In a post made less than four hours after the programme Buckhead posted the following message: 'Howlin, every single one of these memos to file is in a proportionally spaced font, probably Palatino or Times New Roman. In 1972 people used typewriters for this sort of thing, and typewriters used monospaced fonts ... I am saying these documents are forgeries, run through a copier for 15 generations to make them look old. This should be pursued aggressively.'

of it coordinated through Blogs and discussion fora. CBS News reacted to the challenge by initially supporting their story, but in the face of mounting evidence gathered by right wing Blogs such as 'Rathergate', allegedly fed by sources such as the Media Research Center[90] and by Creative Response Concepts, the same public relations firm that promoted the campaign of Swift Boat Veterans for Truth, they were forced on 20 September to publicly apologise, including an on-air apology from Dan Rather saying he had been misled as to the source of the documents.

The debate about the veracity of the documents has raged on between conservative and liberal bloggers, long after the votes were counted. Whether or not the documents were forged is unimportant, what is important is that conservative Blogs and fora won a major victory over a mainstream media station. This incident more than any other of the 2004 election campaign demonstrated the power of the Blog, as a decentralised, disintermediated political speech outlet for the twenty-first century.

Although we in the UK have not yet experienced such an effect of web 2.0 political speech it is only a matter of time.[91] The question remains though how we are to deal with organised online campaigns such as the Blogs for Bush campaign. Should we protect the content of such campaigns as free political speech or should we classify it as electioneering by proxy and seek to control it, at least during elections? The Electoral Commission promised in 2003 to 'continue to track the use of online campaign techniques by political parties and candidates, and assess the impact of online activities on the campaign environment'.[92] It may be the time is now ripe for a further review, perhaps also encompassing the effects of private political commentaries in the election process.

6.5 **Hate speech**

While we seek to protect political speech we seek to restrict hate speech. Sometimes there is a fine line between political speech and hate speech. For example should the YouTube channel for the British National Party be protected as political speech or banned as hate speech? We have already touched upon these issues in our discussion of the distinctive approaches to be found in the US and Europe to potentially harmful speech, and in the analysis of the *Licra et UEJF v Yahoo! Inc.* litigation in France and the US. The entire issue is one which is swathed in social responsibility. Every society suffers from bigotry and ignorance and in every society it is easy for the socially disenfranchised to blame another social, racial, or religious group. In a civilised society

---

[90] The Media Research Center is a conservative group that seeks to neutralise its impact of liberal bias in the media on the American political scene and to bring balance and responsibility to the news media. (Taken from 'About the Media Research Center': http://www.mediaresearch.org/about/aboutwelcome.asp).

[91] In the 2008 Presidential election right-wing commentators in the blogosphere again attempted to leverage their power. A 'blogs 4 McCain' organisation attempted to replicate the success of blogs for Bush. They attempted to tie Barack Obama to William Ayers and Bernardine Dohrn, members of the 1960's anti-war terrorist group the Weather Underground (see http://newsbusters.org/blogs/john-stephenson/2008/02/23/will-media-ignore-obamas-terrorist-ties) and revealed that Pastor Jeremiah Wright, Barack Obama's pastor in Chicago, had preached controversial sermons denouncing the US as racist (see http://blogs4mccain.com/2008/03/19/how-do-you-solve-a-problem-like-jeremiah-wright/).   [92] Electoral Commission, above n. 84, 4.

though these views are marginalised and mainstream public and media opinion is ranged against those who hold such socially harmful opinions. The internet, though, empowers those marginalised by mainstream society and it is not always to the benefit of society as a whole.

6.5.1 **Hate speech and society**

Digital media, and in particular web 2.0 technologies are allowing extremist viewpoints from all ends of the spectrum to proliferate. White supremacists find themselves online alongside Islamic fundamentalists, while homophobes find themselves alongside radical homosexual groups that fight for the removal of all restrictions on homosexual activity including the liberalisation of laws which prevent sexual relations between adult and minor males.[93] Those operating these sites do so without regard to their social responsibility: they view their right to represent their views and opinions as paramount. The problem is that in so doing they may cause harm to others. This is why the UK has taken steps to restrict such speech. Racially offensive speech is prohibited by the Public Order Act 1986,[94] as is the possession with intent to publish of material which is racially offensive.[95] Also prohibited by the Public Order Act is speech which is religiously offensive. The new Part 3A of the Act, introduced by the Racial and Religious Hatred Act 2006, extends the protections previously only available to racially abusive material to prohibit the use of words or actions designed to stir up religious hatred[96] and the publication of material designed to stir up religious hatred.[97] In turn, these provisions have recently been further extended by Schedule 16 of the Criminal Justice and Immigration Act 2008 to cover hatred on grounds of sexual orientation.[98]

The question of compatibility of such laws with Article 10 of the ECHR is unsurprisingly common. In two key cases though the European Court of Human Rights have found provisions such as those found in the Public Order Act to be in compliance with the Convention. In *Jersild v Denmark*[99] the Court found that a Danish conviction of a journalist for aiding the distribution of race hate speech infringed Article 10. This was though on the narrow decision that in so doing they prevented a journalist from discharging his duty to aid discussion of matters in the public interest. As for the Danish law itself they found that the state was within the exceptions found in Article 10(2) in passing a law which prohibited remarks which were insulting to members of targeted groups. In fact the Court noted such a law was required by Denmark's obligations under the 1965 International Convention on the Elimination of all Forms of Racial

---

[93] The author has visited sites representing all these views. It is not the role of an academic text to publicise these views by listing the web sites which promote them. In accordance with good research practice a record of the sites visited is kept by the author and may be supplied on request.   [94] Public Order Act 1986, s. 17.

[95] Public Order Act 1986, s. 23.   [96] Public Order Act 1986, s. 29B.

[97] Public Order Act 1986, s. 29C.

[98] Although it should be noted that a strong Christian lobby secured an exemption in Parliament. The new s. 29JA of the Public Order Act states: 'In this Part, for the avoidance of doubt, the discussion or criticism of sexual conduct or practices or the urging of persons to refrain from or modify such conduct or practices shall not be taken of itself to be threatening or intended to stir up hatred'.   [99] (1995) 19 EHRR 1.

Discrimination. More recently in the case of *Lehideux & Isorni v France*[100] the Court found that Article R.645-1 of the French Penal Code (Restriction on Holocaust Denial Speech) is compatible with Article 10.

6.5.2 **Inter-state speech**

With European lawmakers extending ever further the protections afforded to marginalised sections of society, in the UK the progression has been from racial hate speech to religious hate speech and most recently to sexual orientation hate speech; gender hate speech may be next, and with the constitutional principles of the US protecting all but the most immediately harmful speech a rise in conflicts between US based content and European based consumers becomes more likely in the web 2.0 environment. We have already visited at length the best known example of this ideological conflict, *Licra et UEJF v Yahoo! Inc. and Yahoo! France*. This lengthy litigation produced a most unsatisfactory outcome which demonstrates that attempts to reach international consensus on this issue are unlikely to succeed. With the US Supreme Court ruling in *Reno v ACLU*[101] that the First Amendment applies to internet communications the US government finds that it cannot enter into any international treaty or agreement which would conflict with its duty to uphold the US Constitution.[102] This was demonstrated in the negotiations of the Council of Europe Convention on Cybercrime.[103] The Convention which aims to provide a framework for the development of a common policy against all aspects of Cybercrime including internet pornography, computer hacking, and distribution of malicious code was signed by the Council of Europe states and several invited non-member states including the US. It was the intent of the drafters that that Convention would have an article dealing with hate speech but the US delegation stated that due to the effect of *Reno v ACLU*, they would be unable to sign a convention which restricted free expression. Because of this, and because the framers of the Convention wanted the US to sign all references to hate and xenophobic speech were removed from the main Convention and were placed into a separate Additional Protocol to the Convention on Cybercrime Concerning the Criminalisation of Acts of a Racist and Xenophobic Nature Committed Through Computer Systems.[104] This additional protocol was not signed by the US.[105]

We may never find common ground between the US and other leading democratic states including EU states on this issue, but as Douglas Vick points out 'it is far from certain that sexism, racism, homophobia or religious intolerance are greater problems in the US than in countries with well-developed anti-hate legislation'.[106] When the Programme in Comparative Media Law and Policy concluded its three-year research

---

[100] (2000) 30 EHRR 365.   [101] 521 US 844 (1997).   [102] See Vick, above n. 38.
[103] CETS No. 185, Budapest, 23.XI.2001.   [104] CETS No. 189, Strasbourg, 28.I.2003.
[105] It should be noted that the UK also did not sign the Protocol.
[106] Vick, above n. 22, 51.

project into industry self regulation and content,[107] it concluded that data havens were not unusual in digital communications, with Europe and in particular the UK, acting as a similar 'offshore centre' for online gambling for citizens of the US. Thus short of blocking access to US-based websites which breach the Public Order Act, it appears UK regulators and UK citizens may have to accept that while as noted by District Judge Fogel in *Yahoo Inc. v LICRA* 'the Internet in effect allows one to speak in more than one place at the same time'[108] individuals will in most cases be subject only to the effective jurisdiction of the place where they are domiciled or ordinarily resident.[109] This means we may find more a more US-style marketplace of speech occurs online as US citizens debate sensitive subjects from behind the shield of the First Amendment.

6.6 **Commercial speech**

One area in which the US First Amendment is less strongly applied is in the field of commercial speech. Commercial speech, sometimes known as promotional or advertising speech, is speech expressed on behalf of a company or individual for the intent of making a profit. It is economic in nature and usually has the intent of convincing the audience to follow a particular course of action, often purchasing a specific product.

6.6.1 **Commercial speech and the First Amendment**

The concept of commercial speech, in First Amendment Jurisprudence, was introduced in the case of *Valentine v Chrestensen*.[110] The respondent had purchased a former US Navy submarine which he toured around the US for exhibition. He had brought the submarine to New York and had moored it at State pier in the East River. To promote his exhibit he prepared and printed handbill advertising the boat and soliciting visitors for a stated admission fee. On attempting to distribute the bill in the city streets, he was advised by the petitioner, the Police Commissioner, that this activity would violate section 318 of the New York Sanitary Code which forbad distribution in the streets of commercial and business advertising matter. Mr Chrestensen argued the city ordinance was in breach of the First Amendment but the Supreme Court ruled that the Constitution does not protect commercial speech.

Although the Chrestensen principle has been questioned over the years, and has been somewhat diluted, the Supreme Court continues to recognise that commercial speech does not receive the same level of Constitutional protection as other forms of speech.[111] This must come as somewhat of a relief to anyone who operates an email account, discussion board, blog, or other interactive service.

---

[107] Programme in Comparative Media Law and Policy, *Self-Regulation of Digital Media Converging on the Internet: Industry Codes of Conduct in Sectoral Analysis* (2004). Available from: http://pcmlp. socleg.ox.ac.uk/selfregulation/iapcoda/0405-iapcode-final-execsummary.pdf.

[108] 145 F. Supp. 2d 1168 (ND Cal. 2001), 1192.

[109] For more on jurisdiction see Ch. 16, below.   [110] 316 US 52 (1942).

[111] See *Ohralik v Ohio State Bar Association* 436 U.S. 447 (1978) c/f *44 Liquormart Inc. v Rhode Island* 517 US 484 (1996).

6.6.2 **Commercial speech and the information society**

The digital environment is awash with unsolicited commercial communications, colloquially known as spam.[112] Accurate statistics on spam are difficult to source. The internet appears equally awash with a variety of spam statistics making reliable data almost impossible to source.

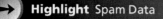

Highlight Spam Data

Symantec-MessageLabs recorded that in November 2008 spam had fallen to a level of 58% from a 2008 high of 78%. The most recent (unconfirmed) figures for July 2009 put the level at 56%. Meanwhile Barracuda puts the level of spam for July 2009 as high as 92%.

The true figure is somewhere between the two but with reports of up to 200 billion spam messages being sent daily the problem is clearly of a massive scale.[113] Somewhat surprisingly there have been few surveys of consumer responses to spam, but in 2002 a Harris Poll revealed that 80% of those surveyed said that they found spamming very annoying and 74% favoured making spam illegal.[114] Why then do spammers continue? There are two predominant reasons for this. The first is that unlike traditional unsolicited commercial communications, digital commercial communications benefit from the all the advantages discussed in Part I. It is infinitely replicable, easy to store and the key for spammers, almost costless to send. As any internet user knows you only pay for your access cost. Once you are connected to the network the costs of carrying data across the network are borne by the telecommunications providers, not the customer. Excepting issues of bandwidth availability it costs no more to send one million emails than to send one. The same is not true of traditional media. One million telephone calls will cost in or around one million times the cost of a single telephone call and one million letters will cost (bulk discounts aside) one million times the cost of a single letter. Thus it seems email is almost designed for spam messages. For the spammer there are almost no overheads and massive reach. But if everyone just filters and deletes their spam why do spammers

---

[112] Unsolicited Commercial Communications are colloquially known as spam because of the Monty Python sketch in which a couple go into a restaurant and the wife tries to get something other than spam. In the background are a bunch of Vikings that sing the praises of spam. Pretty soon the only thing you can hear in the sketch is the word 'spam'. That same idea would happen to the internet if large scale inappropriate postings were allowed. You couldn't pick the real postings out from the spam.

[113] SC Magazine, *200 billion spam messages sent daily as spammers change tactics for 2009*, 16 December 2008. Available from: http://www.scmagazineuk.com/200-billion-spam-messages-sent-daily-as-spammers-change-tactics-for-2009/article/122908/.

[114] Harris Interactive, *Large Majority of Those Online Wants Spamming Banned*, 3 January 2003. Available from: http://www.harrisinteractive.com/harris_poll/index.asp?PID=348.

keep doing it? Well a surprising statistic from internet security company Marshal shows that 29% of internet users have purchased something advertised in a spam message.[115]

6.6.3 **Regulating spam in Europe**

Despite the obvious appeal of spam to a number of people the question of how to regulate spam is clearly a major issue. Steps have been taken in both the European Union and the US to control spam. The EU began consultation on spam regulation in summer 2000 when they began to consider the Commission proposal for a Directive on privacy and electronic communications. In their explanatory memorandum the Commission noted that: 'Four Member States already have bans on unsolicited commercial e-mail and another is about to adopt one. In most of the other Member States opt-out systems exist. From an internal market perspective, this is not satisfactory. Direct marketers in opt-in countries may not target e-mail addresses within their own country but they can still continue to send unsolicited commercial e-mail to countries with an opt-out system. Moreover, since e-mail addresses very often give no indication of the country of residence of the recipients, a system of divergent regimes within the internal market is unworkable in practice. A harmonised opt in approach solves this problem'.[116]

On the basis of this the Commission proposed that the draft privacy in electronic communications Directive use an opt in approach where only those persons who had given prior consent to the receipt of unsolicited messages could lawfully receive them. This approach is highly controversial, not least with the business community and during the Parliamentary hearings on the draft Directive this was replaced with an opt out approach instead. However at the last stage of the co-decision procedure the Council reinstated the opt in proposal and the final wording as passed in the *Directive on Privacy and Electronic Communications*[117] states:

> **Highlight** Article 13(1) of the *Directive on Privacy and Electronic Communications*
>
> 'Electronic mail for the purposes of direct marketing may only be allowed in respect of subscribers who have given their prior consent'.

Ian Lloyd points out it may seem that the term 'prior consent' could allow for an opt out system rather than an opt in one, where failure on the part of the user to indicate a preference could be taken to equate to consent.[118] But as Lloyd himself approves the Directive makes clear this cannot be so.

---

[115] Marshal, *Sex, Drugs and Software Lead Spam Purchase Growth*, 19 August 2008. Available from: http://www.marshal.com/pages/newsitem.asp?article=748&thesection=news. Although this may seem a surprisingly high percentage it does in fact tie in with other surveys which show a spam response rate of between 20–30%.   [116] http://www.euro.cauce.org/en/bground.html.
[117] Dir. 2002/58/EC, Official Journal L 201, 31/07/2002 P. 0037–0047.
[118] I. Lloyd, *Information Technology Law* 5th ed. (2008), 177.

Recital 40 makes clear that 'prior *explicit* consent of the recipients is obtained before such communications are addressed to them', the use of the term explicit making clear that an opt out system is incompatible with the Directive. There remains though one important exception to Article 13(1). Under Article 13(2) if there has been a prior commercial relationship between the sender of the communication and the recipient thereof the communication may be sent without prior explicit consent 'provided that customers [are] clearly and distinctly are given the opportunity to object, free of charge and in an easy manner, to such use of electronic contact details when they are collected and on the occasion of each message in case the customer has not initially refused such use'. In effect what Article 13(2) says is that if you have a prior commercial relationship the opt in requirement is reversed and it becomes an opt out requirement.

The Directive was given effect in the UK on 11 December 2003 when *The Privacy and Electronic Communications (EC Directive) Regulations 2003* came into force. By Regulation 22(2) it becomes a harm to: 'transmit, or instigate the transmission of, unsolicited communications for the purposes of direct marketing by means of electronic mail unless the recipient of the electronic mail has previously notified the sender that he consents for the time being to such communications being sent by, or at the instigation of, the sender'. The Article 13(2) exception is given effect in Regulation 22(3).

Rather disappointingly for many anti-spam campaigners it is not an offence to send spam; rather Regulation 30(1) states that: 'a person who suffers damage by reason of any contravention of any of the requirements of these Regulations by any other person shall be entitled to bring proceedings for compensation from that other person for that damage'. The trouble with this is that it effectively makes it a tort claim and in most cases where individuals receive spam messages the harm or damage suffered is either unquantifiable or of such low value as to be *de minimis*. That is not to say the Regulations are unenforceable.

Case Study *Roberts v Logistics UK*

In December 2005 Nigel Roberts, a businessman from Alderney, lodged a claim under the Regulations in Colchester County Court against Logistics UK, a Stirlingshire based company. Logistics UK did not defend the action and agreed to pay Mr. Roberts £270 in damages and £30 in costs.

Case Study *Dick v Transcom*

In March 2007 it was reported that Gordon Dick, an electronic marketing specialist from Edinburgh, won £750 in damages and costs of £616.66 when he pursued Henley-on-Thames based Transcom under the Regulations.

It would appear therefore that Courts are not averse to finding damage does occur without the need to demonstrate network failure or other physical or network damage caused by the spam messaging in question. Interestingly though the largest award made in the UK against an individual sending spam messages was not made under the 2003 regulations.

In September 2006 it was reported that Microsoft has reached an out of court settlement with Paul Fox, a UK based spammer who used spam to promote his pornographic websites, under which Mr Fox would pay £45,000 by way of damages and as a contribution to Microsoft's legal costs. Rather than attempt to pursue Mr Fox under the Regulations though Microsoft chose to file a complaint that he had breached the terms and conditions of their Hotmail service, which state: 'You may not use any Microsoft Services to send Spam. You also may not deliver Spam or cause Spam to be delivered to any of Microsoft's Services or customers'. It is also abundantly clear several years on from the enactment of the Regulations that they are having little, if any, effect on the volume of spam sent and received in the UK or the EU. The reason for this is clear when you look at where most spam originates.

In their May 2009 spam report online security company Symantec report that eight of the top ten spam producing nations are outwith the EU,[119] with the worst offender, the US, estimated to produce 24% of all spam messages.[120] This again illustrates the problem first seen in the *Yahoo!* case and discussed further under the hate speech head: the spammer may be addressing individuals in the UK, but he is most likely to be found in the US. To have any hope of reducing the volume of spam we must get to its root in the US.

6.6.4 **Regulating spam in the US**

Fortunately, as we have seen commercial speech is not afforded the same level of protection under the First Amendment allowing Congress to take steps to limit spam messages. This was achieved in 2003 when Congress passed the Controlling the Assault of Non-Solicited Pornography And Marketing Act of 2003 (the CAN-SPAM Act). The Act came into force on 16 December 2003 and regulates what the Act calls a 'commercial electronic mail message', that is 'any electronic mail message the primary purpose of which is the commercial advertisement or promotion of a commercial product or service (including content on an Internet website operated for a commercial purpose).'[121]

The Act permits email marketers to send unsolicited commercial email as long as it adheres to three basic compliance requirements defined in the Act: opt out, content, and sending behaviour compliance. Opt out compliance requires the initiator of spam messages to: (1) include a visible and operable unsubscribe mechanism in all emails, (2) honour consumer opt out requests within 10 days, and (3) use opt out lists only used for compliance purposes.[122] Content compliance requires the initiator of spam

---

[119] Symantec, *The State of Spam: A Monthly Report—February 2009*. Available from: http://eval. symantec.com/mktginfo/enterprise/other_resources/b-state_of_spam_report_06-2009.en-us.pdf. The ten were: The US, Brazil, China, India, South Korea, Russia, Turkey, Poland, Columbia and Romania.   [120] *ibid*, 12.   [121] 15 USC §7702.   [122] 15 USC § 7704(4).

messages to provide: (1) accurate sender information, (2) accurate and relevant subject lines (which must be relative to offer in body content and not be deceptive), and (3) a legitimate physical address of the publisher and/or advertiser.[123] Finally, the sending behaviour requirement prohibits the initiator of spam from: (1) relaying or retransmitting messages through a computer or network he has no permission to use,[124] or (2) sending messages to a harvested email address.[125]

There have been several high profile prosecutions under the Act. Most famously Robert Soloway, the self-styled 'King of spam' was sentenced to forty-seven months in prison in 2008 for multiple breaches of the Act.[126] The Soloway case was the second CAN-SPAM Act case to secure a prison term. The first was a case brought in 2007 against Jeffrey Kilbride and James Schaffer, two spammers who bought lists of email addresses and sent the owners links to pornographic websites. They were both sentenced to five years in prison.[127] Despite these and other high profile cases such as the *ValueClick* case which saw ValueClick fined $2.9 million for sending deceptive emails suggesting the user had won valuable prizes,[128] the MySpace case which saw MySpace win a total of $234 million in damages from Sanford Wallace and Walter Rines who had spammed 700,000 MySpace accounts,[129] and most recently the massive $834 million in total damages handed down in *Facebook Inc. v Adam Guerbuez and Atlantis Blue Capital*,[130] the number of spam emails sent year on year in the US continues to rise.[131] Why should this be given such high profile actions? Critics have pointed out that far from outlawing the practice of spam, the CAN-SPAM Act 'essentially legalizes and regulates spam messages in the United States'.[132] In addition by affording an opt out procedure rather than the European opt in procedure it allows spammers to continue unhindered in their activity provided they comply with the regulatory requirements of the Act. Even where the spammer is compliant with the Act in every way they are unlikely to receive many opt out requests as expert advice on spam is to never reply to an opt out service or to use an opt out link as this merely confirms a live address has been found which may in fact lead to an increase in spam received.[133]

It appears legal regulation of spam in unlikely to be effective. Even in the event the US passed European style opt in legislation today spam would almost certainly continue

---

[123] 15 USC § 7704(1)–(3).   [124] 15 USC § 7704(6)(3).   [125] 15 USC § 7704(6)(1).

[126] Paul Shukovsky, 'Spam King gets nearly 4 years in prison', *Seattle PI*, 22 July 2008. Available from: http://seattlepi.nwsource.com/local/371772_spamking23.html.

[127] T. McVeigh, 'Porn spammers jailed for five years', *The Observer*, 14 October 2007. Available from: http://www.guardian.co.uk/technology/2007/oct/14/internet.crime.

[128] J. Cheng, 'CAN-SPAM violations cost online ad firm $2.9 million', *Ars Technica*, 17 March 2008. Available from: http://arstechnica.com/tech-policy/news/2008/03/can-spam-violations-cost-online-ad-firm-2-9-million.ars.

[129] *MySpace Inc. v Wallace et al.* No. CV-07-1929 ABC (AGRx) (CD Cal. May 12, 2008). Available from: http://www.spamsuite.com/webfm_send/309.

[130] Case No. 5:08-cv-03889-JF (ND Cal. Nov. 21, 2008). Available from: http://docs.justia.com/cases/federal/district-courts/california/candce/5:2008cv03889/206207/25/0.pdf.

[131] Sophos, *Security threat report: 2009*. Available from: http://www.sophos.com/sophos/docs/eng/marketing_material/sophos-security-threat-report-jan-2009-na.pdf.

[132] R. Ford, 'Preemption of State Spam Laws by the Federal CAN-SPAM Act', 72 *University of Chicago Law Review* 355 (2005).

[133] Spamhaus, *Spam Unsubscribe Services*. Available from: http://www.spamhaus.org/removelists.html.

to rise with growing markets including Brazil, China, Russia, and India filling any gap left by a drop in US based spam. Although spam may be one form of speech we do not support it appears that for the near future at least we must continue to rely on technical solutions such as spam filters and blacklists to stem the tide of spam.

6.7 Conclusion: cyber-speech and free expression

The internet is the most perfect communications medium yet designed. For the first time an individual can address large groups and can do so without regard for traditional borders or nation states. Although we must view this as being on the whole positive the breaking down of borders has affected the ability of nation states to protect their community values in the online environment. This legal-regulatory failure was first predicted in 1996 by David Johnson and David Post,[134] but it is only now we are seeing the effects of this. Speech in cyberspace is speech which crosses borders like the flow of a river, and just as the government of France can do little to stop the waters of the River Rhone crossing the border from Switzerland into France there is little they can do about content hosted on US based servers being available to the citizens of France. The effect of this is that governments are being asked to reconsider if and how they wish to regulate expression.

The major challenges are in the three key areas outlined in this chapter: (1) political speech, (2) extremist/hate speech, and (3) spam. It is likely that the first will, in the UK at least, remain subject to light touch regulation for as long as traditional media outlets TV, Radio, and Press, remain the primary focus of electioneering for UK political parties. But we must learn from the experiences of the US, particularly their experience in the 2004 presidential election. There is a balance to be struck between allowing individuals to critique and comment on mainstream media coverage at election time and allowing them to set the media agenda.

The regulation of spam is probably another area which will continue to see light touch legal controls. Major revisions to *The Privacy and Electronic Communications (EC Directive) Regulations 2003* are unlikely in the foreseeable future. This is because as we have seen legal controls are largely ineffective in dealing with spam: much more effective are technical controls such as filtering and blocking.

The area of major tension in the next few years is likely to remain extremist and hate speech. The Yahoo! case is unlikely to be the last word on this, although it also demonstrated the futility of localised legal enforcement proceedings unless the defendant is domiciled in or has assets domiciled in the jurisdiction in question. These challenges will continue to grow in the web 2.0 environment where individuals rather than corporations play a greater role in media content production.

Whatever the future holds in all these areas we should remember that the positive effects that digital communications have had on free expression and the free, full, and frank exchange of views and ideas between individuals far outweigh the negative; but it is to be hoped that those engaged in online expression remember their social responsibilities as well as their rights.

---

[134] Johnson & Post, above n. 64, and accompanying text.

FURTHER READING

Books

Eric Barendt, *Freedom of Speech* 2nd ed. (2005)

Frederick Schauer, *Free Speech*, (1982)

Cass Sunstein, *Republic.com* 2.0 (2007).

Brian Winston, *Messages: Free Expression, Media and the West from Gutenberg to Google*, (2005)

Chapters and Articles

Matthew Fagin, 'Regulating speech across borders: technology vs values' (2003) 9 *Michigan Telecommunications and Technology Law Review* 395

Douglas W. Vick, 'Regulating Hatred' in Mathias Klang & Andrew Murray (eds) *Human Rights in the Digital Age* (2005)

Douglas W. Vick, 'The Internet and the First Amendment' (1998) 61 Modern Law Review 414

Defamation

Although the UK recognises and seeks to protect the individual rights found in Article 10 of the European Convention on Human Rights and Article 19 of the Universal Declaration of Human Rights, one form of speech which has continually found itself subject to strict regulation in the UK is defamatory speech: that is speech harmful to the reputation of others. Defamation occurs when one publishes, or makes public, a statement which damages a person's reputation and tends to lower him in the estimation of right-thinking members of society. Defamatory statements are commonplace. Co-workers tend to defame other co-workers, students often defame lecturers, and individuals in pubs and bars defame a variety of public figures from footballers to actors to politicians. As an experiment think back to the last time you said something about someone that you either knew or suspected not to be true, or about which you were recklessly unaware of its veracity, and which was likely to lower the reputation of that person among those present.

It is a fact of life that we like to 'gossip' about other people,[1] and the best gossip as we all know is salacious and shocking gossip. This causes people to exaggerate, or even to make up stories about others to attain or secure social status. This was not an issue where the nature of discourse was just gossip. When gossip was passed over pints of beer or glasses of wine in the local pub or exchanged over coffees in Starbucks it was ephemeral: it was in the air for a second and then gone again. Actionable defamation, that is the type of defamatory statement which causes an action to end up before a judge, was a world away from gossip. It tended to be statements published in the press or broadcast on television or radio. This is partly due to the extensive audience such statements could reach and partly due to the fact that a publisher or broadcaster indicated deep pockets which could be called upon to fulfil a damages award. As is the common theme of this book the nature of digital communication and the information society has changed all this. As was discussed at length in Chapter 6 the nature of digital communications is that individuals now possess the broadcast abilities of the traditional mass media/broadcast sector. Further, as discussion fora, blogs, video-blogs, and social network updates provide a semi-permanent record of statements, they lose the character of ephemera that gossip has. Finally entries on blogs, social network sites, and

---

[1] It is reported by the Social Issues Research Centre at the University of Oxford that gossip accounts for 55% of male conversation time and 67% of female time. See K. Fox, *Evolution, Alienation and Gossip: The role of mobile telecommunications in the 21st century*, SIRC: http://www.sirc.org/publik/gossip.shtml.

video sharing sites require the assistance of commercial internet service providers and content hosts which assure the availability of deep pockets. It is therefore unsurprising that a number of defamation cases arising both from traditional media sites and from user generated media entries have been brought in the UK and further afield.

7.1 **The tort of defamation**

The tort occurs when one individual makes a defamatory statement about another in which the defamed party may be identified.[2] The defamatory statement must be 'published' that is, it must be communicated to at least one other person. You may defame a natural person, although they must be a living person,[3] or a corporation,[4] although in English Law it is against the public interest for local authorities, government-owned corporations, and political parties to bring defamation actions,[5] while trade unions[6] lack personality to raise actions. English Law makes a distinction between libel: that is a written or recorded defamatory statement including a statement made in a broadcast and slander: a spoken or otherwise transient defamatory statement. In general libel is treated more strictly by the courts than slander, at least in part on the basis that a recorded statement is more likely to be damaging than a transitory one.

Modern telecommunications and mass communication technologies have tended to blur this line somewhat. A statement made on a live television broadcast could reach a far greater audience than a statement written in a local newspaper or in an academic textbook and thus modern telecommunications caused an imbalance in the respective potential effects of libel and slander. Because of this s. 1 of the Defamation Act 1952 states that: 'For the purposes of the law of libel and slander, the broadcasting of words by means of wireless telegraphy shall be treated as publication in permanent form'. Digital communications have, of course, caused further imbalances in traditional defamation principles. As almost all content in the digital environment is recorded there can be little doubt that any defamatory statement contained therein would be subject to an action in libel rather than slander. The only exception may be a live webcast. The law is not clear as to whether a defamatory statement made in a live webcast would be determined to be libel or slander. Should such an event occur it would be for the court to determine whether or not s. 1 of the Defamation Act 1952 applied.[7]

---

[2] It is irrelevant whether or not you intended to identify the defamed party. If they *can* be identified they may then claim for defamation.

[3] Famously in *Rex v Ensor* (1887) 3 TLR 366 Stephen J stated: 'The dead have no rights and can suffer no wrongs. The living alone can be the subject of legal protection, and the law of libel is intended to protect them'. For a critique of this see F. Cameron, 'Defamation Survivability and the Demise of the Antiquated "Actio Personalis" Doctrine', 85 *Columbia Law Review* 1833 (1985).

[4] *Jameel v Wall Street Journal* [2007] 1 AC 359.

[5] *Derbyshire v Times Newspapers Ltd* [1993] AC 534; *Goldsmith v Boyrul* [1997] 4 All ER 268. However, it should be noted that individuals working within such organisations whose reputation is impaired can still commence proceedings. See *Reynolds v Times Newspapers Ltd* [1999] 4 All ER 609.   [6] *EETPU v Times Newspapers Ltd* [1980] 1 All ER 1097.

[7] It is suggested that following the decision of the Scottish Court of Session in *Shetland Times v Wills* [1997] FSR 604, a UK court is unlikely to find a webcast to be a 'means of wireless telegraphy' meaning that s. 1 would not apply to live webcasts.

7.1.1 **Statements, publication, and defences**

When a defamatory statement is made several issues arise. There are questions of who may be liable in damages, questions of when and where the statement was made, issues surrounding defences and the role and potential liability for distributors of the defamatory statement. Although the law of defamation is well established and we have the assistance of the Defamation Act 1996 in interpreting the various roles and potential liabilities involved in an action for defamation we find these issues have become extremely complex when dealing with a media that is capable of crossing borders, which keeps a constant record of all 'discussions' and which allows individuals access to a mass communication channel.

The first issue to address is who is responsible and potentially liable for an online defamatory statement? Primary liability for any defamatory statement rests with the author of the statement: that is the person who made the utterance or who wrote the defamatory text. Liability does not only rest with the author. Liability also arises for editors, publishers, and distributors of a defamatory statement. Distributors and publishers of defamatory statements have always proven to be popular defendants, or co-defendants, as they possess deep pockets, a character often not true of the author or even of the editor of the original libel. As distributors are in a particularly perilous position, distributors are rarely aware of all the content of the material they distribute, and even if they were they have little opportunity of knowing the veracity of statements made in material they distribute; they are offered a particular defence in s. 1 of the Defamation Act 1996, known somewhat unimaginatively as the distributor defence. This states that a distributor of a defamatory statement has a defence if he shows that he took reasonable care in relation to its publication, and he did not know, and had no reason to believe, that what he did caused or contributed to the publication of a defamatory statement. This defence, as we shall see below, is important for ISPs and hosting services who cannot possibly be aware of all the content they host, and or, supply.

The next issue is where the harm occurs; although there are special considerations which arise with internet publication, which will be discussed in detail below, the general rule on jurisdiction and harm is complex enough as was demonstrated in the case of *Berezovsky v Forbes, Inc. (No.1)*.[8]

Case Study *Berezovsky v Forbes, Inc. (No.1)*

Mr Berezovsky is a Russian businessman, who although now resident in Britain was at the time of the alleged defamation living and working in Russia. In 1996 Forbes magazine published an article claiming that Mr Berezovsky was involved in criminal activity and labelling him as a Russian mafia godfather and insinuating that he was involved in the murder of television producer Vladislav Listiev.

Mr Berezovsky decided to litigate claiming the article to be defamatory; surprisingly he chose to litigate in England. This seems a remarkable decision. Mr Berezovsky was

[8] [2000] 1 WLR 1004; 2000 WL 544123.

living and working, at this time, in Russia, he was in fact a member of the Russian government holding the office of Deputy Secretary of the Security Council of the Russian Federation, while the magazine was published in the US. England therefore seemed an unusual forum for this dispute, but of course English libel laws are famously accommodating of plaintiffs, leading to complaints about so-called libel tourism. Unsurprisingly the defendant challenged the jurisdiction of the English courts. Evidence was laid before the court showing that of the 788,346 copies of the issue in question only 1,915 (0.25%) were sold in England and Wales with over 98.9% of the issues being sold in the US and Canada. Forbes claimed that as Mr Berezovsky was not resident in England and Wales and as the magazine was published in and marketed towards and overwhelmingly sold in the North American market the correct forum for this dispute was either Russia or the US. Mr Berezovsky countered that he had a considerable reputation to protect in England and Wales. He explained in an affidavit that 'Over the past several years I have had extensive contacts with England, in business, in government service and personally. During the years in which I pursued my career in international business and finance, I worked frequently in London and with persons and companies based in London. This is entirely understandable, given London's status as the international business and financial capital of Europe, where all of my business interests have been based, and of which Russia is an increasingly important part'.

In the High Court Popplewell J placed a stay on proceedings on the basis that Russia was the better forum for the claim as Mr Berezovsky's links to England and Wales were not strong. The case went to the Court of Appeal. Hirst LJ found that Mr Berezovsky amply met the criteria for a hearing in England and Wales and with the agreement of May LJ and Sir John Knox, reversed the decision of Popplewell J. The case eventually ended up before the House of Lords. There Forbes's appeal was dismissed. In the leading judgement Lord Steyn noted that: 'In 1994/5 he [Berezovsky] visited London on 22 occasions and in 1996/7 on 9 occasions, the reduced rate being due to his involvement in government. He kept an apartment in London. His wife from whom he has separated lives in London with their two children. He also had two daughters from a previous marriage at Cambridge University. As Hirst LJ observed it was surprising on this evidence that the judge found that Mr Berezovsky's connections with England were tenuous. The new material admitted in the Court of Appeal included concrete evidence from three independent sources as to the effect of the Forbes article on Mr Berezovsky's business reputation. The three deponents were a commercial solicitor, the managing director of a Swiss company, and the managing director of a Russian oil company. It is not necessary to set out their evidence in detail. It is sufficient to say that the Forbes article was known to executives of financial institutions and deterred them from entering or continuing London-based negotiations with Mr Berezovsky'.[9] On this basis Lord Steyn found the necessary connection with the jurisdiction of the court was made.

Lord Steyn then dealt with three challenges to the assumption that the courts of England and Wales were the correct forum for the case, all of which are of key

---

[9] *ibid*, 1010–1011.

importance when dealing with issues of online jurisdiction as we shall see later when we discuss cases such as *Dow Jones v Gutnick*[10] and *Jameel v Dow Jones*.[11] The first of these was whether Russia was a better forum for the case to be heard. Lord Steyn rejected this claim on the basis that 'only 19 copies [of the relevant issue of Forbes Magazine] were distributed in Russia ... and most importantly ... it is clear that a judgment in favour of the plaintiffs in Russia will not be seen to redress the damage to the reputations of the plaintiffs in England'.[12] Next on the claim that the US was the better jurisdiction Lord Steyn noted that: 'the connections of both plaintiffs with the United States are minimal. They cannot realistically claim to have reputations which need protection in the United States. It is therefore not an appropriate forum'.[13] Finally, and most importantly Lord Steyn addressed a claim raised by counsel for the appellant that 'the correct approach is to treat multi-jurisdiction cases like the present as giving rise to a single cause of action and then to ascertain where the global cause of action arose'.[14] Lord Steyn rejected this. He found that such an argument 'runs counter to well established principles of libel law. It does not fit into the principles so carefully enunciated in *Spiliada*.[15] The present case is a relatively simple one. It is not a multi-party case: it is, however, a multi-jurisdictional case. It is also a case in which all the constituent elements of the torts occurred in England. The distribution in England of the defamatory material was significant. And the plaintiffs have reputations in England to protect. In such cases it is not unfair that the foreign publisher should be sued here'.[16]

This last point is particularly important when dealing with online publication. Lord Steyn is directly rejecting a claim that when publication is of a global nature it is the role of the court to identify a single cause of action and raise a single claim where that cause arose, in the *Berezovsky* case this would probably be the US. Instead he reaffirms the principle of *lex loci delicti*: that is wherever harm has occurred those who are victims of that harm may raise an action. Thus a webpage which is accessible worldwide may lead to an action in any jurisdiction in which the claimant's reputation has suffered.[17] This is an application of the multiple publication rule (to which we will return below). It states that whenever a new publication or republication of a defamatory statement takes place, a fresh cause of action arises wherever and whenever that occurs. This rule made sense in the real world when to republish a statement usually meant taking some form of affirmative action such as paying for redistribution or reprinting of the statement. In the digital environment though it has taken on a new dimension as material hosted on a single web server anywhere in the world may be continually republished in a variety of jurisdictions by the simple act of a new reader visiting the webpage and downloading the defamatory statement to his computer screen. As we shall see below this has caused great difficulty for authors and publishers online. Such is the extent of the perceived injustice to online publishers caused by this rule the Ministry of Justice has issued a consultation paper on *Defamation and the Internet: The multiple*

---

[10] [2002] HCA 56.   [11] [2005] 2 WLR 1614.
[12] *Berezovsky v Forbes, Inc. (No. 1)*, above n. 8, 1014–1015.   [13] *ibid*, 1015.   [14] *ibid*, 1011.
[15] *Spiliada Maritime Corp v Cansulex Ltd (The Spiliada)* [1987] AC 460.
[16] *Berezovsky v Forbes, Inc. (No. 1)*, above n. 8, 1012–1013.
[17] This will be discussed in depth below.

publication rule.[18] This is part of a proposed reform of defamation law and asks whether the multiple publication rule should be retained? and if not, should a single publication rule be introduced? As will be seen below this change, if implemented, would allow online publication to be treated in a fashion more akin to traditional publishing both in terms of place of publication for jurisdictional purposes but also in relation to date of publication for the purposes of limitation. At the time of writing the consultation remains open. A Report on the consultation may be expected in early 2010.

The final general issue is to examine when defences may be raised to a claim in defamation. There are several defences; the most complete defence is *veritas*, that the statement made was true.[19] As a defence if *veritas* is raised it is for the defendant to establish on the balance of probabilities that the statement is true. This indicates that if you have no evidence to support the statement you should refrain from making it in public even if you believe it to be true. There are though further defences which may be brought to bear even if *veritas* cannot be established.

An alternative is 'fair comment'. This defence may be available if the statement is expressed to be a personal opinion on some matter of public interest. Thus should I comment that 'the Prime Minister's approach to banking regulation is ludicrous and lacking direction or form' I may be able to claim fair comment. Fair comment is famously not available if the statement in question is a matter of fact rather than opinion, whether it is in the public interest or not. It is also clear that the public interest is not the same as of interest to the public. In *London Artists v Littler*,[20] Lord Denning said that for a matter to be in the public interest, it had to concern something which would affect people at large. 'The salacious activities of television presenters, for example, may be of interest to a large segment of the population, but it is probably not in the public interest to publish them, because these activities do not have any direct effect on people's lives'.[21]

The other true defence open to the author of a defamatory statement is the public interest defence (not to be confused with the public interest element of the fair comment defence). In recent years the public interest defence has become known as 'the Reynolds defence' after the case that established the principles under which it may be raised. The case was *Reynolds v Times Newspapers Ltd and Others*,[22] and the principle established was that the public interest defence could be raised when a newspaper or other media organisation published a defamatory statement if they could prove it was in the public interest to publish it and that it was the product of responsible journalism.[23] There are

---

[18] Consultation Paper CP20/09, 16 September 2009: http://www.justice.gov.uk/consultations/docs/defamation-consultation-paper.pdf.

[19] *M'Pherson v Daniels* (1829) 10 B&C 263. Note: it is not necessary that the defamatory statement be perfectly true in all respects; it will suffice as a defence if is substantially true—*Alexander v North Eastern Railway* (1865) 6 B&S 340.   [20] [1969] 2 QB 375.

[21] *ibid*, 391.   [22] [1999] UKHL 45; [1999] 4 All ER 609; [1999] 3 WLR 1010.

[23] Lord Nicholls set out ten factors which should be taken account of in determining whether responsible journalism was practiced. They are: (1) The seriousness of the allegation. The more serious the charge, the more the public is misinformed and the individual harmed, if the allegation is not true. (2) The nature of the information, and the extent to which the subject-matter is a matter of public concern. (3) The source of the information. Some informants have no direct knowledge of the events. Some have their own axes to grind, or are being paid for their stories. (4) The steps taken to verify the information. (5) The status of the information. The allegation may

two further privileges, rather than defences which may be brought to the assistance of a defendant in a defamation action. There are absolute privileges for fair and accurate statements made in judicial proceedings[24] and contemporaneous reports of such proceedings,[25] and for statements made in either House of Parliament.[26] Qualified privilege is awarded for fair reports of judicial proceedings, Parliamentary proceedings, and public meetings and notices.[27]

7.2 Digital defamation: publication and republication

It is clear that publication in an online forum or via sms or mms would qualify as publication for the law of defamation. It is equally clear that in all cases except live (and unrecorded) webcast or other live digital broadcasts such as internet radio transmissions the publication would be of the nature to raise an action in libel rather than slander.[28] The first major issue raised by digital distribution of defamatory material is the method of distribution and what this means for publication and republication.

As we have already seen in Lord Steyn's judgement in *Berezovsky v Forbes*, the standard usually employed by a court in taking jurisdiction over a defamation action is that of *lex loci delicti*. This means that wherever a claimant suffers a loss or harm to his reputation an action may be raised. Traditional media outlets could take steps to limit their exposure to overseas actions. As we saw in Chapter 6, traditional media outlets could have defined or specific markets where they would broadcast or distribute their content. By targeting their publications or broadcasts to specific jurisdictions they could avoid extraterritorial actions as they would be in a position to establish that as publication took place only within a specific jurisdiction harm could not have occurred outwith that jurisdiction. This principle would defend publishers and broadcasters even if a few copies of the defamatory material crossed borders in the bags or suitcases of travellers between states. Obviously, and as illustrated by *Berezovsky v Forbes*, once the publisher or broadcaster actively distributes his product in other states he runs the risk of facing a libel action in any state in which he markets his product. In *Berezovsky*, a key piece of evidence throughout was that Forbes Magazine had 566 subscribers in England and Wales and the issue in question sold a further 1,349 copies at newsstands. Thus traditional media publishers could balance the risks of being pursued in an overseas jurisdiction against the commercial benefits of trading in the jurisdiction.

---

have already been the subject of an investigation which commands respect. (6) The urgency of the matter. News is often a perishable commodity. (7) Whether comment was sought from the claimant. He may have information others do not possess or have not disclosed. An approach to the plaintiff will not always be necessary. (8) Whether the article contained the gist of the claimant's side of the story. (9) The tone of the article. A newspaper can raise queries or call for an investigation. It need not adopt allegations as statements of fact. (10) The circumstances of the publication, including the timing.

   [24] *Watson v McEwan* [1905] AC 480.   [25] Defamation Act 1996, s. 14.
   [26] Bill of Rights 1689. Although this may be waived under s. 13 of the Defamation Act 1996.
   [27] Defamation Act 1996, Sch. 1.
   [28] The question of whether a live webcast or an internet (and therefore cable carried) radio station would qualify as broadcasting by means of wireless telegraphy under s. 1 of the Defamation Act 1952 has been discussed above.

The online distribution model is very different. A static or dynamic digital space (web page, user generated content site, bulletin board, or broadcast site) is stored and updated via a server. That server may then be accessed anywhere in the world, and at any time unless access to the server is blocked. At the risk of sounding repetitive it is the same central issue which has driven the discussion in Chapters 4 and 6: digital communications cross borders without challenge and may be stored and recovered at any time. The effect of this, when faced with the challenges raised by the law of defamation, is though potentially paralysing. Whereas previously publishers or broadcasters could choose to extend the audience for their publication or broadcast by entering a new market, or jurisdiction depending on whether you view this as a commercial or legal development, the suggested implication of digital publishing is that any publisher, no matter how small or localised their intended audience may be, could potentially be seen to publish simultaneously in every country worldwide where their content could be read, and even more potentially damaging: applying the principle in *Berezovsky*, every time their content was accessed by any user worldwide it would count for defamation law purposes as a republication of that content in the place where the user accessed it. Could defamation law really be that strict? If so would anyone publish anything which was remotely at risk of a defamation suit online given that they could potentially have to defend themselves in any court in any jurisdiction worldwide?

7.2.1 **Dow Jones v Gutnick**

The answer to some of these questions came in the winter of 2002 when the High Court of Australia handed down the long anticipated judgement in *Dow Jones & Co. Inc. v Gutnick*.[29] This case has many factual similarities to the *Berezovsky* case but was the first defamation case to answer the question 'does internet publication qualify as publication within a jurisdiction?'

✎ **Case Study** *Dow Jones & Co. v Gutnick*

On 30 October 2000 Barrons Magazine published an article entitled 'Unholy Gains' and placed a copy on the Barrons Online website.

The article in raised a number of allegations about Mr Gutnick, a well-known Melbourne entrepreneur. It claimed that he was involved in the manipulation of stock prices, warning readers to avoid investment products with which the plaintiff was associated and calling for an investigation into the plaintiff's conduct by US securities regulators. It also questioned Mr Gutnick's connection with a convicted money-launderer and tax evader called Nachum Goldberg and suggested that Mr Goldberg assisted Mr Gutnick in a tax evasion scheme by laundering money through religious charities.

Mr Gutnick raised a statement of claim in the Supreme Court of Victoria. In this he claimed he had been defamed within the State of Victoria both in print and online.

---

[29] [2002] HCA 56; 210 CLR 575.

Unlike *Berezovsky*, it seems a very small (though unspecified) number of physical copies of the magazine were distributed in Victoria.[30] Instead Mr Gutnick's claim focussed upon the *Barrons Online* site. He produced evidence that there were 550,000 subscribers to the *Barrons Online* website worldwide at the relevant time: when questioned the defendant conceded that of that number 1,700 subscribers had paid by credit card from Australia, including several hundred subscribers in Victoria.

As with the *Berezovsky* case the defendant applied to have the proceedings stayed on the basis of the doctrine of *forum non conveniens*. The defendant claimed that the article was published in the US, specifically New Jersey, and that that was the correct forum for this claim. In particular Howard Gold, the editor of *Barrons Online*, in an affidavit to the court stated that: 'stories which were written and edited in New York are transmitted by a dedicated computer to [our] corporate campus in New Jersey. There the data is transferred from Barrons' two computers in New Jersey on to six further servers which hold the stories or articles. All six servers are physically located in New Jersey'.[31] At trial Hedigan J, dismissed the defendant's claims citing with approval Lord Steyn's judgement in *Berezovsky*. Dow Jones sought leave to appeal to the Victoria Court of Appeal, but this was refused. Almost three months later, Gleeson CJ and Hayne J granted special leave to appeal to the High Court of Australia.

The key issues in dispute in *Dow Jones* are exactly the same as in *Berezovsky*, but with the focus being on digital publishing rather than print publication. Firstly the court had to decide whether the article had been 'published' in Australia generally and Victoria in particular. The court examined both sides of the argument: the single publication argument put forward by Dow Jones which claimed that publication was a single event which took place in New Jersey and the multiple publication argument put forward by Mr Gutnick which argued that publication occurred wherever the consumer read the material and concluded that: '[b]ecause publication is an act or event to which there are at least two parties, the publisher and a person to whom material is published, publication to numerous persons may have as many territorial connections as there are those to whom particular words are published'.[32] Having established the multiple publication rule should apply equally to online publications as to other types of publications they then turned their attention to the question of when an article was published in a given territory if it is made available via a web server in another jurisdiction.

➡ Highlight Gutnick before the High Court of Australia

Defamation is to be located at the place where the damage to reputation occurs. Ordinarily that will be where the material which is alleged to be defamatory is available in comprehensible form assuming, of course, that the person defamed has in that place a reputation which is thereby damaged. It is only when the material is in comprehensible form that the damage to reputation is done and it is damage to reputation which is the principal focus of defamation, not any quality of the defendant's conduct.

➡

---

[30] *Gutnick v Dow Jones & Co. Inc.* [2001] VSC 305.   [31] *ibid*, 309.
[32] *Dow Jones & Co. Inc. v Gutnick* [2002] HCA 56, 63.

> →
>
> In the case of material on the World Wide Web, it is not available in comprehensible form until downloaded on to the computer of a person who has used a web browser to pull the material from the web server. It is where that person downloads the material that the damage to reputation may be done. Ordinarily then, that will be the place where the tort of defamation is committed.

The above is the key passage from the decision. It was the key passage both on a micro and a macro level. On the micro level it established that in *this* case the Supreme Court of Victoria was right to find jurisdiction, a finding that led eventually to Dow Jones settling the case for A$180,000 in damages and A$400,000 costs.[33] The effects on the macro level were much greater. The High Court of Australia had said explicitly what everyone had suspected following the *Berezovsky* decision: digital content hosted on a web server would be deemed to be 'published' at the point of access not at the point of storage. Thus a web server hosted in the US could publish material in any country which allowed access to that server. In other words an online publication could lead to litigation for defamation in potentially any jurisdiction worldwide.

Some commentators suggested the potential chilling effects of *Dow Jones* on internet speech would be calamitous. The *New York Times* famously editorialised: 'To subject distant providers of on-line content to sanctions intent on curbing free speech—or even to 190 libel laws—is to undermine the internet's viability'.[34] Others though were more measured, pointing out that all the High Court of Australia had done was apply a well established principle of libel laws that had been seen in a series of previous cases culminating in the *Berezovsky* case.[35] As these commentators pointed out international communications and media had not proven to be hamstrung by the multiple publication rule in the past and there was no reason to suggest that things would be any different with online publications. Although the scale of international publication was undoubtedly magnified by online publishing publishers had little to fear of being dragged before a succession of courts across the globe. As Jonathan Zittrain pointed out there still needs to be a reason for the court to take jurisdiction:

> The Australian court was unpersuaded by the 'pile on' argument that Gutnick could next sue the company in Zimbabwe, or Great Britain, or China. It pointed out that Gutnick himself lived in Australia, and Dow Jones quite explicitly sold subscriptions to the online Barron's to Australians. These facts helped Australia escape the dilemma of justifying almost any country's intervention if it was to justify its own. Without its special if not unique relationship to one party in the case, Australia may well have declined to intervene in the dispute.[36]

[33] ABC News, *Dow Jones settles Gutnick action*, 12 November 2004: http://www.abc.net.au/news/newsitems/200411/s1242115.htm.

[34] Editorial, 'A Blow to Online Freedom', *New York Times*, 11 December 2002: http://query.nytimes.com/gst/fullpage.html?res=9D05E7DE143AF932A25751C1A9649C8B63.

[35] D. Rolph, 'The Message, Not the Medium: Defamation, Publication and the Internet in Dow Jones & Co Inc v Gutnick' (2002) 24 *Sydney Law Review* 263; M. Richardson & R. Garnett, 'Perils of Publishing on the Internet: Broader Implications of Dow Jones v Gutnick' (2004) 31 *Griffith Law Review* 4.

[36] J. Zittrain, 'Be Careful What You Ask For: Reconciling a Global Internet and Local Law' in Adam Thierer (ed) *Who Rules the Net?: Internet Governance and Jurisdiction* (2003).

There is therefore little risk of a greater chilling effect with online speech as with any other form of speech. In fact it can be argued that as we saw in Chapter 6, with the ease of access and widespread audience offered through digital publication, online publishing finds itself protected from the chilling effects of defamation law to a greater extent than other forms of publishing. Additionally as we saw in Chapter 6 in our discussion of the *Licra et UEJF v Yahoo! Inc. and Yahoo! France*,[37] an order of an extra-territorial court can only be enforced against the author of a statement found to be defamatory if either (a) the author is resident in or has assets domiciled within the jurisdiction in question or (b) the local courts where the author is resident recognise the order of the foreign jurisdiction, something which a US court is unlikely to do when faced with libel orders from overseas.[38]

7.2.2 Loutchansky v Times newspapers: republication and limitation

The fall-out from the *Gutnick* decision was predictable. Those states perceived to be plaintiff-friendly in defamation actions found cases were quickly raised following online publication of allegedly defamatory material. At the forefront of this were the courts of England and Wales.

The first of a series of cases which have helped establish the level of connection required for the English courts to take jurisdiction over an international defamation action was *Loutchansky v Times Newspapers Ltd*.[39] The *Loutchansky* case is very similar to the *Berezovsky* case. Dr Loutchansky, a Russian national, claimed that two news stories published in *The Times* newspaper on 8 September 1999 and 14 October 1999 were defamatory. The stories claimed that Dr Loutchansky was the boss of a major Russian criminal organisation and that he was involved in, amongst other things, money-laundering. The defendants accepted that the articles were defamatory of Dr Loutchansky, but argued qualified privilege, and also argued that Dr Loutchansky's action was time barred.

This claim was based on s. 4A of the Limitation Act 1980 which states that in actions of libel or slander 'no such action shall be brought after the expiration of one year from the date on which the cause of action accrued'. Dr Loutchansky had failed to raise the case in time, but he argued that in relation to material *The Times* placed on its web servers that each time the material was accessed by a reader was a fresh publication of the stories, thus allowing him to comply with the Limitation Act. This is another application of the debate between a single publication rule and the multiple publication rule already discussed extensively in *Berezovsky* and *Gutnick*: in this case it is not the place of publication which is in issue it is the time of the publication.

As we have already seen common law courts tend to apply the multiple publication rule when approaching this issue. In this case counsel for the newspaper argued that this approach had been rendered incompatible with the Limitation Act through the application of internet technology. Lord Lester of Herne Hill QC, acting for the

---

[37] Tribunal de Grande Instance de Paris (Superior Court of Paris) 2000.
[38] See *Telnikoff v Matusevitch* 702 A 2d 230 (Md 1997); *Bachchan v India Abroad Publications Inc*, 585 NYS 2d 661 (NY 1992).   [39] [2002] 2 WLR 640; [2002] QB 783.

respondents, argued that the Court of Appeal should adopt a single publication rule on the basis that the emergence of the internet and the extensive period for which material was archived and accessible through online services meant that should the multiple publication rule be endorsed there would be ongoing liability of an open ended nature for material placed online. This he argued was incompatible with the intent of the Limitation Act which was to provide for a limited period following publication for an action to be brought.[40] Lord Lester went on to claim that the existence of internet-based libraries of newspaper stories provided an important public service and it was the law that was out of step with this service. If the law did not change he warned that: 'if a newspaper defendant which maintained a website of back numbers was to be indefi-nitely vulnerable to claims in defamation for years and even decades after the initial hard copy and internet publication, such a rule was bound to have an effect on the preparedness of the media to maintain such websites, and thus to limit freedom of expression'.[41]

The Court considered all Lord Lester's arguments, but ultimately dismissed all his arguments. They did not accept that the effect of the multiple publication rule in the information society was to undermine the intent of the Limitation Act. In the opinion of the Court, given by Lord Phillips of Worth Matravers MR, it was pointed out that an action based on internet publication was subsidiary to the action based on print publi-cation. In other words each publication was a separate action with separate twelve month limitation periods, and essentially with separate quanta of damages attached thereto: as Lord Phillips says, 'the scale of such publication and any resulting damage is likely to be modest compared with that of the original publication'.[42] On this basis the Court dismissed the claim that the multiple publication rule interfered with the work-ing and intent of the Limitation Act.

This only left the claim that the multiple publication rule was out of step with the new order of internet publication and record keeping. The Court quickly rejected this claim as well. Lord Phillips stated that although the Court accepted 'that the maintenance of archives, whether in hard copy or on the Internet, has a social utility ... [we] consider that the maintenance of archives is a comparatively insignificant aspect of freedom of expression. Archive material is stale news and its publication cannot rank in importance with the dissemination of contemporary material. Nor do we believe that the law of defamation need inhibit the responsible maintenance of archives. Where it is known that archive material is or may be defamatory, the attachment of an appropriate notice warning against treating it as the truth will normally remove any sting from the material'.[43] In other words once the publisher of the material becomes aware of the fact that it may be defamatory they may take simple steps to limit their exposure by simply adding an addendum to the archive material informing readers of this. This would work in much the same way as a retraction in print.

The *Loutchansky* case therefore adds further to our understanding of digital defama-tion. Between *Gutnick* and *Loutchansky* it was established that the multiple publication

---

[40] [2002] QB 783, 814.   [41] *ibid*, 817.   [42] *ibid*, 818.   [43] *ibid*, 817–818.

rule applies to internet publications in such a manner that each new access to material held on a server is a new publication both in space and time. It seemed the courts may be swamped by cases of this type.

7.2.3 King v Lewis

The next case to develop this principle was the case of *King v Lewis*.[44] This involved an action brought by Mr Don King, a famous boxing promoter and US resident, against three defendants: Mr Lennox Lewis, a UK citizen, but at the time a US resident, Mr Judd Burstein, a New York based lawyer and US citizen, and Lion Promotions LLC, a Nevada-based promotion company. Mr Lewis and Lion Promotions were suing Mr King and a co-defendant, Mike Tyson, in New York claiming interference with an agreement between Mr Lewis and Mr Tyson in connection with a proposed re-match of their world heavy-weight title contest, claiming $35 million in compensatory damages and $350 million in punitive damages. The New York litigation received a great deal of publicity, at least in part due to Mr Burstein putting the complaint on the boxing website *boxingtalk.com*. The proceedings in London followed the publication of two online articles surrounding the New York litigation. The first appeared on the site *fightnews.com* on 5 July 2003, was written by Mr Burstein and was entitled 'My Response to Don King'. In this Mr Burstein claimed that Mr King had made anti-semitic remarks about him and accused him of bigotry.[45] The second appeared on *boxingtalk.com* on 8 July 2003 and was an interview with Mr Burstein carried out by a Mr Leon. It repeated all the claims made by Mr Burstein in the earlier article.[46] Although it may seem that the Courts of New York were the most appropriate forum for a dispute between three US-based individuals and a US-based corporation involving claims made on US-based websites, Mr King chose to raise his action in England. This is a not uncommon action for individuals with reputations to protect, as we have seen in the *Berezovsky* case, and may be explained in the instant case because to raise an action in the US he would need to overcome the standard in *New York Times v Sullivan*.[47] This states that where a public figure attempts to bring an action for defamation, they must prove that the statement was made with 'actual malice'. This means that the person making the statement must know the statement to be false, or must have issued the statement with reckless disregard as to its truth. In England Mr King did not have to meet the *Sullivan* standard but he did need to show *lex loci delicti*.

In dismissing an appeal from Mr Justice Eady's decision to allow Mr King to serve the claim form out of the jurisdiction, the Court of Appeal examined Mr King's claim to have the case heard in England & Wales. The Court seemed to be convinced that Mr King had a reputation to protect in England,[48] and appeared to be particularly swayed by the fact that Mr King 'would wish to adduce evidence from a number of witnesses based in the UK, on such matters as his reputation and connection with this country and, in particular, his links with Jewish charity work in London'.[49] What is less

---

[44] [2004] EWCA Civ. 1329.   [45] *ibid*, [8].   [46] *ibid*, [9].   [47] 376 US 254 (1964).
[48] [2004] EWCA Civ. 1329, [13].   [49] *ibid*, [38].

satisfactory is that the Court never sought, or was given, any actual evidence of publication occurring in England and Wales. Instead they were content to state that: 'The libels alleged consist in two texts stored on websites based in California. In the ordinary way they can be, and have been, downloaded here. It is common ground that by the law of England the tort of libel is committed where publication takes place, and each publication generates a separate cause of action. The parties also accept that a text on the Internet is published at the place where it is downloaded. Accordingly there is no contest but that subject to any defences on the merits the respondent has been libelled in this jurisdiction'.[50] The Court never investigated the degree of publication in England and Wales. Were the stories downloaded on one occasion or one hundred? We may never know for this dispute was merely about the procedural issue of could the courts of England and Wales issue a claim against the defendants. The Court was not interested in discussing the merits of the case at this time; this would be a matter for later trial.[51] It is unfortunate though that the Court did not consider this issue as on the wording of the decision of the Court of Appeal in *King* a single download within the jurisdiction of England and Wales would be sufficient to enable a libel action to be raised within this jurisdiction if the plaintiff had a reputation to protect in the jurisdiction. This seems close to the tenuous connection or 'pile on' argument which some had predicted would lead to a massive rise in libel tourism and multijurisdictional claims and which had been rejected by Jonathan Zittrain.[52] The next case was to have a significant impact on this.

7.2.4 Dow Jones v Jameel

The next key case as it turned out was *Dow Jones, Inc. v Jameel*.[53] This is another in the long line of cases starting with *Berezovsky* and including *Gutnick* in which an international businessman has challenged stories in US based business-oriented publications which accuse him of links to organised crime. In this case a Saudi businessman Yousef Jameel and his brother Mohammed Jameel were accused in an article in the *Wall Street Journal* of providing financial support for al Qaeda. The story arose when the US obtained secret al Qaeda documents relating to the formation of the al Qaeda movement in 1988. Among these documents was one called 'the Golden Chain' which purported to list 20 Saudi financial backers of Osama Bin Laden: on this list was Mr Jameel.[54] The *Wall Street Journal* published a news story based upon this discovery entitled 'War on Terror' by Glenn Simpson on 18 March 2003 and placed it on the *wsj.com* website. Via the website one could link to the list of names on the Golden Chain.

On 15 April 2003 Mr Jameel's solicitors wrote to Dow Jones asking them to remove the Golden Chain document from their website and warning their client would take action to 'protect his reputation in England'.[55] When Dow Jones refused to do so a claim

---

[50] *ibid*, [2].
[51] There appears to have been no later trial on the merits of the claim. It may be suspected this was a negotiating lever designed to reach a settlement of the dispute in New York.
[52] Above n. 36.   [53] [2005] EWCA Civ 75; [2005] Q.B. 946.   [54] [2005] EWCA Civ 75 [8].
[55] *ibid*, [14].

was raised in the High Court. Mr Justice Eady found in favour of the plaintiff but Dow Jones immediately appealed to the Court of Appeal and it was in the judgement of the Court, handed down by Lord Phillips of Worth Matravers, MR that we see a new approach to internet defamation cases in England and Wales develop.

The question which was to become the focus of much of the Court's time was whether Mr Jameel had suffered any actual harm in England and Wales. While Mr Jameel managed to force an admission from Dow Jones that there were approximately six thousand subscribers to *wsj.com* in England and Wales,[56] Dow Jones countered that only five subscribers had actually followed the hyperlink from the story to read the Goldern Chain document, and that of these five one was Mr Jameel's solicitor, one was a consultant to the claimant's businesses and another was a director of a business associated with Mr Jameel. In the words of Lord Phillips, '[t]hey are members of the claimant's camp'.[57] With only two subscribers having apparently read the defamatory document who were not connected to the litigation the questions for the court were whether a substantial tort had taken place and/or whether an abuse of process would occur should the claim be allowed to proceed. On the former issue Lord Philips concluded that '[i]f the claimant succeeds in this action and is awarded a small amount of damages, it can perhaps be said that he will have achieved vindication for the damage done to his reputation in this country, but both the damage and the vindication will be minimal. The cost of the exercise will have been out of all proportion to what has been achieved. The game will not merely not have been worth the candle, it will not have been worth the wick'.[58] On the latter he concluded:[59]

→ Highlight Defamation and Abuse of Process

It would be an abuse of process to continue to commit the resources of the English court, including substantial judge and possibly jury time, to an action where so little is now seen to be at stake. Normally where a small claim is brought, it will be dealt with by a proportionate small claims procedure. Such a course is not available in an action for defamation where, although the claim is small, the issues are complex and subject to special procedure under the Civil Procedure Rules.

The *Jameel* case adds greatly to our understanding of the tort of defamation in the online environment. We can now see that although a single publication within the jurisdiction of the UK courts may be enough to allow them to take jurisdiction, it is for the plaintiff to establish they have suffered substantial harm, that is harm substantial enough to overcome the *de minimis* rule: failure so to do may lead, as with Mr Jameel, to your case being thrown out as an abuse of process.

---

[56] *ibid*, [16].   [57] *ibid*, [17].   [58] *ibid*, [69].   [59] *ibid*, [70].

7.2.5 **Online defamation post Jameel**

In at least two cases subsequent to the *Jameel* decision the courts have had recourse to the *de minimis* provision set out therein and on both occasions they have upheld and applied the *Jameel* principle.

The first of these cases was *Al Amoudi v Brisard & Anor.*[60] This case involved an Ethiopian-born businessman, Mohammed Hussein Al Amoudi who was normally resident in Saudi Arabia but who spent about two and a half months a year living in England and Jean Charles Brisard a French national resident in Switzerland, an author and international expert and investigator on terrorism financing. It was alleged by Mr Al Amoudi that he was defamed by M. Brisard in two entries he made on his website in which he claimed Mr Al Amoudi was '(i) a knowing participant in the economic, financial and/or terrorist networks of the terrorist Osama Bin Laden and/or is likely to have knowingly facilitated ties with the said network; and/or (ii) that, being himself a part of the vast financing system that is the trade mark of Osama Bin Laden's terrorist operations, he has knowingly financed and/or facilitated the financing of Osama Bin Laden's terrorism'.[61] M. Brisard argued that 'in the relevant period the reports containing the words complained of were not downloaded within this jurisdiction' or in the alternative 'if and in so far as the claimant can prove that the reports were downloaded within this jurisdiction within the relevant period, they were downloaded by lawyers acting for the claimant or for others named in the reports or by persons or friends or business associates of the claimant.'[62] In either case M. Brisard argued the claim was an abuse of process applying the *Jameel* principle. The claim was heard by Mr Justice Gray who concluded that it is for the claimant to prove that the material in question was accessed and downloaded within the jurisdiction of the courts of England and Wales.[63] As the plaintiff had been unable to demonstrate this he refused the plaintiff's application for summary judgement and remanded the case to be heard at a full hearing where the evidence could be fully tested.[64]

Finally there is the case of *Brady v Norman*.[65] This case is rather different from all its predecessors as there is no international element to this case. Both plaintiff and defendant are UK based, with the plaintiff, Mr Brady, being the former general secretary of the rail union ASLEF, and the defendant Mr Norman, the current general secretary. Mr Brady's claim arose out of an article published in the July 2006 edition of *Loco Journal*, the monthly magazine of ASLEF. In the article entitled 'The Brady Era is Over' it was stated that 'the Certification Officer had ruled the previous week that Mr Brady had legitimately been excluded from ASLEF membership for bringing the union into disrepute'.[66] The offending issue of the magazine, as well as being distributed to ASLEF members was placed on the ASLEF website. Mr Brady conceded that ASLEF members, as well as ex-members, officers and their widows, and the

---

[60] [2006] EWHC 1062 (QB); [2007] 1 WLR 113.   [61] [2007] 1 WLR 113, 115.
[62] *ibid*, 116.
[63] 'I am unable to accept that under English law a claimant in a libel action on an Internet publication is entitled to rely on a presumption of law that there has been substantial publication'. *ibid*, 123.   [64] It appears the case never went to trial.
[65] [2008] EWHC 2481 (QB).   [66] *ibid*, [5].

union's professional advisers had a legitimate interest in receiving information about what took place at the union conference,[67] but argued that by placing the *Loco Journal* report on the ASLEF website the union and its officers had made it available to non-privileged individuals who had no interest in the union's activities. Mr Brady's legal team estimated this may have led to 202 further publications which were the publications in dispute.[68] Deputy Judge Richard Parkes QC rejected Mr Brady's claims. He ruled that the court could not infer that just because the material was available to be read online it would be read by members of the public who had no direct interest in the operations of the union. Like Mr Al Amoudi, Mr Brady was asking the court to assume online publication had occurred. The distinction between the *Brady* case and the *Al Amoudi* case was that Mr Brady could establish the article had been accessed online, in this case on 202 occasions, what he could not establish though was that those accessing the online publication were not covered by the same legitimate interest of those receiving the original published version of the magazine. As Richard Parkes QC concludes: 'Without some evidence to justify the inference (for instance, evidence that the ASLEF site and the information contained in it provide an attractive resource for transport enthusiasts generally, rather than simply for members and staff) it seems to me to be no more than pure speculation to infer that an "outsider" would have read the words complained of. An inference is a conclusion reached on the basis of evidence and reasoning: it is not a matter of guesswork. It would not have been right to ask the jury to take a guess. I therefore held that there was no sufficient evidence of website publication to individuals in non-privileged circumstances to leave to the jury'.[69]

7.2.6 **The ministry of justice consultation paper**

The case law has given us a detailed understanding of the application of the multiple publication rule in online defamation. We can say with some degree of certainty that each access and download of a particular article or paper is a single publication (or republication) of that article. We can add to this the knowledge that each new republication begins afresh the one year limitation period contained in the Limitation Act 1980, and that perhaps as little as a single publication/republication in a jurisdiction in which the claimant has a reputation to protect *may* be enough to allow a claim to be brought, but that claim will be subject to an examination for abuse of process which means that to be successful the claimant will have to demonstrate not merely a connection with the jurisdiction in question but a *substantial* connection which may only be demonstrated by showing substantial harm has been, or is likely to be, suffered by the claimant within that jurisdiction.

These developments though have left the publishing industry extremely nervous of online publishing, and in particular the dangers posed by archive materials. As a result the UK Government has taken steps to review the application of the multiple publication rule in the information society. The consultation paper *Defamation and the internet: the multiple publication rule* was published on 16 September 2009 and remains open for

---

[67] *ibid*, [10].   [68] *ibid*.   [69] *ibid*, [26].

comment until 16 December 2009.[70] The consultation asks a series of questions relating to the multiple publication rule as interpreted for online content through the long series of cases discussed in this chapter. The consultation paper notes that the problem of online content, especially archived content is that 'each "hit" on a webpage creates a new publication, potentially giving rise to a separate cause of action, should it contain defamatory material. Each cause of action has its own limitation period that runs from the time at which the material is accessed. As a result, publishers are potentially liable for any defamatory material published by them and accessed via their online archive, however long after the initial publication the material is accessed, and whether or not proceedings have already been brought in relation to the initial publication'.[71] As a result there is a concern that operators of online archives find themselves being placed in a potentially unfair position as 'the accessibility of online archives means that the potential for claims is much greater in respect of material accessed online.'[72]

The consultation paper therefore asks for views on a number of questions. Prime among them is the connected questions 'do you consider in principle that the multiple publication rule should be retained? If not, should a single publication rule be introduced?' In a series of supplementary questions issues such as the interaction between publication and limitation, raised in *Loutchansky*, are examined alongside alternatives to a single publication rule such as perhaps awarding qualified privilege protection to online archives of material. It is far too early at the time of writing to predict the outcome of this consultation but from the structure of the consultation paper and the way the questions are framed it seems that the Ministry of Justice is in favour of replacing the multiple publication rule with a new single publication rule as a way to encourage online publishers to allow access to archive materials. The next stage of the process should see a report in early 2010. Any changes to the law will be after the 2010 general election.

7.3 **Intermediary liability**

Finding a court willing to take jurisdiction over your claim is only the first stage in establishing a successful libel claim. Next you have to correctly identify the author, publisher, or distributor of the defamatory statement and have them brought before the court. In traditional publishing this is usually quite simple. The author often attaches his or her name to the article, by-line, or book in question. The publisher is always identifiable by the addition of publishers' details in nearly all commercially produced material and the distributor will usually include the person who sold you the material in the first place. As with almost everything in the information society the addition of the digital elements of distribution confuses the usual principle. When the author of a defamatory statement signs him or herself as *noxious2256*, and when the site itself is published by an offshore anonymous corporation apparently domiciled in Panama or Russia it can prove difficult, if not impossible, to identify those primarily liable for the

---

[70] Consultation Paper CP20/09, above n. 18.   [71] *ibid*, [3].   [72] *ibid*, [4].

defamatory statement.[73] If you have been defamed online it seems all too often that the only party which can be identified as being liable is the ISP who has carried the defamatory statement, or who has allowed access to it. Thus it is not surprising that an extensive body of litigation has grown up around the liability of ISPs for hosting and carrying defamatory content.

7.3.1 **Early cases: ISPs as publishers**

Early litigation on this issue took place in the US. Possibly the first case to examine the liability of internet hosts was *Cubby Inc. v CompuServe Inc.*[74] This case involved a posting on a Computer Information Service (the predecessor to web forums) forum called 'Rumorville USA'. Rumorville was a journalism forum which published a daily newsletter providing reports about broadcast journalism and journalists. It was published by a private company, Don Fitzpatrick Associates of San Francisco (DFA), on the CompuServe service. Mr Cubby was the developer of a database called 'Skuttlebut' which was designed to publish news and gossip in the television news and radio industries: Skuttlebut was intended to compete with Rumorville. Mr Cubby claimed that on separate occasions in April 1990, Rumorville published false and defamatory statements relating to Skuttlebut, and that CompuServe carried these statements as part of their service.

The allegedly defamatory remarks included a suggestion that individuals at Skuttlebut gained access to information first published by Rumorville through a back door and a description of Skuttlebut as a new start-up scam.[75] By contract with CompuServe, DFA had complete editorial control over the Rumorville pages. For District Judge Leisure this was the key to CompuServe's potential liability. 'CompuServe has no more editorial control over such a publication than does a public library, book store, or newsstand, and it would be no more feasible for CompuServe to examine every publication it carries for potentially defamatory statements than it would be for any other distributor to do so'.[76] On this basis Judge Leisure dismissed the claim against CompuServe on the basis that 'as a news distributor, [they] may not be held liable if [they] neither knew nor had reason to know of the allegedly defamatory statements.'[77] This was a positive outcome for the fledgling internet industry. It suggested that provided they had no actual knowledge of a defamatory statement an internet hosting service would not be held liable for material they hosted on their server. In other words internet hosts were distributors, not publishers and could call upon the 'distributor defence'.

The next major internet defamation case in the US was about to change this though. The case was *Stratton Oakmont Inc. v Prodigy Services Co.*[78] This case centred on a claim that Prodigy was liable as a publisher rather than merely as a distributor for a series of

---

[73] In an interesting recent development Mr Justice Lewison allowed blogger Donal Blaney to serve an order via Twitter which required an imposter to identify themselves. This order was successful in stopping the impersonator from carrying on his actions. Although an order for breach of copyright it could be amended to be used in defamation actions. If parties failed to comply though the usual problems of identification would remain. See F. Gibb, 'High Court to serve injunction through Twitter', *The Times*, 2 October 2009: http://technology.timesonline.co.uk/tol/news/tech_and_web/article6857851.ece.   [74] 776 F.Supp 135 (SD NY 1991).   [75] *ibid*, 136–137.
[76] *ibid*, 139.   [77] *ibid*, 140.   [78] 23 Media L. Rep. 1794 (NY Sup Ct, 1995).

allegedly defamatory statements made by an anonymous user on Prodigy's 'Money Talk' bulletin board. The posts were all made between 23 and 25 October 1994 and claimed that Stratton Oakmont, who were a securities investment firm, and their president Daniel Porush, committed criminal acts in connection with the initial public offering of stock of Solomon-Page Ltd and that Stratton Oakmont were 'a cult of brokers who either lie for a living or get fired'.[79] The problem for the plaintiffs was that applying the logic of the earlier *Cubby* case Prodigy would be held to be only distributors of the statements in question not their author or publisher, and as the author could not be identified they would be left with no recourse. The answer was in the way that Prodigy managed their service. Prodigy advertised that it controlled the content on its boards by deleting language it deemed to be offensive, and had done so through the use of filtering software and by promulgating guidelines that directed board leaders to remove offensive language and content. For Justice Ain this was sufficient evidence that Prodigy maintained enough editorial control over the articles posted on the Money Talk bulletin board to merit being held to a publisher's standard of liability.[80]

These cases produced a surprising outcome. It was clear from reading both authorities that an internet host who took a 'hands-off' approach to hosting content would generally be free from liability unless they had knowledge of the defamatory nature of the statement as they would be treated as distributors, while hosts who monitored, filtered, and edited content would be held to the stricter publisher standard. This posed a problem for Congress who at the time was drafting the Communications Decency Act (CDA).[81] The CDA was designed to clean up the internet. Its primary aim was to control the ready availability of pornographic material on the internet by extending regulation common in broadcast and cable television and making it an offence to carry indecent material across state lines by means of a telecommunications service. The problem for Congress was that for the Communications Decency Act to be effective they needed the support of internet hosts and ISPs who would search for and remove offensive material. In so doing though it appeared from the *Stratton Oakmont* decision that they would then leave themselves at risk of defamation actions for any libellous material they also hosted. To assuage the concerns of ISPs an amendment was made to the original Communications Decency Bill adding a new section, § 230, which provided a safe harbour for ISPs and similar. The key provision of § 230 is § 230(c)(1), which provides that: 'No provider or user of an interactive computer service shall be treated as the publisher or speaker of any information provided by another information content provider'. The effect of § 230(c)(1), seems therefore to be to provide blanket immunity from publisher liability for any provider of an interactive computer service, statutorily overruling *Stratton Oakmont*. In a perverse footnote when the Communications Decency Act was passed it was immediately challenged by a collection of civil liberties groups and it was eventually struck down by the Supreme Court as being incompatible with the First Amendment,[82] § 230 though remained in effect: the online publishing industry was given its good samaritan defence without having to police for indecent content.

---

[79] *ibid*, 1796.   [80] *ibid*, 1797.
[81] The Communications Decency Act was Title V of the Telecommunications Act of 1996, Pub. LA. No. 104-104, 110 Stat. 56 (1996).   [82] *Reno v ACLU* 521 US 844 (1997).

7.3.2 **CDA §230: safe harbour**

The issue became how § 230 would be applied. We did not have to wait long for the early cases to come through and one of the first was *Zeran v America Online*.[83] Shortly after the Oklahoma City bombing, an unknown person posted messages onto an AOL bulletin board purporting to be from Mr Zeran, advertising t-shirts and other items with slogans glorifying the bombing in which 168 people were killed. Mr Zeran received numerous disturbing and threatening telephone calls from people outraged with the posted notice eventually forcing him to go into hiding. He raised a libel action against AOL claiming they were negligent in allowing these notices to remain and reappear on their bulletin board despite having received notice and complaints from him following the appearance of the first advertisement. Here although AOL clearly had notice of the defamatory nature of the statement, and thus would be liable either as a publisher or as a distributor of the defamatory statement, the Federal Court of Appeals for the Fourth Circuit circumvented the publisher/distributor distinction and stated that when Congress was speaking of 'publishers', it meant to include both publishers and distributors.[84] On this basis the Court held that 'Congress was referring to the use of the term publication in defamation law as it is used generally to describe the "communication intentionally or by a negligent act to one other than the person defamed".'[85]

This decision was rightly criticised for extending the § 230 defence further than Congress intended.[86] This did not stop the *Zeran* definition being applied in a series of cases involving among other things, a claim that White House aide Sidney Blumenthal abused his spouse,[87] a failure by Prodigy (who ironically had lost in the *Stratton Oakmont* case to begin this whole process) to prevent an imposter sending abusive emails and making abusive postings in the name of another,[88] and most ironically and worryingly given the reason for the promulgation of § 230 it was held by the Florida courts to protect AOL from liability for failing to monitor and prevent the marketing of child pornography.[89] By the turn of the millennium it seemed that the *Zeran* decision has infected courts across the US: never would a provider of a digital information service be held liable for material they hosted or carried no matter how defamatory or obscene.[90]

Slowly though courts across the US have retreated from the *Zeran* position. In 2003 the US Court of Appeals for the Seventh Circuit expressed their dissatisfaction with the *Zeran* principle. In *Doe v GTE*,[91] despite holding that the defendants in the instant case

---

[83] 129 F 3d 327 (4th Cir. 1997).   [84] *ibid*, 332.   [85] *ibid*.
[86] See, e.g. M. Spencer, 'Defamatory E-mail and Employer Liability: Why Razing Zeran v. America Online Is a Good Thing', 6 *Richmond Journal of Law & Technology* 25 (2000): http://www.richmond.edu/jolt/v6i5/article4.html; I. Ballon, 'Zeran v. AOL: Why the Fourth Circuit is Wrong' (1998) 1 *Journal of Internet Law* 6: http://library.findlaw.com/1999/Feb/2/127916.html.
[87] *Blumenthal* v. *Drudge* 992 F. Supp. 44 (D DC 1998).
[88] *Lunney v Prodigy Services Company* 723 NE 2d 539 (NY Ct. App. 1999).
[89] *Doe v America Online, Inc.* 718 So. 2d 385 (Fla Ct. App. 1998).
[90] See, e.g. D. Rowland 'Free Expression and Defamation' in M. Klang & A. Murray (eds) *Human Rights in the Digital Age* (2005); M. Deturbide, 'Liability of Internet Service Providers for Defamation in the US and Britain: Same Competing Interests, Different Responses' 2000 (3) *The Journal of Information, Law and Technology*. http://www2.warwick.ac.uk/fac/soc/law/elj/jilt/2000_3/deturbide/.   [91] 347 F.3d 655 (2003).

were entitled to the protection offered by §230, the Court asked 'Why should a law designed to eliminate ISPs' liability to the creators of offensive material end up defeating claims by the victims of tortious or criminal conduct?'[92] The Court went on to suggest a better interpretation would be to return to traditional defamation principles: 'perhaps § 230(c)(1) forecloses any liability that depends on deeming the ISP a "publisher"—defamation law would be a good example of such liability—while permitting the states to regulate ISPs in their capacity as intermediaries'.[93]

This case signalled a change of attitude. Many cases have followed the *GTE* position since, including the high profile case of *Chicago Lawyers' Committee for Civil Rights under Law, Inc. v Craigslist, Inc.*,[94] yet despite these 'green shoots' which suggest a relaxation of the hard line interpretation found in *Zeran* it is still extremely difficult to raise a defamation action in the US against any information service provider, and with recent cases such as *Barrett v Rosenthal* suggesting that this immunity may even extend in certain circumstances to individuals who distribute or republish content,[95] it seems it may be as difficult as it ever was to find an information service provider liable for hosting or republishing a defamatory statement in the US.

7.3.3 ISP publisher liability in the UK

The position in the UK is thankfully clearer and more balanced. Rather than giving information service providers blanket immunity we balance the rights and responsibilities of internet hosts and ISPs. The first examination of ISP liability in the UK is to be found in the case of *Godfrey v Demon Internet Service*.[96]

✎ Case Study *Godfrey v Demon Internet Service*

Dr Laurence Godfrey was a lecturer in physics, mathematics, and computer science based in London. On 13 January 1997, a posting, apparently originating in the US, was made to an internet newsgroup *soc.culture.thai* which although we are not told the exact nature of, is referred to by Moreland J as 'squalid, obscene and defamatory of the Plaintiff'.

Demon Internet carried the *soc.culture.thai* forum and stored postings for about a fortnight during which time the posting was available to be read by its customers.

On 17 January 1997, Dr Godfrey sent a fax to Demon Internet informing them that the posting was a forgery and that he was not responsible for its posting and requesting them to remove the posting from their Usenet news server as it was defamatory of him.

The defamatory posting was not removed as requested but remained available on the Demon Usenet server until its expiry on 27 January 1997. As a result of this Dr Godfrey raised a defamation action against Demon Internet.

---

[92] *ibid*, [14].   [93] *ibid*, [15].
[94] No. 07-1101 (7th Cir., March 14, 2008): http://www.ca7.uscourts.gov/tmp/L41FFRTU.pdf.
[95] 51 Cal.Rptr.3d 55 (Cal. Sup. Ct., 2006). This case is discussed further below.
[96] [1999] 4 All ER 342; [1999] EWHC QB 244.

There were two primary questions in issue. The first was, in applying the multiple publication rule were Demon Internet the publishers of the statement on each of the occasions a Demon customer accessed it via the Demon Server? The second was, could Demon avail itself of the defences contained in s. 1 of the Defamation Act 1996? On the first issue Moreland J was clear: 'In my judgment the Defendants were clearly not the publisher of the posting defamatory of the Plaintiff within the meaning of Section 1(2) and 1(3) and incontrovertibly can avail themselves of Section 1(1)(a)'.[97] He was, unfortunately for Demon Internet, equally as unequivocal on the second question: 'However the difficulty facing the Defendants is Section 1(1)(b) and 1(1)(c). After the 17th January 1997 after receipt of the Plaintiff's fax the Defendants knew of the defamatory posting but chose not to remove it from their Usenet news servers. In my judgment this places the Defendants in an insuperable difficulty so that they cannot avail themselves of the defence provided by Section 1'.[98]

In effect the decision of *Godfrey* is to treat information society service providers as akin to distributors, or republishers, that is they are immune from suit, under s. 1 of the Defamation Act 1996, until such time as they are made aware of the nature of the defamatory material. At this point then under s. 1(1)(c), their immunity is stripped and by s. 1(1)(b) they are required to 'take reasonable care in relation to its publication': in practice they must decide whether the statement is likely to be defamatory and if they believe it may be they must take steps to prevent further distribution or republication of the statement or face liability. This provides a balanced approach where information society providers are not expected to actively monitor content they carry and/or host but where, unlike the position in the US following the promulgation of § 230 of the Communication Decency Act, liability may arise from a failure to act once they have been made aware of the defamatory nature of the content in question.

Soon after the *Godfrey* decision a change was made to the UK law in this area. The European Commission had for some time been looking to harmonise European Law in this area and in the Electronic Commerce Directive[99] a number of provisions were brought forward to harmonise the liability of ISPs for (a) carrying, (b) caching, and (c) hosting material including obscene material and defamatory material.

→ **Highlight** E-Commerce Directive Articles 12–14

Article 12: Where an information society service is provided that consists of the transmission in a communication network of information provided by a recipient of the service, or the provision of access to a communication network, Member States shall ensure that the service provider is not liable for the information transmitted.

→

[97] *ibid*, [19].   [98] *ibid*, [20].
[99] Directive 2000/31/EC of the European Parliament and of the Council of 8 June 2000, OJ L 178, 17 July 2000.

> ➡
>
> **Article 13:** Where an information society service is provided that consists of the transmission in a communication network of information provided by a recipient of the service, Member States shall ensure that the service provider is not liable for the automatic, intermediate and temporary storage of that information, performed for the sole purpose of making more efficient the information's onward transmission to other recipients of the service upon their request.
>
> **Article 14:** Where an information society service ... consists of the storage of information provided by a recipient of the service, Member States shall ensure that the service provider is not liable for the information stored at the request of a recipient of the service, on condition that: (a) the provider does not have actual knowledge of illegal activity or information and, as regards claims for damages, is not aware of facts or circumstances from which the illegal activity or information is apparent; or (b) the provider, upon obtaining such knowledge or awareness, acts expeditiously to remove or to disable access to the information.

Article 12 creates a 'mere conduit' defence similar to that given to telecommunications companies and which protects them from slander claims 'published' by the telephone network. This defence will not apply if the ISP originated or modifies the content of the message. Article 13 extends a caching defence. Again there are requirements that the ISP does not originate or modify the content of the message, but with this defence comes a further requirement that 'the provider acts expeditiously to remove or to disable access to the information it has stored upon obtaining actual knowledge of the fact that the information at the initial source of the transmission has been removed from the network, or access to it has been disabled, or that a court or an administrative authority has ordered such removal or disablement'.[100] This requires ISPs who retain cache copies of web pages or other content to remove such copies from their system once they become aware that the original has been removed for whatever reason. Failure to do so may expose such ISPs to liability for the content they cache. Article 14 provides that ISPs who host material have a form of distributor defence not dissimilar to that seen in *Godfrey*. In harmonising the rules for liability of information society service providers the E-commerce Directive does remarkably little to change the previous UK Law, with perhaps the only major change being the introduction of the take-down requirement for cache copies found in Article 13(1)(e).

The UK gave effect to the E-commerce Directive in the E-Commerce (EC Directive) Regulations 2002.[101] Regulations 17, 18, and 19 repeat the wording of the Articles 12, 13, and 14 almost verbatim. A significant addition to the Directive's provisions is though to be found in reg. 22. Reflecting criticisms made of the Directive in an earlier DTI consultation, reg. 22 attempts to address the issue of what constitutes 'actual knowledge' for the purpose of regs 18 and 19. This provides an illustrative list of factors which a court

---

[100] Art. 13(1)(e).   [101] SI 2002/2013.

may consider in determining whether a service provider has received notice through any means of contact that the service provider has made available, as required by reg. 6(1)(c).[102] To date the Regulations appear to have functioned extremely smoothly. Despite some initial concerns that the Regulations may be abused by individuals and organisations who sought to use the notification procedure to take down critical comment this appears not to have been the case. In fact to date only two significant cases which review intermediary liability under the Regulations have reached the courts.

The first is *Bunt v Tilley & Ors*.[103] Mr Bunt claimed that Mr Tilley and two other individuals had made defamatory statements about him using online services. He wished also bring proceeding against three information service providers on the basis that the individual defendants published the offending words 'via the services provided' by their ISPs, although as Eady J pointed out he did not plead that any of the three corporate defendants had at any stage hosted any website relevant to the claims.[104] The foundation of Mr Bunt's claims against the ISPs seemed to be that they had enabled the individuals in question to publish the allegedly defamatory statements by providing them a connection to the internet. This claim raised substantial points of significance as to the basis upon which a provider of such services could, if at all, be liable in respect of material which is simply communicated via the services which they provide. Should Eady J side with Mr Bunt's interpretation of the Regulations, ISPs could be liable for any material they carried across their network, even if they themselves did not host said material should they become aware of the nature of the material their customer was publishing and fail to take steps to block their customer from continuing to use their service. Fortunately for the information service industry Eady J dismissed Mr Bunt's claims. He held that ISPs fell within the definition of 'information society service' provider by applying the definition of an information society service given in reg. 2(1) of the E-Commerce (EC Directive) Regulations.[105] They were therefore able to rely upon defences within regs 17–19 and the claims against the ISPs were accordingly struck out. In a sense *Bunt* merely confirms what we thought we already knew; that the Regulations prevent the attribution of liability to telephone companies or other passive telecommunications providers (such as ISPs) for the distribution of defamatory material over their communication networks.

The second, more recent, case is *Metropolitan International Schools Ltd v Designtechnica Corp*.[106] Here, the claimant claimed that the first defendant hosted several web fora in which threads were hosted which accused the claimant (a distance learning operator) of a number of faults including providing poor value for money, exploiting students and being 'little more than a scam'. The third defendant in the action was search engine giant Google. The claimant claimed they were jointly liable as they: 'published or caused to be published at www.google.co.uk and/or www.google.com a search return for the Train2Game thread which ... set out the following words defamatory of the Claimant as the third and fourth highest search result: "Train2Game new SCAM

---

[102] Reg. 6(1) obliges an ISP to make certain information available to the end user 'in a form ... which is easily, directly and permanently accessible'. Regulation 6(1)(c) refers to the service provider's contact details, including email addresses, which facilitate rapid and direct communication with the ISP.   [103] [2006] EWHC 407 (QB); [2006] 3 All ER 336.   [104] *ibid*, [5].
[105] *ibid*, [41].   [106] [2009] EWHC 1765 (QB).

for Scheidegger"'.[107] Mr Justice Eady was asked by Google to deny a request to serve the order out of jurisdiction on Google. The case therefore became the first UK case to examine the liability of search engine providers for defamation committed on a catalogued website.

At the heart of the claim were Google's previews. Each search return displays not only a link to the page but also one or two lines of text which preview the page. It was these previews which contained the defamatory material referred to above. Eady J began by distinguishing the decision in *Godfrey*. He found that Google was not the 'publisher' of the snippet, noting that: 'A search engine is a different kind of Internet intermediary. It is not possible to draw a complete analogy with a website host. One cannot merely press a button to ensure that the offending words will never reappear on a Google search snippet: there is no control over the search terms typed in by future users. If the words are thrown up in response to a future search, it would by no means follow that the Third Defendant has authorised or acquiesced in that process … [and on this basis] I believe it is unrealistic to attribute responsibility for publication to the Third Defendant, whether on the basis of authorship or acquiescence'.[108]

Eady J went on to consider whether the search engine giant could be liable as an intermediary carrier, and vitally whether the provisions of the E-Commerce (EC Directive) Regulations would apply to them. In the instant case he found no liability for Google on the basis of his previous analysis but found that 'the United Kingdom government has so far taken the view that it is unnecessary or inappropriate to extend protection expressly to search engines. It would not be appropriate, therefore, for me to proceed as though there were a comparable statute in effect in this jurisdiction. I think that, for the Third Defendant to be classified as or deemed a "host", statutory intervention would be needed'.[109] As a first instance decision this case is of influential authority only, although a dearth of alternative authorities suggests that it will be highly influential should similar facts arise. On this basis it is somewhat of a mixed victory for Google, for although Eady J found they were not liable as publishers, and vitally were found to have no duty to 'take down' material under the *Godfrey* principle as they were 'not hosting a website and do not have anything from which to "take down" the offending words',[110] they have been denied entry to the safe harbour provisions found in the Regulations. No doubt Google would argue that it is better to be found not liable in the first place than to have to seek shelter in the safe harbour, and that is undoubtedly true, but to draw a distinction between ISPs and hosts on the one hand and search engine providers on the other may yet have unforeseen consequences.

7.4 **Digital defamation and UGC**

In the web 2.0 environment User Generated Content (UGC) is king. In everything from consumer reviews in sites such as *TripAdvisor* to user generated videos on *YouTube*, the web 2.0 economy is built on UGC. The problem with UGC though is its completely unfiltered nature which increases greatly the risks of defamation occurring.

---

[107] *ibid*, [15] (Scheidegger was the former trading name of the claimant).   [108] *ibid*, [55], [64].
[109] *ibid*, [112].   [110] *ibid*, [78].

An increasing number of cases are being brought against individuals and services which host UGC as web 2.0 services take off. Many cases are minor in nature but demonstrate a propensity for an increase in this type of defamation action. For example a fifteen year old schoolboy in Finland was found guilty of criminal libel for a video he posted on *YouTube* showing his teacher singing at the school party with English subtitles under the headline 'Karaoke of the mental hospital'.[111] Meanwhile in the US a defamation action by literary agent Barbara Bauer against Wikipedia and twenty others over a Wikipedia entry entitled '20 Worst Literary Agents' continues despite Wikipedia wining a summary judgement declaring that it is immune from suit in this matter due to §230 of the Communications Decency Act.[112]

It may be that Wikipedia's co-defendants in this action also find themselves protected by the wide reach of §230. In an earlier Californian case, *Barrett v Rosenthal*,[113] the Supreme Court of California held that an individual who was alleged to have committed libel by maliciously distributing defamatory statements in emails and internet postings could be protected by §230. It must be stressed that in this case the defendant was not the author of the statements in question, only the distributor. The case arose when women's health advocate Ilena Rosenthal posted a controversial opinion piece on a Usenet news group. The piece was written not by Rosenthal, but by Tim Bolen, an outspoken critic of the plaintiffs, Drs Stephen Barrett and Timothy Polevoy, who operate web sites devoted to exposing health frauds. The Court held that in examining distributor liability 'Congress did not intend for an internet user to be treated differently than an internet provider'.[114] Thus, in California at least, an individual who distributes or republishes a defamatory statement is given equal protection with an information service provider who does likewise. It is highly unlikely such a result would occur in the UK given the narrow definition of an information service provider in the E-commerce Regulations. Rather the best advice to give to individuals in the UK is to be cautious in any statement they publish, republish, or otherwise distribute.

The reason for recommending caution is clear from the few UK cases dealing with individual liability for statement made in the online environment. The first reported case was *Keith-Smith v Williams*.[115] This involved a series of claims made on a Yahoo! discussion group called 'In the Hole' by Tracey Williams about Michael Keith-Smith, a UK Independence Party candidate in the 2005 general election. Among other claims Ms Williams suggested that Mr Keith-Smith was a racist, a Nazi, a sex offender, and a sexual deviant. Ms Williams may have thought she was safe from litigation as she did all this hiding behind a pseudonym. Mr Keith-Smith obtained a court order requiring Yahoo! to identify Ms Williams and in an undefended action in the High Court in March 2006 he secured a total award of £10,000 in damages, being £5,000 in compensatory damages and £5,000 in aggravated damages. Although the Judge notes

---

[111] Reuters, *Teen fined for YouTube karaoke video*, 24 August 2007: http://www.reuters.com/article/internetNews/idUSL2478621120070824.

[112] See *Judge Dismisses Bauer Lawsuit Against Wikimedia/Wikipedia*: http://dearauthor.com/wordpress/2008/07/03/judge-dismisses-bauer-lawsuit-against-wikimediawikipedia/.

[113] 51 Cal.Rptr.3d 55 (Cal Sup Ct, 2006).   [114] *ibid*, 87.   [115] [2006] EWHC 860 (QB).

with some regret that 'the defendant possibly, or indeed probably, does not have the means to pay an award of damages or costs',[116] he felt it important to make the award to clear Mr Keith-Smith's reputation.

This case has been followed by a flurry of other cases examining personal liability for postings in internet discussion fora. In *Sheffield Wednesday Football Club & Ors v Hargreaves*,[117] the court was asked to make a so-called 'Norwich Pharmaceutical Order', that is an order that a person who assists another in committing a tort must reveal the identity of the wrongdoer to allow the party who has suffered harm to take action. Mr Hargreaves was the operator of a site called *owlstalk.co.uk* a specialist site for fans of Sheffield Wednesday football club to discuss matters relating to the club. Although Mr Hargreaves himself never posted any inflammatory or defamatory statements several of his users did, including some statements questioning the financial probity of several of the directors of the club. Mr Hargreaves refused to name the individuals without a court order. In discussing whether or not to make the order to identify eleven users of the *owlstalk* board, Judge Richard Parkes QC, noted a balance had to be struck between the rights of those allegedly defamed and the rights of the posters to privacy. Applying this balance he ruled that the identity of seven of the eleven individuals should be protected, stating: 'I do not think it would be right to make an order for the disclosure of the identities of users who have posted messages which are barely defamatory or little more than abusive or likely to be understood as jokes. That, it seems to me, would be disproportionate and unjustifiably intrusive'.[118] The remaining four though had posted statements which Judge Parkes thought 'may reasonably be understood to allege greed, selfishness, untrustworthiness and dishonest behaviour on the part of the Claimants'. He concluded 'in the case of those postings, the Claimants' entitlement to take action to protect their right to reputation outweighs, in my judgment, the right of the authors to maintain their anonymity and their right to express themselves freely'.[119] Thus four users of the *owlstalk* board were identified, although reports in the media suggest no further action was taken.[120]

7.4.1 Facebook libel

Probably the most interesting UK case to date on UGC and libel is the infamous *Facebook* libel case: *Applause Store Productions Ltd & Anor v Raphael*.[121] On 19 June 2007, a false Facebook profile for Matthew Firsht was set up, containing private information including reference to his date of birth, relationship status, purported sexual preferences, and his political and religious views. The following day a Facebook group was set up, with a link to the profile, called 'Has Matthew Firsht lied to you?' This contained material which was defamatory of him and his company Applause Store, indicating he owed substantial sums which he avoided paying with lies and implausible excuses.[122]

---

[116] *ibid*, [15].   [117] [2007] EWHC 2375 (QB).   [118] *ibid*, [17].   [119] *ibid*, [18].
[120] P. Gray, 'UK Libel Law v Freedom of Expression', *Liverpool Daily Post*, 14 October 2008: http://www.thelegalweek.merseyblogs.co.uk/2008/10/blog-uk-libel-law-v-freedom-of.html.
[121] [2008] EWHC 1781 (QB).   [122] *ibid*, [3]–[4].

Mr Firsht discovered the false profile and group page on 4 July 2007 and requested it be removed. It was removed on 6 July 2007 and on 1 August 2007 his solicitors obtained a 'Norwich Pharmaceutical Order' order against Facebook for disclosure of the registration data provided by the creator of the offending material. That evidence indicated that the defendant created both the profile and the group page. The defendant was known to Mr Firsht, being a former close friend of Mr Firsht. This suggested he had indeed set up the profile page as whoever created the profile knew that Mr Firsht had a twin brother, was from Brighton, practised a variety of Judaism, and was familiar with his company and work as well as the unusual spelling of his name.[123]

Mr Raphael denied setting up either the profile or the group page: he suggested he had an alibi but this was rejected by Judge Richard Parkes QC. With this established the Judge looked at the harm caused by the placing of the false statements on the *Facebook* site. The first problem Mr Firsht faced was overcoming the *Jameel* principle as *Facebook* does not store data showing how many users view a profile or group. Therefore he could not produce evidence of publication which extended beyond a small group of six who actually saw the material, all of whom were connected to him in some way.[124] However, Judge Parkes accepted that *Facebook* was a medium in which users regularly searched for the names of others whom they know, and anyone who had done so against Mr Firsht's name in the time between the publication of the false entries and their removal would have found the offending material without difficulty. He judged that it was likely 'a not insubstantial number of people [would] have done so. By that I have in mind a substantial two-figure, rather than a three-figure, number'.[125]

With the *Jameel* hurdle cleared it was necessary to show harm had occurred to Mr Firsht and his company. Judge Parkes, commented that although the libel was 'not at the top end of the scale, it is serious enough to say of a successful businessman that (as I have found the words to mean) he owes substantial sums of money which he has repeatedly avoided paying by lying and making implausible excuses, so that he is not to be trusted in the financial conduct of his business and represents a serious credit risk'.[126] On this basis he awarded libel damages of £15,000 to Mr Firsht, including aggravated damages to reflect the fact that Mr Raphael denied making the remarks and £5,000 to Applause Store Productions.

This is believed to be the first successful claim of *Facebook* defamation worldwide and it provides some valuable cues as to how future claims on social networking sites may be fought.

The first is that the judge was willing to accept that substantial publication had occurred within the jurisdiction of the court without actual evidence of the number of publications being forthcoming. The judge appeared to be particularly swayed on this point by one piece of evidence: 'The fact that the false profile and group were placed on the London network, which then had over 850,000 members, to any of whom they would have been visible. In that connection, [counsel for the Claimant] points to the fact that one Clifford White, who had offices at Elstree Studios, sent an email to the profile less than 30 minutes after it was created, saying that he had just found Mr Firsht on Facebook and wondered if

---

[123] *ibid*, [48].   [124] *ibid*, [70].   [125] *ibid*, [78].   [126] *ibid*, [79].

he would be interested in setting up a Facebook club for "studio residents"'.[127] Does this suggest that if one finds a false and defamatory profile in a smaller network such as a School or University network it will be more difficult to establish 'substantial publication'? With no records kept by Facebook any future litigation of this type will need to rely on circumstantial evidence such as that adduced in the *Applause Store* case.

The second is that the judge was swayed by the easy availability of the false content placing value on the fact that a search against Mr Firsht's name during the period of publication would lead to individuals 'finding offending material without difficulty'. Again one wonders whether Mr Firsht's rather unusual name assisted in this. A quick search of Facebook for the author's name reveals it to be extremely common and groups tend to be dominated by tennis fans. However, one must assume the principle of a simple search facility provided by social networking sites would apply equally no matter how common the name.

Finally, despite there being no evidence of actual financial loss, the judge was willing to make a substantial award of damages. This may be seen to be evidence of the scale of social networking sites. With a potential audience of 850,000 Facebook users and no way to be able to quantify how many of them read the defamatory entries the judge seems to have been sufficiently convinced that any harm suffered may be not insubstantial, hence, at least in part the enhanced reward.

7.4.2 **Libel in the blogosphere**

More recently evidence is emerging of the courts taking a hard line with cases which appear to be abusing the libel procedure. In *Smith v ADVFN Plc & Ors*,[128] Eady J stayed thirty-seven libel actions raised by Mr Smith, arising out of comments made in online fora about Mr Smith's role as coordinator of an action group to recover shareholders investments from the alleged 'Langbar fraud', a City fraud uncovered in 2005. Eady J found that 'in a number of these cases, it is obvious to me that there would be strong defences of qualified privilege or fair comment and, in some cases, arguments running along the lines of "mere vulgar abuse"'.[129]

It appeared Mr Smith was involved in the practice known as 'flaming'—a hostile and insulting interaction between internet users, and would use the responses he received to begin a libel action.[130] Eady J took a dim view of this commenting that 'many would be surprised to see any of this made the stuff of libel proceedings—the object of which is to restore reputation'.[131] In the end Eady J not only stayed the proceedings in the cases before him, he issued a civil restraining order against Mr Smith preventing him from raising any further libel proceedings on the matter before the court without Eady J's permission, this was ordered once Eady J became aware that Mr Smith planned to issue a further twenty-three claims in the next three months. Eady J was though careful to

---

[127] *ibid*, [70].   [128] [2008] EWHC 1797 (QB).   [129] *ibid*, [24].
[130] As Eady J. noted at [18] 'Several of the Defendants have made the point that Mr Smith would be well aware of all this and that he has shown himself to be unrestrained in "dishing it out". Indeed, some of the remarks of which he now complains were themselves prompted by the way he was behaving towards others. In particular, he had been very critical of someone known as "Wiganer". This led in turn to criticisms of his behaviour. This was mainly on the basis that there was in his case plenty of "give" but no willingness to "take"'.   [131] *ibid*, [23].

confine his ruling to the facts, saying that he would not suggest for a moment that '"blogging" cannot ever form the basis of a legitimate libel claim'.[132]

Most recently the courts revisited this issue in *Carrie v Tolkien*.[133] This is a most unusual case as the claimant was complaining about posts made to his blog which he had complete editorial control over. This led Eady J to conclude that Mr Carrie had 'acquiesced in the continuing publications since the original date of publication'.[134] As a result he would only entertain a claim for damages based upon the period of time between initial publication and the when Mr Carrie discovered the posting; a maximum period of four hours and nineteen minutes. With the plaintiff unable to establish that any publication of the statement had occurred in this timeframe, much less substantial publication, Eady J was forced to conclude that 'this would appear to be a suitable case to classify the claim as an abuse of process, in accordance with the *Jameel* doctrine, because of the minimal (if any) level of publication'.[135]

No doubt a considerable body of litigation will build up over the next few years on issues surrounding UGC and defamation in the UK. These five cases represent the tip of the iceberg. A considerable number of actions never reach the courts and those that do often settle before hearing. In addition most of the UK cases to date deal with web 1.0 bulletin board systems, only *Applause Store and Carrie* are true web 2.0 cases. It is to be expected that more cases will arise surrounding blog postings, YouTube postings, and social network entries. It is already known that many celebrity Twitter accounts are in fact operated by imposters,[136] it only seems to be a matter of time until one of these imposters is pursued for making a defamatory statement. Digital defamation may be one of the greatest challenges for high profile individuals and businesses in the information society.

7.5 **Conclusion**

As a communications media the internet is an obvious breeding ground for comment which is harmful. In addition several unique characteristics of cyberspace make the publication of defamatory content more likely online than in any other mass media fora. The impression of anonymity that the internet gives affords people the sense of security that encourages the making of reckless statements, some of which may be defamatory. The cross border nature of the network allows individuals to defame from overseas and to seek the protection of provisions such as the First Amendment to the US Constitution. The internet archives material for later access in a more efficient way than other mass media allowing defamatory statements to be found easily and accessed long after they were originally made, and finally the encouragement to participate and create found in web 2.0 is turning everyone into a social networker or citizen journalist.

While there is no doubt that overall the freedom of expression afforded to individuals via the internet is a force for good in society, we cannot allow individual reputations to be

---

[132] *ibid*, [108].   [133] [2009] EWHC 29 (QB).   [134] *ibid*, [15].   [135] *ibid*, [19].
[136] See, e.g. A. Semuels, 'Dalai Lama imposter escorted from Twitter', *LA Times*, 9 February 2009: http://latimesblogs.latimes.com/technology/2009/02/twitter-dalai-l.html; NME News, *David Bowie: 'I don't have a Twitter account'* 28 January 2009: http://www.nme.com/news/david-bowie/42375.

sullied because of the thoughtless actions of a few. This is the challenge of online defamation. As we have seen throughout this chapter issues such as the multiple publication rule, international and cross-border publications and the liability of intermediaries and carriers have all been to the fore. The application of the multiple publication rule in cases such as *Loutchansky* have challenged the usual rules on both the time and place of publication, arguably rendering the limitation period valueless and extending the availability of forum shopping. Although later cases such as *Jameel* and *Al Amoudi* have taken steps to rebalance the rights of the competing parties it is clear that internet republication has forced a substantial rethink of what is means to publish a statement. This may lead to a substantial change in the fabric of UK law of defamation at the conclusion of the Ministry of Justice consultation on the multiple publication rule. In the interim we may expect more decisions in the style of *Jameel* and *Al Amoudi* as judges attempt to strike a balance between the interests of free expression and the rights of the defamed.

Further, as often online defamation occurs in anonymity, or may be caused by the actions of an individual domiciled overseas where enforcement may prove difficult we are likely to see a continuation of the line of cases on intermediary liability which began in the UK with the *Godfrey* case and which most recently may be seen in the *Designtechnica* case. The UK/EU Law arguably strikes a sensible balance here with the safe harbour provisions found in the European Law much more balanced than their US equivalent in § 230 of the CDA. While US courts have spent much of the last ten years trying to narrow the application of § 230, UK courts have developed a sophisticated jurisprudence surrounding the European safe harbour provisions. It may be argued that Eady J was unsophisticated in his approach in *Designtechnica*, in which he found Google to be not liable as they had no control rather than finding they had the protection of the safe harbour,[137] but despite this the application of the safe harbour principle has been much more successful in the UK than in the US with a balanced and sensible approach to intermediary liability being followed.

Finally we come to the very topical and growing issue of UGC defamation. The explosion of interest surrounding social networking sites such as Facebook, MySpace and Twitter have changed the nature of social interaction. Individuals no longer communicate in small groups in pubs, restaurants or clubs they now socialise online in large groups. While offline statements tended to stay in the ether for a few seconds before disappearing they are now retained in a publicly accessible forum. The growth of social network defamation is likely to be one of the defining points of information technology law in the next ten years. The *Applause Store* case is unlikely to be the last word on this, while impersonators on Twitter may soon also attract the attention of defamation lawyers.[138] This is not necessarily a bad thing. Anything which causes people to show respect and consideration for their fellow user can only be positive.

---

[137] A curious decision for as he pointed out himself 'Google has taken steps to ensure that certain identified URLs are blocked, in the sense that when web-crawling takes place, the content of such URLs will not be displayed in response to Google searches carried out on Google.co.uk': *Metropolitan International Schools Ltd v Designtechnica Corp*, above n. 106, [57].

[138] In the first Twitter impersonation case Barrister Matthew Richardson used s. 84 of the Copyright, Designs and Patents Act 1988 to prevent an imposter from continuing his pretence of being Blogger Donal Blaney. Equally though anything the imposter tweeted which lowered the reader's opinion of Blaney could have formed the basis of an action in defamation. See n. 73 above.

FURTHER READING

Books

M. Collins, *The Law of Defamation and the Internet* (2 ed., 2005)

D.J. Solove, *The Future of Reputation: Gossip, Rumor, and Privacy on the Internet* (2008)

D. Rolph, *Reputation, Celebrity and Defamation Law* (2008)

Chapters and Articles

J. Zittrain, 'Be Careful What You Ask For: Reconciling a Global Internet and Local Law' in A. Thierer (ed.), *Who Rules the Net?: Internet Governance and Jurisdiction* (2003)

T. Ludbrook, 'Defamation and the Internet: where are we now and where are we going?' [2004] *Entertainment Law Review* 173, 203

B. Malloy, 'Anonymous Blogging and Defamation: Balancing Interests of the Internet.' 84 *Washington University Law Review* 1187 (2006)

PART III

Digital content and intellectual property rights

Intellectual Property Law as applied to digital goods and services. How laws designed for 'creations of the mind' have been adapted and applied in the digital environment: The challenge of free content vs reward.

8   **Intellectual property rights and the information society**

    8.1 An introduction to IPRs

    8.2 IPRs and digitisation

9   **Software**

    9.1 Protecting software: history

    9.2 Copyright in computer software

    9.3 Copyright infringement and software: literal copying

    9.4 Copyright infringement and software: non-literal copying

    9.5 Copyright infringement and software: permitted acts

    9.6 Patent protection for computer software

    9.7 Conclusion

10 **Copyright in the digital environment**

    10.1 Linking, caching, and aggregating

    10.2 Peer-to-peer networks

    10.3 Information and the public domain

    10.4 Conclusion

11 **Databases**

    11.1 Copyright and the database right

    11.2 The database right

    11.3 Databases and the information society

12 **Branding and trade marks in the information society**

    12.1 Trade marks and branding

    12.2 Trade marks in the global business environment

    12.3 Domain names as badges of identity

    12.4 Trade mark/domain name disputes

    12.5 The ICANN UDRP

    12.6 The nominet DRS

    12.7 Brand identities, search engines and secondary markets

    12.8 Conclusion

Intellectual property rights and the information society

Intellectual property is a subject with a complex and varied history. It can trace its roots back to the late medieval period, but for a long period little interest was shown by the legal profession in this marginal and esoteric subject. It was never taught in the under-graduate LLB syllabus and was rarely seen even at LLM level. Textbooks on intellectual property law were scarce with William Cornish's 1980 text *Intellectual Property* probably the first such book published in the UK. All this was about to change though. With the move from the post-industrial society to the information society interest in intellectual property and intellectual property rights (or IPRs) exploded. The information society and more importantly the information economy placed value in information rather than in physical goods, industrial processes, or even services. The only body of law which had a relationship with information in its pure form was the long neglected intellectual property rights and so lawyers and law schools had to quickly reacquaint themselves with this marginalised subject.

It quickly became apparent that intellectual property and the information society shared a common root: both dealt with protecting the economic value of intangibles. Nothing in the digital environment can be touched, held, or physically possessed. In nature this makes virtual goods similar in form to intellectual property. The parallels with in particular the law of copyright are clear. Copyright is awarded to the expression of an idea, rather than to a thing. But the expression must be recorded in some form for the copyright to take effect. Thus when we think of copyright goods we think of physical items, most commonly books manufactured from paper and binding or music CDs or video DVDs. Of course the physical element of the copyright product is not the part of the product protected by copyright: the book, CD, or DVD is merely a physical carrier for the informational product.[1] The same is true of digital goods in the informa-tion society. As we saw in Chapter 5, digital goods have no weight or form, and to be possessed we need a carrier media for them, usually in the form of a hard drive or an internet server or else in the form of a flash memory card or old fashioned CD or DVD. There is therefore a natural synergy between traditional intellectual goods and modern information goods. The character traits they share mean that as the information society was going through its formative phase, Intellectual Property Rights, or IPRs, became the

---

[1] See J. P. Barlow, 'The Economy of Ideas: Selling Wine Without Bottles on the Global Net', *Wired 2.03*, March 1994.

natural interface between the traditional legal world and the developing informational society. This interface still plays an important role today with copyright forming the backbone of our system for the protection and exploitation of software as well as forming a focal point for the ongoing debate between the rights of artists and creators to be rewarded in the information society and for individuals to share and distribute content of all types. The law of trade marks still drives domain name disputes and search engine keyword disputes, while new forms of IPRs such as the database right have developed to meet some of the unique challenges of the digital society. This section will examine some of the key relationships between IPRs and the information society, beginning here with a short introduction to IPRs, including a short discussion of their role and history.

8.1 **An introduction to IPRs**

Intellectual Property Rights are the collective name given to a suite of legal protections, mostly Statutory, but some at Common Law, which seek to protect the creator, author, or inventor of an intangible creation. There are many theories as to the development and role of IPRs in modern society[2] although the most common theme is the protection of the incentive-innovation-reward cycle.[3] This states that innovations or creations which benefit society as a whole should be encouraged and the creator should be rewarded for their creation. As intellectual property is intangible it would be easy for a free-rider to replicate the valuable creation of the original author or inventor without rewarding him or her for their creativity. Thus the author of a book could find unauthorised copies of their book being printed and circulated with no reward to them for their creativity,[4] or the inventor of a new industrial process could find competitors using their invention to compete against them in the marketplace. As intellectual property can be so easily misappropriated without some form of legal protection for these 'fruits of the mind' there would no incentive to create.

Intellectual Property Rights, by protecting the creator/inventor/author, build a cycle of incentive-innovation-reward which benefits society as a whole. The cycle begins by incentivising creative individuals to spend time indulging their creativity secure in the knowledge that should they produce something valuable they will eventually be rewarded for this. By allowing creative individuals the time to create they produce something innovative, whether that be an innovation capable of industrial application (an invention) or an innovative cultural product (such as a book, film, or music). Knowing that they are protected by IPRs that person then publishes or otherwise exploits their innovative output at which point they are rewarded through means such as royalty

---

[2] See e.g. W. Cornish, *Intellectual Property: Omnipresent, Distracting, Irrelevant?* (2004); W. Landes & R. Posner, *The Economic Structure of Intellectual Property Law* (2003); R. Blair & T. Cotter, *Intellectual Property: Economic and Legal Dimensions of Rights and Remedies* (2005); R. Spinello & H. Tavani, *Intellectual Property Rights in a Networked World: Theory and Practice* (2004).

[3] H. MacQueen, C. Waelde & G. Laurie, *Contemporary Intellectual Property: Law and Policy* (2008), 11.

[4] This often occurred in the nineteenth century USA which failed to recognise the copyright of other states. This policy was attacked by Charles Dickens in his lecture tour of the US in 1842.

payments. The financial security this offers allows them to begin the whole process anew at the incentive stage.

IPRs are an essential part of modern society: they underpin a great number of creative industries including the music and film industries, the computer software and games industries, publishing, dance, theatre and drama, pharmaceuticals, and the computer industry. There are a large variety of IPRs ranging from the three central IPRs: copyright for the original expression of ideas, patents for inventions capable of industrial application, and trade marks for badges or signs capable of distinguishing the operation or product of one business from another, to the newer or less common IPRs including the database right for organised bodies of information, registered and unregistered design rights for industrial and architectural designs, semiconductor topography rights for designs of microchips, and plant variety rights for newly engineered plant varieties. In this text we will focus only on those which have the greatest interaction with informational goods and services: copyright, patents (only in relation to computer software), trade marks, and the database right. In order to provide the backdrop to the chapters which follow there will now follow a short introduction to these four rights.

8.1.1 **Copyright**

Copyright was developed in the sixteenth and seventeenth centuries as a response to the rapid growth of moveable type printing presses which facilitated the production and distribution of printed text. We can think of copyright as the first legal response to a challenge of new technology and the development of copyright may be seen to be analogous to the development of legal rules and principles for the information society. Prior to the development of moveable type printing press technology by Johannes Gutenberg in what is now modern day Germany in the 1440s, the concept of having rights in creative works had never been considered. Creative works were nonrivalrous, meaning that the fruits of the labour of the mind could be shared between many.[5]

The nature of creative works meant that when the concept of exclusive property in land and goods was developed, there was no parallel for works of the mind. Throughout the intellectual highs of the ancient Greek and Roman worlds and the intellectual dark ages which followed, there was no exclusive property in the written or spoken word. During this period creative works were often distributed by travelling storytellers, usually wandering minstrels, who would travel from town to town and engage in singing, acting, storytelling, and comedy. With most citizens unable to read the minstrel was often the only way for individuals to learn the stories from the scriptures, or to hear news of recent events such as famous victories in battle. The concept of anyone 'owning' such knowledge would have been quite impossible for the average mediaeval European to imagine.

The printing press changed all this. It industrialised the process of distribution, replacing the scribe or the minstrel with the press and the bookseller. This meant an industry

---

[5] As famously recounted by Thomas Jefferson in his *Letter to Isaac McPherson*, 13 August 1813, where he notes: 'He who receives an idea from me, receives instruction himself without lessening mine; as he who lights his taper at mine, receives light without darkening me.' Full text: http://odur.let.rug.nl/~usa/P/tj3/writings/brf/jefl220.htm.

grew up around publishing, a profitable industry in which often the profits went to the publisher and the bookseller, not the author, poet, or playwright.[6] For around one hundred years the publishing industry and the authors who supplied it with its raw materials were in dispute over who had the right to issue copies of works to the general public.[7] This dispute was ended in 1710 when the world's first Copyright Act, the Statute of Anne, came into force. This gave to authors of books, including play texts and poems, a monopoly right to control the publication of copies of their work for a period of twenty-one years (if the work was already published when the Act came into force) or fourteen years (for new works).

The Statute of Anne is the foundation of modern copyright law, which for the UK is to be found in Part I of the Copyright, Designs and Patents Act 1988. Today copyright protects a wide variety of expression. It still protects the written word but now also protects music, dance, theatrical performances, works of art, photographs, sound recordings, films (and video recordings), television and radio broadcasts, and cable programmes. Copyright reaches into almost every aspect of our lives. The most common interactions that people have with copyright on a day to day basis are in their use of modern entertainment products. Music is nearly always sold subject to copyright terms. If you buy a CD or download a track from iTunes, you do not own that music. Instead you are awarded a non-exclusive licence to make use of that music. This does not extend to making copies of the music, playing or performing it in public or selling or distributing further copies. You are given a basic right to listen to the music for your own consumption and usually in the modern digital distribution model to make a limited number of copies on MP3 players or similar devices. The same is true of movies or television programmes. You are entitled to watch a television programme or to make a single recording for the purpose of 'time shifting' the broadcast,[8] you are not though entitled to sell, rebroadcast, or distribute any copy you may make.[9] The other primary point of interaction between the general public and copyright law is in relation to computer software. You are unlikely to own any software on your computer. Again like music and movies computer software is licensed to the end user. When you first install any new software on your computer you will be asked to agree to an 'end-user licence agreement'. This lists all the terms and conditions of your agreement with the software developer who owns the copyright. Most people never read these agreements, simply clicking on the 'I accept' button. This is not good practice as these contracts are legally enforceable and usually contain a number of clauses which limit the software developer's liability for damage or harm and require the customer to accept and install software updates. Occasionally end-user licence agreements can even be used to justify the installation of spyware or similar potentially harmful software on to your computer.

---

[6] It is often recorded that William Shakespeare made his fortune through lands he purchased in Stratford-upon-Avon and from performances of his plays. He made little if any money from productions of Folios of his plays.

[7] This dispute which mostly gave the 'copy-right' to publishers during the seventeenth century is discussed in detail in A. Murray, *The Regulation of Cyberspace: Control in the Online Environment* (2007), 169–175. See also R. Deazley, *On the Origin of the Right to Copy: Charting the Movement of Copyright Law in Eighteenth Century Britain (1695–1775)* (2004).

[8] CDPA 1988, s. 70(1).   [9] CDPA 1988, s. 70(2).

Today copyright arises automatically and persists for an extensive period. For Literary, Dramatic, Musical, and Artistic works, including computer software, this period is the lifetime of the author and for seventy years after his or her death. It is clear this period, designed for traditional literary and artistic works, rather overprotects modern copyright works such as computer software and games, which are unlikely to have a commercial lifespan of more than five years, and with hardware upgrades being constantly developed very few digital devices will survive long enough for original software and gamesware to enter the public domain in a meaningful fashion. Also thanks to international cooperation a copyright valid in one Berne Convention state will be recognised and enforced in other Berne Convention states,[10] meaning that copyright protection is extensive, almost global. It allows the copyright holder a series of exclusive rights to: (1) copy the work; (2) issue copies of the work to the public; (3) to rent or lend the work to the public; (4) to perform, show, or play the work in public; (5) to communicate the work to the public; and (6) to make an adaptation of the work or do any of the above in relation to an adaptation.[11] Anyone who commits any of these acts without the copyright holder's permission infringes copyright allowing the copyright holder to enforce their copyright and to seek an award of damages. Copyright is therefore a diverse and long-lasting right. Although not seen as a particularly powerful form of protection, its wide range of protection and lack of a record of pre-existing copyrights and copyright holders causes a high degree of tension in the information society which is a short-term society with emphasis on immediacy and which has a tendency to 'cut & paste' information.

8.1.2 Patents

Patents are quite different to copyright in terms of aim, scope, and history. Patents originated as Letters Patent, a letter from a Monarch or similar overlord issued to a tradesman offering him a monopoly over a process for a period of time in return for services to the State.

> **➡ Highlight** John of Utynam's Patent
>
> The first recorded Letter Patent in England was issued by King Henry VI to John of Utynam in 1449. John was a glazer with a new methodology for producing coloured glass. The King gave John an exclusive grant of use of his methodology in England for a period of twenty years. In payment the King required John to create stained-glass windows for the King's new educational institutions: Eton College and King's College, Cambridge. Under the terms of the letter John had to tutor his assistants in the skills of making coloured glass ensuring that his techniques would become part of the public domain in England once his patent expired.

---

[10] The 'Berne Convention' is the *Berne Convention for the Protection of Literary and Artistic Works* of 1886.   [11] CDPA 1988, s. 16(1).

The idea of Letters Patent was widespread throughout Europe but it is probably Venice which invented the modern patent system when in 1474 it passed a decree that tradesmen who disclosed a new technology would be granted a ten year monopoly over the use of that technology.[12]

The first formal recognition of a patents system in England, as opposed to individual Letters from the Crown, came in the form of the Statute of Monopolies in 1624. This provided that patents would only be available to 'the true and first inventor' of processes and for a period of not more than fourteen years.[13] This is the foundation of the modern patent system but it left the award of Letters Patent to the discretion of the Crown, it was only in the nineteenth century that the modern system of patent law and procedure developed when in 1852 the Patent Office was established and with it a process for the examination of patent applications and the issuing of a UK patent.

The history of patents is therefore longer and more chequered than the history of Copyright. Although Letters Patent predate Copy Rights, the modern system of copyright became established in the eighteenth century, whereas modern patent law owes much to nineteenth century developments. This probably owes much to the technological drivers behind the two systems. Copyright became industrialised with the development of the movable type printing press in the 1440s whereas patents had to await the industrial revolution driven by the invention of the Boulton and Watt Steam Engine in the 1770s to become industrialised. This emphasises the close historical relationship between IPRs and technology.

Modern UK Patent Law is to be found mostly in the Patents Acts 1977 and 2004, with the 1977 Act containing the bulk of the rules on patentability and enforcement. Strangely the Act does not define an invention, merely instead defining the scope of protection offered to an invention.[14] Instead the Act characterises how an invention may be recognised by setting out a test for patentability.[15]

➡ Highlight Test for Patentability

An invention must:

    (a) be new (usually referred to as novel);

    (b) involve an inventive step;

    (c) be capable of industrial application; and

    (d) not be found within the list of excluded matter.

The list of excluded matter is extremely important as within this list we find 'a scheme, rule or method for performing a mental act, playing a game or doing business, or a

---

[12] MacQueen *et al.*, above n. 3, 360.   [13] Statute of Monopolies 1624, s. 6.
[14] Patents Act 1977, s. 125(1).
[15] Patents Act 1977, s. 1(1). For further discussion on the nature of patentability see MacQueen *et al.*, above n. 3, 433–456.

program for a computer'.[16] This represents a longstanding principle that one should not be able to gain a monopoly over an intellectual or business process. The addition of computer software to this category suggests that a computer programme is viewed primarily as a method of conducting business or perhaps as a substitute for a mental process and as a result steps are taken to exclude software from patentability.[17] In addition it should be noted that material which is capable of protection by copyright is generally excluded from patentability[18] and as we have already seen the Copyright, Designs and Patents Act 1988 treats software as a literary work.[19] Thus on two principles, one a direct exclusionary principle, the other an indirect exclusionary principle, software is not to be treated as a patentable invention. As we shall see in chapter nine the application of this principle is not as simple as one may expect.

Should your invention clear all these hurdles you will be granted a patent after a lengthy examination of your patent application, including publication of the application to allow for public scrutiny of it. A patent is awarded for a maximum period of twenty years, although you will need to pay a renewal fee annually after the first five years of the patent's life. Unlike copyright patents do not arise automatically, they must be registered, and unlike copyright patents are not automatically of international effect. A patent application is only valid in the state in which it is made, and claims often seen on consumer items that a 'worldwide patent [is] applied for' are inaccurate. A multinational patent application may be made under the Patent Cooperation Treaty which allows a single application to be made in a PCT signatory state and undergo a single examination before being passed to other PCT patent offices for local registration. Multinational patent applications are very lengthy, complex, and expensive and thus in many ways we can see patents as the antitheses of copyright: they are a strong and effective monopoly right, but are limited both temporally and geographically, with multinational patents usually only preferred for inventions of a high degree of economic potential.

8.1.3 **Trade marks**

Trade marks are a more modern creation. Like the modern patents system they may be seen to be the fruit of the industrial revolution. Trade marks have their roots in the common law of 'passing off', a claim in tort which first appeared in the early nineteenth century.[20] Passing off allowed, and indeed allows, a business enterprise to protect the goodwill it has established in its trading name or brand identity to raise an action in tort against anyone who damages that goodwill by causing the public to confuse their brand, product, or service with that of the claimant.[21] The three essential elements of a passing off claim were, and remain: (1) the establishment that the claimant has goodwill in the name, brand, or identity in question; (2) that there has been a misrepresentation

---

[16] Patents Act 1977, s. 1(2)(c).

[17] It should be noted that the framers of the Patents Act 1977 were bound to implement this exclusion as there was a similar exclusion in the European Patent Convention of 1973 to which the UK was a signatory.   [18] Patents Act 1977, s. 1(2)(b).   [19] CDPA 1988, s. 3(1)(b).

[20] See C. Wadlow, *The Law of Passing Off* 3rd Rev. ed. (2005); H. Carty, *An Analysis of the Economic Torts* (2001).   [21] See *Perry v Truefitt* (1842) 6 Beav 66.

(by the defendant); and (3) that misrepresentation has caused damage to claimant's goodwill.[22]

The problem with relying on the tortious claim was that the claimant always had to first establish goodwill. It would be much easier if the claimant could instead rely upon some form of presumption. This, along with the growing internationalisation of trade in the late nineteenth century,[23] led to the Trade Marks Registration Act 1875. This created a domestic register of trade marks allowing businesses to protect their brand or identity without the need to establish goodwill during a passing off claim. Unlike patents, or even copyright, trade marks are protected for a potentially unlimited term. Provided the mark remains in use and the trade mark holder renews periodically (currently the term is every ten years) the mark may be retained in perpetuity.[24]

The modern law of trade marks is to be found in the Trade Marks Act 1994. This provides that 'any sign capable of being represented graphically which is capable of distinguishing goods or services of one undertaking from those of other undertakings' may be registered as a trade mark.[25] Once registered the mark must be renewed every ten years.[26] The Act protects the trade mark holder against a variety of threats, including piracy (that is the use in the course of trade of a mark or sign which is *identical* to the trade mark and is used in relation to goods or services similar to those for which the trade mark is registered); unfair competition (that is the use of a sign which is similar to the trade mark and used in relation to goods or services identical with or *similar* to those for which the trade mark is registered and there is a likelihood of confusion); and misappropriation (that is the use of a 'famous mark', being a trade mark which has a 'reputation' in the UK in a manner which without due cause, takes unfair advantage of, or is detrimental to, the distinctive character or the repute of the trade mark).[27]

Internationally trade mark protection functions similarly to patent protection. There is no global or even international trade mark.[28] Trade marks like patents are awarded by domestic trade mark registries and are limited in effectiveness to the jurisdictional reach of the office which registered the mark. Like patents there is a procedure to seek a basket of international trade marks through a cooperation procedure. This is managed by a procedure known as the Madrid system which was created under the Madrid Agreement Concerning the International Registration of Marks of 1891. Under the Madrid system a trade mark owner can apply to have their trade mark protected in several countries simultaneously by filing a single application with their domestic trade mark office and electing to have this application forwarded to any number of Madrid protocol

---

[22] See *Erven Warnink BV v J. Townend & Sons* [1979] AC 731; *Reckitt & Coleman Products v Borden, Inc.* [1990] 1 All ER 873.   [23] MacQueen *et al.*, above n. 3, 541–542.

[24] It should be noted that UK Trade Mark No. 1, a Red Triangle registered on 1 January 1876 (the first day of operation of the new register) by Bass Breweries is still in operation and use.

[25] TMA 1994, s. 1(1) , s. 40(1).   [26] TMA 1994, ss. 42, 43.   [27] TMA 1994, s. 10.

[28] There is though a community trade mark which has effect throughout EU member states and is managed by the Office for Harmonization in the Internal Market (Trade Marks and Designs) (OHIM), which is located in Alicante, Spain. This is similar to the European Patent which is administered by the European Patent Office in Munich. The main distinction between the two being that the European Patent Office is not an EU body, it is a treaty body created by the European Patent Convention of 1973.

nations.[29] A trade mark so registered is equivalent to an application or a registration of the same mark effected directly in each of the countries designated by the applicant. If the trade mark office of a designated country does not refuse protection within one year, the protection of the mark is the same as if it had been originally registered with that office. The Madrid system and the PCT system are very similar, and as with the PCT system, Madrid applications are lengthier, more complex and more expensive than a domestic application and tend to be preferred for trade marks and brands inventions of a high degree of economic potential.

8.1.4 **The database right**

Compared to these three traditional IPRs, the database right is a modern development. The database right came into effect following the promulgation of the Database Directive in 1996.[30] The database right, more properly known as the *sui generis* database right to distinguish it from copyright protection of databases, was brought in to meet the challenge of protecting increasingly valuable databases of information which may not qualify for copyright protection.

The information economy places considerable value in databases: everything from customer contact databases to direct marketing databases to databases of customer shopping habits. Although commercially valuable it was not clear that the contents of a database were protected. If a company were to obtain a copy of a competitor's database and were to make use of it for their own commercial gain it was not clear there would be an action open to the original owner of the database. In some EU states, most notably the UK, there was a suggestion that the contents of a database would be protected by copyright law. This is because the UK has a famously low standard of originality requirement for copyright protection of compilations of data.[31] In other states, notably France and Germany, the law of copyright clearly would not protect databases. This divide started to affect the market for database industries with most EU-based database industries deciding to base themselves in the UK. To harmonise the law, and to allow for a free-market in the database industry, the Directive was passed.

The Directive provides for two different forms of database protection. Copyright protection is available where in creating the database the designer of the database displays a high level of skill or originality. This standard is found in the Copyright, Designs and Patents Act which states that copyright protection for databases is available when 'by reason of the selection or arrangement of the contents of the database the database constitutes the author's own intellectual creation.'[32] A database which fails to meet this higher standard will be protected by the *sui generis* database right. This protects the contents of a database for a period of fifteen years from the end of the calendar year in

---

[29] On 27 October 2008 there were 84 Madrid protocol signatories including the EU, the UK, and the US. A full list may be accessed at: http://www.wipo.int/export/sites/www/treaties/en/documents/pdf/madrid_marks.pdf.

[30] Directive of the European Parliament and of the Council of 11 March 1996 on the legal protection of databases, Dir.96/9/EC, OJ L 77, 27 March 1996, 20–28.

[31] See *Ladbroke (Football) Ltd v William Hill (Football) Ltd* [1964] 1 WLR 273 (HL); *Independent Television Publications Ltd v Time Out Ltd.* [1984] FSR 64.

[32] CDPA, s. 3A(2), giving effect to Art. 3(1) of the Database Directive.

which the making of the database was completed.[33] The protection of the database right is afforded to the maker of the database: that is the person 'who takes the initiative in obtaining, verifying or presenting the contents of a database and assumes the risk of investing in that obtaining, verification or presentation'.[34] One peculiarity of the database right is that by reg. 17(3), 'Any substantial change to the contents of a database, including a substantial change resulting from the accumulation of successive additions, deletions or alterations, which would result in the database being considered to be a substantial new investment shall qualify the database resulting from that investment for its own term of protection'.[35] This means that a continually updated database may qualify for permanent protection as at some point during the fifteen years of its original protection the accumulation of changes and amendments made to the database will cause it to qualify for a new, and further, period of protection. The *sui generis* database right protects the maker of the database from unauthorised extraction or re-utilisation of all or a substantial part of the contents of the database.[36] This suggests a level of protection somewhat less than that available at copyright law meaning the *sui generis* database right is rather weak. One advantage offered by the database right is that like copyright it requires no registration or recording by a public office to be of effect. Like copyright law it arises automatically and will be recognised by all states which recognise the database right, in effect all twenty-seven EU states.

8.2 **IPRs and digitisation**

As with all other areas of the law the way we think about and deploy IPRs is being challenged by the information society and the process of digitisation. The interaction between IPRs and the developing discipline of Cyberlaw is though rather different to most other areas of law. At this point in this book we have examined the difficulties that traditional (physical) property law as well as principles of free expression and defamation have had in adapting to the information society. Further on we will look at how criminal law and commercial law are similarly finding the information society to be a challenge but IPRs, founded in the fires of technological developments past, and characterised as the focal point between legal controls and intangible (informational) products and services, are flourishing in the information society. The story of this part of the book is less about the need for the traditional legal rules to develop and evolve to meet the challenges of the information society, but more questioning whether the widespread adaption of traditional intangible property principles, as found in IPRs, are beneficial to the development of the information society.

It has become common to think of information technology law, or Cyberlaw, as applied intellectual property law. Courses in information technology law at both undergraduate and postgraduate level in UK universities tend to devote a large proportion of their time to dealing with the IP/IT interface, looking at copyright in software, patents for software and business methods, trade marks for domain names and as meta tags and search terms, the database right and copyright in cyberspace, including hypertext

---

[33] The Copyright and Rights in Databases Regulations 1997 (SI 1997/3032), reg. 17(1).
[34] *ibid*, reg. 14(1).   [35] *ibid*, reg. 17(3).   [36] *ibid*, reg. 16(1).

linking, deep linking, framing and misappropriation of copyright material. Governments and intergovernmental organisations have also spent a considerable amount of time looking at these issues and the rump of decided cases in Cyberlaw subjects are concerned with the application of IPRs in the digital environment. To observe all these is not to criticise. It is to be expected that when something becomes economically valuable that there will be a move to 'enclose' it using property rights. With digital properties, as we saw in Chapter 5, it was difficult to extend traditional property models and so all parties with an interest turned to the at hand models to protect intangible property which were IPRs. But as Cyberlaw continues to evolve and develop as a cognate discipline critics are now challenging what many perceive as an over-reliance on models developed for another age and for different challenges in dealing with the information economy and the information society.

Chief among these critics is Professor Lawrence Lessig who has campaigned tirelessly against what he sees as the misapplication of copyright law to create what he calls a 'second enclosure movement' in Cyberspace.[37] Professor Lessig believes so passionately in this cause that he, along with likeminded individuals, founded the Creative Commons movement in 2001 to allow individuals the option of permitting certain uses of their creative works including music, video, and photographs, rather than the 'all rights reserved' approach found in copyright law. This system, which Lessig branded 'some rights reserved' has proven to be extremely successful with over 140 million works now estimated to make use of Creative Commons licenses.[38] It is not only copyright law which has attracted criticism in the digital environment. All of our four key IPRs have been the subject of criticism for over-protecting content or systems in the information society. Many commentators have critiqued the US Patent and Trademark Office for awarding patents for software and for business methods which have overprotected the patentee and have chilled innovation,[39] while the heavy handed approach taken by trade mark owners when dealing with individuals who register domain names which are similar to their pre-existing trade mark or which use their trade mark in a domain name as a means of operating a legitimate complaint site (so called 'sucks' sites)[40] have also been critiqued.[41]

What is clear is that there is a tension between what citizens of the information society want and expect: liberty, free use of content and unfettered free expression, and what the intellectual property industry is seeking: protection, control over use and abuse and reward. This tension is not unlike that seen in Chapter 6 between those individuals who argue speech should be free and those who argue that in the interests of society it is necessary to place limits on free expression. It is clear that if the information society is to function a balance must be struck between the interests of IPR holders and the interests of the rest of us to 'rip, mix and burn' digital content.

---

[37] L. Lessig, *Free Culture: How Big Media Uses Technology and the Law to Lock Down Culture and Control Creativity* (2004).

[38] This is the most recent figure available to the author from http://wiki.creativecommons.org/License_statistics#Estimates_over_time.

[39] K. Blind, J. Edler & M. Friedwald, *Software Patents: Economic Impacts and Policy Implications*, (2005).

[40] See, e.g http://www.walmart-really-sucks.com/, http://www.ryanairsucks.com/, or http://www.bmwsucks.com.

[41] M. Mueller, *Ruling the Root: Internet Governance and the Taming of Cyberspace* (2002).

FURTHER READING

Books

H. MacQueen, C. Waelde & G. Laurie, *Contemporary Intellectual Property: Law and Policy* (2008), Part I

W. Cornish, *Intellectual Property: Omnipresent, Distracting, Irrelevant?* (2004)

R. Spinello & H. Tavani, *Intellectual Property Rights in a Networked World: Theory and Practice* (2004)

Chapters and Articles

J.P. Barlow, 'The Economy of Ideas: Selling Wine Without Bottles on the Global Net', *Wired* 2.03, March 1994

L. Lessig, 'Intellectual Property and Code' 11 *St. John's Journal of Legal Commentary* 635 (1996)

L. Lessig, 'The International Information Society' 24 *Loyola of Los Angeles Entertainment Law Review* 33 (2004)

Software

9.1 **Protecting software: history**

The information society is founded upon the symbiotic relationship between hardware devices and the software which operates these devices. Digital hardware cannot function without software, while software, without hardware to implement its commands is merely a series of ones and zeros recorded on a storage device. As hardware without software was valueless computer hardware was originally supplied with software pre-installed and maintained by the hardware manufacturer. Thus if you bought, or more likely given the prohibitive cost leased, an early IBM mainframe computer such as the IBM 1401 the machine would be supplied complete with software, much in the same way a DVD player is sold today.[1] There was no competitive market for the supply of computer software and as a result no software industry or interest in the ownership of IPRs in software. This changed as the 1960s drew to a close. IBM's success in the computer markets of the 1960s led the US Department of Justice to inquire whether IBM was committing antitrust violations both by leasing rather than selling mainframe computers and by selling hardware and software as a 'bundled' single product. As a response to these investigations and in an attempt to head off an antitrust suit IBM announced on 23 June 1969, that it would unbundle much of its software and would price and license that software separately from its hardware and support services. From this date on separate markets for computer hardware and computer software existed. Software was now a standalone product which would require legal protection in the marketplace lest any unscrupulous individual attempt to free ride on the investment of another.

Almost immediately the legal profession became interested in the newly developing market in computer software. There were early questions as to how software should be protected. Should it be by the application of patent law or by the law of copyright or should it be a *sui generis* form of protection? Again, as in many areas of the involving the interface of law and the information society, early jurisprudence on this subject is to be found in the US. In 1972 in the case of *Gottschalk v Benson*,[2] the US Supreme Court ruled that a process which converted binary-coded decimal numbers into true binary

---

[1] A typical IBM 1401 system would have cost about $370,000 if purchased outright in 1961 (the year of its launch). This is the equivalent of around $2,654,000 at 2010 values. To lease an IBM 1401 cost $2,000 per month or $14,350 per month at 2010 values.

[2] *Gottschalk, Commissioner of Patents v Benson et al.* 409 US 63 (1972).

numbers (a process valuable in software development) was not patentable. Justice Douglas in giving the opinion of the court said that this decision should not be seen to deny patentability to all software, and noted that 'It may be that the patent laws should be extended to cover these programs' but that this was 'a policy matter to which we are not competent to speak'.[3] The court revisited this issue only six years later in the case of *Parker v Flook*.[4] Here the court found that the addition of a new software-based system to calculate safety limits in a catalytic conversion process was insufficient to qualify the process as a whole for patent protection, the only novelty being in the software design.

The failure of the fledgling software industry to convince the Supreme Court, or the prior President's Commission on the Patent System,[5] that patents should be extended to software, led to the industry seeking protection elsewhere. Almost as soon as IBM had unbundled its software development arm, Elmer Galbi, a consultant with IBM, had suggested the need for a *sui generis* form of legal protection for computer software based on modification of the patent system.[6] This idea received limited support from the Supreme Court, and led to Congressman Hamilton Fish Jr introducing a Bill which would enshrine *sui generis* software protection in the US Code.[7] The Bill was unfortunately seriously flawed and opponents claimed it was too heavily influenced by proposals emanating from IBM, which risked extending IBM's near-monopoly of the software industry. The Bill was therefore allowed to lapse and while the anti-protectionist movement continued to find success in cases such as *Gottschalk* and *Flook* they saw there was little need to make changes to the law as it stood.

The economic reality thought was that unless some formal system of protection for computer software could be found the fledgling software industry was under threat. With software patents at this point being rejected by the judiciary and the executive and with no realistic prospect of an agreed approach to *sui generis* protection it appeared that copyright offered the only realistic alternative. Copyright expansion was the preferred route of the World Intellectual Property Organisation and offered several apparent advantages. Firstly as copyright law does not require prior registration to be effective the expansion of copyright to software would not increase the administrative burden of patents offices. Secondly, as copyright is a 'soft' protection, with only a broad requirement of originality required to gain copyright protection and no need to establish inventiveness or a development on the prior art there was no need to establish a database of prior art for software. Further, as software, when written as source code, looks like written text it seemed apt to extend copyright, as the natural form of protection for literary works, to software.

[3] *ibid*, 66.   [4] 437 US 584 (1978).

[5] Report of the President's Commission on the Patent System, *To Promote the Progress of Useful Arts*, S. Doc No. 5, 90th Cong., 1st Sess. (1967).

[6] E. Galbi, Proposal for New Legislation to Protect Computer Programming, 17 *Journal of the Copyright Society* 280 (1970); E. Galbi, Software and Patents: A Status Report, 14 *Communications of the ACM* 274 (1971).

[7] See R. Stern, *Computer Law: Intellectual Property Rights in Computer-Related Subject Matter Cases and Materials*, George Washington Law School, Ch. 13: http://docs.law.gwu.edu/facweb/claw/ch-13.htm.

The US introduced a new Copyright Act in 1976 and in this it was made clear that Congress intended to extend copyright protection to software.[8] What was not clear though was how much protection computer programs should be given and whether there should be special exceptions to the exclusive rights of the copyright owners, as with some other types of literary works. Because Congress didn't want to delay the passage of the Act, it appointed the National Commission on New Technological Uses of Copyrighted Works to report back about computer programs and other new technologies and put a placeholder provision in the Act.[9] The Commission reported back in July 1978. Its main recommendation was that a new definition be added to § 101 of the Copyright Act to the effect that: 'a computer program is a set of statements or instructions to be used directly or indirectly in a computer in order to bring about a certain result'. This would fully extend copyright protection to software by affording them the status of 'a literary work'. As this required a change in the law Congress had to pass an amendment to the Copyright Act, and so it came to pass on 12 December 1980 that the US became the first country to formally extend copyright law to computer programs.

Meanwhile the UK had also been considering how to protect computer software. There had been discussions similar to those seen across the Atlantic and the prevailing view was that the listing of the source code of a computer program in a printout would protect that code as a literary work.[10] This assumption was tested in a number of interim hearings such as *Sega Enterprises v Richards*.[11] This case involved the early computer game *Frogger*. Mr Richards was alleged to have copied elements of the *Frogger* source code to produce his own copy of the *Frogger* game system which he then sold in competition to Sega. Mr Richards admitted he copied elements of Sega's code: the only question was whether Sega had copyright protection in their source code. The court examined this question and found that 'copyright under the provisions relating to literary works in the Copyright Act of 1956 subsists in the assembly code program ... the machine code program derived from it by the operation of the part of the system of the computer called the assembler is to be regarded ... as either a reproduction or an adaptation of the assembly code program, and accordingly, for the purposes of deciding this motion ... copyright does subsist in the program'.[12] This decision, although the result of only an interim hearing, is exactly what commentators had predicted. The 1956 Copyright Act was sufficiently flexible to protect software without the need for expensive amendment as the US had done.

---

[8] The definition of literary works found in § 101 of the 1976 Act states that they are 'works, other than audiovisual works, expressed in words, numbers, or other verbal or numerical symbols or indicia, regardless of the nature of the material objects, such as books, periodicals, manuscripts, phonorecords, film, tapes, disks, or cards, in which they are embodied'.

[9] § 117 was the placeholder provision. It stated: 'Notwithstanding the provisions of sections 106 through 116 and 118, this title does not afford the owner of copyright in a work any greater or lesser rights with respect to the use of the work in conjunction with automatic systems capable of storing, processing, retrieving, or transferring information, or in conjunction with any similar device, machine, or process, than those afforded to works under the law, whether title 17 or the common law or statutes of a State, in effect on December 31, 1977, as held applicable and construed by a court in an action brought under this title'.

[10] D. Bainbridge, *Introduction to Information Technology Law* 6th ed. (2008), 34.

[11] [1983] FSR 73.

[12] *ibid*, 75. Nowadays we would tend to refer to the 'assembly code' as the source code.

Despite the limited success of the now well established software industry in cases such as *Richards*, the industry remained nervous. None of the early cases in the UK had gone to a full hearing. Usually when the industry won an interim decision the defendant would settle and would move on to a new project. This was the time when computer games and even business software could be written at home as a hobby and if one project fizzled out another was always just around the corner. Then a case in Australia changed things quite dramatically. The case was *Apple Computers, Inc. v Computer Edge Pty Ltd* and the decision of the Federal Court for New South Wales was exactly what the software industry had feared.[13] Although the decision of Beaumont J. was quickly overruled by the Appeal Court,[14] the damage was done. The first common law case on software copyright outside the US, to go to a full hearing had found that copyright law did not automatically cover computer software. In panic legislatures across the globe moved to place their now economically significant copyright industries on a sound legal footing, as the US had done in 1980. The Federal Australian Government passed the Copyright Amendment Act 1984 and in the UK the Copyright (Computer Software) Amendment Act 1985 finally and formally brought computer software within the protection afforded to a literary work under the Copyright Act 1956.

Case Study *Apple Computers, Inc. v Computer Edge Pty Ltd*

The defendants were importing computers from Taiwan which copied the design of the Apple II minicomputer. They were selling the machines under the name 'Wombat' and claimed the machines had no Apple software installed.

This claim was found to be false when the claimants proved that programs installed on three silicon chips found within the Wombat's hardware contained within them the names of several Apple programmers. The defendants argued that the code contained on the chips was not protected by the Australian Copyright Act 1968.

It fell to Beaumont J to decide the case. He found that none of the programmes are literary works within the meaning of the statute, stating: 'in my view, a literary work for this purpose is something which was intended to afford "either information or instruction or pleasure in the form of literary enjoyment" [whereas] the function of a computer programme is to control the sequence of operations carried out by a computer.' He went on to add that should copyright require to be extended to software this was a decision for the legislature not the judiciary.

9.2 Copyright in computer software

9.2.1 Obtaining copyright protection

The current position UK law holds in relation to copyright for computer software is to be found in the Copyright, Designs and Patents Act 1988 (CDPA), as amended. The key

---

[13] *Apple Computers Inc. v Computer Edge Pty Ltd* [1983] FCA 328.
[14] *Apple Computers Inc. v Computer Edge Pty Ltd* [1984] FSR 481.

provision is s. 3(1)(b) which states that '"literary work" means any work, other than a dramatic or musical work, which is written, spoken or sung, and accordingly includes a computer program'. This means that all the general principles of copyright law developed with respect to literary works over the centuries now apply equally to software: including the requirements for the subsistence of copyright protection and the protection afforded by copyright. To gain copyright protection software is required to fulfil the subsistence requirements of a literary work: they are that it is original,[15] it has been 'recorded'[16] and that it qualifies for protection in the UK.[17]

Originality is in UK law quite a low threshold test which requires that the author of the work has not copied (plagiarised) the work or elements of the work from others. The classic test of originality is drawn from the case of *University of London Press Ltd v University Tutorial Press Ltd*.[18] This case involved exam papers written by academics for the University of London. The question was, were exam questions sufficiently original to allow copyright law to protect them as literary works? Peterson J considered that 'The originality which is required relates to the expression of the thought . . . the Act does not require that the expression must be in an original or novel form, but that the work must not be copied from another work—that it should originate from the author'.[19] This extremely low originality threshold is often called the 'sweat of the brow' standard: the author need not show literary originality, only that he or she expended effort on the creation of the work and that the work is not plagiarised from another source. UK courts continue to apply the 'sweat of the brow' doctrine. In the infamous case of *Ladbroke (Football) Ltd v William Hill (Football) Ltd*,[20] the selection of a number of scheduled football matches for inclusion on a football pools coupon was found to qualify as a literary work due to the degree of skill, judgment, and labour necessary to select the correct combination of matches to allow the best selection for the customer and the bookmaker. There is therefore little doubt that computer software which is not copied or plagiarised from another source will be sufficiently original for copyright protection to subsist. This will apply whatever form the software comes in as the Act does not distinguish between software in higher level source code or machine readable object code. This is deliberate and designed to prevent a repeat of the *Apple Computers, Inc. v Computer Edge Pty Ltd* decision, and also is designed to 'future-proof' the Act against any developments in software design and engineering.

The UK is unusual in applying a 'sweat of the brow' standard. Most states apply a more stringent standard which requires an intellectual contribution from the author. This can be problematic when dealing with software design, in particular the design of operating systems or business software which are required to follow narrow design protocols to ensure interoperability and stability. This distinction between the UK 'sweat of the brow' standard and the higher Continental 'droit d'auteur' standard could have fragmented the European software industry with greater protection being found in the UK than in Continental Europe. The risk of this was highlighted in 1985 when a German court found that to be protected by copyright, a computer program must result from individual creative achievement exceeding the average skills

---

[15] CDPA 1988, s. 1(1).   [16] CDPA 1988, s. 3(2).   [17] CDPA 1988, s. 1(3).
[18] [1916] 2 Ch. 601.   [19] *ibid*, 608–609.   [20] [1964] 1 WLR 273.

displayed in the development of computer programs.[21] This meant a program which automated or replicated an existing process with no special design or technique could not be afforded copyright protection. Fortunately the Software Directive harmonised the originality standard.[22] By Article 1(3) 'a computer program shall be protected if it is original in the sense that it is the author's own intellectual creation. No other criteria shall be applied to determine its eligibility for protection'. Thus, when looking specifically at the originality threshold for software the 'sweat of the brow' standard is exported throughout Continental Europe. The effectiveness of Article 1(3) was confirmed in the post-Directive German case of *Buchhaltungsprogram*,[23] where the Federal Supreme Court of Germany declined to follow *Sudwestdeutsche Inkasso* and instead applied a lower standard of originality based upon Article 1(3). There appears little doubt therefore that following the enactment of Article 1(3) the originality threshold is easily met throughout the EU: to qualify the software must simply be original, in that it was created by the author and was not copied or plagiarised from another source.

The second requirement for copyright protection to arise is that the software must be 'recorded, in writing or otherwise'.[24] To be distributable software must be recorded: thus the very act of making software will usually fulfil this requirement. The manner in which software is recorded is though unusual. Software will usually be distributed as encoded binary data (a series of zeros and ones) either stored magnetically (on a HDD or similar) or as tiny bumps and grooves on the surface of an optical disc (such as a DVD) or even as a series of electrical or optical pulses carried across telecommunications networks (as a download). The obvious question is whether a series of binary representations encoded in this fashion qualifies as being 'recorded, in writing or otherwise'. Section 178 of the CDPA assists slightly by giving a broad definition of 'writing' as 'includ[ing] any form of notation or code, whether by hand or otherwise and regardless of the method by which, or medium in or on which, it is recorded'. Although not definitive, the broad definition of writing given in s. 178 suggests that the courts would have little difficulty in applying this definition to any of the forms of distribution discussed above. In fact there seems little question that even temporary copies of a software file or instruction is sufficient to meet the recording threshold as under s. 17(6) copyright may be infringed by 'the making of copies which are transient'. To state an infringing copy may be transient, is at least strongly indicative that the original may be equally transient.[25]

The final requirement for copyright protection is that the work in question must qualify for protection under the CDPA; this is a requirement of domicile. The copyright holder is required to demonstrate that UK copyright law, as opposed to the copyright

[21] *Sudwestdeutsche Inkasso KG* v. *Bappert and Burker Computer GmbH* (1985) Case 52/83, BGHZ 94, 276.
[22] Council Directive of 14 May 1991 on the legal protection of computer programs (Dir. 91/250/EEC) 1991 O.J. L 122 42.
[23] *Buchhaltungsprogram*, unreported BGH, 14 July, 1993.   [24] CDPA 1988, s. 3(2).
[25] In truth the requirement of recording is as much a requirement of evidence as copyright law. We require fixing of copyright materials in a recorded form so that should an infringement claim arise the court has a fixed record of the original work with which it can compare the allegedly infringing copy. Thus something which was fixed transiently could establish copyright, provided some archive of the event was kept which could be presented to the court.

law of another state should be applied. There are a number of ways a literary work, including software, can qualify for protection under the CDPA. By s. 153, if the author is a British citizen or a citizen of a British overseas territory or was a domiciled British resident at the time the software was made, or is a UK registered company then it any work they produce is eligible for UK copyright protection. Alternatively if the author falls into none of these categories then if the software was first published in the UK it qualifies for UK protection.

It should be noted though that even software which does not meet these strict criteria can qualify for protection in the UK. By s. 155(3) first publication overseas shall not preclude the author from being able to claim 'simultaneous publication' in the UK where the work is published in the UK within thirty days of the original publication. Despite those extremely generous provisions many reading this may assume that the requirement of a UK connection for the work may rule many software products out of UK copyright protection. If we take a computer game for example like the well-known *Call of Duty* series, these are 'authored' by a company called Infinity Ward located in Encino, California and published by a Activision, a company based in Santa Monica, California. Should Activision choose to release the next *Call of Duty* game in the US on a date more than thirty days prior to its UK publication date it does not qualify for UK Copyright protection as the author does not meet the residency requirement and the work does not meet the publication requirement. This would suggest the game was not protected in the UK and would be open to all manner of infringing acts including the making and distributing of illegal (pirate) copies. This, obviously, is not the case as such a rule would affect not only software but movies, music, and works of literature. The truth is that once the work qualifies for US Copyright protection, then under the terms of the Berne Convention,[26] the UK agrees to extend copyright protection to that work as if it were a UK copyright work.[27] The Convention provides a truly global copyright protection with one hundred and eighty-three signatories each recognising the copyright of all the others.[28] Thus once you obtain copyright in any one of the Berne signatory states you are automatically protected in all one hundred and eighty-three. It is therefore almost impossible to imagine that a software work would not be protected in the UK on grounds of qualification.

9.2.2 The scope of copyright protection

Once copyright protection has been obtained in an original piece of software, what rights does this confer on the copyright holder?[29] As a literary work software qualifies for the same protection as books, movies, or music. This affords the copyright owner

---

[26] Berne Convention for the Protection of Literary and Artistic Works 1883.

[27] See Berne Convention, Art. 5(1).

[28] A full list of the UK's bilateral obligations under the Convention may be found in the Schedule to the Copyright and Performances (Application to Other Countries) Order 2008, SI 2008/677.

[29] It should be noted that the copyright owner may be a different person to the author. This is particularly important when dealing with computer software which may be created by a collaborative effort of many hundred programmers. Under s. 11(2) where a literary, dramatic, musical, or artistic work, is made by an employee in the course of his employment, his employer is the first owner of any copyright in the work subject to any agreement to the contrary. Thus although Microsoft may have had several hundred programmers all acting as co-authors on the Windows 7 project the copyright holder will be Microsoft Corp.

four 'restricted acts', actions that only the copyright holder may legally carry out or may permit others to carry out. These are: (1) to make copies of the work;[30] (2) to issue copies of the work to the public;[31] (3) to communicate the work to the public;[32] and (4) to make an adaptation of the work or do any of the above in relation to an adaptation.[33]

These acts all have specific meaning both within the CDPA, and within the broader scope of copyright law. By s. 17(2), copying is defined as 'reproducing the work in any material form'. This extends beyond making complete (or literal) copies of the work and may include copying the structure or plot of a play or story or the use of characters created by another.[34] This is particularly common with computer software as the value of the software is in the structure of the software and what it does rather than in the source or object code which are never usually seen by the consumer. Thus, a software designer may study the structure of an original piece of software; say an original computer game such as Team 17's *Worms*, and then by copying the gaming engine and underlying protocols produce a competing game such as *Snails* a variant on the worms theme produced for mobile phones. As *Snails* will not share any of the original code with *Worms* there can be no question of literal copying. Instead in cases of 'non-literal copying' the question becomes whether the latter piece of software has copied these elements of the original which are afforded protection.[35] As a result much of the case law discussed in the following section will focus on non-literal infringement.[36]

An adaption is specifically defined in relation to software in s. 21(3)(ab) as 'an arrangement or altered version of the program or a translation of it'. Adaptations tend to occur when a piece of software written for one operating system, such as Apple's *Leopard* is rewritten to operate on a different operating system such as Microsoft's *Vista*. Adaptations can also occur when an original piece of software is rewritten, usually by an agent employed by the end-user of the software to allow the end-user to cancel a contractual arrangement with the software vendor and replace the vendor's software with his own. With commercial software often leased at substantial service costs which include fees for maintenance and upgrades it is tempting for end-users to seek to replace supplied software with their own version. This is of course perfectly legal provided the software they develop is neither copied from or is an adaptation of the original

---

[30] CDPA 1988, ss. 16(1)(a), 17.   [31] CDPA 1988, ss. 16(1)(b), 18.
[32] CDPA 1988, ss. 16(1)(d), 20.   [33] CDPA 1988, ss. 16(1)(e), 21.

[34] The use of structure and concepts was discussed in depth in *Baigent & Anor v The Random House Group Ltd (The Da Vinci Code)* [2006] EWHC 719 (Ch), affd [2007] EWCA Civ 247.

[35] For the avoidance of doubt the author does not suggest the producers of *Snails* committed any form of copyright infringement. It is perfectly acceptable and indeed normal practice to be inspired by a successful game and to produce variants on the game idea. For example at the moment the First-person Shooter of FPS seems to be the dominant game variety played on home consoles with a number of competing titles all based on the system pioneered by *Wolfenstein 3D* in 1992 and *Doom* in 1993.

[36] This is not to deny the massive effect software piracy has on the software industry. The *Business Software Alliance 2008 Global Software Piracy Study*, calculated that global software piracy cost the industry $53bn in 2008 with 41% of all software installed being illegal copies. Software piracy is a legally clear issue. The production, distribution, and installation of pirated software are all infringements of copyright, with those who produce and distribute pirated software are committing a criminal offence under s. 107 of the CDPA. The issue with software piracy is one of enforcement, not one of legal certainty.

software. As with non-literal copying there have been several cases on this issue which will be examined below.

The remaining rights reserved to the copyright holder, the right to issue copies of the work to the public and the right to communicate the work to the public are less problematic. These rights allow copyright holders to control the distribution of their work, and ensure that the copyright holder is adequately rewarded for their efforts. There is though one unusual aspect of the right to issue copies of the work to the public which should be highlighted; exhaustion of the right. The right conferred on the copyright holder under s. 18, is only the right to first distribute a copies of the work in the European Economic Area. Once that has been done the right, with respect to *that copy* of the work, is exhausted allowing the owner of that copy of the work to sell it on. This can be clearly seen with an example.

> ### ★ **Example** Exhaustion of the First Sale Right
>
> Ana buys a legitimate copy of a computer program in Portugal. She then imports it into the UK when she moves to London. She later decided to sell her copy of the software on eBay.co.uk. The principle of exhaustion means Ana may legally sell her copy of the software in the UK without the permission of the copyright owner (assuming she removes any installations of the software from her computer).
>
> Bárbara bought her copy of the same software in Brazil. She also moves to London. If Bárbara tries to sell her copy of the software on eBay.co.uk she would technically be in breach of copyright. As Brazil is not an EEA state she may not re-sell her copy legally within the EEA without the permission of the copyright holder.
>
> Similarly the exhaustion of the copyright holder's right to first distribution only gives Ana the right to resell her copy of the software. It does not allow her to rent or lease her copy, nor does it allow her to make additional copies of the software.

9.3 **Copyright infringement and software: literal copying**

To carry out any restricted act without the permission of the copyright holder invites an action for copyright infringement. An action for copyright infringement is usually a civil action, although many people imagine it to be a criminal action due to the language used by the copyright industry in campaigns such as the 'copying is theft' campaign operated by the Federation Against Copyright Theft. In truth only a small number of activities involve the criminal law, most of which involve making literal copies available to the public.[37] In fact the divide between the civil enforcement of copyright infringement and the application of the criminal law follows quite closely the divide between literal, or pirated, copies and non-literal copies.

---

[37] The bulk of criminal copyright offences may be found in ss. 107–112 of the CDPA 1988.

9.3.1 **Offline piracy**

Literal copies, usually known as pirated copies, are precise copies of a work and are usually produced with a view to selling or otherwise distributing them as a substitute for the original. As a complete copy of a work there is no doubt that literal copies infringe. There are a variety of ways in which software piracy may occur. The most simple and obvious being the production of illegal copies on CD or DVD in a backstreet factory which are then sold on in markets, on the street, or in pubs. Although this type of activity is more common overseas it does go on in the UK with reports of individuals being caught in such activity being quite commonplace.[38] Such cases are usually dealt with by either the police or trading standards officers often with the support of the copyright holder or the Federation Against Software Theft. A variant on this theme is the illegal pre-loading of software by hardware suppliers. Here instead of making an illegal copy of the software on a CD or DVD the hardware supplier simply installs the software on to the hard drive of a PC and then sells the computer with the software pre-installed to a customer. This is more common in the UK than the production of pirate CDs and DVDs. Many cases are reported on this practice, including *Microsoft v Electro-Wide Ltd*,[39] in which Laddie J found that 'an original equipment manufacturer who pre-loads software onto a computer for sale to the public needs a relevant licence from the copyright owner each time he loads the software'.[40]

Commonly software piracy in the UK involves a variant of the pre-loading practice. One such variant is multiple installations, or end-user piracy. This occurs where an end user buys a licence which allows him or her to install the software on a limited number of computers (usually one or two), but installs it on a number of computers. With households nowadays often containing several PCs the temptation to install the software on all computers in breach of the license conditions may be overwhelming. For example the version of Microsoft Office most commonly sold to consumers is the Home and Student edition. This version of the software comes with three licenses, but many households contain more than three computers. Having paid around £100 for his purchase the end-user may be tempted to install the software on all his machines. The temptation may be even more acute in small to medium size businesses where there may be a few dozen or a few hundred PCs but not quite as many licenses.[41]

---

[38] See, e.g. 'Businessman was selling illegal software', *The Western Gazette*, 20 February 2009: http://www.thisisdorset.co.uk/westerngazette/dorchester/Businessman-selling-illegal-software/article-715643-detail/article.html; 'Rothwell: Man caught selling fake computer software escapes jail', *Cross Gates Today*, 4 March 2009: http://www.crossgatestoday.co.uk/5311/Rothwell-Man-caught-selling-fake.5033064.jp; A. Savvas, 'Cornish roofer caught for selling rogue software', *Computer Weekly*, 19 November 2007: http://www.computerweekly.com/Articles/2007/11/19/228197/cornish-roofer-caught-for-selling-rogue-software.htm.

[39] [1997] FSR 580.   [40] *ibid*, 582.

[41] The Business Software Alliance periodically audits and fines companies (mostly in the US). In 2005–06 they fined at least twenty-four companies more than $2.4m for having infringing copies of a variety of software. See T. Weiss, 'U.S. Companies Fined for Using Illegal Software', *Computerworld*, 13 January 2006: http://www.pcworld.com/article/124377/us_companies_fined_for_using_illegal_software.html; L. Rosencrance, 'Using Illegal Software May Not Pay', *Computerworld*, 25 July 2006: http://www.pcworld.com/article/126551/using_illegal_software_may_not_pay.html.

This type of infringement is notoriously difficult to track down as it is widespread and usually at a low level, too low in terms of monetary value to pay for a detailed investigation. To combat this problem commercial software manufacturers have employed to a variety of authentication measures. This is usually achieved though a 'product activation key' a unique identifier supplied with the software which the end-user must enter when the software is first installed. Often today these keys require to be registered online with the copyright owner so that they may ensure only the licensed number of copies of the software is currently in use. These systems are though open to attack through the use of key generators, small programs which can mimic the operations of the registration system used by the copyright owner to defeat the activation process. To attempt to defeat the use of key generators some software companies have developed further anti-piracy systems such as Microsoft's Genuine Advantage programme which it uses to protect its Windows and Office systems. This system uses a license validation program which checks a number of details for the relevant Microsoft software on registration and at each update. If the system finds the details to be inaccurate it does not allow the software to update leaving the end user at risk of software failure.

9.3.2 **Online piracy**

More commonly today software piracy in the UK is an online activity. With broadband connection speeds increasing and small and home office wireless networks being simple to install and cheap to operate, two online piracy methods have increased in importance. The first is client-server piracy. This is similar in effect to pre-loading piracy but with the distinction that only a single copy of the software is installed on a server which may then be accessed and used by any user on the network. This type of software installation is usually legal if you have the right form of licence but in some cases the number of end-users exceeds the number of licenses the network operator has purchased. In these cases infringement occurs.

More damaging though in terms of both volume and value is the worryingly commonplace occurrence of file-sharing software. The legal regulation of online copyright infringement will be discussed in greater depth in the following chapter, but here it is worth noting that in the UK the practice of swapping discs or buying illegal copies of software in markets or car boot sales has substantially been replaced with trading illegal files on file sharing technologies such as BitTorrent. The size of the illegal peer-to-peer market should not be underestimated. A recent survey by Ipoque, a company with experience of tracking data packets online found that on average 56.33% of all data traffic was peer-to-peer traffic: this could be compared with 24.58% web traffic.[42]

This has led copyright holders to take action against those who file share software. Most controversially a practice called 'volume litigation' has been pioneered by UK Law Firm Davenport Lyons. This practice, which will be discussed further in

---

[42] *Ipoque Internet Study 2008/09*: http://www.ipoque.com/resources/internet-studies/internet-study-2008_2009.

the following chapter, sees claimants identifying a large number of alleged infringers and then sending out settlement offers, offering to settle the claim for a one-off fee of between £300–£525.[43] Parties who do not settle are offered a second chance to settle for an increased fee, before a claim is lodged. In the first case to reach the county court under this procedure Topware Interactive, the producers of Dream Pinball 3D won more than £16,000 in default damages.[44] Whether this new process, which operates something like a class action in reverse, is successful in the long term remains to be seen. Davenport Lyons has stopped using the process following bad publicity and the very public withdrawal of key client Atari.[45] A new entrant ACS Law is at the time of writing the only UK firm employing the practice. In November 2009 they indicated their intention to send around 15,000 letters before action in early 2010.[46] It is to be imagined that ACS Law may suffer the same problems of proof and concurrent bad publicity suffered by Davenport Lyons. However the ready profitability of this process suggests that that ACS Law will find a steady stream of clients who wish to make use of this process.

9.3.3 Employee piracy

The final, less common, but potentially extremely harmful form of literal infringement is employee piracy. This occurs when an employee leaves their employers employ and takes with them a complete copy, or a copy of a section, of their employer's product, usually with a view to producing a competing product of their own. An example of this type of infringement may be seen in the case of *IBCOS Computers Ltd v Barclays Mercantile Highland Finance Ltd*.[47] This case involved a software developer, Mr Poole, who wrote a suite of programs for his employer IBCOS which handled accounts and payrolls for agricultural machinery dealers. This software called ADS was owned by the plaintiff. Under the terms of Mr Poole's contract he could not develop any competing products within two years of his termination of his contract of employment. After leaving IBCOS Mr Poole wrote a new software suite similar to ADS called Unicorn which he supplied to *Barclays Mercantile* for marketing and sale. Mr Poole was careful to ensure that Unicorn was not marketed until after his two year limitation period had expired.

IBCOS claimed that Mr Poole had used elements of the ADS code in the Unicorn program and raised an infringement action. When the two programs were compared side by side it became clear that Mr Poole had copied elements of the ADS code. There were common errors of punctuation and spelling in the comment lines of the programs[48] and the same programming errors and redundant code were found in the same places.[49]

[43] P. Revoir, 'Up to 25,000 British illegal downloaders sued for £300 as games developers turn to courts', *Daily Mail*, 21 August 2008: http://www.dailymail.co.uk/news/article-1046607/Up-25-000-British-illegal-downloaders-sued-300-games-developers-turn-courts.html.
[44] BBC News, *Game sharers face legal crackdown*, 19 August 2008: http://www.news.bbc.co.uk/1/hi/technology/7568642.stm.
[45] C. Williams, 'Atari dumps Davenport Lyons' piracy nastygram campaign', *The Register* 27 November 2008: http://www.theregister.co.uk/2008/11/27/atari_davenport_lyons/.
[46] J. Fildes, 'Lawyers target thousands of "illegal" file-sharers, BBC News, 27 November 2009: http://news.bbc.co.uk/1/hi/technology/8381097.stm.
[47] [1994] FSR 275.   [48] *ibid*, 297–298.   [49] *ibid*, 299.

Faced with this evidence Jacob J had little difficulty finding that copying had occurred. The only remaining question was whether the copying had been sufficient to qualify as a 'substantial part' of the original.[50] A key question here was whether Jacob J should consider each work separately and individually or whether he could treat the entire ADS software suite which comprised of 335 program files, 171 record layout files, and forty-six screen layout files as a single work.[51] Rejecting an earlier suggestion made in an interlocutory hearing in the case of *Total Information Processing Systems Ltd v Daman Ltd*.[52] that the mere linking of several programs is not in itself an original literary or artistic work, Jacob J found that ADS was a compilation capable of independent copyright protection which existed in addition to and separately from the individual copyrights in each of the elements.[53] With this decided Jacob J then considered whether the evidence indicated that substantial copying had occurred of both the individual elements of ADS and of ADS as a whole. He found substantial elements of the individual programs were repeated in Unicorn and in comparing the overall structure of Unicorn to ADS found that both programs shared: nine levels of security; a unique ability to create different invoice types; a common internal sales system within the ordinary sales ledger package; month end sales audits combined with VAT; a twenty-two character parts description; use of three separate programs for the stock ordering facility; twelve labour rates; five levels of sub-totalling and both had a redundant and unnecessary holiday stamp facility.[54] These common features were in Justice Jacob's view too many in number and too similar in design to be caused by Mr Poole's programming style and his re-use of common routines. He therefore found in favour of IBCOS finding infringement of both the individual elements of ADS and of ADS as a whole.

The principles Jacob J set out in *IBCOS* were later to be applied in the similar case of *Cantor Fitzgerald International v Tradition (UK) Ltd*.[55] Cantor Fitzgerald (CF) are inter-dealer brokers in bonds, which means they act as the middle men in a bond transaction. In September 1991 CF dismissed their Managing Director, Mr Howard, who then approached Tradition with a view to setting up an inter-dealer brokerage for them. To get the Tradition system up and running Mr Howard hired a number of members of staff from CF including Mr Harland, then the head of the Systems Department at CF and almost his entire programming team. CF claimed that in setting up their inter-dealer brokerage Tradition infringed several of CF's copyrights in its brokerage software. They claimed that Tradition had directly infringed by installing copies of the CF brokerage system on their system. This was admitted by Tradition and was easily disposed of. CF further claimed that elements of the CF software had been copied in the design of the new Tradition software. Tradition admitted that they had included some of the CF code in their program but that this accounted for less than 4% of the complete CF code. They therefore argued this was not a 'substantial part' as required by s. 16(3)(a) of the CDPA.

It fell to Pumfrey J to determine whether the elements copied were in fact substantial, and how substantiality should be measured. He first noted that due to the way

---

[50] By s. 16(3)(a) of the CDPA 1988 infringement by copying only occurs where the alleged infringer has copied 'the work as a whole or any substantial part of it'.
[51] Figures from [1994] FSR 275, 289.   [52] [1992] FSR 171.   [53] [1994] FSR 275, 292–293.
[54] *ibid*, 304–305.   [55] [2000] RPC 95.

a computer program operates there is an argument that 'every part of a computer program is essential to its performance, and so every part, however small, is a "substantial part" of the program'.[56] This he rejected as overbroad. Instead he preferred to follow the lead of Jacob J in thinking of computer software as similar to a literary work with the focus of substantiality resting on the quality of what is taken rather than the quantity: 'Substantiality is to be judged in the light of the skill and labour in design and coding which went into the piece of code which is alleged to be copied. It is not determined by whether the system would work without the code; or by the amount of use the system makes of the code'.[57] On this basis Pumfrey J went on to examine the software suites as a whole, and each of their component parts, as Jacob J had done in *IBCOS*. He found that the direct copies of the CF software loaded onto the Tradition system were infringing, but found that mostly because the Tradition programmers had copied small elements of the CF system with a view to developing a better program suite little of the new Tradition software infringed CF's copyright, although on a few key elements including one called LIFFE.BAS there had been infringement. The case therefore brought a mixed result for both parties with CF claiming a partial win but more importantly these two cases *IBCOS* and *Cantor Fitzgerald* have set the standard test for partial literal copying, an activity that tends only to occur in this type of piracy.

9.4 Copyright infringement and software: non-literal copying

Much less common than literal copying, but much more legally complex is the idea of non-literal copying. Non-literal copying occurs when the structure, design, or characterisation of a literary work is copied. Famously in 2006 the High Court had to decide whether Dan Brown's blockbuster novel *The Da Vinci Code* (DVC) had copied elements of a previous non-fiction book *The Holy Blood and the Holy Grail* (HBHG).[58] The claim made by the authors of HBHG was that Mr Brown had copied the central theme (in chronological order) of HBHG, and that without this central theme there is very little structure to be found in either HBHG or DVC. They claimed that this central theme therefore formed a bridge between the two works by which Brown substantially copied HBHG in his own work DVC. This was a complex claim which took up a considerable amount of court time. When Peter Smith J finally produced his lengthy judgement he found against the claimants finding that the shared central theme could not be identified from the evidence and that 'even if there is a Central Theme as alleged by the Claimants in HBHG it ... is merely an expression of a number of facts and ideas at a very general level. There is nothing in them in my view that goes beyond that proposition. It follows therefore that the Central Theme as expressed is not such as to justify being protected against copying'.[59]

---

[56] *ibid*, 130.   [57] *ibid*, 135.
[58] *Baigent & Anor v The Random House Group Ltd (The Da Vinci Code)* [2006] EWHC 719 (Ch).
[59] *ibid*, [259].

The Da Vinci Code case is a typical literary non-literal infringement case. Debates in such cases usually centre on the dividing line between shared ideas (which are not copyrightable) and shared structures, themes, and concepts (which may be). In cases involving literary works there is never any doubt that the reader is able to distinguish between the two works and will experience both rather differently; this is because with books the reader consumes the actual written word. In *The Da Vinci Code* case the issue was not that the consumer may buy DVC in preference to HBHG as one was a non-fiction book and the other a thriller novel, but rather that the author and publisher of DVC had profited from the expressed ideas of the authors of HBHG. With software the issue is very different. The end user rarely sees the source code and will never usually see the object code. The way we consume and experience software is therefore very different to other literary works. We do not consume the protected element of the work as we do with books, films, music, or with artistic works; instead we experience software through the 'user interface', usually a 'graphical user interface' which uses graphical icons, and visual indicators (icons) to control software operations. Because of this unique way we interface with software it is possible for the consumer experience to be replicated without copying any of the underlying code: this is known as 'look and feel infringement'.

9.4.1 Introducing look and feel infringement

Look and feel infringement first came to the attention of the legal establishment in the 1980s. Initially look and feel infringement was driven not as an attempt to avoid the impact of copyright law while free riding on the work of others, but more prosaically because a software program, or suite, written from one operating system (such as windows) would not run on a different operating system (such as IBM's O/S2). Thus a successful piece of software written for one operating system would need to be translated to work on another operating system. In making the translation every effort would be made to ensure the translated program would work in the same way as the original: in other words would have the same 'look and feel'. If such a translation was carried out by the copyright holder there would be no copyright issue, but if a third party decided to translate, or 'port-over' a program without the permission of the copyright holder litigation may follow.

As with almost every area of law and information society, early case law is to be found in the US. Although *Whelan Associates Inc. v Jaslow Dental Laboratory Inc.*,[60] is not the first look and feel case it was the first to be of widespread impact. This case involved a program known as 'Dentlab' written by Ms Elaine Whelan for a client Mr Rand Jaslow. Mr Jaslow ran a dental prosthetics laboratory and in 1978 he realised there could be advantages to computerising his office systems. He therefore bought an IBM Series One computer and attempted to write some software to run his office systems. Finding this beyond his limited computer skills he approached a local software company, Strohl Systems Group to produce the software. Under the terms of their agreement Strohl would write the software and then after installing it in Mr Jaslow's computer they could sell it to other

---

[60] 797 F 2d 1222 (3d Cir. 1986).

dental laboratories. In return for this Mr Jaslow would receive a 10% royalty on each copy sold. Ms Whelan wrote the software and it was installed in Mr Jaslow's computer.

Some time around 1982 Mr Jaslow realised that most dental labs being small operations few could afford the IBM Series of computers that were needed to run Dentlab. He therefore set out to write an alternative program written in BASIC which would run on smaller home computers. He began to market his new product known as 'Dentcom' in 1983. Ms Whelan, who had since left Strohl and had set up her own company Whelan Associates, and who had bought all the rights to Dentlab sued for copyright infringement. As Dentcom was written in a different programming language from Dentlab, the US Court of Appeals for the Third Circuit had to decide how to evaluate the level of copying that Mr Jaslow had committed, if any. To do so the court attempted to distinguish between unprotectable ideas and protectable expression by introducing the 'idea expression continuum'. The continuum is a line with pure ideas at one end and with abstract expression at the other (seen in Figure 9.1). At some point along this line ideas cross over the idea-expression threshold and move from being unprotectable to being protected expression. The only question remaining was where the threshold should be placed when dealing with a utilitarian work such as computer software.

Judge Becker in giving the opinion of the court explained it was an extension of the test set out in the famous US copyright case *Baker v Selden*,[61] and explained it thus: 'the purpose or function of a utilitarian work would be the work's idea, and everything that is not necessary to that purpose or function would be part of the expression of the idea'.[62] Applying this test the court found that the purpose of the programme was to assist in the running of a dental laboratory. As there were many ways a piece of software could be designed to achieve this purpose the structure of the original program was not essential to that purpose and must therefore be an expression of Ms Whelan's originality. As the Dentcom program shared many of the structural elements of Dentlab, and as the look and feel of the two programs were substantially similar, the court found a strong presumption of infringement could be raised. As the respondent was unable to rebut this presumption, the court found that Dentcom had indeed infringed Debtlab's copyright.

The *Whelan* decision was highly controversial and many commentators felt the court had placed the copyright threshold too far to the left of the continuum.[63] With the court

Figure 9.1 The Idea-expression continuum

[61] 101 US 99 (1879).   [62] 797 F 2d 1222, 1236.
[63] M. Chapman, 'Copyright Law - Putting too Much Teeth into Software Copyright Infringement Claims', 12 *Journal of Corporation Law* 785 (1986–1987); T. Gage, 'Copyright Protection for Computer Software Structure - What's the Purpose', *Wisconsin Law Review* 589 [1987]; S. Jones, 'Copyright Protection for the Structure and Sequence of Computer Programs', 21 *Loyola of Los Angeles Law Review* 255 (1987–1988).

drawing the line neatly between the purpose of the software and everything else it meant that anything which was not essential to that purpose was protected expression even if the structure or design used by the copyright holder was the most efficient way of performing a particular task such as storing or transferring data. Commentators felt that *Whelan* had also given software much greater protection than other literary works such as books which tended not to protect structures which were determined by efficiency or expediency.

Despite this controversy *Whelan* continued to be followed. For example in *Lotus Development Corp. v Paperback Software*,[64] Judge Keeton ruled that Paperback's VP-Planner spreadsheet software infringed Lotus's copyright in their 1–2–3 spreadsheet by copying the two-line moving cursor menu system that Lotus used in their 1–2–3 product.[65] He felt that as there were a variety of other methods that could be used to design a spreadsheet menus system, and indeed which were being used, that the 1–2–3 menu was therefore expressive not functional. Decisions like this perpetuated monopolies over functional tools like menu structures. The reason Paperback had copied Lotus's menu system in the first place was that by 1987 Lotus controlled 70% of the spreadsheet market through its 1–2–3 program.[66] To ask people to switch to another spreadsheet program would require them to retrain; this involves switching costs, the cost of switching from one product or service to another. Paperback emulated the Lotus menu to reduce switching costs in an attempt to compete with Lotus.

9.4.2 Look and feel infringement: Computer Associates v Altai

By 1992 the debate on the *Whelan* standard had reached fever pitch,[67] when along came another major look and feel case, *Computer Associates International Inc. v Altai*.[68] The *Computer Associates* (or CA) case offered the US Court of Appeals for the Second Circuit the chance to review *Whelan* and if necessary reset US copyright law. The case involved two pieces of software designed by CA, a mainframe job scheduling program[69] called 'CA-SCHEDULER' and a translator programme[70] called 'CA-ADAPTOR', and two competing products developed by Altai, 'ZEKE' and 'OSCAR'. The CA products had been developed over a period of time by a team of programmers including Claude Arney. In January 1984 Arney left CA and joined Altai to work on their job scheduling program ZEKE, taking with him copies of the source code for ADAPTOR. Using his familiarity

---

[64] 740 F Supp 37 (D Mass, 1990).

[65] Lotus's 'two-line moving-cursor menu,' presented the user with a list of command choices such as 'file', 'copy', 'quit' and a moving cursor to use in entering the user's commands. This was an extremely efficient menu system before the widespread adoption of 'point and click' menus.

[66] Funding Universe, *Lotus Development Corporation*: http://www.fundinguniverse.com/company-histories/Lotus-Development-Corporation-Company-History.html.

[67] Among the relatively small communities of copyright lawyers and software designers at least. It may not have been perceived as a major issue in the populace at large.

[68] 982 F 2d 693 (2nd Cir, 1992).

[69] A mainframe job scheduling program is essentially a piece of software to create a schedule specifying when the computer should run various tasks, and to manage the computer in carrying out these tasks.

[70] A translator program, or to give it its proper name, an 'operating system compatibility component', allows the same piece of software to run on different operating systems. As the IBM 370 computers CA-SCHEDULER was designed to run on could use one of three different operating systems ADAPTOR allowed CA-SCHEDULER to be used with any IBM 370 operating system.

with the CA software, and his copies of the ADAPTOR source code Arney rewrote ZEKE and created OSCAR. All parties agree that 'when the dust finally settled, Arney had copied approximately 30 per cent of OSCAR's code from CA's ADAPTER program.'[71] After release of the OSCAR software CA issued an infringement claim against Altai. Upon receiving the claim Altai, on the advice of counsel, had the entire OSCAR program rewritten by a team of programmers who were not familiar with either OSCAR or ADAPTOR and who had not been involved in the original OSCAR project. This procedure is known as a 'clean room rewrite' and is intended to remove all the tainted code. Once this process was complete Altai re-released OSCAR. The original copyright claim was settled with Altai agreeing to pay CA $364,444 in damages. CA though claimed that the rewritten version of OSCAR remained in breach of their copyright as there remained a substantial similarity between the two programs even after OSCAR was rewritten. The District Court rejected CA's claims and the case went before the Court of Appeals.

The decision in *CA* is one of the most complex judicial rulings in this field. To fully understand the entire scope of the decision requires a close examination of the Judge Walker's opinion. Firstly the court considered whether *Whelan* should be followed. After much discussion the court was clear in its decision: 'We think that Whelan's approach to separating idea from expression in computer programs relies too heavily on metaphysical distinctions and does not place enough emphasis on practical considerations. As the cases that we shall discuss demonstrate, a satisfactory answer to this problem cannot be reached by resorting, *a priori*, to philosophical first principals'.[72] Instead the court proposed a new three step test to be employed in evaluating whether or not infringement has occurred when dealing with non-literal infringement of utilitarian works such as computer software.

→ Highlight The Computer Associates Three-Step Test

1. Abstraction—the reverse engineering of the software design process. The court is to deconstruct the elements of the software from their lowest level (the code) to their highest level (the function of the programme). In so doing to retrace and map the steps taken by the software designer and record the structures and elements of the program at each level of abstraction.

2. Filtration—the separation of protected expression from unprotectable elements. Unprotectable elements to be filtered include ideas, anything dictated by efficiency, anything required by external factors (the so-called scènes à faire doctrine), or anything taken from the public domain. Whatever is left following filtering is known as the core of protectable expression or the 'golden nugget'.

3. Comparison—the court may now compare the alleged infringing software with the 'golden nugget' to determine whether a substantial piece of the original protected expression has been copied.

---

[71] 982 F 2d 693, 702.   [72] *ibid*, 706.

Applying this test the court found that the amended version of OSCAR did not infringe CA's copyright in ADAPTOR.

This three stage test is certainly more precise than the rather loose idea expression continuum found in *Whelan*. It should in theory prevent copyright from being used to protect essential elements of a program such as the menu system, as seen in *Lotus v Paperback*, or in program interfaces which are essential for interoperability. The problem with this test though is its complexity. The process of abstraction in particular is very poorly defined. Walker J describes it in his judgement thus:

> As applied to computer programs, the abstractions test will comprise the first step in the examination for substantial similarity. Initially, in a manner that resembles reverse engineering on a theoretical plane, a court should dissect the allegedly copied program's structure and isolate each level of abstraction contained within it. This process begins with the code and ends with an articulation of the program's ultimate function. Along the way, it is necessary essentially to retrace and map each of the designer's steps—in the opposite order in which they were taken during the program's creation. As an anatomical guide to this procedure, the following description is helpful: At the lowest level of abstraction, a computer program may be thought of in its entirety as a set of individual instructions organized into a hierarchy of modules. At a higher level of abstraction, the instructions in the lowest-level modules may be replaced conceptually by the functions of those modules. At progressively higher levels of abstraction, the functions of higher-level modules conceptually replace the implementations of those modules in terms of lower-level modules and instructions, until finally, one is left with nothing but the ultimate function of the program.... A program has structure at every level of abstraction at which it is viewed. At low levels of abstraction, a program's structure may be quite complex; at the highest level it is trivial.[73]

Even to a highly skilled lawyer trained in the process of forensic enquiry this description of the abstraction process is extremely difficult to process. With many judges of the period fundamentally unfamiliar with the process of software design and engineering it made the application the abstraction-filtration-comparison test extremely difficult. As we shall see below when English judges first wrestled with the test they got it spectacularly wrong, but it also meant that the test, if it was to survive needed to be developed by further case law if it was to be of use.

9.4.3 **Look and feel infringement: Lotus v Borland**

Whether or not the abstraction-filtration-comparison test was to succeed therefore depended upon the next major non-literal copying case in the US. This turned out to be *Lotus Development Corp. v Borland International Inc.*[74] This case is similar to the *Lotus v Paperback* case discussed above and is centred on the same issue of copyright protection for the menu system of the Lotus 1–2–3 spreadsheet. The court was faced with many questions but central among them was how to use the *Altai* test.

Having been asked to apply *Altai*, the court rejected its application finding that '[w]hile the Altai test may provide a useful framework for assessing the alleged nonliteral copying of computer code, we find it to be of little help in assessing whether the literal copying of

---

[73] *ibid*, 706–707.   [74] 49 F 3d 807 (1st Cir, 1995).

a menu command hierarchy constitutes copyright infringement'.[75] If the court had left its examination at this point we may have thought little about this: the court having distinguished *Altai* for the purposes of the case at hand, but Stahl, J went on: 'In fact, we think that the *Altai* test in this context may actually be misleading because, in instructing courts to abstract the various levels, it seems to encourage them to find a base level that includes copyrightable subject matter that, if literally copied, would make the copier liable for copyright infringement'.[76] This astute observation showed *Altai's* fatal flaw. *Altai* in asking judges to abstract the software and its supporting documentation assumed that at some level idea became expression and that some of the abstracted material would be protected as such. What the court in *Borland* discovered is that with some aspects of software there is no expressive element whatsoever and nothing for copyright to protect. In the instant case they were being asked to protect a menu command system which the court felt was a functional interface rather than a measure of expression.

➡ Highlight The *Borland* Functionality Test

In many ways, the Lotus menu command hierarchy is like the buttons used to control, say, a video cassette recorder (VCR). A VCR is a machine that enables one to watch and record video tapes. Users operate VCRs by pressing a series of buttons that are typically labelled 'Record', 'Play', 'Reverse', 'Fast Forward', 'Pause' and 'Stop/Eject.'

   That the buttons are arranged and labeled does not make them a 'literary work,' nor does it make them an 'expression' of the abstract 'method of operating' a VCR via a set of labeled buttons. Instead, the buttons are themselves the 'method of operating' the VCR.

Per Stahl J

The decision on *Borland* appears to have stopped the widespread adoption of the *Altai* test in the US. Although there have been a number of look and feel cases since *Borland*,[77] the application of the *Altai* test has been rare. Rather unusually the *Altai* test has arguably had greater effect on UK copyright policy with regard to non-literal software infringement than it had on US policy.

9.4.4 Look and feel before the UK courts

Altai was to have significant effect on early UK jurisprudence on look & feel infringement, due to the decision of the High Court in *John Richardson Computers Ltd v Flanders (No.2)*.[78] The facts of *Richardson* are quite similar to the earlier US case of *Whelan*. Mr Richardson was a pharmacist who had written a program which would print labels

---

[75] *ibid*, 815.   [76] *ibid*.
[77] See, e.g. *Blue Nile Inc. v Ice.com and Odimo, Inc.* 478 F.Supp.2d 1240, (WD Wash., 2007).
[78] [1993] FSR 497.

for dispensed drugs and keep a stock count of prescription drugs in a small dispensing pharmacy. This program was written in BASIC and could be used on Tandy and Video Genie machines. Although his program was successful Mr Richardson realised he was not a professional programmer and his program had some shortfalls. He therefore set up a company, John Richardson Computers (JRC) and employed Mr Flanders, a professional programmer. Mr Flanders rewrote the original program for the new BBC microcomputer with great success.

After leaving JRC's employ in 1986, Mr Flanders began work on a new program called 'Pharm-Assist' for the IBM series of computers. It was this subsequent program which led JRC to take action against Mr Flanders. This was the first major non-literal software copyright case in the UK. The case was allocated to Ferris J who had to both decide the scope and limits of copyright protection under the CDPA, and how to develop a test for infringement applicable to the UK. Following an analysis of the facts Ferris J concluded that there were six issues which he needed to address:

(1) Does copyright subsist in a computer program?

(2) If it does, is the copyright in the BBC program vested in the claimant?

(3) Assuming the above, what ought to be the approach of the Court to the appraisal of an allegation of breach of copyright in a computer program where it is not claimed that the source code itself has been copied?

(4) Are there objective similarities between the BBC program and the defendant's program which enable the defendant's program to be regarded in any respect as a copy of the BBC program?

(5) Were any such similar features in fact copied from the BBC program?

(6) Is any copying which may be found to have occurred the copying of a substantial part of the BBC program?[79]

Having established the first two questions were to be answered in favour of the claimant Ferris J turned his attention to the key question 'what ought to be the approach of the court to the appraisal of an allegation of breach of copyright in a computer program where it is not claimed that the source code itself has been copied?' He reviewed prior English authorities on non-literal copying of literary works, and the US case law on non-literal copyright infringement, culminating, at that time, in the case of *Altai* before concluding that '[there is] nothing in any English decision which conflicts with the general approach adopted in the Computer Associates case'.[80] Ferris J did though make one concession to the long line of prior authority on non-literal copying before the English courts. He felt that the 'golden nugget' was a peculiarity of the US jurisprudence: 'I think that in preference to seeking the "core of protectable expression" in the plaintiff's program an English court will first decide whether the plaintiff's program as a whole is entitled to copyright and then decide whether any similarity attributable to copying which is to be found in the defendant's program amounts to the copying of a substantial part of the plaintiff's program'.[81] As a result of this Ferris J established a new four-part UK test for non-literal infringement.

---

[79] Adapted from [1993] FSR 497, 515.   [80] *ibid*, 526–527.   [81] *ibid*, 527.

> ### ➜ **Highlight** The John Richardson Four-Part Test
>
> 1. Was the plaintiff's work protected by copyright?
> 2. Were there similarities between the plaintiff's and the defendant's programs?
> 3. Were these similarities caused by copying or were other explanations possible?
> 4. In the event copying is established did the copied elements constitute a significant part of the original work?

It was only at stage four, the test of significant copying that the *Altai* abstraction-filtration-comparison test would be employed, the other three stages being determinable by traditional non-literal infringement standards found in works of literature. This multi-faced test may be seen as a great improvement on the original *Altai* test. It predicts some of the issues raised later in the US in *Borland* and predicts the problem of over-protection the *Borland* court identified. The test though remained extremely complex, and some critics believe Ferris J never fully understood the complexities of the filtration stage in particular.[82]

These criticisms crystallised in the later case of *IBCOS Computers Ltd v Barclays Mercantile Highland Finance Ltd*.[83] This case, which was discussed previously under the literal infringement heading, found Jacob J highly critical of Ferris J's approach noting that: 'For myself I do not find the route of going via US case law particularly helpful.'[84] In particular Jacob J was concerned that the abstraction-filtration-comparison approach may be too strict for UK copyright law, noting that 'United States copyright law is not the same as ours, particularly in the area of copyright works concerned with functionality and of compilations ... United States case law has, ever since *Baker v Selden*, been extremely careful to keep copyright out of the functional field, either by saying there is no copyright in, or that copyright cannot be infringed by taking, the functional ... I doubt that would have happened here.'[85] With this in mind Jacob J suggests an alternate four-part test:

> ### ➜ **Highlight** The IBCOS Four-Part Test
>
> 1. What are the work or works in which the claimant claims copyright?
> 2. Is each such work 'original'?
> 3. Was there copying from that work?
> 4. If there was copying, has a substantial part of that work been reproduced?

---

[82] R. Arnold, 'Infringement of Copyright in Computer Software by Non-Textual Copying: First Decision at Trial by an English Court *John Richardson Computers* v. *Flanders*' [1993] EIPR 250; D. Rowland and E. MacDonald, *Information Technology Law* (3rd ed., 2005), 40; S. Lai, *The Copyright Protection of Computer Software in the United Kingdom* (2000), 33.

[83] [1994] FSR 275.   [84] *ibid*, 302.   [85] *ibid*, 292.

Unlike Ferris J, Jacob J did not propose the use of the *Altai* test at any point, instead trusting judges to apply their forensic skills in the same way a judge would be asked to in a non-literal literary infringement case. It has been argued that these two decisions are compatible with each other as *Ibcos* was a literal infringement case, while *Richardson* was a case on non-literal infringement.[86] This cannot escape the fact though that in *Ibcos* Jacob J clearly stated that 'going via the complication of the concept of a "core of protectable expression" merely complicates the matter so far as our law is concerned. It is likely to lead to overcitation of US authority based on a statute different from ours'.[87] Clearly therefore *Richardson* and *Ibcos* suggest two different tests for non-literal infringement in English law and as both cases were decided before the High Court, neither had greater authority. For a period therefore there were two equally valid tests at English Law. This remained unresolved until Pumfrey J in the later literal infringement case, *Cantor Fitzgerald International v Tradition (UK) Ltd.*[88] elected to follow the approach of Jacob J in *Ibcos*. Although *Cantor Fitzgerald* was again a High Court decision and could not overrule or enshrine either of the tests Pumfrey J made it clear that in his view the *Ibcos* standard was to be preferred. This case probably signalled the end of the brief flirtation the English courts had with the *Altai* test, but they do not signal the end of the development the law in relation to of non-literal infringement of computer software.

9.4.5 Look and feel: Navitaire v easyJet

In 2004 came probably the most significant non-literal infringement case in the UK to date: *Navitaire Inc. v easyJet Airline Co. & Anor.*[89] This involved an attempt by a customer to reverse engineer and replicate a piece of proprietary software. The software in question, called 'OpenRes'; was supplied under licence by the claimant to the defendant for use on their website. It allowed them to take bookings online and operate flights without the need to issue a physical ticket. By 1999 it became clear that easyJet wanted to radically overhaul their booking software to offer further routes, greater language support, and easier operability. easyJet negotiated with Navitaire about this upgrade but no agreement could be reached. Instead easyJet approached the second defendant, BulletProof Technologies with the request that BulletProof should write a new booking system which would allow easyJet to install these much needed upgrades but which would operate in all other respects exactly the same as OpenRes. This was important for easyJet for two reasons. Firstly they did not want to have to retrain all their ticketing agents on a new booking interface and secondly they wanted to migrate databases held on the OpenRes system to the new system.

BulletProof worked closely with easyJet's IT department over an extended period to create a new booking system 'eRes'. In designing eRes BulletProof did not examine or make use of the OpenRes code, instead they worked from an operational copy of OpenRes, copying the structure of the software and emulating the functions of OpenRes. Because none of the code had been directly copied Navitaire raised a non-literal infringement

---

[86] D. Bainbridge, *Introduction to Information Technology Law* (6th ed., 2008), 50.
[87] [1994] FSR 275, 302.   [88] [2000] RPC 95.   [89] [2004] EWHC 1725 (Ch) (2004).

claim focussing upon eRes's emulation of OpenRes command codes used by operators,[90] as well as emulations of the screen displays used particularly in the report screens and the underlying business logic of the OpenRes system.

Pumfrey J examined each of these claims in turn and in depth. He rejected Navitaire's claim that their command codes were protectable forms of expression. He found that the use of 'single [command] words in isolation are not to be considered as literary works' and that as a result 'the individual command words and letters do not qualify.'[91] This is based upon a decision in an earlier case *Exxon Corp. v Exxon Insurance Consultants International Ltd*,[92] which had ruled that single words are unlikely to be sufficiently original to qualify for copyright protection unless sufficient skill, labour, and judgement has been expended on the creation of the word. He then examined whether strings of command codes such as; 'A13JUNLTNAMS' could qualify for protection. Again the answer was in the negative these were not 'recorded' in the program code, rather they were commands entered by the user. In any event, Pumfrey J. noted that Recital 13 of the Software Directive[93] appeared to forbid protection of user interfaces meaning that the command codes could not be protected.[94] He then went on to consider whether Navitaire had copyright in the screen displays produced by the OpenRes software. He found that there were two types of screen display: one a simple text based display which provided an interface for the input of data, and the second more dynamic graphical user interface screens which made use of icons. The former he held were not protectable, but the latter were protectable and to the extent that the defendants had substantially copied these there was an infringement of copyright.

The key claim though was the final one; that in copying the look and feel of the OpenRes system the defendants had infringed the underlying business logic of the OpenRes system. This was the most important aspect of this case. To the end-user OpenRes and eRes were substantively the same. They looked the same, they operated in the same way and they produced the same results. eRes was a direct emulation of OpenRes. Whether or not this was a breach of copyright was likely to have far-reaching consequences. Pumfrey J described this as a question of 'copying without access to the thing copied, directly or indirectly'.[95] He noted that this claim was moving away from the literary element of software to its functional element: 'The claim depends first upon the contention that the manner in which a machine behaves under the control of a program represents part of the skill and labour that went into the program. This is not an unreasonable observation. On the contrary, it is the whole object of the programmer to get the computer to behave in the required manner'.[96]

---

[90] 'Command codes' are strings of characters which function as a type of shorthand in the booking system. They are explained by Pumfrey J at [26]: 'For example, in OpenRes, the command A13JUNLTNAMS (where the flight date is 13 June, the originating airport is Luton (LTN) and the destination airport Amsterdam (AMS)) should produce a screen displaying the available flights on that day'.   [91] *ibid*, [80].   [92] [1982] RPC 69.   [93] Above, n. 22.
[94] Recital 13 reads 'Whereas, for the avoidance of doubt, it has to be made clear that only the expression of a computer program is protected and that ideas and principles which underlie any element of a program, including those which underlie its interfaces, are not protected by copyright under this Directive.'   [95] [2004] EWHC 1725, [113].   [96] *ibid*, [114].

Despite seeing the merit of the claim Pumfrey J. was not willing to extend copyright protection in this manner:

> The questions in the present case are both a lack of substantiality and the nature of the skill and labour to be protected. Navitaire's computer program invites input in a manner excluded from copyright protection, outputs its results in a form excluded from copyright protection and creates a record of a reservation in the name of a particular passenger on a particular flight. What is left when the interface aspects of the case are disregarded is the business function of carrying out the transaction and creating the record, because none of the code was read or copied by the defendants. It is right that those responsible for devising OpenRes envisaged this as the end result for their program: but that is not relevant skill and labour. In my judgment, this claim for non-textual copying should fail. I do not come to this conclusion with any regret. If it is the policy of the Software Directive to exclude both computer languages and the underlying ideas of the interfaces from protection, then it should not be possible to circumvent these exclusions by seeking to identify some overall function or functions that it is the sole purpose of the interface to invoke and relying on those instead. As a matter of policy also, it seems to me that to permit the 'business logic' of a program to attract protection through the literary copyright afforded to the program itself is an unjustifiable extension of copyright protection into a field where I am far from satisfied that it is appropriate.[97]

Pumfrey J closes his analysis with an analogy which is extremely helpful in understanding his logic. 'Take the example of a chef who invents a new pudding. After a lot of work he gets a satisfactory result, and thereafter his puddings are always made using his written recipe, undoubtedly a literary work. Along comes a competitor who likes the pudding and resolves to make it himself. Ultimately, after much culinary labour, he succeeds in emulating the earlier result, and he records his recipe. Is the later recipe an infringement of the earlier, as the end result, the plot and purpose of both (the pudding) is the same? I believe the answer is no.'[98]

9.4.6 Look and feel in the UK after navitaire

The outcome of *Navitaire* was widely predicted[99] and has been widely welcomed.[100] The US jurisprudence of the late 1980s and early 1990s had long been identified as being over expansive in terms of the copyright protection offered to software developers. *Whelan*, for example, had been seen as a thorn in the side of software developers ever since its date of publication. The US courts had though over time taken steps to reduce the chilling effects decisions such as *Whelan* had on the software industry through a series of cases culminating eventually in *Borland* which reduced copyright protection for software to a manageable and balanced level. Unfortunately for the courts of

---

[97] *ibid*, [129]–[130].   [98] *ibid*, [127].

[99] Computer Weekly, *EasyJet software case 'a complete nonsense'*, 19 May 2003: http://www.computerweekly.com/Articles/2003/05/19/194648/easyjet-software-case-a-complete-nonsense.htm; J.C. Perez, 'Developer sues Accenture subsidiary', *Infoworld*, 6 MY 2003: http://www.infoworld.com/article/03/05/06/HNaccenturesued_1.html.

[100] S. Stokes, 'The Development of UK Software Copyright Law: From John Richardson Computers to Navitaire' [2005] 11 *Computer and Telecommunications Law Review* 129; M. Heritage & P. Jones, 'The End of "Look and Feel" and the Invasion of the Little Green Men? UK Copyright and Patent Protection for Software after 2005', [2006] 12 *Computer and Telecommunications Law Review* 67.

England and Wales early look and feel cases were heavily influenced by the expansive protection set out in *Altai* which assumed copyright protection must be afforded at some level to software. With few look and feel cases in the UK it took until 2004 for the UK to completely rid itself of the influence of the early US case law, despite Jacob J's best efforts. With *Navitaire* UK copyright law had now been rebalanced.

Before leaving non-literal copying and the approach of the Courts in England and Wales it falls upon us to consider one last case. This is the first case to reach the level of the Court of Appeal and involves a dispute over a series of arcade games; it is the case of *Nova Productions Ltd v Mazooma Games Ltd.*[101]

Nova Productions designs, manufactures, and sells arcade games. It brought two actions for infringement of copyright in one of its pool-based arcade games, Pocket Money. The first action was against Mazooma in relation to the creation and use of software for a game called Jackpot Pool. The second action was against a company called Bell Fruit in relation to a game called Trick Shot. Both claims alleged infringement in artistic works, being the graphics and the frames generated and displayed to the user of the game, and the computer program as a literary work.

At first instance, Kitchin J found for the defendants. He concluded there was no reproduction of any artistic copyright work, first because the features of similarity relied upon were either implemented quite differently or were different in appearance and, secondly, because those features represented ideas expressed at a very high level of generality or abstraction with no meaningful connection with the artistic nature of the graphic works relied on.[102] Applying the principles of *Navitaire*[103] he then rejected the software claim on the basis that any similarities derived were cast at such a level of abstraction and were so general that they could not amount to a substantial part of the computer program.[104]

On appeal it agreed that the individual frames stored in the memory of a computer were 'graphic works' within the meaning found in the CDPA.[105] However, save for the fact that they were of a pool table with pockets, balls, and a cue, nothing of the defendants' screens amounted to a substantial reproduction of a corresponding screen in Nova's game.[106] Nova though argued that there was a further artistic work in the screen graphics, that being: 'something beyond individual freeze-frame graphics ... there is a series of graphics which show the "in-time" movement of cue and [power] meter ... what the defendants had done was to create "a dynamic re-posing" of the [original]— one in which the detail of the subjects had changed, but an essential artistic element of the original was carried through to the Defendants.'[107]

Jacob LJ in giving the leading judgement rejected both claims. He found there was no reproduction of a substantial part of the screen display,[108] and further there was

[101] [2007] EWCA Civ 219 (March 14, 2007).
[102] *Nova Productions Ltd v Mazooma Games Ltd & Ors* [2006] EWHC 24 (Ch) (20 January 2006), [245].   [103] *ibid*, [248].   [104] *ibid*, [253].   [105] s. 4(1).
[106] *Nova Productions Ltd v Mazooma Games Ltd & Ors* [2007] EWCA Civ 219 (14 March 2007), [12].
[107] *ibid*, [13].   [108] *ibid*, [18].

also no foundation for Nova's 'in-time' argument.[109] With the artistic copyright claim quickly disposed of the Court could turn its attention to the claim that the defendants' programs infringed Nova's copyright in the Pocket Money program itself. Nova tried to persuade the Court that notwithstanding the decision in *Navitaire* someone who copies the function of a computer program to write his own program to achieve the same result is clearly appropriating part of the skill and labour expended in designing the program.[110] Jacob LJ rejected this submission. He also saw nothing in the Software Directive to suggest, as Nova contended, that the preparatory design work of a computer program should be protected as such, even if it consisted only of ideas as to what the program should do. It was clear to Jacob LJ from the Directive that for computer programs as a whole, including the preparatory design work, ideas were not to be protected. What was protected by way of preparatory design work was that work as a literary work, the expression of a design which was to go into the ultimate program, not the ideas themselves.[111]

What is most important about the *Nova* decision is not the actual outcome, which could have been confidently predicted prior to the first instance hearing in the High Court, but the very definite response of the Court of Appeal to a challenge to the principles of *Navitaire*. Nova made an early attempt to have the case referred to the European Court of Justice on the basis that there was a need to interpret the Software Directive's references to 'literary works' and 'preparatory design material for a computer program'. This was robustly rejected by the Court.[112] The Court then took an equally robust view of attempts to reinterpret *Navitaire*. In so doing they have given *Navitaire* a stamp of authority which allows us to imagine this will remain the UK 'gold standard' test with respect to non-literal software copyright infringement for the foreseeable future.

9.5 Copyright infringement and software: permitted acts

Not all activities involving the reproduction of elements of computer software infringe the rights of the copyright holder: some acts are permitted by the CDPA. Firstly there are a wide range of acts classified as 'fair dealing'. These are permitted activities, regulated by the Act, which apply to all literary works, software included.

The list of permitted acts is all contained in Chapter III and covers an extensive variety of activities. In terms of software the most commonly useful fair dealing defences are likely to include the right to make copies for the purpose of private study[113] and copying

---

[109] At [16] Jacob LJ notes: 'Graphic work is defined as including all the types of thing specified in s. 4(2) which all have this in common, namely that they are static, non-moving. A series of drawings is a series of graphic works, not a single graphic work in itself. No-one would say that the copyright in a single drawing of Felix the Cat is infringed by a drawing of Donald Duck. A series of cartoon frames showing Felix running over a cliff edge into space, looking down and only then falling would not be infringed by a similar set of frames depicting Donald doing the same thing. That is in effect what is alleged here.'   [110] *ibid*, [48].   [111] *ibid*, [50].
[112] *Nova Productions Ltd v Mazooma Games Ltd & Ors* [2006] EWCA Civ 1044 (25 July 2006).
[113] CDPA 1988, s. 29.

in the course of criticism, review, or news reporting.[114] The private study exception allows an individual to make a copy of a literary work 'for the purposes of research for a non-commercial purpose'. This allows individuals to study the work, but crucially in relation to software does not allow the user to 'convert a computer program expressed in a low level language into a version expressed in a higher level language'[115] or to 'observe, study or test the functioning of a computer program in order to determine the ideas and principles which underlie any element of the program.'[116] The reason for these exceptions is that there are specific fair use provisions for software found elsewhere in the Act which deal with these activities, and which will be discussed below.

The other general fair dealing right which may be implemented in relation to software is the criticism or review right. This allows the reviewer to carry out restricted activities in relation to the work for the purpose of 'criticism or review, of that or another work or of a performance of a work provided that it is accompanied by a sufficient acknowledgement'.[117] This right may be useful in particular when reviewing features of a piece of software in an online review or similar. Fair dealing rights also extend to a number of specific situations such as the use of copyright material in education and examinations,[118] libraries and archives,[119] and in the administration of justice,[120] but by far the most interesting section of the Act for those who deal with software design and development are the provisions contained in ss. 50A–50C, entitled: 'computer programs: lawful users'.

Sections 50A–50C contain four permitted acts specifically designed to allow for fair use of and development of computer software. These are the back-up right, the decompilation right, the study and testing right, and the adaptation right. The simplest of these rights, and the most useful for an end-user rather than developer, is the back-up right contained in s. 50A. This allows a lawful user of a copy of a computer program to 'make any back up copy of it which it is necessary for him to have for the purposes of his lawful use'. This allows a lawful user[121] to make a copy of their software to be stored in case the software requires to be reinstalled at some point in the future should the original installation become corrupt. When this right was first introduced by the Copyright (Computer Programs) Regulations 1992[122] it was envisaged that the back-up copy would be on a removable media such as a floppy disk but today with software usually requiring to be installed on to the HDD of the user before it can be used the 'back-up' copy is usually the original installation disc. This raises the interesting, and as yet unanswered question of whether an end-user could use s. 50A to allow them to install software on their hard drive.[123]

The remaining three rights are of greater use to software developers than users. The decompilation right contained in s. 50B, allows a lawful user of a copy of a computer

---

[114] CDPA 1988, s. 30.   [115] CDPA 1988, s. 29(4)(a).   [116] CDPA 1988, s. 29(4A).
[117] CDPA 1988, s. 30(1).   [118] CDPA 1988, ss. 32–36A.   [119] CDPA1988, ss. 37–44A.
[120] CDPA 1988, ss. 45–50.
[121] Helpfully defined in the Act as a person who 'has a right to use the program (whether under a licence to do any acts restricted by the copyright in the program or otherwise)', s. 50A(2). In effect this means anyone who has bought or otherwise licensed a legal copy of the software.
[122] SI 1992/3233.
[123] Although as yet unanswered the author is of the view that it is unlikely a judge would view an installed copy of a piece of software as a 'back-up' as it would be the primary use piece of software.

program expressed in a low level language (i.e. in object code) to convert it into a version expressed in a higher level language, (i.e. source code) or incidentally in the course of so converting the program, to copy it.[124] This right is subject to quite strict restrictions. One may only decompile for the purposes of the permitted objective 'to obtain the information necessary to create an independent program which can be operated with the program decompiled or with another program.'[125] Decompilation may only therefore be carried out to allow for interoperability of programs. The reason for the introduction of s. 50(B) is to ensure that software developers with a dominant position in either the operating systems market or part of the applications software market cannot use their market dominance to prevent competition. The fear was that dominant market players such as Microsoft would be able to prevent new entrants into the market by not revealing vital information about the file extensions used by the dominant software or about digital rights management systems they use to recognise and allow access to content. Imagine if you will a company wishes to produce a new word processing program. When they launch this program they want their customers to be able to access and edit files sent by friends and colleagues using the market leading Microsoft Word program, also they want files produced on their word processor to be equally accessible to users of Microsoft Word. This is interoperability, the ability of one program to interface with another. Without the ability to access the protocols Microsoft uses in its file extensions such interoperability would be impossible. This is remedied by s. 50B, which allows developers, when the designer of the original software withholds such information, to dissect the code of the original program to allow interoperability to take place.

The third permitted right is the right to 'observe, study or test the functioning of the program in order to determine the ideas and principles which underlie any element of the program if he does so while performing any of the acts of loading, displaying, running, transmitting or storing the program which he is entitled to do.'[126] This section may seem to be rather superfluous. It suggests a lawful user may study a copy of their own software, surely something that sensibly shouldn't worry the courts? The reason for s. 50BA is though twofold. Firstly it reinforces and gives some guidance as to the application of the idea/expression dichotomy which courts have had some difficulty with in relation to software. It also allows developers to produce software designs which emulate installed software as in the *Navitaire* case provided they do not copy the code of the original.

The final permitted right is the right for the lawful user of a piece of software to copy or adapt that software, including for the purpose of error correction.[127] Often the end-user licence supplied with a piece of software precludes the end-user from carrying out repairs or corrections to the software. This may be problematic, particularly if the copyright holder elects to end technical support for that piece of software or if the commercial relationship between the software supplier and the end-user breaks down. There are some inherent ambiguities in s.50C, in particular what is the exact meaning

---

[124] CDPA1988, s. 50B(1). [125] CDPA 1988, s. 50B(2)(a). [126] CDPA 1988, s. 50BA(1).
[127] CDPA 1988, ss. 50C(1), (2).

of 'necessary' found in s. 50C(1)(a)[128] and what qualifies as an 'error' for the purpose of s. 50C(2). Some guidance on the latter point may be gleaned from Jacob J's decision in *Mars UK Ltd v Teknowledge Ltd*.[129]

This was a case involving the upgrade of software on vending machines. Mars provide software on a programmable memory chip which allows vending machine operators to ensure only legal coins are accepted by their machines. This is done via a complex set of measurements including weight, size and electrical resistance of coins. When coinage changes, as with the introduction of new 5p, 10p, and 50p coins in the 1990s these coin-sorter units must be reprogrammed. Mars produce a reprogramming unit and license agents to carry out reprogramming on their behalf. Teknowledge are a private company who in the 1990s reverse engineered Mars's *Cashflow* software which managed most modern coin-sorter units. Mars claimed this was a breach of their copyright, Teknowledge claimed that they were permitted to produce a 'spare part' for replacement or repair, a common law defence found in an earlier House of Lords case, *British Leyland v Armstrong*.[130] In evaluating this claim Jacob J had to evaluate whether this common law defence had survived the passing of ss. 50A–C of the CDPA. In finding the common law defence no longer applied he also seemed to indicate that the error correction defence was different to a repair or update defence. Thus it seems that 'error correction' is limited to correcting errors in coding which directly interfere with the operability of the software: anything which requires to be carried out to update or repair software caused by environmental changes (as in *Mars*) is not error correction. Thus if you need to upgrade software because of the development of a new virus threat, the development of a new standard protocol or simply to reflect changes in operating practice this appears not to be error correction and not permitted by the s. 50C exception.

9.6 Patent protection for computer software

Section 1(2)(c) of the Patents Act 1977 is quite clear: 'the following (among other things) are not inventions for the purposes of this Act, that is to say, anything which consists of a scheme, rule or method for performing a mental act, playing a game or doing business, *or a program for a computer*'. Equally clear is Article 52(2)(c) the European Patent Convention, 'the following in particular shall not be regarded as inventions ... schemes, rules and methods for performing mental acts, playing games or doing business, *and programs for computers*'. With two such unarguably clear statements of the law at both European and UK level it may be assumed that this final section of this chapter would be necessarily short but unfortunately the law on patent protection for computer software is less clear than one might hope. Software developers have long sought patent protection for their output. As previously discussed as

---

[128] S.50C(1)(a) states: 'It is not an infringement of copyright for a lawful user of a copy of a computer program to copy or adapt it, provided that the copying or adapting is necessary for his lawful use'. [129] [1999] EWHC 226 (Pat). [130] [1986] AC 577.

early as 1972 in the case of *Gottschalk v Benson*,[131] the US Supreme Court examined the patentability of computer software, a question they were to return to in 1978 in the case of *Parker v Flook*.[132]

The UK courts had begun looking at the patentability of software processes even earlier. In *Gevers' Application*[133] the court examined whether a data processing operation using punch cards was a 'manner of manufacture' under the Patents Act 1949. Mr Gevers had designed an index of word trade marks using punched cards and a processing system which allowed use of these cards to check for similarity between applications for trade marks and previously registered marks. Graham J allowed Mr Gevers' application finding that his punched cards shared a similarity to a cam control for a lathe and could be distinguished from a card which contained written or printed information intended to convey information to the human eye or mind.[134] In the later case of *Burrough's Corporation (Perkin's Application)*,[135] the Court held that 'computer programmes which have the effect of controlling computers to operate in a particular way, where such programmes are embodied in physical form, are proper subject matter for letters patent'.[136] Although it may be assumed that the 1977 Patents Act statutorily overruled these early cases[137] software designers have continued to seek patent protection for their output. This is because the level of protection offered by patent law is much greater than that offered by copyright law, with the core idea of the software being protectable by patent and although patents are of a short lifespan, only twenty years as opposed to copyright's seventy years plus, this is more than sufficient when dealing with most software applications which tend to be of a short shelf life. Further the recent retreat from expansive look and feel protection seen in both the US and the UK has increased demand for software patents.

There is a problem with the wording of the Patents Act. There is a deliberate ambiguity designed to allow a patent to be awarded to an invention which contains a software element, but is not solely software-based. This ambiguity can be seen if you look at s. 1(2)(c).[138]

→ Highlight Patents Act 1977, s. 1(2)(c)

It is hereby declared that the following (among other things) are not inventions for the purposes of this Act, that is to say, anything which consists of a scheme, rule or method for performing a mental act, playing a game or doing business, or a program for a computer; but the foregoing provision shall prevent anything from being treated as an invention for the purposes of this Act only to the extent that a patent or application for a patent relates to that thing as such.

---

[131] Above n 2.   [132] Above n. 4.   [133] [1969] FSR 480.   [134] *ibid*, 486–487.
[135] [1973] FSR 439.   [136] *ibid*, 450.   [137] On which see *Gale's Application* [1991] RPC 305.
[138] The wording of the European Patent Convention is again similar. It states: 'The following in particular shall not be regarded as inventions ... schemes, rules and methods for performing mental acts, playing games or doing business, and programs for computers ... only to the extent to which a European patent application or European patent relates to such subject-matter or activities as such'—Article 52.

This ambiguity requires patent examiners to walk a very fine line. It is designed to ensure that patents may be awarded for inventions which rely upon software as an element of their design, think engine management systems or today even the humble washing machine, but to exclude pure software inventions such as hyperlinking or 'cut and paste'. The problem is that courts are required to develop tests which allow the patentable 'software-related invention' through, but which prevent the patenting of software. With such high values at stake it is no surprise that this fine distinction has come again and again under attack. The first attempt to define where this line should be drawn was the case of *VICOM/Computer-related Invention*.[139]

9.6.1 **VICOM/computer-related invention**

This was an application to the European Patent Office (EPO) under the Convention. It related to a new processing system for digital images, the process itself being described a series of mathematical algorithms.

The Appeal Board of the EPO decided that a claim for a technical process, carried out under the control of a programme cannot be regarded as related to a 'computer program as such'. They reached this decision in applying an approach which became known as the 'technical effect' approach. It asks judges or patent examiners to examine the application as if the excepted element (the software) were not present. Then ask 'does the application without the excepted element meet the standard of patentability?' If the only novel or original element is in the excepted element the answer will be no and the application should be refused. If the software element is merely part of the novelty of the invention the answer will be yes and a patent should be awarded.

In allowing VICOM's appeal the Board noted that: 'the computer program referred to ... merely serves to calculate the element values of the small generating kernel and the weighting values. It does not form part of the image processing methods claimed, nor is it embodied in the apparatus claims. Indeed such a program would not be patentable in view of the Board's foregoing considerations'.[140] The Board also gave some helpful pointers as to what would be patentable and what not:

1. A computer of known type set up to operate according to a new program cannot be considered as forming part of the state of the art.

2. A claim directed to a technical process which process is carried out under the control of a program (whether by means of hardware or software), cannot be regarded as relating to a computer program as such.

3. A claim which can be considered as being directed to a computer set up to operate in accordance with a specified program (whether by means of hardware or software) for controlling or carrying out a technical process cannot be regarded as relating to a computer program as such.

The *VICOM* decision was highly influential both before the Board of Appeal of the EPO and before the UK courts. It was applied by the Court of Appeal in *Merrill Lynch's*

---

[139] [1987] 2 EPOR 74.   [140] *ibid*, [18].

Application,[141] in which the court rejected Merrill Lynch's application to patent a system for automating market trades. The court found that that the inventive step of Merrill Lynch's system was contained in the software which tracked the market and executed trades: as such the 'invention' was not patentable. Repeatedly throughout the late 1980s and 1990s *VICOM* was followed by the UK courts in a series of cases including *Genentech Inc.'s Patent,*[142] *Gale's Application,*[143] *Wang Laboratories Inc.'s Application,*[144] and *Fujitsu Ltd's Application.*[145] It appeared a clear and simple test to determine the patentability of software related inventions, as opposed to pure software had been achieved. Yet even as this stability had established itself activities were taking place elsewhere which threatened to undermine it.

9.6.2 **The effect of State Street Bank**

In the US the decision in *Borland* had reduced considerably the scope of look and feel protection. Further it had indicated that functional elements of software such as command systems or interfaces were unlikely to be protectable. This led to a new wave of patent applications for software elements.

In *State Street Bank & Trust Co. v Signature Financial Group,*[146] the US Court of Appeals for the Federal Circuit found that a patent application which was to all intents and purposes the amalgamation of two excluded subject-matters, computer software and a method of doing business was patentable. The application involved a claimed invention of a 'Data Processing System for Hub and Spoke Financial Services Configuration'. In layman's terms this was a computerised system for moving funds within a series of accounts managed by the applicants. The case therefore shares many similarities with the English case of *Merill Lynch.* In a departure from the previous case law the court found that systems such as these were patentable if it produces 'a useful, concrete and tangible result'.[147] Almost immediately the US Patent and Trademark Office issued new guidelines to examiners indicating that software which produced such a result may be patentable.[148] With the US Patent and Trade Mark Office now entertaining patent applications for software inventions pressure grew on other jurisdictions to follow suit. The EPO was well placed to consider an expansion of patent policy.

In February 1999 the Board of Appeal considered the case of *IBM's Application.*[149] This involved an application to patent a data processing system for windows based computers such that any information displayed in one window which is obscured by a second window is automatically moved to allow the first window to be clearly displayed. In a paradigm shifting ruling, perhaps influenced by the *State Street* ruling in the US, the Board ruled that a computer program was not excluded from patentability *per se.*

---

[141] [1989] RPC 561.   [142] [1989] RPC 147.   [143] Above n 136.   [144] [1991] RPC 463.
[145] [1997] RPC 608.   [146] 149 F 3d 1368 (Fed. Cir. 1998).
[147] *ibid,* 1374. It should be noted that in the recent case of *In re Bernard L. Bilski and Rand* 88 U.S.P.Q.2d 1385 (2008), the US Court of Appeals for the Federal Circuit overruled parts of the *State Street* test noting that 'those portions of our opinions in State Street and AT&T relying solely on a "useful, concrete and tangible result" analysis should no longer be relied on.'
[148] H. Rockman, *Intellectual Property Law for Engineers and Scientists* (2004), 229–230.
[149] [1999] RPC 861.

It stated that 'the exclusion from patentability of programs for computers as such (Article 52(2) and (3) of the EPC) may be construed to mean that such programs are considered to be mere abstract creations, lacking in technical character. The use of the expression "shall not be regarded as inventions" seems to confirm this interpretation. Programs for computers must be considered as patentable inventions when they have a technical character.'[150]

> **→ Highlight** Decision of the Board of Appeal in IBM's Application
>
> A patent may be granted not only in the case of an invention where a piece of software manages, by means of a computer, an industrial process or the working of a piece of machinery, but in every case where a program for a computer is the only means, or one of the necessary means, of obtaining a technical effect, where, for instance, a technical effect of that kind is achieved by the internal functioning of a computer itself under the influence of said program.

In short, the Board found that if the effect of the software was to cause a computer to function in a novel and inventive manner that software may be patentable.

This was to be the first in a long line of cases in which the EPO and the Board of Appeal gave ever narrower interpretations of the meaning of Article 52(2)(c) of the Convention. In *PBS Partnership/Controlling pension benefits systems*,[151] the Board of Appeal held that a program which calculated pension benefits and life assurance benefits could be patentable, despite the fact that the program itself would usually be excluded subject matter under Article 52 as well as the operation it was performing. This is an extremely complex decision. The process that the program was performing was a method of doing business which is excluded from patentability by Article 52(2)(c), and the system or apparatus that was to be protected was software which was similarly excluded. But by a tortuous process of interpretation the Board found that although business practices were not patentable under the Convention and that a non-technical process for carrying out that activity was similarly not protected, 'An apparatus[152] constituting a physical entity or concrete product suitable for performing or supporting an economic activity, is an invention within the meaning of Article 52(1) EPC'.[153] This is extremely difficult to conceptualise. While both the operation itself and software in the abstract were excluded subject matters, the design of a software-based system to carry out the process could be patentable:[154] as David Bainbridge notes: 'it seemed to diminish the exclusion of computer programs as such from inventions almost to vanishing point'.[155]

---

[150] *ibid*, 870.   [151] [2002] EPOR 52.
[152] Being an organisational structure, including a suitably programmed computer or system of computers.   [153] [2002] EPOR 52, [5].
[154] Although in this case it was not as it lacked the necessary inventive step.
[155] Bainbridge, above n. 10, 155.

9.6.3 **De facto software patents under the european patent convention**

From this position it was a simple step to allow *de facto* software patents while the Convention retained the fiction that they were excluded subject matter. In *HITACHI/ Auction method*[156] the Board considered a patent for an online Dutch auction system. The auction would start with a preliminary data exchange between the bidder's computers and the server (auction) computer in order to collect bids from the participants. Each bid would comprise two values, a 'desired price' and a 'maximum price in competitive state'. Once this was complete the auction would run automatically and requires no further bidder interaction. An auction price is set and successively lowered until it reaches the level of the highest bid or bids as determined by the 'desired price'. In the case of several identical bids the price is increased until only the bidder having offered the highest 'maximum price' is left who is then declared successful.[157] The Board found that there are three requirements which must be fulfilled for a claim of this nature to be patented:

1. It should be an 'invention'. That is it must be new, inventive, and industrially applicable.

2. The term 'invention' is to be construed as 'subject-matter having technical character', and

3. Verification that the claimed subject-matter is an invention within the meaning of Article 52(1) EPC must be done before performing the three other tests, i.e. the novelty, the inventive step and the industrial applicability tests.[158]

The Board then confirmed the fact that a mixture of a technical and non-technical feature may be patentable, finding that 'contrary to the examining division's assessment, the apparatus of claim three is an invention within the meaning of Art. 52(1) EPC since it comprises clearly technical features such as a "server computer", "client computers" and a "network"'.[159] Although the application in the instant case was ultimately rejected as it lacked an inventive step, this, like the *Pension Benefits Case* before, it is an incredible decision. It seems to suggest that the clothing of a business method, or perhaps even a mathematical formula or a scheme for carrying out a mental act in a technical apparatus may be patentable.

The Board seems to accept that this approach is controversial, perhaps even counter to the original intent of the drafters of the Convention, in noting that: 'The Board is aware that its comparatively broad interpretation of the term "invention" in Art. 52(1) EPC will include activities which are so familiar that their technical character tends to be overlooked, such as the act of writing using pen and paper. Needless to say, however, this does not imply that all methods involving the use of technical means are patentable. They still have to be new, represent a non-obvious technical solution to a technical problem, and be susceptible of industrial application.'[160]

---

[156] [2004] EPOR 55.   [157] Adapted from [2004] EPOR 55, [19].   [158] *ibid*, [20].
[159] *ibid*, [26].   [160] *ibid*, [34].

The high water point, at the date of writing, in this expansive interpretation of Art. 52 is to be found in the connected cases of *MICROSOFT/Clipboard formats I*[161] and *MICROSOFT/Clipboard formats II*.[162] Both cases involved patent applications made by Microsoft to cover aspects of their Windows clipboard system in particular allowing non-file data to be transferred from one application to another via the clipboard. The Board followed *Hitachi* and found that a method applying technical means was an invention and that a computer system was a technical means. The Board emphasised the difference between a computer system and a computer program:

> The Board would like to emphasise that a method implemented in a computer system represents a sequence of steps actually performed and achieving an effect, and not a sequence of computer-executable instructions (i.e. a computer program) which just have the potential of achieving such an effect when loaded into, and run on, a computer. Thus, the Board holds that the claim category of a computer-implemented method is distinguished from that of a computer program. Even though a method, in particular a method of operating a computer, may be put into practice with the help of a computer program, a claim relating to such a method does not claim a computer program in the category of a computer program.[163]

This is the clearest exposition to date of the distinction between computer programs, which are excluded from patentability and a computer-implemented method, which is not. Although the computer-implemented method may just describe the operation of the software it is seen as distinct from the software. Again patent examiners are being asked to walk a very fine line.

9.6.4 **Aerotel Ltd v Telco and Macrossan's Application**

The UK courts have watched all these developments with interest. Although the Board of Appeal has no authority over UK patent law, the relationship between a UK patent and a European patent is such that decisions of the EPO, and its Board of Appeal, are highly influential on UK patent law and policy. This tension between the newly expansive European approach and the UK approach which was still heavily influenced by *VICOM* came to a head in *Aerotel Ltd v Telco and Macrossan's Application*.[164]

The case concerned two inventions; one a system allowing for pre-paid calls to be made from any telephone (Aerotel), the other an automated method of acquiring the documents necessary to incorporate a company through the use of an online database (Macrossan). In giving the judgement of the court Jacob LJ spent a considerable amount of time examining the prior UK case law, including *Merrill Lynch, Gale and Fujitsu* and the Board of Appeal decisions including *Pensions Benefits, Hitachi* and *Microsoft*. It was clear from his examination that little common ground now lay between the two jurisdictions and Jacob LJ found it was incumbent upon the court to review and modernise the UK law.

---

[161] [2006] EPOR 39.   [162] [2006] EPOR 40.   [163] *ibid*, [42].
[164] [2006] EWCA Civ 1371, [2007] 1 All ER 225.

> **→ Highlight** The Macrossan Test
>
> The new test came in two stages.
>
> 1. UK authority should be preferred over the recent EPO line of authority. Jacob LJ was quite forthright in his view on this: 'The fact is that this court is bound by its own precedent: that decided in Merrill Lynch, Gale and Fujitsu—the technical effect approach with the rider.'
> 2. A clear and simple test which brought the *Merrill Lynch* test up to date should be used. This involved the development of a new four-stage test:
>   a. Construe the claim;
>   b. Identify the contribution;
>   c. Ask; is the contribution solely of excluded matter? and
>   d. Check whether the contribution is technical.

Macrossan may be seen as either an attempt to entrench the *VICOM* 'technical effect' approach, something to be criticised,[165] or as an attempt to bridge the divide between the UK approach and the European approach by inviting the Board of Appeal to reconsider post *VICOM* developments in light of the fact that *VICOM* has never been expressly overruled.[166] It is clear the court in *Macrossan* intended the latter. At paragraph 29 Jacob LJ invites the Board of Appeal to reconsider their recent jurisprudence:

> We are conscious of the need to place great weight on decisions of the Boards of Appeal, but, given the present state of conflict between the old (*Vicom* etc.) and the new (*Hitachi etc.*) approaches, quite apart from the fact that there are three distinct new approaches each to some extent in conflict with the other two, it would be premature to do so. If and when an Enlarged Board rules on the question, this Court may have to re-consider its approach. If such a ruling were to differ from what this court had previously decided a question would arise as to what should be done: should this court (and first instance courts) follow the previous rulings in our courts, leaving it to the House of Lords (or the future Supreme Court) to decide what to do or should the new ruling of the Enlarged Board be followed? It may be that the better course then would be for a decision of the first instance court to be 'leapfrogged' to the House of Lords or Supreme Court. For the present we do not have to decide this. All we decide now is that we do not follow any of the trio. The fact that the BGH has already declined to follow Pension Benefits reinforces this view—doing so will not lead to European consistency.

Unfortunately this request initially fell on deaf ears. The President of the Board of Appeal refused to acknowledge the differences in approach between the EPO and UK courts[167] and a clear distinction remained. The UK courts continue to apply the *Macrossan* test, most recently in *Re AT&T Knowledge Ventures LP*[168] and most importantly to date in the

---

[165] See, e.g. Bainbridge, above n. 10, 157.
[166] See, e.g. D. Booton, 'The Patentability of Computer-implemented Inventions in Europe' [2007] *Intellectual Property Quarterly* 92.
[167] Letter from Professor Alain Pompidou President of the EPO Board of Appeal to Lord Justice Robin Jacob (undated): http://www.ipo.gov.uk/p-pn-subjectmatter-letter.htm.
[168] [2009] EWHC 343 (Pat).

Appeal Court in *Symbian Ltd v Comptroller General of Patents*.[169] Then came an interesting development: in summer 2007 Professor Pompidou, the President of the Board of Appeal who had refused Lord Justice Jacob's request, was replaced by Alison Brimlow. Ms. Brimlow had been the Comptroller General of the UK Patent Office and so was familiar with the perceived divide between the *VICOM* approach and the *HITACHI* approach. On 22 October 2008 she referred a number of questions to the Enlarged Board of Appeals of the EPO concerning the patentability of computer software.[170] At the time of writing the decision of the Board is pending but the questions demonstrate that Ms. Brimlow, unlike her predecessor, believes there is a clear distinction between the *VICOM* and *HITACHI* approaches. Among the questions asked are: 'Can a claim in the area of computer programs avoid exclusion under art. 52(2)(c) and (3) merely by explicitly mentioning the use of a computer or a computer readable storage medium?' and 'Does the activity of programming a computer necessarily involve technical considerations?'. The answer to these questions, and the others posed by the President, will shape the next stage of software patents.

9.7 **Conclusion**

Of all the areas where law and the digital society interface the question of how the law should protect computer software is probably the most complex. This is due to many factors. Firstly there is the long history: the software industry was the first fully-formed digital industry, emerging in the 1970s before digital entertainment media, digital criminal activity, or e-commerce. Secondly the product of the software industry is both traditionally the most valuable of any digital industry and the most complex. The software industry emerged before the legal system could adapt meaning that software has never had a planned legal response in the way that computer crime, electronic contracting, or databases have. Whereas it may be argued that software is a unique product, and would have been suited to a *sui generis* form of protection it has instead fallen between two stools: copyright protection designed primarily for artistic expression not functional goods, and patents which seek to protect inventions, not systems of performing human acts. We now stand at a crossroads, the second in the short lifespan of this industry. In the 1980s any hope of a software patent law was abandoned in favour of expansive look and feel copyright protection. The 1990s and the 2000s have seen a shift back towards software patents both explicitly (as in the US) and implicitly (in Europe). The President's reference to the Enlarged Board of Appeal takes on particular significance against this background, particularly at a time when the US is also reviewing the role of software patents following the *en banc* decision of the US Court of Appeals for the Federal Circuit in *In re Bernard L. Bilski and Rand*.[171]

---

[169] [2008] EWCA Civ 1066. For a discussion of the *Symbian* case see C. De Mauny, 'Court of Appeal Clarifies Patenting of Computer Programs' (2009) 31 *European Intellectual Property Review* 147. [170] *President's Reference/Computer Program Exclusion* [2009] EPOR 9.
[171] Above n. 146.

Whatever method of protection is followed, copyright law or patent law, the value of the software industry to the GDP of developed nations ensures some form of protection will be afforded to software. It is essential however that whatever form the next generation of software protection takes we do not repeat the mistakes of the look and feel cases of the 1980s in providing a form of protection that is either under or over inclusive. Competition within the industry requires that innovation is not stifled by the application of IPRs, while free riders must be discouraged. Protecting software products has proven to be one of the most intractable problems of the information society, a problem we have yet to fully deal with.

FURTHER READING

Books

P. Leith, *Software and Patents in Europe* (2007)

S. Lai, *The Copyright Protection of Computer Software in the United Kingdom* (2000)

D. Bainbridge, *Software Licensing* (1999)

Chapters and Articles

S. Stokes, 'The Development of UK Software Copyright Law: From John Richardson Computers to Navitaire' (2005) 11 *Computer and Telecommunications Law Review* 129

D. Booton, 'The Patentability of Computer-implemented Inventions in Europe' [2007] *Intellectual Property Quarterly* 92

K. Moon, 'The nature of computer programs: tangible? goods? personal property? intellectual property?' (2009) 31 *European Intellectual Property Review* 396

10

Copyright in the digital environment

The move from physical to digital distribution models and the development of the internet are two of the most disruptive events of the twentieth century. They have affected the lives of billions of people globally and changed the way the developed world trades, communicates, and socialises. But as with all disruptive technologies the positive benefits they bring are tinged with negative effects. As well as allowing people to keep in touch over long distances and allowing new models of commerce to develop they have also allowed the internet to become the largest and most efficient copying machine built by man. This development is not accidental it is in the DNA of the internet that it copies and distributes digital information.

When built in 1969 the difficulty that the designers of the ARPANET had to overcome was how to supply data from one computer to another in a remote location. This entailed copying the data, splitting it into packets, and delivering these packets to remote locations: in essence the building of a platform for the copying and distribution of digital content. While computers were expensive and network connections slow, this was not a problem. The very idea that someone would pay several thousand dollars for a computer to allow them to download and store copies of music, movies, or games across a network connection which operated at 9,600 bits per second,[1] was frankly laughable. But in the last twenty years the costs of computers, storage media, and high speed downloads have tumbled as the information society has become part of our everyday lives. This, coupled with an explosion of digital consumer devices such as CD/DVD players, MP3/MP4 players, Smart Phones such as the multifunctional Apple iPhone, games systems, and other electronic consumer devices such as the Sony eBook Reader has created a new marketplace for digital consumer entertainment products, products that are at extreme risk of piracy and given the nature of the internet as a copying and distribution device have been pirated extensively. This increase in piracy is occurring at a time when producers of digital consumer goods are trying to establish new delivery models for their products through direct download delivery sites such as Apple's iTunes, Amazon's Kindle Store, and Netflix Download. When they are asked to compete against free services such as BitTorrent it is hard for them to develop their market: what rational person is going to pay £10.99 to download a movie from iTunes if they can get it for free via a BitTorrent client?

---

[1] To underline how much download speeds have accelerated in the last twenty years a standard 9600 bps modem in use in 1990 would take about 85 minutes to download a 6mb MP3 music file, today an 8MB/s broadband connection would take around 7–10 seconds.

This chapter focuses on the battle between producers of content and free riders; between the copyright industries and their own consumers; between taking profit from content and making it free. It is a battle fought on many levels, an economic level, an artistic level, a legal level, and an ideological level. Some people believe passionately that the copyright industries are profiteering, charging on average £7.99 for a full album download on iTunes which involves no cost of physical production (no need for a CD case, album sleeve or even a CD), no distribution costs (no need for fleets of vans to deliver CDs to shops) and no overheads for the retailer (iTunes has no shops on which it needs to pay rent, rates, heating, or staff costs). Others believe equally passionately that failure to control peer-to-peer file sharing will have long term deleterious effects for all copyright industries. Some believe passionately that the internet allows an artistic freedom which was impossible in the old distribution model when artists needed to be signed to a music label before their music could reach the shops; others worry about an explosion of mediocre music, films, and video games. Some believe that the illegal file sharing of copyright protected media is the single biggest threat the copyright industry has faced. They believe there is a need to review, rewrite, and extend copyright protection to afford additional protection to copyright holders in an attempt to rebalance the interests of copyright holders and users. They argue this is necessary because the level of protection copyright holders had before the advent of the information society has been eroded by the simple, free, and (mostly) anonymous practice of file sharing. Others believe the copyright industry is seeking to extend copyright protection in a way which may prove harmful to society at large. Finally some believe that in the digital environment with its limitless supply of ones and zeros information wants to be and should be free. Others disagree. This will be the story of this chapter but before we get to the heart of the modern debate about file sharing and free riding copyright content we must begin with an analysis of how the internet has challenged the application and development of copyright law.

10.1 Linking, caching, and aggregating

When ARPANET was designed and built in the 1960s few considerations were given to copyright issues. As the network was designed only to connect research computers the copyright in the material accessible on ARPANET was usually owned by the university or research centre where the mainframe computer could be found. As all involved in the ARPANET project were entering the project with the express aim of sharing research materials and findings there was no conceptualisation of copyright infringement being pursued for any ARPANET activity.

Copyright became more of an issue as the network deregulated; the advent of private Internet Service Providers saw copyright issues came to the fore. In particular the World Wide Web posed a major challenge to established copyright orthodoxy. It is founded upon hyperlinking: the very nature of its DNA being the ability to join together original content, or to draw original content from one place and place it in another (as is done with embedded images). This, coupled with the widespread geographical reach of the web and its foundations as an easy to use and easy to access platform, meant that quickly copyright law and web-based applications came into direct competition with each other.

10.1.1 **Web-linking**

First among common web-copyright issues was the issue of linking. It may seem clear that when one places original material on a web site that it is the intent of the copyright holder that, absent a password protection system to control access, the material may be accessed and read (including making a cache copy of the content in the end-user's browser cache),[2] but this is only part of the issue. Web pages function by getting referrals from other pages (links), these links are what make the web dynamic, and so one may assume that as well as implying that placing content on a public web page allows for reading and caching of that content it also allows for linking to that content. This is not the case.

This issue came to a head in 1996 in the case of *Shetland Times Ltd v Wills*.[3] The pursuer was an established newpaper publisher producing a local newspaper servicing the Shetland Isles. Some time prior to October 1996 they began publishing an online version of their newspaper on the expectation that once this became popular they would be able to sell advertising space on the front page of the site. Dr Wills operates a web-only news publication, *The Shetland News*. In October 1996 it became clear to the pursuers that *The Shetland News* was embarking upon a programme of so-called deep linking: this is linking directly to pages in the body of a site bypassing the front page. Their activities are described by Lord Hamilton:

> Since about 14 October 1996 the defenders have included among the headlines on their front page a number of headlines appearing in recent issues of *The Shetland Times* as reproduced on the pursuers' web site. These headlines are verbatim reproductions of the pursuers' headlines as so reproduced. A caller accessing the defenders' web site may, by clicking on one of those headlines appearing on the defenders' front page, gain access to the relative text as published and reproduced by the pursuers. Access is so gained and subsequent access to other such headlines also gained without the caller requiring at any stage to access the pursuers' front page. Thus, access to the pursuers' items (as published in printed editions and reproduced by them on their web site) can be obtained by bypassing the pursuers' front page and accordingly missing any advertising material which may appear on it.[4]

The final sentence here demonstrates the crux of the case. By deep-linking to *Shetland Times* news stories *The Shetland News* was misappropriating the advertising revenue from these stories. *The Shetland Times* sought an interim interdict (the Scottish equivalent of an injunction) to prevent *The Shetland News* from using any of their headlines on its site or from linking directly to any of their content other than their home page.

---

[2] For those unfamiliar with the operations of web browsers a cache copy is a stored copy of a web page previously visited by the user. These are used to reduce the amount of information that needs to be transmitted across the network during a browsing session as information previously stored in the cache can often be reused by the browser. This reduces bandwidth and processing requirements of the web server, and helps to improve responsiveness for users of the web. Modern browsers employ a built-in cache, but some ISPs also use a caching proxy server, which is a cache that is shared between all users of that network. Thus if a customer of O2 broadband visits http://www.bbc.co.uk/news, O2 will cache a copy in its server, then when the next customer requires http://www.bbc.co.uk/news instead of calling upon the BBC server to deliver the page O2 will supply the copy from its server. The server periodically checks with the BBC server to see if a page update is needed.

[3] 1997 SC 316.   [4] *ibid*, 318.

Lord Hamilton had two decisions to make, (1) did a newspaper headline qualify as a 'literary work' under s. 17 of the Copyright, Designs and Patents Act, and (2) whether a web page constituted a 'cable programme' under s. 20 of the Copyright, Designs and Patents Act as then worded.[5] He evaluated both claims in an interim hearing. Due to the nature of the hearing no authority was laid before the court making the opinion of little authority, however he found that:

> While literary merit is not a necessary element of a literary work, there may be a question whether headlines, which are essentially brief indicators of the subject matter of the items to which they relate, are protected by copyright. However, in light of the concession that a headline could be a literary work and since the headlines at issue (or at least some of them) involve eight or so words designedly put together for the purpose of imparting information, it appeared to me to be arguable that there was an infringement, at least in some instances, of s. 17.[6]

This at the time was of passing interest. The question of replicating headlines or short descriptions of text was no doubt important especially when one is creating a link to content on another site; the real question though was whether Lord Hamilton felt a web site was itself capable of copyright protection. Although the wording of s. 20 has changed since the case, the decision on this final issue was of widespread importance. This may only have been an interim hearing, and the jurisdiction of the court may have been limited, but this was the first time a judge anywhere in the world had been asked to rule on the copyright status of a web site. Lord Hamilton found that a web page operated by sending information across a network which fitted with the definition of a cable service as then defined as 'a service which consists wholly or mainly in sending visual images, sounds or other information by means of a telecommunications system, otherwise than by wireless telegraphy'.[7] On this basis, and on the basis that at an interim hearing the pursuer only needs to demonstrate a 'balance of convenience' in their favour, he found that 'the pursuers have, in my opinion, a *prima facie* case that the incorporation by the defenders in their web site of the headlines provided at the pursuers' web site constitutes an infringement of s. 20 of the Act by the inclusion in a cable programme service of protected cable programmes'.[8]

The *Shetland Times* case was at once unimportant and yet of international influence. As an interim hearing it carried almost no precedence, yet as the first published judicial opinion on copyright protection for web content, this four page decision which discussed no previous authority was discussed and analysed globally.[9] Lord Hamilton was often, and unfairly given the nature of the hearing, criticised for extending the definition of a cable programme to cover a web site. Most critics attacked his interpretation

---

[5] It should be noted s. 20 of the CDPA 1988 has been completely rewritten since this case was heard. With new text being introduced by *The Copyright and Related Rights Regulations* 2003 (SI 2003/2498).   [6] 1997 SC 316, 319.

[7] This was found in s. 7(1) of the CDPA 1988. This section was repealed in whole by *The Copyright and Related Rights Regulations* 2003.   [8] 1997 SC 316, 319.

[9] Just a few of these papers include: H. MacQueen, 'Copyright in Cyberspace' [1998] JBL 297; J. Adams, 'Trespass in a digital environment', [2002] IPQ 1; J. Connolly & S. Cameron, 'Fair Dealing in Webbed Links of Shetland Yarns' 1998 (2) JILT: http://www2.warwick.ac.uk/fac/soc/law/elj/jilt/1998_2/connolly/; and S. Pitiyasak, 'Does Thai law provide adequate protection for copyright infringement on the Internet?' [2003] 25 EIPR 6.

that a web site could operate as a cable program. They pointed out that the definition of a cable program as one which 'sends visual images, sounds or other information' suggested a push media system, a type of media platform where a broadcaster sends programmes or other content unbidden (such as TV or Radio), whereas a web site is a pull media system, the customer must select what to receive and ask for it. Whatever the critics thought Lord Hamilton had decided both that the contents of web pages could be protected by copyright law and that deep linking without the permission of the copyright holder could infringe copyright. In making this decision the door had been opened for further copyright challenges to web based content and as may be expected a number of cases followed looking at how copyright law should deal with linking and in particular deep linking.

Across Europe claims were raised against deep linking. One of the earliest cases was the French case of *Havas Numerique et Cadre On Line v Keljob*.[10] This case involved two online job agencies and the operator of a specialised jobs search engine. The claimants, the job agencies, claimed that in offering direct links from their search results to particular pages within the claimants' sites the defendant was in infringement of their copyright and database rights. At an interim hearing the Tribunal de Commerce de Paris distinguished between simple hyperlinks and the practice of deep linking. The court observed that linking was implicitly permissible and even encouraged providing only that the link is via the homepage. The court found though that links which appropriate the referenced site's contents mask the URL of the linked site or fail to inform the user that he or she has transferred to the site of a different content provider infringes the property rights of the linked website owner. Accordingly, the court found the defendant's deep links to be parasitical and an unlawful appropriation of the claimants' work. On appeal though this decision was reversed.[11] The Grande Instance de Paris found that Keljob merely operated a search engine which provided results to its users and openly redirected them to pages within the claimants' sites. Resultantly, there was no copying and no distribution in any manner which was unfair.

A similar case was heard in Germany where the Landgericht (District Court) of Cologne heard the case of *Stepstone v Ofir*.[12] This was a case involving two competing online job agencies. The defendant would routinely deep-link to job details held on the claimant's website. The claimant claimed copyright infringement; the defendant argued that by placing information on a publicly accessible web page the claimant had given an implied license to link to it. The court held that the defendant, in deep linking to content within the claimant's site, had infringed the claimant's exclusive right of copying, distribution, and representation, in particular the distribution right.[13] Most cases to

---

[10] Tribunal de Commerce de Paris, 26 December 2000: http://www.legalis.net/cgi-iddn/french/affiche-jnet.cgi?droite=decisions/dt_auteur/ord_tcomm-paris_261200.htm (in French only).

[11] *Cadremploi v Keljob*, Tribunal de Grande Instance de Paris, 5 September 2001: http://www.juriscom.net/txt/jurisfr/da/tgiparis20010905.pdf (in French only).

[12] Landgericht, Köln, February 28, 2001: 28 O 692/00. Discussed in G. Smith, *Internet Law and Regulation* 4th ed. (2007), 70.

[13] Stepstone also pursued Ofir in France. On this occasion the Nanterre Tribunal of Commerce held that the actions of Ofir did not infringe Stepstone's copyright. See *SARL Stepstone France v SARL Ofir France* Tribunal de Commerce de Nanterre 8 November 2000: http://www.legalis.net/breves-article.php3?id_article=83 (in French only).

date have though dealt with news aggregation sites which act in a similar fashion to the *Shetland News*. These sites copy headlines from a variety of news sites and then deep link to stories within these sites: currently the best known news aggregator is Google News.

Probably the earliest such case arose in The Netherlands where in the case of *PCM v Kranten.com* the court held that deep linking was not a reproduction of the copyright work and as a result no copyright infringement occurred.[14] The headlines which were copied in the form of the links were also found not to infringe as there is a specific journalistic exception in Dutch copyright law which allows reproduction of copyright work in a press report provided the original source is acknowledged.[15] A contrary position was though taken in Denmark in the case of *Danish Newspaper Publishers Association v Newsbooster.com*.[16] Newsbooster operated a subscription news service. The subscriber would choose a number of keywords, and then Newsbooster would select news stories of interest to him based upon these keywords and would send to him links in the form of email messages. The emails would contain a précis of the story and a deep link to the story on the originator's site. The Publishers Association, representing the news originators, demanded that the group negotiate payments with them, or remove links to its sites. In a claim similar to the *Shetland Times* one, the Publishers Association argued that Newsbooster was a direct competitor of the newspapers and by bypassing their front pages, Newsbooster's links deprived them of advertising revenue and violated the newspapers' copyright as well as database rights. The court found that Newsbooster had infringed the newspapers' copyright and issued an injunction, noting that 'Newsbooster repeatedly and systematically reproduces and publishes the newspapers' headlines and articles'.[17]

These cases suggested a split approach was developing. In France and The Netherlands authorities were in place suggesting that deep-linking was not an infringement of copyright,[18] while in Germany and Denmark a contrary position had developed. Of course it is not this simple; each case must be measured on its merits and it is clear for instance that the actions of Keljob in providing a job search engine were very different from those of Newsbooster in providing direct emailed links to news stories.

Latterly though it seemed as though some form of consensus approach had developed. In Germany the decision in *Stepstone* has been rendered less influential by the decision of the Bundesgerichtshof (Federal Court of Germany, Germany's highest court) in *Paperboy*.[19] Paperboy offered a news aggregation service comprising elements of a mainstream aggregation page, as previously seen in *Kranten*, and a personalised email service, similar to that seen in *Newsbooster*. The court in a very different decision to the previous German law found that 'Where a hyperlink is made to a page on a third party's website which constitutes a work protected by copyright, the making of that hyperlink does not infringe the right of reproduction of that work'[20] and further that

---

[14] Sub nom. *Algemeen Dagblad BV v Eureka Internetdiensten* [2002] ECDR 1.
[15] Interestingly for a UK audience a similar 'fair dealing' provision is found in s. 30(2) of the CDPA 1988.   [16] [2003] ECDR 5.   [17] *ibid*, [16].
[18] Similar authority had been seen in Austria. See *Meteodata v Bernegger Bau* (Unreported, 17 December 2002, Supreme Court of Austria), discussed in Hobinger, 'Austria: Deep Linking: Copyright Note Allows Display of Foreign Contents on Website' 2003 (4) *World Internet Law Report* 18.
[19] Sub nom. *Verlagsgruppe Handelsblatt GmbH v Paperboy* [2005] ECDR 7.   [20] *ibid*, [H7].

'a copyright owner who makes available on the internet a work protected under copyright law, without technological protection measures, must be taken to have enabled any use which an on-demand user can make. In general, there is no infringement of copyright where access to a work is facilitated by the setting of hyperlinks, whether in the form of ordinary links or through the use of deep links.'[21]

The Danish courts also moved away from the hard-line position found in *Newsbooster* in the case of *Home A/S v Ofir*.[22] Ofir operates an internet portal site linking to such items as job adverts and homes for sale. In 1998, the parent company of Ofir had contacted Home, an online real estate portal similar to the UK site primelocation.com, offering them free advertising in national newspapers to the value of kr250,000, in exchange for the right to get data from their servers to be used in the real estate section of Ofir's portal. Home indicated they were not interested as they felt it would be self-cannibalising. Ofir later launched their estate agency portal. In operating this portal they used a search robot to update their database daily. This robot obtained thirteen essential items of information on a daily basis from Home's database. The Ofir database was arranged and compiled without favouring any particular broker. The real estate broker's name was given and when the user clicked on the property, he was transferred either to the broker's homepage or directly to the property. Home claimed Ofir's actions were in breach of copyright and raised an action. In contradistinction to the earlier *Newsbooster* case the court found that Ofir's deep linking to Home's database did not infringe Danish Copyright Law. In particular the court noted that deep linking was a generally desirable function of the internet as a medium for searching and exchanging an incredibly extensive and steadily increasing quantity of information, stating that: 'it should be an ordinary practice that search engines make available deep links which allow the user to access the required information in an effective manner. Parties, including providers in the Internet, should thus expect that search services will establish links to these pages which are published.'[23]

10.1.2 **Google Inc. v Copiepresse SCRL**

By 2006 it appeared that a clear consensus had developed in Continental Europe: deep linking would be allowed, and should be expected except in those occasions where one party has acted in a manner which may be deemed to unfairly compete with the activities of another. Recently though the whole debate on linking has been reopened by the Belgian case of *Google Inc. v Copiepresse SCRL*.[24]

The case surrounds two aspects of the Google search engine/portal. The first is the Google cache facility which Google offers on all its catalogued entries. You may or may not have noticed the Google cache in your everyday use of Google. This is a small link which sites to the bottom left of your search returns. When you search for a keyword or phrase Google returns a number of results but all are displayed in a similar fashion: the page header will be displayed in large font, in bold blue and this

---

[21] *ibid*, [H8].
[22] Unreported, 24 February 2006, Danish Maritime and Commercial Court, discussed in Mercado-Kierkegaard, 'Clearing the legal barriers—Danish court upholds "deep linking" in Home v. Ofir', (2006) 22 *Computer Law and Security Report* 326.   [23] *ibid*, 332.
[24] [2007] ECDR 5.

is the main link you usually click on. Beneath the link is a short two line description usually taken from the meta description of the page or from the first two lines of text if there is no meta description, below this is the URL of the page, usually displayed in green. Directly right of the URL are two active hyperlinks. These are internal links which link to pages within the Google site: the first is 'cache' link, the second the 'similar pages' link. The operation of these two links is very different. The 'similar pages' link will, when selected, return a further set of search returns based upon sites that Google has classified as being related to the site originally returned. The 'cache' link on the other hand takes you to a locally stored facsimile of the original site as it was catalogued by the Google robot. The cache facility was described in some detail to the court in *Copiepresse*; the claimants argued that in making and then offering to their users access to the Google cache Google were reproducing and/or communicating to the public works (or parts of works) protected by copyright without having the authorisation of the copyright holder.

> **→ Highlight** The Google Cache Facility
>
> When Google crawls the Web it creates a copy of each page examined and stores it in a cache memory, which enables it to consult that copy at any time, and in particular when the original (or Internet) page becomes unavailable. When you click on the link 'cached copy' of a web page, Google displays that page in the form that it was found the last time that it was indexed. Furthermore, the cached material forms the basis for a determination by Google as to whether a page is relevant to your search. When a cached page is displayed, it is preceded by a framed heading which reminds you that this is a cached copy of the page and not the original page and citing the search terms which led to its inclusion in the research results.
>
> Copiepresse at [68]

The second issue was the operation of the 'Google News' service or on the Google.be site 'Google.Actualités'. Google News is a relatively new addition to the Google portfolio. It is available as an option at the very top of the Google Search page. This is a cross between a search engine and a news aggregator offering specialised topical searches. If you click on the Google News link without entering a search term you are given a newspaper style offering of topical news stories, with acknowledgement of the source of each story and in traditional Google style a clear hyperlink taking you to the original version of the story. Like a traditional internet news site there are a variety of sub-headings a user may select such as 'World News', 'Technology', and 'Sport'. For this reason the claimants argued that Google News was more than a search facility, it was an information portal, not unlike *www.bbc.co.uk*. The expert appointed by the court agreed. He felt that as 'the user finds articles without any action being necessary on his part and is not obliged to undertake a specific search ... the Google News site is thus a portal for information drawn from the press.'[25] On this basis the claimants also contended that the Google

---

[25] *ibid*, [92].

News site was also in breach of Belgian copyright law as again, through this facility, Google were reproducing and/or communicating to the public works (or parts of works) protected by copyright without having the authorisation of the copyright holder. At an earlier interlocutory hearing the court found that Google had infringed both the copyright and database right of the newspaper publishers, Google appealed that decision and it was this hearing before President of the Court Magerman and Deputy Registrar Wansart which examined the issues in depth.

First the court examined the operation of the Google cache facility. They found that as the cache function operated by allowing a user access to a version of the original website held on the Google server rather than directing the user to the original site (as a hyperlink would do) the cache was 'a physical reproduction of the work and a communication of it to the public within the meaning of Art.1 of the Law on copyright'.[26] The next question was whether or not Google had made the copy. In their defence Google claimed that as it only copied the HTML code for the page (a code which only contains the text and no image), they never created a copy of the page. Rather, the internet user creates a copy of the work when she accesses the cache. As such the user is the author of any reproduction or communication to the public, the only act undertaken by Google being the provision of a facility allowing or enabling a communication to be made to the public by internet users.[27] The court quickly dismissed this tortuous interpretation of the manner in which the copy was made, finding that 'Google stores in its memory a copy of webpages. The fact that that copy preserves the HTML code of those pages—i.e. that it is converted into computer language—does not seem particularly relevant'.[28] In summary the court held that Google's cache operation was both an act of reproduction and a communication to the public.

The court next turned to the Google News site. Google argued that Google News was not an information portal, rather it was 'search engine … specialised in news material, which allows internet users easily to identify the news articles which may be of interest to them among the headlines published on the internet in the last 30 days and to consult them, at source, by going to the sites of the publishers making those articles available with just one mouse click'.[29] The court felt the distinction between an information portal and a search engine was unimportant as the same questions were raised however the Google News site was characterised.[30] The true question was about the nature of the Google News operation. The claimants argued that in producing the Google News service Google had specifically infringed their copyright by reproducing headlines and extracts drawn from their copyright work. This then raised the question of whether headlines could be protected at copyright law; one of the same questions Lord Hamilton had wrestled with over ten years previously. Google argued that headlines used in press articles are not original at all, claiming them to be merely turns of phrase in current use in language, citing by way of example 'The King visits Sweden' or 'Tom Boonen, world champion'. The Court

---

[26] *ibid*, [71].   [27] *ibid*, [72].   [28] *ibid*, [74].   [29] *ibid*, [86].
[30] 'In relation to the argument that "Google Actualités" or "Google News" service is not a "mere search engine service" but is an "information portal", the court noted that it is settled law that a hyperlink referring to a work protected by copyright is not a reproduction and that if there is a reproduction, it is the work of the internet user. However, this is not the case here as Google News reproduces and communicates to the public, on the homepage of its website, the headlines of press articles and an extract from those articles.' *Ibid*, [H12].

rejected this claim finding that: 'while not all the news article headlines can be considered as original—some of them in fact appear to be purely descriptive and do not therefore show the distinctive stamp of their author—nevertheless one cannot assume that a press article headline would never be sufficiently original to benefit from the protection of the Law on Copyright'[31] and went on to note that the short extract, usually the first two lines of the story, which was displayed alongside the link was equally susceptible to copyright protection.[32] The Court therefore found that Google News did reproduce and distribute copyright protected works.

With the *Copiepresse* case established Google needed to bring forward a defence which would allow them to continue their activities. They laid two main defences: (1) Freedom of Expression under the ECHR and (2) Fair Dealing. Google firstly argued that the Google News service was protected by Article 10 of the European Convention on Human Rights, arguing that freedom of expression protects the various aspects of the communication process, those being the freedom to receive and to communicate information.[33] Google recognised that the freedom to receive and to communicate information can be limited in order to protect the rights of others, including copyright, but argued nevertheless the restriction of the right of freedom of expression sought by the claimants was disproportionate as Google News was a free tool for access to information and did nothing more than perform a sign-posting function to facilitate research for information on the internet.[34] The court rejected this claim. It noted that copyright is based on a balance between, on the one hand, recognition of the legitimate interests of authors and, on the other hand, of the interests, which are also legitimate, of the public and of society in general and that copyright law had already been designed to take account of this balance by allowing fair dealing exceptions. Thus, Google could not claim a blanket Article 10 exception; they would need to establish that they fell within a fair dealing exception.[35]

This left only one line of defence for Google to run. They offered two alternate Belgian fair dealing defences which mirror UK provisions: (1) quotation for the purpose of critique, argument, review, or teaching,[36] and (2) fair dealing in reporting the news.[37] The court rejected both defences. In response to the critique, argument, or review defence it noted that 'the Google News service is based on the automated indexing of news articles made available to the public on the internet by a robot. The classification of the articles by theme is done automatically, without any human intervention.'[38] Therefore 'Google News does not undertake any analysis, comparison or critique of those articles, which are not the subject of any commentary at all'.[39] In regard to the news defence the court first noted that 'This argument by Google seems to contradict the argument presented previously when describing the Google News service, when Google presented its

---

[31] *ibid*, [105].
[32] '[I]n order to infringe the author's exclusive right, a reproduction does not need to be complete and may be merely partial, provided that there is some "borrowing", whether complete or partial, of that which makes the work "original".' *Ibid*, [109].   [33] *ibid*, [53].
[34] *ibid*, [54].   [35] *ibid*, [56]–[62].   [36] For a similar UK provision see s. 30(1) of the CDPA.
[37] For a similar UK provision see s. 30(2) of the CDPA.   [38] [2007] ECDR 5, [130].
[39] *ibid*, [138].

activity as a specialised search engine service and not as an information portal.'[40] This dry observation by the court preceded their coup-de-grâce:

> One should observe the justification for this exception. As noted by Google in its written arguments, the purpose of this exception is to enable the media to react rapidly to news events, the rapidity with which the information has to be reported not enabling them to seek the prior consent of the author. That is not the situation in which Google finds itself. It would be permissible for Google—which draws up a list of information, from around 500 information sources in French, refreshing that information every 15 minutes—to obtain, in advance, the agreement of the publishers of the website on which that information was collected. Google cannot therefore rely on the exception for news reporting.[41]

Google therefore was found to be in breach of copyright in the operations of both its cache operation and its Google News operation. Google immediately announced its intention to appeal,[42] but then brought to bear its commercial might in the hope of forcing a settlement on the issue. Google removed the offending material from the Google News site and their cache, as required by the judgement, but also the company removed the newspapers represented by Copiepresse from the main Google index meaning they were no longer visible to users of Google worldwide.[43] This had an obviously deleterious effect on the online business model of the newspapers in question forcing them to seek a partial settlement with Google. This involved newspapers tagging material they do not want cached with a 'noarchive tag'. The settlement seems uneasy. Copiepresse continue to press for damages,[44] while Google have decided elsewhere to license content for their Google News service rather than risk further litigation.[45] Successes elsewhere in Europe have convinced the Society of Editors in the UK to press the Culture Secretary to 'look urgently for effective ways in which Google and others could be prevented from profiting from third party content without recompense to or consent from those who generated the material'.[46] But with almost no UK case law on news aggregation and deep linking are they right to assume UK copyright law is on their side?

The question is how would a UK court receive the continental line of authority? The authority of the *Shetland Times* case has been statutorily overruled: cable programmes have had no separate copyright protection since the Copyright and Related Rights Regulations 2003 came into effect. The question now would be whether the defendant had infringed copyright by communicating the infringing article to the public or (in relation to headlines and cache copies) had reproduced the original works.

---

[40] *ibid*, [143].   [41] *ibid*, [147]–[149].

[42] R. Whetstone, 'About the Copiepresse Decision' *The Official Google Blog*, 13 February 2007: http://googleblog.blogspot.com/2007/02/about-copiepresse-decision.html.

[43] N. Anderson, 'Belgian Newspapers back on Google, but stay out of Google News', *Ars Technica*, 3 May 2007: http://arstechnica.com/tech-policy/news/2007/05/belgian-newspapers-back-on-google-but-stay-out-of-google-news.ars.

[44] E. Heald, 'Google News and newspaper publishers: allies or enemies?' *Editors Weblog*, 11 March 2009: http://www.editorsweblog.org/analysis/2009/03/google_news_and_newspaper_publishers_all.php.

[45] Associated Free Press, *Google News, EPA members in partnership agreement*, 17 March 2009: http://www.google.com/hostednews/afp/article/ALeqM5iOKGNolLjGQJ3iUJL0Dt-4DEYxUg; C. McCarthy, 'Agence France-Presse, Google settle copyright dispute', *ZDNet News*, 6 April 2007: http://news.zdnet.com/2100-9588_22-151774.html.

[46] Letter from the Society of Editors to Culture Secretary Andy Burnham dated 24 March 2009: http://www.societyofeditors.co.uk/page-view.php?page_id=139&parent_page_id=0&news_id=1236&numbertoprintfrom=1.

The recent case of *Union Des Association Europeenes De Football & Ors v Briscomb & Ors*[47] may assist us in these questions. Mr Briscomb and his co-defendants were streaming live Champions League football matches via the website *www.sportingstreams.com*. The claimants claimed that in so doing the defendants infringed their copyright in their broadcasts by communicating them to or authorising their communication to the public contrary to s. 20 of the Copyright, Designs and Patents Act. Lindsay J held that the claimants had made good this claim, as well as a claim in the alternative that the defendants infringed the claimants' copyright in the broadcasts made by copying them contrary to s. 17 of the Act. In a similar fashion to the *Shetland Times* case *Briscomb* is a summary judgement meaning the action was undefended, leading to an unchallenged analysis of the law. This is disappointing as while there have been cases across Europe which have gone to appeal we have to make do with a mix of interim and summary hearings.

What can we read into all this then? Firstly, and most importantly, there is no UK case law which stands in opposition to the decisions found in Continental Europe on these issues. The scant case law we have in *Shetland Times*, and *Briscombe* seems to follow a similar line of approach as the Continental cases on deep linking and on caching and aggregating. Lord Hamilton's decision in *Shetland Times* that a newspaper headline could qualify for copyright protection mirrors the much later *Copiepresse* decision, while Lindsay J's decision in *Briscombe* that making content available via a web page may constitute making available to the public, and that should that act involve copying this would also infringe the right to make copies, also mirrors the approach of the court in *Copiepresse*. Secondly, much of the law applied in the later deep linking cases such as *Paperboy* and *Home A/S v Ofir* and of course in *Copiepresse* comes from a common root, the Directive on the Harmonisation of Certain Aspects of Copyright and Related Rights in the Information Society,[48] which was given effect in the UK by the Copyright and Related Rights Regulations 2003.[49] This allows us to imagine that a UK court would come to a position similar to those found in other EU states post 2003. We can say therefore with some degree of confidence that should similar cases arise in the UK, a judge would most likely rule that simple hypertext linking, whether it is surface linking or deep linking, is not an infringement of copyright applying principles similar to those seen in Germany in *Paperboy* and Denmark in *Home A/S v Ofir*. Equally we can predict with some degree of confidence that a British judge is likely to follow the principles seen in *Copiepresse* when faced with cases involving caching and aggregation. Google may therefore have cause to negotiate with the UK news industry.

10.2 Peer-to-peer networks

Linking, caching, and aggregation are not usually the first thing people think about when they are asked for their views on copyright in the digital environment. Although these issues are of vital import to the future development of network design and functionality most media coverage of online copyright issues focusses on illegal file sharing and the harm it may cause to copyright industries. This is perhaps not surprising; much

---

[47] [2006] EWHC 1268 (Ch).   [48] Dir. 2001/29/EC.   [49] SI 2003/2498.

early high profile litigation focussed on this issue, and indeed still does with the most recent focus being on the high profile *Sweden v Neij et al.* (*The Pirate Bay case*).[50] The problem is that, as stated at the outset of this chapter, the internet is to date the largest and most efficient copying machine built by man. In addition most users access the internet from home in what they imagine is anonymity. Although in practice they can be traced, for the average user the idea that law enforcement agencies or copyright holders will track their activities while they are safely in their own bedrooms seems remote. It is not surprising therefore that the internet is used extensively to share music, movies and games without the permission of the copyright holder. The technology behind file sharing, and the ways file sharing systems have attempted to get around copyright law have both grown in sophistication as the years have gone by. To date there have been at least four generations of file sharing technologies, as well as a raft of litigation in the US, The Netherlands, Australia and Sweden. Surprisingly, like linking, caching, and aggregating, to date there has not been a full hearing on file sharing and copyright infringement in the UK.

10.2.1 **Early cases**

Probably the first case to examine file sharing technologies was *UMG Recordings v MP3. Com*.[51] MP3.com offered an exciting new service. They were digitising all music available on CD in the US with a view to offering a service known as My.Mp3.com. This would allow subscribers to listen to an MP3 version of music they owned from any computer anywhere in the world. It worked by storing MP3 copies of the music on a web server which could be accessed by the subscriber across a network connection. To prevent subscribers illegally accessing music they did not own, MP3.com required their customers to prove ownership of a copy of a particular music track by either inserting their copy of the original CD into their CD-Rom, allowing the MP3.com software to confirm the authenticity of the CD, (this was called the 'Beam-it Service') or they must purchase the CD from one of defendant's online retailing partners (the 'Instant Listening Service'). A group of music publishers including UMG, Sony, and Warner raised a claim against MP3.com claiming that both their processes of digitisation and distribution were in infringement of copyright. MP3.com claimed their process was protected by Fair Use (the US equivalent of Fair Dealing). They relied in particular on two earlier decisions, *Sony Corporation of America v Universal City Studios, Inc.*,[52] and *Recording Industry Association of America v Diamond Multimedia Systems Inc.*[53]

Sony v Universal is the famous 'Sony Betamax' case. It was a claim centred on the legality of the home video cassette recorder (VCR). Universal, alongside a host of other movie studios and the Motion Picture Association of America, argued that the Sony Betamax VCR was a device which could be used to infringe copyright in their content and that Sony by knowing what use their customer would make of the device were

[50] Stockholms Tingsrätt, No. B 13301-06, 17 April 2009: http://www.icmpecho.com/defavgdok.pdf (in Swedish). Discussed in greater depth below.
[51] 92 F Supp 2d 349 (SDNY 2000).   [52] 464 US 417 (Sup. Ct 1984).
[53] 180 F 3d 1072 (9th Cir. 1999).

secondarily liable for any primary infringement carried out by their customers.[54] This was a long, complex, and ultimately ground breaking case when after eight years of litigation the US Supreme Court ruled by a narrow 5–4 majority that Sony were protected from liability as their Betamax VCR had a protected fair use, to be used for the purpose of 'time shifting'. This is described by the court as the practice of 'the average member of the public [using] a VCR principally to record a program he cannot view as it is being televised and then to watch it once at a later time'.[55] The court found that although there was a risk that some time shifting practices may cause harm to copyright holders 'the record and findings of the District Court lead us to two conclusions. First, Sony demonstrated a significant likelihood that substantial numbers of copyright holders who license their works for broadcast on free television would not object to having their broadcasts time-shifted by private viewers. And second, respondents failed to demonstrate that time-shifting would cause any likelihood of nonminimal harm to the potential market for, or the value of, their copyrighted works. The Betamax is, therefore, capable of substantial noninfringing uses. Sony's sale of such equipment to the general public does not constitute contributory infringement of respondents' copyrights.'[56]

A similar principle was sought by the defendants in the *RIAA v Diamond* case. Diamond produced the Rio Mp3 player, one of the first commercially available portable MP3 players. The Rio was first marketed in 1998 and it allowed the customer to carry with them 32MB of MP3 music (about 10–12 tracks). Although this seems quite unremarkable in the current MP3 market the Rio was groundbreaking in several ways, including a 12 hour playback time on a single battery and the first music download store 'RioPort' which was the first to license commercial downloads. The RIAA took action against Diamond as the Rio was not compatible with the terms of the Audio Home Recording Act 1992, a piece of protectionist legislation which required digital music device manufacturers to install a system known as Serial Copy Management System.[57] Although ultimately the case was decided on a different point one of the defences put forward by Diamond was that the Rio was a device to allow users to 'space shift' copies of their music. Building upon the 'time shifting' defence seen in *Sony*, Diamond argued that the Rio 'merely makes copies in order to render portable, or "space-shift," those files that already reside on a user's hard drive'.[58] The court agreed finding that 'Such copying [space shifting] is paradigmatic noncommercial personal use entirely consistent with the purposes of the Act'.[59]

This 'space shifting' defence was again raised in the *MP3.com* case. The defendant argued that all the My.Mp3.com service offered was the opportunity for the user to listen to their music at any place where they had internet access without the need to carry the original copy of the CD with them. They argued that as the user was required to demonstrate that

---

[54] This secondary infringement claim was made under the US copyright principles of vicarious and contributory infringement. These will be discussed extensively when the *Napster* case is discussed below.   [55] 464 US 417, 421.   [56] *ibid*, 456.

[57] Serial Copy Management System is a copy protection scheme that was created in response to the digital audio tape (DAT) invention. In order to prevent DAT recorders from making second-generation or serial copies, SCMS sets a 'copy bit' in all copies of original recordings. This prevents anyone from making further copies of those copies, or serial copies.

[58] 180 F 3d 1072, 1079.   [59] *ibid*.

they owned the original recording through either the 'Beam-it' or 'Instant Listening' service there was little risk of the copyright holder suffering harm. On this occasion though the court disagreed with this line of defence. The key distinction between *MP3.com* and the previous *Sony* and *Diamond* cases was where the primary infringement occurred. In both the previous cases the device supplier merely supplied a device which was capable of being used for infringing copyright which could then be used for fair (therefore protected) or unfair (therefore unlawful) purposes; in the case of MP3.com, they were committing the primary infringement (copying) therefore the fair use defence of space shifting, which was available to their users only (if anyone) did not extend to them. The court summed this up simply: 'Although defendant recites that My.MP3.com provides a transformative "space shift" by which subscribers can enjoy the sound recordings contained on their CDs without lugging around the physical discs themselves, this is simply another way of saying that the unauthorised copies are being retransmitted in another medium—an insufficient basis for any legitimate claim of transformation'.[60] The court found that what MP3.com was doing was transforming the copyright protected music files which were encoded on CDs in CD-DA[61] format into MP3 format in a process known as 'ripping'. They were then retransmitting the 'ripped' MP3 file to their subscribers. As MP3.com was committing the infringement for a commercial purpose they could not be defended by the 'space shifting' exception. The simplicity of this distinction allowed the judge, District Judge Rakoff, to pithily dispose of the case saying '[t]he complex marvels of cyberspatial communication may create difficult legal issues; but not in this case'.[62]

Judge Rakoff has been proven correct in his prediction. While the *MP3.com* case may have proven to be somewhat of a damp squib, legally speaking, it was merely a precursor to a number of cases involving the transformation and retransmission of a variety of video, audio, and software files both in the US and internationally. This series of cases encompasses some of the most celebrated internet law cases including *MGM Studios, Inc. v Grokster, Ltd*,[63] *Sweden v Neij et al.*,[64] *Universal Music Australia Pty Ltd v Sharman License Holding Ltd*,[65] *Viacom International, Inc. et al v Youtube, Inc. et al*,[66] and possibly most famously of all *A&M Records, Inc. v Napster, Inc.*[67]

10.2.2 **A&M records, Inc. v Napster, Inc.**

The *Napster* case is possibly the most famous information society case to date. The facts have been widely discussed in the media and online, but the detail of the case is often missing in the broad brush approach taken by the media and therefore a close discussion of the facts of the case remains valuable.

Napster was created by Shawn Fanning a seventeen year old freshman (first year student) at Northeastern University in 1999. The idea that Fanning had was to create a music community site where fans of bands or singers could go, chat, and share music with each other.[68] The file sharing aspect of Napster did not seem to hold

---

[60] 92 F Supp 2d 349, 356.   [61] Compact Disc Digital Audio.
[62] 92 F Supp 2d 349, 351.   [63] 545 US 913 (2005).   [64] Above, n. 50.
[65] [2005] FCA 1242.   [66] Case no. 1:2007cv02103, Filed: 13 March 2007.
[67] 239 F 3d 1004 (9th Cir. 2001).
[68] Renee Ambrosek, *Shawn Fanning: The Founder of Napster* (2006), 30.

primacy in Fanning's original design, rather his focus was on creating a music community, but as part of his design he included the ability for users to directly swap MP3 files with each other. In so doing, without perhaps realising the groundbreaking nature of this development he created the first fully functional peer-to-peer protocol, the Napster protocol. To explain the contribution of the Napster protocol we need to examine the distinction between Peer-to-Peer (or P2P) file sharing and traditional server-client file systems.

Prior to Fanning's development of the Napster protocol online file transfers had always followed a web 1.0 model where the file was stored on a web server which could be accessed by anyone with the requisite permission and then downloaded from that server. MP3.com had used a model such as this with their fêted (and fated) My.Mp3. com service. This model remains familiar to us today and is used by services as diverse as Apple's iTunes Store, BBC's iPlayer, YouTube, and streamed music systems such as Last. fm or Spotify. Fanning though introduced the concept of P2P file sharing to the masses. This operates very differently from traditional server-client file transfers. Instead of operating a central server containing all the files available for download a P2P system stores the files on the hard drives of the network subscribers. Subscribers choose which files they will share and these are placed in a 'shared' folder. The P2P software can access this folder and may transfer data out of this folder to another user by creating a network connection between the users or 'peers'.

★ Example Shawn Fanning's Party Analogy

Fanning described the difference between client server networks and the Napster network by using an analogy of attending a party.

In the client-server party each guest turns up empty handed to the party and all the food and drink is supplied by the host. To get a drink you must ask the host to supply it and you can only have what the host has supplied. Your host may be efficient but he has to serve everybody and you may have to wait in a queue.

At a Napster party all the guests bring their own food and drink. There is still a host, but all he does is greets you at the door and takes a note of what you have brought. Then anytime anyone wants a drink they can ask the host who has brought a particular product. The host can check his list and put them in touch with the right person and they can then exchange drinks directly with each other.

The Napster party works as long as people are not too greedy and are willing to share.

Peer-to-peer systems seemed to offer a solution to the *MP3.com* problem. Like *Sony* and *Diamond* it is the end-user who does the copying of files, not the service provider. This seemed to offer Napster a degree of protection against copyright infringement claims. The first line of defence was that they did not commit primary infringement any sharing (and therefore copying) of files was done by their customers. Secondly, their customers would, it was imagined, be deemed to be acting in a non-commercial capacity allowing them to claim fair use defences such as time and space shifting should the copyright holders decide to pursue a claim.

There were though two problems with the Napster concept and design. The first was one that Shawn Fanning could not have imagined in the spring of 1999: Napster became a global phenomenon. Jupiter Media, the respected media research agency reported that by February 2001 Napster had 26.4 million users,[69] a remarkable reach for a program only released in June 1999. Although this may at first seem a positive outcome for Fanning and his internet start-up Napster, Inc. it meant that the music publishing industry and the Recording Industry Association of America quickly focussed their attention on this fledgling company. The second was a design problem which was ultimately to prove to be Napster's downfall. If you recount the party host analogy given by Shawn Fanning he explains that at the Napster party there is a host who keeps track of what each person has brought and who introduces guests to each other. In the Napster environment this function was fulfilled by 'the Napster server'. When a new user first downloaded and installed the Napster software, the software would catalogue the MP3files she held on her computer and would place copies of these (with the user's permission) into a shared music folder. Then when the user first logged on to the Napster exchange site the Napster server would log her IP address (to allow sharing of files later) and the files which were in her shared music folder. The Napster server would then add this information to its search-able database allowing other users to discover what files the user had available for shar-ing. A keyword search of that database would return a list of users with file names which matched that keyword as well as details of how fast a connection they could offer. Thus a user searching for 'Backstreet Boys' (this was 2000 remember) would have returned a list of available files and users. They would then select one user, or peer, before the Napster server would instigate a digital handshake allowing the transfer to take place between users or peers. The Napster server meant that Napster always knew what files their sub-scribers were sharing and technically, as the Napster server had to make that digital hand-shake, could prevent the sharing of files between users of the service.

These two factors led a number of music publishers to file a complaint with the District Court for the Northern District of California on 6 December 1999. The plain-tiffs contended that Napster's activities constituted 'contributory and vicarious federal copyright infringement'.[70] On 26 July 2000, the District Court granted the plaintiffs' motion for a preliminary injunction. The injunction was slightly modified by written opinion on 10 August 2000. The District Court preliminarily enjoined Napster 'from engaging in, or facilitating others in copying, downloading, uploading, transmitting, or distributing plaintiffs' copyrighted musical compositions and sound recordings, pro-tected by either federal or state law, without express permission of the rights owner.'[71] Napster appealed to the Federal Court of Appeals for the Ninth Circuit. The case was heard on 2 October 2000 by Chief Judge Schroeder and Circuit Judges Beezer and Paez. On 12 February 2001 Judge Beezer issued the opinion of the Court.

---

[69] Comscore Inc., *Global Napster Usage Plummets, But New File-Sharing Alternatives Gaining Ground, Reports Jupiter Media Metrix*, 20 July 2001: http://www.comscore.com/press/release.asp?id=249.

[70] Contributory and vicarious copyright infringement are two different forms of secondary infringement actionable under the Federal Copyright Act 1976. Although we have no direct equiv-alents in the UK ss. 22–26 of the CDPA 1988 cover much of the same ground and many similar concepts are discussed in *CBS Songs Ltd v Amstrad Consumer Electronics Plc* [1988] AC 1013.

[71] *A&M Records, Inc. v Napster, Inc.* 114 F. Supp. 2d 896 (N.D. Cal. 2000), 927.

The Court examined each of the plaintiffs' claims as well as three affirmative defences put forward by Napster. Firstly, Judge Beezer examined the claim that 'Napster users are engaged in the wholesale reproduction and distribution of copyrighted works, all constituting direct infringement'.[72] Although the plaintiffs accepted that Napster never actually copied any of the files in issue, the plaintiffs had to establish primary infringement on the part of Napster's users as without a primary infringement there could be no secondary infringement by Napster. Factually it was clear that the activities of Napster users were clearly in breach of the exclusive rights of the copyright holders; users were copying copyright protected music files and they were distributing them. It seemed all the copyright holders had to establish was that they were the rights holders to the music in question to establish primary infringement had occurred, but Napster felt their customers could have an affirmative fair use defence and presented to the Court three such defences: (1) Sampling, (2) Space Shifting, and (3) Use with Permission.

Napster firstly claimed that its users 'download MP3 files to "sample" the music in order to decide whether to purchase the recording'.[73] Napster further argued that the District Court had erred in refusing a sampling defence as it '(1) erred in concluding that sampling is a commercial use because it conflated a noncommercial use with a personal use; (2) erred in determining that sampling adversely affects the market for plaintiffs' copyrighted music, a requirement if the use is noncommercial; and (3) erroneously concluded that sampling is not a fair use because it determined that samplers may also engage in other infringing activity'.[74] Judge Beezer rejected this claim noting that '[e]vidence relied on by the District Court demonstrates that the free downloads provided by the record companies consist of thirty-to-sixty second samples or are full songs programmed to "time out," that is, exist only for a short time on the downloader's computer. In comparison, Napster users download a full, free and permanent copy of the recording. The determination by the District Court as to the commercial purpose and character of sampling is not clearly erroneous.'[75]

Napster then attempted to run a variant of the *Diamond* space shifting defence. They argued that 'Space-shifting occurs when a Napster user downloads MP3 music files in order to listen to music he already owns on audio CD.'[76] Again the court was not impressed, with Judge Beezer noting that 'Both Diamond and Sony are inapposite because the methods of shifting in these cases did not also simultaneously involve distribution of the copyrighted material to the general public; the time or space-shifting of copyrighted material exposed the material only to the original user. In *Diamond*, for example, the copyrighted music was transferred from the user's computer hard drive to the user's portable MP3 player. So too Sony, where "the majority of VCR purchasers did not distribute taped television broadcasts, but merely enjoyed them at home". Conversely, it is obvious that once a user lists a copy of music he already owns on the Napster system in order to access the music from another location, the song becomes available to millions of other individuals, not just the original CD owner.'[77] This only left the defence of use with permission but as Judge Beezer pointed out the 'plaintiffs did not seek to enjoin this and any other noninfringing use of the Napster system',[78]

---

[72] 239 F 3d 1004, [17].   [73] *ibid*, [39].   [74] *ibid*.   [75] *ibid*, [40].   [76] *ibid*, [44].
[77] *ibid*, [45].   [78] *ibid*, [46].

thus this defence was also ruled out. The court therefore established that Napster users did not have a fair use defence and that the plaintiffs would likely succeed on a claim for copyright infringement against Napster users. On this basis the court moved on to examine the plaintiffs' claims for secondary infringement against Napster.

The court first examined whether Napster had committed contributory copyright infringement. Contributory infringement is established by the application of a two part test. The defendant must (1) know, or have reason to know of the direct infringement and (2) materially contribute to the infringing activity. This is where the Napster server proved to be Napster's downfall. As the Napster server recorded all files available for distribution in real time, and as many of these files contained material that was clearly being offered in breach of copyright Napster could have knowledge of the infringing activity of its subscribers. The court though was careful to tread a fine line. They did not want to outlaw P2P systems just because they could be used for copyright infringement. Judge Beezer explained that 'if a computer system operator learns of specific infringing material available on his system and fails to purge such material from the system, the operator knows of and contributes to direct infringement. Conversely, absent any specific information which identifies infringing activity, a computer system operator cannot be liable for contributory infringement merely because the structure of the system allows for the exchange of copyrighted material. To enjoin simply because a computer network allows for infringing use would, in our opinion, violate *Sony* and potentially restrict activity unrelated to infringing use'.[79] Nevertheless this did not assist Napster as 'We nevertheless conclude that sufficient knowledge exists to impose contributory liability when linked to demonstrated infringing use of the Napster system. The record supports the district court's finding that Napster has *actual* knowledge that *specific* infringing material is available using its system, that it could block access to the system by suppliers of the infringing material, and that it failed to remove the material'.[80] As the Napster software and server hardware was essential to the swapping of copyright protected files the court therefore had little difficulty in finding the second arm of the test also proven: Napster were found liable for contributory infringement.

The court then turned to the question of vicarious infringement. Vicarious infringement requires the application of a three part test: (1) there has been a direct infringement; (2) the vicarious infringer is in a position to control the actions of the direct infringer and (3) the vicarious infringer benefits financially from the infringement. The first element of the test had already been established so the court focussed on the remaining questions. Napster argued they did not benefit financially; they did not charge subscribers for either the software or access to the service, in fact Napster argued they made no money at all through the availability of infringing files on the Napster network. The court disagreed. It felt that without the availability of infringing files Napster would not have grown at the phenomenal rate at which it grew. This, the court felt was a direct financial benefit, '[f]inancial benefit exists where the availability of infringing material "acts as a draw for customers." Ample evidence supports the district court's finding that Napster's future revenue is directly dependent upon "increases in userbase." More users register with the Napster system as the "quality and quantity

---

[79] *ibid*, [56].   [80] *ibid*, [57].

of available music increases." We conclude that the district court did not err in determining that Napster financially benefits from the availability of protected works on its system.'[81] This left only one final question, had Napster been in a position to control its users? Again the Napster server was the Achilles heel of the Napster operation; the court found that through it Napster had 'the ability to locate infringing material listed on its search indices, and the right to terminate users' access to the system'.[82]

There remained one crumb of solace for Napster. The court recognised that merely indexing file names did not mean that Napster had to have knowledge of what these files contained, as Judge Beezer explained: 'we recognize that the files are user-named and may not match copyrighted material exactly (for example, the artist or song could be spelled wrong).'[83] However this was not enough to save Napster. The Appeals Court did vary the terms of the injunction as they felt that the injunction of the District Court that 'Napster ensures that no "copying, downloading, uploading, transmitting, or distributing" of plaintiffs' works occur on the system' was over-broad. Instead the Appeals Court placed the burden of establishing infringement on the plaintiffs who were required to 'provide notice to Napster of copyrighted works and files containing such works available on the Napster system before Napster has the duty to disable access to the offending content.'[84] As this order seemed to offer Napster the opportunity to continue to operate Napster remained in operation. A cat and mouse game developed between copyright holders and Napster users. The copyright holders gave Napster details of tens of thousands of infringing files which it was required by the injunction to block. Users would then change file names allowing the injunction to be circumvented and the whole process would begin anew. It proved impossible though for Napster to continue to meet the demands of the injunction and in July 2001 the Napster service was closed down.[85] Following protracted discussions to try and save Napster, including a reported deal to sell the company to German music publisher Bertelsmann for $85 million, Napster eventually went into liquidation. Its trade marks and brand name were bought at a bankruptcy auction by Roxio Inc. and they rebranded their pressplay music service 'Napster 2.0'. Today Napster operates as a leading legal download service specialising in music for mobile phones through its 'Napster To Go' service. Napster is now a subsidiary of US retail giant Best Buy.

10.2.3 Post Napster: MGM Studios, Inc. v Grokster, Ltd

The music industry had claimed a victory, but at what cost? It seemed the Court of Appeals had suggested the P2P technology Napster had used was not in of itself illegal (and in fact was not dissimilar to traditional search engines which also may assist

---

[81] *ibid*, [61].   [82] *ibid*, [67].   [83] *ibid*.   [84] *ibid*, [86].
[85] On the last day of service the ten most downloaded tracks were reported to be: (1) Everly Brothers—Bye Bye Love; (2) The Clash—I fought the law (and the law won); (3) Jerky Boys—Fanning my balls (a play on Shawn Fanning's name); (4) Judge Jules—Gatecrasher; (5) Warren Zevon—Send Lawyers, Guns and Money; (6) Jimmy Buffet—A pirate looks at 40; (7) Metallica—Seak and Destroy; (8) Dr Dre—Bang Bang; (9) Red Hot Chili Peppers—Give it away; and (10) Doobie Brothers—Listen to the music.

individuals in obtaining illegal materials), but rather the problem was the Napster server which allowed Napster a high degree of oversight and control. If a P2P system could be designed which did not use a central index server it seemed its implementation would not infringe US copyright law.

Two such systems were quickly developed. One was to design a decentralised P2P network which operates more like the internet. This does away with the need to have a central server. Instead when one logs in to the network a connection is made to the nearest active user, or node, on the network. As this node already has onward connections any requests may be forwarded throughout the network without the need for a central server. If we return to Shawn Fanning's party analogy, this is a party without a host. The new arrival joins at the fringes of the party and talks to the person nearest to them. If they have a request for a particular food or drink they ask the person they are talking to for it. Assuming this person does not have what the user requests he passes this request on to anyone he is within speaking distance of (in network terms has a network communication with) and the request spreads across the room as it passes from person to person growing exponentially as it goes. Eventually one person responds saying she has the item requested and the response is relayed back across the same route the request took allowing the requester and the provider to be introduced. The transfer then takes place in the usual way. Decentralised P2P systems have some advantages but also some strong disadvantages. As they are completely decentralised there can be no claim of a controlling mind and they are (in theory at least) difficult to disrupt. But they can be extremely slow and they carry a large amount of network traffic as requests are sent and replies received.

A better system, technically, is the semi-structured system allowed by the use of so-called 'supernodes'. A semi-structured system combines the advantages of the centralised and decentralised systems. Instead of having a central server, semi-structured P2P systems use a number of users as temporary information hosts, or supernodes. The easiest way to explain is to return to the party analogy one last time. Now when a new guest arrives at the party he is met by a host but this host is one of many hosts and no one host is in control of the party or the venue. Hosts are chosen because of their ability to connect quickly with a group of guests and when a new guest joins the party the nearest host to them meets them and asks them to give them details of what they have brought to the party and what they want to eat or drink. Their (local) host can then tell them immediately if anyone in their immediate circle of guests can supply them with what they want by checking their list of available food and drinks. If no-one within the host's immediate circle has what the guest is looking for they ask the hosts nearest to them to check their lists and so the request is transferred on in the same way it was in the decentralised party but here the communications are only between hosts. These hosts, or supernodes, thus act as local search servers and provide the backbone of the network. Cleverly though a supernode can leave at any time and she will be immediately replaced by whichever guest is best placed to fill the gap. The semi-structured network in effect decentralises the server function as well as the file transfer and search functions.

Several P2P providers began offering either decentralised or semi-structured P2P services. Famous brand names to use one or other of these technologies included Kazaa, eMule, EDonkey, Gnutella, Grokster, and Morpheus. Users quickly migrated to these new P2P systems, many of which had been developed outside the US;[86] it seemed that the music industry had won the battle but lost the war. Even worse for copyright holders while Napster had only allowed the sharing of MP3 audio files these new services allowed sharing of any type of file meaning Hollywood movie studios, television networks, and software developers were now all affected. The copyright holders began afresh. In spring 2003 a number of entertainment industry plaintiffs[87] raised an action Groskter Ltd and Streamcast Ltd suppliers of leading P2P technologies Grokster and Morpheus.[88]

Initially the legal omens looked good for the P2P service providers. At a preliminary hearing before Judge Steven Wilson of the US District Court for the Central District of California a motion by the defendants for summary judgement in their favour was granted.[89] Although Judge Wilson recognised that customers of Grokster and Streamcast were engaging in unlawful activities he could see nothing to suggest either of the defendants had knowledge of their customers' activities or had the ability to control them. He noted that '[although] the Court is not blind to the possibility that Defendants may have intentionally structured their businesses to avoid secondary liability for copyright infringement, while benefiting financially from the illicit draw of their wares . . . the Court need not decide whether steps could be taken to reduce the susceptibility of such software to unlawful use'.[90] He went on to note that although he shared some sympathy with the plight of the plaintiffs 'to justify a judicial remedy, however, [the] Plaintiffs invite this Court to expand existing copyright law beyond its well-drawn boundaries'.[91]

By removing the element of control and knowledge that the Napster central server offered the second generation P2P providers had escaped potential contributory or vicarious liability. The copyright holders appealed to the Court of Appeals for the Ninth Circuit. The appeal was heard by Circuit Judges Boochever, Noonan, and Thomas, with Judge Thomas issuing the opinion of the Court on 19 August 2004. The Court affirmed Judge Wilson's decision finding that 'the defendants are not liable for contributory and vicarious copyright infringement.'[92] As with the earlier opinion of Judge Wilson, Judge Thomas was sympathetic to the plight of the copyright holders but noted that the defendants could not be held liable for either contributory or vicarious copyright infringement without the court expanding the scope of either or both forms of infringement.[93] At appeal the plaintiffs attempted to have the court extend the scope of vicarious liability by arguing that the defendants had 'turned a blind eye to detectable acts of infringement for the sake of

[86] For instance Kazaa was owned and operated by Dutch Company Consumer Empowerment, while Grokster Ltd, creators of Grokster, was registered in Nevis, West Indies.

[87] The plaintiffs fell into two camps. (1) the motion picture industry plaintiffs: MGM; Columbia Pictures; Disney Enterprises; New Line Cinema; Paramount Pictures; Time Warner Entertainment; Twentieth Century Fox; and Universal City Studios; and (2) the music industry plaintiffs: Arista Records; Atlantic Records; Bad Boy Records; Capital Records; Elektra Entertainment; Hollywood Records; Interscope Records; LaFace Records; London—Sire Records; Motown Records; BMG Entertainment; Rhino Entertainment; Sony Music Entertainment; UMG Recordings; Virgin Records America; Walt Disney Records; Warner Brothers Records; WEA International; WEA Latina; and Zomba Recording.

[88] *MGM Studios, Inc. v Grokster, Ltd* 259 F. Supp. 2d 1029 (CD Cal. 2003); *MGM Studios, Inc. v Grokster, Ltd* 380 F.3d 1154 (9th Cir. 2004); *MGM Studios, Inc. v. Grokster, Ltd* 545 US 913 (2005).

[89] *MGM Studios, Inc. v Grokster, Ltd* 259 F. Supp. 2d 1029 (CD Cal. 2003).

[90] 259 F. Supp. 2d 1029, 1046.   [91] *ibid.*

[92] *MGM Studios, Inc. v Grokster, Ltd* 380 F.3d 1154 (9th Cir. 2004).

[93] 380 F.3d 1154, 1160–62.

profit'.[94] The court though rejected this claim. Judge Thomas was clear that any expansion of the law of copyright should come from Congress, not through judicial activism:

→   Highlight Judge Thomas in *MGM* v *Grokster*

The introduction of new technology is always disruptive to old markets, and particularly to those copyright owners whose works are sold through well established distribution mechanisms. Yet, history has shown that time and market forces often provide equilibrium in balancing interests, whether the new technology be a player piano, a copier, a tape recorder, a video recorder, a personal computer, a karaoke machine, or an MP3 player. Thus, it is prudent for courts to exercise caution before restructuring liability theories for the purpose of addressing specific market abuses, despite their apparent present magnitude.

Indeed, the Supreme Court has admonished us to leave such matters to Congress. In Sony the Court spoke quite clearly about the role of Congress in applying copyright law to new technologies. As the Supreme Court stated in that case, the direction of Article I is that Congress shall have the power to promote the progress of science and the useful arts. When, as here, the Constitution is permissive, the sign of how far Congress has chosen to go can come only from Congress.

[380 F.3d 1154, 1167]

The decision of the Court of Appeals for the Ninth Circuit is interesting on several levels. Judge Thomas and his brethren were sending a message to both the plaintiffs and to Congress. At the time of the *Grokster* case Congress was considering a revision to US copyright law, Judge Thomas was suggesting both that the plaintiffs would make better use of their time in lobbying Congress, and that Congress was the proper forum to review, and if necessary amend the Copyright Act. Also he was expressing the need for copyright law to balance the interests of traditional copyright industries and the need to ensure new technology is allowed space to develop given the monopolistic nature of copyright law. Finally he was making a thinly veiled comment that the Supreme Court should not intervene given the current interest of Congress in the matter. Despite Judge Thomas's comments the plaintiffs appealed to the Supreme Court who agreed to hear the case.

The case was argued before the Supreme Court on 29 March 2005, with the decision of the court issued on 27 June 2005. The Justices of the Supreme Court were unanimous that the decision of the Court of Appeals should be overturned. Between the Ninth Circuit hearing and the Supreme Court hearing the plaintiffs had developed their 'turning a blind eye' argument. They presented the Justices with the argument that Grokster and StreamCast had 'clearly voiced the objective that recipients use it to download copyrighted works, and each took active steps to encourage infringement'.[95] By making this claim the plaintiffs were inviting the Justices to extend a principle from patent law, known as the 'active inducement' principle to copyright law.[96] The court was willing to hear this

---

[94] This was a development of part of the *Napster* decision. See *A&M Records, Inc. v Napster, Inc.,* 239 F.3d 1004, 1023.   [95] 545 US 913, 919.

[96] For a discussion of this see P. Samuelson, 'Legally Speaking: Did MGM Really Win the Grokster Case?' 48 *Communications of the ACM* 19 (October 2005).

argument. Justice Souter, who gave the opinion of the court,[97] noted that 'The rule on inducement of infringement as developed in the early [patent] cases is no different today. Evidence of active steps ... taken to encourage direct infringement'.[98] Justice Souter was encouraged that there was a tradition of borrowing from patent law in cases such as this. He noted that '*Sony* took the staple-article doctrine of patent law as a model for its copyright safe harbour rule, the inducement rule, too, is a sensible one for copyright'.[99]

➡ Highlight The Active Inducement Principle

We adopt it here, holding that one who distributes a device with the object of promoting its use to infringe copyright, as shown by clear expression or other affirmative steps taken to foster infringement, is liable for the resulting acts of infringement by third parties.

[Justice Souter, *MGM v Grokster* at 932]

In making this decision the Supreme court had ignored its previous direction from *Sony* that courts should not intervene to extend the scope of copyright protection, and the plea from Judge Thomas that new technologies should be allowed to develop. The court did not clearly define when active inducement would be found, instead the court gave guidance as to what may or may not constitute 'active inducement'. Justice Souter noted that 'mere knowledge of infringing potential or of actual infringing uses would not be enough here to subject a distributor to liability. Nor would ordinary acts incident to product distribution, such as offering customers technical support or product updates, support liability in themselves. The inducement rule, instead, premises liability on purposeful, culpable expression and conduct, and thus does nothing compromise legitimate commerce or discourage innovation having a lawful promise'.[100] What is clear therefore is that there must be some form clear campaign or inducement which incites infringement to occur. Had the defendants been involved in such a campaign?

Justice Souter examined the evidence: of Streamcast he noted that they 'beamed onto the computer screens of users of Napster-compatible programs ads urging the adoption of its OpenNap program, which was designed, as its name implied, to invite the custom of patrons of Napster, then under attack in the courts for facilitating massive infringement'.[101] Meanwhile Grokster were 'distribut[ing] an electronic newsletter containing links to articles promoting its software's ability to access popular copyrighted music.'[102] In particular he found three things on the record to be damning of both defendants: (1) 'each company showed itself to be aiming to satisfy a known source of demand for copyright infringement, the

---

[97] Concurring opinions were also issued by Justice Ginsberg and Justice Breyer. The reason for the concurring opinions is that some Justices were split over whether the case differed substantially from the *Sony* case. Justice Ginsburg, joined by Justice Kennedy and Chief Justice Rehnquist, felt that 'this case differs markedly from Sony' based on insufficient evidence of noninfringing uses. Justice Breyer, joined by Justices Stevens and O'Connor, felt that 'a strong demonstrated need for modifying Sony (or for interpreting Sony's standard more strictly) has not yet been shown.'

[98] 545 US 913, 931.   [99] *ibid*, 932.   [100] *ibid*, 932–933.   [101] *ibid*, 933.

[102] *ibid*.

market comprising former Napster users;'[103] (2) 'neither company attempted to develop filtering tools or other mechanisms to diminish the infringing activity using their software';[104] and (3) 'StreamCast and Grokster make money by selling advertising space, by directing ads to the screens of computers employing their software. As the record shows, the more the software is used, the more ads are sent out and the greater the advertising revenue becomes. Since the extent of the software's use determines the gain to the distributors, the commercial sense of their enterprise turns on high-volume use, which the record shows is infringing.'[105]

Following the decision of the Supreme Court the defendants followed different paths. Grokster closed its site on 7 November 2005. A note on its home page reads: 'The US Supreme Court unanimously confirmed that using this service to trade copyrighted material is illegal. Copying copyrighted motion picture and music files using unauthorized peer-to-peer services is illegal and is prosecuted by copyright owners. There are legal services for downloading music and movies. This service is not one of them. YOUR IP ADDRESS IS XXXXX AND HAS BEEN LOGGED. Don't think you can't get caught. You are not anonymous'.[106] Streamcast, however, continued to fight the suit on remand and on 27 September 2006, the US District Court for the Central District of California granted summary judgment in favour of the plaintiffs.[107] Streamcast promised to appeal the decision,[108] but on 22 April 2008, Streamcast Networks filed for Chapter 7 Bankruptcy.[109] Other P2P network providers fearing lawsuits similar to the *Grokster* one began either shutting down their services or taking steps to make them legal. Sam Yagan, president of MetaMachine, announced in a congressional hearing that they were closing their eDonkey and Overnet P2P systems following the *Grokster* decision.[110] Others followed suit with Kazaa migrating to a paid model[111] and LimeWire creating a filtering system which allows copyright holders to blacklist their protected content[112] and instigating a legal download store.[113]

10.2.4 **Peer-to-peer litigation outwith the US**

Litigation has not been restricted to the US. Major cases have taken place, and indeed are still taking place, in The Netherlands, Australia, Denmark, Italy and Sweden. Technology has also moved on with most people now using BitTorrent technology to fuel their demand for illicit copies of copyright protected content. One of the most interesting international actions was raised in The Netherlands.

---

[103] *ibid*, 934.   [104] *ibid*, 935.   [105] *ibid*.   [106] From http://www.grokster.com/.
[107] From: http://w2.eff.org/IP/P2P/MGM_v_Grokster/motion_summary_judgement.pdf.
[108] M. Hickins, 'StreamCast Up Streaming Creek', *Internet News* 28 September 2006: http://www.internetnews.com/bus-news/article.php/3634866.
[109] Bitplayer, 'Morpheus throws in the towel', *Los Angeles Times* 1 May 2008: http://opinion.latimes.com/bitplayer/2008/05/morpheus-throws.html.
[110] US Senate Committee on the Judiciary, *Testimony of Sam Yagan, President MetaMachine, Inc. (developer of eDonkey and Overnet)*, September 28, 2005: http://judiciary.senate.gov/hearings/testimony.cfm?id=1624&wit_id=4689.
[111] Kazaa will be discussed further below. Kazaa eventually reached a $100m settlement with copyright holders before becoming a legal download service. See BBC News, *Kazaa site becomes legal service*, 27 July 2006: http://news.bbc.co.uk/1/hi/technology/5220406.stm.
[112] See http://register.limewire.com/filter/.
[113] Available at: http://www.store.limewire.com/store/app/pages/Home.

Arguably the best known P2P system to arise out of the ashes of Napster was Kazaa. It was designed by the Scandinavian design team of Niklas Zennström, Janus Friis, and Priit Kasesalu who would go on to develop Skype and Joost and was distributed by their Dutch registered company Consumer Empowerment. In September 2000 Consumer Empowerment had written to Buma/Stemra (the Dutch licensing and collecting society for performers and composers) seeking a licence for the use of music by the users of the Kazaa software. Consumer Empowerment believed such a licence would protect them from *Napster* style litigation. Over the course of the following year though the negotiations broke down and eventually Consumer Empowerment (now renamed Kazaa BV) raised an action in an attempt to compel Buma/Stemra to continue negotiations. Buma/Stemra entered a counter-claim that Kazaa be compelled to take steps to prevent the distribution of works in the Buma/Stemra repertoire.[114]

On 29 November 2001 the President of the District Court of Amsterdam found partly in favour of Consumer Empowerment but ordered that 'Kazaa to take such measures within 14 days after service of this judgment that no longer, by means of the computer program provided by it, copyright infringing publications and reproductions with respect to musical works that are part of Buma/Stemra's repertoire can take place, on forfeiture of a penalty of 100,000 Guilders per day with a maximum of 2,000,000 Guilders'.[115] Both parties appealed to the Amsterdam Court of Appeal but perhaps fearful of the financial risks involved Kazaa BV sold the Kazaa application to a complicated mesh of offshore companies, primarily Sharman Networks, a company headquartered in Australia and incorporated in Vanuatu, and designed specifically to act as an offshore safe haven for applications like Kazaa. On appeal Kazaa BV won an unlikely victory.[116]

> **➜ Highlight** *BUMA & STEMRA v Kazaa*
>
> Insofar as there are acts that are relevant to copyright such acts are performed by those who use the computer program and not by Kazaa BV. Providing the means for publication or reproduction of copyrighted works is not an act of publication or reproduction in its own right. Also, it is not true, that is for the moment it cannot be assumed to be true, that the Kazaa computer program is exclusively used for downloading copyrighted works.
>
> In its appeal, Kazaa presented a large number of examples of works that were distributed by means of Kazaa either with the author's permission or that are part of the public domain, or that are not copyrighted or of which the distribution is permitted under a legal limitation to copyright. Buma/Stemra claims that the sole essential function of the Kazaa computer program is to allow users to exchange copyrighted works, however, this claim, which Kazaa contested with good reasons, was not further substantiated.

[114] In his judgement of 29 November 2001 President of the Court Orobio de Castro gives a full account of the background to the case. A unofficial English translation: http://w2.eff.org/IP/P2P/BUMA_v_Kazaa/20011112_kazaa_complaint.html.

[115] *ibid.*

[116] *BUMA & STEMRA v Kazaa*, Amsterdam Court of Appeal, 28 March 2001. Unofficial translation: http://w2.eff.org/IP/P2P/BUMA_v_Kazaa/20020328_kazaa_appeal_judgment.html.

The court also considered whether, as with Napster, Kazaa BV should be required to monitor and filter their users. Here, the lack of a central server meant Kazaa was to be treated differently: 'With the present state of standardisation it is not possible to technically detect which files are copyrighted and which are not. Thus, it is not possible for Kazaa (or any other software) to incorporate a blockage against the unlawful exchange of files'.[117] This could be seen as a bittersweet victory for Kazaa: they had won the legal battle but had moved ownership of their Kazaa software offshore. Later an appeal by Buma/Stemra to the Supreme Court of the Netherlands would confirm the decision of the Appellate Court:[118] the actions of Kazaa were not unlawful in Dutch Law as their service allowed for the transmission of all types of digital content, some protected by copyright, some not, some there with the permission of the copyright holder, some not.

As there was no way for Kazaa to directly control the activities of their customers or to have knowledge of what these customers were doing no liability arose. The *Buma/Stemra v Kazaa* litigation is little analysed by UK commentators, at least in comparison to its more famous US counterpart *Grokster* but it is submitted that it is of key importance for our understanding of the law in the UK. The Dutch Law, like the UK Law is heavily influenced by EU harmonisation efforts and like the UK has, as yet, no principle of 'active inducement' in copyright infringement. Although one cannot be sure that a UK court faced with a scenario similar to the Kazaa case would find similarly it demonstrates that a different approach to the *Groskster* one is available. That being said, the Kazaa story is only partly told. With the Kazaa software now owned by Sharman Networks the focus of litigation moved to Australia.

On 5 February 2004 thirty applicants, all involved in music production and distribution, raised an action in the Federal Court of Australia against Sharman Networks and several other respondents. The applicants argued that ninety-eight sound recordings, in which they owned the copyright, had been available for download, and had been downloaded, from the Kazaa system. Sharman ran a defence similar to the Kazaa BV one in The Netherlands: (1) that Kazaa is capable of being used, and is used, to make available and download files which do not involve any infringement of the applicants' or anyone else's copyright; (2) the software is content neutral and Sharman do not and are unable to control either the files (whether video, music, text, or otherwise) which users might make available by placing them in their My Shared Folder or the content which they search for and choose to download using the software; and (3) in the context of 'authorisation' there is a critical distinction between giving a person the power to do an infringing act and purporting to grant a person the right to do that act.[119]

Mr Justice Wilcox was faced with a variety of international approaches to the issue of illegal file sharing on decentred P2P systems. The US Supreme Court had ruled that Streamcast and Grokster could be held liable for illegal file sharing where they actively induced such sharing. The Dutch Supreme Court had though ruled that Kazaa could not be held liable for the actions of their customers as there was no way for Kazaa to directly control the activities of their customers or to have knowledge of what these customers were doing. This was the first time a common law court with close jurisprudential links to the UK was asked to weigh up both sides of the argument.

---

[117] *ibid*.

[118] *BUMA & STEMRA v Kazaa*, Supreme Court of The Netherlands, 19 December 2003, Case No. C02/186HR. Unofficial translation: http://www.muddlawoffices.com/RIAA/cases/Netherlands.pdf.

[119] *Universal Music Australia Pty Ltd v Sharman License Holdings Ltd* [2005] FCA 1242, [52].

Justice Wilcox wrote a long and detailed judgement in which he acknowledged the potential influence of the US Supreme Court in cases outwith their jurisdiction, noting: 'there was a question in my mind as to whether the Supreme Court's decision provided any guidance to the resolution of this case. On 30 June 2005, I invited the parties to comment about that matter'[120] before concluding 'much of the Australian statutory law had no counterpart in US law … Grokster [is] of little assistance to me'.[121] Although there is no doubt that the US Supreme Court decision did not directly influence Justice Wilcox's decision on the law it is cited several further times in his judgement, usually in reference to an argument made by counsel for either the applicants or respondents, it is clear therefore that counsel for both sides attempted to use parts of the US Supreme Court decision to shape policy.

Following extensive analysis Justice Wilcox found that Sharman Networks had infringed copyright in the named recordings and further that they were likely to infringe copyright in other recordings.[122] He based these findings on three key principles which emerged during the trial:

→ **Highlight** Justice Wilcox's Principles in *Sharman Networks*

1. Despite the fact that the Kazaa website contains warnings against the sharing of copyright files, and an end user licence agreement under which users are made to agree not to infringe copyright, it has long been obvious that those measures are ineffective to prevent, or even substantially to curtail, copyright infringements by users. The respondents have long known that the Kazaa system is widely used for the sharing of copyright files.

2. There are technical measures (keyword filtering and gold file flood filtering) that would enable the respondents to curtail—although probably not totally to prevent—the sharing of copyright files. The respondents have not taken any action to implement those measures. It would be against their financial interest to do so. It is in the respondents' financial interest to maximise, not to minimise, music file-sharing. Advertising provides the bulk of the revenue earned by the Kazaa system, which revenue is shared between Sharman Networks and Altnet.

3. Far from taking steps that are likely effectively to curtail copyright file-sharing, Sharman Networks and Altnet have included on the Kazaa website exhortations to users to increase their file-sharing and a webpage headed 'Join the Revolution' that criticises record companies for opposing peer-to-peer file-sharing. They also sponsored a 'Kazaa Revolution' campaign attacking the record companies. The revolutionary material does not expressly advocate the sharing of copyright files. However, to a young audience, and it seems that Kazaa users are predominantly young people, the effect of this webpage would be to encourage visitors to think it 'cool' to defy the record companies by ignoring copyright constraints.

---

[120] *ibid* [30].   [121] *ibid.*

[122] At [517] Justice Wilcox gives his disposition: 'I propose to make two declarations concerning those respondents. One declaration will state that the six respondents have infringed the copyright in each of the Defined Recordings by, first, authorising Kazaa users to make a copy of the said recording and to communicate the recording to the public, in each case without the licence of the relevant applicant; and, second, by entering into a common design to carry out, procure or direct that authorisation. The other declaration will be that the six respondents threaten to infringe the copyright of the applicants in other sound recordings in the same way.'

This decision is extremely instructive from a UK perspective. Justice Wilcox held that Sharman provided the facilities for another person to infringe copyright which was a potential breach of s. 101 of the Copyright Act 1968 which states that: 'Subject to this Act, a copyright subsisting by virtue of this Part is infringed by a person who, not being the owner of the copyright, and without the licence of the owner of the copyright, does in Australia, *or authorizes the doing in Australia* of, any act comprised in the copyright.'[123] He held that by 'authorising Kazaa users [in Australia] to make copies of [protected] sound recordings and to communicate those recordings to the public' s. 101 was infringed.[124] It should be noted there is no precise UK equivalent to s. 101 of the Copyright Act 1968. Sections 23–26 of the Copyright, Designs and Patents Act provide a series of grounds for secondary infringement claims but all are rather more precise than the generic provision of s. 101 of the Australian Act. It is impossible to say for certain how a UK judge would approach this issue but it may be assumed that the general policy move in common law courts in recent years has been to favour the copyright holder, as seen in the US in *Grokster* and in Australia in *Sharman*. This suggests that there are several approaches a UK judge may follow. They may find a P2P provider to be 'dealing' in infringing copies in breach of s. 23(c).[125] Although it may be seen to be a stretch to define a P2P provider as a 'distributor' in this fashion it does mirror the analysis found in both Grokster and Sharman where the courts were heavily influenced by the at very least tacit knowledge of the P2P providers and the profit motive which fuelled their activities. Alternatively they may find a P2P provider to be transmitting infringing copies of the work in breach of s. 24(2).[126] Whichever section of the Act was employed it is likely a UK judge would follow the approach taken by Justice Wilcox in *Sharman* and find P2P file sharing technologies to be in infringement of the rights awarded by the Copyright, Designs and Patents Act, but with no major file sharing technologies domiciled in the UK it is unlikely we shall see this thesis tested in court.

10.2.5 **Sweden v Neij et al. (The pirate bay case)**

Before leaving the case-law on P2P technologies we must finally review the most recent act of this ongoing legal drama which has been played out in Sweden. It involves the most recent and popular form of file sharing technology BitTorrent. BitTorrent works in a completely different manner to both centralised and decentralised P2P technologies. BitTorrent is an internet protocol, similar in function to File Transfer Protocol. To use the BitTorrent protocol you need a BitTorrent client, a specialised program which allows the transfer of files using the BitTorrent system. These BitTorrent clients are well known and

---

[123] Copyright Act 1968, s. 101(1) (emphasis added).   [124] [2005] FCA 1242, [420].
[125] S. 23(c) states: 'The copyright in a work is infringed by a person who, without the licence of the copyright owner in the course of a business exhibits in public or distributes an article which is, and which he knows or has reason to believe is, an infringing copy of the work'.
[126] Section 24(2) states: 'Copyright in a work is infringed by a person who without the licence of the copyright owner transmits the work by means of a telecommunications system (otherwise than by communication to the public), knowing or having reason to believe that infringing copies of the work will be made by means of the reception of the transmission in the United Kingdom or elsewhere.'

include 'BitTornado', 'µTorrent' and 'BitLord'. These have a similar relationship to the BitTorrent protocol as web browsers such as Internet Explorer and Firefox have to HTTP. Once installed a BitTorrent client allows for the uploading and downloading of BitTorrent files. To obtain a file via BitTorrent the user first has to obtain a small file called a Torrent file. This contains metadata used by the BitTorrent client to obtain the location of the file. What makes BitTorrent both efficient and attractive is its method of sharing files. Instead of the file transfer taking place between two users (a Peer-to-Peer transfer) it allows for an interaction between several users simultaneously (a Multi Peer transfer) by breaking large files down into smaller chunks and having different users transmit each chunk independently. Thus if we return to (and stretch) Shawn Fanning's original party metaphor BitTorrent is an extremely large and unmanaged party. When a new guest arrives they may want a cocktail, perhaps a Cosmopolitan. They look at a 'guest book' at the door which lists those party guests who have the component parts of their drink. They can then search out these individuals who each supply one component (vodka, triple sec, cranberry juice and lime juice) and once complete they can assemble the completed cocktail. In truth BitTorrent is much more complex than this as people are simultaneously uploading (seeding) and downloading (leeching) file chunks. The key to a fast download is to find a Torrent which tracks many seeders and fewer leechers. For the purposes of our analysis though the key part of the analogy is the operation of the guest book which is analogous to these small Torrent files which are essential to finding all the parts of your larger music, video, or software file. These tend to be made available though BitTorrent indexes, sites which specialise in tracking and listing available Torrent files. The largest and best known index is the Swedish site *The Pirate Bay*, which due both to its high profile and popularity as a Torrent index has had several confrontations with law enforcement authorities and copyright holders.

On 31 May 2006 *The Pirate Bay* was raided by Swedish Police officers who removed all of *The Pirate Bay's* servers and questioned three of *The Pirate Bay's* 'stewards' Gottfrid Svartholm, Mikael Viborg, and Fredrik Neij on suspicion of operating a business infringing copyright. This, in Sweden, as in the UK, may be a criminal offence.[127] The site was offline for three days and the Motion Picture Association of America claimed victory with MPAA chairman Dan Glickman announcing that 'The actions today taken in Sweden serve as a reminder to pirates all over the world that there are no safe harbors for internet copyright thieves.'[128] Despite this reports of *The Pirate Bay's* death were premature. The site was up and running again on 2 June 2006, their logo amended to depict their traditional pirate ship firing cannonballs at the Hollywood sign. The investigation continued throughout 2006 and 2007 and eventually on 31 January 2008 *The Pirate Bay's* operators Gottfrid Svartholm, Fredrik Neij, Peter Sunde, and Carl Lundström were charged with 'promoting other people's infringements of copyright laws'.[129]

---

[127] The UK equivalent provision may be found in CDPA, s. 107.

[128] This quote, and all other factual data about *The Pirate Bay* raid is drawn from: Quinn Norton, 'Secrets of the Pirate Bay', *Wired*, 16 August 2006: http://www.wired.com/science/discoveries/news/2006/08/71543?currentPage=all.

[129] L. Larsson, 'Charges filed against the Pirate Bay four', *Computer Sweden*, 31 January 2008: http://www.idg.se/2.1085/1.143146.

Two specific charges were levied: (1) 'complicity in the production of copyrighted material' and (2) 'complicity to make copyrighted material available'.[130] The first related to making copies available via *The Pirate Bay* site, the second to making and indexing Torrent files via the site. The trial began on 16 February 2009 and on day two of the trial the state prosecutor Håkan Roswall dropped the charge of 'complicity in the production of copyrighted material', this was reported to be in response to evidence given on day one about the technical operations of *The Pirate Bay*.[131] The second, lesser charge remained.

The defendants argued that the actions of *The Pirate Bay* were no different to those of other indexing and search websites such as Google, Yahoo!, or Microsoft's Live search. Those sites provide a search facility for HTML-based content which may or may not be made available in breach of copyright. There is no doubt that a proportion of content available on the web is there without the permission or license of the copyright holder, but Google and others do not take steps to positively identify which content is in breach of copyright and which is not. This, the defendants argued, reflected also how *The Pirate Bay* functioned. Torrents may contain material made available with the permission or licence of the copyright holder, or they may contain content made available in breach of copyright, all *The Pirate Bay* does is index torrents; it does not question their content. The prosecution responded that unlike Google *The Pirate Bay* actively use their technology to assist in the commission of copyright infringement and they directly profit from this. Mr Roswall said he was not asking the court to rule on the legality of BitTorrent itself, but rather what the defendants did with the technology. He said that the Swedish Supreme Court had previously ruled that someone running a Bulletin Board which shared copyright material had been found guilty of assisting copyright infringement and that *The Pirate Bay* should be viewed in this light. He went on to estimate that the site had made between 5 million and 10 million kroner (£400,000–£800,000), turnover directly attributable to illegal file sharing.[132] In making his case the prosecutor was clearly drawing on the same principles which had led the US Supreme Court to find that Grokster/Streamcast had actively induced copyright infringement, and which had led the Federal Court of Australia to find that Sharman Networks had infringed the Copyright Act 1968.

On 17 April 2009 the District Court of Stockholm announced its decision.[133] All four accused were found guilty of complicity to make copyright material available, the Court having rejected the defendant's 'Google defence'. They were each sentenced to one year in prison and collectively found liable for damages totalling 30m Swedish krona (around £2.4m).[134] The defendants immediately indicated they would appeal

---

[130] K. Fiveash, 'Pirate Bay prosecutor tosses infringement charges overboard', *The Register*, 17 February 2009: http://www.theregister.co.uk/2009/02/17/pirate_bay_half_charges_dropped_report/.   [131] *ibid.*
[132] Information and data drawn from *The Pirate Bay Trial Day 10: Calls for Jail Time*: http://torrentfreak.com/the-pirate-bay-trial-day-10-calls-for-jail-time-090302/.
[133] Stockholms Tingsrätt, No. B 13301-06, 17 April 2009: http://www.icmpecho.com/defavgdok.pdf (in Swedish).
[134] The damages are awarded in varying amounts to a number of claimants. Sony Music Entertainment (Sweden) €41,467; Universal Music €73,782; Playground Music Scandinavia AB €28,159; Bonnier Amigo Music Group AB €4,290; EMI Music Sweden €162,988; Warner Music Sweden €146,484; Yellow Bird Films 3,150,000 kr; Nordisk Film Valby 225,000 kr; Warner Bros Entertainment Inc. 2,484,225 kr; Metro-Goldwyn-Mayer Pictures Inc. & Columbia Pictures Industries Inc. 5,579,325 kr; Twentieth Century Fox Film Corporation 10,822,500 kr; Warner Bros Entertainment Inc. 414,000 kr; and Twentieth Century Fox Film Corporation & Mars Media Meteiligungs GmbH Film Productions 4,495,950 kr.

the verdict[135] a process which could take several years. Until then it seems likely *The Pirate Bay* will continue to operate rendering the legal success of the copyright holders somewhat bittersweet.[136]

Despite the successes of copyright holders in cases such as *Napster, Grokster, Sharman*, and *The Pirate Bay* the popularity of peer-to-peer file sharing continues to grow with no apparent limit on its popularity. The number of Torrent indexes has grown since *The Pirate Bay* action first commenced in 2006 while Pirate Bay was on 16 April 2009 the 105th most visited site on the web with a reach of .676% (or about 11 million visits per day).[137] This may fall far short of Google.com's 30.73% (or about 490 million visits per day) but ranks ahead of well known mainstream web sites such as eBay UK, Metacafe, Bebo, and Digg. Even if Swedish prosecutors were able to close down *The Pirate Bay* permanently, which seems unlikely,[138] other Torrent indexes would quickly fill the void. The days of closing down a few P2P site operators being an effective method to control the illegal trade in copyright protected music, video, and software files appear long gone in the completely decentralised world of BitTorrent. New techniques have therefore been developed in an attempt to stem the tide of illegal files. One technique is to seek to block access to sites which offer file sharing technology or indexes. Much of this activity has focussed recently on *The Pirate Bay*. In August 2008 an Italian judge ordered all Italian ISPs to block access to *The Pirate Bay* as part of a probe into copyright law violation.[139] Interestingly it was reported that traffic to *The Pirate Bay* from Italy actually increased following the implementation of the ban as users found ways around the block including the use of proxy sites and mirror sites.[140] *The Pirate Bay* appealed and on 24 September the ban was lifted by the Tribunal de Bergamo.[141] It should be noted thought that the ban was lifted on a technical point of Italian law and it should not be assumed that all blocks will be equally voided.[142]

On 28 January 2008 the Eastern High Court of Denmark also ordered Danish ISP Tele2 to block access to *The Pirate Bay* following an application from IFPI. The Court found that *The Pirate Bay* is indisputably a means to traffic copyrighted materials between users and that

---

[135] http://trial.thepiratebay.org/2009/03/05/exclusive-interview-with-brokep-today-at-12-cet/.4
[136] See D. Ionescu, 'Hollywood's Victory Over The Pirate Bay Will Be Short-Lived', *PC World*, 18 April 2009: http://www.pcworld.com/article/163366/hollywoods_victory_over_the_pirate_bay_will_be_shortlived.html.; a planned purchase of *The Pirate Bay* which would have turned it into a legal download site seems to have failed. See: http://www.wired.com/threatlevel/2009/09/pirate-bay-purchase-sinking/.
[137] On 20 April, i.e. three days after the Stockholm District Court verdict *The Pirate Bay* was ranked 106th by Web Ranking service Alexa.com. Although it had fallen one place in the overall rankings from 16 April (the day before the verdict) it now had a reach of .721% or about 11.5 million visits per day, up 4.5% from 16 April.
[138] While the appeal is ongoing the original verdict remains suspended under Swedish Law. In addition it is widely reported that following the original raid in 2006 Pirate Bay servers were moved from Sweden to The Netherlands. See Ionescu, above n. 136.
[139] AP, 'Italy Blocks The Pirate Bay', *The Age*, 15 August 2008: http://www.theage.com.au/news/web/italy-blocks-the-pirate-bay/2008/08/15/1218307210151.html.
[140] *The Pirate Bay Sees Boost in Italian Traffic Following 'Block'.*: http://torrentfreak.com/the-pirate-bay-sees-boost-in-italian-traffic-following-block-080815/.
[141] Decision: http://blog.brokep.com/wp-content/uploads/2008/09/ricorso-tpb.png.
[142] The technical point being that the original order was a seizure warrant and under Italian law, a seizure cannot be interpreted as forcing somebody to do something (in this case ISP's to filter user's traffic).

Tele2 was responsible for making the site freely available to its customers. On this basis the court found that Tele2 assisted copyright infringement in breach of s. 2(2) of the Danish Copyright Act.[143] Initially *The Pirate Bay* shrugged off this attempt to block access. The order only related to one Danish ISP and with the publicity surrounding the case visitors to the site from Denmark actually went up.[144] But as time went on other ISPs began to block access to *The Pirate Bay* and in February 2009 the Court has ruled that all Danish ISPs would have to do the same, or potentially face a fine.[145] At the time of writing an appeal is being prepared by the ISPs who claim that ISPs should be neutral in the issue and that the matter should be sorted out between content owners and those that host it.[146] Whether the Danish appeal is success-ful or not the use of blocks to prevent file sharing is unlikely to be any more successful than direct attacks on those who provide file sharing technology or indexes. It still requires cases to be raised on a provider by provider basis. All a blocking application does is relocate the action to another jurisdiction by using ISPs as a proxy. Blocking access to *The Pirate Bay* or *Sumotor-rent* (another popular Torrent index) will not deal with the root of the problem: individuals sharing copyright protected content with other individuals. Is there a solution for this?

10.2.6 Other methods to prevent illegal file sharing: technical measures

Copyright holders seem to be trialling two alternate solutions in the UK at the moment; both aimed at the individual copyright infringer rather than the P2P provider. One is a development of the blocking approach seen in Denmark, the other a variation of the class action strategy which has attracted the name 'volume litigation'.

The first is the more mainstream approach. Working with the Departments of Cul-ture Media and Sport and Business Innovation and Skills, the copyright industries are attempting to develop a partnership with the UK Government and ISPs for a self regu-latory system. This system is modelled on a proposal first developed in France and included in the French 'law favouring the diffusion and protection of creation on Internet'.[147] The idea is a 'three strikes and you are out' system where ISPs act as agents for copyright holders. The original UK proposal, based on the French Law, would have seen copyright enforcement authorities gathering IP address data of individuals shar-ing copyright protected material and then passing it on the ISPs for action. The ISPs

---

[143] An English translation of the Court's decision is available at: http://piratgruppen.org/spip.php?article872.

[144] J. Cheng, 'Pirate Bay to IFPI: Danish ban has led to even more traffic', *Ars Technica*, 12 February 2008: http://arstechnica.com/tech-policy/news/2008/02/pirate-bay-to-ifpi-danish-ban-has-led-to-even-more-traffic.ars.

[145] *Danish ISPs to Fight the Pirate Bay Block*: http://torrentfreak.com/danish-isps-to-fight-the-pirate-bay-block-090205/.   [146] *ibid.*

[147] The Law's proper name is 'Projet de loi favorisant la diffusion et la protection de la créa-tion sur Internet'. It was originally passed on 13 May 2009, having previously been rejected by the Assemblee Nationale. It was then struck out by the Conseil Constitutionnel (Constitutional Court of France) on 10 June 2009 for the Law 'violated the 1789 Declaration of the Rights of Man and of the Citizen, and in particular the presumption of innocence, separation of powers and free-dom of speech'. The Assemblee Nationale passed an amended version of the Law (15 September 2009). It came into force on 1 January 2010.

would then identify customers based upon this data and would send them a warning letter (in practice probably a warning email), informing them that their activities were unlawful and were being monitored. In the event the customer continued to share copyright material despite this warning a second letter would be sent informing the customer that they were in breach of their terms and conditions of service and that if they persisted they would be disconnected. If the customer still persisted the ISP would then be expected to disconnect the customer. The original French proposal has been highly controversial,[148] and in the UK opposition to the proposal quickly emerged.

One of the most vociferous opponents was Charles Dunstone, CEO of Carphone Warehouse a major UK ISP. In a statement Mr Dunstone stated that 'we are the conduit that gives users access to the internet, we do not control the internet nor do we control what our users do on the internet. I cannot foresee any circumstances in which we would voluntarily disconnect a customer's account on the basis of a third party alleging a wrong doing.'[149] Mr Dunstone here captures the essence of the problem with three-strike policies. While the economic benefit accrues to the copyright holder, the cost of enforcement rests with the ISP: it is the ISP who must pay the administrative costs of identifying and writing to customers, and ultimately it is the ISP who may lose paying customers, especially where some ISPs agree to support the policy and others do not. Without the support of Carphone Warehouse any agreement was likely to be undermined, the copyright industry representatives returned to the negotiating table. Following further discussion a Memorandum of Understanding (MoU) was agreed between the BPI, Motion Picture Association, the Departments for Business, Enterprise & Regulatory Reform, Innovations, Universities and Science, and Culture, Media and Sport and six leading UK ISPs.[150] The MoU stated that 'parties agree that the objective of this MOU is to achieve within two to three years a significant reduction in the incidence of copyright infringement as a result of peer to peer file-sharing and a change in popular attitude towards infringement.' To achieve this outcome five principles were agreed between signatory parties:

1. Signatories agree to work together with each other and with Ofcom to agree codes of practice.

2. Signatories, led by the creative industries, will work together to ensure that consumers are educated to respect the value of the creative process.

3. Signatories agree on the importance of competing to make available to consumers commercially available and attractively packaged content in a wide range of user-friendly formats as an alternative to unlawful file-sharing, for example subscription, on demand, or sharing services.

4. Signatories will work together on a process whereby internet service customers are informed when their accounts are being used unlawfully to share copyright

---

[148] See, e.g. C. Kowaliski, 'Ignorance, legislative stupidity, and the French three-strikes piracy bill', *The Tech Report*, 3 April 2009: http://techreport.com/discussions.x/16691.

[149] S. Turton, 'Carphone Warehouse blasts "three strikes" proposal', *PC Pro News*, 4 April 2008: http://www.pcpro.co.uk/news/184431/carphone-warehouse-blasts-three-strikes-proposal.html.

[150] The six being BSkyB, BT, Carphone Warehouse, Orange, Tiscali, and Virgin Media. The MoU comprises Annex C of BERR/DCMS/DIUS, *Copyright in a Digital World: What Role for a Digital Rights Agency?*: http://www.ipo.gov.uk/digitalbritain.pdf.

material and pointed towards legal alternatives. In the first instance ISP signatories will each put in place a three month trial to send notifications to 1000 subscribers per week identified to them by music rights holders, to agreed levels of evidence, as having been engaged in illicit uploading or downloading. Based on evidence from the trial, which will be analysed and assessed by all Signatories, Ofcom will agree with Signatories an escalation in numbers, widening of content coverage, and a process for agreeing a cap.

5. Signatories will be invited by Ofcom to a group to identify effective mechanisms to deal with repeat infringers. In addition, rights holders will consider prosecuting particularly serious infringers in appropriate cases.

As can be seen the MoU falls far short of the three-strike proposal. Instead of suggesting users be disconnected by ISPs it places the emphasis on education and reform of the digital distribution model. The key aspects are that ISPs assist copyright holders in a campaign of education and will warn customers who engage in file sharing that their activities have been noted. Essentially, however, the primary enforcement role remains with the copyright holders who agree to 'consider prosecuting particularly serious infringers in appropriate cases'.

The copyright industries were though extremely unhappy with the settlement achieved via the MoU. In particular the British Phonographic Institute (BPI) felt that the two to three year timeframe in the MoU was unacceptable. They argued that by 2012 many millions of pounds would be lost to UK creative industries and that a more immediate response was required. They caught the ear of the Department of Business, Innovation and Skills which on 16 June 2009 issued a further consultation on this matter entitled *Consultation on Legislation to Address Illicit Peer-to-peer (P2P) File Sharing.*[151] The consultation, which closed on 15 September 2009, noted that despite the MoU 'Government has been convinced of the need for some legislative baseline to change the behaviour of the majority of file-sharers via an obligation on ISPs to notify broadband subscribers that their account has been identified as responsible for a copyright infringement'.[152] The consultation proposed two obligations on ISPs which form part of the Digital Economy Bill introduced into Parliament in the 2009-10 session. The first is the 'notification obligation', which will oblige ISPs 'to notify an account holder, upon receipt of appropriate evidence (standards to be set by the code) from a rights holder of an alleged copyright infringement on that account, of the existence of such evidence'.[153] This is proposed in the belief that a large percentage of individuals (possibly as high as 70%) will stop file sharing upon receipt of such a notification. In addition to merely informing the user that evidence has been gathered against them the notification will also provide 'advice and guidance on securing wireless networks where appropriate; a statement that the notification is sent pursuant to the legislation; advice on how/where to access legitimate content; information about copyright and why it is important; and anything else specified by the code'.[154]

One issue of particular interest, given the problems of volume litigation practice (discussed below) is the standard of proof required. This is set out in paragraph 4.14: 'The

---

[151] Available from: http://www.berr.gov.uk/files/file51703.pdf.   [152] *ibid*, [2.11].
[153] *ibid*, [4.9].   [154] *ibid*, [4.12].

standard of evidence required from rights holders should, as a minimum, establish an infringement on the balance of probabilities. The template used by the BPI in the MOU trial should serve as a model for this as it has proved satisfactory to all the ISPs in the trial and has not provoked any particular concerns by consumers affected. This will need to be defined by the code'. This suggests the widespread adoption of an extremely low standard of proof, something that caused concern to several who replied to the consultation.[155]

If users continue to share files after receiving notification they are moved to 'serious infringer' status. This triggers a further obligation for their ISP to maintain a register of the number of notifications sent to the user with the view that copyright holders may use that as evidence in a case against the user.[156] This all sounds perfectly innocent to date and one may question why the proposals have been greeted with a howl of media and consumer group outrage[157] as all ISPs are being asked to do is tell customers that someone holds evidence they are file sharing and to maintain a database of such notifications. This is because at paragraph 4.23 it is proposed that 'Ofcom should have a power to require ISPs to take technical measures (which will be specified in the legislation) against serious repeat infringers aimed at preventing, deterring or reducing online copyright infringement, such as: Blocking (Site, IP, URL); Protocol blocking; Port blocking; Bandwidth capping (capping the speed of a subscriber's internet connection and/or capping the volume of data traffic which a subscriber can access); Bandwidth shaping (limiting the speed of a subscriber's access to selected protocols/services and/or capping the volume of data to selected protocols/services); and Content identification and filtering'. The BPI have been keen to stress these options do not include user disconnection as has been widely, and erroneously, reported,[158] but it should be noted that the consultation paper merely lists these technical responses as examples of the types of measures which the legislation may contain. In addition paragraph 4.23 goes on to make a thinly veiled argument for extending a disconnection principle: 'It is entirely possible that the obligations on notification and collection of anonymised information on repeat infringers that may lead to legal actions taken by rights holders that we set out here will not, by themselves, deter some infringers. If that is established it is important that Ofcom should have the ability to take further steps to reduce copyright infringement significantly, in line with the long term objective'.

It is expected that despite strong objections to the proposals from a variety of viewpoints including ISPs, consumers rights groups, open information groups and even

---

[155] See Response by Consumer Focus: http://www.consumerfocus.org.uk/media/viewfile.aspx? filepath=1_20090514114916_e_@@_P2P311008.PDF&filetype=4.

[156] *Consultation on Legislation to Address Illicit Peer-to-peer (P2P) File Sharing*, [4.19–4.21].

[157] See, e.g. BBC News, *Anger at UK file-sharing policy*, 25 August 2009: http://news.bbc.co.uk/1/ hi/8219652.stm; C. Williams, 'UK.gov revives net cut-off threat for illegal downloaders', *The Register* 25 August 2009: http://www.theregister.co.uk/2009/08/25/p2p_disconnection/; Open Rights Group response to the Consultation Exercise: http://www.openrightsgroup.org/uploads/081030_ berr_p2p.pdf.

[158] Speech of Kiaron Whitehead to the 4th Annual SCL Conference 21 and 22 September 2009. Copy on file with author.

artists themselves,[159] the Digital Economy Bill will lead to enforcement powers substantially in the form set out in the Consultation Paper. While these may not lead to disconnection of users as the French Law does there is little doubt that many tens of thousands of notices will follow and that many of these will accuse innocent people of file sharing due to the weaknesses in the collection of evidence that we have already seen in the practice of volume litigation.

10.2.7 Other methods to prevent illegal file sharing: volume litigation

Volume litigation is a highly controversial and relatively new tactic introduced into the UK by law firm Davenport Lyons (DL), and now practiced exclusively by a niche firm ACS Law. The practice first came to light in March 2007 when DL sent letters to five hundred individuals who, they claimed, had shared a computer game called Pinball Dreams 3D. The letters offered to settle the claim in return for a payment of in the region of £600, failure to settle would lead to DL taking further action.[160] This practice may be seen as a twist on the class action lawsuit where a collection of individuals bands together to pursue a corporation: here the corporation is ameliorating the costs of pursuing hundreds of actions by packaging them together and launching a 'volume' case. Details about the success, or otherwise, of volume litigation are sketchy. Firms involved in volume litigation do not reveal how many cases settle for payment or how many are abandoned: for example the DL website merely refers to an award of £16,000 damages awarded to Topware Interactive, copyright holders of Pinball Dreams 3D, by the Patents County Court in London in August 2008.[161] What is not clear though from this update is that the case was undefended, as were a series of smaller awards also mentioned in the update. To date no law firm has prosecuted a defended action before the UK courts. This suggests the tactic in this form of action is to try and force settlements rather than to pursue litigation. The few cases which have gone to court have all been undefended leading to the award of default judgements: what is not clear is whether there has been any attempt to enforce any of these judgements.

The practice of volume litigation was initially attractive to copyright holders. As well as Topware Interactive, DL were retained by Codemasters, Reality Pump, Techland, and Atari to pursue claims relating to games titles such as *The Lord of the Rings,* the *Colin McRae Rally* series, and *Operation Flashpoint.*[162] Recently though a stream of bad publicity had dogged the practice. First it became clear that claims were being made based on IP address data alone. This meant individuals who may not have adequately secured their

---

[159] See statement of The Featured Artists Coalition, the British Academy of Songwriters, Composers and Authors, and the Music Producers Guild at: http://musically.com/blog/2009/09/04/uk-musicians-and-composers-slam-governments-anti-piracy-consultation/.

[160] M. Ballard, 'Games firm pursues 500 pinball 'pirates' through UK courts', *The Register*, 28 March 2007: http://www.reghardware.co.uk/2007/03/28/uk_share_hunt/.

[161] Davenport Lyons, *Illegal File-Sharer Ordered to Pay £16,000 By Judge*: http://www.davenportlyons.com/html/legal_services/articles/it_newmedia/file_sharing.html.

[162] A. Mostrous and J. Richards, 'Computer games industry threat to downloaders: "pay up or we'll sue"', *The Times*, 20 August 2008: http://technology.timesonline.co.uk/tol/news/tech_and_web/gadgets_and_gaming/article4569180.ece.

wireless servers could find themselves receiving demands for the actions of individuals who had illegally piggy backed on their server.[163] The bad publicity surrounding what many saw as strong arm tactics reached a head in late 2008 with two separate episodes.

Case Study Ken and Gill Murdoch

In October 2008 Davenport Lyons sent a letter on behalf of Atari to Ken and Gill Murdoch of Inverness accusing them of sharing Atari's *Race 07* game. Ken (66) and Gill (54) said that they had never played a computer game before and contacted *Which?* The story quickly became a minor cause célèbre with Davenport Lyons dropping the claim but not before their tale was reported by *The Daily Express*, the *BBC*, and *The Daily Mail*.

Case Study Davenport Lyons and Smut

Davenport Lyons decided to represent the copyright holders of several hardcore pornographic titles. A substantial number of claim letters were issued in late 2008 relating to a number of film titles, all of which appear to be material which it would be illegal to trade in, or potentially even possess, in the UK. Quite apart from the question as to whether a Court of Equity would entertain an application from a copyright holder who is seeking to enforce their copyright in obscene material, Davenport Lyons had unfortunately sent several of their claims letters to respectable elderly citizens leading to a further round of bad publicity. This bad publicity led to Atari severing relations with the firm, while the tactics caused *Which?* to report the firm to the Solicitors' Regulatory Authority.

At the time of writing DL have suspended indefinitely their practice of volume litigation. The bad publicity surrounding these two events seems to have discouraged them from the practice. The practice is now solely employed by in the UK by niche firm ACS:Law. Whether or not ACS:Law ultimately succeeds in making the volume litigation model work for them remains to be seen. The concept of volume litigation is extremely strong, however it is to be suggested that to be effective those operating volume litigation services need to learn from the early experiences of DL. It is suggested that if volume litigation is to go mainstream every step must be taken to ensure a solid infringement case is in place *before* issuing letters of claim, and the tone of letters should be less confrontational. It is impossible to predict whether or not volume litigation will become popular among copyright holders of what remains a niche operation seen as similar to that of ambulance chasing personal injury lawyers, but it must be recognised as another potential weapon in the arsenal of copyright holders.

---

[163] It is illegal under s. 125 of the Communications Act 2003 to 'dishonestly obtain an electronic communications service', this includes making use of another's wireless internet connection without permission. See J. Leyden, 'UK war driver fined £500', *The Register*, 25 July 2005: http://www. theregister.co.uk/2005/07/25/uk_war_driver_fined/.

10.3 **Information and the public domain**

After a lengthy analysis of the measures taken by copyright holders in an attempt to prevent the unlawful distribution of their protected content via the web and file sharing systems it is a relief to conclude this chapter by examining some of the positive benefits the internet offers for the publication and distribution of creative content. One such benefit may be seen in the European i2010 Digital Libraries Initiative. This is a Commission project with the aim of creating a virtual European library, to make Europe's cultural and scientific resources uniformly accessible.

The library was first proposed in April 2005 in a letter to the Presidency of Council and to the Commission from six Heads of State and Government.[164] The Commission formalised the proposal and presented *the i2010: communication on digital libraries*.[165] This asked member states to comment on proposals for the formation of such a library including asking whether the mass digitisation process involved in the creation of such an institution would comply with copyright law. The Commission noted that: 'Digitisation presupposes making a copy, which can be problematic in view of intellectual property rights (IPR). Directive 2001/29/EC on the harmonisation of certain aspects of copyright and related rights in the information society foresees an exception for specific acts of reproduction by publicly accessible libraries, educational establishments, museums or archives. The exception is however not mandatory and has led to different implementations in the Member States. The limited use that can be legally made of the resulting digital copies is a further disincentive for digitisation'.[166]

> **Highlight** The European Digital Library
>
> Following extensive consultation the Commission proposed in summer 2006 that member states: 'promote a European digital library, in the form of a multilingual common access point to Europe's distributed digital cultural material, by: (a) encouraging cultural institutions, as well as publishers and other rightholders to make their digitised material searchable through the European digital library, and (b) ensuring that cultural institutions, and where relevant private companies, apply common digitisation standards in order to achieve interoperability of the digitised material at European level and to facilitate cross-language searchability.
>
> [Commission Recommendation of 24 August 2006 on the digitisation and online accessibility of cultural material and digital preservation, Recommendation 5]

Throughout the Commission recognised the challenge that copyright law offers to this project, noting that 'Europe's cultural heritage should be digitised, made available and preserved, while fully respecting Community and international rules on copyright and

---

[164] About the EC i2010 Digital Libraries Initiative: http://www.theeuropeanlibrary.org/portal/organisation/cooperation/archive/edlproject/digital_libraries.php.
[165] COM(2005) 465 final.   [166] *ibid*, 6.

related rights'.[167] As a first stage the European Digital Library Project provides a portal for access to the bibliographic catalogues and digital collections of the National Libraries of Belgium, Greece, Iceland, Ireland, Liechtenstein, Luxembourg, Norway, Spain, and Sweden. To make such projects succeed in the medium to long term though libraries must be able to provide digital materials within the boundaries of copyright law.

Currently under the Copyright, Designs and Patents Act librarians do not have permission to digitise copies of published works, but interestingly s. 44A of the Copyright, Designs and Patents Act allows the Secretary of State to make regulations allowing legal deposit libraries[168] to make a deposit copy of material published on the internet if the material or the person publishing it is connected to the UK.[169] Unfortunately to date no such regulations have been made. It seems unlikely therefore that the rights of archivists and librarians will be extended anytime soon. This suggests that UK participation in the i2010 project is likely to be limited to works in the public domain, or under Crown copyright or works which have been digitised with the permission of the copyright holder. A further provision in the Legal Deposit Libraries Act which would allow Deposit Libraries to obtain copies of published non-print (i.e. digital) publications remains, like s. 44A of the CDPA, disappointingly undeveloped with again a failure by the Secretary to State to proscribe Regulations meaning it is not of any effect several years after the Act received Royal Assent.

The balance between the rights of copyright holders and the community at large is a difficult one to achieve. It is essential that copyright holders are afforded an opportunity to be rewarded for the work they put in to creating their outputs. As an author myself I am acutely aware of this. However projects such as i2010 offer both an exciting glimpse of what is possible and make one consider how much of today's digital only online publishing will be preserved for future generations. Perhaps the answer is to allow authors to indicate at publication if they object to their work being archived, redistributed, or even altered or remixed. This is the view of one particular organisation: the Creative Commons movement.

10.3.1 **Creative commons**

The Creative Commons movement started in 2001 when a group of individuals with the support of the Center for the Study of the Public Domain at Duke University came together with a view of finding a way to free digital content from the constraints of a copyright law designed for the atomic environment. The Creative Commons project is closely linked to US law professor Lawrence Lessig who set out his vision for Creative Commons in a 2004 paper simply entitled *The Creative Commons*.[170] In this Lessig describes the Creative Commons movement as 'a kind of environmentalism for culture',[171] the idea being 'to build a layer of reasonable copyright law'.[172]

---

[167] *ibid*, 5.
[168] Legal Deposit Libraries are defined in s. 14 of the Legal Deposit Libraries Act 2003. They are the British Library, The National Library of Scotland, The National Library of Wales, Trinity College Library, Dublin, the Bodleian Library, and University Library, Cambridge.
[169] CDPA 1988, s. 44A(b).
[170] L. Lessig, 'The Creative Commons', 65 *Montana Law Review* 1 (2004).   [171] *ibid*, 11.
[172] *ibid*.

The reason why the Creative Commons movement came about is the Lawrence Lessig and co-founder James Boyle (among others) believed that a rebalancing of copyright interests was necessary in the information society. They had seen in the previous ten years what Lessig described as two extremes: firstly 'in the beginning of the Internet the architecture of the Internet disabled any ability to control the distribution of copyright works ... The architecture meant that copyright was not respected because anybody could copy and perfectly distribute any copyrighted work without control'.[173] However in 1995 the copyright industry responded to this threat: 'the copyright industry ... in response to the Internet launched a campaign to change the technical and legal infrastructure that defined the Internet from an architecture of no control to an architecture of total control ... we have thus moved from one extreme to the other'.[174]

Lessig and Boyle believed neither of the extremes represented the interests of most internet users. They felt most people wanted to make use of copyright material without the strict restrictions the copyright industry was seeking to implement for commercially valuable copyright content while ensuring that commercially valuable content was protected, or to put it in Lessig's own words 'But the world is divided not into two, but into three. There are those who believe in all rights reserved, those who believe in no rights at all, but there are also many who believe that some rights should be controlled but not all'.[175] This third group is represented by Creative Commons, its famous strap-line is 'some rights reserved' a reflection of this balance between the extremes. Creative Commons does not seek to overthrow or subvert copyright law,[176] but rather allows copyright holders to embed permissions into their copyright material allowing others to reuse, share, or copy that material without seeking the active permission of the copyright holder. Creative Commons achieves this through the application of six mainstream licences. These are:

1. Attribution (BY): This license lets others distribute, remix, tweak, and build upon the work, even commercially, as long as they credit the author for the original creation.

2. Attribution-Share Alike (BY–SA): This license lets others remix, tweak, and build upon the work even for commercial reasons, as long as they credit the author and license their new creations under the identical terms. All new works based on the original will carry the same license, so any derivatives will also allow commercial use.

3. Attribution-No Derivatives (BY-ND): This license allows for redistribution of the work, commercial and non-commercial, as long as it is passed along unchanged and in whole, with credit to the author.

4. Attribution-Non-Commercial (BY-NC): This license lets others remix, tweak, and build upon the work non-commercially, and although their new works must also acknowledge you and be non-commercial, they don't have to license their derivative works on the same terms.

---

[173] *ibid*, 10.   [174] *ibid*.   [175] *ibid*.
[176] An alternate movement 'copyleft' seeks to subvert copyright by forcing release of content into the public domain. Copyleft principles inform the GNU Free Documentation License, details from: http://www.gnu.org/licenses/licenses.html#FDL.

5. Attribution-Non-Commercial-Share Alike (BY-NC-SA): This license lets others remix, tweak, and build upon the work non-commercially, as long as they credit the author and license their new creations under the identical terms.

6. Attribution-Non-Commercial-No Derivatives (BY-NC-ND): This license is the most restrictive of the six main licenses. This license is often called the 'free advertising' license because it allows others to download the work and share it with others as long as they mention the author and link back to them, but they can't change the work in any way or use it commercially.

To use a Creative Commons license the author visits the Creative Commons website[177] and answers a series of questions including which jurisdiction they reside in and what they want others to be able to do with the work. Based on answers to these questions they will be recommended a Creative Commons license for their work. The Creative Commons License is actually the three part document: there is the commons deed (human readable code); the legal code (lawyer readable code) and the metadata (machine readable code).

The Commons Deed is a summary of the key terms of the actual license (the Legal Code). It states simply and clearly, what others can and cannot do with the work.[178] The Commons Deed itself has no legal value, and its contents do not appear in the actual license.

The Legal Code is the actual license. Licences must be specifically tailored to each separate jurisdiction to ensure that they comply with local copyright law. At the time of writing there are fifty-two jurisdictions using Creative Commons licenses, including England and Wales and Scotland with seven more in development. In each of these jurisdictions a Legal Project Lead has drafted local versions of the main (US) licence to ensure they comply both with local copyright law and the ethos of the Creative Commons movement. The metadata describes the key license elements that apply to a piece of content to enable discovery through creative content enabled search engines.[179] Once the license is attached others may then use the work within the confines of what is permitted by the licence without requiring to ask for the permission of the copyright holder. The idea is that content is made available to be shared and reused while allowing the copyright holder to set limits that she is comfortable with. Creative Commons has been remarkably successful.

As has already been stated Creative Commons licenses are available in fifty-two jurisdictions and to date over 100 million Flickr images are licensed under a Creative

---

[177] Some sites such as Flickr offer a license tool which assists the author in obtaining a CC License.

[178] For example the CC BY (Version 3.0) Code states: 'You are free: to Share—to copy, distribute and transmit the work; to Remix—to adapt the work. Under the following conditions: Attribution—You must attribute the work in the manner specified by the author or licensor (but not in any way that suggests that they endorse you or your use of the work). For any reuse or distribution, you must make clear to others the license terms of this work. The best way to do this is with a link to this web page. Any of the above conditions can be waived if you get permission from the copyright holder. Nothing in this license impairs or restricts the author's moral rights.'

[179] Both Google and Yahoo! allow for specialised creative commons searches. Either may be accessed via http://www.search.creativecommons.org/.

Commons licence[180] the substantial part of the estimated 150 million total Creative Commons licensed works of all types.[181] To date Creative Commons licenses have twice been the subject of court actions. In 2006 the District Court of Amsterdam upheld a challenge by former MTV VJ Adam Curry against a Dutch tabloid newspaper that had reprinted photographs from his Flickr stream which were licensed under an attribution-non-commercial-share alike licence. The Court held that 'in principle, Curry owns the copyright in the four photos, and the photos, by posting them on that website, are subject to the Creative Commons License. Therefore [the defendant] should observe the conditions that control the use by third parties of the photos as stated in the License'.[182] In the other action Lower Court number six of Badajoz rejected a claim by the main Spanish collecting society: Sociedad General de Autores y Editores (SGAE) against a local bar owner for back payment of performing licence fees when the bar owner managed to prove that all the music performed in the bar had been licensed for public performance under Creative Commons licenses.[183] The judge noted that 'The author possesses some moral and economic rights on his creation. And as the owner of these rights, he can manage them as he considers appropriate, being able to yield the free use, or hand it over partially. Creative Commons licenses are different classes of authorizations that the holder of his work gives for a more or less free or no cost use of it ... They allow third parties to be able to use music freely and without cost with greater or minor extension; and in some of these licenses, specific uses require the payment of royalties. The defendant proves that he makes use of music that is handled by their authors through these Creative Commons licenses'.[184]

Creative Commons therefore is a flourishing and successful, as well as legally recognised, alternative to the 'all rights reserved' copyright model contained in the Copyright, Designs and Patents Act. It is not expected to replace all rights reserved copyright, and the Creative Commons movement acknowledges that for some it will not be the appropriate model of protection: particularly for creators who wish to commercially exploit their works.[185] However for the vast majority of internet users who wish merely to allow their photographs, music, and videos to be seen, heard, or viewed, or who are happy for their work to be reused, remixed, and reworked Creative Commons provides a real alternative to the statutory copyright scheme. While the i2010 project may find it difficult to catalogue and store copyright work, a Creative Commons i2010 remains entirely possible.

---

[180] See http://www.creativecommons.org/weblog/entry/12540.

[181] See http://www.wiki.creativecommons.org/Metrics.

[182] Taken from M Garlick, *Creative Commons Licenses Upheld in Dutch Court*: http://www.creativecommons.org/press-releases/entry/5822. The full text of the decision (in Dutch) may be accessed at: http://www.rechtspraak.nl/ljn.asp?ljn=AV4204.

[183] The decision (in Spanish) may be accessed at: http://www.internautas.org/archivos/sentencia_metropoli.pdf.

[184] Taken from M Garlick, *Spanish Court Recognizes CC-Music*: http://www.creativecommons.org/weblog/entry/5830.

[185] However the three non-commercial licences can allow an author or creator to publicise and share their work while retaining the commercial interests in it.

10.4 **Conclusion**

This chapter has covered substantial ground. At the heart of the information society is a conflict between a culture of free use and access, of 'rip, mix, and burn' and of remixing and mashing and the culture of creative reward, publication, and commercial exploitation. This conflict is driven by the very nature of the information society in general and the internet in particular. The information society is built upon the sharing and exploitation of information, while copyright law is about the protection and control of information. One is about exploitation the other reward. The internet is, when one thinks about in simple terms, just a massive device for the copying and distribution of information: in a very real sense it is designed to massively infringe copyright. For the past fifteen years, and no doubt for at the very least the next fifteen, lawyers, judges, and lawmakers have been trying to establish where the legal balance in interests between these two extremes are to be struck. Some companies have become famously successful by trading in information, prime among these is Google. Some people see the activities of Google in not only cataloguing websites but also caching data, digitising books, and appropriating newspaper headlines as being in breach of copyright and its values,[186] while others see it as the greatest success story of the information society thus far.[187] This frames the predicament faced by judges, lawyers, and lawmakers: when is the exploitation of other people's data lawful and when, at copyright law is it unlawful? In essence what makes Google different from *The Pirate Bay*?[188]

These questions will no doubt continue to challenge lawyers and lawmakers as the information society is still in its formative phase. Eventually we may find YouTube regulated as a TV broadcaster, Google may have to licence all content for its Google News service, and we may even succeed in regulating peer-to-peer file sharing sites, but these things will not happen overnight.

FURTHER READING

Books

L. Lessig, *Free Culture* (2005)

C. Doctorow, *Content: Selected Essays on Technology, Creativity, Copyright and the Future of the Future* (2008)

N. Netanel, *Copyright's Paradox* (2007)

M. Boldrin, *Against Intellectual Monopoly* (2008)

---

[186] See, e.g. H. Porter, 'Google is just an amoral menace', *The Observer*, 5 April 2009: http://www.guardian.co.uk/commentisfree/2009/apr/05/google-internet-piracy.
[187] See, e.g. D. Vise & M. Malseed, *The Google Story: Inside the Hottest Business, Media and Technology Success of Our Time* (2008).
[188] This question was raised by Carl Lundström at the conclusion of *The Pirate Bay* trial.

Chapters and Articles

S. Klein, 'Search Engines and Copyright' 39(4) *IIC* 451 (2008)

V. Testa, 'Twenty Years of Walls—the Fall of the Local, Rise of the Global and the Triumph of the Immaterial Content Empire' [2009] *Entertainment Law Review* 274

R. Piasentin, 'Unlawful? Innovative? Unstoppable? A Comparative Analysis of the Potential Legal Liability facing P2P End-users in the US, United Kingdom and Canada' [2006] *International Journal of Law and Information Technology* 195

Databases

One clearly identifiable effect the information society has had on the law is the introduction of a new, *sui generis*, form of intellectual property protection in the form of the database right. Databases are structured collections of records or data stored in an indexed filing system usually, although not necessarily, held on a computer system. The structure is achieved by organising the data according to a database model which allows data to be accessed, cross-referenced, recompiled, and extracted according to data labels. Databases are diverse in design and scope. At the most basic level a telephone directory may be classified as a database: it is ordered using an alphabetical structuring and data may be retrieved by users accessing at the correct page. At the other end of the scale are massive digital databases such as the Lexis/Nexis database which catalogues and cross references case law, commentaries, newspaper reports, and statutory material from a number of jurisdictions. The Lexis/Nexis database also requires a much more sophisticated approach from the user as instead of merely following an alphabetical listing the user will use keywords and search phrases to find and extract the data they need. Technically the internet itself, or at very least the web, is a database with search engines such as Google, Yahoo!, and Bing providing the means to locate and extract data: few would think to classify the web as such though.

The database right is designed to protect the investment made in the gathering and indexing of data or files within a database model. It shares some similarities with copyright but is distinctively its own form of protection and has different boundaries to copyright protection. The database right was introduced throughout European Union member states following the promulgation of Directive 96/9/EC of the European Parliament and of the Council of 11 March 1996 on the legal protection of databases.[1] In the UK the Directive was implemented by the Copyright and Rights in Databases Regulations 1997,[2] which made some amendments to the Copyright Designs and Patents Act 1988 to more clearly define the boundaries between copyright and *sui generis* database protection, and separately introduced the database right into the UK effective from 1 January 1998.

---

[1] OJ L.077, 27/03/1996.   [2] SI 1997/3032.

11.1 **Copyright and the database right**

The roots of the *sui generis* database right are to be found in copyright law. As we have seen throughout Chapters 9 and 10 the relationship between informational products and copyright law is a fraught one. Although copyright protection has the required flexibility to allow it to be moulded to new types of creative output such as software or web pages it also often conflicts with the values or practices seen in the start-up industries which surround such new products. Thus many of the early software cases such as *Whelan v Jaslow*,[3] or *John Richardson Computers v Flanders*,[4] reflected the conflict between the expansive protection copyright offered and the practice of translating software between operating systems common at the time, while recent case-law involving Google suggest a current conflict may be brewing between the 'information wants to be free' ethos of the internet and the values protected by copyright.[5]

A similar conflict of values arose with regard to the protection of databases in the early 1990s. A database as a collection of (usually written) material seemed to naturally fall under copyright protection: a parallel could be drawn with anthologies of poetry or essays for which the publisher obtains copyright protection.[6] Databases became common, and valuable, from the early 1980s as the cost of personal computers fell and major organisations saw the benefits of moving from old-fashioned paper-based records to the modern computer records.[7] With database contents being of potentially great value, both internally as a business asset and on the open market as a commodity, businesses sought legal protection of their databases through the application of copyright law.

Within the UK this seemed perfectly possible for a database could be categorised as a compilation under s. 3(1)(a) of the Copyright, Designs and Patents Act, which meant that if it fulfilled the requirements of originality and connection to the UK it would be protected as a copyright work. In the UK these requirements are not particularly onerous. The connection requirement may simply be achieved as under s. 154(1)(c) of the Copyright, Designs and Patents Act: 'A work qualifies for copyright protection if the author was at the material time a qualifying person, that is a body incorporated under

---

[3] *Whelan Associates Inc. v Jaslow Dental Laboratory Inc.*, 797 F 2d 1222 (3d Cir. 1986). Discussed fully above, see p. 197ff.

[4] *John Richardson Computers Ltd v Flanders (No. 2)* [1993] FSR 497. Discussed fully above, see p. 202ff.

[5] *Google Inc. v Copiepresse SCRL* [2007] ECDR 5. Discussed fully above, see p. 228ff.

[6] Anthologies will usually be classified as 'compilations' under CDPA, s. 3(1)(a). The editor or publisher will be awarded copyright protection for the original elements of the compilation (the selection and ordering of the works for instance), although copyright in the works themselves will remain with their original authors.

[7] The benefits of digitisation of records are multipart. Three benefits identified by Fred Cate in his book *Privacy in the Information Age* (1997) are: (1) it is easier to generate, manipulate, transmit and store information; (2) the cost of collecting, manipulating, storing and transmitting data is lowered; and (3) electronic information, due to its very nature, has developed an intrinsic value not found in analogue information, i.e. because digital information is cheaply processed and stored, it attracts a premium in the marketplace. Andrew Murray in his contribution to M. Klang & A. Murray (eds), *Human Rights in the Digital Age* (2005) identifies a fourth benefit: convergent media platforms allow digital information to be reutilised across several platforms at little extra cost.

the law of a part of the United Kingdom.' Thus any UK incorporated corporation would have the protection of the Copyright, Designs and Patents Act extended to their databases in the event they were deemed to be original. This meant the application of the 'sweat of the brow' test discussed previously in chapter nine. This test is drawn from the case of *University of London Press Ltd v University Tutorial Press Ltd.*[8] in which Peterson J stated that 'the Act does not require that the expression must be in an original or novel form, but that the work must not be copied from another work–that it should originate from the author'.[9] This means any original database, that is one in which the creator of the database has expended skill, labour, and judgement in its creation rather than simply copying it from another source, would be protected by copyright law in the UK.

It is important to be clear what is actually protected by this copyright. It is the design and structure of the database itself, not the individual contents of the database which may be separately protected by their own copyright as literary, artistic, or musical works. Thus if an individual were to create a database of photographs of cityscapes (a so-called photo-library), they could obtain copyright protection of the database as a whole (its structure, its selection of contents, and its 'model') while the copyright in each image in that database would remain with the original photographer. This means that a competing, and almost identical database may be built by a competitor provided they put in the work of gathering and cataloguing the images.

11.1.1 **The listings cases**

The application of the Copyright, Designs and Patents Act to listings of information in the form of a simple database was confirmed by two cases involving the publisher of a directory of solicitors and barristers in the late 1980s. The first was the case of *Waterlow Publishers Ltd v Rose.*[10] The plaintiff under, contract to the Law Society of England and Wales, compiled and arranged for publication *The Solicitors' and Barristers' Directory and Diary* which contained a geographical listing of solicitors and barristers by region. To enable them to produce this publication the Law Society gave to the plaintiffs a list of all solicitors. The publishers then supplemented and verified this data by sending questionnaires to all firms asking for further data including areas of practice specialism. Prior to 1984 the defendant owned a printing company which printed copies of the directory; this work was then transferred to another firm. Following this the defendant resolved to publish his own competing directory entitled *The Lawyers' Diary*. To launch his diary the defendant began by using a copy of the *Solicitors' Diary* to obtain the information he needed which in his defence he said was necessary as 'it would have been impossible to do otherwise because the 1984 Solicitors' Diary was the only list of solicitors available'.[11] The defendant sent to solicitors copies of their entries in the current edition of the *Solicitors' Diary* and asked them to confirm whether the data was accurate and to make any necessary changes. The plaintiff argued that this action was in breach of their copyright in the *Solicitors' Diary*.

---

[8] [1916] 2 Ch. 601. Discussed fully above, see p. 187.   [9] *ibid*, 608–609.
[10] [1995] FSR 207. NB the case was actually decided on 27 October 1989 and was reported at the time in *The Independent* and *Times* newspapers. It was not formally reported in the Law Reports though for some time.   [11] *ibid*, 212.

The Court of Appeal had to decide three factors: (1) was the *Solicitors' Diary* protected as a copyright work, (2) was the plaintiff the author of that work, and (3) did the defendant's actions breach copyright in the work. Slade LJ made short work of the first question, finding that 'Section 48(1) of the Copyright Act 1956 (the 1956 Act) defines "literary work" as including "any written table or compilation". The "literary work" in which Waterlow claims copyright by its pleading is thus the "compliation" consisting of section 5 of the Solicitors' Diary 1984'.[12] Was the plaintiff the author of the work though? Here Slade LJ was less sure. He believed that the plaintiff was either the author or co-author of the work, 'I think it clear that if one accepts Laddie's definition of the author of a "compilation", Waterlow, if not the sole author, was at least a co-author of that compilation.'[13] In either event it did not matter as the plaintiff 'had a good cause of action for infringement of the copyright either as author or as co-author or by virtue of the presumption contained in section 20(4).'[14]

Slade LJ then turned his attention to the final question. Had the defendant infringed the plaintiff's copyright? Slade LJ noted that the defendant claimed that '[he was] designing his own directory on different lines and with a different layout from that of Waterlow's production, and [in] exercising his own independent skill and judgment in arranging the material, he would not be infringing'.[15] However this was rejected as 'these submissions afford no valid defence to the claim of infringement: Mr Rose's suggestion that the database which he was in the process of constructing for his own directory was based solely on the material supplied to him by the solicitors with whom he had communicated is unsustainable. In 20 per cent of the cases where he sent out forms to individuals or firms, the recipients ignored them. The judge rejected his evidence that in such cases he proposed simply to omit them from the directory, and Mr Rose has not sought to challenge this rejection before this court. Furthermore, it has been common ground before this court that in 60 per cent of the cases the forms would be returned unaltered so that the material contained in them would be unchanged.'[16] The Court therefore found in favour of the plaintiff and in so doing clearly established the principle that databases were protected as compilations under English Law, and that the correct standard of originality was therefore the literary standard of the 'sweat of the brow'.

A similar decision was reached in the following case of *Waterlow Directories Ltd v Reed Information Services Ltd.*[17] This High Court case arose from the same publication, the *Solicitors' Diary*. The defendants on this occasion published another competing directory, the *Butterworths Law Directory*. In 1990 in order to update its directory, the defendant compared the *Solicitors' Diary* with their directory and highlighted those names and addresses which appeared in the *Solicitors' Diary* but not *Butterworths Law Directory*. The highlighted names and addresses were copied onto a word processor which was then used to produce letters inviting those solicitors and barristers to appear in the new edition of *Butterworths Law Directory*. Out of 12,620 firms of solicitors in the *Solicitors' Diary* about 1,600 were highlighted in this way.

The plaintiff argued this infringed their copyright in the *Solicitors' Diary*. Aldous J agreed finding that 'it is accepted that copyright subsists in the plaintiff's directory

---

[12] *ibid*, 214.   [13] *ibid*, 217–218.   [14] *ibid*, 218.   [15] *ibid*, 222.   [16] *ibid*.
[17] [1992] FSR 409.

and that the plaintiff owns that copyright. Further, it is accepted that the defendant, using the plaintiff's directory, copied onto a word processor about 1,600 out of 12,600, names and addresses of solicitors and the names and addresses of organisations onto a computer. Thus it appears to me there has been reproduction and infringement if the amount reproduced constitutes a substantial part of the work. What is a substantial part of a work is a question of degree, depending on the circumstances, and it is settled law that the quality of that which is taken is usually more important than quantity. In the present case, it is a reasonable inference that the parts reproduced by the defendant were important in that they enabled the defendant to carry out a comprehensive mailing ... That benefit was perceived to be substantial and at this stage of the action I hold that there is a strong case that the part taken by the defendant was a substantial part'.[18]

On this basis Aldous J held that 'it was clear that a person could not copy entries from a directory and use such copies to compile his own directory. Even if it was correct that a person could use the information in a directory to compile another directory provided that reproduction did not take place, that was not the case before the court. The defendant had reproduced the names and addresses from the plaintiff's directory onto a word processor and a computer'.[19] The second *Waterlow* case confirmed that extraction of data for a different application (in this case to turn directory entries into a mailing list) was an infringement of copyright. By the time of this second judgement (October 1990) it was clear that the Copyright, Designs and Patents Act provided considerable, perhaps even comprehensive, protection to original databases.

11.1.2 The database directive

The UK standard was causing difficulties at a European level. As we saw in Chapter 9, the UK is unusual in applying a 'sweat of the brow' standard. Most states apply a more stringent standard which requires an intellectual contribution from the author. This distinction between the UK 'sweat of the brow' standard and the higher Continental 'droit d'auteur' was leading to a fragmentation of the European database industry: with greater protection being found in the UK than in Continental Europe.[20] This was in turn affecting the internal market, with companies who deal in databases and their contents being more likely to set operations in the UK than in Continental Europe.[21] To remedy this situation, and to harmonise legal protection of databases throughout the EU, the Commission issued a formal proposal for a Directive on the legal protection of databases.[22] Following some amendment the proposal was passed on 11 March 1996 as Directive 96/9/EC, usually known simply as 'the Database Directive'.

---

[18] *ibid*, 414.   [19] *ibid*, 410.

[20] This is acknowledged in the text of the Directive where at Recital 1 it states 'Whereas databases are at present not sufficiently protected in all Member States by existing legislation; whereas such protection, where it exists, has different attributes.' Dir. 96/9/EC of the European Parliament and of the Council of 11 March 1996 on the legal protection of databases, Recital 1.

[21] This is also acknowledged in the Directive: 'Whereas such differences in the legal protection of databases offered by the legislation of the Member States have direct negative effects on the functioning of the internal market as regards databases and in particular on the freedom of natural and legal persons to provide on-line database goods and services on the basis of harmonized legal arrangements throughout the Community', *ibid*, Recital 2.

[22] Proposal for a Council Directive on the Legal Protection of Databases, 35 OJ C 156/4 (1992).

The Directive creates a two-tier approach to database protection by firstly creating a pan-European copyright in some databases, and then supplementing this with the *sui generis* database right where copyright does not apply. Article 1 defines a database (for the purposes of the Directive) as 'a collection of independent works, data or other materials arranged in a systematic or methodical way and individually accessible by electronic or other means'.[23] Article 1 also clarifies that a program used to build, access, or update the contents of the database is to be distinct from the database itself, stating that '[p]rotection under this Directive shall not apply to computer programs used in the making or operation of databases accessible by electronic means'.[24] Thus if a software developer is asked to design a bespoke database management tool that is not part of the database: the database consists only of the data stored in the database. The software will though qualify separately for copyright protection, or perhaps even patent protection, as discussed in chapter nine.

The distinction between copyrightable databases and other databases is to be found in Art.3(1): 'databases which, by reason of the selection or arrangement of their contents, constitute the author's own intellectual creation shall be protected as such by copyright. No other criteria shall be applied to determine their eligibility for that protection.' The essential characteristic of copyright protected databases therefore is they must be 'the author's own intellectual creation'. This suggests a standard higher than the traditional UK standard of 'sweat of the brow', but unfortunately the Directive does not develop this further.

The UK Government has implemented Article 3(1) by way of the new s. 3A of the Copyright, Designs and Patents Act, introduced by reg. 6 of the Copyright and Rights in Databases Regulations 1997.[25] Section 3A(2) implements Article 3(1) almost word for word stating that: 'For the purposes of [copyright law] a literary work consisting of a database is original if, and only if, by reason of the selection or arrangement of the contents of the database the database constitutes the author's own intellectual creation'. What does this mean? The UK courts have had little interaction with s. 3A to date. In *Navitaire Inc. v easyJet Airline Co. & Anor*[26] Pumphrey J touched upon s. 3A in dealing with the extraction of data from an airline booking system. He seemed quite perplexed as to how to interpret s. 3A(2) within the spirit of the Directive finding that 'I cannot help but feel that section 3A is directed to the contents of the database. The one pointer against this conclusion is to be found in the European Parliament and Council Directive (96/9/EC) of 11 March 1996 on the Legal Protection of Databases ("the Database Directive") which section 3A is intended to implement. Recital 15 says "Whereas the criteria whether a database should be protected by copyright should be defined to the fact (sic: the French text is "devront se limiter au fait que", which is clearer) that the selection or the arrangement of the contents of the database is the author's own intellectual creation; whereas such protection should cover the structure of the database." In an electronic database, there is no compelling need to view the programs or scripts creating the database as part of the database, even though they define its "arrangement" and "structure". Anyway, they acquire copyright even if no database is ever generated from them, and my inclination would be to say that they do so by virtue of the fact that they are computer programs.'[27]

---

[23] Dir. 96/9/EC, Art. 1(2).   [24] *ibid*, Art. 1(3).   [25] SI 1997/3032.
[26] [2004] EWHC 1725 (Ch) (2004).   [27] *ibid*, [274].

In the later case of *Pennwell Publishing (UK) Ltd v Ornstien & Ors*[28] Deputy Judge Fenwick QC, disappointingly did not engage fully with s. 3A(2) when invited to do so, but did comment that: 'it is not necessary, in the light of my other findings, for me to reach a conclusion as to whether the database either in its form on the Outlook system or in the form of the JuniorContacts.xls spreadsheet was an original work within the meaning of the Copyright Designs and Patents Act 1988, but it is right to indicate that I was far from persuaded that the exercise of assembling a list of contacts addresses would be sufficient to qualify.'[29]

This leaves us with a rather confused picture. We know that copyright can arise in a sufficiently original database, but are unsure where that originality is to be found. Pumphrey J assists by perhaps clarifying that the originality must be in some form of authorial selection or organisation of the data rather than in some form of separate 'database design' which is dictated or expressed through software design. Deputy Judge Fenwick assists by expressing a view that what one may call a standard database structure such as the alphabetical ordering of contacts is also insufficient. These all suggest that to gain copyright protection for a database one must attain the higher, continental 'droit d'auteur' standard of originality. Such a result would be entirely consistent: the reason for the introduction of the Database Directive in the first place was to harmonise copyright protection standards for databases throughout Europe. That they should be harmonised at the 'droit d'auteur' standard is entirely logical given that the Directive also creates a new, arguably lesser *sui generis* database right which mirrors quite closely the UK 'sweat of the brow' standard. In fact this outcome is entirely the one sought by the UK Government in making the Copyright and Rights in Databases Regulations.[30] At the time the Regulations were introduced in Parliament the Minister of State, Ian McCartney, was clear on the Government's intent.

> Some people felt that no amendment of the Copyright Designs and Patents Act 1988 was needed to introduce the test, and that the current test of originality for literary works was enough. The Government do not share that view. The directive is clear. It requires copyright protection for databases 'which, by reason of selection or arrangement of their contents, constitute the author's own intellectual creation.' This is intended to exclude so-called sweat-of-the-brow databases—that is, ones that involve time, money or effort, but no intellectual creativity, such as the white pages telephone book that I mentioned earlier. Such sweat-of-the-brow databases would still be eligible for database right; the main purpose of the directive was to provide this form of protection. In practice, it is likely that many databases will continue to be protected by copyright, as well as by the new database right.[31]

Thus copyright will only be available for databases where the creator, or author, of the database has shown the higher continental standard of 'droit d'auteur' in the selection or arrangement of the contents of the database. This requires the author to demonstrate (in the terms of the French Law), an œuvre de l'esprit, (a work of the mind). This is an extremely high standard for a database whose contents are usually gathered rather than created to attain. If this is the standard the UK courts are to apply, then the author must respectfully disagree with Mr McCartney's view that 'many databases will continue to be protected by copyright'. The *sui generis* database right has become the overwhelming method of protection for databases.

---

[28] 2007 EWHC 1570 (QB).   [29] *ibid*, [107(f)].   [30] Above n. 25.
[31] Fourth Standing Committee on Delegated Legislation, 3 December 1997: http://www.publications.parliament.uk/pa/cm199798/cmstand/deleg4/st971203/71203s01.htm.

11.2 **The database right**

The *sui generis* database right was introduced in Chapter III (Arts 7–11) of the Database Directive. The right is awarded on creation of the database to the 'maker' of the database; in the Directive this is defined simply as the person who 'takes the initiative and the risk of investing'.[32] The UK Regulations give a far greater definition of a maker in reg. 14. The maker of a database is defined there as 'the person who takes the initiative in obtaining, verifying or presenting the contents of a database and assumes the risk of investing in that obtaining, verification or presentation'.[33] This is subject to several exceptions and limitations: (1) Where a database is made by an employee in the course of his employment, his employer shall be regarded as the maker of the database, subject to any agreement to the contrary;[34] (2) where a database is made by Her Majesty or by an officer or servant of the Crown in the course of his duties, Her Majesty shall be regarded as the maker of the database;[35] (3) Where a database is made by or under the direction or control of the House of Commons or the House of Lords the House by whom, or under whose direction or control, the database is made shall be regarded as the maker of the database, and if the database is made by or under the direction or control of both Houses, the two Houses shall be regarded as the joint makers of the database;[36] and finally (4) a database is made jointly if two or more persons acting together in collaboration take the initiative in obtaining, verifying, or presenting the contents of the database and assume the risk of investing in that obtaining, verification, or presentation.[37] The UK Regulations make clear that the maker of the database will be the first owner of the database right.[38]

Once the maker of the database has been identified, and for simplicity's sake we may assume that this is usually the person who pays for the database to be constructed, what rights does database right afford to the maker? The protection afforded by the *sui generis* right may be found in Articles 7(1) and 7(5) of the Directive.

> **→ Highlight** Database Directive: Article 7(1)
>
> Member States shall provide for a right for the maker of a database which shows that there has been qualitatively and/or quantitatively a substantial investment in either the obtaining, verification or presentation of the contents to prevent extraction and/or re-utilization of the whole or of a substantial part, evaluated qualitatively and/or quantitatively, of the contents of that database.

Some of these key terms are further defined: 'extraction' means 'the permanent or temporary transfer of all or a substantial part of the contents of a database to another medium by any means or in any form', while 're-utilization' means 'any form of making available to the public all or a substantial part of the contents of a database by the distribution of copies, by renting, by on-line or other forms of transmission. The first

---

[32] Dir. 96/9/EC, Recital 41.   [33] SI 1997/3032, reg. 14(1).   [34] *ibid*, reg. 14(2).
[35] *ibid*, reg. 14(3).   [36] *ibid*, reg. 14(4).   [37] *ibid*, reg. 14(5).   [38] *ibid*, reg. 15.

sale of a copy of a database within the Community by the rightholder or with his consent shall exhaust the right to control resale of that copy within the Community'.[39]
Article 7(5) supplements the protection found in Article 7(1).

> **→ Highlight** Database Directive: Article 7(5)
>
> The repeated and systematic extraction and/or re-utilization of insubstantial parts of the
> contents of the database implying acts which conflict with a normal exploitation of that
> database or which unreasonably prejudice the legitimate interests of the maker of the database
> shall not be permitted.

Collectively the effect of Articles 7(1) and 7(5) are to ring fence the contents of a
database: their aim is to prevent competitors from either substantially recreating a
protected database by the extraction of a substantial part of the original, or a series of
insubstantial extractions, or from making use of a substantial part of database without
the permission of the database maker or owner.

The UK has implemented these provisions by reg. 16. The implementation of Article
7(1) is found in reg. 16(1) which states: 'Subject to the provisions of this Part, a person
infringes database right in a database if, without the consent of the owner of the right,
he extracts or re-utilises all or a substantial part of the contents of the database.' Regulation 16(2) implements Article 7(5): 'for the purposes of this Part, the repeated and
systematic extraction or re-utilisation of insubstantial parts of the contents of a database
may amount to the extraction or re-utilisation of a substantial part of those contents.'
The final part of the implementation jigsaw is found in reg. 12(1) were 'substantial' is
defined as 'substantial in terms of quantity or quality or a combination of both.'

The *sui generis* right is therefore rather different to a copyright. It has a different standard of originality, and protects in quite a different way. It is not copying *per se* which is
restricted but rather *substantial* or *repeated* extraction or reutilisation of the database contents. Also there are many restrictions contained within the Directive and given effect in
the Regulations which limit the scope of the *sui generis* right. Article 8(1) provides that:
'[t]he maker of a database which is made available to the public in whatever manner may
not prevent a lawful user of the database from extracting and/or re-utilizing insubstantial parts of its contents, evaluated qualitatively and/or quantitatively, for any purposes
whatsoever'[40] while Article 9 provides three 'fair dealing' exceptions.

Member States may stipulate that lawful users of a database which is made available to the
public in whatever manner may, without the authorization of its maker, extract or re-utilize a
substantial part of its contents:

(a) in the case of extraction for private purposes of the contents of a non-electronic database;

(b) in the case of extraction for the purposes of illustration for teaching or scientific
research, as long as the source is indicated and to the extent justified by the
non-commercial purpose to be achieved;

---

[39] Dir. 96/9/EC, Art. 7(2).   [40] Given effect by Reg 19(1).

(c) in the case of extraction and/or re-utilization for the purposes of public security or an administrative or judicial procedure.[41]

The term of protection is also less than with Copyright Law. By Article 10(1) the right 'shall expire fifteen years from the first of January of the year following the date of completion', unless the database is subsequently made available to the public during this period in which case 'the term of protection by that right shall expire fifteen years from the first of January of the year following the date when the database was first made available to the public.'[42] There is though one substantial qualification to these terms. By Article 10(3) 'Any substantial change, evaluated qualitatively or quantitatively, to the contents of a database, including any substantial change resulting from the accumulation of successive additions, deletions or alterations, which would result in the database being considered to be a substantial new investment, evaluated qualitatively or quantitatively, shall qualify the database resulting from that investment for its own term of protection.' Neither the directive, nor the UK Regulations, has a full and satisfactory definition of when a change is 'substantial'. One assumes though this is to be the same definition found as applied in reg. 7(1) for which there is some degree of case-law discussed below. In any event given that a database has to be continually updated to remain useful it seems likely that most databases will undergo 'substantial' amendment in the fifteen years that protection runs. For example if you were to update as little as 0.01% of the database on a daily basis you would cumulatively update over 54% of the database over a fifteen year period. Thus it seems that for any managed database perpetual protection will be available.

11.2.1 The fixtures marketing cases

With a completely new form of IP protection it is not surprising that the courts have been busy trying to set the limits of what is permissible and what is not. A series of questions arose in several national courts, almost all of which were eventually referred to the European Court of Justice for interpretation. These questions included: (1) What amounts to a substantial investment for qualification of the right? (2) Does the right accrue where the database is a 'spin-off' from investment in another field—e.g. where broadcasters schedule television programmes the 'spin-off' is a database of scheduled television programmes? (3) What amounts to repeated and systematic extraction? And (4) Does the right cover instances where information is generated/created and cannot be obtained from alternative sources? Many of these questions arose initially in a series of cases arising from the rights to football fixtures lists. These cases, known collectively as the 'Fixtures Marketing' cases included *Fixtures Marketing Ltd v Organismos Prognostikon Agonon Podosfairou (OPAP)*,[43] *Fixtures Marketing Ltd v Oy Veikkaus AB*,[44] and *Fixtures Marketing Ltd v Svenska Spel AB*.[45]

All three involved material extracted from a database of football fixtures created by combining the individual fixtures lists of the English Premier League, the English Football

---

[41] Given effect variously by SI 1997/3032, Sch. 1 and reg. 20(1).
[42] Dir.96/9/EC, Art. 10(2).
[43] [2005] 1 CMLR 16. Case originated in The Athens Court of First Instance, Greece.
[44] [2005] ECDR 2. Case originated in The Vantaa District Court, Finland.
[45] [2005] ECDR 4. Case originated in The District Court, Gotland, Sweden.

League, the Scottish Premier League, and the Scottish Football League. This database was then managed by Fixtures Marketing on behalf of the leagues with a view to commercially exploiting the contents of the database. All three of the respondents had in various ways made use of details from the relevant fixtures lists without the permission of the claimant. OPAP were using fixtures drawn from the database on fixed odds betting coupons and an online betting site in Greece, Oy Veikkaus were using fixtures from the database for their football pools coupon in Finland and Svenska Spel were doing likewise in Sweden. All three cases were heard together before the European Court of Justice.

The questions referred varied from case to case but the key questions were asked in the OPAP reference which simply asked: '(1) What is the definition of database and what is the scope of Directive 96/9 and in particular Art.7 thereof which concerns the sui generis right? (2) In the light of the definition of the scope of the directive, do lists of football fixtures enjoy protection as databases over which there is a sui generis right in favour of the maker and under what conditions? and (3) How exactly is the database right infringed and is it protected in the event of rearrangement of the contents of the database?' Although wide in scope these are key questions. The judge of the Athens Court of First Instance is inviting the ECJ to clarify the scope of the directive and to determine what may amount to 'a substantial investment' under reg.7(1), whether or not a 'spin-off' database may qualify for protection at all and finally what amounts to 'extraction and/or re-utilization a substantial part'.

The court gave full consideration to all these issues with a very full opinion given by Advocate-General Stix-Hackl. As to the initial question, that of what qualifies as a 'database' under Article 1(2), the court first noted that 'nothing in the directive points to the conclusion that a database must be its maker's own intellectual creation to be classified as such ... the criterion of originality is only relevant to the assessment whether a database qualifies for the copyright protection'.[46] This confirmed the widely held view that the 'droit d'auteur' standard of an œuvre de l'esprit (in English usually referred to as a 'spark of originality') was not applicable to the *sui generis* database right. From here the court went on to answer the question finding that 'classification of a collection as a database requires that the independent materials making up that collection be systematically or methodically arranged and individually accessible in one way or another.'[47]

→ Highlight Definition of a Database (from *Fixtures Marketing*)

Any collection of works, data or other materials, separable from one another without the value of their contents being affected, including a method or system of some sort for the retrieval of each of its constituent materials.

This makes clear that that the definition of a database is to be interpreted broadly, certainly broad enough to cover everyday directories such as telephone directories or legal directories such as were seen in the *Waterlow* cases. This led on to the second element of the first question: what may amount to 'a substantial investment' under reg. 7(1)?

---

[46] [2005] 1 CMLR 16, [26].   [47] *ibid*, [30].

> **Highlight** Definition of a Substantial Investment (from *Fixtures Marketing*)
>
> The expression 'investment in ... the ... verification ... of the contents' of a database must be understood to refer to the resources used, with a view to ensuring the reliability of the information contained in that database, to monitor the accuracy of the materials collected when the database was created and during its operation. The expression 'investment in ... the ... presentation of the contents' of the database concerns, for its part, the resources used for the purpose of giving the database its function of processing information, that is to say those used for the systematic or methodical arrangement of the materials contained in that database and the organisation of their individual accessibility. Investment in the creation of a database may consist in the deployment of human, financial or technical resources but it must be substantial in quantitative or qualitative terms. The quantitative assessment refers to quantifiable resources and the qualitative assessment to efforts which cannot be quantified, such as intellectual effort or energy.

Thus to qualify for protection under Article 7(1) the maker of the database must have invested substantially, either in financial terms, or in terms of effort, skill, and manpower, and that investment *must* be made to ensure the database is accurate and/or functional. The investment cannot be for any other purpose such as commercialising or marketing the database or for some other reason unrelated to the creation of the database itself.

The court then answered the second question. It noted that given the wide interpretation of Article 1(2) that it had indicated that 'the date and the time of and the identity of the two teams playing in both home and away matches are covered by the concept of independent materials within the meaning of Art. 1(2) of the directive in that they have autonomous informative value ... [as such] it follows that a fixture list for a football league such as that at issue in the case in the main proceedings constitutes a database within the meaning of Art.1(2) of the directive.'[48] It also answered the question of whether a 'spin-off' database could ever be protected.

> **Highlight** Protecting 'Spin-off' Databases (from *Fixtures Marketing*)
>
> The fact that the creation of a database is linked to the exercise of a principal activity in which the person creating the database is also the creator of the materials contained in the database does not, as such, preclude that person from claiming the protection of the sui generis right, provided that he establishes that the obtaining of those materials, their verification or their presentation, in the sense described at above, required substantial investment in quantitative or qualitative terms, which was independent of the resources used to create those materials.

---

[48] *ibid*, [33], [36].

This ultimately proved to be Fixtures Marketing's downfall. The makers of the database were the professional football leagues of England and Scotland. The database was created as part of their primary function: the setting of league fixtures for the football season. Further as they were the originators of the contents of the database they did not need to verify the accuracy of the database. As the Court recorded:

> Finding and collecting the data which make up a football fixture list do not require any particular effort on the part of the professional leagues. Those activities are indivisibly linked to the creation of those data, in which the leagues participate directly as those responsible for the organisation of football league fixtures. Obtaining the contents of a football fixture list thus does not require any investment independent of that required for the creation of the data contained in that list. The professional football leagues do not need to put any particular effort into monitoring the accuracy of the data on league matches when the list is made up because those leagues are directly involved in the creation of those data. The verification of the accuracy of the contents of fixture lists during the season simply involves, according to the observations made by Fixtures, adapting certain data in those lists to take account of any postponement of a match or fixture date decided on by or in collaboration with the leagues. Such verification cannot be regarded as requiring substantial investment. The presentation of a football fixture list is closely linked to the creation as such of the data which make up the list. It cannot therefore be considered to require investment independent of the investment in the creation of its constituent data.

Ultimately therefore the database of football fixtures created by the football leagues and distributed under license to Fixtures Marketing did not qualify for Article 7 protection because the makers of the database had not 'substantially invested qualitatively and/or quantitatively in either the obtaining, verification or presentation of the contents.' With this decision made the Court, unfortunately declined to answer the third question.[49]

11.2.2 **British Horseracing Board Ltd v William Hill**

The Fixtures Marketing cases are an extremely important series of cases which usually would have been met with a fanfare at their outcome. The Court had examined the scope of the Database Directive and had given guidance on the application of Article 7(1), but they were little commented upon by the profession, academics, or the media for the same day the European Court of Justice had given its opinion an almost identical case, which had been bundled together with the *Fixtures Marketing* cases and which answered the third question that the Court had declined to answer in the *OPAP* case: this was the case of *British Horseracing Board Ltd v William Hill Organization Ltd*.[50]

The facts of this case are extremely similar to the *Fixtures Marketing* cases, and it is for this reason that *William Hill* was disposed with jointly with the *Fixtures Marketing* cases. William Hill operate a chain of high-street betting shops which among other things allow for betting on horse racing, an operation known as 'off-course bookmaking'. For many years William Hill had been operating their high street bookmaking shops using information supplied from Weatherbys a private company who compiled the Jockey Club database which contained advance information about race meetings, runners, and riders. In 1999 the Jockey Club database was merged with the British Horseracing Board (BHB)

---

[49] *ibid*, [54].   [50] [2005] 1 CMLR 15; [2005] RPC 13.

database, although Weatherbys continued to supply data to William Hill's high street operation under a licence. The issue though was William Hill's website. They had no licence or permission to use data from the BHB database for online gambling. William Hill began to operate an internet gambling site in May 1999. It offered a variety of daily bets using information that had originated in the BHB database. William Hill argued they did not need a separate licence for this operation as the information they used was not subject to database protection, in particular William Hill argued that the information had been made publicly available via newspapers, teletext, and the specialist betting information service Satellite Information Services Limited ('SIS') which provides a raw data feed of all races taking place that day to all its subscribers, which includes William Hill. BHB argued that the database was a major part of their operation. It was estimated to contain some 800,000 entries and cost some £4m per annum to maintain, over 25% of BHB's entire annual expenditure.[51] BHB argued that by extracting the daily data for races to be run that day William Hill extracted and re-utilised a 'substantial part' of the database. Their argument was based on the principle that Article 7(1) states 'substantial' is to be evaluated 'qualitatively and/or quantitatively'. Although the data extracted each day may be so small in proportion to the overall size of the database so as to be quantitatively insubstantial, it was, argued BHB, qualitatively substantial as the data extracted each day was the only data of commercial value for that day: by extracting that data William Hill effectively were avoiding payment to use the only commercially valuable part of the database for that day. In the alternative BHB argued that by making daily extractions from the BHB database William Hill were actively involved in systematic extraction and/or re-utilisation of insubstantial parts of the contents of the database in breach of Article 7(5).

BHB launched their case in summer 2000 and the initial hearings were before Laddie J on 12–14 December 2000. Laddie J's judgement was issued on 9 February 2001.[52] In this he found that 'Article 7(1) provides that substantiality is to be assessed by looking at the quantity and quality of what is taken but it does not require them to be looked at separately. It contemplates looking at the combination of both … Here what the defendant is doing is making use of the most recent and core information in the BHB Database relating to racing. William Hill is relying on and taking advantage of the completeness and accuracy of the information taken from the [Raw Data Feed], in other words the product of BHB's investment in obtaining and verifying that data. *This is a substantial part of the contents.*'[53] With regard to the subsequent claim under Article 7(5), Laddie J found that 'William Hill's borrowing from [the database] from day to day comes within Article 7(5) as repeated and systematic extractions and re-utilizations of parts of its contents.'[54]

Unsurprisingly William Hill appealed this decision. The appeal was heard by the Court of Appeal (Peter Gibson, Clarke & Kay LJJ) who stayed proceedings on 31 July 2001 to refer the case to the ECJ.[55] The Court of Appeal referred eleven questions to the ECJ, some similar to those raised elsewhere in the *Fixtures Marketing* cases but many were important and were either unique to this reference or had not been answered

[51] [2005] 1 CMLR 15, [32].
[52] *British Horseracing Board Ltd & Ors v William Hill Organization Ltd* [2001] EWHC 517 (Patents).
[53] *ibid*, [53].   [54] *ibid*, [73].
[55] *British Horseracing Board Ltd & Ors v William Hill Organization Ltd* [2001] EWCA Civ 1268.

elsewhere.[56] In a groundbreaking judgement the Court substantially disregarded the opinion of Advocate-General Stix-Hackl, the same Advocate-General who had advised them on the *Fixtures Marketing* cases. The Court went through the reference in great detail answering all the questions closely. It began by answering the prior questions:

> (2) What is meant by 'obtaining in Article 7(1) of the Directive? In particular, are the facts and matters in [issue in the case] capable of amounting to such obtaining? and (3) Is 'verification' in Article 7(1) of the Directive limited to ensuring from time to time that information contained in a database is or remains correct?

The Court applied the reasoning seen in the *Fixtures Marketing* cases in answering these questions. It ruled that 'investment in the selection, for the purpose of organising horse racing, of the horses admitted to run in the race concerned relates to the creation of the data which make up the lists for those races which appear in the BHB database. It does not constitute investment in obtaining the contents of the database. It cannot, therefore, be taken into account in assessing whether the investment in the creation of the database was substantial.'[57]

This is an application of the 'spin-off' principle discussed above. While BHB were creating data for another purpose the database was merely a spin off from that purpose. Therefore the investment made in creating the data could not count towards a 'substantial investment' in the database: that would require to come from further investment in gathering or generating external data (i.e. data not required for the purpose of running BHB operations) or verifying the data.

This led to question 3, how high is the verification standard? The Court unfortunately did not answer this directly, but they did indicate what did not qualify as verification: 'the process of entering a horse on a list for a race requires a number of prior checks as to the identity of the person making the entry, the characteristics of the horse and the classification of the horse, its owner and the jockey ... However, such prior checks are made at the stage of creating the list for the race in question. They thus constitute investment in the creation of data and not in the verification of the contents of the database.'[58] At this point the Court could have concluded its analysis by finding in a similar fashion to the *Fixtures Marketing* cases that the BHB database was merely a 'spin-off database' and as such did not qualify for protection because the makers of the database had not 'substantially invested qualitatively and/or quantitatively in either the obtaining, verification or presentation of the contents'. Fortunately though the Court, perhaps influenced by the number of references which had been made under the Directive went on to analyse the remaining questions.

The Court next addressed the seventh, eighth, and ninth questions together. These were:

> (7) Is 'extraction' in Article 7 of the directive limited to the transfer of the contents of the database directly from the database to another medium, or does it also include the transfer of works, data or other materials, which are derived indirectly from the database, without having direct access to the database? (8) Is 're-utilisation' in Article 7 of the directive limited to the

---

[56] The eleven questions may be found at [2005] 1 CMLR 15, [AG27].   [57] *ibid*, [38].
[58] *ibid*, [39], [40].

making available to the public of the contents of the database directly from the database, or does it also include the making available to the public of works, data or other materials which are derived indirectly from the database, without having direct access to the database? and (9) Is 're-utilisation' in Article 7 of the directive limited to the first making available to the public of the contents of the database?

These questions all came about because of William Hill's practice of drawing the information it needed for its online betting sites not from the BHB database directly, but from third party sources such as the SIS Raw Data Feed and newspaper listings such as *The Racing Post*. The Court began with a general observation that '[t]he use of expressions such as "by any means or in any form" and "any form of making available to the public" indicates that the Community legislature intended to give the concepts of extraction and re-utilisation a wide definition ... those terms must therefore be interpreted as referring to any act of appropriating and making available to the public, without the consent of the maker of the database, the results of his investment, thus depriving him of revenue which should have enabled him to redeem the cost of the investment.'[59]

Following this the Court went on to find that '[s]ince acts of unauthorised extraction and/or re-utilisation by a third party from a source other than the database concerned are liable, just as much as such acts carried out directly from that database are, to prejudice the investment of the maker of the database, it must be held that the concepts of extraction and re-utilisation do not imply direct access to the database concerned.'[60] The Court therefore found that 'The terms "extraction" and "re-utilisation" in Art.7 of the Directive must be interpreted as referring to any unauthorised act of appropriation and distribution to the public of the whole or a part of the contents of a database. Those terms do not imply direct access to the database concerned. The fact that the contents of a database were made accessible to the public by its maker or with his consent does not affect the right of the maker to prevent acts of extraction and/or re-utilisation of the whole or a substantial part of the contents of a database.'[61]

Finally the Court turned to the key questions:

(1) May either of the expressions: 'substantial part of the contents of the database'; or 'insubstantial parts of the contents of the database' in Article 7 of the Directive include works, data or other materials derived from the database but which do not have the same systematic or methodical arrangement of and individual accessibility as those to be found in the database? (4) What is meant in Article 7(1) of the directive, by the expressions: 'a substantial part, evaluated qualitatively ... of the contents of that database'? and 'a substantial part, evaluated quantitatively ... of the contents of that database'? (5) What is meant in Article 7(5) of the directive, by the expression 'insubstantial parts of the database'? (6) In particular, in each case: does 'substantial' mean something more than 'insignificant' and, if so, what? does 'insubstantial' part simply mean that it is not 'substantial'? and (10) In Article 7(5) of the directive what is meant by 'acts which conflict with a normal exploitation of that database or unreasonably prejudice the legitimate interests of the maker of the database'? In particular, are the facts [of this case] capable of amounting to such acts?

---

[59] *ibid*, [51].   [60] *ibid*, [53].   [61] *ibid*, [67].

While the preliminary issues were valuable, in particular the answer to questions seven, eight, and nine, what the Court was about to do in answering these five questions was interpret the key provisions of Articles 7(1) and 7(5), in particular what amounted to a 'substantial part' for Article 7(1) and when would repeated extractions under Article 7(5) infringe the maker's database right?

The Court first turned to Article 7(1) and sought first to clarify what constituted a 'substantial part' of a database.

> **→ Highlight** A 'Substantial Part' (from *BHB*)
>
> The expression 'substantial part, evaluated quantitatively', of the contents of a database within the meaning of Art.7(1) of the Directive refers to the volume of data extracted from the database and/or re-utilised, and must be assessed in relation to the volume of the contents of the whole of that database. If a user extracts and/or re-utilises a quantitatively significant part of the contents of a database whose creation required the deployment of substantial resources, the investment in the extracted or re-utilised part is, proportionately, equally substantial.
>
> The expression 'substantial part, evaluated qualitatively', of the contents of a database refers to the scale of the investment in the obtaining, verification or presentation of the contents of the subject of the act of extraction and/or re-utilisation, regardless of whether that subject represents a quantitatively substantial part of the general contents of the protected database. A quantitatively negligible part of the contents of a database may in fact represent, in terms of obtaining, verification or presentation, significant human, technical or financial investment.
>
> [at 70–71]

This was a surprising outcome. While the definition of a 'substantial part, evaluated quantitatively' was in line with predictions the definition of a 'substantial part, evaluated qualitatively' was not what had been expected. It had always been imagined that a 'substantial part, evaluated qualitatively' would refer to the commercial value of that part of the database as against the database as a whole. So for example in the current case the data for that day's race meetings would qualify as a substantial part of the database as a whole evaluated qualitatively. What the ECJ said though was it was not the value of the data at extraction which was to be measured it was the value of the data at its addition to the database. Thus data which was difficult or costly to obtain or verify would be 'qualitatively substantial' whether or not this was subsequently of any greater value commercially than the rest of the database. As BHB had expended no greater effort or money in obtaining the data for the current day's races than for any other data in the database the Court held that 'those materials do not represent a substantial part, in [quantitative or] qualitative terms, of the BHB database.'[62]

---

[62] *ibid*, [74], [80].

Finally the question of whether William Hill had infringed Article 7(5) was addressed.

> → **Highlight** Purpose of Article 7(5) (from *BHB*)
>
> The purpose of Art.7(5) is to prevent circumvention of the prohibition in Art.7(1) of the Directive. Its objective is to prevent repeated and systematic extractions and/or re-utilisations of insubstantial parts of the contents of a database, the cumulative effect of which would be to seriously prejudice the investment made by the maker of the database just as the extractions and/or re-utilisations referred to in Art.7(1) of the Directive would.
>
> [at 86]

In other words the purpose of Article 7(5) is not to prevent users repeatedly accessing a database to extract or reutilise insubstantial parts of the database, as William Hill was doing; it was to prevent the cumulative construction of a competing database, or the accumulation of data from a database over a period of time which would lead to a cumulative 'substantial part'. Again this was somewhat surprising and had not been widely predicted. It made the application of Article 7(5) extremely narrow, so narrow as perhaps to be of little practical application.

The end result of the immediate case was that BHB lost. On nearly every point the ECJ ruled against them. Their database was not sufficiently original to qualify for database protection as there had been no independent significant investment in the obtaining or verification of the data. Even if the database were protected the actions of William Hill were not infringing: they neither extracted or reutilised a substantial part of the database nor did they make repeated extractions or reutilisations which 'conflict with a normal exploitation of that database or which unreasonably prejudice the legitimate interests of the maker of the database' under Article 7(5). The case was remanded back to the Court of Appeal for disposal and on 13 July 2005 the Court of Appeal gave judgement in favour of William Hill but not without reservation.[63] Lord Justice Clark observed that 'I am conscious that in doing so I have agreed to allowing an appeal against a decision which I was inclined to think was correct when the case was last before the Court of Appeal in July 2001. The reason for my change of view is of course the decision and reasoning of the ECJ.'[64]

11.2.3 **After *BHB***

The immediate fall out of the decisions of the European Court of Justice of 9 November 2004, and in particular the *BHB* decision, was a concern that by interpreting Articles 7(1) and 7(5) so narrowly the court had effectively undermined the protection offered by the *sui generis* database right. In the immediate aftermath of the decision news reports and professional journals reported that the effect of the decision was to effectively

---

[63] *British Horseracing Board Ltd & Ors v William Hill Organization Ltd* [2005] EWCA Civ 863.
[64] *ibid*, [37].

narrow the protection afforded to makers of databases.[65] This in time led to a number of academic articles which suggested similarly.[66] The common view of many of these comments is that the court had been forced to narrow the scope of the Directive for there was a danger that 'this new property right would arise virtually everywhere there was a website'.[67] In time though a clearer view of the decisions of 9 November developed, at least in part formed by the Commission Evaluation of the Database Directive which was carried out immediately after these decisions.[68]

The Report set out to evaluate three particular criticisms of the *sui generis* database right: (1) its scope is unclear and it is poorly targeted; (2) the database right 'locks up' data to the detriment of research and the academic community; and (3) the database right is too narrow in scope and fails to protect investors.[69] In evaluating these claims the Commission examined (1) the impact of the 9 November 2004 judgements; (2) whether there was an indication that the academic community and the research community at large were paying unnecessary costs to access data; and (3) the measure of the size of the EU database community.[70]

The outcome was rather surprising, in particular for critics of the *Fixtures Marketing/BHB* decisions. In response to the question 'Has the ECJ's interpretation of the scope of the "sui generis" right devalued the uniform levels of protection achieved for "non-original" databases?', the findings of an online survey found that '43% of the respondents believe that the legal protection of their databases will be the same as before the ECJ rulings (or even reinforced); only 36% believe that the scope of protection will be either weakened or removed.'[71] Although this is not a statistically significant result it was not what may have been expected in the immediate aftermath of the November 9 decisions. Further it appeared that a majority of respondents actually welcomed the effect of the decisions: 'most respondents to the Commission services' on-line survey believe that the protection of databases is stronger than before adoption of the Directive. However, a majority of respondents feel that, after the ECJ's rulings, fewer databases will be protected by the "sui generis" right. This allays fears of monopoly abuses which were usually expressed with respect to "single-source" databases (databases where the database maker and the proprietor of the underlying information are the same person or entity).'[72] This suggests that many even within the industry were unhappy with the idea of a broad database right which would have protected spin-off, or in the Commission's terms 'single-source' databases. There was an obvious concern about market abuse with such databases, a concern allayed by the decisions of 9 November 2004.

---

[65] See e.g. T. Frederikse, 'Database Protection Narrowed: British Horseracing Board v William Hill', *Swan Turton e-bulletin*, 10 November 2004: http://www.swanturton.co.uk/ebulletins/archive/TAFDatabaseProtection.aspx; R. Kemp, D. Meredith and C. Gibbons, 'Database Right and the ECJ Judgement in BHB v William Hill: Dark Horse or Non-Starter?', *Kemp Little Bulletin*: http://www.kemplittle.com/PDFs/ECJ-JudgeWilliam%20Hill-05.pdf?SESSIONFRONT=2d26af134666b6b7ed6cc523849f37c3; William Hill wins horseracing database appeal, *Out-Law*, 19 July 2005: http://www.out-law.com/page-5922.

[66] See, e.g. R. Kemp and C. Gibbons, 'Database Right After BHB v. William Hill: Enact and Repent at Leisure', [2006] 22 *Computer Law and Security Report* 493; S. Kon & T. Heide, 'BHB/William Hill—Europe's Feist' [2006] 28(1) *EIPR* 60; T. Aplin, 'The ECJ elucidates the database right', (2005) 2 *IPQ* 204.

[67] Taken from Kemp, Meredith & Gibbons, above n.65, [48].

[68] Commission of the European Communities: *First evaluation of Directive 96/9/EC on the legal protection of databases*, 12 December 2005: http://ec.europa.eu/internal_market/copyright/docs/databases/evaluation_report_en.pdf.

[69] *ibid*, [1.2]. [70] *ibid* [4.1.4]. [71] *ibid*, [1.2]. [72] *ibid*.

In response to the other questions the Commission found the database right to be functioning well. They found that the research and academic communities were still able to access data and that the 9 November decisions had assisted in this[73] and that the database industry in Europe was healthy both before and after the 9 November decisions.[74] Thus the Commission Evaluation suggested that the decisions of the ECJ had actually proved positive for both our understanding, and the health of the database right. By narrowing the scope of the right the ECJ had actually restored confidence in the right, and had prevented overprotection of spin-off, or single source databases which may have harmed the competitiveness of European data industries as end-users would have had to pay for access to single source data which would have led to potential market abuse from companies in a dominant position. Following the publication of the Evaluation the views of commentators softened with the November 9 decisions now seen as broadly positive and reinforcing of the *sui generis* right, with most noting that the narrow interpretation promulgated has assisted all sides in the database industry, with the obvious exception of single source database makers.[75]

11.3 **Databases and the information society**

Before leaving databases we must look at one final issue unique to online databases. With more databases publicly accessible via a web portal there is an increased risk of unauthorised linking to the contents of these databases. This raises issues similar to those discussed in the *Linking, Caching, and Aggregating* section of Chapter 10.[76] Many of the cases discussed in that section including *Stepstone v Ofir,*[77] *Havas Numerique et Cadre On Line v Keljob,*[78] and *Google Inc. v Copiepresse SCRL*[79] involved claims not only of copyright infringement but also claims of unauthorised extraction and/or reutilisation in breach of the database directive. Most of these cases though, with the obvious exception of *Google v Copiepresse,* were decided prior to the decisions of the ECJ on 9 November 2004. The issue of online linking to database contents without the permission of the database maker has thought recently been thoroughly reviewed by the Arnhem District Court of The Netherlands in the case of *NVM Estate Agents v ZAH.*[80] This case is similar to the *Home A/S v Ofir*[81] case discussed in Chapter 10 in that both involve accessing online real estate databases.

---

[73] *ibid* [4.3].   [74] *ibid* [4.2].
[75] See, e.g. M. Prinsley, 'An Opportunity to Improve Protection for Databases in Europe?' (2006) 6(3) *World Data Protection Report* 3; C. Waelde, 'Databases and Lawful Users: the Chink in the Armour', (2006) 3 *IPQ* 256; A. Masson, 'Creation of Database or Creation of Data: Crucial Choices in the Matter of Database Protection' [2006] 28(5) *EIPR* 261.   [76] See pp. 223–233.
[77] Landgericht, Köln, February 28, 2001: 28 O 692/00. Discussed in full above at p. 226.
[78] Tribunal de Commerce de Paris, 26 December 2000. Discussed in full above at p. 226.
[79] [2007] ECDR 5. Discussed in full above at pp. 228–232.
[80] 136002/ KG ZA 06-25, LJN AV5236, 16 March 2006.
[81] Unreported, 24 February 2006, Danish Maritime and Commercial Court. Discussed in full above at p. 228.

In The Netherlands all estate agents who are members of the Dutch Association of Estate Agents (NVM) provide information on their websites detailing houses sold through them. This information is then aggregated on a single website operated by NVM allowing for a single search portal for all NVM member sites. ZAH operates a search engine that daily browses through almost all estate agent websites collecting data on houses that are put up for sale, and then offering access to this aggregated data via its own websites. The information that ZAH places on its website is obtained by means of deep linking to the estate agent website which is currently advertising the property. ZAH did all of this without permission. NVM sought an injunction, accompanied by periodic penalty payments, for ZAH to refrain from deep linking on the grounds that ZAH's actions infringed both their database rights and copyrights. First the court addressed the question whether a catalogue of houses for sale on a website constituted a database. The court found that NVM had failed to make a reasonable case that they had made a qualitative or quantitative substantial investment. In effect the NVM 'database' was a 'spin-off' database. The operation of the member estate agents was to sell properties, to make this possible they had to advertise the properties on their website, they had not therefore 'made a substantial investment in either the obtaining, verification or presentation of the contents' of the database. Further as NVM had merely aggregated the data without verifying or otherwise investing in the data the aggregated database was similarly not protected. The court concluded that the collections of data did not amount to a legal database under Section 2 of the Dutch Database Act.[82] The decision of the District Court was appealed to the Arnhem Court of Appeal who on 4 July 2006 dismissed the appeal and confirmed the District Court's findings.[83]

This decision, along with decisions such as *Home A/S v Ofir* and *Paperboy*[84] suggests that the decisions of 9 November 2004 have allowed for a free 'movement of information' within the EU. Whereas prior to the *Fixtures Marketing/BHB* cases there was a real risk of the *sui generis* database right being applied to any aggregation of data on a webpage, an outcome which would lead in Europe at least to a *de facto* 'sweat of the brow' standard of originality for the protection of all online aggregations of data, the decisions of 9 November have removed this spectre. Online databases are still adequately protected. In the event that there has been 'a substantial investment in either the obtaining, verification or presentation of the contents' as defined in *Fixtures Marketing/BHB* they will gain the protection of the *sui generis* database right. What will not be allowed is for individual organisations to claim database protection for 'spin off' databases such as listings of job adverts, homes for sale, or television or sporting listings. This seems a reasonable balance, and with *Copiepresse* reinforcing copyright law in the arena of deep linking creators of original content may still rely on copyright law to protect their work where appropriate. With the value of data ever increasing it seems fair to predict though that *NVM* v. *ZAH* is unlikely to be the last word on this subject.

---

[82] Case discussed in depth in R. Clark,'*Sui Generis* Database Protection: a New Start for the UK and Ireland?' (2007) 2 *Journal of Intellectual Property Law and Practice* 97.

[83] *NVM* v. *Zoekallehuizen.nl*, 06/416, LJN AY0089.

[84] Sub nom. *Verlagsgruppe Handelsblatt GmbH v Paperboy* [2005] ECDR 7.

FURTHER READING

Books

E. Derclaye, *The Legal Protection of Databases: a Comparative Analysis* (2008)

Chapters and Articles

C. Waelde, 'Databases and Lawful Users: the Chink in the Armour' (2006) 3 *IPQ* 256

A. Masson, 'Creation of Database or Creation of Data: Crucial Choices in the Matter of Database Protection' [2006] 28(5) *EIPR* 261

C. Colston, 'Protecting Databases—a Call for Regulation' (2007) *Denning Law Journal* 85

S. Corbett, 'A Human Rights Perspective on the Database Debate' [2006] 28(2) *EIPR* 83

Branding and trade marks in the information society

As the value of online commerce continues to grow the importance of protecting one's trading identity online is magnified, leading to an increased use of traditional branding techniques, such as trade marks, in the online environment. In this chapter we will discuss the traditional role of trade marks within the creation of brand portfolios and examine the roles trade marks play in the online environment, both as traditional brands and as internet addresses or domain names. We begin with a short discussion of branding and the role of trade marks.

12.1 Trade marks and branding

The issue of 'branding' is one which lawyers have traditionally remained apart from: instead choosing to focus on the narrow legal question of protection of trade marks. One lawyer who though does examine branding is Professor Cornish in his 2002 Clarendon Lectures.[1] His view is that branding and trade marks share a common foundation: 'branding is the watchword of marketers; lawyers talk of trade marks and associated get up. By these terms the two groups mean broadly the same phenomenon; but each inclines to a contemptuous view of what the other contributes to business functioning and general welfare.'[2] A general definition of branding given by Colin Bates of 'BuildingBrands', a UK brand consultancy, is that it is 'a collection of perceptions in the mind of the consumer', which he goes on to develop saying: 'a brand is very different from a product or service: a brand is intangible and exists in the mind of the consumer'.

If this is the definition of branding as found in the marketing and branding industry what is a trade mark as defined by the legal services industry? The answer is to be found in s. 1 of the Trade Marks Act 1994 (TMA) which defines a trade mark as: 'any sign capable of being represented graphically which is capable of distinguishing goods or services of one undertaking from those of other undertakings.' It appears from this that Professor Cornish is correct: there is little substantive difference between the marketing concept of branding and the legal concept of a trade mark. Both are intangible, both are distinctive, both are capable of definition and recording. Yet despite these superficial

---

[1] *Intellectual Property: Omnipresent, Distracting, Irrelevant?* (2004).   [2] *ibid*, 73.

similarities, the two live in very different environments, and an understanding of the conflict between the role of brands and trade marks is essential for the discussion that follows in this chapter, for it is this conflict which has been at the heart of a significant amount of litigation and arbitration.

In the modern consumer-driven society brands have developed a purpose much greater than that intended for trade marks. To understand this purpose take a second, look up from this book and look around (and at) yourself. Chances are you, and the surrounding environment, are emblazoned with brand identities. Sony, Apple, Dell, and HP proclaim you buy their electronics while Ralph Lauren, Hugo Boss, Abercrombie & Fitch, and others proudly proclaim that you choose their clothes. You proudly wear these brands to identify yourself with a brand image: Prada, Louis Vuitton, and Versace (aspirational); Hugo Boss, Zara, and Paul Smith (professional); Marks and Spencer, Next, and Principles (practical); Topshop, French Connection, and H&M (fashionable). You may prefer an Apple laptop to a Dell one as Apple portray themselves as creative and 'outside the box', you probably choose which car you drive as much for the badge on the bonnet as for the practicalities of what it does.

The development of this 'brand society' and its interaction with the legal process was examined by Neil MacCormick in his paper *On the Very Idea of Intellectual Property: An Essay According to the Institutionalist Theory of Law*[3] where he notes that intellectual property rights (IPRs) when viewed as a legal concept display three properties:[4]

> **→ Highlight** MacCormick's Three Legal Properties of IPRs
>
> 1. They prescribe the circumstances in which the IPR comes into being and vests in a particular person;
> 2. The law provides what privileges and other rights belong to the holder of the IPR; and
> 3. The law must specify how and IPR is extinguished and how it can be transferred from one person to another.

This is what MacCormick describes as the 'institutional facts' of IPRs. What is abundantly clear though is that this is a lawyer seeking to rationalise what intellectual property rights are from a legal perspective. He fails to capture, and indeed does not seek to, the complexity of trade marks as cultural icons. This is a weakness of the legal analysis. The lawyer talks of 'badges of identity', 'trade mark registries', and 'infringement and enforcement', whereas the brand consultant talks of 'aspiration values', 'target audiences', and 'lifestyle choices'. The current value of trade marks is not measured in terms of brand recognition, as was the case in the past, but by brand identity. This means we no longer value brands by their ability to distinguish goods and services as being provided by a particular company or individual but by the lifestyle offered by that brand. This has allowed brands to develop quite astonishing dollar values. In 2009 BusinessWeek valued each of the top twenty global brands as being worth in excess of

---

[3] [2002] *IPQ* 227.   [4] *ibid*, 136.

$15bn each, with the global number one brand *Coca-Cola* being valued at a staggering $68bn.[5] With such vast sums of money involved and with more and more business being conducted in the online environment it is only to be expected that both brand owners and their legal advisors would soon turn their attention to brand protection and development in the online environment. This has clear potential for a clash of cultures and it is this which forms the core of this chapter. The following discussion is split into three sections. Firstly we will analyse the UK law on trade mark protection. From here we move on to a discussion of brand identity in the online environment before we conclude with an analysis of the legal conflicts which have arisen from these culture clashes and the proposed legal solutions to these conflicts.

12.2 Trade marks in the global business environment

The legal system takes a narrow view of the role of trade marks, viewing a trade mark as a tool of brand recognition rather than brand identity. There are two varieties of trade mark, the Registered Trade mark (or true trade mark) and the common law of passing off (sometimes referred to as unregistered trade marks).[6] The more familiar of these to most people is the registered trade mark which is sometimes referred to in literature by the addition of a commonly recognisable symbol ® or ™. The addition of such symbols is not though a prerequisite to a registered trade mark and therefore one should never assume that an unadorned name or mark is not a registered trade mark.

12.2.1 Registered and unregistered trade marks

In the UK registered trade marks are regulated by the Trade Marks Act 1994, which implemented the First Trade Marks Directive.[7] By s. 63 of the Act, the Registrar of Trade Marks is required to maintain a register, which contains a record of all registered trade marks. To gain registration in the register an applicant must make an application under s. 32. The procedure is governed by a set of rules which require the Registrar to examine each application to see whether it complies with the Act and Rules. If it does, he publishes it whereupon anyone objecting to the application may oppose it or make observations as to whether or not it should be granted. If no notice of opposition is given or all opposition proceedings are withdrawn or decided in the applicant's favour the Registrar registers the mark unless it appears to him that, having regard to matters coming to his notice since accepting the application, that it was accepted in error. If accepted onto the register the mark is registered for a period of 10 years from the date of registration in the first instance,[8] which may be renewed for further

[5] BusinessWeek *The 100 top Brands 2009*: http://bwnt.businessweek.com/interactive_reports/best_global_brands_2009/.
[6] For more detail on both these see L. Bently and B. Sherman *Intellectual Property Law* (2nd ed., 2004) Ch. 31.
[7] Directive 89/104/EEC of the Council, of 21 December 1988, to approximate the Laws of the Member States relating to Trade Marks and gives effect to the Madrid Protocol for the International Registration of Marks.   [8] TMA, s. 42(1).

periods of ten years.[9] Once registered the proprietor of a registered trade mark has exclusive rights in the trade mark that are infringed by its use in the UK without his consent.[10] Those rights have effect from the date of filing of the application for registration,[11] however, no action may be taken before the date on which a trade mark is registered and no offence is committed by anything done before publication of the registration.

Infringement of a registered trade mark is regulated by s. 10 of the Act. This states that a trade mark may be infringed by using in the course of trade a sign: (a) which is identical with the registered trade mark in relation to goods or services which are identical with those for which the mark is registered;[12] (b) where, because the sign is identical with the registered trade mark and is used in relation to goods or services similar to those for which the mark is registered, or, because the sign is similar to the registered mark and is used in relation to goods or services that are identical with or similar to those for which that mark is registered, there exists a likelihood of confusion on the part of the public, which includes the likelihood of association with the registered mark;[13] or (c) which is identical with or similar to the registered trade mark and is used in relation to goods or services which are not necessarily similar to those for which the trade mark is registered, where the trade mark has a reputation in the UK and the use of the sign, being without due cause, takes unfair advantage of, or is detrimental to, the distinctive character or repute of the trade mark.[14] Use for these purposes includes affixing a sign to goods or their packaging, offering or exposing goods for sale, putting them on the market, stocking them for those purposes under such sign, offering or supplying services under the sign, importing or exporting under the sign, or using it on business papers or in advertising.[15] Sections 11 and 12 of the Act provide that a trade mark is not infringed, *inter alia*, by the use: (a) by a person making use of his own name or address;[16] (b) of indications concerning the kind, quality, quantity, intended purpose, value, geographical origin, time of production of goods or rendering of services or other characteristics of goods or services;[17] or (c) of the trade mark where it is necessary to indicate the intended purpose of a product or service.[18]

Unregistered trade marks function similarly (without the registration process of course). The correct legal term for the protection of an unregistered trade mark is 'the tort of passing off'. Unlike registered trade marks which are a creature of statute, passing off is a common law invention. The modern law is to be found in a handful of cases of which the most recent are the decisions of the House of Lords in *Reckitt & Colman Products Ltd v Borden Inc*[19] and *Erven Warnink BV v J Townend & Sons*.[20] In the first of those cases, Lord Oliver set out what is known as the 'Classic Trinity' which lies at the root of the modern English Law of Passing Off. He said that a claim may be brought where: (a) the claimant's goods or services have acquired a goodwill

   [9] *ibid*, s. 42(2). The oldest trade mark in the Registry is Trade Mark No. 1 of 1876 (the year the register was created). It is the red triangle logo of the Bass brewery.
   [10] *ibid*, s. 9(1).   [11] *ibid*, s. 9(3).   [12] *ibid*, s. 10(1).   [13] *ibid*, s. 10(2).
   [14] *ibid*, s. 10(3).   [15] *ibid*, s. 10(4).   [16] *ibid*, s. 11(2)(a).
   [17] *ibid*, s. 11(2)(b). This includes terms such as 'Scotch' Whisky or 'Lion Quality' Eggs.
   [18] *ibid*, s. 11(2)(c). This includes terms such as 'Ford' exhausts or games controllers for 'Sony Playstation3'.
   [19] [1990] RPC 341.   [20] [1979] AC 731.

or reputation in the market and are known by some distinguishing feature; **and** (b) there is a misrepresentation by the defendant (whether or not intentional) leading or likely to lead the public to believe that goods or services offered by the defendant are goods or services of the claimant; **and** (c) the claimant has suffered, or is likely to suffer, damage as a result of the erroneous belief engendered by the defendant's misrepresentation.[21]

12.2.2 **Trade mark characteristics**

Both registered trade marks and the law of passing off share common characteristics of domesticity and specificity. Domesticity is the provision that a trade mark will only be protected within the jurisdiction in which it is registered or used. For registered trade marks domesticity can be established by reference to the TMA: s. 9(1) states, 'The proprietor of a registered trade mark has exclusive rights in the trade mark which are infringed by use of the trade mark *in the United Kingdom* without his consent.' There is no cross border protection of UK registered trade marks. The concept of domesticity in trade marks is reflected throughout the globe. There is no such thing as an 'international trade mark'. Although two international agreements create provisions for the international protection of trade marks, the Paris Convention for the Protection of Industrial Property and the Madrid Agreement/Protocol, neither creates a truly international trade mark as both require recognition by national governments and/or the domestic registrar of trade marks.

Unregistered trade marks also display domesticity. The clearest example of such a provision in the UK, is the case of *Anheuser-Busch v Budejovicky Budvar*.[22] In this case the Court of Appeal followed the so called 'hard-line' school of passing off in determining that goodwill, a necessary prerequisite for an action of passing off, has a territorial component. There is a separate 'soft-line' school of thought which is recognised in Australia.[23] This school claims to protect the unregistered trade marks of commercial organisations that do not trade within the jurisdiction in question.[24] Does this mean that unregistered trade marks, at least in some corners of the globe, do not demonstrate domesticity? The answer is no. In those cases where the soft-line approach is followed the court will look for evidence of reputation in the trade mark within the jurisdiction in question.[25] The soft-line/hard-line dichotomy is not about domesticity, it is rather a question of whether the court is to look for goodwill on the part of the trade mark holder or merely reputation. Whichever approach is correct, in both schools of thought unregistered trade marks benefit from domesticity.

The second characteristic of trade marks is specificity. Put simply, you only gain protection if there is a likelihood of confusion on the part of the consumer. As the consumer is unlikely to be confused by similar trade marks on entirely dissimilar products, such as Penguin chocolate biscuits and Penguin books, protection is limited to those

---

[21] [1990] RPC 341, 406.   [22] [1984] FSR 413.

[23] See H. Carty, 'Passing Off and the Concept of Goodwill' (1995) *Journal of Business Law* 139; F. Martin, 'The Dividing Line Between Goodwill and International Reputation' (1995) *Journal of Business Law* 70.

[24] See, e.g. the case of *Conagra Inc. v McCain Frozen Foods (Aust) Pty* (1991) 23 IPR 193.

[25] See Lockhart J in *Conagra v McCain, ibid,* 237.

products which share characteristics with the trade mark owner's product. In the UK, for registered trade marks, this is assured by categorising all applications into one of forty-five classes of goods/services.[26] The classification of the register in this manner ensures adequate protection for the trade mark owner, no-one else can use that mark for similar goods/services, while allowing others the right to make use of popular trade names/marks in different sectors of the economy where the public are unlikely to be confused.

Specificity of trade marks has a basis in equity, something which can clearly be seen when one looks at the common law protection offered to unregistered trade marks. Passing off as a common law delict/tort has a basis in equity. The concept of specificity has developed here also under a different title, 'the common field of activity.'[27] The common field of activity ensures that you cannot claim goodwill in your trade name/mark out-with the class of goods or services in which you trade. It is designed to ensure one person does not gain a complete monopoly over a name or mark which would unfairly restrict others gaining access to a (different) market. Domesticity and specificity help create the 'one mark many owners' ethos. It has proved to be an extremely efficient method for regulating trade marks, allowing adequate protection but also free access. The Internet DNS, though, uses a 'one mark one owner' ethos which is alien to experienced trade mark practitioners. This clash of cultures has led many domain name/trade mark disputes.

12.3 Domain names as badges of identity

The domain name system, or DNS, is the system of global navigation used on the internet. Each page of information, each image, and each file is given an address called a Uniform Resource Locator (URL) which, like the address of every home, office, or shop, must be unique if the user is to locate it. This address is made up of several sections illustrated below.

→ Highlight Properties of a Uniform Resource Locator (URL)

http://www.lse.ac.uk/law

The above is the homepage of the Law Department at the London School of Economics. The URL may be broken down as follows:

http://—This page uses hypertext transfer protocol.

www.—This page is found on the World Wide Web.

lse.ac.uk—The unique address of the London School of Economics. This is made up of two domain names; a top level domain and a second level domain. Internet addresses are read right **→**

---

[26] Full classificatory list at: http://www.ipo.gov.uk/t-class.htm.
[27] See *Rolls Razor Ltd v Rolls (Lighters) Ltd* (1949) 66 RPC 137: *Fortnum & Mason plc v Fortnum Ltd.* [1994] FSR 438.

> →
> to left, the top level domain is the .ac.uk section of the domain. This tells the user the address
> is used by a UK registered academic organisation. The second level domain comes to the left of
> the first period, i.e. lse. This is the identifier of the site operator. As a whole the domain name
> must be unique. There can be only one lse.ac.uk address, although variations such as lse.com,
> or lse.co.uk are possible. Before they can be used second level domains require to be registered,
> of which more below.
>
> **law**—This is a tertiary or third level domain. Any text which follows the top level domain is used
> to identify individual pages of information within the site managed by the owner of the domain
> name. Such tertiary domains do not require registration and will not be discussed further.

The key aspect of a domain name is the second level domain. Second level domains are available on a first-come first serve basis, and may be obtained through any one of a number of domain name registries. Registries are private companies who have been accredited by the relevant Registrar[28] and may usually offer registration in any one of a number of top level domains.[29] Registration of a second level domain is extremely cheap and simple with a .co.uk registration costing as little as £2.74 per annum and a .com registration available for as little as £8.97 per annum. To get a second level domain all you need to do is fill out an online form and give the registry your credit card details.

Although functionally domain names once registered are addresses of pages of information in the online environment there is an important distinction between these domain names and traditional addresses in that the makeup of a domain names, in particular the exact nature of the second level domain, is chosen by the registrant. This is quite unlike a traditional address and more like a trade mark registration in that the registrant has control over the allocation of the identifier. Thus while McDonalds may have a restaurant in your town or city, when searching for that restaurant you will navigate in part by an assigned address (such as 36 South Street) and in part by the familiar, and protected, brand identifiers of McDonalds such as the Golden Arches. You would not expect your local McDonalds to have a specific address such as 1 McDonald Road, but due to the way domain names are allocated you do expect McDonalds online presence to be at specific domains including *mcdonalds.com* and *mcdonalds.co.uk*.

Due to this dual nature of domain names as both address tools and brand identifiers some domain names have attracted high values, and many domain names have been litigated over. The most valuable domain names are varied, but tend to show two characteristics: (1) They are located in the .com top level domain, which is the prime real-estate

[28] A Registrar, as distinct from a Registry, is the regulatory authority tasked with the role of overseeing a particular TLD. The key Registrar is the Internet Corporation of Assigned Names and Numbers (ICANN) which manages the generic Top Level Domains. Country Code TLDs such as .uk, .jp, and .fr are managed at a national level. The .uk Registrar is Nominet UK. We will examine the roles, and rules, of ICANN and Nominet UK below.

[29] Any individual may register in any ICANN regulated generic TLD. Some Country Code TLDs are restricted to citizens of that country such as the Greek country code TLD (.gr). Others such as the UK's .uk are open to registration by anyone in a similar manner to the generic TLDs.

of the domain name world,[30] and (2) the second level domain is usually a short, generic, English-language term. Thus, according to the Guinness Book of Records the most expensive internet domain name sold to date, is *business.com* which was sold in 1999 for $7.5 million,[31] with other high value transactions including the domain names *CreditCards.com* which sold for $2.75 million in July 2004, *Wine.com* which sold for: $2.9 million in September 1999 and *Beer.com*, bought in 2004 for a staggering $7 million. It may not surprise anyone though that the most valuable domain names reflect those popular online activities sex and gambling. A recent development of the explosion of interest in online gambling is that 'online poker' has now overtaken 'online sex' as the most searched for term on the internet. This may explain why recently it was reported in the media that the domain name *Poker.com* had been sold in a silent auction for a world record $22 million, but as speculation surrounding the sale grew it appeared the sale failed to complete.[32] That leaves the two most expensive domain names actually sold to date as being two relating to the adult services industry. The second most valuable sale was the transfer of *Porn.com* in May 2007 from domain name reseller Moniker.com to Detroit-based MXN Ltd for $9.5m.[33] The current world-record holder is though the $12 million price tag paid for *Sex.com* in 2005, about which there is an interesting tale.

12.3.1 **Sex.com**

In 1994 an internet entrepreneur Gary Kremen registered the domain name *sex.com* with .com registry Network Solutions Inc. Kremen, as was common at the time, 'warehoused' the domain name, meaning that he retained his registration but did not develop a site at that address. In October 1995 Network Solutions transferred the domain to a competing net entrepreneur Stephen Cohen. Cohen had been trying to gain control of the domain for some time thorough phone calls, emails, and forged letters to Network Solutions. It appears he eventually persuaded an employee of Network Solutions to change the ownership details by using a fake fax, although this was not entirely clear during most of the legal proceedings that followed. After gaining control of the domain name, Cohen developed it, producing an advertising site which gained up to 25 million hits a day. It was reported that Cohen was making between $50,000 to $500,000 every month through payments for click-throughs and other advertising hosted on the site.

Gary Kremen then took steps to recover the domain name through litigation. The ensuing case *Kremen v Cohen*[34] was to be one of the longest running, most malicious

---

[30] In an earlier paper the author referred to the .com top level domain as 'the electronic equivalent of Rodeo Drive or Bond Street'. See A. Murray, 'Internet Domain Names: The Trade Mark Challenge' [1998] *International Journal of Law and Information Technology* 285, 301.

[31] The domain name having previously been sold for only $150,000 two years earlier. This deal was though not as profitable as was suggested at the time as the domain name was bought with stock options, not cash. Later the stock was redeemed for $2 million. Source: S. Levy, 'Sticking to the Business', *Newsweek*, 16 October 2006.

[32] See Gambling 911, *Poker.com Domain Sale a Bust?*, 30 May 2007: http://www.gambling911.com/Poker.com-Domain-Name-053007.html.

[33] See PC Advisor, *Porn.com sale misses net record*, 17 May 2007: http://www.pcadvisor.co.uk/news/index.cfm?newsid=9388.

[34] *Kremen v Cohen*, 99 F.Supp. 2d 1168 (N.D. Cal. 2000); *Kremen v Cohen*, 2002 WL 2017073 (9th Cir. 2002); *Kremen v. Cohen*, 325 F.3d 1035 (9th Cir. 2003); *Kremen v Cohen*, 337 F.3d 1024 (9th Cir. 2003).

court actions of recent US legal history.[35] In November 2000, the US District Court in San Jose found the letter Cohen had used to obtain the *Sex.com* registration was fraudulent and therefore the transfer of *Sex.com* from Kremen to Cohen was void.[36] This may have been felt to be the end of the dispute, but Cohen argued that the forged letter and therefore the court's view on it were irrelevant. He claimed *Sex.com* was his long before Network Solutions registered it on behalf of Gary Kremen. In fact, Cohen said he had been using the Sex.com name as long ago as 1979. Before spending some time in federal prison in the early 1990s for fraud, Cohen had run a bulletin board for swingers and operated it from 1979 into the 1980s. One of the areas on the bulletin board used the three-letter file extension '.com' and was preceded by the word 'sex'. As we have seen one can obtain an unregistered trade mark by developing goodwill in a name or identity, and citing this Cohen claimed that since he had used the term *Sex.com* since 1979, the domain name was rightfully his.

At the following hearing Judge Ware rejected this claim and ordered Cohen to place $25 million in the court's control, pending final judgment and assessment of damages. In defiance of this order, Cohen transferred money to accounts outside of the US. Cohen was held in contempt on 5 March 2001 for violating the court's order and for failing to appear in court on another date. In April 2001, the Californian District Court awarded Kremen an additional $40 million for lost earnings, making the total damages $65 million. Cohen appealed the judgement, but refused to allow assessment of his business, providing false information or none at all, declaring most of his companies bankrupt and moving assets out of the US jurisdiction.[37] Finally an arrest warrant was issued and Cohen fled the country to Mexico. Kremen offered a $50,000 reward for information leading to his arrest, but Cohen remained at large. Cohen continued to file appeals but they were rapidly rejected.[38] Finally in October 2005, Cohen was arrested in Mexico for immigration violations, and was handed over to US authorities. In December 2006 Cohen was released from prison, still having never paid Kremen one cent of the damages. For Kremen the only recompense he received was the $12 million he received for the domain name in December 2005. This falls far short of the damages Stephen Cohen was due to pay, and far short of the perhaps fanciful valuation of $85 million placed on the domain name by Gary Kremen in 2001.

This tale makes clear some key concepts. Firstly domain names have brand values which far exceed their role as mere internet addresses. This reflects their selection rather than allocation. Domain names have much more in common with trade marks than with addresses. They are selected and registered much like a trade mark. In addition they are developed to reflect brand identities in a similar way to trade marks. Some of the most famous brand identities of our age are based upon domain names. The 'old-world' identities of *Coca-Cola*, *Mercedes* and *Tesco* have been joined by *Amazon.com*, *eBay.com* and *Google.com*. Secondly, the *sex.com* controversy showed that domain names could be treated as traditional property. In *Kremen v Cohen*,[39] the court considered

[35] The full story is in K. McCarthy, *Sex.com* (2007).
[36] *Kremen v Cohen*, 99 F.Supp. 2d 1168 (N.D. Cal. 2000).
[37] *Kremen v Cohen*, 2002 WL 2017073 (9th Cir. 2002).
[38] *Kremen v Cohen*, 325 F.3d 1035 (9th Cir. 2003).
[39] *Kremen v Cohen*, 337 F.3d 1024 (9th Cir. 2003).

the question whether a domain name was intangible property. The Court of Appeal for the 9th Circuit stated that a domain name is a form of intangible property because (i) it represents an interest of precise definition, (ii) it is subject to exclusive possession or control, and (iii) a registrant has a legitimate claim to exclusivity.[40] Thus more and more domain names start to look like trade marks. They have value, they are registrable, and they are (legally) intangible property rights. The key difference with domain names is that they are awarded purely on a first-come first-serve basis with no examination of the application as found with trade marks. This vastly increases the risks of names being registered which are in breach of a trade mark of another business or individual, or even given the low cost and simple process of registration, the risk that individuals or companies will deliberately register marks similar to those of famous or well-known brands (such as *coca-coladrinks.net*, or *barclaysbank-online.co.uk*), a process known as cybersquatting, or based on misspellings of well known marks (such as *macdonalds.com* or *eboy.com*), a process known as typosquatting. Thus risks surround trade marks in the online environment at every turn.

12.4 Trade mark/domain name disputes

12.4.1 Early disputes in the US

This conflict of values quickly led to disputes over rightful ownership of domain names. These issues were first brought to the attention of the wider public by a journalist for *Wired* magazine named Joshua Quittner. Mr Quittner while preparing a story for *Wired* on the potential value of commercially recognisable domain names,[41] registered the domain name 'mcdonalds.com' in an attempt to illustrate the risks faced by the owners of famous or well-known names. After a short flurry of communications between Mr Quittner and McDonalds (and their lawyers) Mr Quittner assigned the name to the McDonalds Corporation in return for a donation towards computer equipment for a primary school.[42] While the actions of Mr Quittner may be seen to be harmless the US courts were suddenly abuzz with trade mark lawyers seeking to reclaim valuable cyber-property that their clients had failed to secure.

A series of cases were begun in US courts. The first is most probably that of *Princeton Review v Stanley H. Kaplan Educational Center Ltd*[43] In this case, the educational test prep-aration company Princeton Review opened a web site under the domain name *kaplan.com* which appeared to refer to its competitor the Stanley H. Kaplan Educational Center. Users who reached the site, expecting that it was sponsored by Kaplan, found instead messages disparaging Kaplan's services and praising those of Princeton Review. Kaplan

---

[40] It should be noted this was not the first decision to set out this position. Domain names had previously been found to be a form of intangible property in the cases of *Caesars World Inc. v Caesars-Palace.com*, 112 F Supp 2d 502 (ED Va. 2000) and *Online Partners.com Inc. v Atlanticnet Media Corp* 2000 US Dist LEXIS 783, 101242 (ND Cal 2000).

[41] J. Quittner, 'Billions Registered', *Wired* Issue 2.10 October 1994: http://www.wired.com/wired/archive/2.10/mcdonalds.html.

[42] For more on the actions of Mr Quittner see *The Daily Telegraph*, 14 January 1997.

[43] 94 Civ. 1604 (MGC) (S.D.N.Y., filed March 9, 1994).

having refused Princeton Review's 'generous' offer to relinquish the domain name in exchange for a case of beer, sued. The case was resolved when an arbiter ordered Princeton Review to surrender the domain name.

A similar case involving the misdirection of internet users by using another's name or mark was the immediately following case of *Planned Parenthood Federation of America v Richard Bucci*.[44] This case involved more difficult issues than the Kaplan case. Planned Parenthood is a well known, charitable reproductive health organisation which offers advice on contraception and abortion. It, like Kaplan, found itself the target of efforts by a 'competitor' to divert attention away from it using the *plannedparenthood.com* domain name. The defendant, Mr Bucci, an anti-abortion and anti-birth control advocate, set up a web site using the domain name *plannedparenthood.com*. The site, which carried an opening banner which read, 'Welcome to the Planned Parenthood Home Page,' provided information on and promoted sales of an anti-abortion book. Mr Bucci admitted that he intentionally chose the domain name *plannedparenthood.com* to divert internet users who were seeking Planned Parenthood's website to his own website.

The court found Mr Bucci's actions were a breach of Planned Parenthood's trade mark rights despite a strong defence that he was making use of the Planned Parenthood trade mark in a non-commercial sphere and that he was protected by the right to free speech guaranteed under the First Amendment to the US Constitution. The court stated that Mr Bucci's website was a 'commercial use' of the trade mark, as his use affected the plaintiff's activities. Firstly, the defendant had appropriated the plaintiff's mark in order to reach an audience of internet users who want to reach plaintiff's services, intercepting them and misleading them in an attempt to offer his own political message. Secondly, his appropriation not only provided internet users with competing and directly opposing information, but also prevented those users from reaching the plaintiff and its services and message. In that way, the court found that Mr Bucci's use of the 'Planned Parenthood' name was classically competitive: he had taken the plaintiff's mark as his own in order to purvey his internet services to an audience intending to access the plaintiff's services. Around the time the US Courts were dealing with these cases of 'competitor misappropriation' they were also being asked to deal with simpler cases of 'Cybersquatting' or the misappropriation and storage of well known names with a view to selling them on in the future to either the rightful holder or another at a profit.

Most domain name disputes were not such 'competitor disputes'. The majority involved the warehousing and selling of domains. Because domain names are assigned without substantive review or clearance, the appropriation of the domain names of famous trade marks or trade names by unrelated parties is common. There is no way of knowing how often companies in this situation made nominal or not so nominal payoffs to cybersquatters in order to obtain ownership of domain names containing their marks or brands. But as the courts began to weigh in on such disputes, it became clear that trade mark owners have legal remedies, for the courts have consistently ruled against individuals who obtained domain names for purposes of re-selling them to others.

In the famous case of *Panavision International v Toeppen*,[45] an attempt by the well-known cybersquatter Dennis Toeppen to make use of his *panavision.com* registration by

---

[44] 42 USPQ2d (BNA) 1430, U.S. Dist. LEXIS 3338 (SDNY 1997).   [45] 141 F.3d 1316 (1998).

displaying on the associated website an aerial photograph of the city of Pana, Illinois (as he argued in court a vision of Pana—a Pana vision) was doomed to failure with the 9th Circuit finding that Mr Toeppen had 'made commercial use of Panavision's trade marks and his conduct diluted those marks'. More importantly arguably was the ruling that a domain name was not simply an address: 'We reject Toeppen's premise that a domain name is nothing more than an address. A significant purpose of a domain name is to identify the entity that owns the web site. A customer who is unsure about a company's domain name will often guess that the domain name is also the company's name. A domain name mirroring a corporate name may be a valuable corporate asset, as it facilitates communication with a customer base'.[46]

Some cybersquatters attempted to exert pressure on trade mark holders only to find they fell afoul of anti-dilution provisions. In *Hasbro v Internet Entertainment Group*,[47] Hasbro, the owner of a well-known children's game which it sells in the US under the brand *Candyland*, was disturbed to learn of an adult website plying under the domain name *www.candyland.com*. Although no one would be so confused as to believe that Hasbro might also be the source of online pornographic images, Hasbro reasonably feared that its valuable mark would be damaged by the creation of a new, sexual association with the mark. The District Court agreed and issued a restraining order and preliminary injunction, precluding the defendant from continuing to use the *candyland.com* domain name. Under the dilution doctrine, Hasbro, as the owners of a famous mark did not have to show that a cybersquatter's actions created a likelihood of confusion, as this element of a trade mark infringement claim is not required for a dilution claim.

It was still not entirely clear that traditional dilution doctrine would provide a remedy against individuals who were making no trade mark use of a famous mark, but were instead merely 'warehousing' the names. Could mere registration of a famous mark, without use essentially amounting to nothing but denial of use of the domain name by the trade mark owner be said to blur or tarnish famous marks? This question was answered in a series of further cases involving Dennis Toeppen. In *American Standard v Toeppen*,[48] Mr Toeppen was enjoined from using the *American Standard* trade mark and the *americanstandard.com* domain name and was ordered to transfer the domain name to the plaintiff. He lost again a few months later, in a suit over his registration of the domain name *intermatic.com*.[49] The plaintiff in this case had used its *Intermatic* trade name and mark in connection with its electronics business since 1941, and sued Toeppen for dilution and trade mark infringement. The court granted summary judgment against Toeppen, holding that his registration and use of the *intermatic.com* domain name constituted dilution of a famous mark. His third loss came against Panavision International in the case previously mentioned.

Collectively these cases established that US Trade mark Law, and in particular the Lanham Act,[50] applied to domain names in all circumstances. Domain names were clearly not in law (or US Federal Law at least) just addresses, they were clearly capable of trade mark infringement. Further it was clear that the US courts were willing to act to protect trade marks, both famous marks and simple trade marks. Cybersquatters

---

[46] At 1327.   [47] 40 USPQ2d (BNA) 1479 (1996).
[48] 96 CV 02147 (1996).   [49] *Intermatic, Inc. v Toeppen*, 947 F.Supp. 1227 (1996).
[50] The Lanham Act (title 15, chapter 22 of the US Code) is the US federal trade mark statute and dates from 1946.

were not able to rely on simply warehousing and not using names as a defence. Equally they had found that spurious claims as to use would be 'pierced' by the courts to reveal their true activities but it was not just US courts, and not just cybersquatters and green eyed competitors who were at the heart of the development of the law in this complex arena, the UK courts were also active and some of their claims were much more complex and subtle.

12.4.2 **Early disputes in the UK**

The UK courts first wrestled with this matter in the case of *Pitman Training Ltd v Nominet UK*.[51] The dispute in this case centred around the right to use the domain name *pitman. co.uk*, and the competing interests of two parties, Pitman Training Ltd and Pearson Professional Ltd.[52] Both the training company and the publishing company had at one time been owned by a single company, but in 1985 they had demerged and Pearson Professional had bought the publishing business. As part of the demerger, Pitman Training Ltd agreed not to use the name Pitman, except in relation to their core business. The problem arose when the two companies, who had coexisted peacefully in the actual world for eleven years, tried to register their presence on the internet.

On 15 February 1996, Pearson registered the domain name *pitman.co.uk*, but took no action to develop their web presence. Then, on 15 March 1996, Pitman Training Ltd also registered the domain name with Nominet UK.[53] They went on to establish a web presence in July 1996. Pearson had no knowledge of the Pitman Training website until December 1996, but immediately upon discovering the Pitman Training website they contacted both Pitman Training and Nominet UK, demanding that the right to use the domain name be reassigned to them. On 4 April 1997 Nominet, following threats of legal action from Pearson's lawyers, agreed to reassign the domain name to Pearson, a transfer affected on 7 April. On 9 April, Pitman issued a writ against Pearson and Nominet requiring the immediate reinstatement of their rights to the domain name.

The problem for the judge was each party was entitled to make use of the Pitman trade name in their respective fields. Trade marks, registered or unregistered, benefit from specificity. In virtual reality though there is no specificity of domain names: there can be only one *pitman.co.uk* and there is no method of differentiating between Pitman Training and Pitman Publishing. It was this lack of specificity which led to the dispute before the court. The decision of the court was that the plaintiffs had no viable or reasonably arguable cause of action against the second defendant (Pearson) and the interim injunction was lifted, allowing Nominet to ratify the transfer of registration to Pearson. The impact of this case in UK law that the High Court was willing to uphold the policy of Nominet that registration of second-level domain names should be allowed on a first-come first-serve basis.

The second case to impact on the UK Law in this area was *Prince plc. v Prince Sportswear Group Inc.*[54] Prince plc. were a UK-registered information technology company who

---

[51] [1997] EWHC Ch 367.

[52] Pearson Professional own Pitman Publishing Ltd who produce academic/student texts.

[53] Nominet is the .uk registrar meaning they oversee the allocation of all .uk top level domain registrations. Such a duplication of registration should not have occurred. In the event of parties who have equal claim to second level domain names Nominet runs a 'first come, first serve policy' see: Nominet UK: Rules for the .uk domain and sub-domains.   [54] [1998] FSR 21.

specialised in desktop migration and IT training. As a leading IT company they developed their web presence at an early stage, and had since February 1995 been using the domain name *prince.com*. Prince Sportswear is a US registered sporting goods company who own the registered trade mark 'Prince' in relation to tennis and squash racquets and other items of sportswear. Prince Sportswear have registered trade marks with both the US and UK Patents Offices, and elsewhere. On 16 January 1997 attorneys representing Prince Sportswear sent a letter to Prince plc. indicating that in their opinion Prince plc.'s use of the *prince.com* domain name constituted infringement and dilution of their client's registered trade marks under the Lanham Act. This triggered the .com registry at that time, Network Solutions Inc.,[55] to write to Prince plc. indicating that unless Prince plc. exhibited a trade mark registration of their own or they produced evidence they had 'filed a suit in any court of competent jurisdiction', their domain name registration would be suspended. Unable to exhibit the former Prince were forced to follow the latter route.

On 28 April they filed a suit in the High Court seeking declaration that their use of the *prince.com* domain name did not infringe Prince Sportswear's UK registered trade mark and an injunction to prevent Prince Sportswear from threatening further proceedings in relation to the *prince.com* domain name.[56] On 30 July Mr Justice Neuberger found in favour of Prince plc. The court had been asked to rule upon two distinct issues, but unfortunately, following the decision in the first issue: unwarranted threats of litigation in breach of s. 21 of the Trade marks Act 1994, Neuberger J felt it unnecessary to rule on the second issue: a declaration that the use of the domain name *prince.com* did not infringe Prince Sportswear's registered trade mark.

On the question of unwarranted threats, Neuberger J found that Prince plc. were entitled to protection under s. 21. It had been argued by Prince Sportswear that s. 21 did not apply to the case in issue as they were seeking only to protect US registered trade marks under the Lanham Act. The judge, though, disagreed, finding a reference to Prince Sportswear's UK registration in their initial letter to Prince plc. to be proof of their intention to protect their UK trade mark. More interesting in relation to domain names was the judge's ruling on the claim of Prince Sportswear that the .com name reflects a US limited name. Neuberger J. pointed out that Prince plc. made use of the *prince.com* domain name from the UK and that Prince Sportswear were objecting to the use of the prince name in a domain name 'in any country'; their objection was not limited to any individual market.

Like the *Pitman* case, the dispute in issue in the *Prince* case is of key importance to the development of the UK Law. The interesting aspect of the *Prince* case, and what it added to the evolving jurisprudence of internet law was its international dimension. Although the case came before an English court, and was decided on provisions of the UK Trade marks Act, the issue for Prince Sportswear was access to the US marketplace. This was made clear by the initial letter to Prince plc. which referred to their US registered trade marks, and sought to invoke the (American) Lanham Act. Although the existence of the *prince.co.uk* domain would have been a problem for Prince Sportswear's UK operation, it was the *prince. com* domain which they sought. The reason is the global nature of the .com domain, and its special place in relation to the US market. Prince Sportswear were forced into taking action because there was only one recognised domain name which suited their company,

---

[55] See below: *The ICANN UDRP.*   [56] Under s. 21 of the TMA 1994 (unwarranted threats).

the *prince.com* domain. This issue is at the heart of the domain name/trade mark nexus. Like *Pitman* the dispute in the *Prince* case arose because companies, who had relied for years on specificity and domesticity of trade marks, found the internet to be the first truly global marketplace. For the first time established businesses found they must compromise their interests. The answer to this problem was for trade mark holders to lobby for extra-judicial private dispute resolution services which allowed for an internationalised process separate to domestic trade mark law to regulate this complex extra-territorial system. The resolution to this was the creation of private dispute resolution systems which would provide an alternative to full-blown legal actions with all the concomitant delays and costs. The two most important private dispute resolution procedures (from a UK perspective) the ICANN Uniform Dispute Resolution Procedure (UDRP) and the Nominet Dispute Resolution Service (DRS) are discussed in depth below, but before we get to them we need first to examine how the UK courts have dealt with cybersquatters.

12.4.3 Cybersquatting before the UK courts

The UK courts have dealt with dozens of actions in cybersquatting. Probably the first such case is that of *Harrods Ltd v UK Network Services Ltd*[57] This case involved a well-known UK cybersquatter, Mr Michael Lawrie. Mr Lawrie registered the domain name *harrods.com* which he then warehoused. The court determined that Mr Lawrie's possession of the domain name, and the potential use he may make of it, constituted trade mark infringement and passing off. Unfortunately, Mr Lawrie did not turn up in court; the arguments to support this contention were not outlined and discussed in full. This though was quickly remedied by what is still the key decision on cybersquatting in the UK, *British Telecommunications plc. and Ors v One in a Million Ltd and Ors*.[58]

This was an appeal to the Court of Appeal by the defendants against summary judgment given to a number of leading British companies in a series of actions against the same defendants. The defendants dealt in domain names. They specialised in registering well-known names and trade marks without the consent of the person or company owning the goodwill in the name or mark and offering those names for sale to the owners of such goodwill. They registered *burgerking.co.uk* which they offered to Burger King for £25,000 and *bt.org* which they offered to British Telecommunications for £4,700. The plaintiffs objected to the defendants' registration of *marksandspencer. com, marksandspencer.co.uk, britishtelecom.co.uk, britishtelecom.net, britishtelecom.com, bt.org, ladbrokes.com, sainsbury.com, sainsburys.com, j-sainsbury.com, cellnet.net, and virgin. org*. At trial the Judge, Jonathan Sumption QC, had granted injunctions to restrain the defendants from such registration and dealings, explaining that: (a) it was enough for a plaintiff to show that a defendant intended to infringe the plaintiff's rights in future even though the mere registration of a deceptive company name or a domain name did not amount to passing-off; and (b) the use of a trade mark in the course of the business of a professional dealer for the purpose of making domain names more valuable and extracting money from the trade mark owner amounted to 'use in the course of trade'.

---

[57] Unreported, (High Court, Ch D December 9, 1996).
[58] [1999] 1 WLR 903, [1998] EWCA Civ 1272, [1998] 4 All ER 476.

The appellants appealed on the basis that the action was premature. They submitted that if a name could be used for a legitimate purpose, it was not an instrument of fraud and relief should not be granted unless it was established that the defendant either threatened to pass-off or was, with another, part of a common design to pass-off. They said that in their case they registered domain names with a view to making a profit either by selling them to the owners of the goodwill, using the blocking effect of the registration to obtain a reasonable price, or, in some cases, selling them to collectors or to other persons who could have a legitimate reason for using them. They submitted that could amount neither to passing-off, or a threat to pass-off.

In dismissing the appeal, Aldous LJ analysed several strands of authority which had held that in the law of passing off injunctive relief may be granted before the harm occurs.[59] His Lordship discerned from those cases that the court has jurisdiction to grant injunctive relief where a defendant is equipped with or is intending to equip another with an instrument of fraud. He added that the question whether a name is an instrument of fraud must depend upon all the circumstances: for instance, a name which by reason of its similarity to another name will inherently lead to passing-off is such an instrument but not if it would not inherently lead to passing-off. The court should consider the similarity of the names, the intention of the defendant, the type of trade, and all the surrounding circumstances. If, after taking all the circumstances into account the court should conclude that a name was produced to enable passing-off, was adapted to be used for passing-off and, if so used, was likely to be fraudulently used, an injunction would be appropriate.

He identified three categories of cases in which a court would grant an injunction: 'First, where there is passing-off established or it is threatened; second, where the defendant is a joint tortfeasor with another in passing-off either actual or threatened, and third, where the defendant has equipped himself with or intends to equip another with an instrument of fraud.'[60] After reviewing the party to party correspondence and other dealings between the parties, Aldous LJ concluded:

> In my view there was clear evidence of systematic registration by the appellants of well-known trade names as blocking registrations and a threat to sell them to others. No doubt the primary purpose of registration was to block registration by the owner of the goodwill ... The registration only blocks registration of the identical domain name and therefore does not act as a block to registration of a domain name that can be used by the owner of the goodwill in the name. The purpose of the so-called blocking registration was to extract money from the owners of the goodwill in the name chosen. Its ability to do so was in the main dependent upon the threat, expressed or implied, that the appellants would exploit the goodwill by either trading under the name or equipping another with the name so he could do so.[61]

As for trade marks, his Lordship was satisfied that threats to infringe had been established. The defendants sought to sell domain names that were confusingly similar to registered

---

[59] In *Farina v Silverlock* (1855) 1 K&J 509 the defendant sold materials for an infringing product. An injunction was granted *inter alia* to prevent the defendant from enabling passing-off; in *John Walker & Sons Ltd v Henry Ost & Co Ltd* [1970] RPC 489 an injunction was granted to prevent the supply of bottles and labels to facilitate passing-off abroad, and in *Glaxo Plc v Glaxowellcome Ltd* [1996] FSR 388 where the defendant had incorporated a company combining the name of two well-known public companies just prior to their merger. These cases collectively are sometimes known as 'instruments of fraud cases'.
[60] [1999] 1 WLR 903, 927.   [61] *ibid*, 934.

trade marks. Those domain names indicated origin, which was the purpose for which they were registered, and they were to be used in relation to the services provided by the registrant who trades in domain names. The Court of Appeal concluded that the deputy judge's analysis in respect of passing off and trade mark infringement had been correct.

12.4.4 **Phones4u Ltd v Phone4u.co.uk**

BT v One in a Million is still the leading UK case-law on both passing off and trade mark infringement in the case of cybersquatting and domain name warehousing, but one further decision should be analysed before we move on to look at the extra-judicial procedures which have extensively replaced court actions in such circumstances and that is the case of *Phones4u Ltd v Phone4u.co.uk.*[62]

Phones4u Ltd is a UK chain of mobile phone retailers. It adopted the name Phones4u for some of its stores and its mail order business in 1995, and changed its corporate name and other shop names in 1997. By 1999 the company enjoyed an annual turnover of nearly £44 million and the red, white, and blue Phones4u logo appeared on most of Phones 4u's 63 shops countrywide. By 2004 the number of such shops exceeded 350. Phones4u registered the domain name *phones4u.co.uk* in 1999, and launched its website in October 2000. The second defendant was an individual, Abdul Heykali, who had worked for a small mobile phone retailer in London. Towards the end of 1999, Mr Heykali set up a mobile phone retail business called Mobile Communication Centre. In August 1999, he registered the domain name *phone4u.co.uk*. In November 1999, the site read, 'this site will be going mobile soon … Up and running by 1st of January 2000.' By September 2000, however, the site's content was merely an image of a phone followed by '4U.co.uk.' The site finally went live in July 2001. At that time, a disclaimer appeared: *Phone4U.co.uk are solely an Internet based company and do not have the costs associated with running high street shops … Phone 4U.co.uk is NOT connected with the high street mobile phone retailer Phones 4U.*

Although some key facts were disputed, the judge accepted that Mr Heykali had chosen *phone4u.co.uk* at the recommendation of a shadowy foreign friend and in ignorance of the claimants' business for use in connection with an internet-based mobile phone company. The court was persuaded that Mr Heykali thought it common practice on the internet to combine descriptive words with the phrase '4U'. However, by February or March 2000 Mr Heykali had become aware of the claimants while searching for a Vodaphone dealership which he obtained from the claimants themselves in March 2000. The claimants by then knew of Mr Heykali's domain name and expressed concern that emails intended for them were being misdirected to Mr Heykali. In response to a cease and desist letter from the claimants, Mr Heykali incorporated a company under the name Phone4U Ltd (later changed to Phone4u.co.uk Internet Ltd) and denied any wrongdoing. He also recognised that his domain name was potentially very valuable. The court found that he deliberately exaggerated the number of misdirected emails he had received, and falsely suggested to the claimants that he had already been offered £100,000 for the domain name.

---

[62] [2006] EWCA Civ 244.

For reasons that were never adequately explained, the claimants took no further steps to stop Mr Heykali's activities until proceedings were issued in February 2004. Following a decision of the High Court in March 2005, in which the court found that the claimants had no goodwill in the mark 'Phones4U' at August 1999 when the domain name was registered, and that there had been no deception in the use of the domain name across the five year period it had been in use, the claimants appealed to the Court of Appeal. The lead judgment was that of Lord Justice Jacob. He found that the test for passing off was that of the *Jif Lemon* decision: '(a) reputation, i.e. goodwill; (b) misrepresentation; and (c) damage or its likelihood.' The court went on to state that there did not have to be evidence of direct diversion of sales caused by misrepresentation in order to prove damage. Jacob LJ adopted the 'more modern' definition of damage: '(a) by diverting trade from the plaintiffs to the defendants; (b) by injuring the trade reputation of the plaintiffs whose [goods are] admittedly superior in quality to that of the defendants; and (c) by the injury which is inherently likely to be suffered by any business when on frequent occasions it is confused by customers or potential customers with a business owned by another proprietor or is wrongly connected with that business.'[63]

The court agreed with the appellants on the four arguments raised in support of their appeal namely that: (1) The judge applied the wrong test in deciding whether or not the appellants had protectable goodwill. Jacob LJ was convinced that the appellants had sufficient goodwill by the relevant date to found a claim in passing off. Looking at the evidence he stated that 'To infer from all that, that hardly anyone knew the name, that the name was not "an attractive force which brings in custom" by August 1999 is simply untenable.'[64] The court held that the judge had incorrectly applied the test for distinctiveness required to obtain a trade mark registration in holding that the phrase 'Phones4u' was not inherently distinctive and had muddled the test for registration with the test for goodwill sufficient for passing off. (2) At the date of registration of 'phone4u.co.uk' an instrument of fraud had been created. (3) The judge wrongly characterised a large number of instances of deception as 'mere confusion'. The defendants' email evidence showed that customers of the appellant thought they were communicating with those who owned and ran the Phones4u shops. Examining the evidence, Jacob LJ could see 'clear and convincing evidence of damage to goodwill ... the emails collectively tell a clear story of people trying to contact and deal with or complain to or make inquiries of, Phones4u—the chain of shops they already knew.'[65] (4) The judge erred in placing significance on the parties' coexistence for five years without deception without first considering the extent of the defendants' use of the mark during that time which had been almost non-existent. Turning finally to the trade mark infringement claim, the court considered the effect of the colour limitations on the registration. Jacob LJ sought the view of the Registry before formally delivering the judgment. The Registry replied that the registrar has always regarded colour limitations on the face of the register to be a limitation of rights. On this advice, the court held that, despite the original certificate of registration and the original entry being in monochrome, the colour limitation stated on the register was effective to limit the registrations to the colours claimed. Had there not been such a limitation, Jacob LJ stated that the defendants' use of the words 'Phones4u' or a trivial variant would have infringed the appellant's trade mark.[66]

---

[63] per Slade LJ in *Chelsea Man v Chelsea Girl* [1987] RPC 189 at 202.
[64] [2006] EWCA Civ 244, [31].   [65] *ibid*, [37]–[38].   [66] *ibid*, [49]–[50].

Thus the appellants were ultimately victorious in their passing off claim but Jacob LJ criticised the long delay of four years between the original complaint and the commencement of proceedings. He quoted the words of James LJ in 1879: 'the very life of a trade mark depends on the promptitude with which it is vindicated'.[67] This decision tells us the courts are still willing to apply both trade mark law and the law of passing off to protect businesses from cybersquatters but the evolution of extrajudicial dispute resolution procedures has taken most claims outwith the judicial process.

12.5 **The ICANN UDRP**

The increasing numbers of domain name/trade mark disputes that were being taken to the courts in both the US and the UK had led to calls for a cheaper, more efficient, and more streamlined system of dispute resolution to be put in place. The opportunity to review the dispute resolution procedure applicable to the generic top level domains (including essentially the *.com* domain) arose in the late 1990s during a wide-ranging review of the management of generic top level domains.

From 1991, the registrar for generic top level domains had been a small private contractor called Network Solutions Inc. who had a complete monopoly over registrations in the *.com, .net,* and *.org* domain name space. By the mid 1990s, this monopoly was being challenged by campaigners who believed it was unsuitable given the developing commercial value of, in particular, *.com* domains. The campaigners proposed that Network Solutions monopoly be broken up, and that a not-for-profit organisation known as the Internet Society take over regulation of the domain name registration process.[68] To give effect to these proposals the Internet Society created a working group to take them forward. The group known as the International Ad-Hoc Committee announced they would create seven new top-level domain names which would compete with *.com* and Network Solution's monopoly.[69] The US Federal Government then entered the debate by directing that the Domain Name System should be privatised and that competition within the domain name system should be increased.[70] The campaigners for reform started working alongside the US National Telecommunications and Information Administration, the body was given management of the Federal domain name project, and between them they drew up the Bylaws for a new regulatory authority and set out that the body should have responsibility for, among other things, internet protocol addresses and domain names. On 1 October 1998, the new regulatory and management body for internet addressing was named: it would be known as the Internet Corporation for Assigned Names and Numbers (ICANN). The new regulator would be an American not-for-profit corporation managed by a representative Board of Directors drawn from

---

[67] *Johnston v Orr-Ewing* (1879) 13 Ch.D 434, 464.

[68] J. Postel, *New Registries and the Delegation of International Top Level Domains* (1996): http://www.watersprings.org/pub/id/draft-postel-iana-itld-admin-01.txt.

[69] *Final Report of the International Ad Hoc Committee: Recommendations for Administration and Management of gTLDs*, 4 February 1997: http://www.iahc.org/draft-iahc-recommend-00.html.

[70] The White House, *A Framework for Global Electronic Commerce*, 1 July 1997: http://www.technology.gov/digeconomy/framewrk.htm.

around the world.[71] By the terms of its Articles of Association it was authorised to take responsibility for several key areas of internet stability and governance.

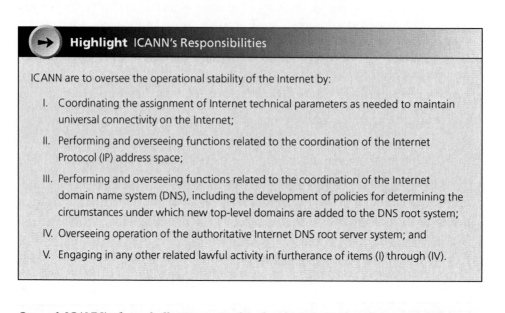

Highlight ICANN's Responsibilities

ICANN are to oversee the operational stability of the Internet by:

I. Coordinating the assignment of Internet technical parameters as needed to maintain universal connectivity on the Internet;

II. Performing and overseeing functions related to the coordination of the Internet Protocol (IP) address space;

III. Performing and overseeing functions related to the coordination of the Internet domain name system (DNS), including the development of policies for determining the circumstances under which new top-level domains are added to the DNS root system;

IV. Overseeing operation of the authoritative Internet DNS root server system; and

V. Engaging in any other related lawful activity in furtherance of items (I) through (IV).

One of ICANN's first challenges was the development of policies regulating the management and allocation of domain names to allow for competition in the registry market for the generic Top Level Domains *.net*, *.org*, and *.com*. To this end, ICANN set to work on its first active project; creating a register accreditation system that would allow new registries to enter the market. Trade mark holders were understandably apprehensive about any changes to be introduced into the market for domain names. They were concerned that by creating competition in the market for the generic Top Level Domains alternative routes for cybersquatting would open up. As a result of their fears trade mark holders sought specific assurances that the deregulation of the generic Top Level Domain market would not allow for the creation of alternative generic Top Level Domains[72] without systems having first been put in place to assure their marks adequate

---

[71] By section 6 of the Original Bylaws as passed on 6 November 1998, 'In order to ensure broad international representation on the Board, no more than one-half of the total number of At Large Directors serving at any given time shall be residents of any one Geographic Region, and no more than two of the Directors nominated by each Supporting Organization shall be residents of any one Geographic Region. As used herein, each of the following shall be a "Geographic Region": Europe; Asia/Australia/Pacific; Latin America/Caribbean Islands; Africa; North America. The specific countries included in each Geographic Region shall be determined by the Board, and this Section shall be reviewed by the Board from time to time (but at least every three years) to determine whether any change is appropriate.' See http://www.icann.org/general/archive-bylaws/bylaws-06nov98.htm.

[72] Alternative gTLDs such as .biz, .info, and .name had long been proposed as a simple way to create new markets and therefore competition. It was envisaged by many that Network Solutions could retain their monopoly in .com while alternate domains such as .biz were promoted by competing registries. Unfortunately the market penetration of the .com brand meant this was unlikely to succeed.

protection within these new markets.[73] In an attempt to meet these concerns the US Department of Commerce placed the trade mark holders' concerns at the centre of its proposed reforms, and made trade mark dispute resolution a key part of ICANN's mandate. The result was the creation of a new alternate dispute resolution (ADR) system applicable to those cases where the intellectual property right holder can establish that the domain name registration of the current holder is 'abusive'.[74]

→ Highlight Abusive Registration (ICANN Rules)

An abusive registration occurs when 'the domain name is identical or misleadingly similar to a trade or service mark in which the complainant has rights; and

(i) the holder of the domain name has no rights or legitimate interests in respect of the domain name; and

(ii) the domain name has been registered and is used in bad faith'.

The new policy, known as the ICANN Uniform Domain Name Dispute Resolution Policy (UDRP) was formally adopted on 24 October 1999. Although called the ICANN UDRP the dispute resolution component of the Policy is not to be supplied by ICANN itself. Rather it uses 'approved dispute-resolution service providers' who supply the panellists to hear claims and who manage the administration of complaints. ICANN announced on 29 November 1999 that the first approved dispute-resolution service provider would be the World Intellectual Property Organisation, who have since been joined by the National Arbitration Forum,[75] the Disputes.org/eResolution consortium,[76] the CPR Institute for Dispute Resolution,[77] and the Asian Domain Name Dispute Resolution Centre.[78] The first UDRP claim was raised on 9 December 1999, the domain name in dispute being worldwrestling-federation.com, an action which led to success for the claimant on 14 January 2000.[79]

The UDRP is a 'mandatory administrative procedure' meaning that all registrants who have registered in the generic top level domains administered by ICANN, are required to submit to the UDRP if a challenge is raised to their registration.

---

[73] World Intellectual Property Organisation, *The Management of Internet Names and Addresses:Intellectual Property Issues: Final Report of the WIPO Internet Domain Name Process*, 30 April 1999, Ch.5: http://arbiter.wipo.int/processes/process1/report/pdf/report.pdf; US Department of Commerce, *Management of Internet Names and Addresses*, Docket Number: 980212036-8146-02, 5 June 1998 at para.8: http://www.icann.org/general/white-paper-05jun98.htm.

[74] WIPO, *The Management of Internet Names and Addresses: Intellectual Property Issue, Final Report of the WIPO Internet Domain Name Process*, 30 April 1999, at [152]–[228]. Report at: http://arbiter.wipo.int/processes/process1/report/pdf/report.pdf.   [75] Approved on 23 December 1999.

[76] Approved on 1 January 2000. eResolution stopped accepting proceedings under the UDRP on 30 November 2001.

[77] Approved on 22 May 2000.   [78] Approved on 28 February 2002.

[79] *World Wrestling Federation Entertainment Inc v Michael Bosman* Case No. D99-0001: http://arbiter.wipo.int/domains/decisions/html/1999/d1999-0001.html.

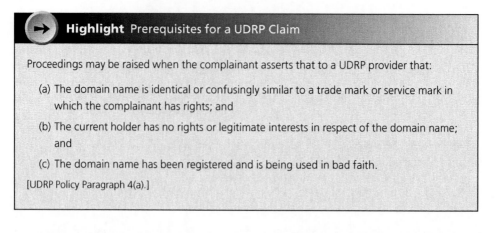

Highlight Prerequisites for a UDRP Claim

Proceedings may be raised when the complainant asserts that to a UDRP provider that:

(a) The domain name is identical or confusingly similar to a trade mark or service mark in which the complainant has rights; and

(b) The current holder has no rights or legitimate interests in respect of the domain name; and

(c) The domain name has been registered and is being used in bad faith.

[UDRP Policy Paragraph 4(a).]

The key aspect of this requirement is part (c), the question of whether the registrant is *mala fides*. This is explained further in paragraph 4(b) of the UDRP Policy where it is stated that a panellist may use as evidence that the registration and use of a domain name is in bad faith: (a) circumstances indicating that the registrant has registered or acquired the domain name primarily for the purpose of selling, renting, or otherwise transferring the domain name registration to the complainant who is the owner of the trade mark or service mark or to a competitor of that complainant, for valuable consideration in excess of documented out-of-pocket costs directly related to the domain name; or (b) the registrant has registered the domain name in order to prevent the owner of the trade mark or service mark from reflecting the mark in a corresponding domain name, provided that the registrant has engaged in a pattern of such conduct; or (c) the registrant has registered the domain name primarily for the purpose of disrupting the business of a competitor; or (d) by using the domain name, the registrant has intentionally attempted to attract, for commercial gain, internet users to their web site or other on-line location, by creating a likelihood of confusion with the complainant's mark as to the source, sponsorship, affiliation, or endorsement of their web site or location or of a product or service on their web site or location.

When faced with a complaint the registrant (or formally under the Policy the respondent) has a variety of defences set out in paragraph 4(c) of the Policy. These are: (a) the respondent has made use of, or demonstrable preparations to use, the domain name or a name corresponding to the domain name in connection with a bona fide offering of goods or services; or (b) the respondent has been commonly known by the domain name, even if they have not acquired any trade mark or service mark rights; or (c) the respondent is making a legitimate non-commercial or fair use of the domain name, without intent for commercial gain to misleadingly divert consumers or to tarnish the trade mark or service mark at issue.

The process itself is quick and simple. The complainant opens the dispute by filing a complaint with the provider of his choice and sending a copy to the respondent at the address shown on the Whois database.[80] At this point, the provider reviews

---

[80] See http://www.whois.net/.

the complaint for compliance with the UDRP rules. If the complaint is in compliance, the proceeding continues; if the complaint is noncompliant, the complainant has five days to remedy the deficiencies or the complaint will be deemed withdrawn. Within twenty calendar days of the complaint, the respondent must respond specifically to the allegations in the complaint and offer any defences which allow for the retention of the domain name (see above). The respondent will be deemed to have defaulted if no response is filed within this twenty day window. Assuming the respondent responds, after the receipt of the response, the provider has five days to appoint a panel to hear the dispute. The panel is usually made up of one independent panellist, but under certain conditions may consist of a panel of three panellists. The make-up of panels is detailed in paragraph 6 of the ICANN Rules for Uniform Domain Name Dispute Resolution Policy.[81] Basically this sets out that if neither party seeks the appointment of a three-member panel then a single panellist will be appointed by the dispute resolution provider.[82] However, under paragraph 6(c) if either the complainant or the respondent elects to have the dispute decided by a three-member panel, then the dispute resolution provider is required to convene a three-member panel consisting of one member selected by the complainant, one selected by the respondent and the third being appointed by then the dispute resolution provider.[83] Once appointed the panel decides the complaint by electronic communications and is required to make a decision within fourteen days of appointment, this decision to be notified to the parties within three days of being made. There is no right of appeal under the ICANN UDRP, although recourse may of course be made to the courts.

Since the first ICANN UDRP decision was issued in January 2000, the UDRP has handled over 18,500 complaints involving over 34,000 domain names.[84] This makes the UDRP by far the most successful and far-reaching aspect of ICANN's functions. Despite its popularity though, the UDRP has been heavily criticised. The most vociferous critic of the UDRP has probably been Professor Milton Mueller of Syracuse University. In his book, *Ruling the Root*, he describes the UDRP as: 'heavily biased in favour of complainants. It allows the trade mark holder to select the dispute provider, thereby encouraging dispute resolution providers to complete for the allegiance of trade mark holders. The resultant forum shopping ensures that no defendant friendly service provider can survive.'[85] This may explain the pre-eminence of the WIPO UDRP service, which is seen to be sympathetic towards trade mark holders' interests, which at 20 May 2005 had provided 6548 UDRP decisions (61% of all decisions), while collectively the other four UDRP providers had provided only 4185 decisions (39%). Another critic, Professor Michael Froomkin, focuses on the

---

[81] At: http://www.icann.org/dndr/udrp/uniform-rules.htm.
[82] *Rules* para. 6(b). Note: further the cost of appointing the panellist will be met by the complainant. There is no cost to the respondent under this scenario.
[83] The regulations on the selection and appointment of panellists in such cases are contained in *Rules* Paragraph 6(e). The fees for a three-member Panel shall be paid in their entirety by the complainant, except where the election for a three-member Panel was made by the respondent, in which case the fees shall be shared equally between the Parties.
[84] A survey of the decisions reported on the ICANN List of Proceedings under the Uniform Domain Name Dispute Resolution Policy website (http://www.icann.org/en/udrp/proceedings/date-index.html) on 27 April 2009 revealed that 18,754 proceedings had been raised involving 34,027 domain names.
[85] M. Mueller, *Ruling the Root: Internet Governance and the Taming of Cyberspace* (2002), 193.

procedure's failure to comply with some of the basic principles of natural justice. He notes that the UDRP 'would have little chance of surviving ordinary "arbitrary and capricious" review, because it denies respondents minimal levels of fair procedure that participants would be entitled to expect … three aspects of the UDRP are particularly troubling: (1) the incentive for providers to compete to be "complainant friendly"; (2) its failure to require actual notice combined with the short time period permitted for responses; and (3) the asymmetric consequences of a decision.'[86] Elsewhere, the current author has focussed upon the lack of training or experience of UDRP panellists, noting that 'almost half of all panellists employed by the two major UDRP providers[87] are untrained and inexperienced in adjudication'[88] and the potential bias of panellists noting: 'the WIPO UDRP panel contains a high proportion of intellectual property practitioners. Of the 193 WIPO panellists currently practicing within the legal profession 110 (57%) list a specialism in intellectual property. In addition, of the 41 academic lawyers listed, 22 (53.7%) are listed as intellectual property professors or lecturers. Although it is to be expected that a high proportion of UDRP panellists would be experienced in intellectual property law given the nature of the disputes in question, and although there is no claim here made of individual bias by panellists in favour of intellectual property rights holders, for those panellists involved in the practice of IP law it may be difficult to maintain neutrality as the major aspect of their full-time vocation is the protection of IP rights from erosion and this might be expected to mean that certain "habits of thought" are prevalent.'[89] The UDRP may therefore be classified as a policy which has been successful and popular with the community at large, but one which is controversial. But with much of ICANN's public image tied to the UDRP, ICANN has had to do everything possible to support the UDRP and its service providers.

12.6 **The nominet DRS**

Nominet UK set up their dispute resolution procedure in autumn 2001, with the first published 'Expert' decision coming on 15 November 2001.[90] Although based in part on the ICANN UDRP, there are essential differences between the Nominet DRS and the UDRP, most obviously the opportunity to obtain summary decision where the complaint is undefended, the addition of a mediation procedure in defended complaints, and the opportunity for an appeal against the decision of a Nominet Expert.

To raise a complaint the complainant must file a complaint with Nominet, either physically, or via the Nominet website.[91] The rules governing the complaint (and the response if one is forthcoming) are then to be found in the 'Procedure for the conduct

---

[86] M. Froomkin, 'Wrong Turn in Cyberspace: Using ICANN to Route around the APA and the Constitution', 50 *Duke Law Journal* 17, 136 (2000).

[87] The two major UDRP providers being WIPO and the National Arbitration Forum.

[88] A. Murray, 'Regulation and Rights in Networked Space' (2003) 30 *Journal of Law and Society* 187, 203.   [89] *ibid*, 216.

[90] *Eli Lilly & Company v Clayton* [2001] DRS 1.

[91] Although it should be noted a physical (signed) copy of the Complaint still requires to be lodged with Nominet.

of proceedings under the Dispute Resolution Service' (the Procedure).[92] Paragraph 3(c) of the Procedure sets out in full the requirements of the complaint document. There is a strict word limit of 5000 words (not including annexes and appendices);[93] it must specify how and where the complainant may be contacted;[94] specify (where known) the respondent's contact details;[95] set out the domain name which is the subject of the dispute and the name or mark which is identical or similar to the domain name and in which the complainant asserts it has rights;[96] and describe in accordance with the Dispute Resolution Policy the grounds on which the complaint is made including in particular: what rights the complainant asserts in the name or mark; why the domain name should be considered to be an Abusive Registration in the hands of the respondent; and discuss any applicable aspects of paragraph 3 of the Policy, as well as any other grounds which support the complainant's assertion.[97] This complaint if found to be valid is then sent by Nominet's DRS team to the respondent who has fifteen days to respond.[98] If no response is forthcoming the complainant can seek a summary decision.[99] If a response is received the complainant is then given a final five days to submit to them a reply to the respondent's response.[100] At the end of submission of the documents of pleading Nominet will (if both sides are engaged) refer the dispute to informal mediation under paragraph 7 of the Procedure. The mediation procedure is done by telephone and email and may last for up to ten days.[101] If mediation is unsuccessful, or if there is no reply to the complaint making mediation impossible, then the dispute may be referred to an independent 'Expert', who acts as an arbiter and decides the dispute under the DRS Policy.

To succeed under the DRS Policy a complainant must establish two things (1) that they have rights in respect of a name or mark which is identical or similar to the domain name;[102] and (2) that the domain name, in the hands of the respondent, is an Abusive Registration.[103] The first limb of this test is relatively easy to establish with the Appeal Panel in *Seiko UK Ltd v Designer Time/Wanderweb*, noting that '[t]he requirement to demonstrate "rights" is not a particularly high threshold test',[104] with among others personal names,[105] and registered company names[106] being sufficient to establish this limb of the test.

The second limb is more testing. To establish an Abusive Registration the complainant is referred to paragraph 3 of the Policy. Paragraph 3 sets out a number of situations in which Abusive Registration will be deemed to have occurred.

---

[92] Available from http://www.nominet.org.uk/disputes/drs/procedure/.
[93] DRS Procedure para.3(c)(i).   [94] *ibid*, [3(c)(ii)].   [95] *ibid*, [3(c)(iii)].
[96] *ibid*, [3(c)(iv)].   [97] *ibid*, [3(c)(v)].   [98] *ibid*, [5(a)].   [99] *ibid*, [5(e)].
[100] *ibid*, [6(a)].   [101] *ibid*, [7(e)].
[102] DRS Policy para. 2(a)(i). Note 'Rights' are defined as: 'rights enforceable under English law. However, a Complainant will be unable to rely on rights in a name or term which is wholly descriptive of the Complainant's business' in para. 1 of the Policy.
[103] *ibid*, para.2(a)(ii). Note an 'Abusive Registration' is defined as: 'a Domain Name which either: (i) was registered or otherwise acquired in a manner which, at the time when the registration or acquisition took place, took unfair advantage of or was unfairly detrimental to the Complainant's Rights; OR (ii) has been used in a manner which took unfair advantage of or was unfairly detrimental to the Complainant's Rights' in para.1 of the Policy.
[104] [2002] DRS 248,[9].   [105] *Stoneygate 48 Ltd v Rooney* [2006] DRS 3844.
[106] *J F Home Improvements Ltd v Giddy* [2005] DRS 3051.

> **→ Highlight** Abusive Registration (Nominet Rules)
>
> Abusive Registration occurs when there are:
>
> i. Circumstances indicating that the Respondent has registered or otherwise acquired the Domain Name primarily for the purposes of selling, renting, or otherwise transferring the Domain Name to the Complainant or to a competitor of the Complainant, for valuable consideration in excess of the Respondent's documented out-of-pocket costs directly associated with acquiring or using the Domain Name; OR as a blocking registration against a name or mark in which the Complainant has Rights; OR for the purpose of unfairly disrupting the business of the Complainant;
>
> ii. Circumstances indicating that the Respondent is using the Domain Name in a way which has confused people or businesses into believing that the Domain Name is registered to, operated or authorized by, or otherwise connected with the Complainant;
>
> iii. The Complainant can demonstrate that the Respondent is engaged in a pattern of registrations where the Respondent is the registrant of domain names which correspond to well known names or trade marks in which the Respondent has no apparent rights, and the Domain Name is part of that pattern.
>
> In addition, under Paragraph 3(c), Cybersquatters who are engaged in the process of warehousing domain names are caught by a specific provision that 'there shall be a presumption of Abusive Registration if the Complainant proves that Respondent has been found to have made an Abusive Registration in three or more Dispute Resolution Service cases in the two years before the Complaint was filed.

Once the complainant has established a *prima facia* case the burden of proof switches to the respondent. Paragraph 4 of the Policy contains a non-exhaustive list of factors which may be evidence that the domain name is not an Abusive Registration. These are: Before being aware of the complainant's cause for complaint, the respondent has used or made demonstrable preparations to use the domain name or a domain name which is similar to the domain name in connection with a genuine offering of goods or services; OR the respondent has been commonly known by the name or legitimately connected with a mark which is identical or similar to the domain name; OR the respondent made legitimate non-commercial or fair use of the domain name; OR the domain name is generic or descriptive and the respondent is making fair use of it.[107]

Perhaps unsurprisingly these defences have been the subject of a great degree of criticism and discourse. Possibly the most controversial decision was that of *Ryanair Ltd v Coulston*.[108] The respondent in that dispute was an individual called Michael Coulston. Mr Coulston once had a bad experience when travelling with Ryanair in which his luggage was temporarily lost and his holiday ruined, since when he devoted some considerable time and energy to publicising what he perceives as deficiencies in the way in

---

[107] In relation to fair use para. 4(b) of the Policy states: 'Fair use may include sites operated solely in tribute to or in criticism of a person or business.'   [108] [2006] DRS 3655.

which Ryanair deals with problems and complaints by its customers. He does this under the campaign name the 'Ryanair Refund Campaign'. As part of his activities he registered the domain name *ryanair.org.uk* on 20 September 2003 and used it as the address for his campaign by hosting a site critical of Ryanair.

Mr Coulston claimed he made a non-commercial fair use of the name as permitted under paragraph 4 of the Policy. Ryanair claimed that the actions of Mr Coulston were designed to confuse Ryanair customers (and potential customers) and as such were for the purpose of unfairly disrupting the business of the complainant in breach of paragraph 3. In deciding the dispute the Expert, Anna Carboni, found that 'Although I do not have full details of the chronology of statements and information posted to the Respondent's website, it is probable—as he asserts—that his initial purpose in registering the Domain Name was to tell his own story of the lost baggage and to comment on the Complainant's customer complaints policies. Nevertheless, my findings in relation to the inherent likelihood of confusion in adopting an essentially identical Domain Name to the mark Ryanair, lead me to conclude that the Domain Name was from the start registered in a manner which took unfair advantage of and was unfairly detrimental to the Complainant's Rights and, as such, was an Abusive Registration.'

Unsurprisingly there has been a great deal of criticism of this decision with many commentators suggesting that it somehow is a restriction on the right to free speech. But if one examines the decision closely it is clear that it turned on some very narrow facts. Mr Coulston lost because the domain name *ryanair.org.uk* was simply too close in character to the complainant's *ryanair.co.uk* and customers were being confused. Mr Coulston admitted in his evidence that the emails he received at *ryanair.org.uk* were predominantly (in descending order of frequency): (1) Spam; (2) messages from people who urgently need to change or correct booking details; (3) messages from people who have not received a confirmation of a booking; (4) messages from people with general Ryanair questions (e.g. about baggage allowances); (5) messages from people wanting to criticise Ryanair; and (6) messages from people wanting to praise Ryanair. Thus it is clear people were confusing his site with the official Ryanair site when it came to opening communications with the airline.[109] The decision of the Expert was really that Mr Coulston's name selection for his site was deliberately chosen to mirror the name of the 'official' website which directly caused confusion. Mr Coulston was free to choose a more fitting domain name for his site such as *ryanaircampaign.org*, which he did and which following a further complaint by the airline to the ICANN UDRP was ruled not to be in bad faith.[110]

Once an Expert decision is made either party then has fifteen days to lodge an appeal.[111] If an appeal is made an appeal panel of three Experts is convened. The appeal panel considers all the evidence laid before the Expert at the original hearing and may additionally consider two further documents, an appeals notice and an appeal notice response, both of which are limited to one thousand words. The panel has complete discretion to review all evidence from the original hearing and may make decisions

---

[109] Admittedly this may have been out of frustration as Ryanair offer no means of communication except by premium rate telephone number.
[110] *Ryanair Ltd v Michael Coulston* WIPO Case No. D2006-1194 (December 12 2006).
[111] DRS Procedure, para. 18.

by majority.[112] Once the appeal decision is made the DRS is closed and the only route of further recourse open to the parties is to refer their dispute to the courts.

12.6.1 Reviewing the nominet DRS

The DRS has proven to be extremely robust. It has dealt with 6,998 disputes (to 20 April 2009), with 1,042 cases being referred to an independent Expert for decision. Very few cases have left the DRS for the courts and in the one case where an attempt was made to bypass the DRS procedure by seeking a judicial review of the DRS it met dismal failure. That case involved the domain name *itunes.co.uk* which had been registered by a company called Cyberbritain Group Ltd. A DRS Claim was raised by Apple Computer Inc., owners of the iTunes brand. The *itunes.co.uk* registration had been made before the UK trade mark application was published. However, Apple Computer Inc's complaint related only to the later use of the name. In her decision the independent Expert, Claire Milne, found that following the launch of Apple's iTunes music download service this use included: (1) direction of traffic on the domain to a website owned by an associate company of Cyberbritain Group Ltd; (2) an offer to sell the domain name to Napster; (3) direction of traffic to Napster under an affiliate scheme (from which profit would be generated); and (4) an offer to sell the domain name for £50,000. On the basis of these findings, the Expert found that the registration was abusive and ordered transfer.

Mr Cohen (the owner of Cyberbritain Group Ltd) stated following the decision that he would not use the DRS appeals procedure but instead he intended to apply for judicial review. Cyberbritain Group duly started judicial review proceedings. Apple Computer, Inc. joined as an interested party and Nominet argued that (a) they were not subject to judicial review and (b) failure to use the appeal stage of the DRS barred Cyberbritain from seeking judicial review. Apple Computer, Inc. also argued that Cyberbritain had waited too long to apply. At an initial hearing the judge rejected the application to judicially review Nominet, citing the failure to use the appeal process and the delay. He avoided the question of whether they were judicially reviewable, as he did not need to decide it. The domain name has since been transferred to Apple Computers, Inc. as decided by the Expert. Thus the DRS is a success story, and with the recent review of the DRS conducted by Nominet promising further developments of the DRS procedure,[113] it may be recorded as one of the success stories of internet regulation.

12.7 Brand identities, search engines and secondary markets

Although the ADR procedures offered by among others ICANN and Nominet remain the most commonly employed procedures with respect to online content with on average 293 cases raised per month under the ICANN UDRP alone in 2009, much recent focus

---

[112] To date (April 2009) there have been only twenty-seven appeals. Of these the original decision has been upheld in fourteen cases and overturned in thirteen.

[113] See http://www.nominet.org.uk/policy/consultations/updatedrs/.

on the interaction between trade marks and the digital environment has been on the employment of marks by search engines and secondary markets such as eBay. This is due to a greater reliance on search engines such as Google when locating data leading to a diminution of the role of domain names.

12.7.1 **Secondary markets**

There has been a recent explosion of litigation globally in this subject with much of the early case law being found in the US and in France. In particular France, as home of many luxury goods brands, has been at the forefront of these claims. In the past three years luxury goods brands Louis Vuitton Malletier, Christian Dior Couture, SA Parfums Christian Dior and Hermes have won a series of cases in France against eBay for the misuse of their trade marks on the eBay site to describe counterfeit goods. In June 2008 in particular a series of cases established the liability of eBay for allowing the abuse of trade marks in this fashion on their eBay France site. On 4 June at the Tribunal de grande instance de Troyes, in the case of *Hermes v eBay*,[114] eBay was found to have 'committed acts of counterfeit' and 'prejudice' by failing to monitor the authenticity of goods being sold on its web site by a user identified as 'Mrs. Cindy F'. As a result they were ordered to pay Hermes damages of €20,000 and to block the user from the eBay site.

This case was though a mere appetizer for the later joined cases of *Louis Vuitton Malletier v eBay*; *Christian Dior Couture v eBay* and *SA Parfums Christian Dior v eBay*.[115] In all three cases eBay were found to have operated a site which supported both the trade in counterfeit goods and the illegal sale of genuine goods without a license of the trade mark holder. The cases related to a number of luxury goods brands and items including Dior and Louis Vuitton handbags and clothes as well as Guerlain, Givenchy and Kenzo perfumes and cosmetics. In total damages amounting to €38.6 million were awarded to the claimants and eBay were banned from selling four perfumes—Christian Dior, Kenzo, Givenchy and Guerlain in France. It appears the court was swayed by two particular facts. The first was that although eBay were aware that up to 90% of Louis Vuitton bags and Dior perfumes advertised on its site were counterfeit they took no steps to police the practice apart from issuing guidance to customers on how to spot fakes. The second is that eBay would advertise on their home page that they had for sale the items in question, thus attracting trade to their site. Both sides have appealed the decision (the claimants on the basis that the court should have ordered eBay to stop all trade in all listed trade marks) and at the time of writing the appeal is pending, but even as this chapter is finalised more decisions come out of France enhancing the position taken in the LVM cases. On 18 September 2009 the Tribunal de Grande Instance de Paris awarded damages of €80,000 to LVM for trade mark infringement. This award was very different to the previous awards as it related not to the practice of selling counterfeit goods but rather to the eBay's use of LVM's trade marks in buying Google Ads. In making this decision the French court is acting quite unilaterally and in breach of a recent European ruling in the case of *Google France v Louis Vuitton Malletier* discussed below.[116]

---

[114] Decision available in French from: http://www.legalis.net/jurisprudence-decision.php3?id_article=2320.   [115] Tribunal de Commerce de Paris, 30 June 2008.

[116] Joined Cases C-236/08, C-237/08 and C-238/08: http://curia.europa.eu/jurisp/cgi-bin/gettext.pl?lang=en&num=79909077C19080236&doc=T&ouvert=T&seance=CONCL

France is famously protective of luxury brands with a high proportion of global brands domiciled there. Attempts by LVM, and others, to extend the principles seen in the French jurisprudence to other jurisdictions have met with less success. An action by luxury jeweller Tiffany against eBay before the US District Court for the Southern District of New York saw eBay found not liable for the misuse of the Tiffany trade mark on counterfeit items sold via eBay.com.[117] District Judge Sullivan found that 'Tiffany has failed to demonstrate that eBay knowingly encouraged others to dilute Tiffany's trademarks. Rather, to the extent that eBay may have possessed general knowledge of infringement and dilution by sellers on its website, eBay did not possess knowledge or a reason to know of specific instances of trademark infringement or dilution as required under the law.'[118] At the time of writing this case is also subject to an appeal, with the Second Circuit Court of Appeal hearing argument in July 2009 and a decision expected soon. Counsel for Tiffany argued that eBay's institutional efforts to root out counterfeits fail to do enough to fight the sale of counterfeit goods. This, Tiffany claims harms both eBay's customers and Tiffany's reputation for quality jewellery. The outcome of the appeal will rest upon the Court's interpretation of the decision of the US Supreme Court in *Inwood* v. *Ives*,[119] which renders a third party liable if they 'intentionally induce another to infringe a trademark or if they continue to supply their product to one whom it knows or has reason to know is engaging in trademark infringement.' Counsel for eBay is arguing that while *Inwood* does apply in this case, it is the decision's finding relative to a third party's 'specific knowledge' that is most relevant. In that regard eBay argues that *Inwood* supports its position that it acts appropriately when notified about specific suspicious goods.

This issue has also been visited by the UK courts. In the recent decision in *L'Oreal v eBay*,[120] Mr Justice Arnold was asked to rule on whether eBay's failure to prevent the sale of counterfeit L'Oreal products, as well as the use of L'Oreal trade marks in both Google advertisements and on the eBay front page infringed L'Oreal's rights under the TMA. In an extensive and wide-ranging judgement he considered a number of issues:

1. Were the goods sold by the fourth to tenth defendants infringing goods?
2. Are eBay Europe jointly liable for any infringements committed by the fourth to tenth defendants?
3. Are eBay Europe liable as primary infringers for use of the Link Marks in relation to infringing goods?
4. Do eBay Europe have a defence under Article 14 of the E-Commence Directive?
5. Do L'Oréal have a remedy under Article 11 of the Enforcement Directive?
6. Are the Distance Selling Regulations relevant to any of the foregoing issues, and if so how?

The key issues for our purposes are issues 2–5. In relation to issue 2, Arnold J found that 'as a matter of domestic common law, eBay Europe are under no legal duty or obligation to prevent infringement of third parties' registered trade marks.'[121] This decision was

---

[117] *Tiffany v eBay* 576 F.Supp. 2d 460 (2008).   [118] *ibid*, 523.
[119] *Inwood Laboratories v Ives Laboratories* 456 US 844 (1982).
[120] [2009] EWHC 361 (Ch).   [121] *ibid*, [375].

reached after a lengthy examination of eBay's responsibilities under the common law of tort as interpreted in cases such as *CBS Songs Ltd v Amstrad Consumer Electronics plc.*[122] and *Unilever plc. v Gillette (UK) Ltd.*[123] Interestingly though Arnold J noted that he must 'qualify my answer ... because eBay Europe may come under such a duty or obligation with regard to future infringements as a result of the operation of Article 11 of the Enforcement Directive, but that does not affect their liability for past infringements.'[124]

This leads to issue 5, will eBay be held liable under Article 11 of the Enforcement Directive? It was noted by Arnold J that the UK has not fully implemented Article 11, which arguably means UK law is not fully compliant with the Directive: 'the United Kingdom has not taken any specific steps to implement the last sentence of Article 11, but instead has relied upon its pre-existing law as being in compliance with that provision. It is not entirely clear, however, that English law is fully compliant with that provision.'[125] Counsel for L'Oreal argued that an injunction may be granted 'on a somewhat obscure equitable principle known as the equitable protective jurisdiction as set out by Buckley LJ in *Norwich Pharmacal Co v Customs & Excise Commissioners* [1974] AC 133 that 'If a man has in his possession or control goods the dissemination of which, whether in the way of trade or, possibly, merely by way of gifts will infringe another's patent or trade mark, he becomes, as soon as he is aware of this fact, subject to a duty, an equitable duty, not to allow those goods to pass out of his possession or control at any rate in circumstances in which the proprietor of the patent or mark might be injured by infringement ensuing. The man having the goods in his possession or control must not aid the infringement by letting the goods get into the hands of those who may use them or deal with them in a way which will invade the proprietor's rights. Even though by doing so he might not himself infringe the patent or trade mark, he would be in dereliction of his duty to the proprietor. This duty is one which will, if necessary, be enforced in equity by way of injunction.'[126] Arnold J considered that on this basis he should apply Article 11, but noted that he was not giving it direct effect,[127] but upon examining case law on Article 11 from across Europe concluded that 'the scope of the obligation placed on Member States by the third sentence of Article 11, and in particular the scope of the injunction which it requires to be available against intermediaries, is unclear.'[128] On this basis he decided he could not make an injunction without first referring the case to the European Court of Justice.

Turning to issue 3 Arnold J determined that in his opinion the display of the sponsored links to users does constitute use of the signs in question by eBay, that they were carried out in the course of trade and that they were used in the UK.[129] Did their use infringe? Arnold J felt it was likely they did but noted this was not *acte clair* and so noted this was also an issue for the ECJ. In particular he was influenced by the fact that the ECJ is considering the joined cases of *Google France v Louis Vuitton Malletier*,[130] which deal with precisely this issue. These cases, Arnold J noted, were also dealing with issue 4, the question of whether intermediaries such as eBay or Google may have a defence under Article 14 of the e-commerce directive. For this reason he ruled these issues should both be referred to the ECJ.

---

[122] [1988] AC 1013.   [123] [1989] RPC 583.
[124] [2009] EWHC 361 (Ch), [375].   [125] *ibid*, [447].   [126] *ibid*, [452].   [127] *ibid*, [454].
[128] *ibid*, [465].   [129] *ibid*, [384–412].   [130] Above n. 116.

As a result of the number of matters Arnold J found not to be *acte claire* the central outcome of the case was a referral to the ECJ. A number of findings and references were ultimately made:

(i) eBay Europe are not jointly liable for the infringements committed by the fourth to tenth defendants.

(ii) Whether eBay Europe have infringed the Link Marks by use in sponsored links and on the Site in relation to infringing goods again depends upon a number of questions of interpretation of the Trade Marks Directive upon which guidance from the ECJ is required.

(iii) Whether eBay Europe have a defence under Article 14 of the E-Commerce Directive is another matter upon which guidance from the ECJ is needed.

(iv) As a matter of domestic law the court has power to grant an injunction against eBay Europe by virtue of the infringements committed by the fourth to tenth defendants, but the scope of the relief which Article 11 requires national courts to grant in such circumstances is another matter upon which guidance from the ECJ is required.

The final outcome of the case will therefore not be known for some time. It seems though that as UK Law stands the activities of secondary market operators such as eBay do not in themselves breach the provisions of domestic or European trade mark law, although active support of an illegal trade in either counterfeit or black market goods would. In contradistinction though, Arnold J suggests that the use of trade marks in advertising and promotion without the authorisation of the trade mark holder may infringe the rights of the trade mark holder, but this he concedes is a matter best dealt with by the ECJ. At several points in his judgement he mentions that there is a case already before the ECJ on this issue. This case is, at the time of writing, not concluded, but we do have the opinion of the Advocate General which usually points to the outcome of the case.

12.7.2 Search engines

The case referred to by Arnold J is *Google France v Louis Vuitton Malletier.*[131] This involved three references from the Cour de Cassation all relating to the same issue and involving substantively the same parties. Each reference involved the use by Google of trade mark terms in generating sponsored adverts in relation to keywords used in searches, such as adverts for eBay in relation to the search term 'Vuitton'. In particular the claimants objected to Google listing their trade marks as trigger words to prospective advertisers: thus an advertiser seeking to promote her site selling designer handbags would be advised by Google to buy the trigger term 'Vuitton'. At the heart of the case was a common question in all three references: 'Is there the possibility of a trade mark infringement consisting in allowing the selection of keywords which corresponded to those trade marks, and in advertising sites offering identical or similar products.'

---

[131] *ibid.*

As mentioned a ruling in the case is not yet available but on 22 September 2009 the Advocate General, AG Maduro, issued his opinion in the cases. He found that 'The selection by an economic operator, by means of an agreement on paid internet referencing, of a keyword which will trigger, in the event of a request using that word, the display of a link proposing connection to a site operated by that economic operator for the purposes of offering for sale goods or services, and which reproduces or imitates a trade mark registered by a third party and covering identical or similar goods, without the authorisation of the proprietor of that trade mark, does not constitute in itself an infringement of the exclusive right guaranteed to the latter under Article 5 of First Council Directive 89/104/EEC of 21 December 1988 to approximate the laws of the Member States relating to trade marks.'[132] In other words, the actions of Google in using a trade mark as a keyword trigger for a targeted advertisement does not constitute trade mark infringement unless there is some aggravating factor. He goes on to explain that the actions of Google may be seen to be similar to comparative advertisement: 'Article 5(1)(a) and (b) of Directive 89/104 and Article 9(1)(a) and (b) of Council Regulation (EC) No 40/94 of 20 December 1993 on the Community trade mark must be inter- preted as meaning that a trade mark proprietor may not prevent the provider of a paid referencing service from making available to advertisers keywords which reproduce or imitate registered trade marks or from arranging under the referencing agreement for advertising links to sites to be created and favourably displayed, on the basis of those keywords. In the event that the trade marks have a reputation, the trade mark propri- etor may not oppose such use under Article 5(2) of Directive 89/104 and Article 9(1)(c) of Regulation No 40/94.'[133]

This is an extremely robust opinion of the AG. He is suggesting that rules on dilution, as well as rules on infringement may not be used to simply defeat the appli- cation of a trade mark as a keyword trigger for online advertising either through search engines such as Google or in price comparison sites such as Pricerunner. It is a com- plete defeat for the trade mark holder. The only grain of comfort is the suggestion that if the information intermediary acts in a manner which demonstrates they intend to abuse the trade mark they cannot gain protection under Article 14 of the e-commerce Directive.[134]

This opinion should be treated with some caution as the full decision is yet to be published. It is possible that the Justices of the ECJ will depart from the opinion of AG Maduro. However this decision accords with the previous UK decision in *Wilson v Yahoo!*,[135] in which Morgan J applied the principle from *Arsenal Football Club plc v Reed*,[136] that 'The proprietor may not prohibit the use of a sign identical to the trade mark for goods identical to those for which the mark is registered if that use cannot affect his own interests as proprietor of the mark having regard to its functions',[137] to decide that Mr Wilson, holder of the trade mark 'Mr Spicy' could not object to its use by Yahoo! and Pricegrabber in sponsored advertising and price comparison.

---

[132] *ibid*, [155].   [133] *ibid*.
[134] AG Maduro notes [at 155] 'The provider of the paid referencing service cannot be regarded as providing an information society service consisting in the storage of information provided by the recipient of the service within the meaning of Article 14 of Directive 2000/31/EC.'
[135] [2008] EWHC 361 (Ch).   [136] [2003] ETMR 19.   [137] *ibid*, [54].

The combined effect of these decisions suggests that both when the ECJ gives its full opinion in *Google France* and when it considers the reference in *L'Oreal* it is likely that the practice of using trade marks in targeted advertisements, price comparison listings and front page promotional advertising will be found to be permissible unless there is additional evidence to suggest specific abuse of the trade mark has taken place. Further the decision in *L'Oreal*, as well as the recent *Tiffany* decision in the US, suggests that the hard-line approach against secondary market operators seen in France is out of step, a fact perhaps confirmed by the recent decision of the Brussels Court of Appeal in the case of *Ralph Lauren v eBay*[138] which held eBay did not infringe RL's trade marks in purchasing Google adwords in Belgium. It seems likely therefore that once all this settles down the ECJ will harmonise the law in line with what we have seen in *L'Oreal* and *Ralph Lauren* and the hard line French approach will be confined. There is little doubt that the issue of secondary markets and paid for advertising will continue to the form the focus of online trade mark disputes in the foreseeable future but it is likely a commonsense approach, along the lines of that set out by Arnold J. in *L'Oreal* will eventually come to the fore.

12.8 **Conclusion**

To suggest that domain names and brand identifiers such as trade marks fulfil the same function is wrong, but to say they have similar functions (and often values) is right. The protection of brand identity, and brand values, online has been at the forefront of much litigation in recent years. The incredible growth of the domain name system caught out those who seek to protect traditional IP portfolios and those who regulated the domain name system were caught out by the huge potential values of what they had on offer. The early cases of cybersquatting, domain name warehousing, and concurrent use demonstrated a 'clash of cultures' between the two. The arrival of the extrajudicial dispute resolution procedures at the turn of the millennium have done much to solve this problem. Although neither the ICANN UDRP, nor the Nominet DRS are perfect they are bridging the divide between the two cultures and may be put down as one of the few successes of 'internet law'.

More recently the focus of trade mark holders has therefore turned to the invisible use of the brands and marks in search engine listings, particularly sponsored advertisements, and to the regulation of secondary markets which arguably support a trade in counterfeit goods. With no common approach a divide has grown, in particular between the French hard line approach and the approach of most other jurisdictions. The decision of the ECJ in *Google France* will go some way to harmonising things at a European level, but until the ECJ also rules on secondary market infringement, probably in the *L'Oreal* referral there will remain a divide between France and the rest of Europe on the regulation of secondary market providers, and in particular eBay. The next five years should see much development of the law in this area.

---

[138] Brussels Court of Appeal, 11 February 2009, 2008/AR/719.

FURTHER READING

Books

M. Mueller, *Ruling the Root: Internet Governance and the Taming of Cyberspace* (2002)

T. Willoughby, S. Abel & T. Bettinger, *Domain Name Law and Practice: an International Handbook* (2005)

Chapters and Articles

M. Froomkin, 'Wrong Turn in Cyberspace: Using ICANN to Route around the APA and the Constitution' 50 *Duke Law Journal* 17

A. Murray, 'Internet Domain Names: The Trade mark Challenge' [1998] *IJLIT* 285

S. Dogan & M. Lemley, 'Trademarks and Consumer Search Costs on the Internet' 41 *Houston Law Review* 777 (2004)

A. Cheung & K. Pun, 'Comparative Study on the Liability for Trade Mark Infringement of Online Auction Providers' [2009] *EIPR* 559.

J. Cornthwaite, 'AdWords or bad words? A UK Perspective on Keywords and Trade Mark Infringement' [2009] *EIPR* 347

PART IV

Criminal activity in the information society

The information society offers opportunities for criminals as well as law abiding citizens. How does the law reduce the risks of criminal activity in the information society?

13 Computer misuse

13.1 Hacking

13.2 Viruses, criminal damage, and mailbombing

13.3 Denial of service and supply of devices

14 Pornography and obscenity in the information society

14.1 Obscenity

14.2 Pornography

14.3 Child abuse images and pseudo images

14.4 Age play

14.5 Extreme pornography

14.6 Private regulation of pornographic imagery

14.7 Conclusions

15 Crime and law enforcement in the information society

15.1 Fraud and identity theft

15.2 Grooming, harassment, and cyberstalking

15.3 Cyberterrorism

15.4 Bandwidth theft

15.5 The convention on cybercrime

15.6 Conclusion

Computer misuse

Computer misuse is the collective term for a number of criminal offences committed by means of a computer, often through access to the internet and which are regulated by the Computer Misuse Act 1990 (as amended). These include computer hacking (unauthorised access); the creation and distribution of computer viruses and other malware; and denial of service attacks. The need for specific legislation in this area became clear in the winter of 1984 when two computer hackers Stephen Gold and Robert Schifreen gained unauthorised access to the BT Prestel computer network and successfully accessed several secure areas of the service.[1]

Their story began in spring 1984 when they obtained a Prestel username and password. There are a variety of tales as to how they did this, and neither has ever confirmed the truth. What does appear to be the case is that they did not obtain these details by watching a Prestel engineer enter his username and password at a trade show as is widely reported on some internet sites.[2] It would appear the password and username were either obtained through the acquisition of a private phone book belonging to a BT engineer[3] or by the actions of Robert Schifreen attempting a variety of passwords and usernames until one was accepted, a so-called 'brute force attack'.[4] Whatever approach was used it appears Prestel did not take security seriously. The Prestel network required that a username was always a ten-character string of letters and/or numbers, and that a password was a four-character string. The username/password combination discovered by Gold and Schifreen was 2222222222/1234. Using this new found information Gold and Schifreen spent a considerable amount of time on the Prestel network. They identified

---

[1] Prestel was an early commercial computer network service in the UK. Prestel was a 'Videotex' system: that is a system similar to traditional teletext systems operated by terrestrial TV broadcasters. It could carry text and simple graphics across telephone lines for display on a domestic TV via a Prestel terminal. It was operated by the Post Office (BT) and allowed access to a wide range of Prestel content supplied by the Post Office and by third parties as well as allowing for emailing between Prestel customers. Prestel was for a while an important commercial service used by banks, financial institutions, travel agents, and media organisations to supply and trade data and to carry out transactions. It even led to the first online banking service in the UK, Homelink, a cooperation between the Nottingham Building Society and the Bank of Scotland.

[2] See Wikipedia, *Entry for Computer Misuse Act*, http://en.wikipedia.org/wiki/Computer_Misuse_Act; Micro Mart, *Whatever Happened to Prestel?*: http://www.micromart.co.uk/features/article/default.aspx?id=22625.

[3] Hugo Cornwall, *The Hacker's Handbook* (1995), 209. Hugo Cornwall was the pseudonym of Peter Sommer, now Research Fellow in Information Systems Security at the London School of Economics.

[4] P. Mungo & B. Glough, *Approaching Zero: The Extraordinary Underworld of Hackers, Phreakers, Virus Writers and Keyboard Criminals* (1993), 34.

several weaknesses in Prestel's security and gained system manager-level access when, in October 1984, in another security breach, a BT engineer left his log-in details on his log-in page.[5] They soon learned how to enter subscription-only areas of Prestel, accessing valuable commercial services providing investment advice for clients of the stockbroker Hoare Govett and commentaries and news reports on international currency markets supplied by the Financial Times, as well as accessing the Homelink internet banking system.[6] Their most infamous act though was to begin their downfall. They managed to gain access to subscribers' personal email accounts, including the email account of the Duke of Edinburgh. One hacker (it is not clear which) sent an email, allegedly from the Duke to the Prestel System Manager, saying 'I do so enjoy puzzles and games. Ta ta. Pip! Pip! HRH Hacker.'[7] This act, along with a further act which could only have been carried out by a Prestel engineer with the highest network clearance (or a hacker with similar clearance)[8] caused BT to reset all system manager passwords and then set a trap for the hackers. They were soon identified and were arrested on 10 April 1985.

The problem for the authorities was what were they to be charged with? It was not clear that they had committed a criminal act. There was no theft or damage to property and although there was deception it was not clear they had committed fraud. The authorities could not simply let them go for that would send the signal that hacking was okay. Eventually it was decided that they would be charged under s. 1 of the Forgery and Counterfeiting Act 1981, which states: 'A person is guilty of forgery if he makes a false instrument, with the intention that he or another shall use it to induce somebody to accept it as genuine, and by reason of so accepting it to do or not to do some act to his own or any other person's prejudice.' The argument of the Crown was that the defendants had infringed this provision as when asked to log in to the Prestel network they had given false details. In the words of counsel for the Crown '[t]he relevant instrument was the control area of the user segment of the relevant Prestel computer whilst it had recorded and/or stored within it the electronic impulses purporting to be a customer identification number and customer password.'[9]

The problem for the Crown was the definition of 'instrument' found in s. 8 of the Act. This states than an 'instrument' is 'any document, whether of a formal or informal character . . . [including] any disc, tape, sound track or other device on or in which information is recorded or stored by mechanical, electronic or other means.'[10] This suggests a degree of permanence is required, but in the Prestel system the username and password were only held for a fraction of a second while the system authenticated them.

---

[5] Cornwall, above n. 3, 209.

[6] *ibid*, 210–211. It was noted though that they could not transfer money on the Homelink system due to external security measures put in place by the Nottingham Building Society and the Bank of Scotland. It is not clear whether they attempted to do so.

[7] *ibid*, 211. In another 'prank' they managed to issue a FT newsflash claiming that the pound was worth fifty dollars on international currency exchanges.

[8] The act itself was a minor one. It was the nature of the way it was carried out which forced Prestel to act. It is reported by Mungo & Glough, above n. 4, in some detail: 'When subscribers dial into Prestel, they immediately see page one, which indexes all other services. Only the system manager can alter or update listings on this page, but [Schifreen], exploiting his [system manager] status, made a modest change and altered the word Index to read Idnex. Though it was perfectly harmless, the change was enough to signal to Prestel that its security had been breached. The other pranks had been worrisome, but altering the first page was tantamount to telling Prestel that its entire system was insecure.': 36.   [9] *R. v Gold and Schifreen* [1988] 1 AC 1063, 1064.

[10] Forgery and Counterfeiting Act 1981, s. 8(1)(a), (d).

At trial the defendants were found guilty and fined.[11] Both immediately appealed and before the Court of Appeal argued, among other things that 'in the context of section 8(l)(d), storage does not include temporary storage in the input buffer because it is immediately passed elsewhere; and (b) the instrument is not *ejusdem generis* with disc, tape and sound track since there was no evidence that the device was in any way physically altered. The impulses always remained separate from the device itself.'[12] The Court of Appeal upheld their claim. In giving the judgement of the Court Lord Lane CJ found that 'the user segment in the instant case does not carry the necessary two types of message to bring it within the ambit of forgery at all. Moreover, neither the report nor the Act, so it seems to us, seeks to deal with information that is held for a moment whilst automatic checking takes place and is then expunged. That process is not one to which the words "recorded or stored" can properly be applied, suggesting as they do a degree of continuance.'[13] On this basis the Court found that 'the language of the Act was not intended to apply to the situation which was shown to exist in this case ... It is a conclusion which we reach without regret. The Procrustean attempt to force these facts into the language of an Act not designed to fit them produced grave difficulties for both judge and jury which we would not wish to see repeated.'[14]

The Crown appealed to the House of Lords, but were unsuccessful in their attempts to have the decision of the Court of Appeal overturned. Lord Brandon of Oakbrook gave the opinion of the Court that 'section 8(l)(d) contemplates that information may be recorded or stored by electronic means on or in (i) a disc, (ii) a tape, (iii) a sound track (presumably of a film) and (iv) devices other than these three having a similar capacity. The words "recorded" and "stored" are words in common use which should be given their ordinary and natural meaning. In my opinion both words in their ordinary and natural meaning connote the preservation of the thing which is the subject matter of them for an appreciable time with the object of subsequent retrieval or recovery. Further, in relation to information recorded or stored on or in a disc, tape or sound track, that is the meaning of the two expressions which appears to me to be clearly intended. For both these reasons I have reached the conclusion that the respondents' case on the first question is right and that the Crown's case on it is wrong.'[15] He then went out of his way to criticise the Crown for prosecuting this case in this manner.

> **→ Highlight** Lord Brandon's Rebuke
>
> I share the view of the Court of Appeal (Criminal Division), as expressed by Lord Lane CJ, that there is no reason to regret the failure of what he aptly described as the Procrustean attempt to force the facts of the present case into the language of an Act not designed to fit them.

The Crown had lost the first case on computer hacking in the UK and had done so in a blaze of publicity and with a stinging rebuke from both the Court of Appeal and the House of Lords. There was a great deal of concern both that the UK was unable to deal

---

[11] *R. v Gold and Schifreen* [1987] QB 1116, 1117.   [12] *ibid*, 1118–1119.   [13] *ibid*, 1124.
[14] *ibid*.   [15] *R. v Gold and Schifreen* [1988] 1 AC 1063, 1072–1073.

with the growing threat of computer hacking and that the outcome of this case may encourage others to take up hacking as a hobby.[16] Against this background moves were made to introduce a new Act which would close this loophole in the Criminal Law. The Law Commission and the Scottish Law Commission produced a joint report recommending that a new offence of unauthorised access to computer data be created,[17] and in the next Parliamentary sitting Conservative MP Michael Colvin sponsored a Private Member's Bill which would give effect to the Law Commissions' recommendations: the Bill, supported by the Government, became the Computer Misuse Act 1990.

13.1 **Hacking**

The Act in its original form was remarkably concise comprising only eighteen sections with no Schedules. This may be due to the origins of the Act as a Private Member's Bill rather than as a Government Bill. The meat of the Act was in its part I (ss. 1–3) entitled 'Computer Misuse Offences'. Here were to be found three new criminal offences, the unauthorised access offence; the aggravated unauthorised access offence; and the unauthorised modification offence. The first two of these were designed to deal with computer hacking.

Section 1, the main hacking provision, is a well designed criminal law provision. It does not use colloquial terms such as 'hacking',[18] 'phreaking',[19] or 'cracking'[20] and instead simply defines the illegal activity. It states:

> **→ Highlight** Computer Misuse Act, s. 1
>
> A person is guilty of an offence if:
>
> (a) he causes a computer to perform any function with intent to secure access to any program or data held in any computer;
>
> (b) the access he intends to secure is unauthorised; and
>
> (c) he knows at the time when he causes the computer to perform the function that that is the case.

[16] It is suggested by Mungo & Glough that the outcome of this case encouraged another young hacker Nick Whitely to begin a campaign which included wiping data from university networks as well as computer firm ICL, a practice which led to him being dubbed 'the Mad Hacker' Mungo & Glough, above n. 4, 39–41.

[17] Law Commission Report No. 186, *Computer Misuse* (Cm. 819), 1989.

[18] Strictly speaking a hacker is anyone who displays skilled software development. They are not always malicious and the term is often applied to skilled programmers working in all aspects of software development.

[19] Phreaking is using a computer or other device for tricking telephone systems to obtain free calls. Phreaking used to be common when internet access was obtained on a cost-per-minute dial-up account. It is less common now with ADSL and similar packages.

[20] A cracker, rather than a hacker, is someone who breaks into someone else's computer system, bypasses passwords or licenses in computer programs; or in other ways intentionally breaches computer security.

Despite its clarity and brevity several questions remained. The first was what was meant by unauthorised access generally: was this an offence designed to prevent hacking as portrayed in the media, that is using one computer to gain access to another, or could the unauthorised access be simply the obtaining of access to a single computer by accessing it directly without permission? In other words to commit the section one offence did one need to hack into a computer or network from an external source? Guidance could be found in s. 17(5) which stated that:

Access of any kind by any person to any program or data held in a computer is unauthorised if—

(a) he is not himself entitled to control access of the kind in question to the program or data; and

(b) he does not have consent to access by him of the kind in question to the program or data from any person who is so entitled.

This seemed to clearly suggest the latter approach was correct and that access could include direct access to a single computer. This, though, was thrown in doubt when the case of *R. v Cropp* was heard before Snaresbrook Crown Court.[21] Mr Cropp was charged with unauthorised access to a computer with intent to commit a further offence under s. 2 of the Computer Misuse Act 1990. He had returned to the premises of an ex-employer to purchase goods on behalf of his current employer. When left alone by the salesperson for a few minutes Mr Cropp entered a discount code onto the Point of Sale computer effecting a 70% discount on the goods sold meaning that his new employer was invoiced for only £204.60 (plus VAT) instead of £710.96 (plus VAT). His activity was traced and he was charged but when he came to trial the defence counsel entered a plea of no case to answer. The grounds for this claim were that in order to contravene s. 1(1) (and therefore s. 2(1)) of the Act the prosecution had to establish that the accused had used one computer to gain access to another computer. Somewhat surprisingly the judge upheld the submission, finding that: 'It seems to me, doing the best that I can in elucidating the meaning of s. 1(1)(a), that a second computer must be involved. It seems to me to be straining language to say that only one computer is necessary when one looks at the actual wording of the subsection: "Causing a computer to perform any function with intent to secure access to any program or data held in any computer."'

This outcome caused consternation for the Crown. It had been assumed that unauthorised access meant any access: this decision threatened to limit the scope of the Act extensively. As a result the Attorney-General sought clarification of this issue from the Court of Appeal by way of an Attorney-General's reference.[22] The Court of Appeal ruled that the judge in *Cropp* had erred. Lord Taylor, CJ gave the opinion of the Court.

The ordinary cannons of construction require this court to look at the words of the section and to give them their plain and natural meaning. Doing that, we look again at the relevant words. They are, 'he causes a computer to perform any function with intent to secure access to any program or data held in any computer.'

Mr Lassman argued successfully before the judge and sought to argue before this court, that the final phrase, 'held in any computer' should really be read as 'held in any other computer' or alternatively should be read 'held in any computer except the computer which has performed the function'.

---

[21] *R. v Cropp*, Snaresbrook Crown Court, 5 July 1991, unreported, but see case note at (1991) 7 CLSR 168.   [22] *AG's Reference No. 1 of 1991* [1992] 3 WLR 432.

To read those words in that way, in our judgement, would be to give them a meaning quite different from their plain and natural meaning. It is a trite observation, when considering the construction of statutes, that one does not imply or introduce words that are not there when the plain and natural meaning is clear. In our judgement there are no grounds whatsoever for implying or importing the word 'other' between 'any' and 'computer' or excepting the computer which is actually used by the offender from the phrase 'any computer' at the end of subsection 1(a).[23]

This was a relief for the law enforcement bodies. If the Court of Appeal had confirmed the original outcome of the case the Computer Misuse Act could have been emasculated at its first application.[24] As it was by confirming that the unauthorised access offences could be committed on a single computer they opened up a further role for ss. 1 and 2. They had confirmed it could be used not only to prosecute the traditional computer hacker as imagined and portrayed in the media it could also be applied to employees who accessed data held on their employer's computers without permission.

13.1.1 **Employee hackers**

In the few years following promulgation of the Computer Misuse Act there were a number of cases involving employee misuse of their employer's resources: many centred on abuse of the Police National Computer system (PNC) by serving police officers and civilian support staff.

The first was *R. v Bennett*.[25] Superintendent Bennett used the PNC to identify his ex-wife's new partner by using details he had gathered on him by observation. Superintendent Bennett pled guilty to a breach of s. 1 and was fined £150. Several subsequent cases followed including *R. v Bonnett* in which a special constable was convicted under s. 1 for unlawfully accessing the PNC without authority to find out who owned the car registration number BON1T, because he wanted to buy it,[26] and *R. v Begley*, in which a WPC used the PNC to access records in an attempt to track down a woman who had had a relationship with her boyfriend.[27] These cases, and many similar cases from the private sector,[28] were easily dealt with by the courts. They were simple criminal prosecutions where the only question was whether or not the accused had committed the infringing act. The first major challenge to the application of ss. 1 and 2 to these 'insider hackers' was to come in the case of *DPP v Bignell*.[29]

---

[23] *ibid*, 437.
[24] E. Dumbill, 'Computer Misuse Act 1990—Recent Developments', (1992) 8 *Computer Law and Practice* 105.
[25] Unreported, Bow Street Magistrates' Court, 10 October 1991.
[26] Unreported, Newcastle-under-Lyme Magistrates' Court, 3 November 1995.
[27] Unreported, Coventry Magistrates' Court. This case, and the others discussed in this section are discussed in M. Wasik, 'Computer misuse and misconduct in public office', (2008) 22 *International Review of Law, Computers & Technology* 135.
[28] Private sector cases included *R. v Borg* in which a computer officer at a financial services firm was cleared of unlawfully accessing her employer's system with a view to defrauding £1 million, and *R. v Speilmann* in which an ex-employee of a financial news service was found guilty of a breach of s. 1 in accessing his ex-employer's system to modify and delete emails. Details of these unreported cases, and many others may be found at *http://www.computerevidence.co.uk/Cases/CMA.htm*.
[29] [1997] EWHC Admin 476; [1998] Cr.App.R. 1.

Bignell was another in the series of cases involving misuse of the Police National Computer. The respondents were two married police officers Paul and Victoria Bignell. They accessed the PNC to extract details of motor vehicles owned by a Mr Howells, the new partner of PC Bignell's ex-wife for purposes not entirely clear from the case report. At trial at Bow Street Magistrates' Court both defendants were found guilty of breaching s. 1 of the Computer Misuse Act and were fined. As a conviction would mean though that they were both likely to lose their jobs as police officers they appealed this decision. On appeal they challenged the decision of the Stipendiary Magistrate on the basis that 'their use of the computer, even if it was found to be for private purposes, was not within the definition of "unauthorised access" provided by s. 17(5) of the Act because the access had been with authority even though that authority was used for an unauthorised purpose.'[30]

This extremely complex and convoluted defence became known as the defence of 'authorised access for unauthorised purpose'. Basically the respondents were arguing that despite the fact they were using the PNC for purposes for which they were not authorised to use it, they did have authority to use the computer system meaning that broadly their access was authorised, it was only their purpose which was not. As the Act states that the s. 1 offence is committed when 'the access he intends to secure is unauthorised'[31] no offence was committed.

This appeal was upheld at Southwark Crown Court in September 1996 but the Crown appealed to the Divisional Court. The appeal was heard by Astill J and Pill LJ. On 16 May 1997 they issued their judgement: they would reject the appeal and uphold the decision of the Crown Court. The decision of the Court was given by Astill J. He examined both the original Law Commission Report and the wording of s. 17 before concluding that the respondents were entitled to access data contained on the PNC as part of their normal duties as Police Officers; therefore they were entitled to access the data, although their purpose for accessing it may have been unauthorised. Astill J attempted to quell concerns that this left employers with little control over how employees used their computer systems by pointing out that 'The authority of the Commissioner is not undermined because the respondents remain subject to internal disciplines. The use of the computer for an unauthorised purpose involves the use of a false Reason Code and that is a matter subject to disciplinary procedures. In addition the respondents could have been prosecuted under the Data Protection Act 1984.'[32]

There has been a considerable amount of analysis of the *Bignell* decision.[33] While some acknowledge that the Crown may have erred in not raising a prosecution under the Data Protection Act,[34] most commentators were highly critical of the outcome.

---

[30] [1997] EWHC Admin 476, [4].   [31] Computer Misuse Act 1990, s. 1(1)(b).
[32] [1997] EWHC Admin 476, [17].
[33] See, e.g. C. Gringras, 'To be great is to be misunderstood: the Computer Misuse Act 1990' (1997) 3 *Computer and Telecommunications Law Review* 213; Z. Hamin, 'Insider Cyber-threats: Problems and Perspectives' (2000) 14 *International Review of Law, Computers and Technology* 105; Wasik, above n.27.
[34] To be fair to the Crown an earlier attempt to prosecute a serving Police Officer under the Data Protection Act 1984 for extracting data from the PNC with a view to passing it on to a friend who worked for a debt collection agency had failed. See *R. v Brown* [1996] 1 AC 543.

The problem was the way Astill J. had interpreted ss. 17(2) and 17(5). Section 17(2) states that:

> A person secures access to any program or data held in a computer if by causing a computer to perform any function he—
>
> (a) alters or erases the program or data;
>
> (b) copies or moves it to any storage medium other than that in which it is held or to a different location in the storage medium in which it is held;
>
> (c) uses it; or
>
> (d) has it output from the computer in which it is held (whether by having it displayed or in any other manner);

While s. 17(5) states:

> Access of any kind by any person to any program or data held in a computer is unauthorised if:
>
> (a) he is not himself entitled to control access of the kind in question to the program or data; and
>
> (b) he does not have consent to access by him of the kind in question to the program or data from any person who is so entitled.

Astill J concluded that 's. 17(2)(a) to (d) sets out four ways in which a person secures access. S. 17(5)(a) and (b) define unauthorised access by reference to access "of the kind in question". That refers to the four kinds of access set out in s. 17(2)(a) to (d) and the respondents did have authority to secure access by reference to s. 17(2)(c) and (d) at least. It therefore follows that "control access of the kind in question" in s. 17(5)(a) must apply to the respondents because they were authorised to secure access by s. 17(2) (c) and (d).'[35] Thus for Astill J s. 17(5) is tied to s. 17(2), but as has been pointed out by several commentators this should not be the case.

Clive Gringras notes that 'the Bignells instructed that a false "reason code" be typed into the police national computer. Why? They wanted the computer to perform this function to allow them to gain access to data which were "not necessary for the efficient discharge of genuine police duties". In other words, they were not authorised to secure access to the data. The offence should have been made out. The reason that the court did not come to this conclusion was because they did not restrict their analysis of the facts with the precise wording of the statute. The Act is drafted in terms of "causing a computer to perform a function" together with the intention to "secure unauthorised access to any program or data". It is therefore an error in law for the court of have provided a judgment littered with references to "accessing a computer". The Act does not sanction those who access computers; it sanctions those who use computers to secure access to data and programs. This difference is fundamental and because it was not appreciated by the Divisional Court we, those who rely on the safety of the material stored by computers, are left again waiting for an appeal to set straight the Act.'[36]

David Bainbridge was equally forthright, 'As part of their normal duties, the police officers were entitled to access such computer information. *But being entitled to access computer material is not the same as being entitled to control access to such material. This is an important and crucial distinction which the court failed to make.*'[37] What Astill J had

---

[35] [1997] EWHC Admin 476, [17].   [36] Gringras, above n. 33, 215.
[37] D. Bainbridge, *Introduction to Information Technology Law* (6th ed., 2008), 443 (emphasis added).

failed to do was distinguish between 'access to data', as defined under s. 17(2) which forms the *actus reus* of the offence under s. 1(1)(a) and '*unauthorised* access' as defined by s. 17(5) and which forms the *mens rea* of the offence under s. 1(1)(b). In effect the Divisional Court had fused the two elements together leaving what David Bainbridge called 'an unsatisfactory gap in the Computer Misuse Act 1990'.[38]

The opportunity for the courts to revisit *Bignell* came quickly. Sometime between January 1996 and March 1997 Joan Ojomo, an employee of American Express working in the credit section of the company's office in Florida, gained access to customer accounts and extracted confidential information which she passed on to others, including a Mr Adeniyi Allison who was resident in London. The information she gave to him and others was then used to encode other blank credit cards which could then be used fraudulently to buy goods and to obtain money from ATMs. Miss Ojomo was arrested, and as a result of the subsequent investigation Mr Allison was arrested and held in London on suspicion of conspiracy to: (1) secure unauthorised access to the American Express computer system with intent to commit theft; (2) secure unauthorised access to the American Express computer system with intent to commit forgery, and (3) cause unauthorised modification to the contents of the American Express computer system. At committal the Magistrate declined to commit Mr Allison on the first two charges but did commit him on the third. The US Government then sought extradition of Mr Allison, while Mr Allison brought a *Habeas Corpus* claim on the basis that none of the offences were extradition offences. A series of cross appeals from both the US Government and Mr Allison emerged before on 13 May 1998 the Divisional Court certified a question of law of general public importance:

> Whether, on a true construction of s. 1 (and thereafter s. 2) of the Computer Misuse Act 1990, a person who has authority to access data of the kind in question none the less has unauthorised access if:
>
> (a) the access to the particular data in question was intentional,
>
> (b) the access in question was unauthorised by a person entitled to authorise access to that particular data,
>
> (c) knowing that the access to that particular data was unauthorised.

The case, *R. v Bow Street Magistrates Court and Allison, ex parte Government of the US of America*,[39] was heard on 13 July 1999 with the full judgement issued on 5 August 1999. This was remarkable timing. It had been just over two years since the *Bignell* decision and now the House of Lords had been referred a case on exactly the same point of law. The decision of the House was given by Lord Hobhouse. He found first of all that offences committed under ss. 2 or 3 were clearly extraditable as s. 15 of the Act clearly stated that they were to be so.[40] The question then remained had there been an offence under either of these sections? It was clear that in her daily work it was possible for Miss Ojomo to access all customer accounts held on the American Express database but she was only authorised to access those accounts that were assigned to her. However she had accessed various other accounts and files which had not been assigned to her and

---

[38] *ibid.*   [39] [2000] 2 AC 216.   [40] *ibid*, 222–223.

which she had not been given specific authority to work on. This meant the Court had to revisit the *Bignell* decision and determine whether these activities of Miss Ojomo were in breach of s. 2.

Lord Hobhouse was extremely critical of the approach taken in *Bignell*, he found that the decision of Astill J 'introduces a number of glosses which are not present in the Act. The concept of control is changed from that of being entitled to authorise to authorised to cause the computer to function. The concept of access to a program or data is changed to access to the computer at a particular "level" [and] he characterised the defendants as persons who had "control access" (using the word "control" as a noun) "of the kind in question." It was this use of language, departing from the language of the statute and unnecessary to the decision of that case, which misled the magistrate and the Divisional Court in the present case.'[41] The actual interpretation of 'control' and 'access' was in his Lordship's opinion much simpler:

> Section 17 is an interpretation section. Subsection (2) defines what is meant by access and securing access to any programme or data. It lists four ways in which this may occur or be achieved. Its purpose is clearly to give a specific meaning to the phrase 'to secure access.' Subsection (5) is to be read with subsection (2). It deals with the relationship between the widened definition of securing access and the scope of the authority which the relevant person may hold. That is why the subsection refers to 'access of any kind' and 'access of the kind in question.' Authority to view data may not extend to authority to copy or alter that data. The refinement of the concept of access requires a refinement of the concept of authorisation. The authorisation must be authority to secure access of the kind in question. As part of this refinement, the subsection lays down two cumulative requirements of lack of authority. The first is the requirement that the relevant person be not the person entitled to control the relevant kind of access. The word 'control' in this context clearly means authorise and forbid. If the relevant person is so entitled, then it would be unrealistic to treat his access as being unauthorised. The second is that the relevant person does not have the consent to secure the relevant kind of access from a person entitled to control, i.e. authorise, that access.
>
> Subsection (5) therefore has a plain meaning subsidiary to the other provisions of the Act. It simply identifies the two ways in which authority may be acquired—by being oneself the person entitled to authorise and by being a person who has been authorised by a person entitled to authorise. It also makes clear that the authority must relate not simply to the data or programme but also to the actual kind of access secured. Similarly, it is plain that it is not using the word 'control' in a physical sense of the ability to operate or manipulate the computer and that it is not derogating from the requirement that for access to be authorised it must be authorised to the relevant data or relevant programme or part of a programme. It does not introduce any concept that authority to access one piece of data should be treated as authority to access other pieces of data 'of the same kind' notwithstanding that the relevant person did not in fact have authority to access that piece of data. Section 1 refers to the intent to secure unauthorised access to any programme or data. These plain words leave no room for any suggestion that the relevant person may say: 'Yes, I know that I was not authorised to access that data but I was authorised to access other data of the same kind.'[42]

Bignell was overruled and a commonsense approach prevailed. Lord Hobhouse clearly set out the different roles of s. 17(2) and s. 17(5). Authority to access data was to the specific data, or for a specific purpose, there was to be no aggregation of data as 'data of a specific

---

[41] *ibid*, 225.   [42] *ibid*, 223–224.

kind' as set out in *Bignell*. Because Miss Ojomo had no permission to access the specific data in question her access was unauthorised and therefore in breach of section 1. Further because this access was secured with the intent to go on and commit fraud this was an extraditable offence under s. 2.

Allison remains the leading case on unauthorised employee, or insider, hacking. Employees who access data without authority risk prosecution under the Computer Misuse Act, even if they are authorised to access other data of that type. The *Allison* principle has been applied in several subsequent but unreported cases including *R. v Culbert*,[43] in which an ex-employee of Associated Newspapers pled guilty to two counts of making an unauthorised modification to a computer system and one of gaining unauthorised access after he offered to damage his employer's computerised print centre in return for £600,000, and *R. v Carey* in which a computer engineer deleted a number of design drawings over a dispute about payment.[44] The risk of insider hacking remains high as was recorded in recent reports by the Audit Commission[45] and the Office of the Information Commissioner,[46] but prosecution for more serious breaches continues to discourage this type of attack.

13.1.2 **External hackers**

Of course when the Computer Misuse Act was passed it was external hackers in the mould of Stephen Gold and Robert Schifreen which most people had in mind. The Act has also been successfully applied to a variety of such attacks in the twenty years it has been in force. Following the *Cropp* decision a number of cases followed including *R. v Goulden*[47] in which a software contractor in dispute with a client over unpaid fees 'locked' the client's computer system by installing a security program and refusing to hand over the password until his fees were paid was fined £1,650 and *R. v Pryce*[48] in which teenage hacker Richard Pryce, aka the 'Datastream Cowboy' pled guilty to twelve charges of unlawful access after accessing websites operated by among others, Lockheed Martin and the US Air Force.

The most famous early case was probably the 'addicted hacker' case *R. v Bedworth*.[49] Paul Bedworth, along with co-accused Karl Strickland and Neil Woods, was charged under ss. 1 and 3 of the Computer Misuse Act. Together they formed a group called Eight Legged Groove Machine (8LGM). They gained access to a number of high pro-file networks including JANET (the Joint Academic Network), the National Assessment Agency, BT, The Financial Times, and the European Commission. Once in they often left messages signed 8LGM or 'eight little green men'. They did not meet, or even know each other or their real names until they were introduced by the arresting officers; all contact was by bulletin boards. Strickland and Woods entered guilty pleas and both

[43] Unreported, Southwark Crown Court, 13 October 2000.
[44] Unreported, Hove Crown Court, 19 September 2002.
[45] The Audit Commission, *ICT Fraud and Abuse*, June 2005.
[46] Office of the Information Commissioner, *Annual Report 2004*, July 2004, 34–36.
[47] Southwark Crown Court, *The Times*, 10 June 1992.
[48] Unreported, Bow Street Magistrates' Court, 21 March 1997.
[49] Unreported, Southwark Crown Court 21 May 1993.

were sentenced to six months in prison.[50] Bedworth however pled not guilty. For some reason the prosecution had charged him with conspiracy to commit offences under ss. 1 and 3 of the Computer Misuse Act, rather than the direct offences. Why this was done is not clear as he appeared to be equally culpable with his co-accused. In any event Bedworth claimed he was addicted to computer use and by virtue of that addiction was unable to form the necessary intent. The defence called expert witnesses to impress upon the jury that Bedworth had an addiction described as 'computer tendency syndrome' and the jury duly acquitted, despite the fact that the Judge had made it clear to the jury that obsession and dependence were no defence to criminal charges. This outcome was surprising, and was heavily criticised.[51] It appears though to be a unique case. At the time there was a considerable amount of concern that the case would establish a precedent which would be followed by other defendants, but this has not turned out to be the case, instead it seems that the jury was influenced by the defendant's background: at the time he was eighteen and about to start university. If so he can count himself most fortunate.

Cases of external attacks prosecuted under ss. 1 and 2 continue to be seen with some regularity. Few are reported but the evidence suggests that although incidences of external hacking attacks remain high the law is quite effective in dealing with offenders. Some recent cases have helped clarify a few of the remaining ambiguities surrounding s. 1. In *Ellis v DPP (No. 1)* the appellant appealed against three convictions under s. 1.[52] Mr Ellis was an ex-student and alumnus of the University of Newcastle upon Tyne. On three occasions he had used non-open access computers on campus to browse the internet. Mr Ellis did this knowing he was not permitted to use these computers for this purpose having been previously advised by an administrative officer at the university that as an alumnus he could only make use of public access computers in the library. On each occasion Mr Ellis did not enter a false password or make any other false declaration to gain access to the computers as they had been left logged in by authorised users who had failed to log out after using them.[53] The question for the court was whether using a logged in terminal without permission was unauthorised access under s. 1. Judgement was given by Lord Woolf, CJ. He found that s. 1 was 'sufficiently wide to cover the use which was made of the computers by the appellant',[54] and that the 'evidence of Mr Hulme, the administrative officer, was perfectly satisfactory evidence on which the magistrates could decide that the appellant was aware that he was unauthorised to use the computers in the way which he did.'[55] As a result the Divisional Court upheld Mr Ellis's convictions.

A further ambiguity was clarified in the later case of *R. v Cuthbert*.[56] Mr Cuthbert made a donation through the Disasters Emergency Committee (DEC) website to support the Asian Tsunami Appeal in the aftermath of the natural disaster on 26 December 2004 but

---

[50] *R. v Strickland, R. v Woods*, Unreported, Southwark Crown Court 21 May 1993.

[51] See among others: Computer Weekly, *The Case of the Artful Dodger*, 25 March 1993; C. Christian 'Down and Out in Cyberspace', (1993) 90 *Law Society Gazette* 2; A. Charlesworth, 'Addiction and Hacking' (1993) *New Law Journal* 540.

[52] *Ellis v DPP (No.1)* [2001] EWHC Admin 362.

[53] Mr Ellis in interview drew an analogy between what he did with the computers and picking up someone else's discarded newspaper to read. *Ibid*, [8].   [54] *ibid*, [16].

[55] *ibid*, [17].   [56] Unreported, Horseferry Road Magistrates' Court 6 October 2005.

became suspicious as to the veracity of the site when he did not receive an immediate acknowledgement of his donation. As he was a freelance information security consultant he decided to test the security of the website by increasing his privileges to see if he could find anything amiss. In so doing he was caught by the site's security measures and reported to the authorities. Given that Mr Cuthbert's actions were in good faith he was surprisingly prosecuted and at trial he was fined £400 plus costs.[57] In sentencing, District Judge Purdy said that it was 'with some considerable regret' that he passed down a guilty verdict, but the Act made it quite clear that Cuthbert had knowingly performed unauthorised actions against DEC's systems.[58] This case makes clear that intent does not affect the applicability of section 1. Although Mr Cuthbert was of good intention, he was still strictly guilty of the unauthorised access offence. This has led some commentators to suggest that professionals involved in testing security systems could find themselves liable to prosecution under the Computer Misuse Act, but as Richard Walton points out 'penetration testing for security purposes is a legitimate and legal activity. The starting point for all such testing is the cooperation and authorisation of the owners of the system under test. No unauthorised activity is involved and so no breach of the CMA can occur. Uninvited security testing is a form of vigilanteism that is not legitimate and clearly breaches the CMA. Professionals avoid this sort of behaviour.'[59]

Recently focus on ss. 1 and 2 of the Computer Misuse Act have been on two very different issues. The Police and Justice Act 2006 has made several amendments to ss. 1–3 of the Computer Misuse Act.[60] The new provisions came into force on 1 October 2008 at the date of writing had not been applied by the courts.[61] The key change made by the amendment is that penalties for the s. 1 offence are increased with considerable extensions to penalties available for cases prosecuted on indictment. When the Computer Misuse Act was introduced s. 1 was a summary offence only with the maximum penalty being 'imprisonment for a term not exceeding six months or to a fine not exceeding level 5 on the standard scale or to both'.[62] This was quite different to the s. 2 offence which carried much heavier penalties on indictment 'on conviction on indictment, to imprisonment for a term not exceeding five years or to a fine or to both.'[63] With the enactment of s. 35 of the Police and Justice Act 2006 the s. 1 offence is now indictable with a maximum penalty much closer to the s. 2 offence of 'imprisonment for a term not exceeding two years or to a fine or to both.'[64] The reason for this

[57] He also lost his job as a freelance information security consultant at ABN Amro Bank.
[58] Reported in R. Walton, 'The Computer Misuse Act' (2006) 11 *Information Security Technical Report* 39, 43.   [59] *ibid*, 43–44.
[60] The bulk of the amendments are to s. 3 and the introduction of a new s. 3A. These will be discussed below.
[61] They were brought into force by The Police and Justice Act 2006 (Commencement No. 9) Order 2008, SI 2008/2503.   [62] s. 1(3).
[63] s. 2(5)(b). Section 2 could also be charged as a summary offence in which case the maximum penalty would be 'imprisonment for a term not exceeding six months or to a fine not exceeding the statutory maximum or to both', s. 2(5)(a).
[64] s. 1(3)(c). It should also be noted that in England and Wales the maximum sentence on summary procedure is now 'imprisonment for a term not exceeding 12 months or to a fine not exceeding the statutory maximum or to both' (s. 1(3)(a)), this perversely means that on summary procedure the maximum penalty under the basic unauthorised access offence (the s. 1 offence) is now greater than the maximum penalty under the ulterior intent offence (the s. 2 offence) as the Police and Justice Act leaves s. 2 unamended.

extension is to be found in the All Party Internet Group Report: *Revision of the Computer Misuse Act.*[65] There they outline that 'Raising the tariff to one year would make the offence extraditable. Making s. 1 indictable would make it possible to prosecute for a criminal attempt at the offence, viz: it would not have to actually succeed.'[66] Thus by making s. 1 an indictable offence with a maximum penalty of two years imprisonment it achieves this double aim. This has not been uncontroversial, particularly against the highly charged political debate surrounding the Computer Misuse Act and extradition centred on the Gary McKinnon case.

13.1.3 **The McKinnon case**

Gary McKinnon is at the centre of much current debate of the scope and application of anti-hacker legislation. McKinnon is a UK hacker who gained access to a number of US military sites including the Department of Defense, the US Army, Navy, and NASA. He appears to have been originally motivated by a desire to discover evidence of extraterrestrial visits and technologies which he, in common with other UFOlogists, believes are held in US military files. Whatever his original motivation McKinnon gained entry to a number of sensitive systems including 53 Army computers, 26 Navy computers, 16 NASA computers, and one at the Department of Defense. It is alleged he gained access to administrative accounts and installed unauthorised remote access and administrative software called 'remotely anywhere' that enabled him to access and alter data upon these computers at any time and without detection by virtue of the program masquerading as a Windows operating system. He appears to have become more political in his intentions as time went by posting a message on one computer 'US foreign policy is akin to Government-sponsored terrorism these days … It was not a mistake that there was a huge security stand down on September 11 last year … I am SOLO. I will continue to disrupt at the highest levels … '[67]

McKinnon was tracked down by the UK National Hi-Tech Crime Unit and was arrested in March 2002 for breaches of the Computer Misuse Act.[68] He was bailed to appear before the courts on 9 October 2002 but was informed in September 2002 that he would not need to appear as the US authorities had decided not to proceed with an extradition request.[69] Then in June 2005 he was arrested pursuant to an extradition request from the US Government. By then the controversial Extradition Act 2003 had been brought into force making it easier for the US authorities to extradite McKinnon. Between June 2005 and summer 2010 McKinnon and his supporters have repeatedly challenged the right of the US authorities to extradite him, which if successful could see him charged under USA-PATRIOT Act of 2001 which could lead to a maximum prison sentence of seventy

---

[65] All Party Internet Group, *Revision of the Computer Misuse Act*, June 2004: http://www.apcomms.org.uk/apig/archive/activities-2004/computer-misuse-inquiry/CMAReportFinalVersion1.pdf.

[66] *ibid*, [93].

[67] *McKinnon v Government of the USA and Secretary of State for the Home Department* [2007] EWHC 762 (Admin), [8].

[68] I. Grant, 'US took 39 months to demand McKinnon's extradition', *Computer Weekly*, 19 January 2009: http://www.computerweekly.com/Articles/2009/01/19/234303/us-took-39-months-to-demand-mckinnons-extradition.htm.   [69] *ibid*.

years in prison. He has to date unsuccessfully challenged the Home Secretary's decision to issue a extradition certificate before the Divisional Court[70] and the House of Lords.[71]

Following his defeat in the House of Lords McKinnon signed a statement admitting offences under the Computer Misuse Act, including under s. 2 and s. 3. He hoped that this may convince the Crown Prosecution Service to prosecute him in the UK under UK Law. Following this his case was referred to the Director of Public Prosecutions, but on 26 February 2009 the CPS issued a statement: 'Having reached our conclusions on these matters, as is our wider duty in accordance with the Attorney General's guidance for handling criminal cases in the USA, we also reconsidered in which jurisdiction the case is best prosecuted—and that remains the US.'[72] Currently McKinnon is only one step away from extradition; this is the outcome of a final Judicial Review action in which McKinnon's legal team argue that due to his recently diagnosed Asperger's Syndrome, the decision to certify his extradition is illegal as the Secretary of State failed to account for this supervening event which affects McKinnon's human rights as he was required to do under s. 6 of the Human Rights Act 1998.[73] If McKinnon loses this review, which seems likely, he is likely to be extradited.

This case has been highly controversial for many reasons. Most commentaries focus on the long delay between McKinnon's first arrest in 2002 and his subsequent arrest in 2005. This also meant that the 2003 Extradition Act applied to the eventual extradition request, an Act which itself has been the subject of controversy for the procedure it put in place wherein at the extradition hearing stage requests from the USA, Canada, Australia, and New Zealand are no longer required to be supported with evidence of a *prima facia* case against the accused. The key controversy though is why McKinnon was never charged under the Computer Misuse Act. There is no doubt the UK authorities could have charged McKinnon in 2002 or subsequently. For the Act to apply the act must have a connection with the UK, this is defined under s. 5(2) as being *either* '(a) that the accused was in the home country concerned at the time when he did the act which caused the computer to perform the function; or (b) that any computer containing any program or data to which the accused secured or intended to secure unauthorised access by doing that act was in the home country concerned at that time.' As McKinnon was in London at the relevant time he is clearly liable to the regulation of the Computer Misuse Act 1990 under s. 5(2)(a), even though the computers he hacked into were in the US. Further as he has admitted offences under ss. 1–3 there is no need for a long and costly trial. Although the harm may have occurred in the US there is no barrier to simply disposing of the McKinnon case at very little further cost to the public purse by having him tried in the UK where he would admit the charges.

It is certainly not unusual for UK hackers to be prosecuted here for harm which they have caused overseas. In *R. v Caffrey*[74] a UK teenager was charged, and later cleared, of

---

[70] *McKinnon v Government of the USA and Secretary of State for the Home Department* [2007] EWHC 762 (Admin).   [71] *McKinnon v Government of the US of America and another* [2008] UKHL 59.

[72] S. Ragan, 'UK refuses to charge McKinnon—NASA hacker one step closer to extradition', *The Tech Herald*, 26 February 2009: http://www.thetechherald.com/article.php/200909/3063/UK-refuses-to-charge-McKinnon-%E2%80%93-NASA-hacker-one-step-closer-to-extradition.

[73] *McKinnon v Secretary of State for the Home Department* [2009] EWHC 170 (Admin).

[74] Unreported, Southwark Crown Court, 17 October 2003. See R. Allison, 'Youth cleared of crashing American port's computer', *The Guardian* 18 October 2003: http://www.guardian.co.uk/technology/2003/oct/18/uknews.onlinesupplement.

an offence under s. 3 of the Computer Misuse Act for a Distributed Denial of Service Attack carried out on the Port of Houston Authority, while in *R. v McElroy*[75] another UK teenager who hacked into a US Department of Energy Research Lab was given 200 hours community service under the Computer Misuse Act. Why the UK authorities refused and refuse to charge McKinnon is a mystery, especially as hundreds of thousands of pounds of costs accumulate as he continues to fight extradition.

13.2 Viruses, criminal damage, and mailbombing

13.2.1 Early cases: the Mad Hacker and the Black Baron

Section 3 is deliberately vague and has been the subject of a great deal of speculation and recent development. As originally passed in 1990 s. 3 stated:

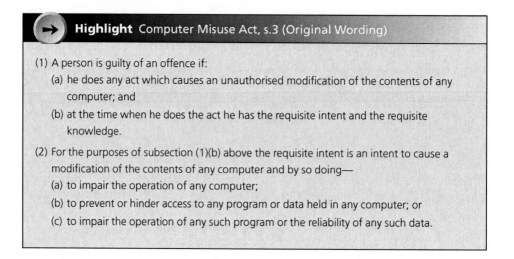

Highlight Computer Misuse Act, s.3 (Original Wording)

(1) A person is guilty of an offence if:
   (a) he does any act which causes an unauthorised modification of the contents of any computer; and
   (b) at the time when he does the act he has the requisite intent and the requisite knowledge.

(2) For the purposes of subsection (1)(b) above the requisite intent is an intent to cause a modification of the contents of any computer and by so doing—
   (a) to impair the operation of any computer;
   (b) to prevent or hinder access to any program or data held in any computer; or
   (c) to impair the operation of any such program or the reliability of any such data.

This offence, known rather unimaginatively as the 'unauthorised modification' offence was to fulfil three separate roles: (1) it was to regulate and control the production and distribution of computer viruses and other malware by making it an offence to distribute software which impaired the performance of any computer; (2) to formalize the law on 'digital criminal damage'; and (3) to criminalise the installation of software devices such as Trojans which allow hackers backdoor access to computers and computer networks almost at will.

One of the first challenges for s. 3 was to clarify the law with relation to 'digital criminal damage', this is when someone directly amends or erases data held on a computer without permission. While the pre Computer Misuse Act case of *Gold and Schifreen* had clearly demonstrated that the pre-existing law could not adequately deal with

---

[75] Unreported, Southwark Crown Court, 3 February 2004. See J. Leyden, 'Victory for commonsense in nuke lab hacking case', *The Register* 4 February 2004: http://www.theregister.co.uk/2004/02/04/victory_for_commonsense_in_nuke/.

computer hacking the pre-existing law on criminal damage was unclear. The Criminal Damage Act 1971 states that 'a person who without lawful excuse destroys or damages any property belonging to another intending to destroy or damage any such property or being reckless as to whether any such property would be destroyed or damaged shall be guilty of an offence.'[76] The definition of property may be found in s. 10 which states it is to be 'property of a tangible nature, whether real or personal, including money.'[77] This would seem to suggest that it would not cover information which by nature is intangible but this was rejected in the case of *Cox* v. *Riley*.[78] Here the accused erased programs from a printed circuit card used to control his employer's computer controlled saw. He was charged under the Criminal Damage Act 1971 but argued that the programs were not tangible property within the meaning of the Act. Nevertheless, he was found guilty on the basis that the printed circuit card had been damaged and was now useless. This approach was confirmed in the later case of *R. v Whitely*.[79]

> **Case Study** The Mad Hacker
>
> Nicholas Whitely was a 21 year old hacker known as the 'mad-hacker'. He was charged with ten offences of intending or recklessly damaging property by hacking into various university computer networks via the Joint Academic Network (JANET) between March and July 1988. He deleted and added files, made sets of his own users and then deleted any files which would have recorded his activity. He managed to attain the status of a system operator which enabled him to act at will without identification or authority. As a result of his actions, computers failed, were unable to operate properly, or had to be shut down for periods of time.

He was found guilty at Southwark Crown Court on 24 May 1990 and appealed to the Court of Appeal. By the time his appeal was heard the Computer Misuse Act was in force but as his charges predated the Act the question remained had Mr Whitely breached s. 1 of the Criminal Damage Act? Lord Lane CJ gave the judgement of the Court. He dismissed the appeal, stating that 'the Act required that tangible property had been damaged, not that the damage itself should be tangible.'[80] He added that 'there could be no doubt that the magnetic particles upon the metal discs were a part of the discs and if the defendant was proved to have altered the particles in such a way as to cause an impairment of the value and usefulness of the disc to the owner, there would be damage within the meaning of section 1',[81] before citing with approval the judgement of Auld J in *Cox v Riley* that 'the term "damage" for the purpose of this provision, should be widely interpreted so as to include not only permanent or temporary physical harm, but also permanent or temporary impairment of value or usefulness.'[82] Thus despite the Criminal Damage Act appearing to be restricted to tangible property the courts had interpreted it widely as applying to data stored on disks and servers.

[76] Criminal Damage Act 1971, s. 1(1).   [77] Criminal Damage Act 1971, s. 10(1).
[78] (1986) 83 Cr App R 54.   [79] *R. v Whitely* (1991) 93 Cr App R 25.
[80] *ibid*, 28.   [81] *ibid*.   [82] *ibid*, 29.

It was the intent of the Law Commission that s. 3 should replace the Criminal Damage Act when dealing with damage to computer data. In its report *Computer Misuse*,[83] the Law Commission came to the conclusion that clarification of the pre-existing law was required. They looked at the definition of property in the 1971 Act and concluded that 'for the commission of a criminal offence to depend on whether it can be proved that data was damaged or destroyed while it was held on identifiable tangible property not only is unduly technical, but also creates an undesirable degree of uncertainty in the operation of the law.'[84] The promulgation of s. 3 had the desired effect for although the Criminal Damage Act remained a possible alternative method to prosecute acts of digital criminal damage subsequent cases have all been decided under the Computer Misuse Act and a recent amendment introduced by the Police and Justice Act 2006 seeks to remove any confusion by introducing a new s. 10(5) into the Criminal Damage Act which reads: 'For the purposes of this Act a modification of the contents of a computer shall not be regarded as damaging any computer or computer storage medium unless its effect on that computer or computer storage medium impairs its physical condition.'

A number of cases have been successfully prosecuted under s. 3 dealing with both criminal damage and the creation and sending of viruses. One of the first was *R. v Goulden* which had been previously discussed.[85] As well as being found to have infringed s. 1 Mr Goulden was found to have infringed s. 3 by installing the security program which he used to lock his client's computer. Also found to have infringed s. 3 were Gareth Hardy, a computer engineer who 'time locked' his employer's computers so that one month after his employment was ended all data became encrypted,[86] Jeremy Feltis, a computer operator who worked for Thorn UK, who 'sabotaged' his employer's computers by disconnecting vital connections,[87] and Alfred Whittaker who installed bespoke software on a client machine with a hidden time lock which locked the client's computers when he was not paid on time.[88]

Without doubt though the first cause célèbre of s. 3 was the case of the 'Black Baron'.[89]

Case Study The Black Baron

Christopher Pile was a self-taught computer programmer who became fascinated with the design of computer viruses. He designed several viruses including the infamous SMEG.Pathogen and SMEG.Queeg viruses, named after expressions from the BBC television series 'Red Dwarf'. The reason Pathogen and Queeg were seen to be so dangerous was they were early examples of polymorphic viruses, viruses which can mutate to take on different forms in an attempt to defeat anti-virus software. The SMEG part of the virus referred to an encryption code system which could change the shape and nature of the virus at each infection: this was made available by Pile to other virus writers as part of a toolkit.

---

[83] Law Commission Report No. 186, above n. 17.   [84] *ibid*, [2.29].
[85] Above, n.47.   [86] *R. v Hardy* Unreported, Old Bailey, 1992.
[87] *R. v Feltis* [1996] EWCA Crim 776.
[88] *R. v Whittaker* Unreported, Scunthorpe Magistrates Court, 1993.
[89] *R. v Pile* Unreported, Plymouth Crown Court, 15 November 1995.

Pile was traced and arrested by officers from the Computer Crime Unit (the forerunner of the National Hi-Tech Crime Unit). He pled guilty to five charges under s. 2 and five of unauthorised modification of data under s. 3 and was sentenced to eighteen months imprisonment. Pile was the first virus writer to be successfully prosecuted under s. 3 and prosecutions for the writing and distribution of viruses remain rare with the only recent cases being of an individual found guilty of sending a computer virus to a competitor by way of an email attachment[90] and a designer of mass mailing viruses who infected thousands of computers.[91]

13.2.2 Later cases: web defacement and mailbombing

The value of section three's wide definition came to be recognised as new forms of attacks developed. In 1997 the first successful prosecution for web defacement took place. Two defendants, Ian Morris and Richard Airlie, hacked into the website of an estate agency and replaced pictures of homes for sale with pornographic images. They were convicted under ss. 2 and 3 and were fined £1250 and sentenced to 100 hours community service.[92] In 2006 another individual was sentenced to eight months' imprisonment, suspended for two years, and given a two year supervision order for defacing members' profiles on loveandfriends.com dating website.[93]

Section 3 has also been applied to 'mailbombing' attacks. These occur when the attacker sends huge volumes of email to an address in an attempt to overflow the mailbox or overwhelm the server where the email address is hosted. To mailbomb one merely sends tens, or even hundreds of thousands of emails simultaneously to the same email server causing the server to fail thereby denying the lawful user of the server the ability to use it: thus denial of service.

The first mailbombing prosecution in the UK took place in 2005 when David Lennon, a 16 year old from London, was charged under s. 3 for mailbombing the network of Domestic and General Group Plc. Lennon had been employed by D&G for three months but then had been dismissed. He decided to take revenge by mailbombing the D&G network by using an automated mail sender to send email messages purporting to come from D&G's HR manager to random recipients within the company. By using this methodology he managed to generate in excess of five million emails which caused network failures in the D&G network. He was arrested and charged.

Following his arrest he admitted sending the emails but said that his intention was to cause a 'bit of a mess up' in the company; that he did not consider what he was doing was criminal; and it was not his intention to cause the damage to D&G.[94] On 2 November 2005 District Judge Kenneth Grant, sitting as a Youth Court in Wimbledon,

---

[90] *R. v Brogden* Unreported, Exeter Crown Court 19 April 2001. Report at: http://www.sophos.com/pressoffice/news/articles/2001/04/va_comserve.html.

[91] *R. v Vallor* Unreported, Southwark Crown Court 21 January 2003. Report at: http://news.bbc.co.uk/1/hi/wales/2678773.stm.

[92] *R. v Morris and Airlie*, Unreported, Cardiff Crown Court, 1997.

[93] *R. v Byrne* Unreported, Southwark Crown Court 7 November 2006. Report at: http://cms.met.police.uk/news/convictions/computer_crime/computer_hacker_jailed.

[94] *DPP v Lennon* [2006] EWHC 1201 (Admin).

ruled that there was no case to answer on the basis that s. 3 was intended to deal with the sending of malicious material such as viruses, worms, and Trojan horses which corrupt or change data, but not the sending of emails.[95] The Director of Public Prosecutions appealed to the Divisional Court where Jack J gave the leading opinion:

> It is not in dispute, that the owner of a computer which is able to receive emails is ordinarily to be taken as consenting to the sending of emails to the computer. His consent is to be implied from his conduct in relation to the computer. Some analogy can be drawn with consent by a householder to members of the public to walk up the path to his door when they have a legitimate reason for doing so, and also with the use of a private letter box. But that implied consent given by a computer owner is not without limit. The point can be illustrated by the same analogies. The householder does not consent to a burglar coming up his path. Nor does he consent to having his letter box choked with rubbish. That second example seems to me to be very much to the point here. I do not think that it is necessary for the decision in this case to try to define the limits of the consent which a computer owner impliedly gives to the sending of emails. It is enough to say that it plainly does not cover emails which are not sent for the purpose of communication with the owner, but are sent for the purpose of interrupting the proper operation and use of his system. That was the plain intent of Mr Lennon in using the Avalanche program. The difference can be demonstrated in this way. If Mr Lennon had telephoned Ms Rhodes and requested consent to send her an email raising a point about the termination of his employment, she would have been puzzled as to why he bothered to ask and said that of course he might. If he had asked if he might send the half million emails he did send, he would have got a quite different answer. In short the purpose of Mr Lennon in sending the half million emails was an unauthorised purpose and the use made of D&G's email facility was an unauthorised use.[96]

Keene LJ agreed stating that: 'The critical issue is that of "consent" as that word is used in s. 17(8) of the Act. I, for my part, see a clear distinction between the receipt of emails which the recipient merely does not want but which do not overwhelm or otherwise harm the server, and the receipt of bulk emails which do overwhelm it. It may be that the recipient is to be taken to have consented to the receipt of the former if he does not configure the server so as to exclude them. But in my judgment he does not consent to receiving emails sent in a quantity and at a speed which are likely to overwhelm the server. Such consent is not to be implied from the fact that the server has an open as opposed to a restricted configuration.'[97] With the ruling of the Divisional Court clear the case was remitted back to Wimbledon Youth Court, and on 23 August 2006 Lennon was sentenced to a two month curfew with electronic tagging.[98]

13.3 **Denial of service and supply of devices**

Mailbombing is though only one type of denial of service (DoS) attack. More sophisticated attacks can take down complete networks and/or web servers rendering websites unavailable. There are a variety of DoS techniques which all take the form of asking the

---

[95] *ibid*, [7].

[96] *ibid*, [9]. It should be noted that although Jack J refers to half a million emails in fact five million were sent.   [97] *ibid*, [14].

[98] J. Oates, 'Kid who crashed e-mail server gets tagged', *The Register* 23 August 2006: http://www.theregister.co.uk/2006/08/23/e-mail_bomber_guilty/.

recipient server to deal with more requests for information than it can deal with causing it to overload.[99] There are two basic varieties of DoS attack, the standard DoS attack where one individual with considerable resources, or more likely a number of individuals acting in a coordinated fashion attacks a single server or web server and Distributed Denial of Service attacks (DDoS) where malicious code such as a Trojan is used to create a network of 'slave' computers under the control of one operator which can all be triggered at one time to carry out the attack.

Under the Computer Misuse Act as passed DoS attacks were probably not illegal, while those engaged in DDoS attacks would probably only be liable for the installation of the Trojan software not the actual attack itself, meaning the authorities would need to track down at least one infected 'zombie' computer to introduce as evidence. This is because s. 3 as originally enacted required the accused to carry out an act of 'unauthorised modification of the contents of any computer' but a DoS, or even a DDoS attack, does not modify the contents of any computer; it merely stops it from functioning while the attack is ongoing and once an attack concludes the server is released and returns to service.[100]

This raised several problems both legal and practical. Practically it meant that it would prove to be extremely difficult to prosecute for a DoS, or even a DDoS in the UK unless either some further offence was committed (such as blackmail or fraud) or unless the prosecuting authorities could establish either a s. 1 or s. 2 offence, or they could find evidence of unauthorised modification of contents. Legally this meant the UK was failing in its duties under the Council of Europe Convention on Cybercrime.[101] Articles 4 and 5 of the convention, on data interference and system interference, were much more widely drawn than s. 3 of the CMA. In particular, Article 5 required signatory states to 'adopt such legislative and other measures as may be necessary to establish as criminal offences under its domestic law, when committed intentionally, the serious hindering without right of the functioning of a computer system by inputting, transmitting, damaging, deleting, deteriorating, altering or suppressing computer data'. This is clearly aimed at DoS attacks in any form.

Faced with both a clear failure in the current law, and the demands of the international community the UK All Party Internet Group (APIG) reviewed the scope of s. 3 as part of their 2004 revision of the Computer Misuse Act.[102] They reported evidence from the Association of Remote Gambling Operators that criminal DDoS attacks were being made on gambling websites accompanied by monetary demands to make the attacks stop.[103] They reported a split in opinion as to whether s. 3 was adequate as it stood to deal with DoS attacks noting that 'almost every respondent from industry told us that the CMA is not adequate for dealing with DoS and DDoS attacks ... We understand

---

[99] For a quick primer on denial of service attacks see US Computer Emergency Readiness Team, *Cyber Security Tip ST04-015: Understanding Denial-of-Service Attacks*: http://www.us-cert.gov/cas/tips/ST04-015.html. For greater detail see R. Overill, 'Computer Crime: Denial of Service Attacks: Threats and Methodologies', (1999) 6 *Journal of Financial Crime* 351.

[100] There is a difference with a mailbombing attack (as Mr Lennon found to his cost) as the emails themselves are stored in the mailserver and as such may be an 'unauthorised modification of the contents of any computer'.

[101] CETS No. 185, Budapest, 23.XI.2001.   [102] All Party Internet Group, above n.65.

[103] *ibid*, [59].

that this widespread opinion is based on some 2002 advice by the Crown Prosecution Service that s. 3 might not stretch to including all DoS activity. Energis and ISPA told us that they knew of DoS attacks that were not investigated because "no crime could be framed"',[104] while 'the Government, many academic lawyers and also, we understand, the NHTCU, believe that s. 3 is sufficiently broad to cover DoS attacks. In April 2003 the Internet Crime Forum (ICF) Legal Subgroup pointed out that s. 3 did not require unauthorised access, merely unauthorised "modification of the contents of any computer". They expressed the opinion that the test applied would be whether the attack had rendered unreliable the data stored on a computer or impaired its operation.'[105] This inherent uncertainty was enough to convince APIG to recommend that 'the Home Office rapidly bring forward proposals to add to the Computer Misuse Act an explicit "denial-of-service" offence of impairing access to data. The tariff should be set the same as the s. 1 "hacking" offence. There should be a further "aggravated" offence along the lines of the current s. 2 where the denial-of-service is merely one part of a more extensive criminal activity.'[106]

These proposals eventually formed part of the review of the Computer Misuse Act found in ss. 35–38 of the Police and Justice Act 2006. Section 3 was substantially rewritten to ensure it criminalises all forms of DoS attack. The new wording states:

> ➡ **Highlight** Computer Misuse Act, s. 3 (New Wording)

(1) A person is guilty of an offence if—
  (a) he does any unauthorised act in relation to a computer;
  (b) at the time when he does the act he knows that it is unauthorised; and
  (c) either subsection (2) or subsection (3) below applies.

(2) This subsection applies if the person intends by doing the act—
  (a) to impair the operation of any computer;
  (b) to prevent or hinder access to any program or data held in any computer;
  (c) to impair the operation of any such program or the reliability of any such data; or
  (d) to enable any of the things mentioned in paragraphs (a) to (c) above to be done.

(3) This subsection applies if the person is reckless as to whether the act will do any of the things mentioned in paragraphs (a) to (d) of subsection (2) above.

The 'unauthorised amendment' offence has been replaced with an 'unauthorised impairment' offence which clearly covers all forms of DoS attack. The new provision only came into force on 1 October 2008 and to date the courts have not had to get to grips with it.[107] It has been highly controversial both in the planning and the execution. One of the most trenchant critics of international attempts to criminalise DoS attacks is the Swedish academic Mathias Klang. As he wrote in his essay *Virtual Sit Ins, Civil*

---

[104] *ibid*, [60].   [105] *ibid*, [61].   [106] *ibid*, [75].
[107] Like the changes to s. 1 discussed above this was brought into force by The Police and Justice Act 2006 (Commencement No. 9) Order 2008, SI 2008/2503.

Disobedience and Cyberterrorism,[108] 'the present legislative trend which criminalises DoS attacks … are much too far reaching and seriously hamper the enjoyment of individuals' civil rights'.[109] Klang's argument is that a DoS attack can, and should be allowed to, function as a form of virtual sit-in. When protestors wish to be heard on a variety of issues from equality and civil rights to enfranchisement or to protest the actions of government, one well known approach is to occupy a public place to make themselves heard and to reach the media.[110] Klang draws a parallel between the activities of non-violent activists in the real world and groups such as the electrohippies, an online activist group that use DoS attacks as part of their portfolio of nonviolent protest. He records how 'in an attempt to create a dialogue on the subject of the use of DoS as a political activism tool, the electrohippies have employed the sit-in as a metaphor and they term their attacks virtual sit-ins. Since they use the client-side method they do not employ zombie machines, and without zombies their actions must be supported by those willing to carry them out. One of their claims of legitimacy is that they have the popular support of the protesters: "Our method has built within it the guarantee of democratic accountability. If people don't vote with their modems (rather than voting with their feet) the action would be an abject failure."'[111] As an example of the type of action undertaken by the electrohippies he reports that 'in March 2003, virtual sit-ins organised by the electrohippies against the war in Iraq managed to disrupt the Prime Minister's website (www.number-10.gov.uk), causing it to be unavailable on several occasions. In response to criticism, they argued that their actions did not prevent any communications between the allies but were intended to show the use of official websites as a part of the propaganda directed at "seeking to sanitise their violation of International human rights law".'[112]

With the changes to s. 3 made by s. 36 of the Police and Justice Act these activities are now clearly illegal in the UK. The question is should we be worried about this development? If Klang is right a serious restriction on civil liberties has occurred: as well as criminalising DDoS attacks which, unlike the electrohippies' client-side attack do not require a coordinated effort from many thousands of individuals, or attacks designed for criminal purposes such as fraud or blackmail, as reported by the Association of Remote Gambling Operators, the new s. 3 also prevents the use of DoS as a peaceful tool of protest. While clearly Klang is right to draw our attention to this, it may be argued that the outcome of the new s. 3 is not as dark as Klang suggests. Sit-ins are not protected speech in UK Law and a sit-in which occupies private property, or which blocks a public highway may be broken up with protestors arrested. Further a virtual sit-in is not akin to a real world sit-in. A real world sit-in has a highly visible presence where the protestors may be seen and heard: in fact this it may be argued is the prime import of the sit-in,

---

[108] M. Klang, 'Virtual Sit Ins, Civil Disobedience and Cyberterrorism' in M. Klang & A. Murray (eds) *Human Rights in the Digital Age* (2005).   [109] *ibid*, 145.
[110] Klang notes that: 'While the origins of the sit-in are difficult to locate, a popular point of origin stems from 1960 when four African American college students in Greensboro, North Carolina protested against the whites-only lunch counter by sitting there every day. After the publication of an article in the New York Times they were joined by more students and their actions inspired similar protests elsewhere.' *Ibid*, 138.
[111] *ibid*, 141.   [112] *ibid*, 142.

it is less about appropriation of place and more about communication of a message. A virtual sit-in affected through a DoS attack is very different. There is no visible presence, rather the opposite: the webpage or server in question merely lists an error message when sought without explanation of why the error occurs. In a real world equivalent it is like protestors building some form of barrier around a property which screens it from public view without explanation as to why they have done it. Further the internet as a whole is a communications media; there are much more effective means for protestors to be heard online than through a DoS attack. They may set up a protest site, buy advertising through Google or similar, or make themselves heard through social network sites such as Facebook, Twitter, MySpace, or YouTube. A DoS attack is an extremely damaging form of attack, especially for e-commerce sites, it does not seem unreasonable to criminalise those involved in such an assault.

13.3.1 **Section 3A**

The Police and Justice Act also added a new provision to the Computer Misuse Act, s. 3A:

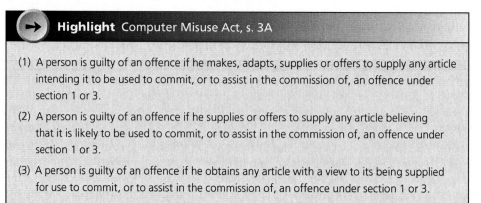

> **Highlight** Computer Misuse Act, s. 3A
>
> (1) A person is guilty of an offence if he makes, adapts, supplies or offers to supply any article intending it to be used to commit, or to assist in the commission of, an offence under section 1 or 3.
>
> (2) A person is guilty of an offence if he supplies or offers to supply any article believing that it is likely to be used to commit, or to assist in the commission of, an offence under section 1 or 3.
>
> (3) A person is guilty of an offence if he obtains any article with a view to its being supplied for use to commit, or to assist in the commission of, an offence under section 1 or 3.
>
> (4) In this section 'article' includes any program or data held in electronic form.

Section 3A, like the changes to s. 3; was been introduced to meet the UK's international commitments under the Cybercrime Convention. Article 6 requires signatory states to criminalise the production and distribution of devices designed to circumvent security protection or to facilitate in attacks on computers and computer systems. The aim of Article 6, and therefore s. 3A, is to criminalise so called 'hacking tools', these are software tools which make it easier to infiltrate computer networks or to design and build viruses, Trojans, and other malware. This seems like a pretty straightforward issue but it has in fact proven to be extremely controversial.

When APIG reviewed the CMA in 2004 they recommended that the UK use an opt-out in Article 6 to not implement it in full.[113] The reason for this recommendation was that 'such offences would result in significant difficulties because almost all these tools

---

[113] All Party Internet Group, above n. 65, [82].

are "dual use" and are widely employed by security professionals and system administrators'.[114] These concerns led the House of Lords Committee on Science and Technology to note that s. 3A left 'security researchers ... at risk of being criminalised because of the recent amendment to the Computer Misuse Act.'[115] The Government replied that this was not the case as 'those in the legitimate IT security sector, who make, adapt and supply tools as part of their daily work should have confidence that the new offence will be used appropriately and be assured that their practices and procedures fall within the law.'[116] The Government stated that the security industry would be protected in CPS guidelines to be issued when the new law came into force. This guidance was duly published on the CPS website.[117] It states that the following factors, among others, should be taken into account by prosecutors when considering a prosecution under s. 3A CMA.

> Section 3A(2) CMA covers the supplying or offering to supply an article 'likely' to be used to commit, or assist in the commission of an offence contrary to section 1 or 3 CMA. 'Likely' is not defined in CMA but, in construing what is 'likely', prosecutors should look at the functionality of the article and at what, if any, thought the suspect gave to who would use it; whether for example the article was circulated to a closed and vetted list of IT security professionals or was posted openly.
>
> In determining the likelihood of an article being used (or misused) to commit a criminal offence, prosecutors should consider the following:
>
> > Has the article been developed primarily, deliberately and for the sole purpose of committing a CMA offence (i.e. unauthorised access to computer material)?
> >
> > Is the article available on a wide scale commercial basis and sold through legitimate channels?
> >
> > Is the article widely used for legitimate purposes?
> >
> > Does it have a substantial installation base?
> >
> > What was the context in which the article was used to commit the offence compared with its original intended purpose?

This guidance appears to do little to protect IT security professionals. One specialist website for such professionals notes that 'sadly the CPS guidance, far from clarifying the matter, at first sight seems likely to increase the confusion. It offers examples where there is little or no ambiguity. But it apparently fails to address the hugely important grey area of security testing tools that by definition can also be exploited maliciously.'[118] Like the reworded s. 3 it is too early to say how s. 3A will be applied by the CPS and interpreted by the courts. It seems unlikely that IT security professionals will be arrested, much less charged for possession of scripts and tools such as PERL which may used for

---

[114] *ibid*, [80].
[115] The Government Reply to the Fifth Report from the House of Lords Science and Technology Committee, Session 2006-07 HL Paper 165, 3: http://www.official-documents.gov.uk/document/cm72/7234/7234.pdf.   [116] *ibid*.
[117] At http://www.cps.gov.uk/legal/a_to_c/computer_misuse_act_1990/index.html.
[118] The H-Security, *UK Crown Prosecution Service publishes Computer Misuse Act guidance*: http://www.h-online.com/security/UK-Crown-Prosecution-Service-publishes-Computer-Misuse-Act-guidance-/news/101286.

both legitimate and unlawful purposes, but the very fact that the Home Office and the CPS allow this ambiguity to remain despite the reports of both APIG and the House of Lords Committee on Science and Technology is worrying. The very nature of offences committed against computer and information systems requires precise accuracy in the wording of the law for it is easy for an individual to inadvertently stray beyond their authorised access or purpose, as we have seen in several cases from *Bignall* onwards. For this reason the law must be precise and clear in its boundaries and applications. The Computer Misuse Act has failed in this from its inception, and with newly added ambiguities in both the reworded s. 3 and the new s. 3A it may continue to do so for many years to come.

FURTHER READING

Books

S. Fafinski, *Computer Misuse* (2009)

H. Cornwall, *The Hacker's Handbook* (1995)

J. Erickson, *Hacking: the Art of Exploitation* (2003)

Chapters and Articles

M. Klang, 'Virtual Sit Ins, Civil Disobedience and Cyberterrorism' in M. Klang & A. Murray (eds) *Human Rights in the Digital Age* (2005)

C. Gringras, 'To be Great is to be Misunderstood: the Computer Misuse Act 1990' (1997) 3 *CTLR* 213

Z. Hamin, 'Insider Cyber-threats: Problems and Perspectives' (2000) 14 *IRLCT* 105

M. Wasik, 'Computer misuse and misconduct in public office', (2008) 22 *IRLCT* 135.

Pornography and obscenity in the information society

The human obsession with pornography and obscenity is as old as society itself.[1] Erotic imagery is common in all cultures and societies including ancient Rome[2] and Greece,[3] to the India[4] and China and Japan[5] of the Middle Ages and the early modern period up to the present day. In common with this cultural obsession one of the first roles played by any new technology has been to improve and streamline the distribution and production of erotica and pornography. As soon as humans divined how to make cave paintings they produced erotic images. With the process of industrialisation more efficient methods of producing images and text were developed and at every development erotica and pornography seemed to lead the way. Early photography produced the first nude and erotic images[6] leading to the development and sale of the infamous 'French Postcards' of the latter part of the nineteenth century. Then moving image began to take over from the still image. Again erotica and pornography was at the forefront of developments with the introduction of 'stag' films such as 'Red Headed Riot' and burlesque films such as 'Peeping Tom's Paradise'.

Through the first half of the twentieth century the main outlets for pornography remained these film rolls and still photographs. Then in the 1940s photomagazines began to be produced culminating the in launch of *Playboy* in 1953. Basically the technology behind pornography remained unchanged until the development of home

---

[1] Erotic cave paintings found across Europe which are estimated to be up to 40,000 years old depict highly realistic drawings of sexual activity including recreational (i.e. non-reproductive) sexual activity. See *Cave paintings show aspects of sex beyond the reproductive*: http://www.dominicantoday.com/dr/this-and-that/2006/5/2/12982/Cave-paintings-show-aspects-of-sex-beyond-the-reproductive.

[2] A number of erotic frescoes have been discovered preserved in Herculaneum and Pompeii.

[3] Erotic images are often found on Greek vases and Greek plays and texts often contain erotic themes.   [4] Most famously recorded in the Kama Sutra.

[5] China and Japan shared an erotic art tradition known as Shunga. It can be traced back to fourteenth century China but has its peak in Japan in the seventeenth to nineteenth centuries.

[6] In *Nude Photography, 1840–1920*, Peter Marshall notes: 'In the prevailing moral climate at the time of the invention of photography, the only officially sanctioned photography of the body was for the production of artist's studies. Many of the surviving examples of daguerreotypes are clearly not in this genre but have a sensuality that clearly implies they were designed as erotic or pornographic images': http://web.archive.org/web/20070218141330/http://photography.about.com/library/weekly/aa013100a.htm.

video cassettes. This allowed people to watch pornographic films in the comfort of their own home for the first time without needing specialist equipment. In the 1970s it was the porn industry in America that is widely credited with the eventual success of the VHS video format over rival Betamax,[7] although it should be noted that other factors contributed to VHS's eventual success. The home VCR began a 'golden age of porn' where the industry grew to a massive size.[8] The adult content industry continues to embrace new technologies making greater use of DVD technology than Hollywood though a series of 'interactive' DVDs[9] and moving to HD at an early stage of its development. It is no surprise therefore that the internet with its unique ability to host and distribute text, video, audio, and image has proven to be an attractive home for modern producers and distributors of pornography. When the accessibility and reach of the internet is paired with the economic benefits of convergence for the producers of pornographic content (video cameras are now available on mobile phones given away for free and HD-Camcorders are on sale for less than £130) it is no surprise that there has been an explosion of the availability of pornographic and obscene images: the question is how does the law deal with this?

14.1 **Obscenity**

As erotica started to give way to pornography and obscenity the law became involved in the control of pornographic goods. The law intervenes in several ways. Firstly it draws a line between types of erotica: erotic content (such as erotic art or literature—this is material produced around a sexual theme but not produced wholly or principally for the purpose of sexual arousal); pornographic content (this is material produced solely or principally for the purpose of sexual arousal);[10] obscene material (this is material likely to deprave and corrupt persons);[11] and extreme content (this includes child abuse images and violent or extremely obscene content). The law then intervenes to determine how each class of erotic, pornographic, or obscene content is to be controlled.

Erotic material may, in general, be sold and distributed freely and usually with few controls.[12] Bookshops often have an erotic literature section and there is no law which prevents a bookseller selling a 15 year old a copy of *Fanny Hill* or *Tropic of Cancer* (although many booksellers may voluntarily refuse to sell such titles to minors). By comparison pornographic content is more closely regulated. It is content which it is legal to sell and distribute but usually within closely restricted channels. For example material rated as R18 (or restricted 18) by the British Board of Film Classification may

---

[7] P. Johnson, 'Pornography Drives Technology: Why *Not* to Censor the Internet' 49 *Federal Communications Law Journal* 217 (1996).

[8] L. Glass 'Second wave: feminism and porn's golden age', *Radical Society,* October 2002 http://findarticles.com/p/articles/mi_qa4053/is_200210/ai_n9085969/.

[9] D. Kennedy 'The fantasy of interactive porn becomes a reality', *New York Times*, 17 August 2003: http://www.nytimes.com/2003/08/17/movies/17KENN.html.

[10] This definition is taken from s. 63(3) of the Criminal Justice and Immigration Act 2008.

[11] This definition is taken from s. 1(1) of the Obscene Publications Act 1959. It should be noted this is not restricted to sexually obscene material. This definition would also includes violent material such as snuff movies and other such content.

[12] Although, as we shall see below, this was not always the case.

only be shown to adults in specially licensed cinemas, and videos/DVDs may only be supplied to adults in licensed sex shops and not by mail order.[13] By comparison obscene content may not legally be imported, published or supplied in the UK[14] although it may be legally possessed provided there is no intent to publish, whereas extreme content may not be imported, supplied, published, or possessed.[15]

14.1.1 **The Hicklin principle**

The way the law has traditionally dealt with pornography and obscenity is illuminating. The UK common law standard is known as the 'Hicklin principle' after the case of *R. v Hicklin*.[16] Here Lord Cockburn CJ famously stated that the test was whether there is a tendency 'to deprave and corrupt those whose minds are open to . . . immoral influences, and into whose hands a publication of this sort may fall.'[17] According to *Hicklin* the essence of corruption is the suggestion of impure thoughts. Moreover publications likely to have this effect on young or other vulnerable people are to be ruled obscene irregardless of the literary or artistic merits of the work.

The *Hicklin* principle was voraciously applied and led to works such as *Lady Chatterley's Lover*, *The Well of Loneliness*, and *Tropic of Cancer* being banned from publication in the UK. This did not prevent publication of these books in English elsewhere (both Lady Chatterley and Tropic of Cancer were published in Paris) but to import such editions was in itself an offence under s. 42 of the Customs Consolidation Act 1876. The dual effect of banning the publication of obscene material in the UK and banning the importation of obscene material from outwith the UK allowed the state to control quite strictly the availability of obscene content. Prior to 1959 little distinction was drawn between erotic, pornographic, and obscene content with almost all sexually explicit content likely to be classified as obscene under the *Hicklin* standard. But that year the obscenity laws were relaxed slightly. Following recommendations from a House of Commons Select Committee the Obscene Publications Act was passed. Although it retained the spirit of the *Hicklin* principle it changed it in one key aspect. Section 1(1) of the Act states an article is deemed to be obscene if:

> its effect or (where the article comprises two or more distinct items) the effect of any one of its items is, if taken as a whole, such as to tend to deprave and corrupt persons who are likely, having regard to all relevant circumstances, to read, see or hear the matter contained or embodied in it.

---

[13] Video Recordings Act 1984, s. 12.

[14] Obscene Publications Act 1959, s. 2; Customs Consolidation Act 1876, s. 42.

[15] Currently in the UK it is illegal to view or possess images of child abuse under s. 160(1) of the Criminal Justice Act 1988, while by s. 45 of the Sexual Offences Act 2003 a child is defined as anyone under 18 years of age. It is further illegal to possess 'extreme pornography' under s. 63 of the Criminal Justice and Immigration Act 2008. 'Extreme pornography' is defined as an image which portrays either (a) an act which threatens a person's life, (b) an act which results, or is likely to result, in serious injury to a person's anus, breasts, or genitals, (c) an act which involves sexual interference with a human corpse, or (d) a person performing an act of intercourse or oral sex with an animal (whether dead or alive). For more on s. 63 see A. Murray, 'The Reclassification of Extreme Pornographic Images' (2009) 72 *MLR* 73.   [16] (1868) LR 3, QB 360.

[17] *ibid*, 371.

The key change in the new test is it asks the jury to consider the effect of the content on persons who are likely to see the content in question (i.e. adults) rather than 'those whose minds are open to immoral influences' i.e. children or other vulnerable groups. Following the entering into force of the 1959 Act a number of important cases clarified that the new obscenity standard was indeed distinct from indecency (the usual standard of pornographic material) including most famously *R. v Penguin Books Ltd.*[18]

14.1.2 **The obscene publications acts**

The law on obscenity has remained mostly unchanged since 1959, the only amendments being the addition of a number of extreme obscenity offences which criminalise possession, rather than the importation, sale, or possession with intent to supply materials.[19] To control the supply of pornography, and to restrict the supply of obscene content the UK law enforcement authorities continued to rely on a mixture of border controls and supply controls. By restricting the availability of pornographic content to licensed sex shops the authorities could oversee the type of content that was being made available to ensure it did not breach the Obscene Publications Act; additionally it meant that pornography produced in the UK, for the most part met community standards. Further by strictly enforcing border controls the authorities could restrict the supply of unclassified (and often obscene) materials.[20]

The arrival of the internet has changed the nature of the distribution model for all forms of content including pornographic content. Like other entertainment products including music, film, and video games much so called 'adult entertainment' is now produced and distributed in a disintermediated digital format. Although there remains a market for physical product distribution in the form of DVDs, the demand for purely digital distribution of adult content has, like music and mainstream film and TV, increased exponentially in the last ten years and has particularly increased with the availability of high speed ADSL connections and the development of streaming technology similar to that used by YouTube. This has left our border authority quite impotent for, as predicted by David Post and David Johnson in 1996, the borderless nature of the internet undermines effective border controls.[21]

This loss of ability to adequately police our borders has by turn rendered the Obscene Publications Act impotent. For while the Obscene Publications Act remains

[18] [1961] Crim LR 176.
[19] These will be discussed in full below. Further it should be noted that as obscenity is tested on the so-called community standard the classification of obscene materials has weakened over the years. In 2004 for the first time a movie which portrays actual sex between actors was given an '18' certificate. The movie *9 Songs* attracted little public outcry, a considerable change from the controversy surrounding *Women in Love* which in 1969 portrayed male full frontal nudity for the first time or *Last Tango in Paris* which in 1972 had portrayed anal sex on screen.
[20] The Courts would tend to strictly apply the provisions of the Obscene Publications Act when dealing with material seized at the border. See, e.g. *R. v Uxbridge Justices, ex parte David Webb* [1994] 2 CMLR 288.
[21] 'Law and Borders—The Rise of Law in Cyberspace' 48 *Stanford Law Review* 1367 (1996): http://www.cli.org/X0025_LBFIN.html.

enforceable its focus on the supply or possession with intent to supply obscene material within the UK is undermined by the fact that the vast majority of indecent and obscene material to be found online is hosted overseas. This is why it is not surprising to find that despite surveys which show more than 10 million UK adults visit pornographic websites,[22] and that 57% of British nine to nineteen year olds who go online at least once a week have come into contact with online pornography,[23] there have been no prosecutions in England and Wales under either the Customs Consolidation Act or the Obscene Publications Act 1959 for privately viewing obscene material using an internet connection. The authorities have instead focussed their meagre resources on extremely obscene material and UK distributors of obscene material with, to date, nearly all prosecutions for internet obscenity centring on the storing and distribution of child abuse images,[24] or the prosecution of those who run pornographic websites from overseas servers but who are resident in the UK and profit from this activity.[25]

With the removal of the physical border between the UK and the rest of the world internet users were afforded the opportunity to access and view pornography held overseas in the blink of eye and with little opportunity for the authorities to intercept the content *en route*. This caused a huge upsurge in consumption and left the authorities with a difficult decision to make. They could either invest large sums to attempt to enforce the law in the digital environment,[26] or they could *de facto* deregulate adult pornography and focus their attentions on more pressing problems such as child pornography. The UK authorities recognising the limits of the law in relation to this subject chose to focus their resources on only the most harmful content.

14.2 **Pornography**

The dividing line between indecent content and obscene content is a vital one. Although pornographic content may be either indecent or obscene it is only obscene content which may not be published, supplied, or imported: in other words one may legally trade in indecent content, provided all necessary regulations are complied with, but one cannot legally trade in obscene content.

---

[22] A. Barnes & S. Goodchild, 'Porn UK', *The Independent on Sunday*, 28 May 2006: http://www.independent.co.uk/news/uk/this-britain/porn-uk-480084.html.

[23] S. Livingstone & M. Bober, *UK Children Go Online* (LSE Department of Media & Communication, 2005: http://www.lse.ac.uk/collections/children-go-online/UKCGOfinalReport.pdf.

[24] See *R. v Barry Philip Halloren* [2004] 2 Cr App R (S) 57; *R. v. Snellman* [2001] EWCA Crim 1530 and *R. v James* [2000] 2 Cr App R (S) 258.

[25] See *R. v Ross Andrew McKinnon* [2004] 2 Cr App R (S) 46 and *R. v Stephane Laurent Perrin* [2002] EWCA Crim 747.

[26] This could either be achieved by the investment of these funds into additional law enforcement personnel or by using the funds to design a technological solution to the problem such as a national firewall or filtering system which would in effect rebuild the natural border in Cyberspace. For an excellent discussion of this subject see R. Deibert & N. Villeneuve, 'Firewalls and Power: An Overview of Global State Censorship of the Internet' in M. Klang & A. Murray (eds), *Human Rights in the Digital Age* (2005).

14.2.1 **The UK standard**

As already discussed the dividing line between indecency and obscenity is defined by a community standard. Since 1959 that standard has been to determine whether the content in question will tend to deprave and corrupt persons who are likely to read, see, or hear the content. This line is not fixed and will vary with changes in society. In 1961 the focus of the test was on literary works such as *Lady Chatterley's Lover* when famously counsel for the prosecution Mervyn Griffith-Jones, asked if it were the kind of book 'you would wish your wife or servants to read'. The jury on that occasion found Penguin Books not guilty of a breach of s. 1 of the Obscene Publications Act 1959, but today the very concept that a publisher may be tried for obscenity for publishing a book of the nature of *Lady Chatterley's Lover* seems nonsensical: society has moved on. Even the publication of Bret Easton Ellis's 1991 novel *American Psycho* with its graphic descriptions of sexual abuse, torture, and murder did not cause the UK authorities to consider a prosecution under the Obscene Publications Act; although the novel was subject to restrictions in other parts of the world.[27]

Similarly standards in mainstream films have moved on considerably. In 1969 a film adaptation of DH Lawrence's *Women in Love* sparked a great deal of controversy when the British Board of Film Censors (later to become the British Board of Film Classification) passed it for cinema display. The film contained the first full frontal male nude scene as Oliver Reed and Alan Bates wrestled naked. A few years later a great deal of controversy (although no prosecutions for obscenity) dogged films like *A Clockwork Orange*, *Straw Dogs*, and *Last Tango in Paris*. Today mainstream movies frequently portray sex and often sex and violence are mixed in so called 'torture porn' movies such as *Hostel*. Despite some controversy there is little call for these movies to be banned. Also the way sex is portrayed in mainstream movies shows how community values have changed. It had always been assumed that the portrayal of the erect male member would automatically rule a film unclassifiable as certificate 18 but that changed in 1999 when Catherine Breillat's movie *Romance* became the first movie to display an erect penis to be passed for cinema display. Since then several movies which portray actual sexual intercourse between actors have been passed for display including Mike Winterbottom's *Nine Songs* which in 2004 became the first film certified 18 to show full sexual intercourse including ejaculation.

This change in community values also led to the creation of the R18 certificate in 1982 for adult movies which may be supplied through licensed sex shops and displayed in licensed 'adult only' cinemas. The number of R18 titles has increased dramatically since 2000 when Mr Justice Hooper upheld a decision of the Video Appeals Committee of the British Board of Film Classification that R18 certificates should not be withheld to adult entertainment products on the basis that they had the potential to cause

---

[27] In Germany, the book was deemed harmful to minors, and its sales and marketing were severely restricted from 1995 to 2000. In Australia, the book is sold shrink-wrapped and is classified R18. The book may not be sold to those under 18. Along with other Category 1 publications, its sale is theoretically banned in the state of Queensland. In New Zealand, the Government's Office of Film & Literature Classification has rated the book as R18. The book may not be sold or lent in libraries to those under 18.

harm to children.[28] Hooper J (in a finding not dissimilar in effect to the move from the *Hicklin* standard to the new Obscene Publications Act standard in 1959) held that 'the risk of [the videos in question] being viewed by and causing harm to children or young persons is, on present evidence, insignificant'[29]

It is clear that the UK has become a more permissive society in relation to indecency and obscenity in the fifty years that the Obscene Publications Act has been in force. The problem with internet pornography is that the UK community standard is in danger of being overtaken by outside values. While UK community standards have moved on considerably the UK is still strict in its application of both indecency regulations (such as the R18 standard) and obscenity laws. So called 'hard core' pornography (*Nine Songs* aside) may only legally be supplied by licensed sex shops and only strictly to those over the age of eighteen and never by mail order. 'Soft' pornography is more widely available with newsagents permitted to sell so called 'top shelf' magazines, again though only legally to those over eighteen. The internet is, however, at least in relation to pornography, a case study in cyberlibertarianism.[30]

As we saw in Chapter 4 the Cyberlibertarian ethos that traditional lawmakers could not enforce their laws against citizens of Cyberspace due to the nature of Cyberspace as a unique and separate jurisdiction has been widely debunked by the Cyberpaternalist school which demonstrated that control of content and the actions of persons could be effected in Cyberspace through code (or design based) controls. But to effect such controls requires a degree of cooperation among lawmakers. In some areas cooperation has been forthcoming, as with regulation of the domain name system discussed in Chapter 12 or in relation to hacking and other computer misuse offences discussed in Chapter 13, but with pornography and in particular the dividing line between indecency and obscenity there is a problem.

As we have seen the line between indecency and obscenity is a community standard and the internet plays host to individuals from many social backgrounds in one place. Lawmakers across the globe cannot agree a common standard: what is considered sexually explicit but not obscene in England may well be considered to be obscene in the Republic of Ireland, and almost certainly material considered obscene in the Islamic Republic of Iran or in the Kingdom of Saudi Arabia would not be felt to be noteworthy in England. Similarly material which would be considered to be obscene in England would probably not be censored in Germany, Spain, or Sweden where a more tolerant approach to erotica and pornographic material is taken. What we are seeing in these differences is a spectrum of obscenity which ranges from extremely conservative to extremely liberal, and upon which individual states position themselves. In general this system has functioned quite effectively in the real world due to the existence of physical borders and border controls. These traditional measures are predicated though upon the assumption that the items in question will be fixed in a physical medium, and that they will require physical carriage to enter the state. With the advent of the digital age both these assumptions have been rendered null. The development of a

---

[28] *R. v Video Appeals Committee of British Board of Film Classification, ex parte British Board of Film Classification* [2000] EWHC Admin 341. [29] *ibid*, [47].
[30] Above, Ch. 4, 'Can we regulate the Digital Environment?'

global informational network has dismantled traditional borders: a point which was so eloquently made by David Post and David Johnson in their seminal paper *Law And Borders—The Rise of Law in Cyberspace*.[31]

> Cyberspace has no territorially-based boundaries, because the cost and speed of message transmission on the Net is almost entirely independent of physical location: Messages can be transmitted from any physical location to any other location without degradation, decay, or substantial delay, and without any physical cues or barriers that might otherwise keep certain geographically remote places and people separate from one another. The Net enables transactions between people who do not know, and in many cases cannot know, the physical location of the other party. Location remains vitally important, but only location within a *virtual* space consisting of the 'addresses' of the machines between which messages and information are routed. [32]
>
> The Net thus radically subverts a system of rule-making based on borders between physical spaces, at least with respect to the claim that Cyberspace should naturally be governed by territorially defined rules.[33]

Thus the traditional concept of border controls is undermined in the digital environment, making it very difficult for individual states to enforce and protect their community standard in the face of competing community standards found elsewhere. This can be demonstrated with an example.

✱ Example Access

Richard is a UK resident accesses and downloads pornographic images held on a server based in Sweden. The image is in compliance with the Swedish community standard but arguably is in breach of the UK community standard.

To consider a prosecution against Richard the UK prosecuting authorities would first have to identify that the item is obscene by applying the UK community standard.[34] If the image was found to be 'obscene' under the UK community standard they would next have to prove that either Richard imported the item in breach of s. 42 the Customs Consolidation Act 1876, or that he possessed the item with intent to publish in breach of s. 2 of the Obscene Publications Act 1959. Neither of these claims would necessarily succeed. The second claim would only succeed in relation to members of communities which trade or share images or files: for individuals who merely access and view pornographic websites there would be no intent to further publish or distribute, and therefore no offence under the Obscene Publications Act. The former claim is one mired in extreme complexity. Whereas identification of an importer was relatively straightforward when dealing with physical goods, it becomes much more complex in relation to digital information. The question is: does the consumer import the image into the UK, or is the image imported into the UK by the supplier, or even their ISP, who

---

[31] Above n. 21.   [32] *ibid*, 1370–1371.   [33] *ibid*, 1370.
[34] If they could not establish the item to be in breach of s. 1 of the Obscene Publications Act, then he would be entitled to view the item under Art. 28 of the EC Treaty. See *Conegate Ltd v HM Customs & Excise* [1987] QB 254 (ECJ); *R. v Forbes* [2002] 2 AC 512 (HL).

then makes it available to the consumer? The answer may at first seem straightforward: if Richard downloads an obscene image from a Swedish website then he should be deemed to be the importer. But what if the website appears to be from the UK? Perhaps the supplier is using a UK based domain name like www.gbporn.co.uk,[35] and seems to be implying they are based in the UK. In such circumstances does Richard exhibit sufficient intent and knowledge to be classed as an importer? As UK border controls are nullified the consumption of pornography is *de facto* deregulated meaning that the point of control over pornographic content is at its point of supply: as very little online pornographic content is hosted in the UK this means that we are reliant upon the community standards found elsewhere.

14.2.2 **A global standard?**

Pornography is hosted on web servers sited across the globe; there is no one community standard that prevails, but one community has greater impact than any other. Although there are no completely reliable statistics detailing where most pornographic websites are hosted it is clear that the US hosts substantially more sexually explicit web pages than any other state with one survey suggesting it could host as much as 89% of all adult web pages.[36] This means that in effect much of the pornography available in the UK has met the US community standard rather than the UK standard.

The US is in many ways a unique marketplace for the production and distribution of pornography due to the effects of the First Amendment. Whereas UK citizens are willing to accept that free expression does not mean limitless freedom to say or do whatever one wishes, US citizens strongly support their First Amendment right to enjoy freedom of speech, even where that right strays into the potentially destructive areas of pornography and hate speech. The question of whether it is appropriate to apply the First Amendment to pornographic content has long vexed US scholars and judges. Some scholars have argued that there can never be a true marketplace of speech in relation to pornographic imagery because there is no real freedom of speech for women in a country in which women are relegated to the particular gender roles that society gives them,[37] others, though, argue that pornographic magazines 'consciously attempt to express a view of social and sexual life'.[38] Whatever position one holds on the validity of First Amendment protection for pornographic imagery the law is quite clear. Material of a sexual nature will be protected by the First Amendment unless that material is determined by the court to be obscene.[39] The current US standard of obscenity was set out in the landmark case of *Miller v California.*,[40] wherein the Supreme Court established a three part test for obscenity.

---

[35] At the time of writing no site or registration existed in relation to this address.

[36] J. Ropelato, 'Internet Pornography Statistics', *Internet Filter Software Learning Center*: http://internet-filter-review.toptenreviews.com/internet-pornography-statistics.html.

[37] This is known as the MacKinnon/Dworkin debate and is found most clearly in the work of Catherine MacKinnon and Andrea Dworkin. See C. MacKinnon, *Feminism Unmodified: Discourses on Life and Law* (1987), 127–213; A. Dworkin, 'Against the Male Flood: Censorship, Pornography, and Equality' *8 Harvard Women's Law Journal 1* (1985).

[38] W. Brigman, 'Pornography as Political Expression' 17 *Journal of Popular Culture* 129 (1983). See also A. Dershowitz, 'Op-Ed' *New York Times*, 9 February 1979.

[39] *Roth v US*, 354 US 476 (1957).   [40] 413 US 15 (1973).

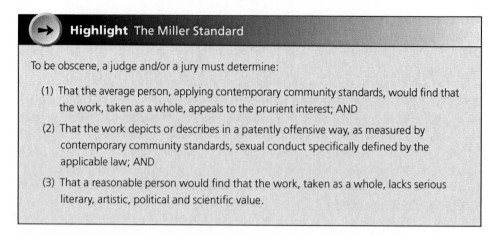

Highlight The Miller Standard

To be obscene, a judge and/or a jury must determine:

(1) That the average person, applying contemporary community standards, would find that the work, taken as a whole, appeals to the prurient interest; AND

(2) That the work depicts or describes in a patently offensive way, as measured by contemporary community standards, sexual conduct specifically defined by the applicable law; AND

(3) That a reasonable person would find that the work, taken as a whole, lacks serious literary, artistic, political and scientific value.

Chief Justice Burger went on to make clear that 'Under the holdings announced today, no one will be subject to prosecution for the sale or exposure of obscene materials unless these materials depict or describe patently offensive "hard core" sexual conduct specifically defined by the regulating state law, as written or construed.'[41] Although at the time it was felt that such a widely drawn standard would lead to wide local differences in obscenity laws this did not turn out to be the case. The scope of community standards was narrowed the next year in *Jenkins v Georgia*,[42] when the Court found that the film Carnal Knowledge could not be found to be patently offensive to the local community. Later further guidance would come in the case of *Pope v Illinois*,[43] which found that the test for literary, artistic, political, or scientific value, had to be based upon national, not local, standards.

Cyberspace not only removed the barriers between states, it also broke down barriers between communities. The US's approach to policing obscenity, much like the UK's, was predicated on the existence of a product fixed in a physical medium and sold or displayed through a physical outlet. The digitisation of pornography rendered the *Miller* concept of 'contemporary community standards' redundant. This first became clear in case of *US v Thomas*.[44]

Robert and Carleen Thomas operated a for fee Bulletin Board Service called *Amateur Action* which allowed members to download pornographic materials including materials depicting among other things, bestiality, oral sex, incest, and sado-masochistic abuse. To view and download these images users had to pay a $55 membership fee and fill out and sign an application which included their name and geographic address. In July 1993, a US Postal Inspector David Dirmeyer, received a complaint regarding the Amateur Action BBS from an individual who resided in the Western District of Tennessee. Dirmeyer investigated the complaint and using an assumed name joined the BBS and successfully downloaded content from the Amateur Action BBS to his home computer. As a result of Agent Dirmeyer's investigation the Thomases were indicted by a grand jury in the Western District of Tennessee and were charged with knowingly using a facility and means of interstate commerce (in this case, the combined computer/telephone system) for the purpose of transporting obscene materials.

---

[41] *ibid*, 27.   [42] 418 US 153 (1974).   [43] 481 US 497 (1987).
[44] 74 F 3d 701 (6th Cir. 1996).

The Thomases argued that they should not be subject to the community standards of Tennessee as they were based in California and in California the materials they posted were not obscene under local community standards (they had purchased the material in local sex shops) and as such they did not and could not know they were committing an offence in Tennessee. Further, they argued that if any community standards other than those of California were to be applied they should be that of the online community, a community based on Cyber-spatial rather than geographical connections among people. Both these claims were rejected by both the Distinct Court and the Court of Appeals for the Sixth Circuit, with the Court of Appeals finding that 'obscenity is determined by the standards of the community where the trial takes place' and that 'it is not unconstitutional to subject interstate distributors of obscenity to varying community standards.'[45]

Essentially the decision in the *Thomas* case was simplified by the fact that the Thomases knew images hosted on their BBS were being accessed and downloaded in Tennessee (and elsewhere) because they kept a record of subscribers; and in cases where interstate trade occurs with the knowledge of the supplier it has been held to be reasonable to hold them to the standards of that state or community.[46] More worrying cases from the point of view of both lawmakers and parents were, though, about to emerge. In cases where pornographic material was posted onto a publicly accessible BBS or website it was more difficult to prosecute using local community standards, as in these cases it was not possible to show knowledge or intent to trade within a particular community. In fact as cases such as *American Libraries Association et al. v Pataki*[47] and *PSINet v Chapman*[48] were later to demonstrate, attempts to apply local community standards had to be carefully handled lest they be found to be in violation of the implicit confines on state power imposed under the US Constitution's Commerce Clause.[49] In fact during the 1990s, despite the success of a few high profile prosecutions such as the *Thomas* case, the quantity of online publicly available pornographic content grew rapidly through the development of BBS trading communities, free access websites, and fledgling file sharing systems.[50] With more pornography becoming freely available, US lawmakers were faced with a new problem. At least for fee Bulletin Board Services, such as the one in the *Thomas* case, were largely adult environments; the wider internet was less discriminating and children were able to access all content, including adult content, as quickly and easily as adults: for as noted by Lawrence Lessig 'a kid in Cyberspace need not disclose that he is a kid'.[51]

14.2.3 **US statutory interventions**

Faced with a growing problem of children being exposed to online adult content state and federal lawmakers attempted to take legal control of the online environment. In 1996 two such attempts came to public prominence, and provoked controversy. In the State

---

[45] *ibid*, 710.
[46] *United States v Beddow* 957 F 2d 1330 (6th Cir. 1992); *United States v Williams*, 788 F 2d 1213, 1215 (6th Cir. 1986).   [47] 969 F Supp 160 (SDNY 1997).
[48] 63 F 3d 227 (4th Cir. 2004).   [49] Article I, Section 8, Clause 3 of the US Constitution.
[50] D. Thornburgh & H. Lin *Youth, Pornography, and the Internet* (2002), Ch. 3: http://www.nap.edu/openbook.php?record_id=10261&page=71.
[51] L. Lessig, *Code and Other Laws of Cyberspace Ver2.0* (2006), 248.

of New York, Governor George Pataki oversaw the introduction of §235.21(3) to the New York State Penal Code (NYSPC). This made it a crime to disseminate information 'harmful to minors' via a computer system. At the same time the Federal Government introduced the Communications Decency Act 1996 (CDA) as Title V of the Telecommunications Act of 1996. Both measures were felt to be in breach of the First Amendment by free speech advocates and were immediately challenged. §235.21(3) of the NYSPC was challenged by an extensive coalition of groups including the American Library Association, Peace-fire, and the American Civil Liberties Union.[52] They contended that the change in the NYSPC was unconstitutional as it unduly burdened free speech in violation of the First Amendment and it unduly burdened interstate commerce in violation of the Commerce Clause. At a summary hearing on 20 June 1997, the plaintiffs succeeded in their claim and were awarded summary judgement. District Judge Loretta Presky noted that:

> The State asserted that only a small percentage of Internet communications are 'harmful to minors' and would fall within the proscriptions of the statute ... I conclude that the range of Internet communications potentially affected by the Act is far broader than the State suggests. I note that in the past, various communities within the United States have found works including *I Know Why the Caged Bird Sings* by Maya Angelou, *Funhouse* by Dean Koontz, *The Adventures of Huckleberry Finn* by Mark Twain, and *The Color Purple* by Alice Walker to be indecent. Even assuming that the Act applies only to pictures, a number of Internet users take advantage of the medium's capabilities to communicate images to one another and, again, I find that the range of images that might subject the communicator to prosecution (or reasonably cause a communicator to fear prosecution) is far broader than defendants assert. For example, many libraries, museums and academic institutions post art on the Internet that some might conclude was 'harmful to minors.' Famous nude works by Botticelli, Manet, Matisse, Cezanne and others can be found on the Internet. In this regard, I point out that a famous painting by Manet which shows a nude woman having lunch with two fully clothed men was the subject of considerable protest when it first was unveiled in Paris, as many observers believed that it was 'scandalous'. Lesser known artists who post work over the Internet may face an even greater risk of prosecution, because the mantle of respectability that has descended on Manet is not associated with their as yet obscure names ... Individuals who wish to communicate images that might fall within the Act's proscriptions must thus self-censor or risk prosecution, a Hobson's choice that imposes an unreasonable restriction on interstate commerce.[53]

This is an extremely important passage of an extremely important decision in relation to the legal control of internet content. In this passage Judge Presky sets out the boundaries within which State Legislatures must work if they are to produce a set of legal controls which do not offend against the Commerce Clause, and as we can see, she draws these boundaries narrowly. Although State Legislatures, retain the power to control the supply of obscene material, a power which the Supreme Court recognised in *Miller v California*,[54] attempts to control the supply of sexually explicit, though not obscene, material are unlikely to be effective given the *Pataki* decision. The problem faced by State Legislatures was that they could not sufficiently precisely define the terms of the content they were seeking to control, a problem exacerbated by the lack of a common

---

[52] *American Libraries Association et al v Pataki*, above n. 47.   [53] *ibid*, [91].
[54] Above, n. 40. Chief Justice Burger made this clear by stating: 'This Court has recognized that the States have a legitimate interest in prohibiting dissemination or exhibition of obscene material when the mode of dissemination carries with it a significant danger of offending the sensibilities of unwilling recipients or of exposure to juveniles' (at 16).

national standard. As had already been demonstrated by the *Thomas* case what may be deemed to be acceptable in California, may be felt to be unacceptable in Tennessee, and with State Laws requiring individuals to self-censor it is almost impossible to imagine how such regulations could not offend against the Commerce Clause. What was clearly needed was a federal response.

The Communications Decency Act was introduced to the Senate on 1 February 1995 by Senators James Exon, a Democrat from Nebraska and Slade Gorton, a Republican from Washington, in response to the previously discussed fears that internet pornography was on the rise. In March 1995, the Senate Commerce Committee unanimously adopted the Exon/Gorton proposal as an amendment to the in progress Telecommunications Reform Bill. In June 1995, the Senate attached the Exon/Gorton amendment to the Bill by eighty-four votes to sixteen. On 1 February 1996, the Bill was passed by both Houses, becoming law on 8 February 1996.

The introduction of the CDA explicitly outlawed intentionally communicating 'by computer in or affecting interstate or foreign commerce, to any person the communicator believes has not attained the age of 18 years, any material that, in context, depicts or describes, in terms patently offensive as measured by contemporary community standards, sexual or excretory activities or organs.'[55] Opponents of the Act argued that 'just as a librarian cannot be expected to determine the age and identity of all patrons accessing a particular book in the library's collection, the provider of online information cannot be expected to police the usage of his or her online offerings. To impose such a requirement would result in reducing the content of online material to only that which is suitable for children.'[56]

A campaign against the Bill began on its introduction and by 1 February 1996 over 115,000 signatures had been collected on a petition against the Act. On 2 February 1996, in response to the adoption of the Act by Congress, thousands of websites turned black for forty-eight hours as part of the Electronic Frontier Foundation's, 'Turn the Web Black' protest. On 8 February 1996 the EFF launched its blue ribbon 'Free Speech Campaign'. This asked those who ran web pages to display a distinctive blue ribbon logo in support of their campaign against the CDA and almost overnight the Blue Ribbon logo populated the web. Publicity campaigns such as these were though merely a sideshow to the main event. As soon as President Clinton signed the CDA on 8 February, the American Civil Liberties Union and twenty three other co-plaintiffs including the Electronic Privacy Information Center, the Electronic Frontier Foundation, and the Planned Parenthood Federation of America, raised a complaint before the Federal District Court in Philadelphia seeking a temporary restraining order against the implementation of the indecency provisions of the CDA on the grounds that 'the Act is unconstitutional on its face and as applied because it criminalizes expression that is protected by the First Amendment; it is also impermissibly overbroad and vague; and it is not the least restrictive means of accomplishing any compelling governmental purpose.'[57] The Complaint was heard by District Judge Ronald Buckwalter, who, on 15 February, granted the plaintiffs an

[55] § 502(2).

[56] D. Sobel, 'The Constitutionality of the Communications Decency Act: Censorship on the Internet' 1 *Journal of Technology Law & Policy* 2 (1996): http://grove.ufl.edu/~techlaw/vol1/sobel.html.

[57] Complaint filed before the US District Court, Eastern District of Pennsylvania, 8 February 1996, Civ. No. 96-963: http://www.epic.org/free_speech/censorship/lawsuit/complaint.html.

order insofar as the CDA referred to indecent, but not obscene content.[58] With the order in place the plaintiffs then extracted from the Federal Government a stipulation that they would not 'initiate any investigations or prosecutions for violations of 47 U.S.C. Sec.223(d) for conduct occurring after enactment of this provision until the three-judge Court hears Plaintiffs' Motion for Preliminary Injunction.'[59] With this safeguard in place to ensure that the CDA would not be enforced while a question mark remained over its constitutionality the plaintiffs prepared a case to be heard before the District Court.

Hearings were quickly arranged and held over six days from 21 March to 10 May.[60] The decision was given on 11 June and all three Judges agreed that on its face the CDA was unconstitutional. Chief Justice Sloviter reflected the views of the Court in noting: 'I have no hesitancy in concluding that it is likely that plaintiffs will prevail on the merits of their argument that the challenged provisions of the CDA are facially invalid under both the First and Fifth Amendments.'[61] The Federal Government, as expected immediately sought to appeal the decision to the US Supreme Court, and on 6 December 1996 the Supreme Court noted probable jurisdiction and agreed to hear the case on 19 March 1997. The Government filed its brief on 21 January; the plaintiffs' briefs were filed on 20 February. Oral argument was heard, as scheduled, on 19 March, following which everyone waited for the Court's ruling. The Court finally issued its decision on 26 June, and by a seven to two majority it found in favour of the plaintiffs. The first decision the Court had to come to was whether the First Amendment applied in Cyberspace. Here Justice Stevens, who gave the majority opinion, was clear:

> **Highlight** The First Amendment of Cyberspace
>
> The Internet provides relatively unlimited, low-cost capacity for communication of all kinds. The Government estimates that 'as many as 40 million people use the Internet today, and that figure is expected to grow to 200 million by 1999.'
>
> This dynamic, multifaceted category of communication includes not only traditional print and news services, but also audio, video, and still images, as well as interactive, real-time dialogue.
>
> Through the use of chat rooms, any person with a phone line can become a town crier with a voice that resonates farther than it could from any soapbox. Through the use of Web pages, mail exploders, and newsgroups, the same individual can become a pamphleteer. As the District Court found, 'the content on the Internet is as diverse as human thought.'
>
> We agree with its conclusion that our cases provide no basis for qualifying the level of First Amendment scrutiny that should be applied to this medium.
>
> [Reno v ACLU 521 US 844 (1997), 862.]

[58] *ACLU v Reno* 929 F Supp 24 (1996).
[59] Stipulation of 23 February 1996: http://www.epic.org/free_speech/censorship/lawsuit/stipulation.html.
[60] The plaintiffs' case was heard on 21 and 22 March and 1 April while the Government's case was put on 12 and 15 April. closing arguments were heard on 10 May.
[61] *ACLU v Reno* 929 F Supp 824 (1996), 856.

Thus with the prior question of whether First Amendment protection could be applied within Cyberspace clearly answered in the affirmative the Court could go on to assess the constitutionality of the CDA. Again, Justice Stevens was clear:

> In order to deny minors access to potentially harmful speech, the CDA effectively suppresses a large amount of speech that adults have a constitutional right to receive and to address to one another. That burden on adult speech is unacceptable if less restrictive alternatives would be at least as effective in achieving the legitimate purpose that the statute was enacted to serve.[62]

The plaintiffs' success was complete. They had won every round and the Supreme Court had, as they hoped, extended First Amendment protection into Cyberspace. The effect of this decision cannot be overstated. Not only had the narrow victory ensured that the *Miller/Pope* obscenity standard was to be applied in Cyberspace, a much more important victory had been won: the Supreme Court had confirmed that the US Constitution, including the First Amendment protection for indecent but not obscene content, applied to that part of Cyberspace over which the US Government and Courts could exert authority. This meant that two years later when the Clinton administration attempted to resurrect parts of the Communication Decency Act in the Child Online Protection Act 1998 the US Supreme Court again ruled such legislation was unconstitutional.[63]

14.2.4 **The decision heard 'round the world'**

The *Reno* decision had impact not only in the US. As previously established the inability of UK border authorities to prevent the massive influx of digital pornographic content hosted outwith the UK means we are reliant on regulation at the point of supply and/ or production of pornographic content. As a considerable proportion of that content is produced in and hosted in the US the *Reno* decision had massive impact in the UK. Further the impact of *Reno* is more far reaching than may have been initially recognised. On the surface it meant that any producer of pornographic content could use the US as a 'safe haven' for their content as any content hosted on a US based server would effectively gain First Amendment protection provided their material was not obscene applying the *Miller/Pope* standard, a standard which is far more permissive than the UK standard. This suggested if online pornographic content were to be effectively regulated international cooperation would be required as any form of regulation would require the cooperation of enforcement authorities in the US. This though would prove extremely difficult to achieve in the post-*Reno* environment for as explained by Douglas Vick 'The *Reno* decision will constrain the international community's efforts to establish a comprehensive body of common rules for regulating Internet content. Under American law, treaties and other international accords are hierarchically inferior to the

---

[62] *ibid*, 880.
[63] The Child Online Protection Act 1998 attempted a slightly different wording to the CDA by putting more emphasis on knowledge and intent: 'Whoever knowingly and with knowledge of the character of the material, in interstate or foreign commerce by means of the World Wide Web, makes any communication for commercial purposes that is available to any minor and that includes any material that is harmful to minors shall be fined not more than $50,000, imprisoned not more than 6 months, or both.' It was ruled unconstitutional by a 5-4 Supreme Court majority in the case of *Ashcroft v ACLU* 542 US 656 (2004).

provisions of the US Constitution. A treaty provision, just like a congressional statute, is unenforceable if it fails to conform with First Amendment law.'[64]

This handicap could clearly be seen in negotiations to draft the Council of Europe, Convention on Cybercrime.[65] The Convention deals with only one 'content-related offence', that being the production or distribution of child abuse images using a computer system.[66] We know several of the states that took part in the drafting process were keen to include further content related offences, but that these never made the final text. The reason for this is to be found in the Explanatory Report:[67]

> The committee drafting the Convention discussed the possibility of including other content-related offences, such as the distribution of racist propaganda through computer systems. However, the committee was not in a position to reach consensus on the criminalisation of such conduct. While there was significant support in favour of including this as a criminal offence, some delegations expressed strong concern about including such a provision on freedom of expression grounds.[68]

Although the identity of the delegations in question are not revealed, it is clear that at least one of these would be the US delegation: the US delegation could not, as Douglas Vick had predicted, sign the US Government up to any treaty provisions which would conflict with First Amendment protection. With child abuse images being clearly classed as obscene in US law,[69] Article 9 could be left in place, but any attempts to extend the Convention into more general content regulation could not be countenanced by the US delegation because of the principle of the First Amendment.

In the thirteen years since the *Reno* decision sexually explicit content on the internet has been effectively deregulated. This has not led, as some predicted, to the internet becoming mired in obscene content. Sexually explicit content remains a small proportion of internet content and has declined as a proportion of internet content since *Reno*.[70] Although in absolute numbers there may be more sexually explicit images available on the internet in 2010 than in 1997 this reflects the general growth of the internet: the statistics demonstrate that 'adult content' websites are growing at a slower rate than mainstream social networking, P2P, and ecommerce sites.[71] This suggests that end-users may be relied upon to police themselves when dealing with pornographic content; but there remains the problem of the more vulnerable members of

---

[64] D. Vick, 'The Internet and the First Amendment' (1998) 61 *MLR* 414, 419.

[65] Council of Europe, ETS No. 185, *Convention on Cybercrime*, Budapest, 23 November 2001: http://conventions.coe.int/Treaty/en/Treaties/Html/185.htm.   [66] Art 9.

[67] Council of Europe, ETS No. 185, *Explanatory Report on the Convention on Cybercrime*: http://conventions.coe.int/Treaty/EN/Reports/Html/185.htm.   [68] *ibid*, [35].

[69] *New York v Ferber* 458 US 747 (1982).

[70] In November 2006 a US Department of Justice Report reported that about 1 per cent of websites indexed by Google and Microsoft were sexually explicit (see http://www.msnbc.msn.com/id/15721799/). Figures for 1997 could not be located but figures from 1998 are available from the OCLC Web Characterisation Report of 2001 which reports that in 1998 2.3% of public web sites contained sexually explicit images. See http://www.oclc.org/research/projects/archive/wcp/stats/misc.htm.

[71] To support these statistics the author reviewed the list of the Alexa top 500 most popular websites on 15 May 2009. Only 15 of the 500 sites listed seemed to contain sexually explicit images. Although this is higher than the 1% of sites recorded by the US Department of Justice this is to be expected as a vast majority of web pages are personal sites or blog sites which attract only a few visitors.

society, especially children. One of the reasons R18 videos may only be sold through licensed sex shops is to prevent children gaining access to them, but with the internet hard core pornographic content may be streamed directly to the laptop, or even mobile phone of teenagers or even preteens. The focus switches from regulating the supply of pornographic content to the adult population to the protection of minors. There are a variety of techniques used including parental controls on mobile phones, software tools such as CyberSitter and NetNanny and the use of server side controls such as BT Cleanfeed but the legal system is little involved in these self-regulatory regimes. Instead the law has focussed on a small proportion of available online pornographic content: that proportion of content so clearly obscene that in the view of the authorities it must be controlled: this is extreme pornographic material including images of child abuse.

14.3 **Child abuse images and pseudo images**

Child abuse images are the most extreme form of pornographic image and are always obscene no matter which community values apply.[72] There are a number of reasons why child abuse images are treated differently to adult pornography but prime among them are that to produce a child abuse image a child must be abused: thus the image is a record (and evidence) of a crime in a way pornographic images are not. This is known as the 'direct harm rationale'. To produce images of child abuse a child must be harmed: as a result the law must take steps to protect children and to prevent such harm and to do so the production, distribution and even possession of child abuse images is criminalised.[73]

Although nearly all countries agree the need for the criminalisation of child abuse images on the direct harm rationale the enforcement of this agreement is though not as simple as it sounds. Firstly there is the relatively simple question of how old is a child? This is not an issue when one is dealing with young children, all governments and lawmakers agree that a five year old is a child. What, though, about a seventeen year old? Or even perhaps a fifteen year old? A strict application of the direct harm rationale assumes that in the production of a child abuse image a child has been abused: this means the 'child' cannot have legally consented to the production of the image in the way adult performers do. This is true only if the 'child' has not reached the age of consent within their state: once they reach majority they can legally have sex, and equally they can consent to it being recorded without direct harm having occurred to them.

---

[72] There is a debate over terminology for images such as these. The Internet Watch Foundation note on their website that: '"child pornography", "child porn" and "kiddie porn" are not acceptable terms. The use of such language acts to legitimise images which are not pornography, rather, they are permanent records of children being sexually abused and as such should be referred to as child sexual abuse images.' I will refer to these images as 'child abuse images' but may refer to them being of a pornographic nature.

[73] Under s. 1 of the Protection of Children Act 1978 it is an offence to 'take, or permit to be taken, any indecent photograph of a child' and to 'to distribute or show such indecent photographs'. While by s. 160 of the Criminal Justice Act 1988 it is an offence for a person to have any indecent photograph of a child in his possession.

The first problem is that different states have different ages of majority. Until recently the age of consent in Canada was fourteen,[74] while in the UK it is sixteen. Throughout the US it varies from sixteen to eighteen while in some states it is as high as twenty (Tunisia) while in others as low as twelve (Tonga).[75] With child abuse images streaming across borders as easily as other forms of pornographic imagery some form of agreement is needed on this basic issue.

This has been achieved in part though the Convention on Cybercrime.[76] Article 9 seeks to form international agreement and cooperation on 'Offences related to child pornography'. Article 9(3) states: 'For the purpose of [this provision], the term "minor" shall include all persons under 18 years of age. A Party may, however, require a lower age-limit, which shall be not less than 16 years.' Thus although there may be no common agreement on the age of sexual majority between member states there is agreement that when dealing with child abuse images they will adopt a common age of eighteen in most circumstances.[77]

As the majority of child abuse images are consumed in Western Europe, Japan, and the North American states the Cybercrime Convention provides a useful point of commonality among law enforcement authorities who can organise international operations to attempt to break so called 'child pornography rings'. To date there have been several such operations including Operation Ore/Avalanche, a joint UK–US operation which began in 1999 and saw over 1,400 convictions in the UK and more recently Operation PIN, an ongoing operation begun in 2003 and managed by the Virtual Global Taskforce.[78] This involves the creation of websites which purport to offer child abuse images but actually lead to law enforcement websites informing the user that their details have been captured and may be passed on to local law enforcement authorities. It is not the direct aim of Operation PIN to secure convictions but rather to deter users from seeking child abuse images.[79] These operations will be discussed further in chapter fifteen when international cooperation in investigation and prosecution of online crime is examined.

A second problem is that it is not always clear how old a 'child' in an image actually is. Again with young children this is not an issue, but a fourteen year old can look eighteen and vice versa. Should the law ban the production, distribution, and possession of

---

[74] The Tackling Violent Crime Act 2008 raises the legal age of sexual consent in Canada from 14 to 16, the first time it has been raised since 1892.

[75] See CBC News Online, *Age of Consent*: http://www.cbc.ca/news/background/crime/ageof-consent-faq.html.   [76] Above, n 65.

[77] The UK has taken steps to ensure UK law complies with Article 9. In England and Wales s. 45(2) of the Sexual Offences Act 2003 amends s. 7(6) of the Protection of Children Act 1978 to read '"Child" … means a person under the age of 18.' In Scotland the relevant provisions are to be found in the Protection of Children and Prevention of Sexual Offences (Scotland) Act 2005. Interestingly a side-effect of this would be that a couple in a perfectly legal sexual relationship where one (or both parties) were aged between sixteen and eighteen would be unable to make a home sex video or take pictures of their partners in sexually suggestive positions. For this reason the Sexual Offences Act 2003 introduced s. 1A into the Protection of Children Act. This provides that it is not an offence to make or possess a photograph of a child over sixteen if at the time the offence was charged the defendant and the child were either (a) married or (b) living together as partners in an enduring family relationship.

[78] A partnership of the Australian Federal Police, the Child Exploitation and Online Protection Centre in the UK, the Italian Postal and Communication Police Service, the Royal Canadian Mounted Police, the US Department of Homeland Security, and Interpol.

[79] See http://www.virtualglobaltaskforce.com/what_we_do.asp.

images of young adults who appear to be younger than they actually are? Equally should an individual who possesses a pornographic image of a person who appears to be over eighteen face prosecution if it is subsequently established that the person in question is in fact a minor? These are questions that have been faced in courts overseas.

In Sweden a child is defined as 'a person whose puberty development is incomplete, or when it can be discerned from the image or from the circumstances around it, is less than 18 years old'.[80] In a recent case the defendant paid two sixteen year old girls to take part in pornographic films. The girls informed him of their age before filming took place but the films were produced anyway. The Stockholm District Court and the Court of Appeal both interpreted the law to mean that if the age of the girls could not be discerned by the images the man could not be guilty of producing or distributing child pornography despite the fact that he was aware of their age. The Courts found that as the girls had passed through puberty and therefore it was not possible to understand from the images that they were under age these were not images of child pornography as defined in the Criminal Code.[81]

To prevent these issues arising in the US the Child Protection and Obscenity Enforcement Act 1988 requires that producers of pornographic material keep records of all performers engaged by them with proof that they were over eighteen at the time the material was produced.[82] The UK strikes a middle ground between these approaches. There is no requirement of record-keeping but we are less laissez-faire than the Swedish position. By s. 160 it is an offence to possess an image of a person under eighteen, whether or not they look older than they actually are. Therefore in the UK it is not technically illegal to possess an indecent image of a person eighteen or over who looks younger than they are, but it is illegal to possess a computer manipulated or computer generated image which is specifically designed to create the impression that a minor is portrayed: these are so-called pseudo-images.

14.3.1 Policing pseudo-images in the UK

Pseudo-images are a new type of child abuse image. The creation of pseudo-images involves powerful computer software such as Adobe Photoshop or Corel Paint Shop Pro to either create photorealistic images which portray children being abused or to manipulate pre-existing pornographic images to make adult actors appear pre-pubescent by digitally removing pubic hair (and other post-pubescent hair such as chest hair or underarm hair) and the resizing of genitals and breasts. These images raise a number of issues. First among them is the simple question of should we criminalise such images at all? As discussed child abuse images are criminalised under the direct harm principle. Pseudo-images are quite different: in the same way that actors are not actually killed in violent action movies or horror movies no children are harmed in the production of pseudo-images. These images may be thought of as an extension of other 'artistic' forms which may portray violence or abuse towards

---

[80] Swedish Criminal Code Chapter 16, para 10a.
[81] Stockholm District Court Case nr B 7047-01. Discussed in full in M. Eneman, 'The New Face of Child Pornography' in M. Klang & A. Murray (eds), *Human Rights in the Digital Age* (2005).
[82] US Code, Title 18 § 2257.

child-like characters such as Japanese Manga, in particular Hentai. But, there are compelling arguments which suggest we cannot consider pseudo-images so lightly.

There is strong evidence which points to a connection between viewing child abuse images and the act of abuse itself.[83] In current research there are four main hypotheses on the paedophile's use of child abuse images: (1) to develop their sexual motivation, (2) to lower their level of sexual impulse control, (3) as a substitute for sexual contact with a child, and (4) to break down the child's resistance while attempting to seduce the child. A study presented in 2003 showed that two-thirds of perpetrators arrested for internet sex crimes against children also possessed stills pictures and film sequences containing child abuse images.[84] Therefore there is a clear psychological link between the consumption of child abuse images and the act of child abuse; further as most paedophiles do not differentiate between pseudo-images and genuine images and as genuine images are easier to produce than pseudo-images producers will tend to continue to produce genuine images. All of these factors suggest that although children may not be directly harmed in the production of pseudo-images such images do cause indirect harm on several levels.

This 'indirect harm rationale' is applied in Article 9(2)(c) of the Convention on Cybercrime which states that 'the term "child pornography" shall include pornographic material that visually depicts realistic images representing a minor engaged in sexually explicit conduct'. The UK was an early adopter of legislation to criminalise pseudo-images with the Criminal Justice and Public Order Act 1994 extending the ambit of both the Criminal Justice Act 1988 and the Protection of Children Act 1978 to cover such images.[85] The extended wording of s. 1(1) of the Protection of Children Act reads:

It is an offence for a person:

(a) to take, or permit to be taken or to make, any indecent photograph or pseudo-photograph of a child; or

(b) to distribute or show such indecent photographs or pseudo-photographs; or

(c) to have in his possession such indecent photographs or pseudo-photographs, with a view to their being distributed or shown by himself or others; or

(d) to publish or cause to be published any advertisement likely to be understood as conveying that the advertiser distributes or shows such indecent photographs or pseudo-photographs, or intends to do so.

Section 160(1) of the Criminal Justice Act now reads:

It is an offence for a person to have any indecent photograph or pseudo-photograph of a child in his possession.

A pseudo-photograph is defined in s. 7(7) of the Protection of Children Act as 'an image, whether made by computer-graphics or otherwise howsoever, which appears to be a photograph.'

---

[83] See, e.g. C. Bagley & K. King, *Child Sexual Abuse* (1989), 219; C. Itzen (ed.), *Home Truths About Child Sexual Abuse* (2000), ch 7.

[84] J, Wolak, K. Mitchell & D. Finkelhor, *Internet Sex Crimes Against Minors: The Response of Law Enforcement*, Crimes against Children Research Center November 2003, University of New Hampshire: http://www.unh.edu/ccrc/pdf/CV70.pdf.

[85] S. 84 of the Criminal Justice and Public Order Act 1994 made the necessary amendments to s. 160 of the Criminal Justice Act 1988 and ss. 1, 4, 5 and 7 of the Protection of Children Act 1978.

The newly extended scope of s. 160 was examined by the Court of Appeal in *R. v Fellows & Arnold*.[86] Mr Fellows was a computer officer at Birmingham University. Without the knowledge of the university he constructed a large database of child abuse images on the university network and made it available via the internet. Mr Arnold was a 'customer' of Mr Fellows who was granted access to Mr Fellows's database in return for supplying him with further images. Both were prosecuted under the Protection of Children Act and both claimed that the Act did not extend to their activities as 'computer data was not a "photograph" for the purposes of section 1.'[87]

This argument was rejected by Evans LJ. He began by examining the dictionary definition of a photograph as 'a picture or other image obtained by the chemical action of light or other radiation on specially sensitised material such as film or glass': this he said could not apply to an indecent image held on a computer hard drive as 'There is no "picture or other image" on or in the disc; nothing which can be seen.'[88] But, he went on to note that under s. 7(2) a photograph was defined as including 'a copy of an indecent photograph', could the images on the hard drive be such a copy? Evans LJ believed so: 'There is nothing in the Act which makes it necessary that the copy should itself be a photograph within the dictionary or the statutory definition, and if there was, it would make the inclusion of the reference to a copy unnecessary. So we conclude that there is no restriction on the nature of a copy, and that the data represents the original photograph, in another form.'[89]

He then gave an *obiter* opinion on the scope of the new pseudo-photographs provisions. As the appellants had been charged prior to s. 84 of the Criminal Justice and Public Order Act 1994 coming into effect they could not be charged with possession or distribution of pseudo photographs but Evans LJ believed he should examine the scope of the new provision in any event. He noted that it was the view of the Court that '[these new provisions] seem to us to be concerned with images created by computer processes rather than the storage and transmission by computers of images created originally by photography.'[90] Thus the collective view of the *Fellows* court was that digitised images held on hard drives were not photographs but were copies of photographs originally taken in the traditional manner and that pseudo-images were only images created by computer and could not be images stored on computer.

If the law had been left in this form it could have caused substantial difficulties for the prosecuting authorities. A completely digital picture (taken with a digital camera and then downloaded onto a hard drive) would appear to fall between these two definitions: being neither a photograph or a copy of a photograph nor a pseudo-image. In one of those strange twists that often occurs though when new legislation is introduced there remain outstanding appeals on the old legislation. Even as Evans LJ gave the judgement of the Court in *Fellows* he knew that it had already been replaced by statutory developments, for his judgement was given on 27 September 1996 while the wording of s. 7(4) of the Protection of Children Act had been changed on 3 February 1995 to read 'references to a photograph include (a) the negative as well as the positive version; and (b) data stored on a computer disc or by other electronic means which is capable of conversion into a photograph.' Therefore while Evans LJ had to follow a complicated line of reasoning to find that data held on a hard drive could be a copy of a photograph, the

---

[86] [1997] 2 All ER 548; [1997] 1 Cr App R 244.   [87] [1997] 1 Cr App R 244, 245-246.
[88] *ibid*, 253.   [89] *ibid*, 254.   [90] *ibid*, 255.

new wording of s. 7(4), if it had applied in the case before him, would have allowed him to simply find the appellants guilty of distribution of 'indecent photographs'.

The UK continues to take a hard line with the possession of both actual and pseudo-images being aggressively prosecuted.

Highlight Prosecuting Possession of Child Abuse Images

Yaman Akdeniz reports that between 1988 (when the possession offence was introduced) and 2004 there were 1,831 prosecutions under s. 160 (with 1,267 convictions) and 624 police cautions. Meanwhile between 1980 and 2004 there were 4,771 prosecutions under s. 1 of the Protection of Children Act with 3,789 convictions and 732 police cautions.

[Y. Akdeniz, *Internet Child Pornography and the Law* (2008), 25]

It may be that the law enforcement authorities prosecute aggressively because the courts have indicated they take a hard-line stance in enforcing the provisions of both s. 160 and s. 1. Many cases of what would usually be thought of as possession of child abuse images are being prosecuted under s. 1 of the Protection of Children Act for the more serious offence of making indecent images.

This follows the decision of the Court of Appeal in *R. v Bowden*. [91]

Highlight *R. v Bowden*

A person who either downloads images on to disc or who prints them off is making them.

The Act is not only concerned with the original creation of images, but also their proliferation. Photographs or pseudo-photographs found on the Internet may have originated from outside the United Kingdom; to download or print within the jurisdiction is to create new material which hitherto may not have existed therein.

The impact of this decision is that anyone who 'saves' an indecent image (even if the copy is merely in their browser's cache) is deemed to have 'made' an image under s. 1: this does seem to stretch the framer's original intent in framing both s. 1 and s. 160 and given that the s. 1 offence carries a maximum term of imprisonment of ten years, as compared to five years under s. 160, seems to suggest this was intended to prevent the more serious offence of *original* creation of indecent images. But *Bowden* demonstrates the hard-line approach taken in the UK. We can see this at work again when dealing with pseudo-images. In *Goodland v DPP*, the Divisional Court suggested that the creation of a crude pseudo-photograph by Sellotaping two images together and then photocopying the resultant gestalt image, could trigger the Protection of Children Act.[92]

---

[91] [2001] QB 88.   [92] [2000] 1 WLR 1427, 1442, per Simon Brown LJ.

14.3.2 **Policing pseudo-images internationally**

Elsewhere though, the regulation of pseudo-photographs has proven much more controversial. While the UK has taken a clear view that the risk of indirect harm to children is too great to allow any form of pseudo-photograph to be possessed and/ or distributed other states take different views. In the US attempts to regulate pseudo-images have run up against the First Amendment with campaigners claiming that as there is no direct harm to children pseudo-images are to be afforded the same artistic protections as classical paintings which often portray naked infants and cherubs. The claims of artistic and free speech activists and the state came to a head in *Ashcroft v Free Speech Coalition*,[93] a challenge to the constitutionality of the Child Pornography Prevention Act 1996.

In 1982 in the case of *New York v Ferber*,[94] the US Supreme Court held that it was not a breach of the First Amendment to restrict the distribution of child abuse images as the restriction on free expression was reasonable to protect children from the harm inherent in making such images. This principle had later been extended in the case of *Osborne v Ohio*,[95] to further cover the mere possession of child abuse images. But the Supreme Court had been clear in both decisions that the restriction of the First Amendment was reasonable because of the risk of direct harm to children. The Child Pornography Prevention Act sought to extend the *Ferber/Osborne* principle significantly. It sought to extend the definition of 'child pornography' to include: 'any visual depiction, including any photograph, film, video, picture, or computer or computer-generated image or picture, whether made or produced by electronic, mechanical, or other means, of sexually explicit conduct, where such visual depiction is, or appears to be, of a minor engaging in sexually explicit conduct.'[96] This would extend the *Ferber/Osborne* principle to cover what in the US is known as 'virtual images', what we call pseudo-images, but as we have seen there is no direct harm in the production of pseudo-images and so the constitutionality of the Act was challenged by the Free Speech Coalition (FSC).

The FSC alleged that by prohibiting images that 'appear to be' children engaged in sexual activity, and prohibiting speech that 'conveys the impression' that the images depict minors engaged in sexual activity, were overbroad, vague, and had a chilling effect on the legitimate work of the adult entertainment industry. The Supreme Court agreed and the Act was struck down. Justice Kennedy gave the leading opinion. He found that despite the fact that 'the sexual abuse of a child is a most serious crime and an act repugnant to the moral instincts of a decent people'[97] there was no evidence of direct harm occurring with relation to virtual images 'While the Government asserts that the images can lead to actual instances of child abuse the causal link is contingent and indirect. The harm does not necessarily follow from the speech, but depends upon some unquantified potential for subsequent criminal acts.'[98] In seeking to prevent the production and distribution of virtual images the Act was overbroad, in Justice Kennedy's words 'the CPPA prohibits speech despite its serious literary, artistic, political, or scientific value. The statute proscribes the visual depiction of an idea—that of teenagers

---

[93] 535 US 234 (2002).   [94] 458 US 747 (1982).   [95] 495 US 103 (1990).
[96] Child Pornography Prevention Act 1996 § 121(2).   [97] 535 US 234, 244.
[98] *ibid*, 250.

engaging in sexual activity—that is a fact of modern society and has been a theme in art and literature throughout the ages.'[99] Thus the CPPA was struck down despite a strong dissenting opinion from Chief Justice Rehnquist who felt that 'Congress has a compelling interest in ensuring the ability to enforce prohibitions of actual child pornography, and we should defer to its findings that rapidly advancing technology soon will make it all but impossible to do so.'[100]

Ashcroft suggested it was impossible for the US Government to restrict the supply of virtual child pornography in the same way *Reno* had made it impossible for them to control the supply of adult content. A subsequent attempt has been made to restrict the availability of virtual images in the Prosecutorial Remedies and Other Tools to end the Exploitation of Children Today (PROTECT) Act 2003. After a lengthy exposition in § 501 as to why the Supreme Court should not strike out the following provisions, § 502 goes on the ban the production and distribution of virtual images which are 'indistinguishable' from actual images of a minor. It is the hope of Congress that in so limiting the definition of 'virtual images' and by explicitly stating that 'drawings, cartoons, sculptures, or paintings' are explicitly excluded from its scope that the Act will avoid the same fate as the CPPA. To date this provision has not been challenged but at least one commentator believes despite the efforts of Congress it is still unconstitutional.[101] The current position in the US is therefore that only pseudo-images which are indistinguishable from real images of child abuse are illegal;[102] all other forms of pseudo-images are protected by the First Amendment.

This issue has also been extensively reviewed in Canada in the case of *R. v Sharpe*.[103] Although not dealing directly with pseudo-images (Mr Sharpe was charged with possession of pornographic texts and some images) the question before the Canadian Supreme Court was similar to the one in *Ashcroft*: could the Federal Government of Canada restrict the creation, possession, and distribution of material which did not directly harm a child in its production or does such a law infringe the rights of Canadian citizens under the Canadian Charter of Rights and Freedoms? Mr Sharpe argued that the provisions of the Canadian Criminal Code were overbroad as they covered not just child abuse images but also textual representations of sexual relationships between adults and children as well as other materials such as pseudo-images which he argued he should be allowed to possess as part of his freedom of thought and expression.

The Supreme Court was faced with a challenging decision: prior to Mr Sharpe's challenge Canada had developed one of the most hard-line approaches to all forms of child pornography including drawings produced by hand and hand written texts.[104] The issue was that as Mr Sharpe argued this came perilously close to a 'thought crime' as it criminalised the recording of one's own thoughts and expressions. The Supreme Court rejected most of Mr Sharpe's claims finding that the restrictions in the Criminal

---

[99] *ibid*, 246.   [100] *ibid*, 258.

[101] B. Slocum, 'Virtual Child Pornography: Does it Mean the End of the Child Pornography Exception to the First Amendment?' 14 *Albany Law Journal of Science and Technology* 637 (2004).

[102] To be indistinguishable the image must be such that 'an ordinary person viewing the depiction would conclude that the depiction is of an actual minor engaged in sexually explicit conduct.' PROTECT Act § 502(c) (codified as 18 USC § 2256(11)).   [103] 2001 SCC 2.

[104] *R. v Pointon* Unreported Manitoba Provincial Court., October 23, 1997. Discussed in *R. v Sharpe*.

Code were proportional but they did create two narrow exceptions for (1) Self-created expressive material (any written material or visual representation created by the accused alone, and held by the accused alone, exclusively for his or her own personal use) and (2) Private recordings of lawful sexual activity (any visual recording, created by or depicting the accused, provided it does not depict unlawful sexual activity and is held by the accused exclusively for private use). The second of these is similar to the defence found in s. 1A of the Protection of Children Act, the first has no counterpart in UK Law (it would be assumed that the Director of Public Prosecutions would be expected to show discretion in cases such as these).

Pseudo or virtual images have therefore caused a degree of divergence between major common law jurisdictions. While lawmakers in each jurisdiction appear agreed that they should be outlawed on the indirect harm principle, States with strong protections for freedom of thought and expression may be expected to resist attempts to outlaw all but the most clearly obscene examples of pseudo-pornography. This raises the question, if *Reno* effectively deregulated adult content globally why has *Ashcroft* not had the same effect with pseudo-images? The reason is fourfold. Firstly, Congress could take steps to control certain forms of pseudo-imagery through the PROTECT Act. This is because these forms of image are obscene under the *Miller* standard and are therefore not protected by the First Amendment. Secondly, in 'consumer states' like the UK, possession of pseudo-images is illegal. This places it on a different footing to obscene content and means the authorities can easily prosecute consumers of such images here. Thirdly, the size of the available market is smaller making it easier for law enforcement authorities to police; and finally, the cost of production of high quality pseudo-images remains high meaning that simple economics, rather unfortunately, lead suppliers to produce actual images of child abuse which remain illegal in nearly every state worldwide.

14.4 **Age play**

One interesting variation on pseudo child pornography which has developed recently is the arrival to 'online Age Play'. This is a variation of a traditional sexual fetish in which one partner plays the role of a child in a role-play scenario. Online Age Play takes place in massively multiplayer online role-playing games (MMORPGs) such as *Second Life* when one player creates an avatar in the form of a child or teenager and then engages in sexual activities with another player or players. This was most common in the virtual reality game *Second Life* but can exist in any MMORPG which allows players to control the design of their own avatar and which allow for sexual interaction between characters.

The question of whether Age Play should be criminalised is a vexed one. Age Play between consenting adults in the privacy of their own home is legal; should it be any different if they choose to use computer technology and avatars to play out their fantasies? The counter-argument is that like pseudo-images the creation of Age Play scenarios may increase the likelihood of indirect harm to children by encouraging paedophiles to explore and develop their desires by progressing from Age Play to the consumption of actual child abuse images, or perhaps to even actual abuse of a child. The *Second Life* community seems to be strongly united against Age Play within their community, meaning that even within *Second Life* Age Play is an underground activity with few participants in *Second Life* reported to have seen Age Play occurring, although *Second Life* maker and operator Linden Labs confirm that they are aware it does go on.[105]

Is online Age Play legal? It is clear that if Age Play is illegal then it must be under provisions relating to pseudo-images as clearly there is no actual child involved in its production. As Age Play involves avatars it is equally clear that as the law stands in the US Age Play is legal there as it would be protected by the *Ashcroft* decision and as second life avatars are not indistinguishable from real children they are not caught by the PROTECT Act. In the UK the law is less clear cut although the wording of s. 7(7) of the Protection of Children Act suggests that such activity is also legal in the UK.

As you should recall the exact wording of s. 7(7) is '"Pseudo-photograph" means an image, whether made by computer-graphics or otherwise howsoever, *which appears to be a photograph*' (emphasis added). The reason pseudo-photographs are defined in relation to actual photographs is to prevent the inadvertent criminalisation of sculpture, artistic images, or cartoon images such as manga and hentai. As an avatar in an MMORPG bears little direct resemblance (on current technology) to a photograph it is likely that Age Play is not illegal under the Protection of Children Act or s. 160 of the Criminal Justice Act 1988. There remains though one other potential avenue of regulation of such activity: the Obscene Publications Act 1959. Should Age Play images be classified as obscene under the Act then anyone who engages in Age Play may commit the offence of 'publishing an obscene article' under s. 2.[106]

It is highly unlikely that a prosecution under the Obscene Publications Act would succeed suggesting that as the law in the UK is currently framed it is not illegal to engage in online Age Play. This view seems to be confirmed from a series of media reports in early 2007 which suggested that investigators from both Germany and the UK were investigating a paedophile ring based in *Second Life*.[107] The stories all surrounded the alleged trading of real and pseudo-images via *Second Life* as well as Age Play. In each report the focus of the investigation was on the trading of images, not the practice of Age Play, although in one report a spokesman for the UK's Child Exploitation and Online Protection Centre did comment that they did have concerns about Age Play.[108] The investigations seem to have tapered off with no reports of prosecutions in either Germany or the UK.

Despite its apparent legality Age Play continues to offend community values. This had led Linden Labs, the makers and controllers of *Second Life*, to take steps to control Age Play, banning the practice and terminating the accounts of users

---

[105] D. Terdiman, 'Phony kids, virtual sex' *cnet News* 12 April 2006: http://news.cnet.com/Phony-kids,-virtual-sex/2100-1043_3-6060132.html.

[106] For this to be possible the virtual portrayal of child abuse which Age Play depicts would have to be found to be to 'tend to deprave and corrupt persons who are likely, having regard to all relevant circumstances, to read, see or hear the matter contained or embodied in it' (s. 1(a)) and it would have to be classified as 'published' which includes the electronic transmission of the data (s. 1(3)(b)). Neither is certain. In particular an adept defence counsel would surely argue that if the image is 'published' it is published by Linden Labs rather than the end user.

[107] Deutsche Welle, *German Prosecutors Pursue Child Porn in 'Second Life'*, 8 May 2007: http://www.dw-world.de/dw/article/0,2144,2481582,00.html; R. Newman, 'Real police enter a fantasy world', *The First Post* 21 May 2009: http://www.thefirstpost.co.uk/6846,features,second-life-police-enter-a-fantasy-world; E. Reuters, 'UK to investigate pedophilia in virtual worlds' *Reuters* 30 October 2007: http://secondlife.reuters.com/stories/2007/10/30/uk-to-investigate-pedophilia-in-virtual-worlds/.   [108] Reuters, *ibid.*

caught involved in the Age Play in *Second Life*.[109] This has led to some suggestions that alternate Age Play MMORPGs may be set up.[110]

For the moment Age Play remains a niche area and for as long as it remains so it is unlikely law enforcement authorities will take steps to regulate it leaving its regulation to communities such as occurred in *Second Life*. If though Age Play were to show evidence of supporting other activities such as the trading in child abuse images, or to be connected to actual abuse then law enforcement authorities may seek to extend the current provisions of the Protection of Children Act to regulate this activity.

14.5 **Extreme pornography**

Extreme pornography is a relatively new term in UK law. It arrived in summer 2005 when the Home Office and the Scottish Executive launched their joint consultation paper: 'Consultation: on the possession of extreme pornographic material'.[111] The consultation was launched after a campaign from Liz Longhurst to ban possession of violent pornography; images portraying sexual asphyxia, necrophilia, and rape, following the rape and murder of her daughter, Jane, in March 2003 by Graham Coutts, a man seemingly obsessed with violent sexual imagery.[112] The consultation process led eventually to the promulgation of s. 63 of the Criminal Justice and Immigration Act 2008 which came into force on 26 January 2009.[113] Section 63 outlaws the possession of extreme pornographic images:

(1) It is an offence for a person to be in possession of an extreme pornographic image.

(2) An 'extreme pornographic image' is an image which is both:

    (a) pornographic, and

    (b) an extreme image.

(3) An image is 'pornographic' if it is of such a nature that it must reasonably be assumed to have been produced solely or principally for the purpose of sexual arousal.

(4) Where (as found in the person's possession) an image forms part of a series of images, the question whether the image is of such a nature as is mentioned in subsection (3) is to be determined by reference to:

    (a) the image itself, and

    (b) (if the series of images is such as to be capable of providing a context for the image) the context in which it occurs in the series of images.

---

[109] 'Linden Lab further clarify ageplay policy', The Metaverse Journal 14 November 2007: http://www.metaversejournal.com/2007/11/14/linden-lab-further-clarify-ageplay-policy/.

[110] T. Nino, 'Wonderland creator promoting new grid', *Massively.com* 6 March 2008: http://www.massively.com/2008/03/06/wonderland-creator-promoting-new-grid/.

[111] Home Office/Scottish Executive, Consultation: on the possession of extreme pornographic material, August 2005: http://www.homeoffice.gov.uk/documents/cons-extreme-porn-3008051/cons-extreme-pornography?view=Binary.

[112] For discussion of the Longhurst campaign and the events surrounding it see A. Murray, 'The Reclassification of Extreme Pornographic Material', above n. 15.

[113] By The Criminal Justice and Immigration Act 2008 (Commencement No. 4 and Saving Provision) Order 2008, SI 2008/2993.

(5) So, for example, where:

    (a) an image forms an integral part of a narrative constituted by a series of images, and

    (b) having regard to those images as a whole, they are not of such a nature that they must reasonably be assumed to have been produced solely or principally for the purpose of sexual arousal, the image may, by virtue of being part of that narrative, be found not to be pornographic, even though it might have been found to be pornographic if taken by itself.

(6) An 'extreme image' is an image which:

    (a) falls within subsection (7), and

    (b) is grossly offensive, disgusting or otherwise of an obscene character.

(7) An image falls within this subsection if it portrays, in an explicit and realistic way, any of the following:

    (a) an act which threatens a person's life,

    (b) an act which results, or is likely to result, in serious injury to a person's anus, breasts or genitals,

    (c) an act which involves sexual interference with a human corpse, or

    (d) a person performing an act of intercourse or oral sex with an animal (whether dead or alive),

and a reasonable person looking at the image would think that any such person or animal was real.

(8) In this section 'image' means:

    (a) a moving or still image (produced by any means); or

    (b) data (stored by any means) which is capable of conversion into an image within paragraph (a).

This is a far reaching addition to the list of banned items. Before January 2009 only child abuse images (and pseudo-images) were proscribed in this manner. Why has the Government extended the law in this fashion? The answer is given in the original consultation paper.[114]

> **→ Highlight** Banning Possession of Extreme Pornography
>
> The issue arises due to the wide range of extreme pornography available via the internet which cannot, in practice, be controlled by our existing laws. Extreme pornography featuring violent rape, sexual torture and other abusive non-consensual acts existed in various forms before the internet but the publication and supply could be controlled by the Obscene Publications Acts 1959 and 1964, the Civic Government (Scotland) Act 1982 and by Customs legislation (the Customs Consolidation Act 1876 and Customs and Excise Management Act 1979). Closing down sources of supply and distribution obviated the need for a possession offence. However, the global nature of the internet makes this approach much more difficult.

---

[114] Home Office/Scottish Executive, Consultation, above n. 111, [1].

This demonstrates the problem highlighted originally by Post and Johnson in 1996,[115] that although the community standards applied in obscenity regulations are local, the internet both fails to respect traditional borders, and is largely given the benefit of the US First Amendment following the *Reno* decision.[116] Faced with the inability to control this most extreme of pornographic content the Government felt compelled to act in light of Mrs Longhurst's high profile campaign. The only effective method of control which they could apply was to pass a possession offence: basically bracketing extreme pornography with child abuse images.

The difficulty with this approach is that while we may justify the criminalisation of the possession of child abuse images on the direct harm rationale (and pseudo-images on the indirect harm rationale) it is more difficult to justify a blanket ban on the possession of extreme images.

An examination of the proscribed content found in s. 63 reveals that it covers four broad headings: (1) snuff and similarly highly violent content; (2) sado-masochism and 'torture porn'; (3) necrophilia; and (4) bestiality. Although all of these acts may themselves be criminal offences if carried out against an unwilling victim, in most cases pornographic content of this nature is produced in much the same way as action movies produce scenes of violence and murder: using actors and careful stage direction. The direct harm approach cannot be therefore justified in all cases. Although there are no doubt cases where actual criminal activity may be recorded in the making of extreme pornography, the definition given in s. 63(7) that the image must 'portray, in an explicit and realistic way' the act in question is too wide to justify the application of the direct harm principle when in most cases these images will be staged by paid actors.[117]

During consultation the Government attempted to make an indirect harm argument, suggesting that 'it is possible to that such material may encourage or reinforce interest in violent and aberrant sexual activity' to the detriment of society as a whole'.[118] The difficulty with this argument is though that while there is extensive statistical data to prove a link between the consumption of pseudo-child abuse images and further offending by paedophiles there is little evidence of a link between consumption of extreme pornography and further offending,[119] a fact admitted by the Government.[120]

The Government therefore took the decision to outlaw the possession of such images on public policy grounds rather than on the harm principle. The policy justification was that 'there is a small category of pornographic material which is so repugnant that, in common with child abuse images, its possession should not be tolerated'.[121] The danger with a public policy argument though is that you must judge the mood of the public

---

[115] Above, n. 21.

[116] In fact it is reported that the UK Government approached the US Government asking them to take steps to close down a number of necrophilia websites at the heart of the Graham Coutts case including 'Necrobabes' which was frequently visited by Coutts ahead of the murder, but were told the sites were protected by the Constitution. See 'Blunkett meets Ashcroft', *Channel 4 News*, 7 March 2004: http://www.channel4.com/news/2004/03/week_1/07_terror.html.

[117] The obvious exception is the bestiality provision as animals like children cannot consent.

[118] Home Office/Scottish Executive, Consultation, above n. 111, [27].

[119] See Murray, above n. 15. See also See M. Popovich, 'Establishing New Breeds of (Sex) Offenders: Science or Political Control?' (2007) 22 *Sexual and Relationship Therapy* 255; A. D'Amato, 'Porn Up, Rape Down' *Northwestern Public Law Research Paper* No. 913013: http://www.ssrn.com/abstract=913013.

[120] Home Office/Scottish Executive, Consultation, above n.111, [31].   [121] *ibid*, [33].

correctly: with s. 63 it is arguable that the Government failed to meet the public mood fully. By outlawing possession of BDSM images an extensive backlash occurred, led by members of the BDSM community who were concerned that the provision would be used to strike at their community. A strong campaign from the BDSM community assisted by anti-censorship groups and human rights organisations forced the Government to make a number of concessions while s. 63 was being debated in Parliamentary Committee.[122] These concessions were designed to allay the fears of the BDSM community that s. 63 would be used as a proxy to clamp down on their lifestyle and activities but may have led s. 63 to miss at least one of its targets.

When consultation began on s. 63 it was clear that the scope of s. 63 was meant to include violent pornography, in particular content which pairs sex and violence such as 'rape images'. But due to concessions made in Committee the original wording of s. 63(7)(a) 'an image of an act which threatens or appears to threaten a person's life' became 'an image [which] portrays, in an explicit and realistic way an act which threatens a person's life'. This substantially narrows the scope of s. 63(7)(a) as violent sexual content, including rape fetish content which does not portray in an explicit and realistic way an act which threatens a person's life is not within the scope of the new offence. The key difference between the original wording and the final version being the removal of the words 'or appears to' which would have allowed authorities to take action against clearly staged violent pornography but which now they cannot. It is unclear why the Government made this change. There are strong public policy grounds for criminalising possession of rape fetish which are seen by society as among the more abhorrent of pornographic images and which may cause indirect harm in the event that actors are coerced in the making of such movies, or may even be actually raped, or in the event that like Graham Coutts a consumer of such images decides to act out his fantasies in real life with tragic consequences. Nevertheless this seems to be the effect of s. 63(7)(a) at least until a court interprets the provision differently.

Section 63 remains a relatively new provision and it will take a few years for its full effect to be measured as courts interpret its provisions and apply them. It seems unlikely that it will have much effect on the large amount of extreme pornographic content available on the internet. As has already been discussed most of this content is hosted in the US where much of it can gain the protection of the First Amendment: therefore s. 63 is unlikely to close down many pornographic websites. The police are unlikely to devote considerable resources to a crime that they see to be of relatively low priority when compared to images of child abuse and in fact the first prosecutions have come as a result of investigations into other matters. The first person charged with possession of extreme pornographic images was investigated after an engineer found the images on his computer while carrying out a repair,[123] while the first person to receive a custodial sentence under s. 63 was arrested on drugs offences with the images in question coming to light in the course of the drugs investigation.[124]

---

[122] A full discussion of the progress of s. 63 through Committee may be found in Murray, above n. 15.

[123] 'Man had "grossly offensive and disgusting" porn images on computer', *St Helens Star* 18 June 2009: http://www.sthelensstar.co.uk/news/4445020.Man_had__grossly_offensive_and_disgusting__porn_images_on_computer/.

[124] J. Ozimek, 'First prison sentence for extreme porn' *The Register*, 29 September 2009: http://www.theregister.co.uk/2009/09/29/newcastle_sentencing/.

It seems likely s. 63 will be more of a political statement than a provision of far reaching legal impact with even the Ministry of Justice estimating a maximum of thirty prosecutions per annum.[125]

14.6 **Private regulation of pornographic imagery**[126]

As the discussion throughout this chapter has demonstrated the development of web hosting and delivery of pornographic content has undermined the effectiveness of states regulators to control their borders and to police the production, distribution, and consumption of pornographic content of in all forms be it indecent, obscene, or extremely obscene. Pornography and obscenity is the area where there is arguably the greatest need for alternative regulatory measures, such as those predicted by Lawrence Lessig in *Code and Other Laws of Cyberspace*,[127] which make use of the design features of the internet to allow for effective regulation. Some such measures have been implemented by Internet Service Providers, mostly designed to restrict the supply of child abuse images and pseudo-images. In the UK a hybrid hierarchical/design control system known as Cleanfeed is used.[128] Cleanfeed is a two part hybrid system: firstly suspect images need to be identified and blacklisted, this is carried out by a private regulatory authority known as the Internet Watch Foundation, then the suspect images, pages, or sites are blocked though the Cleanfeed technical protocol.

Central to the functioning of Cleanfeed is the Internet Watch Foundation (IWF). The IWF was formed in 1996 following agreement between the Government, police forces, and the ISP industry that something had to be done to tackle the problem of child abuse images on the Usenet system. The ISPs suggested a self regulatory body which would operate a 'hotline' to allow members of the public to report potentially illegal images; the experts at the IWF would then establish whether the report had identified an illegal image of child abuse and if they adjudged the image to be illegal they would add it to their blacklist of banned images or sites which ISPs would then block access to, thus protecting them from the risk of being prosecuted for possession of an indecent image of a child under s. 160 of the Criminal Justice Act. Over time, the focus of the IWF's work has moved from Usenet to content hosted on websites and that now forms the bulk of the IWF's day to day work. As well as informing ISPs of material that should be blocked the IWF also passes relevant information to the law enforcement authorities allowing them to take steps to trace the source of the illegal material: material hosted in the UK is reported directly to the relevant local UK police service, the Child Exploitation and Online Protection Centre, or the Serious Organised Crime Agency, whereas material hosted offshore is reported to the Virtual Global Taskforce for investigation.

---

[125] Ministry of Justice, *Criminal Justice and Immigration Bill Regulatory Impact Assessments*, 20 June 2007, 91: http://webarchive.nationalarchives.gov.uk/+/http://www.justice.gov.uk/docs/regulatory-impact-assess-1.pdf.

[126] See also discussion of this issue above at pp. 70–73.

[127] See L. Lessig, *Code and Other Laws of Cyberspace*, (1999); *Code Ver. 2.0* (2006) discussed in depth in Chapter 4, esp. at pp. 62–66.

[128] Cleanfeed is actually the internal BT project name for the system, its actual name is the BT Anti-Child-Abuse Initiative. Over time though Cleanfeed has become the common label of the system.

The IWF is generally well regarded for the work it does and is recognised to have assisted the UK in virtually eradicating child abuse content hosted within the UK.[129] The work of the IWF is not though without controversy. Many commentators have written on the lack of public accountability of the IWF,[130] and in December 2008 the issue of a private regulator with the ability to 'blacklist' content for an estimated 95% of the UK online population became spectacularly newsworthy when the IWF ordered the blocking of the Wikipedia entry for Scorpions album *Virgin Killer.*

Case Study The *Virgin Killer* Affair

'Virgin Killer' is a 1976 album by the German band Scorpions. It is highly controversial due to the nature of the cover art for the album which portrays a ten year old girl posing nude, with a faux glass shatter obscuring her genitalia.

Despite a high degree of controversy the album had been on sale in the UK with the controversial cover and indeed was still available for purchase on Amazon.co.uk at the time. The effect of the IWF block though was much greater than attempted.

When the Cleanfeed system was updated to block access to the Wikipedia page in question ISPs passed all traffic from their customers through a few proxy servers used to manage the Cleanfeed system to ensure the blacklisted page was blocked. This caused problems for users of the site. Wikipedia allows users to anonymously edit its entries but keeps a record of the IP addresses of those who make changes. It may then use this information to selectively block users who vandalise the site or otherwise break its rules. The proxy filtering made it impossible to uniquely distinguish users coming from nearly all UK ISPs.

On discovery of an inordinately high number of requests to edit pages coming from a few IP addresses, and to prevent vandalism, Wikipedia instituted a blanket ban on anonymous edits from the 'big six' ISPs, which account for 95% of British residential internet users.

This had the immediate effect of requiring nearly all registered users in the UK to request the lifting of IP autoblocks on their accounts before they could edit, and the de-facto permanent effect of barring any contributions from people without user accounts on the site. This effect was noticed immediately and complaints to ISPs led to the actions of the IWF being uncovered.

For many people this was the first time they had heard of the IWF (another problem with private/industry regulators) and the public outcry was deafening.[131] The IWF quickly

[129] In 2006, at the tenth anniversary of the IWF it was reported that reported child abuse content hosted in the UK, which was 18% in 1997, had been reduced to 0.2% in 2006. P. Robbins, 'Tackling the threat of child abuse online', *BBC News*, 24 October 2006: http://news.bbc.co.uk/1/hi/technology/6080364.stm.

[130] See, e.g. C.J. Davies, 'The hidden censors of the internet', *Wired 06.09*, 20 May 2009: http://www.wired.co.uk/wired-magazine/archive/2009/05/features/the-hidden-censors-of-the-internet.aspx; C. Doctorow, 'How to make child-porn blocks safe for the internet', *The Guardian* 16 December 2008: http://www.guardian.co.uk/technology/2008/dec/16/cory-doctorow-wikipedia.

[131] See, e.g. R. Cellan-Jones, 'Wikipedia is censored', *BBC dot.life*, 8 December 2008: http://www.bbc.co.uk/blogs/technology/2008/12/wikipedia_is_censored.html (and in particular see the 295 user comments); J. Schofield, 'Wikipedia page censored in the UK for "child pornography"', *The Guardian* 8 December 2005: http://www.guardian.co.uk/technology/blog/2008/dec/08/internet (again read the 114 user comments).

backtracked and referred their decision to their appeals procedure, which upheld the original decision, but faced with rising public anger at their heavy-handed approach, the IWF decided to reconvene to 'consider the contextual issues involved in this specific case' they noted that as the 'IWF's overriding objective is to minimise the availability of indecent images of children on the internet, however, on this occasion our efforts had the opposite effect so the Board decided that the webpage should be removed from the URL list.'[132] The whole affair had an extremely negative effect on public opinion of the IWF and they are having to work hard to restore confidence in themselves. It is noted in the 2008 Annual Report that 'we are committed to improving our services so issues raised by this incident will be addressed, in collaboration with our industry partners, in the year ahead.'[133]

Once a site is blacklisted by the IWF it is passed on to its industry partners for blocking. This is usually achieved through the Cleanfeed content blocking system. The system uses the blacklist and a number of proxy servers to block access to the content in question. For example if there is blacklisted content on the website *yourpiccshere.com/nastynasty/porn*, then when a user requests access to any content on the yourpiccshere.com server that request will be sent to a Cleanfeed server where the blacklist is held. If the content requested is not on the blacklist (say *yourpiccshere.com/holiday/spain*) then the proxy will allow access to the content, though if the customer is seeking to obtain access to the blacklisted content they will be blocked from accessing the site.

A major problem with Cleanfeed is that the end-user does not know that Cleanfeed has blocked his access. There is no 'blocked by Cleanfeed' message, instead the user simply receives a 'not found' error. This means there is no way the average user can tell if content has been blocked by Cleanfeed or is just unavailable, and as the IWF does not publish its blacklist we have no way of knowing how many sites have been blocked in error, or have been blocked in full when only one page or image held on that site is illegal. This would have been the effect of the Wikipedia block if it had not been for Wikipedia's complex editing safeguards designed to prevent defacement of its pages. This raises the question, if, as Richard Clayton of Cambridge University suggests, paedophiles do not routinely publish child abuse images on publicly available websites for fear of being arrested,[134] is the Cleanfeed system an unnecessarily intrusive system allowing too much control into the hands of a few unelected and unaccountable individuals who have the ability to censor almost the entire UK online population for little return? The IWF would, of course, say no and would point to the fact that in 2008 they identified 1,536 unique domains relating to child sexual abuse content, as well as issuing twenty notices under the Protection of Children Act 1978 and thirty-nine notices under the Obscene Publications Acts 1959 and 1964 to UK law enforcement bodies.[135] The problem is that we have no way of knowing how many of the 1,536 domains (which were presumably blacklisted) fell into the same category as Wikipedia and how many were serious paedophile websites.

---

[132] Taken from the 2008 Internet Watch Foundation Annual Report at 9. The 'opposite effect' mentioned is that due to the high level of publicity the affair had sparked, people were searching for the image and were accessing it at a number of sites not yet blocked usually via a search engine like Google or Yahoo!.   [133] *ibid*.

[134] See R. Cellan-Jones, 'Can we block child abuse sites?', *BBC dot.life*, 23 February 2009: http://www.bbc.co.uk/blogs/technology/2009/02/can_we_block_child_abuse_sites.html.

[135] 2008 Internet Watch Foundation Annual Report, 6.

14.7 **Conclusions**

The regulation of pornographic and obscene content is one of the greatest challenges for the information society. As an 'informational product' pornography benefits from the same economies of production and distribution seen in music and video production but with the potential for far greater negative social impact. There are several challenges which will continue to test communities and lawmakers in the next ten to twenty years. First among them is how to prevent children from coming into greater contact with pornography than they already do. With children routinely having their own computer and internet enabled mobile phone from an early age this is becoming a major problem. Secondly is the question of how we wrest back local community values in a place where there is no local community, this may prove impossible, but is certainly worth exploring. Thirdly, is to determine where obscene content becomes unacceptably obscene: this to date has led to the banning of the possession of images of child abuse, and pseudo-images as well as 'extreme pornographic images'. Should we add to this list? Or would it be an infringement of our freedom of thought and expression if we continually grow a list of banned items? Finally we may wish to consider how technology is changing the nature of sexual encounters and question how we wish to deal with online advertising of brothels, and how to deal with new phenomena including sexting, and online grooming. Some of these will be discussed in the next chapter.

FURTHER READING

Books

Y. Akdeniz, *Internet Child Pornography and the Law: National and International Responses* (2008)

D. Thornburgh & H. Lin, *Youth, Pornography, and the Internet* (2002)

A. White, *Virtually Obscene* (2006)

Chapters and Articles

A. Murray, 'The Reclassification of Extreme Pornographic Images' (2009) 72 *MLR* 73

D. Vick, 'The Internet and the First Amendment' (1998) 61 *MLR* 414

J, Wolak, K. Mitchell & D. Finkelhor, Internet Sex Crimes Against Minors: The Response of Law Enforcement, *Crimes against Children Research Center* November 2003

M. Eneman, 'The New Face of Child Pornography' in M. Klang & A. Murray (eds), *Human Rights in the Digital Age* (2005)

15

Crime and law enforcement in the information society

As most online transactions take place with the identity and location of participants hidden behind the computer screen it offers opportunities for those with criminal intent to reach out globally to commit fraud, theft, and harassment; to offer illegal gambling and pornography, and to commit direct cyber-attacks.[1] Although by far the most common form of illegal activity online is simple copyright infringement,[2] there are a growing number of criminal activities being operated through the internet including the unregulated production and distribution of pornography and child abuse images,[3] direct cyber-attacks such as Denial of Service attacks and privacy attacks including hacking, phishing, and the installation of Trojans,[4] computer fraud, online harassment, grooming, and bandwidth theft. Such activities often take place overseas but target UK citizens. The most infamous form of computer fraud is the advance fee fraud (discussed below), which is now so prevalent in Nigeria that it is known internationally simply as the '419 Fraud': 419 referring to the Article of the Nigerian Criminal Code dealing with such fraud.[5] A variation of the 419 Fraud, the 'Russian Scam' targets UK users of online dating sites and is often perpetrated by criminals based in Russia and Eastern Europe, while 'cheque overpayment fraud' or 'criminal cashback' schemes are common on internet auction sites and like the '419 Fraud' often originate in Nigeria. This chapter will look at advance fee fraud as well as a number of other criminal activities common in the information society, including the illegal appropriation of personal data, commonly known as phishing, and offences against the person committed through information and communication technologies including harassment, cyber-stalking, and grooming.

---

[1] Of course IP addresses offer a route to track criminals, but the average computer user does not know how to trace an IP address and even when law enforcement authorities become involved they often find that the address is either 'spoofed' through a re-router or leads to an internet cafe.   [2] Discussed in Ch. 10.   [3] Discussed in Ch. 14.   [4] Discussed in Ch. 13.

[5] Article 419 forms part of Chapter 38, 'Obtaining Property by false pretences; Cheating'. It (along with the rest of the Nigerian Criminal Code) may be found at: http://www.nigeria-law.org/Criminal%20Code%20Act-Tables.htm.

15.1 **Fraud and identity theft**

15.1.1 **Fraud**

The risk of online fraud is extensive. The Home Office estimates that just one type of online fraud, 'card not present' fraud cost the UK economy £212 million in 2006,[6] while a separate study from research group Chatham House estimated that in the same year advance fee fraud cost the UK economy £150 million, with the average victim experiencing a loss of £31,000.[7] Many aspects of fraud are, of course, criminalised with much of the current UK Law to be found in the Fraud Act 2006. The Act was introduced to replace the old deception offences found in the Theft Acts.[8] The problem with the deception offences was that to commit deception it was widely accepted that a human mind had to be deceived. Deception of a computer system which would process an instruction automatically without human intervention was apparently not covered by the Theft Acts.[9]

The Fraud Act 2006 was enacted in response to the growing threat of computer and online fraud, much of which could be operated directly on a computer system. The Act came into force on 15 January 2007: it creates three new forms of fraud and a further offence of obtaining services dishonestly. Section 1 states that a person is guilty of fraud if he commits any of the offences listed in ss. 2–4: these are (1) fraud by making a false representation;[10] (2) fraud by failing to disclose information;[11] and (3) fraud by abuse of position.[12] These new offences, although all still offences of deception, have been extended to clearly cover fraud committed on an automated system. For instance s. 2(5) clearly states that 'a representation may be regarded as made if it (or anything implying it) is submitted in any form to any system or device designed to receive, convey or respond to communications (with or without human intervention).' Thus it will clearly cover all types of electronic communication including email, SMS and IRC, as well as instructions sent to an automated system like an online bank or credit card clearing system. If a UK-based fraudster were therefore to make a false representation, in breach of s. 2, such as to give false credit card details to an online bank or ecommerce site with a view to making a gain,[13] he would commit an offence. This would cover most forms of online fraud, including card not present fraud where the fraudster improperly gains credit card details and uses them to buy goods and services online; asset transfer fraud where a fraudster gains access to online banking services or similar and transfers assets to himself; and most forms of advance fee fraud where the fraudster tricks the victim into advancing them funds in the hope of making a future gain.

---

[6] Home Office, Crime in England and Wales 2006/2007: http://www.homeoffice.gov.uk/rds/crimeew0607.html.

[7] M. Peel, *Nigeria-Related Financial Crime and its Links with Britain* (2006).

[8] These were obtaining property by deception (1968 Act, s. 15); obtaining an money transfer by deception (1968 Act, s. 15A); obtaining services by deception (1978 Act, s. 1); and evasion of liability by deception (1978 Act, s. 2).

[9] In *DPP v Ray* [1974] AC 370, Lord Morris stated: 'For a deception to take place there must be some person or persons who will have been deceived'.

[10] Fraud Act 2006, s. 2.   [11] Fraud Act 2006, s. 3.   [12] Fraud Act 2006, s. 4.

[13] Gain is defined in s. 5(2) as '(a) gain in money or other property; (b) include any such gain or loss whether temporary or permanent; and "property" means any property whether real or personal (including things in action and other intangible property).'

The problem is that in the online environment fraud, like pornography, usually originates overseas but has its effects in the UK. As discussed in the introduction to this chapter the best known is probably the 'Nigerian Advance Fee Fraud', known colloquially as the '419 Fraud'. There are many variations of the 419 Fraud but they all follow a similar pattern.

Case Study The '419' Advance Fee Fraud

The victim receives an email from someone claiming to represent a company or individual with a large sum of money or similar assets which they require to transfer. They claim to have no ability to directly transfer the funds or assets themselves, usually due to banking regulations or some other legal impediment. They ask the victim for their assistance in making the transfer and in return offer them between 10–40% of the value of the asset or funds (usually worth millions of pounds).

When the victim offers to help the fraudster begins to ask for funds to be paid to effect the transfer. These may include small amounts to bribe officials or larger amounts required to show the victim is in good financial standing. Once the funds are transferred the fraudster disappears with the funds.

A variant of the 419 Fraud, popular in Eastern Europe, is the 'Russian Scam'.

Case Study The 'Russian Scam'

The victim is usually selected from a dating site, or singles site. They are contacted by a young woman who claims to be looking to marry a UK citizen. She will often send pictures of herself and will spend some time communicating with the victim by email, IRC, or perhaps even by telephone (although this is unusual as the fraudster is usually a man; women are hired by the fraudsters to make such calls).

The fraudster will then make requests for funds. These may involve payments for medical expenses for the young woman's mother, or for assistance with housing costs. She will then indicate that she is willing to travel to the UK to meet the victim and will ask for expenses for visas, travel tickets, and hotel rooms. The fraudster then disappears with the funds.

Although these frauds have names which reflect where they have recently developed, advance fee frauds can originate anywhere. Many 419 Frauds are now affected from China and former Soviet Bloc countries as well as Nigeria and other sub-Saharan African counties, while Russian Scams often originate in Africa and China as well as in former Soviet Bloc countries. Advance fee fraud is though only one form of internet-based fraud.

Whereas advance fee fraud tends to be practiced in developing nations, other more sophisticated forms of fraud are practiced in Europe and other developed nations.

Here the most common form of dishonest representation is 'card not present' fraud. Like the 419 Fraud there are a variety of ways this is practiced but the end result is usually the same.

Case Study 'Card Not Present' Fraud

The fraudster gets hold of personal credit card details including the name of the account holder, the card number, expiry date, and the CVC or card verification code. This may be acquired in a number of ways: either simply by using discarded credit card receipts, or by 'skimming' a card in a restaurant, bar, or shop, or by 'phishing' for such details online (discussed in greater depth below).

Once these details are known the fraudster may purchase goods or services online. The fraudster may also choose to sell the information on to third parties, this, although not a breach of s. 2 of the Fraud Act, may amount to the common law offence of conspiracy to defraud.

Thus common frauds committed though the application of Information and Communication Technology (ICT) would in most cases be either a breach of s. 2 of the Fraud Act 2006 or one of the subsequent sections, depending upon the nature of the fraud, or may, if involving two or more people amount to conspiracy to defraud at common law. But with so many frauds originating overseas can the international community effectively police this activity?

Some basic standards for international cooperation are found in the Council of Europe Convention on Cybercrime.[14] Article 8 requires that 'Each Party shall adopt such legislative and other measures as may be necessary to establish as criminal offences under its domestic law, when committed intentionally and without right, the causing of a loss of property to another person by: (a) any input, alteration, deletion or suppression of computer data, [or] (b) any interference with the functioning of a computer system, with fraudulent or dishonest intent of procuring, without right, an economic benefit for oneself or for another person.' It is clear though that Article 8 only covers certain forms of fraud. Card not present fraud is covered by Article 8 as it requires the inputting of computer data with fraudulent intent, advance fee fraud though appears not to be covered unless one takes an extremely expansive view of the term 'input of computer data' to cover the contents of emails or instant messages sent by the fraudsters to their victims.

The reason for the narrow scope of Article 8 may be because the Convention is focussed on 'Cybercrime' or as the preamble to the Convention puts it 'the present Convention is necessary to deter action directed against the confidentiality, integrity and availability of computer systems, networks and computer data as well as the misuse of such systems, networks and data by providing for the criminalisation of such conduct.' It is less focussed on traditional criminal activity which makes use of ICT as

---

[14] CETS No. 185, Budapest, 23.XI.2001.

a communications media, and more focussed on new forms of criminal activity which makes use of the unique nature of ICT communications.

The recent growth in advance fee frauds is as a result of the 'globalisation effect' of the information society. Fraudsters, often based in the poorest parts of the world, can use ICT to contact potential victims in the richest nations at a relatively low cost: there is nothing uniquely technology driven about this form of fraud: instead it is an old form of fraud being reborn through the global reach the information society offers.[15] By contrast internet-enabled card not present fraud is a new form of an old fraud. Card not present fraud, as it name suggests, is based on giving false credit or debit card details to a vendor or supplier of services when the card is not available for inspection. As such it tended historically to be carried out by mail or by telephone. Internet-based card not present fraud is a new way of carrying out card not present fraud not previously available: as such it is unlike advance fee fraud as it has created a new way of committing this fraud rather than merely a new way of communicating with victims.

As advance fee fraud is a traditional form of fraud it may be assumed that steps have been taken by states to outlaw the practice: indeed as we have seen it is illegal in the UK under s. 2 of the Fraud Act 2006, and in Nigeria under Article 419 of the Criminal Code. The issue is not the need for further measures, it is rather for international cooperation in the detection and prosecution of such activity.

In 2007 the first fruits of this international cooperation were reported when a joint operation of UK, US, Dutch, Spanish, Canadian, and Nigerian law enforcement agencies led to the arrest of nearly seventy people and the recovery of thousands of forged documents and cheques with a value of £8m.[16] This operation was led by the UK's Serious Organised Crime Agency using intelligence supplied from partner organisations and was carried out in Nigeria with the help of local investigators. This was the first in a series of operations planned to reduce the threat of advance fee fraud from Nigeria. The Serious Organised Crime Agency continues to devote considerable resources to this issue in conjunction with partner institutions and in its 2008 Annual Report it reported that a new partnership with the Nigerian Economic and Financial Crimes Commission had led to a 'successful programme to intercept fraudulent mail in Lagos resulting in Nigerian criminals being displaced to other West African countries, where SOCA and local law enforcement pursued them.'[17] Such partnerships, alongside common legal responses, as seen in Article 8 of the Cybercrime Convention, are essential if law enforcement bodies are to effectively deter fraudulent activity in the information society.

Alongside these common online frauds a number of new frauds have developed, mostly around online auction sites. These include overpayment fraud and escrow fraud.

---

[15] The Advance Fee fraud was originally known as the 'Spanish Prisoner Fraud' and can be dated back to the early 1900s.

[16] BBC News, *UK police in Nigerian scam haul*, 4 October 2007: http://www.news.bbc.co.uk/1/hi/uk/7027088.stm.

[17] Serious Organised Crime Agency, *Annual Report 2008/09*: http://www.soca.gov.uk/assessPublications/downloads/SOCA_AR_2009.pdf, 15.

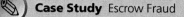

Case Study Overpayment Fraud

This begins when a buyer pays for goods (usually bought via an internet auction site) with a cheque drawn for a higher amount than the agreed price.

The buyer/fraudster will then ask the seller/victim to refund the overpayment by wire transfer. The seller/victim pays the cheque into his bank account and after three or four days assumes the cheque has cleared. He will then usually then send the goods and refund the difference as requested.

After about 16–20 days the seller/victim's bank will bounce the cheque for being a forgery leaving the seller/victim with no payment but having both shipped the goods and paid an amount of cash to the buyer/fraudster. The goods plus cash element of this fraud lead to it being dubbed in some quarters 'criminal cashback'.

Case Study Escrow Fraud

This occurs when a buyer offers to buy a high value item such as a car, boat, or designer watch. The seller will not wish to send the item without knowing the money for payment is secured; the buyer will not want to release the funds until they receive the item in case the seller is fraudulent. The answer is to escrow the funds: putting them in the hands of a reputable third party to hold until such time as the goods are received and the buyer is satisfied they are as described.

This is commonplace and there are a number of reputable escrow agencies but in the case of escrow fraud a fraudulent agency has been set up. The seller then sends the item believing the funds to be safely escrowed, but both the buyer and the escrow agency then disappear.

These are only a few of the number of current online frauds but by far the fastest growing form of online fraud currently is identity fraud.

15.1.2 **Identity theft and identity fraud**

Online identity fraud is now a massive industry. We are particularly susceptible to identity fraud in the information society for a number of reasons but prime among these are: (1) the way information is gathered and stored in the information society and (2) the increased use of identity proxies to prove our identity.

The information society, is as we have seen, both a social and economic market built around the ownership, storage, manipulation, and transfer of data. Much of this data may be used to identify the individual including IP addresses, dates of birth, name, address, telephone number, credit card details, and banking details, among others. There are therefore large amounts of personal data held by companies and organisations with whom we do business. There is always a risk of loss of this data either by the data controller, or in transit between the data subject and the data controller.[18] A loss of data can lead to identity fraud. There is no easy way to prove the identity of an individual when they deal with a website for there are no biometric indicators which we use in real life to establish identity: as Lawrence Lessig says 'In cyberspace … you enter without an identity and you identify only what you want—and even that can't be authenticated with any real confidence.'[19] Thus we use customer IDs, passwords, and passkeys to identify ourselves. Often these passwords and passkeys give access to financial data and resources, in particular online bank accounts or credit card accounts or other payment accounts like PayPal, or they allow others to fraudulently use our accounts to buy or sell goods such as our internet auction accounts.

These proxies for identity are highly prized by the criminal fraternity and have led to the rise of a new form of identity fraud known as 'phishing'.

Case Study Phishing

Phishing is usually carried out by email. An email is sent to many tens of thousands of email accounts at random and says something like the user's account has been suspended due to unusual activity, or that security measures are being upgraded and they need to confirm their details. The email will contain a link which will take the user to a 'shell' website made to look like the genuine site but when they enter their details they are retained by the fraudster who then uses them to gain access to their accounts.

This is again a false representation and is illegal under s. 2 of the Fraud Act 2006.

Like advance fee fraud and card not present fraud phishing represents a real harm to the UK economy with UK banks absorbing losses of over £52m in online banking fraud in 2008.[20] The tactic for dealing with phishing has largely been the same as with other forms of online fraud: suppression in the UK and cooperation on an international level.

On a domestic level the Court of Appeal has recently had its first opportunity to review phishing in the case of *R. v Wellman*.[21] This was an appeal against sentence. Mr Wellman had, along with others, obtained passwords and user IDs for over five thousand individuals by a mix of phishing and Trojans and had compromised over one thousand online bank accounts. He pled guilty at Leeds Crown Court and was sentenced to two terms of six years' imprisonment to run consecutively, a total of twelve years in prison. At appeal this was reduced to one term of four years and one of six to run consecutively, a total of ten years. In giving the judgement of the Court Mackay J noted that 'it is hard to imagine a more sophisticated and determined course of criminal conduct in this sphere of offending.'[22]

---

[18] This will be discussed further in Ch. 18.
[19] L. Lessig, *Code and Other Laws of Cyberspace Ver2.0* (2006), 248.
[20] APACS, *2008 Fraud Figures*: http://www.apacs.org.uk/09_03_19.htm.
[21] [2007] EWCA Crim 2874.   [22] *ibid*, [12].

Sentences such as these demonstrate how seriously the UK courts are taking the risk of phishing, a risk recognised internationally and which has led, like advance fee fraud, to a high level of international cooperation. In 2004 the United Nations organised an expert group on fraud and the criminal misuse and falsification of identity. The group met twice (in March 2005 and January 2007) and recommended that states take steps to update their laws to reflect recent technological developments, that states should ratify or accede to, the United Nations Crime Conventions and Council of Europe Cybercrime Convention, and that states should review rules on territorial jurisdiction to keep pace with ongoing evolution of fraud and identity-related offences and consider establishing extraterritorial jurisdiction in lieu of extradition.[23]

The expert group recommendations have been passed on the United Nations Office on Drugs and Crime, a body that fosters cooperation in the international fight against drug trafficking and organised crime. They have created a further Expert Group on Identity-Related Crime to examine the issue. The third meeting of this group took place in Vienna in January 2009 where they discussed 'legal approaches to criminalize identity theft'.[24] The group reported that they had doubts 'as to whether a single unified offence would be viable in most legal systems, but noted that it should be possible to address the problem through a combination of adjustments to existing crimes and the development of a series of new offences to address the novel forms of crime.'[25] They went on to recommend that 'in developing materials with respect to criminalisation and other legislative responses to identity related crime, it was important to adopt a flexible approach.

They felt it was not necessary to produce fully-developed materials such as model laws, as these were problematic for some Member States and would often not be viable without substantial modifications that would take into account the domestic context and requirements. A better approach was to develop more basic constituent elements which could be used by national authorities to meet their own individual needs, as well as by the secretariat in developing technical assistance materials for use at the national, regional or subregional levels.'[26] In other words the group believes that a set of common principles would provide for a better solution to the problem of phishing and identity fraud than a full set of model laws. This is sensible as most countries have well developed fraud provisions; all that is missing is international cooperation and harmonisation of standards: something a common accord should develop. The report of the expert group was considered at the eighteenth session of the Commission on Crime Prevention and Criminal Justice on 17 April 2009. The findings of the group should eventually lead to proposals to fight the problem being laid at the Twelfth United Nations Crime Congress to be held in Salvador, Brazil in April 2010.[27]

---

[23] Taken from: http://www.itu.int/osg/csd/cybersecurity/pgc/2007/events/presentations/session5-chryssikos-C5-meeting-14-may-2007.pdf.

[24] See, Commission on Crime Prevention and Criminal Justice, *Papers for the Eighteenth Session, Vienna, 16-24 April 2009: Thematic discussion: Economic fraud and identity-related crime*: http://www.unodc.org/documents/treaties/organized_crime/ECN152009_CRP12.pdf.

[25] *ibid*, [6].   [26] *ibid*, [9].

[27] Letter from Antonio Maria Costa, UNODC Executive Director to members of the General Assembly of the United Nations, 3 April 2009: http://www.unodc.org/documents/commissions/CCPCJ-session18/CCPCJ18-Information/CCPCJ18-CU2009-52-E.pdf.

15.2 **Grooming, harassment, and cyberstalking**

As well as offering an opportunity for fraud, the anonymous and intrusive nature of the information society allows users to stalk, harass, and groom others from a distance. We may classify these as offences against the person enabled and supported by ICT. Each of these offences is slightly different and has produced a slightly different legal response. All are illegal in the UK and in many cases the law has recently been amended or updated to account for changes in technology.

15.2.1 **Grooming**

Grooming is the act of befriending or establishing an emotional connection with a child, in order to lower the child's inhibitions in preparation for sexual abuse. Grooming is not new; it existed before the advent of the information society and would be carried out through personal interaction with a child, perhaps at a public place such as a park or by a person with a position of trust such as a teacher, religious leader, or group leader (such as a scoutmaster). The information society makes it easier for strangers to groom children due to the nature of the communications media. First, children are comfortable: they are usually sitting at home and using websites familiar to them such as Habbo, WeeWorld, or Club Penguin, or if older MySpace, Facebook, or Bebo, this causes them to lower their guard. Secondly, internet social networking sites such as the ones mentioned cause children not to recognise 'stranger danger' as easily as they are accustomed to meeting new people in this environment and so do not equate new people to 'strangers'. Thirdly, the anonymity offered by social networking sites allows adults to pose as children so the victim believes they are talking to someone of the same age as them; this again causes them to lower their defences.

Grooming was only formally criminalised in 2003. Prior to the passage of the Sexual Offences Act 2003 law enforcement authorities had to use a hotchpotch of legislation to prosecute many of the acts which the offender may have committed in grooming a child including the Obscene Publications Act 1959 or the Protection of Children Act 1978 (as offenders would often use pornography to convince a child it was okay to engage in sexual conduct); the Malicious Communications Act 1988 (which outlaws the sending of offensive or threatening communications); and the Protection from Harassment Act 1997 (which outlaws activity which the offender knows amounts to harassment).

These were felt to be inadequate to deal with the increased risk of grooming following the development of ICT communications such as email, IRC, and social networking sites. In their famous 2001 report, *Chat Wise, Street Wise*,[28] the Internet Crime Forum reported that a US survey had found that 'Just under one in five of 10–17 year olds surveyed claimed to have received some kind of sexual solicitation on the Internet within the previous twelve months',[29] and that the UK Law as it stood did not adequately deal with the issue of 'online enticement of a child'.[30]

---

[28] Internet Crime Forum, *Chat Wise, Street Wise*, March 2001: http://www.internetcrimeforum. org.uk/chatwise_streetwise.pdf.   [29] *ibid*, [56].   [30] *ibid*, Executive Summary.

The solution was s. 15 of the Sexual Offences Act 2003. This introduces the complicated offence of 'Meeting a child following sexual grooming', a provision which as its name suggests doesn't criminalise the act of grooming itself, but rather the further act of intending to meet a child following grooming. To commit the offence the offender (who must be aged eighteen or over) must either have met or communicated with the child (being a person under sixteen) on at least two previous occasions; the offender must then either meet the child or travel with the intention of meeting the child; and at that time, the offender has the intention of committing a relevant sexual offence (including sexual activity with a child, causing a child to engage in sexual activity, engaging in sexual activity in the presence of a child, or causing a child to watch a sexual act). The reason why the offence is framed in this way is to prevent the risk of criminalising innocent communications with children, by including the final element that the offender must either meet, or travel with intent to meet the minor for the purpose of some form of sexual encounter it removes any element of uncertainty.[31] The new offence has been prosecuted extensively with among others a serving police child protection officer and a priest facing charges.[32] Despite the number of prosecutions, the Court of Appeal is yet to hear an appeal against conviction although it has heard several appeals against sentence including *R. v Mansfield*.[33]

✎ Case Study *R. v Mansfield*

This case was an appeal against a sentence of four years and three months in prison and an extended licence period of three years.

The appellant was a forty-two year old man with no previous convictions. He came in contact with a thirteen year old girl via chatrooms and later by email, text, and mobile phone. He pretended to be seventeen; she told him she was 'nearly sixteen'. Later her mother found a sexually explicit text message on her daughter's phone and told the appellant her daughter's true age.

Despite this the appellant continued to remain in contact with the victim and told her his true age and name. The girl, by now fourteen agreed to meet the appellant in Cambridge. They spent some time together where in evidence she admitted she instigated sexual activity between the two but penetrative sex did not take place.

In giving the judgement of the court Sir Douglas Brown stated that despite the fact 'the girl was compliant and not inexperienced ... the law is there to protect young girls against their own immature sexual experimentation and to punish much older men who take advantage of them. We think that for the sexual offences three years is the correct sentence on all counts.'

---

[31] See House of Commons Select Committee on Home Affairs, Fifth Report, 24 June 2003, Ch. 5: http://www.publications.parliament.uk/pa/cm200203/cmselect/cmhaff/639/63908.htm.

[32] See BBC News, *Priest 'paid for girl's grooming*, 15 May 2007: http://www.news.bbc.co.uk/1/hi/england/merseyside/6657715.stm; Police News, *Child Protection Officer On Grooming Charge*, 29 April 2009: http://www.policeoracle.com/news/Child-Protection-Officer-On-Grooming-Charge_19061.html.   [33] [2005] EWCA Crim 927.

The Crown Prosecution Service sentencing guidelines for s. 15 suggest that where the intent is to commit an assault by penetration or rape the starting point in sentencing should be four years custody if the victim is under thirteen and two years custody if the victim is thirteen or over but under sixteen; and where the intent is to coerce the child into sexual activity the starting point in sentencing should be two years custody if the victim is under thirteen and eighteen months custody if the victim is thirteen or over but under sixteen.[34] This is then subject to aggravating factors such as intimidation or coercion or use of drugs or alcohol.

15.2.2 **Harassment and stalking**

Harassment and stalking are rather different to grooming. Harassment is behaviour intended to disturb or upset, and, which is usually found threatening or disturbing, stalking is an aggravated form of harassment where the victim finds themself followed and continually contacted by the offender. In harassment and stalking cases the victim is usually an adult, although in law it is possible to harass or stalk a minor. In a legal sense there is no distinction between the two both are classified as harassment and are primarily regulated by the Protection from Harassment Act 1997. This provides that a person 'must not pursue a course of conduct (a) which amounts to harassment of another, and (b) which he knows or ought to know amounts to harassment of the other'.[35] This raises the question how one ought to know that their course of action amounts to harassment, given that many harassers/stalkers suffer from mental impairment? This is covered though by s. 1(2) which provides that 'the person whose course of conduct is in question ought to know that it amounts to harassment of another if a reasonable person in possession of the same information would think the course of conduct amounted to harassment of the other'.

If found guilty of harassment the offender may both be charged under s. 2, which can lead to a maximum six months imprisonment and may be issued with a restraining order under s. 5, which if breached may lead to up to five years imprisonment.[36] If the harassment is of such a nature as to put the victim in fear of violence on at least two occasions (this is what the media often colloquially refers to as stalking) then under s. 4 of the Act the offender may be charged with the aggravated offence of 'Putting People in Fear of Violence', this, like breaching a restraining order under s. 5, can lead to imprisonment of up to five years.

In addition to the provisions of the Protection from Harassment Act online harassment (or Cyberstalking as it is usually known) may also lead to prosecutions under the Malicious Communications Act 1988 or the Communications Act 2003. By s. 1 of the Malicious Communications Act 1988 it is an offence to send an indecent, offensive, or threatening letter, electronic communication, or other article to another person. This is a summary offence and as such may only lead to a maximum sentence of imprisonment of six months, as is the offence of improper use of the public electronic

---

[34] CPS, *Sentencing Manual: s.15 Sexual Offences Act 2003*: http://www.cps.gov.uk/legal/s_to_u/sentencing_manual/s15_grooming/.   [35] Protection from Harassment Act 1997, s. 1(1).
[36] Protection from Harassment Act 1997, s. 5(6).

communications system under s. 127 of the Communications Act 2003, which makes it an offence to send, by means of a public electronic communication system, a message or other matter that is grossly offensive or of an indecent, obscene, or menacing character; or which is sent for the purpose of causing annoyance, inconvenience, or needless anxiety to another and which is known to be false. As both these offences are summary in nature, and as the Court cannot issue a restraining order unless the prosecution is brought under the Protection from Harassment Act, the authorities will tend to prosecute under the Protection from Harassment Act rather than the Malicious Communications Act or the Communications Act.

Fortunately harassment and stalking tend to occur locally rather than internationally. With the exception of celebrities who may attract stalkers from any point on the globe, stalkers tend to select their victims from their local community: often stalkers are ex-partners of the victim or they are from within a close social circle such as a work colleague, university colleague, or even from within an extended circle of friends.[37] As such issues of jurisdiction and cross-border enforcement arise less often with harassment and stalking and in general domestic law is in a position to assist the victim and if necessary prosecute the perpetrator.

15.3 **Cyberterrorism**

Cyberterrorism is a newly emergent area of criminal law in the information society. The concept of 'informational warfare', that is states fighting campaigns using informational tools and weapons in addition to traditional ordinance, is well established and dates from at least the early 1990s.[38] The concept of cyberterrorism, that is individuals or groups using the network capabilities of the information society to launch unlawful attacks and threats of attack against computers, networks, and the information stored therein to intimidate or coerce a government or its people in furtherance of political or social objectives, is newer, dating from around the turn of the millennium.[39] Although terrorist acts are clearly criminal, it was not clear initially that the types of activities carried out by cyberterrorists would be illegal. Cyberterrorists may carry out Denial of Service attacks, which as we saw in Chapter 13, were not clearly criminalised until 1 October 2008 when ss. 35–38 of the Police and Justice Act 2006 were brought into force; otherwise they may commit offences of unlawful access to data or unlawful modification of data under ss. 1–3 of the Computer Misuse Act 1990, but often they would simply publish materials in support of terrorist organisations or aims, or incite hatred. Prior to the passage of a series

---

[37] E. Finch, *The Criminalisation of Stalking* (2001).

[38] Information Warfare was first introduced in a formal sense in 1992 in the US Department of Defense Directive TS3600.1. See Kaomea, Hearold & Page, 'Beyond Security: A Data Quality Perspective on Defensive Information Warfare', *MIT Total Data Quality Management Program Working Papers* 1994: http://web.mit.edu/tdqm/papers/other/kaomea.html.

[39] This definition is taken from one of the early discussions of cyberterrorism before the Special Oversight Panel on Terrorism of the US House of Representatives Committee on Armed Services which took place on 23 May 2000. It is taken from the testimony of Dorothy Denning, then Professor of Computer Science at Georgetown University. Testimony at: http://www.cs.georgetown.edu/~denning/infosec/cyberterror.html.

of anti-terror measures from 2000 onward this was not illegal unless the materials were in support of an organisation proscribed by Schedule 1 of the Prevention of Terrorism (Temporary Provisions) Act 1989, a list which predominantly listed Irish dissident groups in a time when the rising risk was from extremist Islamic organisations such as Al-Qaeda.

The law has though changed substantially in the past ten years. The Terrorism Act 2000 introduced several new offences which could take place online. Prime among these were: possession of items for a terrorist purpose; possession of information or documents of a kind likely to be useful to a person committing or preparing an act of terrorism; and inciting terrorism overseas.

Section 57 provides that it is an offence to possess an article in circumstances which give rise to a reasonable suspicion that possession is for a purpose connected with the commission, preparation, or instigation of an act of terrorism. On conviction on indictment, this may lead to a maximum sentence of imprisonment of fifteen years.[40] The wording of the section, and the fact that there was a separate offence of possession of information or documents of a kind likely to be useful to a person committing or preparing an act of terrorism under s. 58, punishable by up to ten years in prison,[41] may lead one to suspect that by 'article' the framers of s. 57 had in mind items such as weapons, bomb making equipment, training video, or similar articles. Unfortunately the definition of 'article' found in s. 121 is extremely vague defining it simply as 'includes substance and any other thing'. This has led the authorities to attempt to prosecute possession of information or data under s. 57.

In the first case of this type, *R. v M*,[42] the prosecution claimed that possession of data stored electronically on computer hard drives or CDs was capable of being an 'article' under s. 57. The prosecution's case was that the s. 57 articles were electronic storage devices such as hard drives, CDs, and DVDs, a USB storage device and a video recording, as well as two documents. At the preliminary hearing, the defendants submitted that 'data' was not an article arguing that the prosecution's interpretation of s. 57 made s. 58(1)(b) completely redundant and made nearly all of s. 58(1)(a) redundant. The defendants argued that the only conduct which would be caught by s. 58 if the prosecution's interpretation was allowed would be collecting information but not writing it down. The Court of Appeal allowed the appeal finding that the issue was whether the items listed were 'articles'. They found that CDs and computer hard drives holding electronic data were capable of being articles within the meaning of s. 57, but that it was clear that Parliament had laid down a different regime for documents and records under s. 58 and 'articles' under s. 57.

This decision which seemed to sensibly delineate the difference between 'articles' and 'data' or 'information', was though unfortunately not followed in the later case of *R. v Rowe* in which a five judge bench found *R. v M* to be *per incuriam*.[43] Mr Rowe had been arrested in possession of a notebook which contained mortar instructions and a substitution code which listed components of explosives and places of a type susceptible to terrorist bombing. The prosecution case was that the appellant was shortly to embark on a terrorist venture and that the notebook and the code were held for terrorist purposes. Mr Rowe was charged and found guilty of possession of a terrorist article under

---

[40] Terrorism Act 2000, s. 57(4)(a).   [41] Terrorism Act 2000, s. 58(4)(a).
[42] [2007] EWCA Crim 298.   [43] [2007] QB 975.

s. 57. Following the decision in *R. v M* he appealed against conviction. On this occasion the Court of Appeal refused his appeal. The judgement of the Court was given by Lord Phillips CJ:

> There is undoubtedly an overlap between section 57 and 58, but it is not correct to suggest that if documents and records constitute articles for the purpose of section 57, section 58 is almost superfluous. Collecting information, which falls within section 58 alone, may well not involve making a record of the information. Equally a person who possesses information likely to be useful to a person committing or preparing an act of terrorism may well not be in possession of it for a purpose connected with the commission, preparation or instigation of an act of terrorism. Sections 57 and 58 are indeed dealing with different aspects of activities relating to terrorism. Section 57 is dealing with possessing articles for the purpose of terrorist acts. Section 58 is dealing with collecting or holding information that is of a kind likely to be useful to those involved in acts of terrorism. Section 57 includes a specific intention, section 58 does not. These differences between the two sections are rational features of a statute whose aims include the prohibition of different types of support for and involvement, both direct and indirect, in terrorism. There is no basis for the conclusion that Parliament intended to have a completely separate regime for documents and records from that which applies to other articles. For these reasons we have concluded that the decision in *R. v. M* was based on false assumptions and false analysis and that it was wrong.[44]

This suggests that possession of data for publication on a website or some other forum may amount to a s. 57 offence if that data or information is of a nature as to be directly associated with a specific terrorist purpose. The nature of s. 57, and s. 58, has though arguably been changed by new provisions introduced by Part I of the Terrorism Act 2006 and we shall return to this analysis below.

The other major provision of the Terrorism Act 2000 which may apply to online activities is the s. 59 offence of inciting terrorism overseas. This formed the focus of one of the most high profile cyberterrorism cases in the UK to date. The case involved a group of young men who operated a network of at least 32 websites and a number of chat forums dedicated to fighting a Jihadist cause, in particular in Iraq. According to evidence:

> the sites included assertions that it was the duty of Moslems to fight armed Jihad against Jews, crusaders, apostates and their supporters in all Muslim countries and that it was the duty of every Muslim to fight and kill them wherever they are, civilian or military. There were also films, much of it emanating from Al-Qaeda in Iraq, posted to the websites showing very explicit acts of terrorist murder, including the beheading of civilian hostages, attacks on the police, government officials and on coalition forces in Iraq. In the internet chat forums individuals disposed to join the insurgency were provided with routes by which to travel into Iraq and manuals of weapons and explosives were requested.[45]

Those involved included Younes Tsouli, a Moroccan born UK resident who called himself Irhabi_007; 'Irhabi' being the Arabic word for terrorist, and '007' a reference to the fictional secret agent James Bond. Tsouli had been among the most wanted supporters of terrorist activity of UK and US Law enforcement agents. All involved were charged under s. 59 for inciting terrorists to commit murder overseas. On 4 July 2007, after

---

[44] *ibid*, 985–986.
[45] *Attorney General's Reference (Nos 85, 86 and 87 of 2007)* [2007] EWCA Crim 3300.

two months at trial, Tsouli and his co-defendants Waseem Mughal and Tariq Al-Daour pleaded guilty to 'inciting another person to commit an act of terrorism wholly or partly outside the UK which would, if committed in England and Wales, constitute murder' and admitted to conspiring together and with others to defraud banks, credit card companies, and charge card companies to pay for the hosting of the web sites and chat rooms. Tsouli was sentenced to ten years' imprisonment, Mughal to seven and a half years, and Al-Daour to six and half years.[46]

The Attorney-General referred these sentences to the Court of Appeal for being unduly lenient, and on 18 December 2007 the sentences of all three men were increased: Tsouli's sentence was increased to sixteen years, Mughal to twelve years, and Al Daour twelve years.[47] In giving the judgement of the Court Gage LJ noted that: 'The offenders' conduct involved the preplanning of a sophisticated and intricate misuse of computers. Its execution was funded by the proceeds of fraud and was carried out with no little technological skills ... their purpose was to facilitate publication of material on the website and in the chat room forums, exhorting in strong terms others to participate in acts of extreme violence on a very large scale. The material which was published leaves no doubt about what was intended. It was also published in the context of the armed conflict in Iraq involving, as it did, British and American soldiers. Their conduct covered a comparatively short period. However, we infer that but for their arrest their conduct would have covered a much longer period.'[48]

The use of the Terrorism Act 2000 to prosecute those operating terrorist websites and chat fora has now arguably been superseded by Part I of the Terrorism Act 2006. By s. 1(2) it is an offence to publish a statement or to cause another to publish a statement which is likely to be understood by some or all of the members of the public to whom it is published as a direct or indirect encouragement or other inducement to them to the commission, preparation, or instigation of acts of terrorism or Convention offences if at the time it is published it is intended to encourage members of the public to be directly or indirectly encouraged or induced to commit, prepare, or instigate acts of terrorism. This offence is punishable on indictment with a prison sentence of up to seven years. In addition there is a separate offence under s. 2 of dissemination of terrorist publications. This makes it an offence to distribute, sell, circulate, offer for sale, or *transmit electronically* material intended to encourage members of the public to be directly or indirectly encouraged or induced to commit, prepare, or instigate acts of terrorism. Like s. 1 the penalty for such an offence may be seven years imprisonment if charged on indictment. Section 3 lays out specific provisions to regulate the publication of terrorist materials via the internet.

Due to the risk of a website being hijacked or defaced without the knowledge of the operator of that site, or of comments made in an unmoderated forum being published without the forum operator's knowledge there is a notification procedure. The procedure requires that a constable gives notice, either in person or by sending it by recorded delivery to the last recorded address of the 'relevant person' (usually the operator of the site),[49] which declares that in the opinion of the constable giving it, the statement or the article or record is unlawfully terrorism-related.[50] The notice requires the relevant

---

[46] *ibid*, [4].   [47] *ibid*, [41].   [48] *ibid*, [40].   [49] Terrorism Act 2006, s. 4.
[50] Terrorism Act 2006, s. 3(3)(a).

person to secure that the statement or the article or record, so far as it is so related, is not available to the public or is modified so as no longer to be so related;[51] warns the relevant person that a failure to comply with the notice within 2 working days will result in the statement, or the article or record, being regarded as having his endorsement;[52] and explains how, he may become liable by virtue of the notice if the statement, or the article or record, becomes available to the public after he has complied with the notice by republication elsewhere.[53] If the recipient of the notice fails to take steps to remove the material or render it inaccessible to the public within two working days then under s. 3(2) the statement is deemed to be 'endorsed by the relevant person',[54] this allows for criminal prosecution under either or both of ss. 1 and 2. Part I came into force on 13 April 2006[55] and to date there have been two opportunities for the Court of Appeal to examine its scope and effect.

In *R. v Rahman and Mohammed* the court reviewed the sentences of two men convicted under s. 2 for separate offences.[56] Mr Rahman had been found in possession of a letter and some video clips held on his computer. He pleaded guilty under s. 2(2)(f) of having terrorist material in his possession which he intended to disseminate. Mr Mohammed was selling Islamic material from stalls at markets in the North of England. Although most of his material was legal some breached the provisions of the Act. He too pled guilty under s. 2 when charged. Mr Rahman was sentenced to six years in prison (near the maximum sentence under the Act), while Mr Mohammed was given a sentence of three years.[57] On appeal these were reduced to five and a half years and two years respectively,[58] with Lord Phillips CJ noting: 'offences under section 2 of the 2006 Act are capable of varying very widely in seriousness and this is reflected by the fact that, while the offence carries a maximum sentence of 7 years imprisonment if tried on indictment, it may be tried summarily.'[59] Despite this the Court felt a sentence of five and a half years was reasonable in Mr Rahman's case even though he had not actually disseminated any of the material. This suggests a hard line will be taken in sentencing under Part I.

The other occasion the Court of Appeal considered Part I is more illuminating. In *R. v Zafar* the Court considered the interplay between s. 57 of the 2000 Act and Part I of the 2006 Act.[60] *Zafar* is the conclusion of the *R. v M/Rowe* line of analysis discussed earlier. The defendants here were the same ones in *R. v M* (that being an earlier interlocutory appeal). All had been charged with the possession of articles for a purpose connected with the commission, preparation, or instigation of an act of terrorism under s. 57, the articles in question being 'documents, compact discs or computer hard drives on which material had been electronically stored. The material included ideological propaganda as well as communications between the defendants and others which the prosecution alleged showed a settled plan under which the defendants would travel to Pakistan to receive training and thereafter commit a terrorist act or acts in Afghanistan.'[61] Following the decision in *Rowe* the Recorder of London gave a further ruling that he would

---

[51] Terrorism Act 2006, s. 3(3)(b).   [52] Terrorism Act 2006, s. 3(3)(c).
[53] Terrorism Act 2006, s. 3(3)(d).
[54] There are defences under ss. 3(5) and 3(6) when a statement is republished without the knowledge or assistance of the original publisher.
[55] The Terrorism Act 2006 (Commencement No. 1) Order 2006, SI 2006/1013.
[56] [2008] EWCA Crim 1465.   [57] *ibid*, [31], [33].   [58] *ibid*, [33], [49].   [59] *ibid*, [8].
[60] *R. v Zafar* [2008] QB 810.   [61] *ibid*, 816–817.

be bound by that decision. That ruling was upheld in a second interlocutory appeal,[62] and at a subsequent trial the accused were found guilty on almost all charges.[63] All appealed against conviction. Their appeal was upheld with Lord Phillips CJ again giving the judgement of the Court. A crucial part of the Court's deliberation was how Part I of the 2006 could be read alongside s. 57 of the 2000 Act. Applying the extremely expansive interpretation of s. 57 found in *Rowe* seemed to suggest Part I of the 2006 Act was unnecessary. Here Lord Phillips noted that 'Parliament, did not envisage that [s. 57] would extend to possessing propaganda for the purpose of incitement to terrorist acts. That belief is strengthened by the fact that Parliament considered it desirable to legislate in relation to possessing propaganda with the intention of inducing acts of terrorism by section 2(2)(f) of the Terrorism Act 2006.'[64]

Where does this leave the interplay between s. 57 of the 2000 Act and Part I of the 2006 Act? It appears that if one possesses documents, including digital data, with the intent to use them to instigate a *specific* terrorist attack (i.e. what may be defined as preparatory materials) this will cause a prosecution to be brought under s. 57. If though the materials are rather in the form of propaganda materials then it falls within the scope of Part I of the 2006 Act. Against this though is the further confusion that the authority of *Attorney General's Reference (Nos 85, 86 and 87 of 2007)* still applies also. This means that if one operates a website which promotes or supports terrorist activity in the widest sense, one would probably be charged under Part I of the 2006 Act. If one offers support or advice, including instruction or maps, via a website or other forum to individuals planning a particular terrorist attack one would probably be charged under s. 57. If, though, as Younes Tsouli and his co-defendants did, one operates a website or forum which provides advice and encouragement to terrorists overseas to commit a terrorist act such as murder or endangerment to life one may be charged under s. 59 which allows for sentences up to a mandatory life sentence.

15.4 **Bandwidth theft**

At first glance bandwidth theft appears to be at the extreme opposite end of the spectrum of criminal activity from cyberterrorism. To an extent this is true but one should not underestimate the dangers of bandwidth theft.

Bandwidth theft is using someone else's broadband connection without their permission. When everyone used fixed line (wired) internet access this was not much of a problem, generally only skilled phreakers could tap into some else's broadband account, but with the ubiquity of wireless internet access today it is relatively easy to piggy back on someone else's account. Usually this is not a major problem: the uninvited user may use the lawful user's bandwidth to download large files like music and movies from peer-to-peer sites or may use it to view pornography or similar; but there are inherent dangers in allowing this activity to go unchecked. At the very least the innocent victim may find his access speeds curtailed by his ISP. This is a common tactic used to dissuade people from abusing their unlimited access rights to continually download large files to the detriment of other users as they use up more of the available bandwidth. This though is the least of the victim's worries.

---

[62] *R. v. M (No. 2)* [2007] 3 All ER 53.   [63] [2008] QB 810, 818.   [64] *ibid*, 822.

As we saw in Chapter 10 there is a new phenomena known as 'volume litigation' which seeks to force early settlements with a large volume of illegal file sharers. This works on the assumption that the IP address to which the illegal file was sent may be used as a proxy for the identity of the illegal downloader: if though the customer using the IP address in question has been the victim of bandwidth theft they will be left with the problem of clearing their name when demands for settlement arrive. Even worse the illegal piggybacker may use the innocent victim's network to download child abuse images, subjecting the victim to a police investigation, or they may access the victim's wireless network with greater criminal intent in mind such as to access the victim's financial accounts or they may use unsecured wireless networks to post material to terrorist websites or other criminal websites making them harder for the authorities to trace.[65] The authorities are therefore keen to crack down on the practice of piggybacking on another's internet access account.

In the UK there a variety of legal tools that may be used to prosecute someone who illegally access the broadband account of another. Obviously to gain access to the internet the broadband 'thief' will be required to connect via the victim's internet router. As a wireless internet router is basically a small computer it would be possible to prosecute under s. 1 of the Computer Misuse Act 1990. Further if the reason access was secured was to commit a further offence, such as downloading child abuse images, then the aggravated access offence found in s. 2 would be committed. Additionally as bandwidth theft usually involves the downloading or uploading of large files the 'thief' is likely to have a detrimental effect on the available speed of the user's network while they remain connected. This is therefore an unauthorised act which is likely to impair the operation of a computer which the 'thief' carries out at least recklessly, if not with intent. This is a breach of s. 3(3) of the Computer Misuse Act. The authorities therefore have a number of options under the Computer Misuse Act (as amended), but to date the few prosecutions for bandwidth theft which have taken place in the UK have been under a different provision.

Under s. 125 of the Communications Act 2003 it is an offence to dishonestly obtain electronic communications services. The offence is committed when one dishonestly obtains access to an electronic communications service with intent to avoid payment for that service. The offence is a serious offence and on indictment may lead to up to five years in prison.[66] Although there have been no reported cases to date there have been several successful prosecutions under s. 125 including that of Gregory Straszkiewicz a 24 year old 'war driver',[67] who was fined £500 under s. 125 at Isleworth Crown Court in July 2005,[68] while many more have accepted a

---

[65] As a basic measure anyone who operates a wireless network should always ensure it is encrypted. This reduces the risk of bandwidth theft but does not eliminate it completely. There are two standards: Wired Equivalent Privacy (WEP) and Wi-Fi Protected Access (WPA2). WPA2 is more secure that WEP which has known weaknesses. Unfortunately in the UK Broadband providers usually supply the weaker WEP protocol as default on their routers. As most people don't know how to change this (or indeed that they need to) most domestic routers in the UK are susceptible to illegal access.   [66] Communications Act 2003, s. 125(3)(b).

[67] Wardriving is the name given to the practice of searching out unsecured wireless hotspots, usually from a moving vehicle with a laptop or palmtop device.

[68] J. Leyden, 'UK war driver fined £500', *The Register*, 25 July 2005: http://www.theregister.co.uk/2005/07/25/uk_war_driver_fined/.

police caution.[69] Although prosecutions under s. 125 remain rare, these cases to date demonstrate beyond doubt that bandwidth theft is clearly illegal in the UK. Many people imagine that piggybacking on another's internet connection is a harmless and legal activity but this is not the case. It should be added though for the sake of completeness that there is a *mens rea* requirement which means that if you have a mobile device such as a laptop, PDA, or internet enabled mobile phone which automatically connects to the strongest available unsecured wireless network you do not commit an offence by innocently using that connection to access the internet. It is only in cases where one *dishonestly* obtains access to an electronic communications service with the intent to avoid payment that the *mens rea* requirement is made out. This means that s. 125 will usually only be applied to cases where the accused has clearly set out to obtain illegal access via someone else's wireless router, perhaps with intent to commit further offences of civil harms such as copyright infringement.[70]

15.5 **The convention on cybercrime**

A common theme across several of the examples of online criminal activity we have examined in this section (hacking and viruses; indecency, pornography, and obscenity; fraud and identity fraud and also cyberterrorism) is that with a truly global network criminals in any part of the world can impact on any other part of the world. Criminal law is the one area where the warnings of the Cyberlibertarian School have been proven substantively correct. There are of course solutions to some of these problems, including the installation of filters, such as the IWF/Cleanfeed filter and localising the offence as the UK has done recently by outlawing the possession of extreme pornography. But to deal with the underlying problem of child abuse images being produced in such diverse places as the Ukraine, the US, and Vietnam or fraud being perpetrated in Nigeria, China, and Russia we need to harmonise law enforcement provisions and seek measures to reduce jurisdictional disputes. In this there have been some successes but also some failures. We have already seen in Chapter 14 that in relation to child abuse images there has been a high degree of international cooperation leading to some spectacular successes in dealing with paedophile rings including Operation Ore/Avalanche, the joint UK–US operation which saw over 1,400 convictions in the UK and more recently the creation of the Virtual Global Taskforce and Operation PIN. To date though international cooperation has been limited in other fields, with only one substantial international convention being agreed, despite some fifteen years of discussion.

Only the Council of Europe Convention on Cybercrime[71] attempts to harmonise international cybercrime laws. As of 1 July 2009 the treaty had been signed by forty-two

---

[69] See, e.g. P. Griffiths, 'Two cautioned over wireless "piggy-backing"', *Reuters*, 18 April 2007: http://www.reuters.com/article/internetNews/idUSL1848090220070418; M. Chapman, 'Man arrested in suspected Wi-Fi theft', *vnuet News*, 23 August 2007: http://www.vnunet.com/vnunet/news/2197280/man-arrested-suspected-wi-theft.

[70] See also L. Eastham, 'Wi-fi Leeching: A Pub Visitor's Guide', *Society for Computers and Law*, 24 August 2007: http://www.scl.org/site.aspx?i=ne9192.   [71] Above, n. 14.

Council of Europe states, including the UK, and four non European states.[72] It had been ratified by twenty-six states, including the US, but not the UK, and has entered into force in these twenty-six states. This raises a number of questions. Why after nearly eight years of being available for ratification have only just over half of signatory states brought the Convention into force? And why has the UK failed to bring the Convention into force in the UK when the US, France, and Germany have all brought it into force?

The problem is not with the substantive provisions which are relatively uncontroversial. They are all found in Chapter II, Section 1 and fall into five subsections: offences against data and systems;[73] computer-related offences;[74] content-related offences;[75] offences related to infringement of copyright;[76] and ancillary offences.[77] The problem is rather with the procedural systems the Convention requires member states to put in place. Mutual assistance and cooperation provisions found in Articles 23 and 25 require states parties to cooperate in the investigation and evidence gathering of convention crimes reported to them by other states partners: or to put it another way, as favoured by critics of the convention 'The treaty requires that [domestic] governments help enforce other countries' "cybercrime" laws—even if the act being prosecuted is not illegal [domestically] ... That means that countries that have laws limiting free speech on the Net could oblige [local law enforcement] to uncover the identities of anonymous [domestic] critics, or monitor their communications on behalf of foreign governments. [Domestic] ISPs would be obliged to obey other jurisdiction's requests to log their users' behaviour without due process, or compensation.'[78]

Although there is some element of truth in these criticisms of the Convention critics have blown the risk out of proportion. Article 25(4) states that 'except as otherwise specifically provided in articles in this chapter, mutual assistance shall be subject to the conditions provided for by the law of the requested Party or by applicable mutual assistance treaties, including the grounds on which the requested Party may refuse co-operation.' This means that the requested state can refuse a mutual assistance request where it exceeds the agreed parameters of the requested state except in specific cases set out, mostly in Article 27, which itself provides safeguards.[79] Nevertheless campaigns

[72] These are: Canada, Japan, South Africa, and the US. Other non European members who have not yet signed are: Costa Rica, Dominican Republic, Mexico, and the Philippines.

[73] These are: Article 2: illegal access (hacking); Article 3 illegal interception of data; Article 4: data interference (criminal damage and viruses); Article 5 system interference (denial of service); and Article 6 production or use of a device for any of the aforementioned purposes.

[74] These are: Article 7: computer-related forgery and Article 8 computer-related fraud.

[75] This is a single offence under Article 9 of production, distribution, or possession of child pornography.

[76] This is a single Article, Article 10 which requires signatories to cooperate in the detection and prosecution of criminal copyright infringement under the Paris Act of 1971, the Rome Convention and the WIPO Copyright and Phonograms and Performances Treaties.

[77] These are: Article 11 attempts and aiding and abetting; Article 12 corporate liability; and Article 13 sanctions and measures.

[78] D. O'Brien, 'The World's Worst Internet Laws Sneaking Through the Senate', *Electronic Frontier Foundation*, 3 August 2006: http://www.eff.org/deeplinks/2006/08/worlds-worst-internet-laws-sneaking-through-senate.

[79] By Article 27(4) 'The requested Party may, in addition to the grounds for refusal established in Article 25(4), refuse assistance if: (a) the request concerns an offence which the requested Party considers a political offence or an offence connected with a political offence, or (b) it considers that execution of the request is likely to prejudice its sovereignty, security, *ordre public* or other essential interests'.

such as the EFF campaign in the US and the Statewatch campaign in the UK have made the Convention highly controversial.[80] This may explain why the UK Government has failed to implement the Convention, even though UK criminal law meets or exceeds the requirements of the Convention on each of the substantive provisions. All we know is that we have yet to implement the convention despite assurances from the Government that it intends to implement the convention 'soon'.

In August 2007 the Government was heavily criticised by the Science and Technology Committee of the House of Lords who noted that 'the United Kingdom has yet to ratify the Council of Europe's 2001 Convention on Cybercrime. This is a matter of concern, particularly as among the provisions in the Convention is a requirement that parties should "afford one another mutual assistance to the widest extent possible for the purpose of investigations or proceedings concerning criminal offences related to computer systems and data, or for the collection of evidence in electronic form of a criminal offence" (Article 25).'[81] Their Lordships went on to note 'When we asked the Minister about the delay in ratification, he confirmed that the Government were "committed to ratifying the Convention". Certain minor legislative changes were required, and these would be completed by means of the Serious Crime Bill [now Act].'[82] Based on this perceived commitment to the Convention, their Lordships recommend that 'the Government to fulfil its commitment to ratify the Council of Europe Cybercrime Convention at the earliest possible opportunity. At the same time, in order to ensure that the UK fulfils the spirit as well as the letter of Article 25.'[83] In its response the Government backtracked from any commitment to implement the Convention in the near future stating: 'in our evidence to the Committee, we discussed the fact that we remain committed to ratifying the Council of Europe Convention on Cybercrime, which we signed in 2001. We have recently legislated, in the Police and Justice Act 2006, to reform the criminal law to ensure that the Computer Misuse Act 1990 is fully compliant, and we will ratify the Convention as soon as possible. However, we will not do so before we implement the Computer Misuse Act changes in April 2008. With regard to Article 25 of the Convention, we are satisfied that provision for mutual legal assistance under the Crime (International Cooperation) Act 2003 is sufficient to respond to requests for help from other countries relating to crimes perpetrated using computers. However, we keep these matters under constant review to determine whether any further measures are necessary and any improvements may be made.'[84]

What causes the Government to continue to backtrack from full implementation of the Convention? This is not clear, continually the Government indicate their intention to ratify the Convention but they never meet the targets they set. Most recently on 27 January 2009 Alan Campbell, Parliamentary Under-Secretary of State

---

[80] For the Statewatch campaign see: 'CoE "cybercrime" convention: legitimising internet surveillance', *Statewatch Bulletin* (November-December 2000): http://www.statewatch.org/news/2001/mar/17b.htm.
[81] House of Lords Science and Technology Committee, *5th Report of Session 2006–07 Personal Internet Security*, HL Paper 165–I, 10 August 2007, [7.61].: http://www.publications.parliament.uk/pa/ld200607/ldselect/ldsctech/165/165i.pdf.   [82] *ibid*, [7.62].   [83] *ibid*, [7.80].
[84] The *Government Reply to the Fifth Report from the House of Lords Science and Technology Committee Session 2006-07: Personal Internet Security*, Cm 7234, August 2007, 11: http://www.official-documents.gov.uk/document/cm72/7234/7234.pdf.

at the Home Office, stated before the Commons that 'the Government are currently following the process for ratification of treaties and we believe that the ratification of the Council of Europe Convention on Cybercrime will be completed by April 2009'.[85] As there is no barrier to the UK ratifying the treaty one may assume that we will eventually do so but it is clear it does not hold a high priority in the Government's legislative programme.

15.6 **Conclusion**

As with all aspects of life the information society offers opportunities for criminal activity to those attracted to that lifestyle. It also offers challenges to law enforcement authorities, courts, and legislators. The challenges are on several levels. The first was that the information society both afforded opportunities for new and unique harms, such as hacking, denial of service, and the writing and distribution of viruses and Trojans. Secondly, it afforded new ways of committing old harms such as the production and distribution of obscene, harmful, violent, or abusive content, fraud and theft, and harassment and stalking. These were issues which called for the law to be updated and the UK Government has been extremely busy over the last twenty years in implementing the necessary changes to the law found in the Computer Misuse Act 1990, the Protection of Children Act 1978, the Police and Justice Act 2006, the Terrorism Acts 2000 and 2006, the Protection from Harassment Act 1997, and the Criminal Justice and Immigration Act 2008 among others. Our laws are among the most well developed for dealing with the threats of e-crimes of all varieties: computer misuse crimes, content-related crimes, and computer-enabled crimes. The next challenge was designing effective law enforcement structures to deal with the challenges of cybercrime. Here too the UK was an early adapter, setting up the National Hi-Tech Crime Unit in 2001 to investigate computer fraud, hacking, data theft, and network attacks, as well as supporting the work of the Internet Watch Foundation in dealing with content-related crime, in particular images of child abuse. Many of these operations have now been assumed under the umbrella of the Serious Organised Crime Agency with the National Hi-Tech Crime Unit becoming SOCA's e-crime unit, while the Child Exploitation and Online Protection Centre, created in 2006 to work with the IWF and Scotland Yard's Child Abuse Investigation Command, also comes within the SOCA framework. We therefore have a highly integrated investigation and evidence gathering organisation in SOCA, but we fail slightly on the final and current challenge: international cooperation. While the UK leads the way in forging international partnerships in dealing with child abuse and child abuse images, and SOCA has provided vital leadership in the international campaign to deal with Nigerian e-fraud, the failure of the UK to ratify the Cybercrime convention means we are unnecessarily delaying full partnership with those countries that have ratified the Convention.

---

[85] House of Commons *Hansard* 27 January 2009, col.288W: http://www.publications.parliament. uk/pa/cm200809/cmhansrd/cm090127/text/90127w0004.htm#column_287W. It may be noted this deadline was not met. In February 2010 the UK still had not ratified the treaty.

FURTHER READING

Books

D. Wall, *Cybercrime: The Transformation of Crime in the Information Age* (2007)

G. Jacobson, *Cybersecurity, Botnets, and Cyberterrorism* (2009)

P. Bocij, *Cyberstalking: Harassment in the Internet Age* (2003)

Chapters and Articles

A. Gillespie, 'Indecent Images, Grooming and the Law' (2006) *Criminal Law Review* 412

P. Romero, 'An Immunological Approach to Counter-terrorism and Infrastructure Defense Law in Electronic Domains' [2006] *IJLIT* 101

A. Gillespie, 'Cyber-bullying and Harassment of Teenagers: the Legal Response' [2006] *Journal of Social Welfare and Family Law* 213

J. Chang, 'An Analysis of Advance Fee Fraud on the Internet' [2008] *Journal of Financial Crime* 71

PART V

Ecommerce

We all want to do business online but how can we be sure we are protected? How do we contract online? How do we make payments and how we sign an agreement?

16 **Electronic contracts**

    16.1 Contracting informally

    16.2 Regulating offer and acceptance

    16.3 Contractual terms

    16.4 Formal contracts

    16.5 Electronic signatures

    16.6 Conclusion

17 **Electronic payments and taxation**

    17.1 A history of international payments methods

    17.2 Electronic payments

    17.3 The electronic money directive

    17.4 Ecommerce taxation

    17.5 Conclusions

16

Electronic contracts

The ability to trade and to make payment is the cornerstone of all modern societies and the information society is no different in this respect. The information society has provided a number of commercial opportunities for entrepreneurs. Most famously software designers Bill Gates, Steve Ballmer, and Paul Allen have become multi billionaires from their Microsoft software packages while their competitors Steve Jobs and Stephen Wozniak made billions from both hardware and software development for Apple. Others such as Michael Dell focussed on producing hardware while the next generation of internet entrepreneurs made money from either selling goods or services in the information society, as demonstrated by Amazon founder Jeff Bezos, eBay founder Pierre Omidyar, or Craigslist founder Craig Newmark, or have simply packaged and sold information as a standalone product as done by MySpace millionaire Tom Anderson, YouTube founders Jawed Karim, Chad Hurley, and Steve Chen, or most famously the Google guys Larry Page and Sergey Brin.

The cornerstone of the ability to extract revenue from all these products and services are two legal principles which underpin all commerce: (1) the binding legal agreement, or contract, and (2) the universal recognition of a form or token of payment. Without the legal certainty offered by a contract, and the recognition and acceptance of a token or form of payment in return for goods and services, all forms of commerce lack the necessary foundations of certainty and liquidity: this is why from earliest times the rules on pacts, or contracts, and token or payment have been at the heart of all trading cultures and communities. This remains true of today's information society. Whatever form business takes, be it the trading of data, entertainment products, news and information, or systems for the management and development of software or hardware these twin requirements of certainty and liquidity remain underpinned by the law of contract and the law relating to payment and payment methods. This chapter and the one which follows will look at how this traditional area of law is reacting to the challenges of digital products and services and virtual payments or payment alternatives.

16.1 Contracting informally

Contracting is one of the most commonplace and simple applications of legal principles. Every day people enter into dozens of legally binding contracts without thinking about it. They enter into contracts of carriage with public transport operators, contracts of sale with shops, garages, and supermarkets, and contracts for the supply of services with hairdressers or dentists. These informal contracts are often entered into without a single word being exchanged, yet a contract is formed all the same.

> ### ✳ **Example** Informal Contracts
>
> Kiera is travelling from home to university for class. She decides to take the bus. She gets on the bus and pays her fare (or shows a pass) and then takes a seat on the bus. She doesn't say anything to the driver; the driver doesn't say anything to her yet a contract has been formed where the customer agrees to pay the fare for the journey undertaken and to comply with the bus company's general conditions of carriage and the driver (as agent for the bus company) agrees to carry the customer in accordance with the same general conditions of carriage.

An equivalent type of transaction takes place daily in supermarkets where the customer offers to buy goods from the supermarket by taking them to the checkout and the checkout operator, as agent for the supermarket, accepts this offer. The customer agrees to pay the advertised price and in return the supermarket agrees to transfer title in the goods to the customer. The reason these contracts may be formed without the exchange of written, or even oral, terms is because these are informal contracts: contracts that have no legally defined form and which may be formed simply by a *consensus ad idem* or a meeting of the minds.

16.1.1 **Contract formation**

The rules for the formation of informal contracts seem extremely simple; to form a contract all parties to the contract must agree on the terms of the contract, and to be bound by these terms. In English Law this is usually assumed to take place when an offer is accepted with consideration,[1] in Scots Law the element of consideration is unnecessary.[2] This apparent simplicity though belies the complexity of contract law and in particular the rules of contract formation. Many of these rules affect the time and even place of formation of the contract and even in informal contracts they prescribe certain conditions for the formation of a concluded contract which are of particular import in dealing with electronic and online contracts.

The basics of any form of contract are that a set of offered terms and conditions must be accepted. The question is how can one recognise an offer and an acceptance? Although this may seem a simple question the intent of parties plays a significant role in determining when, or if, *consensus ad idem* has occurred.

This came to light in a series of shop display cases in the 1950s and 60s. This series began with *Pharmaceutical Society of Great Britain v Boots Cash Chemists (Southern) Ltd.*[3] Boots, the well-known high street pharmacy, had begun a trial of self-service shopping in some of its stores. This allowed customers to buy some pharmacy products by putting them in a basket and taking them to a cashier for payment. The Pharmaceutical Society argued this was in breach of the Pharmacy and Poisons Act 1933 which made it illegal to sell a listed poison without supervision of a registered pharmacist. The question

---

[1] M. Chen-Wishart, *Contract Law* (2nd ed., 2007), Ch. 4.
[2] See H. MacQueen and J. Thompson, *Contract Law in Scotland* (2000).
[3] [1953] 1 QB 401.

before the Court of Appeal was whether the display of goods on the shelf was a standing offer to sell which was accepted by the customer upon placing the drugs in the basket or whether it was merely an 'invitation to treat' with the offer being made by the customer at the till and the acceptance being affected by the cashier. The court found the latter position was preferred with Birkett LJ noting that 'it would be wrong to say that the shopkeeper is making an offer to sell every article in the shop to any person who might come in and that that person can insist on buying any article by saying "I accept your offer." '[4]

This decision was later affirmed and developed in *Fisher v Bell*,[5] in which a shop window display was described as an invitation to treat and *Partridge v Crittenden*,[6] in which a classified advert in a periodical was also similarly defined. These cases are very important in discussing electronic contracting, and in particular online contracts. We can draw on these cases to establish that a display on an ecommerce site such as Amazon should clearly be an invitation to treat and not a standing offer to sell.[7] The offer should come from the customer with the acceptance following at a later stage in the sales process. But one question remains, how should the contract formation process be structured when one of the parties is a computer? Traditionally a contract is formed by a meeting of the minds, meaning both parties must agree to the terms and as a computer cannot form the necessary intent to form the agreement, this suggests that a human agent is required.

Computers are not the first non-human actor to be involved in contract formation. We have used vending machines for decades and ticket machines in stations and in car parks have stood in for human operators for some time. The role of automated ticket machines was reviewed by the Court of Appeal in the famous case of *Thornton v Shoe Lane Parking Ltd*.[8] The case, which is no doubt familiar to any student of English contract law, established the principle that a contractual term displayed or communicated to a contractual counterparty after *consensus ad idem* is reached is not incorporated into the contractual terms. What though is less often analysed in the many discussions of *Thornton* is the approach the court developed for dealing with contract formation and non-human actors. It is perfectly explained in the words of Lord Denning MR:[9]

> **→ Highlight** Lord Denning in *Thornton v Shoe Lane Parking Ltd*
>
> The customer pays his money and gets a ticket. He cannot refuse it. He cannot get his money back. He may protest to the machine, even swear at it. But it will remain unmoved. He is committed beyond recall. He was committed at the very moment when he put his money into the machine.
>
> The contract was concluded at that time. It can be translated into offer and acceptance in this way: the offer is made when the proprietor of the machine holds it out as being ready to receive the money. The acceptance takes place when the customer puts his money into the slot.

---

[4] *ibid*, 407.   [5] [1961] 1 QB 394.   [6] [1968] 2 All ER 421.
[7] But see *Carlill v Carbolic Smokeball Company* [1893] 1 QB 256.   [8] [1971] 2 QB 163.
[9] *ibid*, 169.

This is an important principle. Because a machine lacks the ability to form the necessary intent to conclude a contract the Court has rationalised the display constructed by the machine's operator as a standing offer similar to that found in the much earlier case of *Carlill v Carbolic Smokeball*.[10]

This standing offer reflects the intent of the machine operator and this is then capable of acceptance by the customer who indicates her acceptance of the terms by putting her money in the slot. This principle is assumed to extend to a number of self service operations including vending machines and self service petrol pumps.[11] This would suggest that an online ecommerce site such as Amazon would have to operate under this standing offer principle as they use non-human agents to conclude their contracts. This is at odds with our understanding from cases such as *Boots Cash Chemists, Fisher v Bell*, and *Partridge v Crittenden*, that shop displays, both interactive displays and passive displays, are merely invitations to treat. So the question is, is an ecommerce website like a shop display or like a vending machine?

16.2 Regulating offer and acceptance

With no case law to clarify the issue commentators were left to speculate as to the nature of ecommerce sites. Most agreed that despite the lack of a human actor the interactive nature of websites rendered them more akin to self service shop displays than to vending machines or ticket machines which issued a restricted choice of products.[12] The lack of clarity though raised the spectre of different approaches developing throughout Europe, with some countries taking the standing offer principle while others followed the invitation to treat principle. Such a lack of harmonisation could adversely affect the development of ecommerce in Europe as a significant proportion of both Business to Business (B2B) and Business to Consumer (B2C) transactions were likely to take place across borders.

16.2.1 Articles 9–11 of the electronic commerce directive

To alleviate this risk, and to harmonise some rules on contract formalities, the Commission placed electronic commerce, and electronic contracting at the heart of its fifth framework programme on the information society. The result was the Electronic Commerce Directive.[13] The Directive is a wide ranging document which deals not only with electronic contracting, but also with SPAM emails and protection for ISPs and other third party carriers. The key provisions of interest to contract lawyers are to be found in Articles 9–11.

Upon reading these the first thing which becomes clear is that the Electronic Commerce Directive does not harmonise what is known as the contractual trigger, that is the moment at which *consensus ad idem* is legally deemed to have occurred. In earlier drafts

---

[10] Above, n. 7.   [11] Chen-Wishart, above n. 1, 75.

[12] See, e.g. A. Murray, 'Entering into Contracts Electronically: The Real W.W.W.' in L. Edwards & C. Waelde, *Law and the Internet: A Framework for Electronic Commerce* (2000); D. Bainbridge *Introduction to Information Technology Law* (6th ed., 2007), 363.

[13] Directive 2000/31/EC of the European Parliament and of the Council of 8 June 2000 on certain legal aspects of information society services, in particular electronic commerce, in the Internal Market.

of the Directive it was proposed that this should be done with an original draft version of the Directive suggesting that 'electronic contracts be concluded when: the recipient of the service has received from the service provider, electronically, an acknowledgement of receipt of the recipient's acceptance, and has confirmed receipt of the acknowledgement of receipt.'[14]

This approach was criticised during the legislative passage of the Directive with critics believing that in effect the Directive was seeking to harmonise rules of contractual formation which lie outwith the general competence of the Commission, and certainly well outside the competence of the information society programme. These critiques of the draft led to attempts to define a common contractual trigger being dropped. In their place we have a set of common principles with the key principles being found in Articles 10 and 11.

Article 10 requires transparency in the contract-making process. While there is no common rule of contractual formation, there are a set of common principles which all ecommerce sites have to follow, including essentially by Article 10(1)(a) the provision that the customer be informed of the technical steps she must follow to conclude the contract. Article 10 has been given effect in the UK by reg. 9 of The Electronic Commerce (EC Directive) Regulations 2002,[15] which enacts Article 10 in full and without amendment. The combined effect of Article 10/reg. 9 may be seen on any UK ecommerce website. If one were to visit a well-known internet bookseller's site and were to examine their conditions of use and sale, one would find that condition 14 states:

> When you place an order to purchase a product from [NAME], we will send you an email confirming receipt of your order and containing the details of your order. Your order represents an offer to us to purchase a product which is accepted by us when we send email confirmation to you that we've dispatched that product to you (the 'Dispatch Confirmation Email'). That acceptance will be complete at the time we send the Dispatch Confirmation Email to you. Any products on the same order which we have not confirmed in a Dispatch Confirmation Email to have been dispatched do not form part of that contract.

Thus clearly the customer is informed, in accordance with reg. 9(1)(a) of the UK Regulations, that the webpage operated by this retailer is to be treated as an invitation to treat in accordance with the principles of *Boots Cash Chemist*. The order placed by the customer is then to be treated as an offer to buy. An immediate acknowledgement of this order sent out by this retailer is just that, an acknowledgment of the offer, not an acceptance. Either party remains in a position to withdraw from the contract until such time as the retailer sends their Dispatch Confirmation Email. This forms acceptance and concludes the contract.

At first glance this may seem to favour the retailer as they can withdraw from the contract at any time up to dispatch of the goods, but looking closely it is clear that the customer is also protected as they may withdraw their offer (cancel their order) at any point up to dispatch. This is the common position taken by almost all ecommerce sites. It allows for a human check to be made in the order process before the offer is accepted and the contract finalised. This prevents contracts being formed by non-human actors on erroneous terms as demonstrated in the Argos TV case of 2005 when a processing

---

[14] Draft E-Commerce Directive, Draft E-Commerce Directive, COM (1998) 586 final 18/11/98, Art. 11(1)(a).   [15] SI 2002/2013.

error led to a £350 television set being advertised at only 49p for thirty-one hours leading to 10,000 orders being placed including one order for 80 TVs. Even though customers had completed the check out procedure and had given their credit or debit
card details to pay for the televisions ordered, Argos simply referred to their terms and
conditions and cancelled all orders, refunding all monies paid.[16]

16.2.2 Communicating acceptance

This leaves one final question of contract formation. When, precisely, is acceptance effectively communicated to the offeror? To put it another way does the delivery rule or the
postal rule apply to acceptances which come in the form of a confirmation email? If we
return to the example terms and conditions above we see they say that 'acceptance will be
complete at the time we send the Dispatch Confirmation E-mail to you'. This though is not
the complete picture because for an acceptance to be effective it has to be communicated
to the offeror and there are two general principles which are used to determine when this
is fulfilled. The first is the more commonplace principle that to be effective an acceptance
must be delivered to the offeror. This principle applies in face to face oral negotiations but
also to a number of 'at distance' communications. Most famously in the case of *Entores
Ltd v Miles Far East Corporation*,[17] Lord Denning (as Denning LJ) carried out an extensive
examination of the principle of delivery in relation to an acceptance sent by Telex:

> When a contract is made by post it is clear law throughout the common law countries that the
> acceptance is complete as soon as the letter is put into the post box, and that is the place where
> the contract is made. But there is no clear rule about contracts made by telephone or by Telex.
> Communications by these means are virtually instantaneous and stand on a different footing.
>
> The problem can only be solved by going in stages. Let me first consider a case where two
> people make a contract by word of mouth in the presence of one another. Suppose, for instance,
> that I shout an offer to a man across a river or a courtyard but I do not hear his reply because it
> is drowned by an aircraft flying overhead. There is no contract at that moment. If he wishes to
> make a contract, he must wait till the aircraft is gone and then shout back his acceptance so that
> I can hear what he says. Not until I have his answer am I bound.
>
> Now take a case where two people make a contract by telephone. Suppose, for instance, that
> I make an offer to a man by telephone and, in the middle of his reply, the line goes 'dead' so
> that I do not hear his words of acceptance. There is no contract at that moment. The other man
> may not know the precise moment when the line failed. But he will know that the telephone
> conversation was abruptly broken off: because people usually say something to signify the end
> of the conversation. If he wishes to make a contract, he must therefore get through again so as
> to make sure that I heard. Suppose next, that the line does not go dead, but it is nevertheless
> so indistinct that I do not catch what he says and I ask him to repeat it. He then repeats it and
> I hear his acceptance. The contract is made, not on the first time when I do not hear, but only

---

[16] Argos has a history of pricing errors. In 1999 they offered a £299 television set for £2.99. They
also cancelled these orders. These types of errors are not uncommon. In 2003 Amazon refused
to fulfil orders for a pocket PC on offer for £7.32 instead of £192. In 2002 though Kodak fulfilled
orders for a digital camera sold for £100 instead of its intended price of £329. This was because
Kodak's terms and conditions at the time stated the contract would be concluded when they
sent the order confirmation email, not the later dispatch confirmation stage. Kodak have since
amended their terms and conditions.   [17] [1955] 2 QB 327.

the second time when I do hear. If he does not repeat it, there is no contract. The contract is only complete when I have his answer accepting the offer.

Lastly, take the Telex. Suppose a clerk in a London office taps out on the teleprinter an offer which is immediately recorded on a teleprinter in a Manchester office, and a clerk at that end taps out an acceptance. If the line goes dead in the middle of the sentence of acceptance, the teleprinter motor will stop. There is then obviously no contract. The clerk at Manchester must get through again and send his complete sentence. But it may happen that the line does not go dead, yet the message does not get through to London. Thus the clerk at Manchester may tap out his message of acceptance and it will not be recorded in London because the ink at the London end fails, or something of that kind. In that case, the Manchester clerk will not know of the failure but the London clerk will know of it and will immediately send back a message 'not receiving.' Then, when the fault is rectified, the Manchester clerk will repeat his message. Only then is there a contract. If he does not repeat it, there is no contract. It is not until his message is received that the contract is complete.

In all the instances I have taken so far, the man who sends the message of acceptance knows that it has not been received or he has reason to know it. So he must repeat it. But, suppose that he does not know that his message did not get home. He thinks it has. This may happen if the listener on the telephone does not catch the words of acceptance, but nevertheless does not trouble to ask for them to be repeated: or the ink on the teleprinter fails at the receiving end, but the clerk does not ask for the message to be repeated: so that the man who sends an acceptance reasonably believes that his message has been received. The offeror in such circumstances is clearly bound, because he will be estopped from saying that he did not receive the message of acceptance. It is his own fault that he did not get it. But if there should be a case where the offeror without any fault on his part does not receive the message of acceptance—yet the sender of it reasonably believes it has got home when it has not—then I think there is no contract.

My conclusion is, that the rule about instantaneous communications between the parties is different from the rule about the post. The contract is only complete when the acceptance is received by the offeror: and the contract is made at the place where the acceptance is received.[18]

This extensive analysis brings forth several consequences for electronic contracting. First, it suggests that communications by Royal Mail are a *sui generis* form of communication for the purposes of contract formation rules, and that it is only they which are regulated by the postal rule in place of the delivery rule. This principle was later affirmed in the House of Lords case of *Brinkibon Ltd v Stahag Stahl und Stahlwarenhandels-Gesellschaft*.[19] More recently two Scottish cases, *McIntosh v Alam*,[20] and *Carmarthen Developments Ltd v Pennington*,[21] have suggested that the *Entores/Brinkibon* principle can be extended to facsimile communications. Elsewhere, and before the implementation of the Electronic Commerce Directive, the current author has suggested that email communications may be treated differently to those other forms of telecommunications.

[T]he logical conclusion would be that e-mail acceptances do benefit from the postal rule. The reasons for this are twofold. Firstly, e-mail is not instantaneous like the telephone, telex or fax. With all instantaneous methods of communication, the sender knows immediately whether their transmission has been successful. E-mail is different from these methods of communication. You can ask for a delivery receipt, but this merely signals delivery to a mailbox not a user. In addition, you do not necessarily expect a delivery receipt to be instantaneous and may

---

[18] *ibid*, 332–334.   [19] [1983] 2 AC 34.   [20] 1997 SCLR (Notes) 1171.
[21] [2008] CSOH 139.

therefore delay any follow-up action. Given this, it is submitted an e-mail with a request for a delivery receipt is more analogous with a recorded delivery letter than a fax or telex. As recorded delivery mail benefits from the postal rule so should e-mail.

Secondly, e-mail is much more fragmented than a telephone call or a facsimile transmission. E-mail messages are split into packets and may be sent via several different routes. The sender has no guarantee that the packets will all arrive together or even that all the packets will arrive. As e-mail shows none of the characteristics of the methods of communication which do not benefit from the postal rule, and as it demonstrates many of the characteristics of ordinary mail, it is submitted that the postal rule does apply to e-mail acceptances.[22]

The reason for this argument is apparent. One of the key arguments in support of the postal rule is that the offeror in accepting a posted letter of acceptance accepts the risk of delay or misdirection of a non-instantaneous means of communication.[23] As email displays the characteristics of non-instantaneous communications it must be treated differently to telephone, facsimile, or telex. At the time of writing it is not yet clear if the courts would support the application of the postal rule to any form of electronic communication.

Developments in the Electronic Commerce Directive suggest though it is unlikely. Article 11(1), as given effect by reg. 11(2)(a) of The Electronic Commerce (EC Directive) Regulations, states that 'the order and the acknowledgement of receipt will be deemed to be received when the parties to whom they are addressed are able to access them.' Regulation 11(2)(a) strictly only applies to the offer (termed here the order) and the acknowledgement of receipt of that offer, not to the acceptance, which will usually occur much later when the goods are dispatched. Despite this it is hard to imagine a court accepting an argument that the delivery rule applies to offers and acknowledgements but not to acceptances. Therefore it seems likely that should the question arise a UK court would find that the delivery rule applies to acceptances sent by email which conclude an online commercial transaction, such as a dispatch confirmation email.

Before leaving this issue it is important to note that Article 11 (and Regulation 11(1)) 'shall not apply to contracts concluded exclusively by exchange of electronic mail or by equivalent individual communications.'[24] This means that where email (or some equivalent person to person communication) is the *only* means of communication between the parties the postal rule *may* still have a role to play. But as such contracts are extremely rare we must assume that an informal electronic contract is concluded when the communication designated by the offeree in their terms and conditions, as required by Regulation 9(1)(a), is able to be accessed by the offeror, which in the case of an email will be when it is received in their mailbox as held on their mail service provider's mailserver system.

16.3 **Contractual terms**

Having established when a contract is formed the next question is what are the terms of the contract? The terms of any contract, whether it is an electronic contract or a traditional contract, will be those agreed upon by the parties at the time the contract

---

[22] Murray, above n. 12, 24–25.
[23] See e.g. C. Gringras, *The Laws of the Internet,* (1997), 23; J. Dickie, 'When and Where are Electronic Contracts Concluded?' [1998] 49.3 *Northern Ireland Legal Quarterly* 332.
[24] The Electronic Commerce (EC Directive) Regulations 2002, reg. 11(3).

is concluded. This can clearly be seen in the series of cases known as the ticket cases concluding in *Thornton v Shoe Lane Parking Ltd*.[25] Here Lord Denning led the Court of Appeal in finding that the issue of the ticket by an automated ticket machine was the point at which the contract was concluded, meaning that the terms of issue printed on the reverse of the ticket did not form part of the contract. This is the latest of a long line of ticket cases where terms printed on tickets or receipts have been held only to be validly incorporated into the contract if the terms have been brought to the other party's attention before the contract is concluded.[26] Thus terms not brought to the attention of the counterparty to the contract before the delivery of the final acceptance will not form part of the contract. How does one incorporate terms into the contract? As any student of contract law knows contractual terms usually fall into one of three categories: Express Terms, Terms Incorporated by Reference, and Implied Terms.[27]

16.3.1 **Express terms**

The incorporation of express terms into electronic contracts poses little difficulty. Such terms will be clearly set out in the transmission of information between parties and as such should be easily identified. There are, though, two problem issues regarding express terms which parties should always bear in mind when negotiating an electronic contract. The first is that parties must take care to identify the document or documents which are intended to constitute the contract. This will be more common with contracts concluded by email which have to be individually drafted and which have the potential for prolonged exchanges between the parties at the negotiation stage, than with online contracts. The second potential problem of express terms is their interpretation by the courts in the event of a dispute. Contracting parties should attempt to limit as far as possible any inconsistencies or ambiguities in their contractual terms. In the event of any disagreement between the parties on the terms of the contract the court will apply the established rules of contractual interpretation.[28]

16.3.2 **Terms incorporated by reference**

The structure of the web, with its use of interconnected, hyperlinked pages, lends itself to incorporation by reference.[29] Consequently, terms incorporated by reference are common in relation to electronic contracts. The terms that the contracting party wishes to incorporate are set out in a separate document and are incorporated into the final contract by a reference to this separate document somewhere in the contractual documentation. Commonly this document is a separate webpage hosted on the same server as the online shop or marketplace. This is usually known as the terms and conditions page and is accessible via a hypertext link embedded at several points in the order system usually being expressly referred to during the checkout process.

---

[25] Above n. 8.   [26] See in particular *Parker v South Eastern Railway Co.* (1877) 2 CPD 416.
[27] For detail on these categories see Chen-Wishart, above n. 1, Ch. 10.
[28] See Chen-Wishart, above n. 1, Ch. 11.
[29] As do email systems which support HTML and allow for embedded hypertext links.

To be effectively incorporated the terms must not only be clear and unambiguous they must also clearly have been intended to form part of the contract. This means that the party relying upon these incorporated terms must take all steps to bring them to the attention of the other party before the contract is concluded and in such a manner as to make it clear these terms are intended to be contractual terms.[30] These terms and conditions must therefore be clearly signposted. A passive link to terms and conditions contained on another page will not necessarily be sufficient to incorporate these terms into the contract. To effectively incorporate any external terms and conditions the site operator must offer a clearly marked and prominent link to the specific terms and conditions they wish to incorporate into the contract before the customer makes their offer.

Fortunately the site operator can easily ensure the terms and conditions have been incorporated into the contract by requiring the customer to indicate they have knowledge of, and have accepted, these terms and conditions before processing their order. This is done by requiring the customer to check a box during the check out process acknowledging they have read and accept the terms and conditions or by expressly stating at the submission of the order that the customer agrees to these terms and conditions as a condition of the order being placed. If the customer has acknowledged they are aware of the terms then the terms and conditions will be incorporated into the contract even if the customer has not actually read them.[31]

16.3.3 **Implied terms**

Finally, as with traditional contracts, there may be occasions where terms will be implied into electronic contracts. As implied terms usually come about apart from the contract formation process the fact that a contract has been concluded in Cyberspace will be of no impact to the rules on formation of contract. Implied terms may be implied by fact, such as terms required to give a contract business efficacy,[32] and terms implied on the basis of custom or usage.[33] Additionally terms may be implied by the common law such as the implied term of seaworthiness implied into contracts for the carriage of goods by sea,[34] and the implied rule of non-derogation from grant.[35] As the introduction of these terms is uniform, no matter how the contract was negotiated and concluded, the use of electronic means to conclude the contract will not affect the established rules and reference should be made to traditional contract texts for further guidance on implied terms.[36]

---

[30] Thus courts have continually held that where 'contractual' terms are found in places where the customer would not expect to find them they do not form part of the contract. See *Chapelton v Barry UDC* [1940] 1 KB 532, *Taylor v Glasgow Corporation* 1952 SC 440 (both involving tickets/receipts) and *Lightbody's Trustees v Hutchison* (1886) 14 R 4 (advertising leaflet).
[31] Some terms will require a greater degree of highlighting than others. Exclusionary terms for instance will require a significantly greater degree of explicitness. See Denning LJ in *Spurling v Bradshaw* [1956] 2 All ER 121, 125F, 'Some clauses which I have seen would need to be printed in red ink on the face of the document with a red hand pointing to it before the notice could be held to be sufficient.'   [32] See *The Moorcock* (1889) 14 PD 64.
[33] See *London Founders Association Ltd* and *Palmer v Clarke* (1888) LR 20 QBD 576.
[34] See *Steel v State Line Steamship Co.* (1877) LR 3 App Cas 72.
[35] See *Lyme Valley Squash Club Ltd v Newcastle under Lyme BC* [1985] 2 All ER 405.
[36] Chen-Wishart, above n 1, at 10.4.

16.3.4 **Enforcing terms: consumer protection laws**

Once the contractual terms are agreed and finalised it cannot be assumed that all are enforceable. In a B2C contract some terms may be struck out by consumer protection provisions. When dealing with electronic contract terms in the UK there are three primary sources of consumer protection for contracts concluded online or by email. They are the Unfair Contract Terms Act 1977, The Unfair Terms in Consumer Contracts Regulations 1999, and The Consumer Protection (Distance Selling) Regulations 2000.

The Unfair Contract Terms Act focuses upon attempts by suppliers of goods and/or services to restrict liability for negligence or harm, or to avoid statutory duties. By s. 2 a party to a contract cannot exclude liability for death or personal injury caused by negligence. This applies to all contracts, not only consumer contracts. By s. 3 a business, when contracting with a consumer on standard terms, which is usual for nearly all B2C websites, cannot exclude or restrict liability for loss caused by their having breached the contract, while s. 5 prevents a business when dealing with a consumer from excluding or restricting liability for the supply of defective or unfit goods.

Much of the everyday regulation of consumer contracts is, though, to be found in The Unfair Terms in Consumer Contracts Regulations, in particular reg. 5.

> **Highlight** The Unfair Terms in Consumer Contracts Regulations, reg. 5
>
> 'A contractual term which has not been individually negotiated shall be regarded as unfair if, contrary to the requirement of good faith, it causes a significant imbalance in the parties' rights and obligations arising under the contract, to the detriment of the consumer.'

This means that in any B2C contract concluded on standard terms, if the court finds that term to be biased in favour of the supplier of the goods or services it may be struck out by the court.

The definition of an unfair term was discussed by the House of Lords in *Director General of Fair Trading v First National Bank Plc* where Lord Bingham described it as 'causing a significant imbalance in the parties' rights and obligations under the contract to the detriment of the consumer in a manner or to an extent which is contrary to the requirement of good faith. The requirement of significant imbalance is met if a term is so weighted in favour of the supplier as to tilt the parties' rights and obligations under the contract significantly in his favour. This may be by the granting to the supplier of a beneficial option or discretion or power, or by the imposing on the consumer of a disadvantageous burden or risk or duty.'[37]

Schedule 2 of the Regulations provides an excellent illustrative list of the types of terms which may be found to be unfair. These include terms which 'inappropriately exclude or limit the legal rights of the consumer vis-à-vis the seller or supplier or another party in the event of total or partial non-performance or inadequate performance by

---

[37] [2002] 1 AC 481, 494.

the seller or supplier of any of the contractual obligation' and which 'irrevocably bind the consumer to terms with which he had no real opportunity of becoming acquainted before the conclusion of the contract'.

These Regulations are not, of course, unique to electronic contracts and neither are the final set of consumer protection regulations, The Consumer Protection (Distance Selling) Regulations 2000, although as their name suggests they are unique to contracts agreed where the consumer and the supplier are trading at a distance. The Distance Selling Regulations seek to even out imbalances in information caused by the process of contracting at a distance. By regs 7 and 8 the supplier of goods or services must supply a considerable amount of information before the contract is concluded. This includes the price of the goods or service including all taxes, any delivery costs, arrangements for payment and delivery, and a description of the goods or service. The primary form of consumer protection is though a right to cancel under reg. 10. This provides that the consumer has seven working days beginning with the day after the day on which the consumer receives the goods or service to cancel the agreement.[38] There is no requirement for the consumer to give a reason for their decision to cancel the contract and vitally the consumer cannot be compelled to pay the cost of returning goods. The consumer's only duty is to retain the goods and take care of them and to make them available for collection from her own premises.[39]

To define the enforceable terms of an electronic contract is a complex task. It may be assumed that a well ordered ecommerce site will have a set of clear, and fair, terms, but one can never be sure how the courts will interpret contracts and their terms until long after the contract has been concluded. It should be remembered though that the vast majority of contracts, especially B2C contracts, pass off without problem. Therefore for most contracts the terms of the contract are simply what both parties believe them to be.

16.4 **Formal contracts**

Not all contracts are as simply accommodated into the framework of the information society. While the vast majority of everyday contracts are informal in nature there are a small number of core contractual agreements which require to be formally concluded, usually in writing and sometimes with the requirement of a signature. These contracts tend to be for higher value items or of a nature as to create an ongoing contractual undertaking: they include contracts for the sale or transfer of an interest in land and an application under s. 6 of the Consumer Credit Act 1974.

The initial problem with many formal contracts was that for many there was a statutory requirement that they be 'in writing'. Although one could define an electronic document such as one created on a web page or via email as a written document in the

---

[38] It should be noted that this period assumes the supplier of the goods/service has complied with regs 7 and 8 on the supply of information. If he has failed to do so then the consumer has up to three months to cancel the agreement dependent upon when the supplier finally complied with regs 7 and 8. See regs 11(2) and 12(3). In addition it should be noted that by reg. 13 some contracts cannot be cancelled. These are generally time sensitive or price sensitive contracts and include gambling agreements, the supply of perishables, the supply of personalised goods, newspapers, and periodicals and the supply of audio or video recordings or computer software if they are unsealed by the consumer.   [39] Reg. 17.

colloquial sense there was a degree of debate as to whether it met the statutory definition of writing found in the Interpretation Act 1978 as 'includ[ing] typing, printing,
lithography, photography and other modes of representing or reproducing words in a
visible form.'[40] This rather dated definition of writing as being something in a tangible
form suggested that should the rule of *ejusdem generis* be applied it was unlikely that a
series of binary digits would qualify.

Some form of updating of the law was required and this became urgent when in 1996
the United Nations Commission on International Trade Law (UNCITRAL) adopted its
model law on Electronic Commerce.[41] The Model Law requires all UNCITRAL states
(including the UK) to formally recognise electronic contracts. Article 5 states that 'Information shall not be denied legal effect, validity or enforceability solely on the grounds
that it is in the form of a data message.' Then building upon this principle, the Model
Law goes on to ensure that all supporting principles required to provide for recognition
of electronic contracts are in place. Firstly, Article 6 endows equivalence for electronic
documentation by requiring that, 'where the law requires information to be in writing,
that requirement is met by a data message if the information contained therein is accessible so as to be usable for subsequent reference' and then, through Article 7, it requires
that States give legal recognition to electronic signatures,[42] and finally and perhaps
most importantly, Article 11 formally provides for the legal recognition of electronic
contracts.[43]

As we have seen UK Law could comply with Articles 5 and 11, at least in relation to
informal contracts, but with the Interpretation Act suggesting 'contracts in writing' had
to be in a tangible form and with signatures often required to be 'in writing' there was an
inability to comply with Articles 6 and 7. This led the Department of Trade and Industry
to undertake a review of the UK legal position, a review which concluded that: 'the position on the requirement for information to be "written" or "in writing" ... cannot at present be met using electronic means.'[44] The DTI recognised that 'these uncertainties and
limitations ... are important barriers to the development of electronic commerce',[45] and
opened consultation on the best approach to removing these barriers.[46]

---

[40] Interpretation Act 1978, Sch. 1.
[41] The UNCITRAL Model Law on Electronic Commerce (1996) with additional Article 5 bis
as adopted in 1998 is available at: http://www.jus.uio.no/lm/un.electronic.commerce.model.
law.1996/doc.html.
[42] Art. 7 states: 'Where the law requires a signature of a person, that requirement is met in relation to a data message if: (a) a method is used to identify that person and to indicate that person's
approval of the information contained in the data message; and (b) that method is as reliable as
was appropriate for the purpose for which the data message was generated or communicated, in
the light of all the circumstances, including any relevant agreement.'
[43] Art. 11 states: 'In the context of contract formation, unless otherwise agreed by the parties,
an offer and the acceptance of an offer may be expressed by means of data messages. Where a
data message is used in the formation of a contract, that contract shall not be denied validity or
enforceability on the sole ground that a data message was used for that purpose.'
[44] *Building Confidence in E-Commerce: A Consultation Document*, DTI, 5 March 1999, URN 99/642
at para 16.   [45] *ibid*, [17].
[46] At para. 18 the DTI set out two broad approaches and asked for views to be expressed by
members of the public. The approaches considered were (1) to allow for individual Acts and
Statutory Instruments on a case-by-case basis or (2) allow, through enabling legislation, a power
for Government Ministers to adopt changes through Statutory Instruments where necessary. This
is the approach taken and may be found in s. 8 of the Electronic Communications Act.

This led to the promulgation of the Electronic Communications Act 2000. The Act was designed to ensure the UK complied fully with the UNCITRAL Model Law, and to position the UK to allow for smooth implementation of the Electronic Commerce Directive which was also under construction at this time as a means to ensure the EU, which is a separate UNCITRAL member, also complied with the Model Law. The main provisions of the Electronic Communications Act are ss. 7 and 8. By s. 7(1) 'an electronic signature incorporated into or logically associated with a particular electronic communication or particular electronic data, and the certification by any person of such a signature' shall 'be admissible in evidence in relation to any question as to the authenticity of the communication or data or as to the integrity of the communication or data.' In other words an electronic signature (as defined by the Act) shall be recognised as being the equivalent of a traditional signature.[47] Section 8 is though the key section which allows for electronic documentation to be used in the formation of a contract where some sort of formality is required. It states that Ministers may make subordinate legislation allowing for electronic communications to be used where appropriate to do anything which is 'required to be or may be done or evidenced in writing or otherwise using a document, notice or instrument' or which 'is required to be or may be done by post or other specified means of delivery.'[48]

Immediately it is clear that s. 8 does not give complete equivalence to all 'data messages' in accordance with Article 6. Instead s. 8 enabled Ministers to take a case-by-case approach to equivalence, designing specific rules to allow the integration of electronic data messages into existing statutory schemes with the least disruption. Elsewhere this author has argued that the approach taken in s. 8 was ill founded and failed to comply with the UK's international legal duties to comply not only with Article 6 of the UNCITRAL Model Law, but also saw the UK failing to implement Article 9(1) of the Electronic Commerce Directive.[49] At the time that paper was written the UK Government was part way through the process of amending existing legislation to allow for the use of electronic documentation in the formation of formal contracts, and therefore at that time some formal contracts could be concluded electronically while others could not. This was a very unsatisfactory and unsettled period as contractual counterparties would have to continually check the current settlement to ensure they were permitted to use electronic means to conclude a formal contract. Now, after the promulgation of fifty-three Regulations and Orders in nine years the process of integration is almost complete. Key provisions including The Consumer Credit Act 1974 (Electronic Communications) Order 2004,[50] Part 8 of the Land Registration Act 2002, and The Automated Registration of Title to Land (Electronic Communications) (Scotland) Order 2006[51] now allow everyday transactions such as an application for consumer credit (including a credit card application) and a transfer of an interest in land to be concluded electronically. Finally it may be said that the UK law is arguably in compliance with both the Model Law and the Electronic Commerce Directive, but has the approach taken by the UK Government been desirable?

The UK Government believe this case-by-case approach is desirable as it allows for a tailored response to each type of contract, agreement, or communication. Critics argue

---

[47] Electronic signatures (and s. 7) will be discussed in more depth below.
[48] Electronic Communications Act 2000, s. 8(2) lists a number of 'purposes' for which a Minister may make a s. 8 order.
[49] A. Murray, 'Contracting Electronically in the Shadow of the E-Commerce Directive', in L. Edwards (ed.), *The New Legal Framework for E-Commerce in Europe*, (2005).
[50] SI 2004/3236.   [51] SI 2006/491.

that while the changes are implemented there is an unnecessary degree of uncertainty and that there may be obscure forms of transaction which are missed in the revision process and which without blanket recognition for electronic forms of communication remain impossible to conclude electronically.[52] It must be recognised though that now we are at the end of the revision process the UK case-by-case approach offers a level of certainty not found in the blanket approach seen in other parts of the world including throughout the EU and in the US Uniform Electronic Transaction Act. Now, should a UK-domiciled formal contract be challenged the parties may confidently rely upon specialist legislative rules *before* going to court. This provides a high degree of legal certainty. By contrast countries which have simply adopted the Model Law or Directive by passing a simple permissive provision such as § 7(c) of the US Uniform Electronic Transaction Act which says 'if a law requires a record to be in writing, an electronic record satisfies the law' have back-loaded the costs into the court proceedings.

In other words while the UK approach was originally slow, costly, and cumbersome to design and implement, parties, and the courts, now have a clear framework to apply in the event of a challenge to the legality or enforceability of any formal contract concluded electronically, whereas the simple permissive approach practiced elsewhere, although cheap and simple to originally implement, leads to higher evidentiary costs in court as parties have to establish whether or not their transaction is an 'electronic record' or is 'electronic means' within the meaning of the enacting provision. It appears now, ten years on, that the UK approach is a sound one, but we did have ten years of uncertainty, and a cost of a considerable amount of legislative time to get us to this point.

16.5 **Electronic signatures**

Allowing electronic forms and delivery to be used for formal contracts is only half of the solution to online formal electronic contracting. Most formal contracts not only have requirements of form, they also usually require adoption of the terms of the contract, usually though the addition of a signature, stamp, or seal. This, obviously, proves extremely difficult for an electronic document which has no physical structure upon which a signature may be added. We have had to be extremely inventive in designing structures to replace traditional signatures as there is no way to simply replicate a manuscript signature, which is by far the most common form of signature, when dealing with intangible, digital, documents. To this end a number of techniques were tried in the 1990s, including digitally encoding a signature made with an 'electronic pen and paper system',[53] or even using other biometric data such as fingerprints or iris scans.[54] It soon became clear though that systems such as these attempted to replicate physical signatures instead of seeking to fulfil the function of a signature: in other words systems like these promoted form over function.

---

[52] See Murray, above n. 49. See also A. Murray, 'Regulating Electronic Contracts: Comparing the European and North American Approaches': http://works.bepress.com/cgi/viewcontent.cgi?article=1001&context=andrew_murray.

[53] B. Wright, 'Alternatives for Signing Electronic Documents' [1995] 11 *Computer Law and Security Report* 136.

[54] C. Reed, 'What is a Signature?' 2000 (3) *JILT*: http://www2.warwick.ac.uk/fac/soc/law/elj/jilt/2000_3/reed/.

This was made clear in an excellent article by Professor Chris Reed called 'What is a Signature?' In this Reed distinguishes between the form of a signature: being usually facsimiles of the traditional manuscript signature such as 'the use of initials, marks, seals (for some but not all types of document), the adoption of a printed name and the use of rubber stamps',[55] and the function of a signature. Reed notes that 'the approach adopted by the courts ... was to determine whether the particular form of signature adopted had already been recognised as valid in previous decisions, and if not, to decide whether it was acceptable in the particular circumstances. Often no reasons were given to explain why the signature method in question was legally acceptable; it appears that the judges in each case simply satisfied themselves that the method adopted achieved the same authentication effects as a manuscript signature.'[56]

This, as noted by Reed, is not necessarily the best way to approach the adoption of a system to formalise electronic documents given the radically different nature of the intangible, non-rivalrous, and easily replicable digital document when compared with the tangible, rivalrous, and difficult to reproduce nature of an original manuscript signature, or its facsimiles. Instead Reed suggests we focus on the function of a signature. He identifies three functions of a signature, one of which he defines as primary and two of which are subsidiary.

➡ Highlight The Primary Function of a Signature

The primary function is authentication. This reflects that a signature is an evidentiary tool used to reduce reliance on post-agreement oral evidence which attempts to deny the apparent accuracy of a document or explain its true meaning.

This primary function consists of three 'sub-functions'. These are that a signature provides evidence of:

1. the identity of the signatory;

2. that the signatory intended the 'signature' to be his signature; and

3. that the signatory approves of and adopts the contents of the document.

In addition to this primary function there are two subsidiary functions of a signature: (1) to validate official action (such as a judge signing an order of court) and (2) for consumer protection reasons.[57] Quite rightly Reed suggests that the function of a signature should take priority over its form. There is no need for the traditions of physical signatures being carried over into the information society. Reed argues that the (at that time) newly adopted Electronic Communications Act 2000 and Electronic

---

[55] *ibid.*   [56] *ibid.*

[57] Reed is not strongly in favour of recognising this as a separate function. He notes that 'The consumer's signature merely supplements this method of protection by providing evidence (a) that the other party has supplied the required information, and (b) that the consumer has agreed to the terms. Thus, although signatures have a secondary effect in respect of consumer protection, this effect is achieved through their primary functions as evidence of identity and agreement.'

Signatures Directive[58] shows that the primary method for promulgating electronic signatures is to be through the use of encryption technology.

16.5.1 Formalising electronic signatures

Both the Electronic Signatures Directive and s. 7 of the Electronic Communications Act 2000 were promulgated to meet the requirements of Article 7 of the UNCITRAL Model Law on Electronic Commerce. This required that member states adopt a provision that 'Where the law requires a signature of a person, that requirement is met in relation to a data message if: (a) a method is used to identify that person and to indicate that person's approval of the information contained in the data message; and (b) that method is as reliable as was appropriate for the purpose for which the data message was generated or communicated, in the light of all the circumstances, including any relevant agreement.' Article 7 may be seen as enunciating Reed's primary function of authentication. As with Reed, there is no discussion of form, merely function.

To implement Article 7 the EU enacted the Electronic Signatures Directive 1999. Article 2 introduced two forms of electronic signature.

> **Highlight** 'Standard' Electronic Signatures
>
> A 'standard' electronic signature is one in which 'data in electronic form are attached to or logically associated with other electronic data and which serve as a method of authentication'

> **Highlight** 'Advanced' Electronic Signatures
>
> An 'advanced' electronic signature is an electronic signature which meets the following requirements:
>
> (a) it is uniquely linked to the signatory;
>
> (b) it is capable of identifying the signatory;
>
> (c) it is created using means that the signatory can maintain under his sole control; and
>
> (d) it is linked to the data to which it relates in such a manner that any subsequent change of the data is detectable.

What is the difference between the two? That becomes clear in Article 5 which states that 'Member States shall ensure that *advanced electronic signatures* which are based on a qualified certificate and which are created by a secure-signature-creation device: (a) satisfy the legal requirements of a signature in relation to data in electronic form in the same manner

[58] Directive 1999/93/EC of the European Parliament and of the Council of 13 December 1999 on a Community framework for electronic signatures, OJ L 013, 19/01/2000 P.0012–0020: http://eur-lex.europa.eu/LexUriServ/LexUriServ.do?uri=CELEX:31999L0093:EN:HTML.

as a handwritten signature satisfies those requirements in relation to paper-based data; and (b) are admissible as evidence in legal proceedings.'[59] Meanwhile standard electronic signatures are given lesser recognition 'Member States shall ensure that an electronic signature is not denied legal effectiveness and admissibility as evidence in legal proceedings solely on the grounds that it is: in electronic form, or not based upon a qualified certificate, or not based upon a qualified certificate issued by an accredited certification-service-provider, or not created by a secure signature-creation device.'[60]

The difference between the two is subtle but important. Only the advanced electronic signature is probative or self-proving. This is an essential characteristic of a manuscript signature. A document which is signed by a party is probative; this means the court will assume the document is accurate, and that the party who signed it adopted it in the form signed, unless evidence proves otherwise. By comparison, the adoption of an unsigned document requires to be proven by supporting evidence. A probative document performs the important function of switching the burden of proof from the party seeking to rely upon it to the party seeking to depart from it. What we see in the complex wording of Article 5 is that an advanced electronic signature is to be sufficient to create a probative electronic document while the attachment of any other form of signature is not afforded this value, merely being 'admissible as evidence'. As the point of a signature is to make a document probative anything which is not an advanced electronic signature is of little value as a signature. While it may be valuable for instance for a bank to show that a PIN number was used to authorise a credit card transaction this is only evidence supporting the bank's claim that a party was present and authorised a transaction: the burden of proof remains with the bank. The UK Government implemented Article 5 in s. 7 of the Electronic Communications Act 2000. Again we see the advanced electronic signature is favoured with the Act referring to both a signature and certification of that signature. What then in practice is an advanced electronic signature?

16.5.2 **Advanced electronic signatures**

An advanced electronic signature is a form of electronic signature based in encryption technology. While there are many ways to demonstrate one has accepted the terms of a document and intends to be bound by them all are at risk of forgery or fraud, except for one system known as public key encryption or PKE signatures. The attachment of an unencrypted form of identification risks interception and/or reproduction without authorisation, even a biometric signature could be replicated at a later date by a forger. Further digital documents, unlike physical documents, may be changed with no apparent trace or the change: words could be deleted or altered a value of $1 per unit could be changed easily to $2 per unit without any obvious change on the face of the document. And as a digital document may be signed at a distance there is no way for a counterparty to prove identity without there being some form of third party witness to prove the identity of a signatory.[61]

---

[59] *ibid*, Art. 5(1), emphasis added.   [60] *ibid*, Art. 5(2).

[61] This point may be demonstrated by a short experiment. Should a disgruntled employee of a firm want to take revenge on his employer he may pose as a member of senior management of that firm and enter into an online transaction on unfavourable terms. Assuming the counterparty never meets this person then when he 'signs' the document acting on behalf of the company the counterparty has no reason to suspect anything is amiss. It is only when the contract comes to be fulfilled that the issue will come to light. When dealing at a distance therefore you want some system of independent identification of counterparties.

The system which fulfils all these requirements is a PKE signature. PKE signatures use a particular functionality of encryption technology. Encryption is a well known and tried system for protecting the content of messages, but previously it has not been of much use as a methodology of identifying the originator of the message, or demonstrating their intent to be bound to the message. This was because of the nature of traditional or symmetric key encryption.

When using symmetric keys the originator of the message and the recipient of the message would use the same key to encrypt and decrypt the message.

★ Example Symmetric Encryption

Mario has a message that he must transmit securely to Arianna. To secure the message he uses the Caesar cipher (see Fn 62). He chooses his cipher and sends the key to Arianna. He then separately encodes his message and sends that to Arianna as 'ciphertext'.

Note: Mario and Arianna use the same key to encode and decode the messages.

Thus a basic cipher such as Caesar cipher relied on both the originator and recipient of the message having the same cipher key.[62] This is good for sending messages (assuming the key is kept secure) but no good for proving identity as at least two people have copies of the key. Thus a message sent in encrypted form could be sent by any one of two people (or more depending on how many copies of the key there are).

Asymmetric or Public Key Encryption works differently. Here two keys are created: one known as the private key, the other the public key. The keys are mathematically linked but vitally you cannot discover one key by examining the other, and the keys only work in pairs: that is if you encrypt a message with one key it can only be decrypted by the other. This technology was first suggested in the nineteenth century but was not developed until more powerful computers could be used to create the pairs of keys.

The inventors are widely credited as being James Ellis, Clifford Cocks, and Malcolm Williamson who developed PKE encryption for their employer the Government Communications Headquarters (GCHQ) in the early 1970s. As though they were subject to the Official Secrets Act their work was not acknowledged until much later. Independently their work was replicated by Whitfield Diffie and Martin Hellman in 1976 who published the first schematic for a working PKE system.

PKE is extremely powerful as an encryption tool as one never has to send the decryption key to the message recipient. One weakness of symmetric encryption is that you

---

[62] Caesar cipher is one of the simplest and most widely known encryption techniques. It is a type of substitution cipher in which each letter in the plaintext is replaced by a letter some fixed number of positions down the alphabet. For example, with a shift of +3, A would be replaced by D, B would become E, and so on. Using a +3 shift the message 'attack' becomes 'dwwdfn'. The method is named after Julius Caesar, who used it to communicate with his generals.

must at some point communicate to the recipient of your message the key you are using; this is liable to intercept allowing your enemies to decrypt all your messages.[63] With PKE keys need never be traded in this fashion.

⊛ **Example** Asymmetric PKE Encryption

Mario has another message that he must transmit securely to Arianna. To secure the message he uses the PKE. He takes his message and encrypts it using Arianna's public key. As this message can only be decrypted by the paired key (the private key) the public key may be made publicly available anywhere including on the internet at no risk to the security of the message.

Mario then sends the encoded (ciphertext) message to Arianna, who then decrypts it using his private key. The private key never leaves Arianna's possession making the entire transaction secure.

Note: This time Mario and Arianna use different keys to encode and decode the messages.

This was the reason for the design of PKE. It allowed British agents in Moscow to send messages back to London with no risk of the key being compromised. In addition PKE encryption is extremely resistant to so called 'brute force' attacks making it the preferred choice of encryption today for all secure services and internet sites.[64]

One interesting side effect of PKE though is that it may be used in reverse. An individual who wishes to prove their identity may encrypt a message (or even part of that message) using their private key. They can then send this to someone else and providing the public key they have previously published can decrypt the encrypted part of the message there is overwhelming proof that the message must have been encrypted using the private key, and as the private key is within the possession of one person we therefore have a way of proving identity, and the desire to adopt the contents of a digital document, in other words a signature.

---

[63] There are two very famous examples of intercepted keys from the history books. It is believed that Sir Francis Walsingham, Spy Master of Queen Elizabeth I of England, obtained a secret code used by Queen Mary I of Scotland to communicate with a Catholic nobleman named Anthony Babington from the Tower of London where Mary was being held. This allegedly unearthed a plot to overthrow Elizabeth leading to the execution of Mary. In another example in World War II the German 'Enigma' code was broken by scientists at Bletchley Park with the help of a captured Enigma machine recovered from a German U-boat in 1941. This was later fictionalised in the Hollywood movie 'U-571'.

[64] It is estimates that to break a 128 bit encryption (this is the type used Mozilla Firefox ver.3) it would take a device that could check a billion billion keys (10^{18}) per second about 10^{13} years to exhaust the key space. This is a thousand times longer than the age of the universe, which is about 13,000,000,000 (1.3×10^{10}) years. Even assuming randomness would provide the key in half that time it is still around five hundred times greater than the age of the universe. Much more powerful encryption keys are available for high security and military applications. Fictional books such as Dan Brown's *Digital Fortress* suggest organisations such as the US National Security Agency have supercomputers that can decrypt powerful asymmetric ciphers in a few hours or days. This is not the case.

> ### ✴ **Example** Asymmetric PKE Signatures
>
> Mario now wants to 'sign' a contract with Arianna. To achieve this he encrypts all (or more likely part of) the document using his private key. He then sends the document to Arianna. She then uses Mario's public key to decrypt the encrypted part of the document. If she is successful she knows the document part could only have been encrypted using Mario's private key, and as only Mario has access to that key it is as unique, in evidentiary terms, as a manuscript signature.

The problem with a PKE signature is that by itself it does not prove identity: only possession of a key pair. To explain: there is nothing to stop me from setting up a fake website passing myself off as the UK operation of an international company who does not yet trade in the UK, someone like China Telecom. I then create a matching key pair and place the public key on my website. Then if I induce someone to trade with me I sign all contractual documents using my private key. When my victim checks my signature using my public key it will, of course, demonstrate that the signature is valid, but of course I am not who I say I am. This returns us to the common problem of proving identity when people are in remote locations.

The solution for electronic signatures is to issue a certificate of identity; a virtual ID card for key pairs. To create a certified signature (it should be noted that under Article 5 of the Directive only advanced electronic signatures *which are based on a qualified certificate* are probative) the user either creates her own key pair and sends them to a certification agency such as Verisign or Digi-sign along with proof of identity, or more simply approaches the certification agency and asks them to create a key pair and to issue a certificate at the same time. The certification agency must carry out necessary checks to establish the identity of the individual before issuing the certificate, and may be held liable for damages should someone rely upon that certificate to their loss through any fault of the certification agency.[65] Generally for a low-level personal certificate basic information such as a functioning email address can be enough but for more secure commercial signatures a significant amount of personal information will be required to establish identity.

Now when the signatory signs her message by attaching their private encryption to a portion of the message they also include a copy of the certificate. This shows who issued the certificate, when it was issued and whether or not it is still valid. If the contractual counterparty is at all suspicious they can contact the certification agency and ask for the identity of the signatory to be confirmed. Through the joint use of a secret, and in theory incorruptible, private key and the certificate of identity all of Reed's functions of a signature may be fulfilled, including the two subsidiary functions. In fact in some ways a digitally signed document is preferable to a physical document. A signature is used to authenticate a document but there is a danger of the document being altered. In the real world we use forensics to determine whether a document has been altered

---

[65] See The Electronic Signatures Directive, above n. 58 at Art. 6 and Annexes I and II. See also The Electronic Signatures Regulations 2002, SI 2002/318 regs 3 and 4.

post signature but the risk remains that a page may be removed and replaced by a different page or gaps filled with additional words or numbers. With an electronically signed document we can reduce the risk of such fraud. All electronic documents have an inbuilt integrity check known as a 'checksum' or a 'hash sum'. This is a numerical value of all the data held in the file and is used by computers to check for accidental damage (corruption) or transmission errors in the file. In any complex file that number is uniquely created by the value of the contents of the file and will record any change, no matter how minor in the document, even the addition or removal of a single space. To protect the integrity of a signed document it is commonplace to encrypt the hash value of the document when signing. This both creates the electronic signature and protects the integrity of the document.

Although it is possible to create signed formal documents in purely digital form the uptake of electronic signatures has been somewhat disappointing. Despite the legal framework for electronic contracts and electronic signatures dating from the late 1990s the number of digital contracts formalised by PKE electronic signatures remains low. In 2006 the Commission issued a report on the uptake of electronic signatures in the EU and proposals as part of the Commissions i2010 project. Viviane Reding, Commissioner for information society and media, noted that although the framework provided by the Directive provided 'A reliable system of electronic signatures that work across intra-EU borders' the Commission was not fully satisfied with the take-up of e-signatures.[66] There are many reasons why this may be. The favoured technology of PKE encryption is certainly complex and very unwieldy when one compares it with the simplicity of signing a physical document, while the requirement that one must first obtain a certificate of identity will put off casual users. The Commission though believes that a change may be just around the corner as governments introduce electronic identity cards which could be used to establish identity online, along with a growth in e-government services such as online tax returns, which could be digitally signed using PKE allied to a government identity card. However the potential for e-contracting to grow in all its forms may be limited by other aspects of ecommerce including the ability to make online payments without resorting to the use of credit or debit cards which charge online retailers high transaction fees, improved dispute resolution processes, and streamlined and simplified taxation rules for ecommerce. These will form the focus of our next chapter.

16.6 **Conclusion**

Contract formation is probably the most commonplace legally regulated activity in the online environment. It is at once also the simplest and yet most complex online activity from a legal perspective. As we have seen informal contracts are easily concluded, yet raise a number of issues. Where is the contract domiciled? What are the terms of the contract and when is the contract concluded. These three W's are the WWW of contract lawyers. Traditional rules on contract formation, as seen in cases like *Thornton v Shoe*

---

[66] See 'Electronic signatures: legally recognised but cross-border take-up too slow': http://europa.eu/rapid/pressReleasesAction.do?reference=IP/06/325&format=HTML&aged=0&language=EN&guiLanguage=no.

Lane Parking, and *Entores Ltd v Miles Far East Corporation* assist greatly in the domestic interpretation of these issues. But in the online environment a consumer is just as likely to conclude a contract with an American or French trader as a UK-based trader. Here provisions such as the UNCITRAL Model Law and the E-Commerce Directive assist. Additionally consumer protection laws assist a consumer should they find themselves disputing the position with their counterparty.

This is only part of the story though. Formal contracts have rules as to form and often require a signature, something impossible in the traditional sense when dealing with a digital document. complex rules have been developed as to the form of both documents and signatures, with heavy reliance being placed on highly technical solutions such as PKE encryption technology. Yet despite all these challenges we find in reviewing this chapter an almost complete absence of case law dealing with these subjects. Why is this? It is because on the whole we make it work without the need for legal interventions. Online retailers have extremely detailed terms and conditions and generally those who do not act reasonably and fairly do not last long in the cutthroat online business environment. Although an essential body of law the rules on electronic contract formation and interpretation will, in all likelihood, continue to be little relied upon in court.

FURTHER READING

Books

J. Dickie, *Producers and Consumers* in *EU e-Commerce Law* (2005)

D. Campbell, *E-Commerce and the Law of Digital Signatures* (2005)

L. Edwards (Ed), *The New Legal Framework for e-Commerce in Europe* (2005)

Chapters and Articles

C. Reed, 'What is a Signature?' 2000 (3) *JILT*

A. Murray, 'Contracting Electronically in the Shadow of the E-Commerce Directive', in L. Edwards (ed.), *The New Legal Framework for E-Commerce in Europe,* (2005)

C. Glatt, 'Comparative Issues in the Formation of Electronic Contracts' (1998) *IJLIT* 34

M. Siems, 'The EU Directive on Electronic Signatures—a World Wide Model or a Fruitless Attempt to Regulate the Future?' (2002) *IRLCT* 7

Electronic payments and taxation

The ability to make payment online is the final piece of the ecommerce jigsaw as it allows services to be supplied immediately and orders for products to be processed without delay. The issue of secure payment at a distance, often over borders, is a complex problem and as we shall see the solution used to date has been relatively inelegant, while alternatives have proven difficult to develop and establish.

17.1 A history of international payments methods

The problem of payment at a distance for services or goods rendered and often in different currencies, has been a recurring problem of international trade which has been recently exacerbated by the phenomenal growth of ecommerce. These problems were first tackled by traders in the Eastern Mediterranean in the twelfth to fourteenth centuries with the joint development of the *Lex Mercatoria* and Bills of Exchange. The *Lex Mercatoria*, or Law Merchant, developed between the twelfth and thirteenth centuries and was based upon principles found in the earlier Greek Law of the of The Sea Law of Rhodes.[1] This was a specialist body of law which applied only to merchants (those who traded with others outside their city, state, or province), only in special circumstances (transactions which took place in fairs, markets, or ports) which had a remarkable set of characteristics: (1) it was transnational; (2) its principle source was custom not law; (3) it was administered by merchants not judges; (4) it was procedurally speedy and informal; and (5) it stressed equity as an overriding principle.[2] The trust placed in this regulatory system was enough to convince merchants to trade across extensive distances such as from Venice or Florence to Constantinople (Istanbul) and vitally across jurisdictional boundaries.

In the fourteenth century the *Lex Mercatoria* was supplemented by a payment method that secured both the seller and the buyer in an inter-jurisdictional transaction. The problem was one of common currency. There was no common currency in use across the great trading cities and states of the Mediterranean. Venice used the Venetian Lira, Florence the Florin, and Constantinople the Hyperpyron. To make payment in common currency for goods gold would have to be shipped from one state to another (gold being the store of value and the common form of all three currencies). This of

---

[1] See H. Berman & C, Kaufman, 'The Law of International Commercial Transactions (Lex Mercatoria)', 19 *Harvard International Law Journal* 221, 224 (1978).　　[2] *ibid*, 225.

course was extremely dangerous and left the way open for both thieves and pirates to operate as well as the risk of fraud with the seller either failing to deliver or delivering sub-standard goods.

The introduction of the bill of exchange reduced, but did not eliminate these risks and problems. The bill of exchange was a form of credit note issued by the buyer and despatched to the seller which allowed the seller to receive payment from a merchant local to him.[3]

> ### ✴ Example Payment by Bill of Exchange (original form)
>
> Francesco is a Florentine silk merchant. He imports fine silks from Donus a merchant in Constantinople. Donus is about to send a shipment of silks to Francesco. To arrange payment Francesco sends an agent to Constantinople to inspect the goods and to deliver a letter (a bill of exchange) to Donus authorising him to collect payment from Nilus a tailor based in Constantinople who owes money to Francesco for some fine Italian wool.
>
> Francesco thus substitutes Nilus's debt to him with a debt to Donus and receives goods in return.

This afforded many advantages. Firstly gold or coinage was not shipped from place to place reducing the risk of highway robbery or piracy. Second the transaction could be carried out in local currency. Thirdly, the agent of the buyer could inspect the goods before they made payment ensuring they were in good order. Finally a system of credit could be used where debts were held open to be used to make payment later rather than requiring immediate settlement. The problem was that for the system to work the buyer of goods had to have a local debtor in the place where the seller was based and as many buyers were specifically importers of goods such as silks and spices they had no reason to sell goods back to the place where their seller was based and therefore no local debtors. To get around this problem a group of merchants set themselves up as middle-men. These money exchangers were powerful merchants who would exchange nothing but bills of exchange between each other allowing other merchants to trade without the need of a local debtor.

To return to our earlier example:

> ### ✴ Example Payment by Bill of Exchange (revised form)
>
> Francesco buys another shipment of silk from Donus. This time he had no debtor in Constantinople. He therefore visits Lorenzo, a money exchanger based in Florence. Francesco pays Lorenzo the money he is due to pay Donus plus a small premium for the service.
>
> Lorenzo then issues a bill of exchange drawn on his partner in Constantinople, Theon. Francesco then sends the bill of exchange to Donus in payment for the silk. Donus then presents the bill to Theon for payment.   ➡

[3] See E. Hunt & J. Murray, *A History of Business in Medieval Europe, 1200–1550* (1999), 63–67.

➡

[*Note*: If Francesco did not trust Donus (perhaps it was the first time they had traded) he could ask that payment be delayed until the goods arrive safely and he can inspect them. If all were satisfactory Lorenzo then instructs Theon to pay on the Bill.]

Over time money exchangers became banks and bills of exchange became common forms of payment becoming formalised in the cheque and the banknote.[4]

As we have seen the experiences of these mediaeval merchants have already influenced our understanding of cyberspace and the regulation of actions and transactions therein. As discussed in Chapter 4 Joel Reidenberg made a connection between the development of the custom-based rules of the *Lex Mercatoria* of mediaeval Europe and the custom-based rules that he could identify as developing in chat rooms, user fora, and even early e-commerce sites.[5] Reidenberg recognised that like the merchants of thirteenth century Florence or Constantinople, late twentieth century internet consumers were beginning to dip their toes into uncharted waters. They too were trading more extensively with sellers from outwith their jurisdiction[6] and as with *Lex Mercatoria* Reidenberg believed it was the customary rules that would provide the framework of community regulation.

As we know Reidenberg's principle of *Lex Informatica* was critical in the development of the Cyberpaternalist School of internet regulation, but unlike our appreciation of the role *Lex Mercatoria* could play in understanding a culture and community based on trade and exploration across borders, the application of that other great mediaeval invention the bill of exchange was not championed. Rather, as we enter a new era of international trade where consumers have the opportunity to buy goods from international merchants, bills of exchange seem to be becoming obsolete. The traditional cheque is being phased out and the banknote is less powerful than it has been for hundreds of years. Both are being replaced in the wallets of consumers with card-based payment systems. These systems though were designed for the physical world not the information society. There seemed to be an opportunity, even a need, to design a new form of payment for the new trading community of the twenty-first century: a digital payment system which in its own way could be as groundbreaking as the bill of exchange was in the early fourteenth century.

---

[4] A banknote was (and still is) a specific form of bill of exchange known as a promissory note. It is a bill of exchange drawn directly on a bank where the bank promises to make payment (in gold usually) to the holder of the note. This is why Bank of England banknotes still say 'I promise to pay the bearer on demand the sum of . . .'. Bank of England banknotes are now legal tender in England and Wales under s. 2 of the Currency and Bank Notes Act 1954. Banknotes issued by Scottish and Ulster banks remain promissory notes.

[5] J. Reidenberg, 'Governing Networks and Rule-Making in Cyberspace' (1996) 45 *Emory Law Journal* 911; J. Reidenberg, 'Lex Informatica: The Formation of Information Policy Rules Through Technology' 76 *Texas Law Review* (1998), 553.

[6] This trade was not entirely commercial. It included the exchange of ideas and views.

17.2 **Electronic payments**

17.2.1 **Token payments**

There were a number of forms that a groundbreaking digital payment system could take. The most familiar would be to use a token system. Tokens are the method used in physical currency where a token (a banknote or coin) is exchanged for the supply of goods and services. The token system has a number of benefits which led to it becoming the dominant form of real world currency for over three thousand years.

Firstly, tokens have, over the years, become easily portable and easily stored with banknotes replacing old-fashioned coin-based currency from the eighteenth century onwards. Secondly, tokens such as banknotes and coins are both fungible and divisible. This means that they are interchangeable (one ten pound note is as good as the next) and are capable of subdivision into smaller units (a ten pound note can be divided into two five pound notes or ten pound coins). These functions are essential to liquidity, the function of money that allows it to be traded at a fixed value, including for other currency. This allows for change to be given allowing goods of a lesser value to be traded for a banknote of a higher value with change (tokens of a lower value) being used as the makeweight in the transaction. Thirdly, tokens are a physical store of value. This is vital to retain confidence in a currency and leads to most tokens being secured or guaranteed by the central bank or treasury.

In the UK Bank of England notes are issued by the central bank while coins are issued by the Royal Mint, an executive agency of the Treasury. Unusually the UK also allows some clearing banks to issue their own banknotes. This right is afforded to three Scottish banks: the Royal Bank of Scotland, the Bank of Scotland, and the Clydesdale Bank as well as four Ulster banks: the Bank of Ireland, First Trust Bank, Northern Bank, and Ulster Bank. These banknotes are accepted as currency despite not having been issued by the central bank because (a) none of these seven banks have ever defaulted on payment on any of their tokens and (b) because every note issued by these clearing banks are backed pound for pound by Bank of England notes possessed by the banks in question. Owing to the combined size of these issues (well over a billion pounds) it would be cumbersome for the banks to hold ordinary Bank of England notes as cover. Instead, special one million and one hundred million pound notes, known as Giants and Titans, are used. Unsurprisingly given the face value of these notes they are not for general circulation. The value stored in notes and coins also allows for them to be used to measure the value of competing goods and services, another key function of money. Collectively tokens are an extremely efficient way of fulfilling the three key functions of money:

> **Highlight** The Key Functions of Money
>
> The three key functions of money are to act as:
> (1) a means of exchange;
> (2) a unit of measurement; and
> (3) a comparator of the value of goods and service.

Tokens also fulfil the secondary function of liquidity:

> **Highlight** The Functions of Liquidity
>
> 1) Portability and storability;
> 2) Fungibility; and
> 3) Divisibility.

If any new form of monitory exchange is to replace cash tokens it must at least fulfil these functions.

17.2.2 Alternative payment systems

Several alternatives have developed over the years, mostly based upon substitution of a debt (the original focus of the bill of exchange), novation, and funds transfer. The most common alternative to the token system of currency until recent years was debt substitution. This is where a debt owed to one party is 'paid off' by substituting a debt owed by another. This was the design of the original bill of exchange and over time this became the model of cheque payment wherein a debt owed by the bank to its customer is used to make payment to a third party. Thus a customer has money on deposit with her bank; the bank is her debtor to the value of the money she has on deposit. The customer then buys goods and pays by cheque. In doing so she pays her debt for the goods she has bought by transferring part of the debt the bank is due to her. The bank pays her debt and reduces its indebtedness to her by the same amount.

Debt substitution is a way of reducing the risks associated with carrying money, but it has few of the benefits of cash tokens. It cannot be used as a unit of measurement or as a comparator of the value of goods or services. It is not fungible, is not divisible, and vitally is not as easily transferrable as cash tokens. In other words forms of debt substitution are strictly not money but are a money substitute. The cheque was initially popular for higher value transactions where the allied risks of carrying large amounts of money could be negated. Recently a new phenomenon has seen debt substitution become the dominant form of debt settlement in the UK, due to the replacement of the cheque with the chip and PIN debit card. The general and widespread use of the debit card even for low-value transactions, thanks to the convenience it offers, has seen debt substitution become increasingly popular and now the value of debit card transactions eclipse cash token transactions in the UK high street.[7] Many people refer to chip and PIN debit card transactions as electronic payments, although as we shall see below this is not strictly true, rather they are electronically enabled payments, meaning that chip and pin technology uses digital tools to make the system more reliable and secure, but they are in form debt substitution payments, not true electronic payments.

---

[7] R. Blakely, 'Debit cards overtake cash on the high street', *The Times* 18 April 2006: http://business.timesonline.co.uk/tol/business/industry_sectors/banking_and_finance/article706812.ece.

Another popular payment system, which has proven to be extremely popular with internet transactions, is payment by credit card. Although to the user a credit card transaction may appear to be functionally the same as a debit card transaction—a piece of plastic is handed over and a PIN is used to authorise the transaction—they are in fact very different in function. Whereas a debit card relies upon money the customer has placed with the bank (or perhaps an agreed overdraft) a credit card works by having the credit card company assume the customer's debt for them and then providing the customer with credit to the same value. This uses a principle known as novation: the replacing of one contract or obligation with another. When a customer pays by credit card the credit card company agrees to take on the debt the customer owes to the supplier and makes payment as if it were the customer. It simultaneously issues credit to the customer to the same value as the debt incurred, creating or extending contractual relationships between the credit card company and the supplier, and the credit card company and the customer. In function a credit card payment, like a debit card payment, is a money substitute not a form of money. Like a debit card it offers none of the functions of money. Also in common with a debit card payment, although people often think of credit card payments as electronic payments they are not, they are electronically enabled payments only.

Finally there is payment by fund transfer. This is not an option for traditional high street transactions as it involves a direct transfer from one bank account to another. It tends to be used for high value commercial transactions and for property transactions, as well as for regular payments such as bills and subscriptions. There are a number of names for different types of fund transfer: a standing order is an order to pay a predetermined amount at the instigation of the account holder on a certain date or at a certain frequency; a direct debit allows the payee to debit varying amounts from the payer's account at the payee's request while a CHAPS transfer is a same day inter-account transfer. These types of transfers are often collectively known as electronic fund transfers (EFTs) along with internet account transfers and direct credits. This terminology has also extended to cover credit and debit card purchases with these often being referred to as Electronic Funds Transfers at the Point of Sale (EFTPoS). Again the common message is that none of these alternate payment systems are money in the true sense of the word. Money remains only cash tokens, this being the only form of payment which possesses the functions of money. This raises the obvious question: if more and more trade occurs in a purely digital environment where cash tokens cannot be exchanged and over distances where it is impractical to send cash tokens by traditional means how do we develop a functional currency for the information society?

17.2.3 **Early e-money**

To date the answer to that question has been rather disappointing. The predominant methods of online payment are forms of funds transfer, being a mixture of debit card payments, credit card payments, and funds transfer payments (mostly via eBay subsidiary PayPal). There are obvious reasons for the uptake of funds transfer systems such as credit and debit cards. Firstly, there is a history of using such payment systems for distance selling transactions through 'card not present' systems used previously for telephone or mail order purchases. Secondly, sellers can rely upon guarantees from the card issuer that payment will be made, thus reducing the risk of fraud. Thirdly, buyers (when using credit cards) have guarantees in the event that the goods or services either are not delivered or are of unsatisfactory quality.[8] Also payment by debit or credit card is extremely convenient for consumers as most already have such cards and therefore do not need to take any further action to allow them to make online payments. Thus, until recently, electronic money has tended in reality to mean EFTPoS payments using credit or debit cards. But, as we have already seen such systems are not forms of money, only alternate payment methods.

In the 1990s a number of private organisations did try to develop viable digital cash, or e-cash systems. These came in a variety of forms that tried to copy the functions of money to a greater or lesser extent.

Probably the first system to achieve widespread coverage in the UK was Mondex. Mondex was a smartcard payment system first introduced in 1994. Although still in limited use worldwide Mondex never truly caught the public's imagination. To use Mondex one needed a Mondex card; a smartcard which used an embedded chip as an electronic wallet. One would 'charge up' the card by visiting specially enabled ATM machines and then one could spend amounts from the card by visiting retailers who accepted Mondex. Mondex was a version of electronic cash. It had many of the features of cash tokens: it was easily portable, fungible, and divisible and like cash tokens the Mondex user was anonymous. Mondex style technology is now being used in second generation smartcard systems which we will discuss below including the London Transport Oyster Card and the Hong Kong Transit Octopus Card. The problem with Mondex was it was inconvenient. Only Mondex registered businesses which had installed Mondex readers would accept it for payment. In addition if your Mondex card was lost or stolen then like real cash you lost whatever was charged on to it. Consumers continued to prefer debit cards over Mondex and soon it was removed from the UK market.

Around the same time other e-cash systems were being developed to function purely in the online environment. Digicash was a software-based solution which installed an 'electronic wallet' on your hard drive: a protected space which using encryption technology was secure. The customer could buy Digicash tokens which were simple encrypted files containing some tracking data to prevent forgery (a digital serial number) which was stored in the wallet. When the customer wanted to pay a retailer she could transfer tokens to the value of the goods bought, just like real cash. It functioned like Mondex for online transactions. It fulfilled most of the functions of cash. It was fungible, divisible, and anonymous. It was not though easily portable (it was tied to the wallet, which was tied to the hard drive) but as it was designed as an online currency this did not matter. It did for the first time offer the opportunity to develop a true digital cash system which fulfilled the three key functions of money. It was possible to use Digicash as a means of exchange, a unit of measurement; and as a comparator of the value of goods and service. Digicash spawned a number of imitators including Cyphermint and later Peppercoin a system designed to make so-called micropayments.

---

[8] Under s. 75 of the Consumer Credit Act 1974 if the customer has a claim against the supplier of goods or services which have a value of between £100 and £30,000 and she has paid for these goods or services by credit card, she has an equivalent claim against the credit issuer (her credit card company).

In the 1990s there was a great deal of hope that systems such as Mondex, Digicash, and Cyphermint would soon render traditional cash tokens obsolete.[9] They seemed to offer all the functionality of cash with fewer of the drawbacks. In particular as e-cash was merely a series of data encoded either on a smart card or in a secure wallet on a hard drive there were none of the associated costs absorbed by banks and other financial institutions in transporting cash from site to site. Also stolen 'cash' could, in some circumstances, be remotely deactivated rendering theft of less value while it may even be possible to refund the customer for any loss suffered if it were established that the cash had not been spent or redeemed. Electronic cash also afforded the opportunity for micropayments. These are very small payments of the value of a fraction of a penny.

The idea behind micropayments is that customers for online services such as news services or media services such as music or videogames could choose to pay a small amount each time they used the service rather than paying a subscription. This is only possible with electronic cash as the costs of transacting a traditional fund transfer payment via a credit or debit card far outweigh the value of the transaction. In particular the Peppercoin system was designed for exactly this purpose. The system worked by aggregating a number of micropayments into one large macropayment.[10] Effectively the customer would register with Peppercoin and would then be able to visit Peppercoin merchants and download content for a nominal amount. Over time the amount the customer spent would approach a macropayment trigger—say $10. When the trigger was reached Peppercoin would take the macropayment from the customer's bank or credit card account. Similarly merchants would collect micropayments until they too reached a macropayment trigger. The money would then be transferred to their account by Peppercoin, less of course Peppercoin's fees.

With the development of all these systems in the 1990s why today do we still use banknotes and coins in place of Mondex?[11] Why do we pay for goods online with credit or debit cards instead of Digicash or Cyphermint?[12] And why do we still not have a functioning micropayment system when media moguls such as Rupert Murdoch believe the current free subscription model for internet content does not work?[13] The answers to all these questions demonstrate the complexity of redesigning the centuries old concept of physical cash tokens.

[9] See e.g. S. Levy, 'E-Money (That's What I Want)', *Wired* 2.12, December 1994. Available from: http://www.wired.com/wired/archive/2.12/emoney.html.

[10] See R. Rivest, *Peppercoin Micropayments*: http://people.csail.mit.edu/rivest/Rivest-Peppercoin-Micropayments.ps.

[11] After trials of the Mondex system it was discontinued. The Mondex name was sold to Mastercard who now use it as part of a suite of trade names for second generation smart card payment systems.

[12] Digicash filed for bankruptcy in September 1998. In 2005 it was relaunched as a 'consumer savings concierge'—a way to store and receive online voucher codes. Cyphermint filed for bankruptcy in September 2008. The company relaunched as PayCash Mobile, a company specialising in hardware for mobile payments and kiosk payments. See I. Grigg, 'How DigiCash Blew Everything': http://www.jya.com/digicrash.htm; Mass High Tech, 'Bankruptcy court appoints interim management of Cyphermint', 3 September 2008: http://www.masshightech.com/stories/2008/09/01/daily30-Bankruptcy-court-appoints-interim-management-of-Cyphermint.html.

[13] A. Clark, 'News Corp will charge for newspaper websites, says Rupert Murdoch', *The Guardian* 7 May 2009: http://www.guardian.co.uk/media/2009/may/07/rupert-murdoch-charging-websites. Peppercoin was sold in 2007 to Chockstone a consumer rewards programme operator. The Peppercoin payment system was discontinued and the domain name Peppercoin.com was relaunched as an insurance brokerage.

Firstly, consumers are extremely conservative with cash and payment methods. Given the perceived risks of financial loss consumers tend to trust established names with their money: high street banks such as Barclays, Lloyds, and NatWest are trusted, even after the recent financial crisis, companies with no track record such as Digicash and Cyphermint do not have the same position of trust. Secondly, consumers were happy to use their credit and debit cards both online and offline. The perceived advantage of anonymity offered by e-cash systems was outweighed by the advantage that the card issuer would assume most of the risks of fraud associated with online transactions.[14] It appeared that consumers would even use their credit cards to purchase pornography with little embarrassment leaving few market opportunities for the new entrants.[15] Thirdly the technology was unreliable and untested. Who provided the best system? Which was most secure? There was no way for consumers to know. Fourthly, consumers knew instinctively that micropayments would mean paying for content which was currently available for free. Although in niche markets consumers will adopt micropayments (mostly in online gaming where systems such as Microsoft's 'Points' system used on Xbox Live has been a success) it has never had broad appeal as customers prefer ad-supported content instead. Fifthly and most importantly, all these electronic cash providers were private companies. Nearly all of them were recent start-ups with no record of financial stability. With the exception of a few specialist cases such as the Scottish and Ulster banks, cash tokens are almost exclusively issued by, and guaranteed by, the state. US Dollars are only issued by the US Treasury and the US Mint, Euros are only issued by the European Central Bank or by national mints of Euro states, the Pound as has been discussed before is unusual in allowing private clearing banks to issue notes alongside the Bank of England, but even then this may only be done with a financial guarantee from the Bank of England in the shape of the Bank of England Giant and Titan notes held by the issuers of these banknotes. In short consumers only have confidence in cash tokens issued by, and/or guaranteed by either the central bank or government of the issuing state. This was the problem with cyberspace. There was no government, no central bank, and no pre-existing financial framework: only private organisations and competing technologies. If electronic cash was ever to take off it needed something to boost consumer confidence in e-cash issuers.

17.3 **The electronic money directive**

17.3.1 **E-money issuers**

As part of its information society programme the European Commission had been working on the text of the Electronic Money Directive for some time. It was eventually passed on 18 September 2000 and its aim was to give public confidence in electronic money issuers by implementing strict standards of financial probity. The Directive added a new phrase to our lexicon; an 'electronic money institution':

[14] Grigg, above n. 12.
[15] See S. Lubove, 'Visa's Porn Crackdown', *Forbes*, 1 May 2003: http://www.forbes.com/2003/05/01/cz_sl_0501porn.html.

> **→ Highlight** Electronic Money Institutions
>
> An undertaking or any other legal person, other than a credit institution, which issues means of payment in the form of electronic money.
> [Art.1(3)(a)]

Electronic money institutions are subject to stringent regulation. By Article 1(5) the business of electronic money institutions was tightly restricted.

> **→ Highlight** The Business of Electronic Money Institutions
>
> (1) The issuing of electronic money;
>
> (2) The provision of closely related financial and non-financial services such as the administering of electronic money by the performance of operational and other ancillary functions related to its issuance, and the issuing and administering of other means of payment but excluding the granting of any form of credit; and
>
> (3) The storing of data on the electronic device on behalf of other undertakings or public institutions.

In effect this means that electronic money institutions, unless they were also credit institutions as defined in the Banking Directive, could not undertake any form of business, financial or otherwise, unrelated to their operations as electronic money institutions. This prevented third party businesses such as Microsoft or Cisco from becoming electronic money institutions, leaving the way clear for banks and other credit institutions to occupy the role of electronic money issuers with only specialist niche companies such as Digicash for competition.

To bolster public confidence in electronic money issuers were given strict financial requirements. By Article 4(1) they were required to hold initial capital funds of €1m and were required to retain a funding level of at least that amount for as long as they remained an electronic money institution. Further by Article 4(2) they were required to retain operating funds which were at least equal to the higher of the current value of all electronic money they have in circulation or the average value of their money in circulation in the preceding six months. Further financial controls were to be found in Article 5. Electronic money institutions must have investments which equal their outstanding liabilities (including all electronic money in circulation) and these investments must be in a list of pre-approved low-risk, high liquidity form of investment vehicles.[16] This is a double edged sword. It made electronic

---

[16] For the full list of types of approved investments see Art. 5(1).

money issuers highly secure and highly liquid meaning that an issuer should never find themselves unable to make payment on any call against money tokens they had issued, but it meant that they could not invest in higher return investment vehicles, which carry higher risk but offer better rewards, and vitally they could not lend money received from customers who buy electronic money tokens unless they were approved credit institutions (banks) meaning there was little financial incentive to set up an electronic money institution.[17] The Commission believed these stringent new rules would engender public confidence in electronic money institutions leading to a rapid take-up of e-cash systems and a move away from the reliance placed on credit and debit card payments for online transactions, as well as the possibility of new forms of offline payments technologies. Critics argued that the Directive was too restrictive and that potential electronic money issuers would be put off by the strict require-ments of Articles 4 and 5.[18]

It quickly became clear the critics were right. By 2006 there were only nine active elec-tronic money issuers in the EU, while a further two were licensed but not operating.[19] In addition a further seventy-two bodies were operating under the waiver scheme permit-ted by Article 8. This waiver may be applied where certain narrow exemptions are met. These are either that (a) the total liabilities of the electronic money issuer never nor-mally exceeds €5m and never actually exceeds €6m and the maximum credit per person is €150;[20] or (b) the electronic money issued by the issuer is not of a value of more that €10m, the maximum credit per person is €150 and the electronic money is only accepted by the issuer or any subsidiaries of the issuer which perform ancillary functions related to electronic money issued or distributed by the issuer;[21] or (c) the electronic money issued by the issuer is not of a value of more that €10m, the maximum credit per person is €150 and is accepted as payment only by a limited number of undertakings, which can be clearly distinguished by their location in the same premises or other limited local area; or their close financial or business relationship with the issuing institution, such as a common marketing or distribution scheme.[22] These schemes tend to be for smart-card payment schemes used in gyms, university campuses, or in offices.[23] Wider elec-tronic money schemes tended to be limited to prepay schemes which were exempt from the Directive,[24] the best known such schemes being prepay mobile phones and transport

---

[17] To ensure that these regulations were met electronic money institutions required to hold a license from the relevant state regulator and by Art. 6, and must submit themselves to review at least twice per annum. In the UK the regulator is the Financial Services Authority.

[18] See e.g. M. Kohlbach, 'Making Sense of Electronic Money', 2004 (1) *JILT*: http://www2.war-wick.ac.uk/fac/soc/law/elj/jilt/2004_1/kohlbach/.

[19] European Commission, DG Internal Market, *Evaluation of the E-Money Directive (2000/46/EC) Final Report*, 17 February 2006, 2.2.1: http://ec.europa.eu/internal_market/payments/docs/emoney/evaluation_en.pdf.

[20] Directive 2000/46/EC, Art. 8(1); The Financial Services and Markets Act 2000 (Regulated Activities) (Amendment) Order 2002, SI 2002/682, reg. 9C(4).

[21] Directive 2000/46/EC, Art. 8(2); SI 2002/682, reg. 9C(5).

[22] Directive 2000/46/EC, Art. 8(3); SI 2002/682, reg. 9C(6).

[23] For instance the FSA issued a small e-money issuer certificate to the London Evening Standard for its (now defunct) Eros prepay scheme.

[24] Article 1(3)(b) stated that '"electronic money" shall mean monetary value as represented by a claim on the issuer which is: (i) stored on an electronic device; (ii) issued on receipt of funds

schemes such as Transport for London's prepay Oyster Card. These figures made it clear that by 2006 the Directive had failed. Worse it became apparent that it may be holding back the development of functional electronic money schemes.

In the seven years since the Directive had been promulgated the focus of electronic money had changed radically. When the Directive was designed the focus had been on online payment systems such as Digicash or Cyphermint, but now electronic cash meant convenient real world payment systems including travelcard payment systems such as the Oyster Card, payment by mobile phone, and second generation Mondex technology such as prepay debit cards and traveller's currency cards.

A number of schemes were being planned to make use of the convenience of these technologies. For example, Transport for London had plans to allow the Oyster Card to become a digital wallet which could be used for small value purchases such as newspapers, coffees, or tobacco.[25] The problem for them was that to implement the scheme they would require an electronic money institution license from the FSA as they would no longer be exempted and would be unlikely to qualify for a small e-money license as they would almost certainly exceed the €10m maximum. To try to achieve this they sought partnership with established technology providers such as Barclays, but in 2006 it was announced the scheme would be scrapped.[26] Instead Transport for London licensed Barclaycard to use their Oyster payment technology in the Barclaycard OnePulse credit card.

Another developing scheme was the use of mobile phones to make small payments, usually by SMS payment systems. This is used by the Transport for London to allow for payment of the Central London Congestion Charge by SMS message. It is also used by many local authorities to pay for parking, and in some places you can even pay for goods in vending machines by sending an SMS to the machine operator. The problem with systems which allow SMS payment is that technically it turns a pay-as-you-go mobile phone into a digital wallet for the purposes of the Electronic Money Directive. This is because pay-as-you-go phones store value on them, unlike contract phones in which liabilities are paid at the end of the contract period. This created a potential problem. If mobile phone operators were issuing electronic money, which it seemed they were if they allowed pre-pay customers to pay for third party goods or services using their phone credit, then they would (a) need a license from the FSA, and (b) to comply with Article 1(5) of the Directive they would need to give up all operations other than those relating to their business as an electronic money issuer (including operating a mobile phone network). This outcome was clearly absurd and so the Commission

---

of an amount not less in value than the monetary value issued; and (iii) accepted as means of payment by undertakings other than the issuer.' This is replicated at SI 2002/682, reg. 2. The key phrase (highlighted) makes it clear the pre-pay schemes are not regulated by electronic money regulations.

[25] A. McCue, 'London transport targets Oyster "e-money" trials in 2005', *Silicon.com*, 21 July 2005: http://software.silicon.com/applications/0,39024653,39150647,00.htm.

[26] J. Best, 'Why Oyster's e-money plans hit the buffers', *Silicon.com*, 9 May 2006: http://www.silicon.com/financialservices/0,3800010322,39158733,00.htm.

undertook a review of the Directive in the hope that changes could be made to make the Directive more relevant to electronic money as it was developing in the real world.

17.3.2 Commission review of the e-money directive and the 2009 e-money directive

The review took place between 2004 and 2006. It opened with a review of the application of the Directive to mobile phone operators, which began with a consultation paper in May 2005[27] and led to the publication of the report *Application of the E-Money Directive 2000/46/EC to mobile operators* in January 2005.[28] The report concluded that 'legal uncertainty is damaging the sector, because it prevents investments in new technologies, undermines the consolidation and competitiveness of innovative services as well as the launch of supplementary digital services.'[29] It noted that expert commentators questioned whether it was correct to capture mobile operators within the definition of electronic money institutions, mainly because of a very restrictive interpretation of the conditions listed in Article 1 of the Electronic Money Directive,[30] and recommended that mobile phone operators should benefit from a separate 'risk-based' regulatory structure rather than the strict structural rules which apply to electronic money issuers under the Directive. This, the Commission believed, was possible due to the already strict regulatory structure which surrounds the mobile phone industry and which contains a number of provisions designed to protect the consumer.[31]

These recommendations were taken forward in the subsequent review of the Directive which opened with a consultation paper in July 2005 which asked among other things, 'Should a special EU regime be introduced for institutions issuing E-Money as a non-core part of their business (e.g. mobile operators and other "hybrid" prepaid instrument providers)?'; 'Have the harmonised provisions of the E-Money Directive eliminated legal uncertainty in the field of E-Money?'; and vitally 'Has the Directive encouraged new market entrants?'[32]

This consultation concluded in February 2006 with the publication of a 168 page report, *Evaluation of the E-Money Directive (2000/46/EC) Final Report*.[33] The Report found that in general the uptake of electronic money in the EU had been disappointing, noting that 'e-money market has developed more slowly than expected, and is far from reaching its full potential', and that 'the take-up of card-based e-money has remained low in most EU Member States. Card-based e-purses in many countries have been discontinued,

---

[27] European Commission, DG Internal Market, *A consultation paper on the treatment of mobile operators under the E-money Directive 2000/46/EC*, 10 May 2004: http://ec.europa.eu/internal_market/payments/docs/emoney/2004-05-consultation_en.pdf.

[28] European Commission, DG Internal Market, *Application of the E-Money Directive 2000/46/EC to mobile operators*, 18 January 2005: http://ec.europa.eu/internal_market/payments/docs/emoney/summary_en.pdf.

[29] *ibid*, 2.   [30] *ibid*.   [31] *ibid*, 16–17.

[32] European Commission, DG Internal Market, *Questionnaire on the Electronic Money Directive (2000/46/EC)*, 14 July 2005: http://ec.europa.eu/internal_market/payments/docs/emoney/questionnaire_en.pdf.

[33] European Commission, DG Internal Market, *Evaluation of the E-Money Directive (2000/46/EC) Final Report*, 14 July 2005: http://ec.europa.eu/internal_market/payments/docs/emoney/evaluation_en.pdf.

and for most of those that remain, usage remains very limited ... [as] e-money cards are still used almost exclusively at unmanned stations (public telephones, car parks, vending machines).'[34] The Report does see light at the end of the tunnel noting 'the recent emergence of contactless cards may provide a new impulse to card-based e-money. Such cards are currently issued almost exclusively by public transport providers, and can at present only be used to pay for transport services. However, this may change relatively soon, and there seem to also be significant potential benefits in the use of contactless e-money cards for other types of entities such as financial service providers, retailers, telecoms, utilities, sports stadiums and local councils.'[35]

The Report recognises that these schemes are being held back by the strict rules of the Directive and although it was not within the scope of the Report to formally make recommendations a number of proposals are made to free up the marketplace and to allow for systems such as contactless payment smart cards or payment by mobile phone to develop. These proposals are to be found in two key recommendations: the first that mobile phone operators are either given a blanket waiver or that the waiver provisions in Article 8 be extended to 'closely related third parties (such as third parties delivering mobile content services to customers of the mobile operators)';[36] and the second that the Commission consider 'creating an exemption whereby smartcards that are used exclusively to pay for public transport, but are accepted as payment by more than one transport provider, would not be considered e-money.'[37]

These amendments would have assisted slightly in freeing up the regulation of electronic money issuers in the EU, but these still would fail to address the key critique of the Directive, that the restrictive systemic regulation of electronic money issuers means that they cannot compete with credit institutions (banks and credit card issuers) in the electronic money marketplace. On the vital questions of liquidity and security the Report found that 'there is a considerable degree of support for the idea that certain elements of the regulatory framework are disproportionate to the risks posed by the activities of e-money issuers, and that a less restrictive regime may have been sufficient to ensure the stability and soundness. Many industry stakeholders find the overall set of rules "too blunt", and argue that there is room for adopting a more risk-based approach without endangering the stability of issuers or the adequate protection of consumers.'[38] To this end the Report suggested that a separate study be undertaken looking at the financial and non-financial risks involved in the issuance of e-money.

In many ways the Report was underwhelming and somewhat disappointing. It had never been the aim of the Report to propose widespread changes to the Directive, but with Europe clearly lagging behind the rest of the world in the development of electronic cash tokens it was clear that a Directive which had in mind payment systems in the online world was now holding back the development of electronic cash alternatives in the real world. The Report seemed to suggest the Directive was on the whole working well and only needed a few minor adjustments.

---

[34] *ibid*, 2.2.1.   [35] *ibid*.   [36] *ibid*, 5.4.1.1.
[37] *ibid*, 5.4.1.2. Note this would allow an integrated 'travelcard' system but still would not allow travel payment cards like the Oyster Card to be used to pay for goods or services other than transport.   [38] *ibid*, 5.4.4.2.

Following the Report the Commission continued to review the scope and role of the Directive. Finally in October 2009 after a further three years of development and review the Commission finally the new Electronic Money Directive which came into effect on 30 October 2009.[39] Member states have until 30 April 2011 to give effect to the new Directive. It attempts to codify the (now) extremely complex laws applicable to electronic money issuers. In the period since the original Electronic Money Directive was passed three subsequent Directives have been passed which affect electronic money institutions. These three Directives, the Payment Services Directive[40] and the Capital Requirements Directives (of which there are two),[41] have made major changes to the framework of banking and credit services in the EU.

The Payment Services Directive introduced new liquidity and security regulations for all payment service providers, including electronic money issuers, but also introduced a new form of financial institution—the payment institution.[42] Payment institutions are permitted to make and remit payments on behalf of customers but are not allowed to issue credit (that being the preserve of credit institutions) or issue electronic money (that being the preserve of credit institutions and electronic money institutions). Thus the Payment Services Directive creates a three-tier system with banks and similar institutions (known as credit institutions) at the apex, electronic money institutions in the middle, and payment institutions at the base. The problem with the Payment Services Directive was the very different rules on probity which are now applied to payment institutions when compared to electronic money institutions.

As discussed earlier an electronic money institution was required to hold initial capital of €1m and to retain that level of capital for as long as they remained an electronic money institution. In addition they were required to retain operating funds at least equal to the higher of the value of all electronic money they have in current circulation or the average value of their money in circulation in the preceding six months: these funds to be held in approved low-risk, high liquidity form of investment vehicles.[43] As we have discussed in relation to mobile phone operators, electronic money institutions may not carry out operations not linked to their role as electronic money institutions. By comparison a payment institution under the Payment Services Directive need only provide initial capital of between €20,000 and €125,000 depending upon the type of operation they intend to offer, and they may carry out business operations unrelated to their role as payment institutions. The Commission recognised that these changes made the provisions of the Electronic Money Directive appear punitive by comparison: '[The law provides an] inconsistent legal framework with a disproportionate prudential regime, inconsistent waivers and passporting procedures as well as the application of anti-money laundering

---

[39] Directive 2009/110/EC of the European Parliament and of the Council of 16 September 2009 on the taking up, pursuit and prudential supervision of the business of electronic money institutions amending Directives 2005/60/EC and 2006/48/EC and repealing Directive 2000/46/EC, OJ L267/7: http://eur-lex.europa.eu/LexUriServ/LexUriServ.do?uri=OJ:L:2009:267:0007:0017:EN:PDF.   [40] 2007/64/EC.

[41] Directive 2006/48/EC relating to the taking up and pursuit of the business of credit institutions and Directive 2006/49/EC on the capital adequacy of investment firms and credit institutions.

[42] The Payment Services Directive is outwith the Scope of this analysis. Anyone interested in the detail of the Directive may read D. Mavromati, *The Law of Payment Services in the EU: The EC Directive on Payment Services in the Internal Market* (2008).   [43] Above p. 445.

rules to electronic money services. This overall legal inconsistency will increase once the Payment Services Directive provisions have been implemented (by November 2009), since some of the requirements for the prudential regime of payment institutions differ widely from those applicable today to electronic money institutions.'[44]

To this end the new Electronic Money Directive brings major changes. The initial capital requirement is reduced and the rules on liquidity are changed to bring them more in line with the Payment Services Directive,[45] while vitally the rule restricting electronic money issuers to carry on business as only an electronic money issuer are swept away by Article 6(1).

➡ Highlight Article 6(1)

Institutions shall be entitled to engage in any of the following activities:

   (a) the provision of payment services listed in the Annex to Directive 2007/64/EC;

   (b) the granting of credit related to payment services referred to in points 4, 5 or 7 of the Annex to Directive 2007/64/EC, where the conditions laid down in Article 16(3) and (5) of that Directive are met;

   (c) the provision of operational services and closely related ancillary services in respect of the issuing of electronic money or to the provision of payment services referred to in point (a);

   (d) the operation of payment systems as defined in point 6 of Article 4 of Directive 2007/64/EC and without prejudice to Article 28 of that Directive;

   (e) business activities other than issuance of electronic money, having regard to the applicable Community and national law.

This will finally allow mobile phone operators to be licensed as electronic money institutions without fear of this affecting their ability to carry on their core business.

There is little doubt that this is a long overdue development and by relaxing the key provisions on liquidity and allowing electronic money institutions to carry on unrelated business the millstones around the old Directive will be swept away. What is interesting is what electronic money has become in the nine years between the original Directive and the new one. In 2000 it was envisaged that the problem was with online payments. Customers were relying on credit and debit cards to make payment; this was extremely inefficient with high transaction costs and with no means for micropayments or for consumer to consumer payments. It seemed that what was missing was an internet currency: money rather than payments methods. The Commission believed there was a demand for electronic money to facilitate online electronic commerce and believed that the Electronic Money Directive would provide the framework for this to grow.

---

[44] Proposal for a Directive of the European Parliament and of the Council on the taking up, pursuit and prudential supervision of the business of electronic money institutions, amending Directives 2005/60/EC and 2006/48/EC and repealing Directive 2000/46/EC, above n. 40, 3.

[45] Article 5 has a complex set of principles to be employed in calculating the liquidity principle.

We now know there was no demand for electronic money in the online environment. Customers liked the security and convenience offered by card payments and advertising supported content provided an alternative to micropayments. Even the problem of consumer to consumer cash payments has been solved by a variety of online clearing systems which allow individuals or small businesses to accept credit card payments, or bank transfer payments without the need to enter into partnership with the major card payment clearing services. The success of Google Checkout, and more spectacularly PayPal, seems to suggest we do not need money in the true sense online; payment methods are sufficient.[46]

Instead electronic money has begun to surprisingly flourish in the real world. People carry less cash than they used to as they rely more on payment methods. This means it is more likely that people will not have change for small value transactions such as paying for parking, for transport, or for low value items such as coffee or a newspaper. Additionally for banks and for vendors coins are very inefficient. They cost a lot to transport and need constant security. Conversely at low values payment methods are also inefficient. Debit and credit card companies charge transaction fees which usually have a minimum value of around 15p per transaction meaning that if you use your debit card to pay for a 50p newspaper the vendor receives only 35p (or perhaps even less), this is why many vendors require a minimum £5 spend on cards. Electronic money, although it does still come with transactions costs, is a cheaper simpler method of real world payment and with the further development of both payment by SMS and smart card technologies including further development of near field communication technology it seems likely that the high street, not the internet will be the natural home for the next stage of electronic money development and with the relaxation of the strict rules found in the original Electronic Money Directive the EU will finally be in the right place to reap the rewards of such technologies.

17.4 **Ecommerce taxation**

The final issue that is peculiar to e-commerce is the question of how to tax online transactions. With a high degree of cross-border transactions, and with a number of 'virtual' goods such as MP3 music files, on-demand movies and games, and online business services such as continuing professional education and market research being deliverable at the touch of a button and in a form indistinguishable from non-commercial services such as home movies or personal webpages there is a risk of an extensive amount of taxation revenue being lost. With the vast, and increasing, value of global e-commerce estimated by the OECD to be worth in excess of $2 trillion, the ecommerce sector worldwide could yield taxation revenues worth in excess of $200bn even at a very conservative tax take of 10%. It is not surprising that a number of schemes have therefore been developed to ensure that taxation is collected from all manner of online transactions.

---

[46] The one exception to this is of course 'in game' cash for online games such as 'gold' in World of Warcraft, 'Platinum Pieces' in Everquest, and 'Linden Dollars' in Second Life. These will be discussed below in Chapter 21.

In many ways the easiest taxation problem to solve is the gathering of tax on goods sold online and delivered overseas. Individuals buy goods online from a variety of sources ranging from legitimate ecommerce sites such as Amazon, iTunes, and eBuyer through to illegitimate or even downright illegal offshore sites offering tobacco, alcohol, or jewellery tax-free. To obtain the correct taxation revenue on these goods involves a variety of techniques. Firstly there needs to be international cooperation on the collection and remission of taxation revenues. Obviously the customer pays for goods at their source: thus if a UK customer buys goods from Amazon.com the payment is collected in US Dollars in Washington State. But the goods are destined for the UK marketplace where UK taxation would usually apply. So who collects the tax, the UK or Washington State?, and how much is it—UK VAT rates at 17.5% or Washington State sales tax rates which is 6.5%? Fortunately there are already international agreements which regulate such transactions.

Although the exact provisions of the agreements vary the general provision is that a consumer who buys goods overseas is not liable for local sales tax but will potentially be liable for local sales taxes, as well as import duties and potentially excise duties upon their importation. Thus, to return to our example, the general rule is that a UK customer who buys goods from a US-based website such as Amazon.com is not liable for local sales tax in Washington State but may be liable to pay UK VAT, as well as import duties, when the goods arrive in the UK. This leaves the question of how the UK Revenue and Customs collect their monies. When shipping the goods to an overseas territory the shipper is required to fill out a customs declaration declaring what the goods are and their value. These declarations may be used by HM Revenue and Customs to calculate tax payable on the goods. The shipping company then sends the customer a request for payment for this amount and retains possession of the goods, in bond, until the taxes and duties are paid. If the necessary taxes are not paid the goods cannot be released (and may later be sold by HMRC at an auction).

There are obvious weaknesses with this system as the volume of international business to consumer trade increases through a growth in ecommerce. Firstly, it is extremely labour intensive. It requires shipping companies to hold packages while payments are processed. Secondly, it is incompatible with the European Customs Union, which means goods within the EU may be traded freely. Thirdly, it relies upon parties being honest in their declarations. If the goods are shipped from an unscrupulous international trader he may declare a £500 Louis Vuitton bag as being worth only £25. The only way for the authorities to tell is to open the package and inspect the contents, something they can only afford to do with a small proportion of packages meaning many items slip through.[47]

With traditional ecommerce (i.e. the delivery of physical goods ordered online) the current system was being put under massive strain. But with recent broadband

[47] Although it should be noted that if HMRC open a package and find a false declaration has been made it is the recipient of the goods who is liable for that false declaration, meaning the recipient may be fined as well as having to pay the full cost of the import duties and the VAT. See http://customs.hmrc.gov.uk/channelsPortalWebApp/channelsPortalWebApp.portal?_nfpb=true&_pageLabel=pageVAT_ShowContent&id=HMCE_CL_001454&propertyType=document.

developments allowing for home delivery of digital products such as music, movies, or other information-based products this system ceases to function completely. There is no shipper, no customs declaration, and no chance for customs staff to intercept and check the contents of the delivery. Ecommerce in general and digital delivery of informational goods in particular, meant that new provisions and new agreements on taxation collection and enforcement were required.

To assist with the international collection of sales taxes there have been a series of meetings and agreements. The first major agreement was formulated at an OECD conference in Ottawa in 1998. The Ottawa meeting led to the promulgation of the Ottawa Taxation Framework.[48] It was not the intent of the Ottawa meeting to set out hard rules on the impact of the information society on taxation, rather it sets out a set of principles for OECD nations to apply in relation to issues such as domicile for personal and corporate taxation, electronic tax records and filing and ecommerce. In relation to ecommerce specifically the Framework provides five general principles: [49]

Highlight The Ottawa Framework General Principles

1. *Neutrality*: Taxation should seek to be neutral and equitable between forms of electronic commerce and between conventional and electronic forms of commerce. Business decisions should be motivated by economic rather than tax considerations. Taxpayers in similar situations carrying out similar transactions should be subject to similar levels of taxation.

2. *Efficiency*: Compliance costs for taxpayers and administrative costs for the tax authorities should be minimised as far as possible.

3. *Certainty and simplicity*: The tax rules should be clear and simple to understand so that taxpayers can anticipate the tax consequences in advance of a transaction, including knowing when, where, and how the tax is to be accounted.

4. *Effectiveness and Fairness*: Taxation should produce the right amount of tax at the right time. The potential for tax evasion and avoidance should be minimised while keeping counteracting measures proportionate to the risks involved.

5. *Flexibility*: The systems for the taxation should be flexible and dynamic to ensure that they keep pace with technological and commercial developments.

Different nations took a different view of how best to apply these principles to the collection of sales taxes. Generally the initial response was to treat ecommerce sales as the same as any other form of transaction. Thus in the US the Federal Government

---

[48] http://www.oecd.org/dataoecd/46/3/1923256.pdf.

[49] For a detailed discussion of these principles and their application see OECD, *Taxation and Electronic Commerce* (2001).

passed The Internet Tax Freedom Act,[50] an Act which ensured that States could not pass any new or additional sales taxes on internet commerce over and above those usually applied to mail order transactions. In the EU initially no changes were made to current tax rules and policies. But over time it became apparent that with the rise in digital delivery of goods EU suppliers were at a risk of losing out to international suppliers. This was because under the Sixth VAT Directive,[51] suppliers based in the EU were required to collect VAT at the point of production or distribution on all ecommerce sales (both tangible and digital), including exports to customers outside the EU. By comparison, as we have seen, tangible goods were subject to taxation at their place of consumption, usually at their port of first importation to the EU. But as there were no digital goods at the time this arrangement was formed there was no similar provision for the delivery of digital goods to European customers from suppliers domiciled outwith the EU. This meant that overseas suppliers of purely digital goods and services could undercut EU based suppliers as they had no sales tax liability.

This changed on 1 July 2003 when the VAT on Ecommerce Directive came into force.[52] The Directive, which it is almost impossible to read on its own as it merely makes extensive changes to the Sixth VAT Directive, made widespread changes to the established EU VAT rules. It changed the establishment principle for digital goods: now digital goods are taxed in the state where the customer resides rather than where the supplier is located, in other words at the point of consumption rather than the point of supply. This puts digital goods on to the same footing as physical goods and means that EU suppliers and non-EU suppliers have the same liability to levy VAT payments on EU customers, and conversely it means that EU suppliers no longer have to charge VAT on digital goods or services supplied to non EU customers.

The Directive applies to all services defined as 'electronically supplied services'. These include: (1) the supply of web services such as web-hosting and maintenance of programmes and equipment; (2) the supply of software and updates; (3) the supply of images, text, and information, and making database contents; (4) the supply of music, films, and games (including games of chance), and of political, cultural, artistic, sporting, scientific, and entertainment broadcasts and events; and (5) the supply of distance teaching.[53] In practice what this means is that a supplier of goods and/or services to an EU-based consumer must charge that consumer VAT calculated at the rate payable in the consumer's home country, with the exception that when goods and/or services are supplier by an EU supplier then under the principles of the single market the supplier may charge their local VAT rate.

---

[50] HR 4328 (5 November 1998). Extended as the Internet Tax Nondiscrimination Act 2004 (Pub.L.108–435).

[51] EC (European Community) Sixth VAT Directive, Dir.77/388/EEC.

[52] Council Directive 2002/38/EC of 7 May 2002 amending and amending temporarily Directive 77/388/EEC as regards the value added tax arrangements applicable to radio and television broadcasting services and certain electronically supplied services, OJ L 128/41: http://eur-lex.europa.eu/LexUriServ/LexUriServ.do?uri=OJ:L:2002:128:0041:0044:EN:PDF. Note when first enacted the Directive had a three year 'sunset clause'. This has subsequently been extended three times by Directives 2006/58/EC, 2006/138/EC and 2008/8/EC while drafting changes to the Sixth VAT Directive are finalised.   [53] Taken from Dir. 2002/38/EC, Annex L.

This is extremely complex and is perhaps best described with the aid of an example.

⊛   Example VAT Payments under the VAT on Ecommerce Directive

Let us imagine two customers, one a UK based customer, Andrea, the other a US based customer, Brad.

Both are looking to register for an online seminar on international copyright law. Both have a choice of three suppliers: UK_Copyright (based in the UK); USIP (based in the US) or École Droit d'auteur (based in France).

All three charge the same basic fee of £1,000. Prior to 1 July 2003 the supply of the seminar to Andrea would be based upon the place of production. UK_Copyright would charge Andrea her fee plus the UK VAT rate of 17.5%, giving a total cost of £1,175. USIP would be able to supply Andrea the course with no sales tax charged as she was non-resident in the US making the fee £1,000, whereas École Droit d'auteur would charge her the basic fee plus French VAT at 19.6% making the total cost £1,196.

By comparison the prices offered to Brad would vary little. The prices offered by UK_Copyright and École Droit d'auteur would be the same as those quoted to Andrea due to the principle of VAT being levied at the point of production/supply in the EU at that time. The price quoted by USIP may rise by the addition of state sales tax depending upon which state Brad is resident in. This may add up to 8.25% to his price meaning a total cost of up to £1,082.50.

Following the enactment of the VAT on Ecommerce Directive this position changes dramatically. With regard to Andrea the position of UK_Copyright and École Droit d'auteur remain unchanged. UK_Copyright are already charging her the correct VAT for her place of residence while École Droit d'auteur can take advantage of the common market for goods and services and charge her the local French VAT rate. Now though as a non-EU resident USIP must apply UK VAT to her price meaning USIP now also must quote her a price of £1,175.

The change in position of Brad is though more pronounced. Now UK-Copyright and École Droit d'auteur no longer have to charge him local VAT meaning both can quote him a price of £1,000, whereas the position of USIP remains unchanged.

It is clear is that the new provisions benefit EU suppliers to the detriment of non-EU suppliers, a position which has led to international criticism of the Directive.[54] Despite this the Directive formalises the only functional way to ingather sales tax payments for the delivery of digital goods and services. The actual collection of taxes at the point of consumption is the only possible means to ensure tax is fully accounted for as there is no intermediary in the state of consumption to act as agent for the revenue and it is functionally impossible for HMRC to check imports at the borders.

Why must the tax be levied at the tax rate of the state of consumption rather than the rate in the state of supply? This is because as we have seen at several points in this book previously the consumer has no need of knowing where the supplier of

---

[54] See, e.g. M. Weiss & N. Noto, 'EU Tax on Digitally Delivered E-Commerce', *Congressional Research Service*, April 7 2005: http://ipmall.info/hosted_resources/crs/RS21596_050407.pdf.

the goods is domiciled, all the consumer needs is the domain name of the supplier's site, or the necessary software, such as Apple's iTunes software, to allow him to access the supplier's online store. Applying the principle of regulatory arbitrage,[55] suppliers would certainly relocate to international tax havens such as Nauru which has no sales tax. Applying the tax rate for the state of supply would, in such cases, lead to zero rate taxation for all digital goods and services imported to the EU from such tax havens, a situation the EU is keen to avoid. Thus it is clear that the only formula which can effectively collect sales tax on digital goods and services is the one designed by the EU. It tasks the supplier with the collection duty, a duty they will be willing to take on to allow their business to make sales, while protecting the tax revenues of EU member states by ensuring suppliers cannot simply relocate to tax havens to avoid this duty.

No doubt this rather Heath Robinson system of taxation of ecommerce which relies heavily upon the goodwill of international suppliers and their local law enforcement bodies will over time be subject to change. Although major internet retailers such as Amazon and Apple will happily comply with their duties to levy and remit sales taxes, it is clear that in developing internet powerhouses such as China and India the collection rate is much lower. Perhaps in future we will see the resurrection of an old scheme, the bit-tax scheme which sees end-users pay taxation on each MB of data they consume. A variant of the bit-tax has recently been adopted by the UK Government: this will require all telephone line users to pay £6 per annum to pay for network upgrades. This is a flat rate tax very unlike a true bit-tax which proved popular around the turn of the century as a proposed means to both pay for network upgrades and to discourage illegal file sharing.[56] The bit tax proposal failed at that time because the cost of collection was seen as uneconomic. In addition it was seen as an unfair tax on internet users who were (at the time) paying high costs for access and usually were liable to value added tax on their telecommunications bills. A bit tax was therefore seen as a form of double taxation. Now with broadband access charges much lower and with much more efficient systems for measuring usage a bit tax could be resurrected should revenues from VAT on digital goods fall. At the moment as most ecommerce goods supplied to the UK market, both digital and physical, originate from either the EU or North America there is little demand to change the current settlement. Whether this remains the case depends upon how the ecommerce environment develops in the next few years.

17.5 **Conclusions**

According to the song 'money makes the world go round'. While hopefully we are not so avaricious a society as to be dominated by our desire for money there is no doubt that ecommerce needs to be able to service the basic financial requirements of any commercial sector if it is to continue to grow. Interestingly it was thought in the

---

[55] See above, pp. 58–62.
[56] See, e.g. Bit Tax (Internet Access), *Hansard* HC Deb 18 November 1998 v. 319 c.588W; L. Soete & K. Kamp, 'The "BIT TAX": the case for further research', *Maastricht Economic Research Institute on Innovation and Technology, Research Memoranda 012*: http://ideas.repec.org/p/dgr/umamer/1996012.html.

early days of ecommerce that two competing demands would affect the development of ecommerce. It was thought that the development of ecommerce would be negatively affected by an inability to pay for goods and services online by any means except card payment systems.

Card payments lacked many of the functions of money, in particular they lacked anonymity and they were expensive to operate. The lack of anonymity meant that users would fear identity fraud and would not buy goods or services online which may cause embarrassment and for suppliers the transaction fees meant that they could not be used economically for small value transactions as the fees payable would outweigh the payment received. On the positive side the internet with its lack of recognition of borders would allow parties to arbitrage taxes by relocating servers and offices to tax havens while consumers could buy overseas and attempt to avoid local sales taxes.

All these predictions have proven to be false. Customers have embraced payment by card. They do fear identity fraud, but know their card issuer will reimburse them for any losses they incur. They have no embarrassment about using their cards to make payment because the feeling of anonymity a computer screen gives means they would rather buy Viagra online than in a pharmacy, and in any event goods bought online have to be shipped to their home anyway so why worry about giving your credit card details. Industry, realising that cards were to become the dominant online payment system, developed alternatives to cash payments for low value transactions—using a mixture of subscription services and advertising supported services. The tax authorities did not stay out of cyberspace and over time systems have come to pass to collect all forms of taxation including sales tax on digital goods.

Some things that were not predicted have though come to pass. Electronic money has found a new lease of life in the real world. The convenience of payment by mobile phone being the driving force behind one arm of the technology while the familiarity of smart card systems as a means of payment for public transport is driving another. For all involved in the money supply chain the benefits offered by electronic money are clear. The risks of forgery are reduced, the costs of production are removed, and most importantly there are no cash deposits in banks, stores, or in armoured cars to steal. Money, like music, film, and photographs becomes a series of ones and zeros. Although new risks will arise and there will be a need to protect banking systems from cyberattacks there is little doubt that a wholesale migration to electronic money would reduce traditional forms of criminal activity.

FURTHER READING

Books

S. Basu, *Global Perspectives on E-commerce Taxation Law* (2007)

T. Sabri, *E-payments: A Guide to Electronic Money and Online Payments* (2009)

O. Hance & S. Balz, *The New Virtual Money: Law and Practice* (1999)

D. Mavromati, *The Law of Payment Services in the EU: The EC Directive on Payment Services in the Internal Market* (2008)

Chapters and Articles

M. Kohlbach, 'Making Sense of Electronic Money' 2004 (1) JILT

J. Rogers, 'The New Old Law of Electronic Money' 58 *SMU Law Review* 1253 (2005)

A. Cockfield, 'Designing Tax Policy for the Digital Biosphere: How the Internet is Changing Tax Laws' 34 *Connecticut Law Review* 333 (2002)

A. Guadamez & J. Usher, 'Electronic Money: The European Regulatory Approach', in L. Edwards (ed.), *The New Legal Framework for E-Commerce in Europe* (2005)

PART VI

Privacy in the information society

The financial value of data is such that individual privacy is often set aside in the pursuit of commercial advantage. The information society makes it easy for individuals to be monitored and tracked: how much data are we willing to trade for convenience? How does the law strike a balance between data privacy and data brokering?

18 **Data protection**

    18.1 Digitisation, personal data, and the data industry

    18.2 Data protection act 1998: background and structure

    18.3 The data protection act 1998

    18.4 The data protection principles, processing, and fairness

    18.5 Conditions for processing of personal data

    18.6 Supervision of data controllers: data subject rights

    18.7 State supervision of data controllers

    18.8 Conclusion

19 **Data and personal privacy**

    19.1 Enhanced CCTV

    19.2 RFID tracking

    19.3 Data retention and identity

    19.4 Conclusions

Data protection

As has been alluded to at several points in the previous chapters, one of the effects of the information society is a divorce of identity from the person. Basically this means that with more and more of our everyday lives being ordered or even accessed via a computer and an internet connection we increasingly use proxy data to identify who we are. These include true proxies such as passwords and user IDs, bank or credit card information, email addresses; and personal data such as date of birth, place of birth, mother's maiden name, first school attended or nowadays biometric data such as a digital record of a fingerprint or facial scan data taken from a digital image. This places our identity at unique risk in the modern society as a large proportion of our transactions are validated by reference to proxies rather than to direct identification. This leads to at least two distinct threats to our data, and therefore to our identity. The first is identity theft or identity fraud. This is a malicious assault on our identity proxies carried out with criminal intent. This particular aspect of data harm has been discussed already in Chapter 15. The second is the misapplication, mishandling, or misprocessing of data. This is (usually) innocent and benign in intent, although the impact may not be. This may be something as simple as failing to secure data, a charge laid before the UK Government at several points during 2007 as they in quick succession lost data relating to 25 million child benefit recipients,[1] 3 million candidates for the driving theory test,[2] 168,000 NHS patient records,[3] and 40,000 housing benefit claimants;[4] or it may be that the data is inaccurate or out of date leading to an unfair outcome in a computerised decision making process,[5] or it may be that against the wishes of the data subject the data is sold or transferred to a third party for purposes such as marketing.[6] It is the latter risks that will form the focus of this chapter.

---

[1] For a full discussion of the affair see *The Poynter Report*: K. Poynter, *Review of information security at HM Revenue and Customs: Final Report* (2008: http://www.hm-treasury.gov.uk/d/poynter_review250608.pdf.

[2] H. Mulholland, 'Details of 3m learner drivers lost, government admits', *The Guardian*, 17 December 2007: http://www.guardian.co.uk/uk/2007/dec/17/politics.helenemulholland.

[3] D. Rose, 'More personal data lost as nine NHS trusts admit security breaches', *The Times*, 24 December 2007: http://www.timesonline.co.uk/tol/life_and_style/health/article3090664.ece.

[4] J. Ungoed-Thomas, 'More financial data discs lost', *The Times* 2 December 2007: http://www.timesonline.co.uk/tol/news/uk/crime/article2983759.ece.

[5] Famously lampooned in the Little Britain sketch 'computer says no'. For those on the receiving end of a computerised decision making process though there is little to laugh about. See J. Bing 'Code, Access and Control' in M. Klang & A. Murray (eds), *Human Rights in the Digital Age* (2005).

[6] See D. Garrie & R. Wong, 'The Future of Consumer Web Data: a European/US Perspective' [2007] *IJLIT* 129; G. Gunasekara, 'The "Final" Privacy Frontier? Regulating Trans-border Data Flows' [2007] *IJLIT* 362.

18.1 **Digitisation, personal data, and the data industry**

In Chapter 3 we discussed how digitisation created the information society. Among the issues discussed there was the inherent value of digitised information.[7] As we discovered digital information is commercially more valuable than analogue information. This was first clearly outlined by Professor Fred Cate, who in his book *Privacy in the Information Age* identified four characteristics of digital information and information management which caused this to be so.[8]

> **Highlight** Cate's Four Characteristics of Digital Information
>
> 1. It is that it is easier to generate, manipulate, transmit, and store digital information.
> 2. The cost of collecting, manipulating, storing, and transmitting data is lowered.
> 3. Electronic information has developed an intrinsic value not found in analogue information due to its very nature.
> 4. The operating parameters of computer systems and networks generate additional digital information through back-up copies and cache copies.

Due to these four factors Cate records that 'we are witnessing an explosion in digital data.'[9] To Cate's four factors we can add a fifth factor identified by Andrew Murray in 2005, digital convergence.[10] This allows for digital data to be traded across platforms more easily and like Cate's fourth principle leads to duplication of data as files are held on a number of devices simultaneously. All these principles mean that data is now commercially more valuable than when it was held as discrete analogue packets before the advent of the information society.

A multi-billion pound industry had grown up around this new product. Some companies gather data to act as an advisor to others. An example of such a company would be Experian. Experian are the world's largest credit reference and scoring agency. They ingather data from a variety of sources such as lenders, the electoral roll, and list of County Court judgements and score the risk of lending to individuals. Their services are used by all forms of credit agencies including mortgage lenders and credit card issuers to determine whether to make loans to individuals.

Other companies gather data to improve their service to their customers. Examples of such schemes include customer loyalty cards such as the Tesco Clubcard and the Nectar Card. These gather data on customer buying habits and allow the retailer to tailor their stock and staffing levels accordingly as well as offering customers rewards such as discount vouchers and promoting to customers related goods and services.

A third type of company carries out market research using gathered data with a view to selling their insights, or tailored advertising products, to clients. These include

[7] See above pp. 36–47.
[8] F. H. Cate, *Privacy in the Information Age*, (1997) at 14–15.   [9] *ibid*, 16.
[10] A. Murray, 'Should States Have a Right to Informational Privacy?' in M. Klang & A. Murray (eds), *Human Rights in the Digital Age* (2005).

traditional market research companies like Brand Institute and Neilsen, but more and more includes internet companies with Google being a leading provider in this area. Google gathers vast amounts of search data and then sells specialist online advertising (Google Ads) which are much more focussed on the target market than traditional media advertising. By offering this service Google has become the largest media advertising company globally including in 2007 surpassing ITV1 to become the UK's largest media advertiser.[11]

Fourthly, there are companies which act as information brokers for others. These companies gather information and sell it on as packaged data for the purposes of product development, advertising and promotion, or other purposes. This may include social networking sites such as Facebook, or mobile phone operators or it may be specialist information gatherers such as so-called 'adware' companies such as Gator or When U who gather data on internet habits and then sell that information on to third parties.

Finally there are the organisations on the fringes of what is legal. These are groups that gather data to create massive databases of customer details including mailing lists, email lists, and phone lists. These are then used for direct mailing or cold calling to try to sell goods and services. Some organisations involved in this industry are responsible and act completely legally, such as The Database Manager, Electric Marketing, or even BT. Others though are less responsible and exist at the fringes of what is required under the Data Protection Act.

All these companies want personal data. It is the lifeblood of their operations but it is costly to gather and process. As a result a number of digital processes have been developed to make it easier and cheaper to ingather and store such data, but such automation of data gathering risks our data privacy as computers have no ability to evaluate the nature of data or its sensitivity. As a result a strict legal regime is required to regulate the industry as a whole. This regime needs to ensure that when data is gathered individuals are aware of what data is being gathered, why it is being gathered, and how it will be stored. It needs to ensure that there are standards within the industry to ensure data is accurate, up to date, secure, and fairly processed. Further it needs to ensure that if sold or transferred, data remains protected and cannot be sold or transferred for reasons unconnected with its original gathering. Finally there needs to be an enforcement procedure to ensure all these things are done and that there is oversight of the industry as a whole. All these factors are the principles of the Data Protection Act 1998.

18.2 **Data protection act 1998: background and structure**

The Data Protection Act 1998 is the culmination of many years work in the field of personal data protection. There was no need for data protection rules or principles prior to process of digitisation. Analogue data was inherently protected by its nature: being extremely costly to gather, store, and process, analogue data was only gathered and retained when it was of substantial value. The dawn of the information society saw the first movements to protect personal data.

---

[11] See D. Sabbagh, 'Google shows ITV a vision of the future', *The Times*, 30 October 2007: http://business.timesonline.co.uk/tol/business/industry_sectors/media/article2767087.ece.

The world's first data protection law was probably that passed in the Federal German state of Hesse in 1970.[12] This early piece of legislation which applied to all data, not only data held on computers, proved to be the framework for all European Data Protection Laws which came after it. It heavily influenced the Swedish Personal Data Act of 1973, the world's first national provision on data protection, and several subsequent provisions including the West German Federal Data Protection Act of 1977, the French Act on Data Processing, Data Files and Individual Liberties of 1978, and eventually the British Data Protection Act 1984.[13] A theme common in these provisions was the creation of a supervisory authority (usually independent of government) to oversee a new set of data protection principles designed to protect the individual from unfair or inaccurate data processing. An example of the form common to many of these early provisions is the Data Protection Act 1984 (now repealed).

18.2.1 **The data protection act 1984**

The Act created a supervisory body for businesses that gathered processed and stored data (labelled by the Act as data users). Everyday control of data users was affected by the Data Protection Registrar, whose primary responsibility was to maintain a Register of Data Users under s. 4 of the Act. Under s. 5 it was an offence to process data without being entered on the register. At the time the Act was passed this was a rather effective means of controlling data users. Computers were still rather expensive to install and operate, and as the UK Government at the time had decided to limit the application of the Act to data 'recorded in a form in which it can be processed by equipment operating automatically in response to instructions given for that purpose',[14] in other words to digital data only, this meant a register was an extremely effective way to keep tabs on data users.[15]

The register was though only part of the Registrar's armoury. Just because a company had been registered didn't mean that they were processing personal data fairly and securely. As a result, and in common with most continental data protection laws the Act contained a list of data protection principles in Schedule 1. These were basic principles of fairness, accuracy, and security such as 'personal data shall be processed, fairly and lawfully', 'personal data shall be accurate and, where necessary, kept up to date', and that 'appropriate security measures be taken against unauthorised access to, or alteration, disclosure or destruction of, personal data and against accidental loss or destruction of personal data'. To ensure compliance with these principles the Registrar was given a suite of enforcement rights including the right to issue an enforcement notice under s. 10 which required data users to 'take, within such time as is specified in the notice, such steps as are so specified for complying with the principle or principles in question'. If the enforcement notice failed to bring about the desired effect the Registrar could then issue a de-registration

---

[12] The full text of the Hesse Act and a discussion of it may be found in P. Sieghart, *Privacy and Computers* (1976).

[13] For a discussion of all these developments see A. Warren, 'Right to Privacy? The Protection of Personal Data in UK Public Organisations' (2002) 103 *New Library World* 446.

[14] DPA 1984, s. 1(2).

[15] The UK Government decided to limit the scope of the Act to digital data as it was their belief that pre-existing regulations to deal with analogue data were sufficient. On this one area the UK Law found itself at variance with most continental data protection provisions which tended to protect data in all forms.

notice under s. 11, which would remove the data user from the register, thereby making any further processing by the data user an offence under s. 5. In addition to the Registrar there was set up the Data Protection Tribunal. The Tribunal was to act as an appeals body against any enforcement or de-registration notices issued by the Registrar.

18.2.2 **The data protection directive**

In general the 1984 Act functioned well, though not without criticism,[16] until the early 1990s when the falling prices of computers and storage and the arrival of the World Wide Web changed the landscape. The information society truly came of age during this period and suddenly the use of a registration system to police data users, and the Registrar's enforcement powers, looked rather underpowered. The UK was not the only country within Europe suffering from the massive changes in technology that had occurred between 1984 and 1992. More problematically by 1992 there were eleven different national provisions regulating data protection within the European Economic Area,[17] while a further seven had no data protection laws whatsoever.[18] The position was beginning to mirror that with regard to database contents discussed in Chapter 11: the lack of a harmonised approach was causing harm to a single European market in data as some countries protected all forms of data, some, like the UK, only protected data held in digital form, and some failed to protect data at all. What was needed was a programme which would produce a harmonised approach to data protection across the EU and EEA.

In 1990 the Commission had announced their intent to remove these discrepancies by bringing forth a Directive on 'The protection of individuals with regard to the processing of personal data and on the free movement of such data'.[19] The Directive was eventually brought forward under Article 100A of the Treaty of Rome. This is the internal market protocol. It allows the Council to adopt new measures for 'the approximation of the provisions laid down by law, regulation or administrative action in Member States which have as their object the establishing and functioning of the internal market.' The key to the Article 100A procedure is that by Article 100A(3) 'the Commission, in its proposals envisaged in paragraph 1 concerning health, safety, environmental protection and consumer protection, will take as a base a high level of protection.' This means that when the Article 100A procedure is used the harmonisation occurs at the highest level already operating within the Union. For Data Protection this meant the level found in Germany, which was considerably greater than that found in the UK Data Protection Act 1984, and which, for example, protected data in all forms, not only data held digitally. This meant that when the Directive was finally adopted in 1995 as Directive 95/46/EC of the European Parliament and of the Council of 24 October 1995 on the protection of individuals with regard to the processing of personal data and on the free movement of such data (Data Protection Directive)[20]

---

[16] See I. Walden, 'What Are Your Views?—Monitoring and Assessment of the Data Protection Act 1984', [1988] 4 *Computer Law and Security Report* 32; C. Edwards & N. Savage, 'Implementing the Data Protection Act 1984' (1986) *Journal of Business Law* 103.

[17] The countries with data protection laws were Sweden, Germany, France, Denmark, Norway, Luxembourg, Austria, the UK, Ireland, the Netherlands, and Belgium.

[18] In some states privacy laws may have fulfilled the role of data protection laws, but privacy laws have a different focus and application than data protection provisions. The seven with no specific data protection laws were: Finland, Greece, Italy, Portugal, Spain, Iceland, and Liechtenstein.

[19] OJ 1990 C277/03.   [20] OJ 1995 L 281/31.

the UK Government was required to make extensive changes to the law on data protection. To comply with the Directive these changes had to be implemented within three years. The Government, after due consultation, introduced the new Data Protection Bill in the House of Lords in January 1998 which received Royal Assent on 16 July 1998. Despite this the UK failed to meet the Commission's deadline of 24 October 1998 as the new Act could not take effect until a number of supporting items of secondary legislation were complete. Eventually the Act came into force on 1 March 2000, nearly five years after the Directive was adopted.

18.3 **The data protection act 1998**

18.3.1 **Forms of data**

The Data Protection Act 1998 was substantially longer than the old provision, a reflection of changes in society and the value of data from 1984 to 1998. Whereas the old Act had been forty-three sections and six schedules, the new Act was seventy-five sections and sixteen schedules.

Although much of the structure is similar to the old 1984 Act the Directive required the 1998 Act to be much wider in scope, increasing the role of the Data Protection Registrar, giving more powers of enforcement and extending the definition of protected data and controlled processes. The first change was in the scope of protected data. The new definition, found in s. 1(1):

→ Highlight Data Protection Act 1998, s. 1(1)

'data' means information which:

  (a) is being processed by means of equipment operating automatically in response to instructions given for that purpose,

  (b) is recorded with the intention that it should be processed by means of such equipment,

  (c) is recorded as part of a relevant filing system or with the intention that it should form part of a relevant filing system,

  (d) does not fall within paragraph (a), (b) or (c) but forms part of an accessible record as defined by section 68;

  (e) is recorded information held by a public authority and does not fall within any of paragraphs (a) to (d).

When compared to the old 'data' definition found in the 1984 Act: 'data recorded in a form in which it can be processed by equipment operating automatically in response to instructions given for that purpose', we see a much wider application of data protection law under the new regime. This is required to give effect to the Directive's definition of a 'personal data filing system' as 'any structured set of personal data which are accessible according to specific criteria, whether centralized, decentralized or dispersed on a functional or geographical basis'.[21] The 1998 Act therefore covers data held in manual filing systems as well as digital data. To be covered by the provisions of the Act data has simply to have one of two characteristics: (1) it must be either digital data which is intended to be computer processed; or (2) it is manual data which forms part of a relevant filing system. This means it must be indexed or stored in a fashion which indicates it forms part of an indexed collection of material.[22] If the material held is 'data' for the purposes of the Act there then follows two further sub-divisions.

Personal data is data which 'relates to a living individual who can be identified (a) from those data, or (b) from those data and other information which is in the possession of, or is likely to come into the possession of, the data controller, and includes any expression of opinion about the individual and any indication of the intentions of the data controller or any other person in respect of the individual.'[23] Understanding personal data is the key to understanding the Data Protection Act for it is only the processing of personal data which is controlled. Thus by s. 17 'personal data must not be processed unless an entry in respect of the data controller is included in the register maintained by the Commissioner under section 19', while all the rights awarded to the data subject under Part II (and discussed below) also only apply to personal data. Thus the distinction between data and personal data is key. Only the storage, processing, and transfer of personal data is controlled and regulated.

In addition to personal data the 1998 Act adds a new dimension to data protection by introducing into UK law for the first time a highly protected form of personal data known as 'sensitive personal data'. This is defined in s. 2:

→ Highlight Data Protection Act 1998, s. 2

Sensitive personal data is personal data consisting of information as to:

(a) the racial or ethnic origin of the data subject,

(b) his political opinions,

(c) his religious beliefs or other beliefs of a similar nature,

(d) whether he is a member of a trade union,

(e) his physical or mental health or condition,

(f) his sexual life,

(g) the commission or alleged commission by him of any offence, or

(h) any proceedings for any offence committed or alleged to have been committed by him, the disposal of such proceedings or the sentence of any court in such proceedings.

---

[21] Dir. 95/46/EC, Art. 2(c).

[22] To be precise, s. 1(1) defines a 'relevant filing system' as 'any set of information relating to individuals to the extent that, although the information is not processed by means of equipment operating automatically in response to instructions given for that purpose, the set is structured, either by reference to individuals or by reference to criteria relating to individuals, in such a way that specific information relating to a particular individual is readily accessible.'

[23] DPA 1998, s. 1(1).

The common theme of sensitive personal data is that it is data which may be used to discriminate against an individual. As such there is a special regime for such data both in the Directive,[24] and the Data Protection Act. The Act applies special conditions to the processing of data of this nature in Schedule 3. These conditions will be discussed below when we discuss the Data Protection Principles.

18.3.2 Processing and use of data

The Data Protection Act 1998 also extends protection by extending the definition of 'processing' of data and introducing a definition for 'using' data. These are key data protection terms as it is only when data is processed or used that the regulatory provisions of the Act come into play.

In the 1984 Act processing had been defined as: 'amending, augmenting, deleting or re-arranging the data or extracting the information constituting the data and, in the case of personal data, means performing any of those operations by reference to the data subject'[25] while 'use' was not defined at all. The weakness of these definitions became clear in the case of *R. v Brown*.[26] PC Brown was a police constable with Kent Police. As part of his duties he was entitled to make use of the police national computer (PNC) database for the registered purpose of policing as agent of his Chief Constable, who was registered as a data user under the Data Protection Act 1984. On two occasions, in order to assist a friend who ran a debt-collection agency PC Brown made checks of the PNC on vehicles owned by debtors from whom the agency had been engaged to recover debts. The results of these checks were simply passively displayed on a computer screen for PC Brown to read. On the first occasion the search did not reveal any personal data as defined by the Act as the vehicle was owned by a company. On the second occasion the search revealed personal data but there was no evidence that any subsequent use was made of the information obtained. The defendant was charged with two offences of using personal data held within the memory of the computer for a purpose other than that described in the register, contrary to s. 5 of the Act. At trial the judge directed the jury that on the first count the defendant could only be guilty of an attempt. The defendant was convicted on the first count of an attempt and on the second of the full offence.

He appealed to the Court of Appeal which allowed his appeal against conviction. The case was subsequently appealed by the Crown to the House of Lords. Their Lordships, in a split decision, dismissed the appeal. The lead judgement was given by Lord Goff of Chieveley. He found that as the word 'use' was not defined in the Act 'it must be given its natural and ordinary meaning'.[27] Based on this understanding he then gives a very complex analysis of what it means to 'use' data under the Act.

> Synonyms of the verb 'use' are to 'make use of,' or to 'employ for a purpose.' Here the word is used in relation to 'data,' and data means information recorded in a computer-readable form.

---

[24] Article 8 deals with 'special categories of data'. This provides that 'Member States shall prohibit the processing of personal data revealing racial or ethnic origin, political opinions, religious or philosophical beliefs, trade-union membership, and the processing of data concerning health or sex life' except where special provisions as laid out in Article 8 apply.
[25] DPA 1984, s. 1(7).   [26] [1996] AC 543.   [27] *ibid*, 548.

I must confess that at first sight I would not have thought that simply retrieving such information from the database in which it is stored, so that it appeared on a screen or a printout and could therefore be read by a human being, could properly be described as 'using' the information so recorded. Of course, the computer would be used to retrieve it; but the retrieval of the information would not of itself be 'using' the information so retrieved. It would simply be transferring the information into a different form. This to my mind underlines the fact that the definition of data as information in a computer-readable form does not mean that such information is only data while it is so recorded. It means rather that, if information is so recorded, it becomes data for the purposes of the Act; and if such information from that source is thereafter made use of it is used within the meaning of the Act. So if for example a police constable with the Kent Constabulary operates the police computer to retrieve personal data from the database so that he becomes aware of its contents, and then proceeds to make use of that information, he uses the personal data within the meaning of the statute. In such a case, the retrieval is not the use; it is simply a prerequisite of the use. Moreover if the police officer, who is the servant or agent of the data user, the Chief Constable, knowingly or recklessly puts the information to an improper use, he will be guilty of an offence under the Act. This may occur not only where the police officer retrieves the personal data from the database and then puts the information to an improper use, but also where, for example, he improperly makes use of personal data which has come to his knowledge when he operated the police computer innocently on a previous occasion, or where the data has been communicated to him by a colleague who had innocently operated the computer.[28]

Based on the tortuous reasoning displayed here Lord Goff found that as there was no evidence PC Brown had done anything other than display and consult the data he was not guilty of an offence under s. 5. He noted that:

The above reading of the statute accords not only with the natural and ordinary meaning of the word 'use' in its statutory context, but also with the statutory purpose of protecting personal data from improper use (or disclosure). It is a startling fact that, if the construction urged upon your Lordships by the prosecution were correct, a police officer who idly operated the police computer, retrieving personal data onto the screen without putting it to any use, would not merely be subject to disciplinary action (where appropriate) but would be guilty of a criminal offence; whereas another police officer who learned from a colleague of certain information constituting personal data stored in the database of the police computer and then, knowing of its source, used the information for business purposes would not. This surely cannot be the statutory intention; indeed if it were so, it could give rise to justifiable concern on the part of individuals who are the subject of personal data.[29]

He was joined in this view by Lords Hoffman and Browne-Wilkinson, but Lords Griffiths and Jauncey dissented. Lord Griffiths noted that:

To read the personal data about an individual displayed on a computer screen or in a printout is an invasion of that person's privacy, if there is no legitimate purpose for doing so. I therefore prefer the construction that forbids the illegitimate display of personal data ... It is not straining the meaning of language to say that a person is using the information stored in a computer if he informs himself of its contents. Whether or not he then goes on to apply the information for a particular purpose, and to use it in that sense, will depend on the value of the information to him: but whether or not he applies the information does not alter the fact that he has wrongly invaded the privacy of the individual, and now has the information available to apply at any time in the future.[30]

---

[28] *ibid*, 548–549.   [29] *ibid*, 550.   [30] *ibid*, 555.

This clear divide between the views of their lordships was squarely caused by the inexact language applied in the 1984 Act. By failing to define 'use' and by applying restrictive definitions of 'processing' and 'data' such confusion was almost certain to arise. The 1998 Act meets some of these concerns. As we have already seen data is much more widely defined which means if one were to apply Lord Goff's byzantine analysis to the current definition of data it is likely one would conclude that consulting data was indeed a 'use' of data: more importantly though s. 1 offers a better definition of processing.

> **→ Highlight** Data Protection Act 1998, s. 1
>
> 'Processing', in relation to information or data, means obtaining, recording or holding the information or data or carrying out any operation or set of operations on the information or data, including:
>
> (a) organisation, adaptation or alteration of the information or data,
>
> (b) retrieval, consultation or use of the information or data,
>
> (c) disclosure of the information or data by transmission, dissemination or otherwise making available, or
>
> (d) alignment, combination, blocking, erasure or destruction of the information or data.

This definition makes it clear that mere consultation of data is a data process. The Act though goes further and also defines several other key terms which are applied throughout the Act. 'Use' is now defined alongside 'disclosing' as 'including using or disclosing the information contained in the data'[31] while new terms 'obtaining or recording' are defined as 'including obtaining or recording the information to be contained in the data'.[32] Although these definitions may be criticised as being under-developed and somewhat circular they do assist greatly, in particular with the new offence of unlawfully obtaining personal data under s. 55.

This states it is an offence to 'obtain or disclose personal data or the information contained in personal data, or procure the disclosure to another person of the information contained in personal data.' If PC Brown were to repeat his actions today it is likely he would be charged with this offence. In such a case he would likely be found guilty: he would clearly be found to have 'obtained personal data' even if he did not then act upon that data and given the wider definition of data and processing it seems unlikely judicial interpretation would find otherwise. This leaves one final question. How would Lord Goff feel about this outcome? He did note that he had concerns about the Crown's interpretation of 'use' under the 1984 Act noting that if 'the prosecution were correct, a police officer who idly operated the police computer, retrieving personal data onto the screen without putting it to any use, would not merely be subject to disciplinary action (where appropriate) but would be guilty of a criminal offence.' His concern though seemed to be not that the action itself would be criminalised, but rather that

---

[31] DPA 1998, s. 1(2)(b).   [32] DPA 1998, s. 1(2)(a).

a more serious counter-action would not: 'another police officer who learned from a colleague of certain information constituting personal data stored in the database of the police computer and then, knowing of its source, used the information for business purposes would not.' Applying the 1998 Act though both would appear to be guilty of an offence under s.55. This outcome would also appear to please Lord Griffiths who felt that PC Brown's actions were 'an invasion of privacy'. Perhaps s. 55 has healed the judicial rift evident in the *Brown* decision.

18.3.3 **Personnel of the data protection act**

The remainder of the structural provisions of the 1998 Act are similar to the 1984 Act but with some changes in the language of data protection. Whereas the 1984 Act had 'data subjects' and 'data users' the 1998 Act has a three way split. Data subjects remain unchanged as 'an individual who is the subject of personal data', but the old fashioned definition of a 'data user' as 'a person who holds data' is gone, replaced with 'data controller' being 'a person who (either alone or jointly or in common with other persons) determines the purposes for which and the manner in which any personal data are, or are to be, processed' and 'data processor' being 'any person (other than an employee of the data controller) who processes the data on behalf of the data controller'.[33] This new split of data controller and data processor reflects how the data industries have changed over the years. Whereas in 1984 it was common for companies to process their own data due to the cost and difficulty of transmitting data, by 1998 most data processing was outsourced to specialist companies. The data controller/data processor distinction allows the Act to control both aspects of data management and processing.

The entire regulatory structure is still overseen by a non-governmental public officer and an appeals tribunal. The old fashioned name of Data Protection Registrar (a name which reflected the primary role of the registrar in maintain the Register of Data Users) is gone though replaced with the title Information Commissioner, and to mirror the change in name of the primary regulatory officer the tribunal is also renamed from the Data Protection Tribunal to the Information Tribunal.[34]

This change is much more than cosmetic. Under the 1984 Act the Data Protection Registrar had extensive powers including the right to issue enforcement and de-registration notices and could, under Schedule 4, obtain a warrant to enter premises and make inspections. But the extended powers of the Information Commissioner under the 1998 Act go much further than these. There remains a requirement that data controllers notify the Information Commissioner that they are processing data under the Act,[35] but with nearly every business, charity, and voluntary organisation and a large number of individuals registering with the Information Commissioner the Register is now simply too large to be an effective means of regulation, especially as individuals cannot simply search the register to see what data is being held on

[33] The definition of 'data controller', 'data subject', and 'data processor' are all taken from s. 1(1) of the Data Protection Act 1998. The definition of 'data user' is from s. 1(5) of the Data Protection Act 1984.
[34] For more on the appointment and role of the Commissioner and Tribunal see s. 6 of the Data Protection Act 1998.   [35] DPA 1998, ss. 16 and 17.

them as a publicly accessible register searchable by data subject identity would, rather ironically, be in breach of the Data Protection Act.[36]

Thus the focus of the Information Commissioner's role switches from maintaining the Register to education and enforcement. By s. 51 the Commissioner is given the general duty to promote good practice and to issue information on good practice. This is expanded by s. 51(3) which gives the Commissioner the power to issue codes of practice. To date codes of good practice issued or endorsed by the commissioner include a CCTV code of practice, a framework code for the sharing of information, a code of practice on telecommunications directory information and fair processing, and a code of practice for archivists and records managers. In addition to these codes of practice the Commissioner issues an annual report under s. 52. In this report the Commissioner will usually report on their education activities which include information audits, conferences and colloquia and sponsored research.[37]

18.4 **The data protection principles, processing, and fairness**

Education is not of itself enough to prevent unauthorised or unfair processing of data. The educational role of the Information Commissioner is supplemented by a series of data protection principles applied to data controllers and enforced by the Information Commissioner. These principles form the heart of the Data Protection Act and by s. 4(4) 'it shall be the duty of a data controller to comply with the data protection principles in relation to all personal data with respect to which he is the data controller.' The principles are found in Schedule 1.

➡ Highlight The Data Protection Principles

(1) Personal data shall be processed fairly and lawfully and, in particular, shall not be processed unless:
   (a) at least one of the conditions in Schedule 2 is met, and
   (b) in the case of sensitive personal data, at least one of the conditions in Schedule 3 is also met.

(2) Personal data shall be obtained only for one or more specified and lawful purposes, and shall not be further processed in any manner incompatible with that purpose or those purposes.

➡

---

[36] You can though search the register by Data Controller at http://www.ico.gov.uk/ESDWebPages/search.asp. The results will give you the purposes for which personal data are held by the data controller. A search for 'Oxford University Press' gives six purposes (1) staff administration, (2) Advertising, Marketing and Public Relations, (3) Accounts & Records, (4) Trading / Sharing in Personal Information, (5) Information and Databank Administration, and (6) Journalism and Media. Her Majesty's Revenue and Customs have twelve purposes (which I will not list here).

[37] For example the 2008 Annual report is available from: http://www.ico.gov.uk/upload/documents/library/corporate/detailed_specialist_guides/annual_report_2007_08.pdf.

> ➡
>
> (3) Personal data shall be adequate, relevant and not excessive in relation to the purpose or purposes for which they are processed.
>
> (4) Personal data shall be accurate and, where necessary, kept up to date.
>
> (5) Personal data processed for any purpose or purposes shall not be kept for longer than is necessary for that purpose or those purposes.
>
> (6) Personal data shall be processed in accordance with the rights of data subjects under this Act.
>
> (7) Appropriate technical and organisational measures shall be taken against unauthorised or unlawful processing of personal data and against accidental loss or destruction of, or damage to, personal data.
>
> (8) Personal data shall not be transferred to a country or territory outside the European Economic Area unless that country or territory ensures an adequate level of protection for the rights and freedoms of data subjects in relation to the processing of personal data.

Although all the principles are of equal weight in many ways the key principle is the First Principle. This is the general principle that data processing shall be carried out in a fair and reasonable manner. This is an extremely vague term, which although supported by conditions for the fair processing of data in Schedules Two and Three (discussed below) has caused problems for courts in the UK and further afield.

18.4.1 Processing data: Bodil Lindqvist

The first issue is the rather vague term 'processing'. This is defined by the Directive as 'any operation or set of operations which is performed upon personal data, whether or not by automatic means',[38] while the UK Data Protection Act defines it as 'obtaining, recording or holding the information or data or carrying out any operation or set of operations on the information or data'.[39] This is potentially a very expansive set which could cover anything from hard-core data mining of gathered personal data by commercial organisations to individuals mentioning friends and family on personal web pages without permission or otherwise in accordance with the Directive and Act. Was it really the intent of the Directive to be so widely applied?

The leading case to date on the question of 'processing' in accordance with the Directive is the Swedish case of *Bodil Lindqvist*.[40] Mrs Lindqvist, in addition to her day job as a maintenance worker, worked as a catechist in the parish of Alseda in Sweden. She took a data processing course to allow her to develop an online presence for her church. At the end of 1998, Mrs Lindqvist set up internet pages using her personal computer in order to allow parishioners preparing for their confirmation to obtain information they might need. At her request, the administrator of the Swedish Church's website set up a link between those pages and that site.

The pages in question contained information about Mrs Lindqvist and eighteen colleagues in the parish, sometimes including their full names and in other cases only their first names. Mrs Lindqvist also described, in a mildly humorous manner, the jobs

---

[38] Dir. 95/46/EC, Art. 2(b).   [39] DPA 1998, s. 1(1).   [40] [2004] QB 1014 (ECJ).

held by her colleagues and their hobbies. In many cases family circumstances and telephone numbers and other matters were mentioned. She also stated that one colleague
had injured her foot and was on half-time on medical grounds. It was established that
Mrs Lindqvist had not informed her colleagues of the existence of those pages or
obtained their consent, nor did she notify the Datainspektionen (Swedish supervisory authority for the protection of electronically transmitted data) of her activity. She
removed the pages in question as soon as she became aware that they were not appreciated by some of her colleagues.

Mrs Lindqvist was charged by Swedish authorities with breach of the Swedish Data
Protection Act on the grounds that she had: (a) processed personal data by automatic
means without giving prior written notification to the Datainspektionen; (b) processed
sensitive personal data (injured foot and half-time on medical grounds) without
authorisation; and (c) transferred processed personal data to a third country without
authorisation. Mrs Lindqvist accepted the facts of the case but challenged that her
activities (placing material on a website) did not qualify as 'processing' data under the
Directive and thereby the relevant Swedish law. The Swedish Court of Appeal referred
the case to the European Court of Justice for their interpretation of the Data Protection
Directive.

In a wide-ranging opinion the ECJ found that:

→ **Highlight** The Decision of the ECJ in *Bodil Lindqvist*

(1) The act of referring, on an internet page, to various persons and identifying them by
name or other means constituted the processing of personal data within the meaning of
Art. 3(1).

(2) The processing of personal data such as that described in answer to the first question was
not covered by any of the exceptions given in Art. 3(2).

(3) Reference to the fact that a colleague had injured her foot and was on half time on
medical grounds constituted personal data concerning health within the meaning of Art. 8(1).

(4) Personal data which came from a person who had loaded them onto an internet
site which then appeared on the computer of a person in a third country were not directly
transferred between those two people but through the computer infrastructure of the hosting
provider where the page was stored. Thus, operations such as those carried out by Lindqvist did
not constitute a transfer of data to a third country within the meaning of Art. 25.

(5) The provisions of the Directive did not, in themselves, bring about restrictions which
conflicted with the right to freedom of expression. It was for the national courts responsible
for applying implementing legislation to ensure a fair balance between the rights and interests
in question.

(6) Nothing prevented Member States from extending the scope of national legislation
implementing the Directive to areas not included in the scope thereof provided that no other
provision of Community law precluded it.

This ruling clearly gives an extremely expansive interpretation of 'processing'. Even the simplest act of placing information on a personal web site qualifies. This makes the interpretation of 'fairness' of paramount importance as only when data is processed 'fairly and lawfully' is the first data protection principle met.

18.4.2 Processing data: Johnson v Medical Defence Union

The leading UK case on fairness is *Johnson v Medical Defence Union Ltd*[41] The claimant, Mr Johnson, was a consultant orthopaedic surgeon with over twenty years clinical experience. He was, from 1980, a member of the Medical Defence Union (MDU), a mutual society which provides advice and professional liability insurance cover to its members. He was reported as having 'never been the subject of a claim for alleged professional negligence.'[42] However it was reported that 'over the years he [had] sought advice and assistance from the MDU in relation to professional questions and problems that concerned him, including complaints made against him. His contact with the MDU, and that from others about him, gave rise to the opening at least since 1991 of 17 MDU files.'[43]

As a result of a review of their files the MDU wrote to Mr Johnson in January 2002 informing him they would not renew his membership at the end of his current subscription. The letter gave no reasons. Mr Johnson sought the reasons, but none were provided. As a result of the MDU's actions Mr Johnson claims he suffered damage to his professional reputation and financial loss. He made a claim under s. 13 of the Data Protection Act 1998 seeking compensation for unfair processing of his personal data.

At an initial hearing before Rimer J in 2006 all Mr Johnson's claims were dismissed.[44] In particular he found that:

> [The MDU's risk policy] was formulated against the background of a contractual relationship between the MDU and its members under which the MDU had and has an absolute discretion to terminate a member's membership and in which it was in the interests of all members that it should have a sound risk assessment policy. There might be legitimate scope for disagreement between those competent to judge these things as to whether the MDU risk assessment policy was sound or otherwise, or as to whether it could be improved. But I have no reason to believe that it was arrived at other than after proper consideration and that it was regarded as other than the most appropriate policy for the needs of the MDU ... The MDU could process his data in the circumstances in which it did perfectly fairly without his [Mr Johnson's] input, and the evidence from the MDU witnesses satisfied me that his input would be unlikely to have made any difference to the assessment of his case: because, put shortly, the policy regards a member's input as essentially irrelevant.[45]

Therefore, according to Rimer J., Mr Johnson's suggestion that he 'was entitled to have his data processed and case considered by reference to his own inexpert assertions as to the risk assessment policy that the MDU should apply' should be rejected.[46]

Mr Johnson appealed. His appeal was based on the foundation that the MDU's policy was flawed. In particular he believed two flaws led to his personal data held by the MDU

---

[41] [2007] EWCA Civ 262.   [42] *ibid*, [2].   [43] *ibid*.
[44] *Johnson v The Medical Defence Union Ltd* [2006] EWHC 321 (Ch).   [45] *ibid*, [110].
[46] *ibid*, [202].

being processed unfairly. The first was that the MDU's policy of assessing members according to number of incidents or complaints rather than according to their outcome meant he was penalised and secondly because of that policy, the Risk Assessment Review process used by the MDU did not allow any explanation by the member of the various incidents reported to it.

On 28 March 2007 the Court of Appeal dismissed Mr Johnson's claim. They held that the MDU's processing of Mr Johnson's personal data for the purpose of conducting a risk assessment review was, in relation to all but two of the files in question, fair and lawful under the Act, and dismissed Mr Johnson's claim for compensation. Arden LJ noted that 'Mr Johnson gave his consent to the processing of personal data for a number of purposes, including risk management. The directive requires consent to be unambiguous (Article 7). However, in my judgment, Mr Johnson did not have to know the nature of the MDU's risk assessment policy to give a valid consent for this purpose.'[47] She went on to note 'the judge [Rimer J] did not accept Mr Johnson's submission, either in relation to the lead files or the non-lead files, that the MDU had an obligation to consult Mr Johnson about the processing exercise or to invite his representations upon it. In my judgment the judge was right to hold that the fairness principle did not require this. As a general proposition a party to a contract cannot in my judgment use the fairness principle as a means of upsetting any contractually permitted use of information where, as here, processing was foreseeable. I see no basis for displacing this general proposition in this case.'[48]

The unfair processing of the remaining two files was held not to have caused damage to Mr Johnson. The court paid particular regard to the fact that Mr Johnson had signed-up to the MDU's risk assessment policy and agreed to the processing of his personal data for this purpose, and the court held that the review was carried out within the terms of this policy. In terms of compensation, the court held that even if Mr Johnson had shown there to be a breach of the Data Protection Act, there is nothing within the Act that would give him the right to compensation for a general loss of reputation. The court noted that a defamation claim would be a more appropriate course of action for this; however, the court did note that had the MDU breached the Data Protection Act in processing Mr Johnson's personal data, he would have been able to claim for losses and distress 'by reason of a data controller's contravention of the Data Protection Act'.[49]

What is apparent from these two cases is the complexity of processing in accordance with the regulatory provisions. Mrs. Lindqvist appeared to be engaged in an innocent activity, which she no doubt felt was a private matter. The Medical Defence Union was by comparison involved in high level data processing with the potential to adversely affect the professional career of Mr Johnson and others that were subject to its risk assessment review. Ultimately though we know that Mrs Lindqvist's actions were in breach of the Swedish Data Protection law (and the Directive), while the actions of the Medical Defence Union were fair. How can a data controller process data with confidence given the complexity of the first data protection principle?

---

[47] [2007] EWCA Civ 262, [145].   [48] *ibid*, [148]–[149].   [49] *ibid*, [72].

18.5 **Conditions for processing of personal data**

To assist Data Controllers in fulfilling the First Principle Schedules 2 and 3 list conditions in which the principle is met. Schedule 2 states that with personal data processing should only take place when:

1. The data subject has given his consent to the processing.
2. The processing is necessary:
   (a) for the performance of a contract to which the data subject is a party, or
   (b) for the taking of steps at the request of the data subject with a view to entering into a contract.
3. The processing is necessary for compliance with any legal obligation to which the data controller is subject, other than an obligation imposed by contract.
4. The processing is necessary in order to protect the vital interests of the data subject.
5. The processing is necessary:
   (a) for the administration of justice,
   (aa) for the exercise of any functions of either House of Parliament,
   (b) for the exercise of any functions conferred on any person by or under any enactment,
   (c) for the exercise of any functions of the Crown, a Minister of the Crown or a government department, or
   (d) for the exercise of any other functions of a public nature exercised in the public interest by any person.
6. The processing is necessary for the purposes of legitimate interests pursued by the data controller or by the third party or parties to whom the data are disclosed, except where the processing is unwarranted in any particular case by reason of prejudice to the rights and freedoms or legitimate interests of the data subject.

In cases of sensitive personal data Schedule 3 is applied instead. This states that the processing of sensitive personal data should only take place on one or more of the following occasions:

1. The data subject has given his *explicit* consent to the processing of the personal data.
2. The processing is necessary for the purposes of exercising or performing any right or obligation which is conferred or imposed by law on the data controller in connection with employment.
3. The processing is necessary:
   (a) in order to protect the vital interests of the data subject or another person, in a case where:
       (i) consent cannot be given by or on behalf of the data subject, or
       (ii) the data controller cannot reasonably be expected to obtain the consent of the data subject, or
   (b) in order to protect the vital interests of another person, in a case where consent by or on behalf of the data subject has been unreasonably withheld.
4. The processing:
   (a) is carried out in the course of its legitimate activities by any body or association which:
       (i) is not established or conducted for profit, and
       (ii) exists for political, philosophical, religious or trade-union purposes,

(b) is carried out with appropriate safeguards for the rights and freedoms of data subjects,

(c) relates only to individuals who either are members of the body or association or have regular contact with it in connection with its purposes, and

(d) does not involve disclosure of the personal data to a third party without the consent of the data subject.

5. The information contained in the personal data has been made public as a result of steps deliberately taken by the data subject.

6. The processing:

(a) is necessary for the purpose of, or in connection with, any legal proceedings (including prospective legal proceedings),

(b) is necessary for the purpose of obtaining legal advice, or

(c) is otherwise necessary for the purposes of establishing, exercising or defending legal rights.

7. The processing is necessary:

(a)   for the administration of justice,

(aa) for the exercise of any functions of either House of Parliament

(b)   for the exercise of any functions conferred on any person by or under an enactment, or

(c)   for the exercise of any functions of the Crown, a Minister of the Crown or a government department.

8. The processing is necessary for medical purposes and is undertaken by:

(a) a health professional, or

(b) a person who in the circumstances owes a duty of confidentiality which is equivalent to that which would arise if that person were a health professional.

In this paragraph 'medical purposes' includes the purposes of preventative medicine, medical diagnosis, medical research, the provision of care and treatment and the management of health-care services.

9. The processing:

(a) is of sensitive personal data consisting of information as to racial or ethnic origin,

(b) is necessary for the purpose of identifying or keeping under review the existence or absence of equality of opportunity or treatment between persons of different racial or ethnic origins, with a view to enabling such equality to be promoted or maintained, and

(c) is carried out with appropriate safeguards for the rights and freedoms of data subjects.

10. The personal data are processed in circumstances specified in an order made by the Secretary of State for the purposes of this paragraph.

18.5.1 **Consent**

Most commonly data is processed according to the first condition of processing data. That is 'The data subject has given his consent to the processing' or for sensitive personal data. 'The data subject has given his *explicit* consent to the processing of the personal data.' What in practice does this mean?

We are all familiar with the opt-in and opt-out boxes frequently used by data controllers at the point they gather the data. Is the provision of an opt-out box sufficient to qualify as consent? What about explicit consent for sensitive personal data? Such boxes are commonplace, often with both being used in quick succession such as tick to opt-in to receive data from us and tick to opt-out to us passing data on to third parties. The extensive use of such boxes is enough to tell us that broadly they comply with the first condition (at least for personal data), but there are some limits to their use.

The first thing to note is that neither 'consent' nor 'explicit consent' are defined by the Act. This means in applying these terms courts will as usual refer to the ordinary usage of the terms and, as the Data Protection Act is derivative of the Directive, to the Directive where appropriate. The term consent is defined in the OED as to 'give permission, express willingness or agree' while 'explicit' is defined as 'leaving nothing merely implied'. Applying these definitions it appears that consent may be given by means of an opt-out box remaining unchecked as by not recording dissent permission, willingness or agreement may be applied. Explicit consent though would appear to require some form of positive indication of consent so as to avoid any implication being required to be drawn.

This suggests opt-in boxes are okay but opt-out boxes are not when dealing with sensitive personal data. This interpretation is supported by Article 2(h) of the Directive which states 'the data subject's consent shall mean any freely given specific and informed indication of his wishes by which the data subject signifies his agreement to personal data relating to him being processed.' The only potential difficulty is the question of the use of the term 'informed' in Article 2(h). Informed consent is slightly different to consent and suggests the data subject is given rather more information than is found in a standard opt-out or opt-in box. It is noticeable that the word 'informed' did not make it into either Schedule 2 or Schedule 3. This position is further clouded by an opinion issued by the Article 29 Working Party (an independent review body set up under Article 29 of the Directive). In an opinion issued in 2004 on 'unsolicited communications for marketing purposes' (SPAM) and the application of the Privacy and Electronic Communications Directive,[50] the Working Party found that:

> Consent given on the occasion of the general acceptance of the terms and conditions governing the possible main contract (e.g., a subscription contract, in which consent is also sought to send communications for direct marketing purposes) must respect the requirements in Directive 95/46/EC, that is, be informed, specific and freely given. Provided that these latter conditions are met, consent might be given by the data subject for instance, through the ticking of a box.
>
> Implied consent to receive such mails is not compatible with the definition of consent of Directive 95/46/EC and in particular with the requirement of consent being the indication of someone's wishes, including where this would be done 'unless opposition is made' (opt-out). Similarly, pre-ticked boxes, e.g., on websites are not compatible with the definition of the Directive either.

This suggests opt-out boxes are not compatible with the Directive at any level, but as this decision relates to a reference under the Privacy and Electronic Communications

---

[50] Directive2002/58/EC:http://www.informationtribunal.gov.uk/Documents/decisions/Linguaphone_Institute.pdf.

Directive and as Working Party opinions are advisory not adjudicatory this opinion is of no direct effect on the continued use opt-out boxes. Until a decision of the UK or European courts states otherwise it seems safe to assume that opt-out boxes comply with Schedule 2 at least, although as discussed possibly not with Schedule 3. This does not mean that the use of such opt-outs and opt-ins is completely deregulated. In 1994 the UK Data Protection Tribunal reviewed the use of tools such as these in the case of *Linguaphone Institute v Data Protection Registrar*.[51] The case surrounded order forms contained on direct mail advertisements for the appellants language teaching business. Linguaphone was involved in the practice of list brokering, that is selling customer details to third parties. The form contained an opt-out box for customers who did not want their details to be brokered. It stated '(Please) tick here if you do not wish Linguaphone to make your details available to other companies who may wish to mail you offers of goods or services.' The box was positioned at the bottom of the form, was in small print, and was not terribly prominent. The Tribunal decided that 'the position, size of print and wording of the opt-out box does not amount to a sufficient explanation to an enquirer that the company intends or may wish to hold, use or disclose that personal data provided at the time of enquiry for the purpose of trading in personal information.' Thus opt-out boxes must be sufficiently prominent and must explain what use your data will be put to to be effective.

Once your consent is given the data controller may fairly process the data in accordance with the first condition of data processing, but it should be noted that consent is not permanent. The data subject may withdraw consent at any time. Curiously though this is not directly specified in the Directive or the Act, although ss. 10 and 11 allow the data subject to prevent processing for the purpose of direct marketing or where the processing may cause damage or distress and Article 9 of the Directive on Privacy and Electronic Communications allows consent to be withdrawn at any time in relation to the processing of location data. Consent though is only one of a number of 'fair processing' conditions. Both Schedules 2 and 3 list a number of such conditions which may allow processing without the consent of the data subject.

Most of the conditions set out in Schedule 2 are to allow for the usual functioning of pre-existing legal obligations such as the right to process to conclude or perform a contract, or the right to process to comply with a legal obligation or in the administration of justice. Two interesting conditions are condition four: processing in the vital interests of the data subject and condition six: processing necessary for the purposes of legitimate interests pursued by the data controller. It is difficult to explain with any certainty when either of these conditions is fulfilled given the rather generic nature of these conditions. One can imagine that condition four may be fulfilled by a financial institution or employer who is taking steps to protect the data subject from fraud or identity theft. Thus credit and debit card companies routinely monitor card transactions for evidence that a card has been cloned or stolen. This may qualify under

---

[51] DA/94 31/49/1.

condition four. Condition six is more difficult to pin down. Although the Act states that 'The Secretary of State may by order specify particular circumstances in which this condition is, or is not, to be taken to be satisfied'[52] no such order has been made to date. It is hard to imagine what form of processing may be *necessary* for the purposes of legitimate interests pursued by the data controller rather than merely convenient or expedient. As Professor Lloyd observes 'in general, data controllers might well be advised not to place too much reliance upon this ground.'[53]

18.5.2 Processing sensitive personal data

The conditions found in Schedule 3, are by comparison more focussed upon the type of data which is classified as sensitive personal data. Thus we find processing in relation to employment, processing carried out by trade unions and religious organisations, processing for medical purposes, and processing for the purposes of racial or ethnic monitoring are permitted alongside the usual conditions in favour of processing in the administration of justice and for carrying on the duties of the Crown.

The most interesting conditions in Schedule 3 are condition three: 'The processing is necessary in order to protect the vital interests of the data subject or another person, in a case where consent cannot be given by or on behalf of the data subject, or the data controller cannot reasonably be expected to obtain the consent of the data subject, or in order to protect the vital interests of another person, in a case where consent by or on behalf of the data subject has been unreasonably withheld', and condition ten: 'The personal data are processed in circumstances specified in an order made by the Secretary of State'.

Condition three will probably be applied in emergency medical situations such as where the data subject is unconscious and medical personnel need to consult their medical records or take a medical history from relatives. It would also extend to consulting the data subjects records where that was necessary to treat a third party, perhaps where the third party appears to have contacted a transmittable disease from the data subject and the data subject is unreasonably refusing to allow them access to his records.

Condition ten allows for further conditions which allow sensitive personal data to be processed without the consent of the data subject. It has been used to pass no less than three orders which extend the conditions in which sensitive personal data may be processed. The most extensive of the three is The Data Protection (Processing of Sensitive Personal Data) Order 2000.[54] This Order adds no less than ten additional conditions which allow for the processing of sensitive personal data for the prevention and detection of an unlawful act, to protect against malpractice or misfeasance, to allow for counselling advice and support, for the carrying on of insurance and pensions business, for equal opportunities monitoring including monitoring of religious discrimination and discrimination on health grounds, for monitoring of political opinion by political parties, and 'where processing is necessary for the

---

[52] Sch. 6, para. 6(2).   [53] I. Lloyd, *Information Technology Law* (5th ed., 2008), 102.
[54] SI 2000/417.

exercise of any functions conferred on a constable by any rule of law'. A further extension was provided by The Data Protection (Processing of Sensitive Personal Data) (Elected Representatives) Order 2002.[55] This provides that elected representatives[56] may process sensitive personal data in order to fulfil their function as elected representatives, while The Data Protection (Processing of Sensitive Personal Data) Order 2006[57] extends the grounds still further to allow processing of data relating to payment cards for the purposes of 'administering or cancelling' that card when it has been used in the commission of an offence involving indecent photographs or pseudo-photographs of children. The idea behind this provision is to allow law enforcement authorities to be able to inform card issuers that the card has been used in the commission of an offence thereby allowing the card issuer to cancel the data subject's account. The intent is to make it more difficult for the data subject to be able to use a payment card to obtain harmful materials in future.[58]

What is clear is that the protections afforded by the data protection principles are limited. Processing may take place for any number of conditions listed in Schedules Two and Three without the consent of the data subject, and the Government may at any time extend these conditions by statutory instrument. Although the data protection principles provide a framework that says processing is fair and reasonable, and although they require data to be kept secure and up-to-date, the true means of scrutiny and supervision of data controllers are to be found elsewhere in the Data Protection Act.

18.6 **Supervision of data controllers: data subject rights**

Data controllers are supervised using a variety of means including public scrutiny, oversight by the Information Commissioner, and where necessary the application of the criminal law. As already discussed, the first level of control is that data controllers are required to notify the Information Commissioner *before* they begin to process personal data.[59] This information is then entered onto the publicly accessible Register of Data Controllers, although as already discussed,[60] this is of limited value in a society where nearly almost every commercial organisation will be a data controller. It can though provide a starting point for data subjects who are seeking to ensure that data held on them is accurate, up-to-date, and is being stored and processed fairly. This is essential because the primary control mechanism for day-to-day enforcement of data protection principles is through the actions of data subjects.

---

[55] SI 2002/2905.

[56] Being MPs, MSPs, UK MEPs, Members of the Welsh and Northern Irish Assemblies, Local Authority Councillors, Elected Mayors and Members of the London Assembly and Common Council of the City of London.   [57] SI 2006/2068.

[58] See Explanatory Memorandum to the Data Protection (Processing of Sensitive Personal Data) Order 2006: http://www.opsi.gov.uk/si/em2006/uksiem_20062068_en.pdf.

[59] DPA 1998, ss. 16 and 17.   [60] See above pp. 473–474.

18.6.1 **Subject access: Durant v the Financial Services Authority**

Self policing of personal data is a key aspect of the Act and to assist with this data subjects are given an assortment of low-level enforcement powers. The first is that they may under s. 7 make a subject access request. This requires data controllers to reveal to the data subject if they hold data on them and what use they make of that data. This includes detailing what data the data controller holds, who, if anyone, they disclose that data to, and any information, if available, as to the source of the data. This information should be given to the data subject within forty days of the application being received by the data controller.[61]

The aim of s. 7 is to allow data subjects to check what data is held on them and how that data is being processed and/or transmitted on. This investigatory right then arms data subjects with the necessary information to allow them to take further action such as applying for data to be deleted or corrected, or if necessary to report the actions of the data controller to the Information Commissioner for investigation.

That is not to say this procedure is without risk. It would obviously be a breach of the data protection principles, in particular principle seven, if data were revealed under a s. 7 application to the wrong person.[62] To prevent this there are a number of measures which are designed to protect the data subject. By s. 7(3) the data controller may require the data subject to provide further information to prove his identity and may refuse to comply with a subject access request until this information is supplied. This information may take the form of personal identifiers such as passwords or identification numbers or it may take the form of physical identifiers such as a passport or driving license. Further to this, s. 7(4) deals with conjoined or commixed data. These are forms of data in which the information held on the data subject is linked to data held on other persons.

Conjoined data is data which is held in a single file or folder about two or more data subjects, but which as far as possible treats data subjects separately. An example may be a personnel review file on a sales and marketing team which evaluates each member of the team in comparison with each other rating their relative strengths and weaknesses and evaluating their teamwork. Commixed data is data relating to two or more persons which has come together to form a single file or entry. An example may be a joint mortgage application of two persons which forms a single mortgage file with the lender.

By s. 7(4) 'Where a data controller cannot comply with the request without disclosing information relating to another individual who can be identified from that information, he is not obliged to comply with the request unless: (a) the other individual has consented to the disclosure of the information to the person making the request, or (b) it is reasonable in all the circumstances to comply with the request without the consent of the other individual.' The questions of what qualifies as 'data relating to

---

[61] s. 7(8).
[62] Imagine if you will an investigative journalist obtaining medical details of a well-known political or business figure by means of a false application under s. 7.

another individual who can be identified' and when it is reasonable to comply with a request absent the other data subject's permission, have been considered by the Court of Appeal in *Durant v Financial Services Authority*.[63]

The appellant was an erstwhile customer of Barclays Bank, against whom he had brought proceedings which ended unsuccessfully for the appellant in 1993. Since then he had sought, without success, disclosure of various records in connection with the dispute giving rise to the litigation because he believed that the records might assist him to re-open his claims or to secure an investigation into the conduct of the Bank. In September and October 2001 he made two requests to the FSA in its role as the regulator for the financial services sector, seeking disclosure of personal data held by it, both electronically and in manual files. The FSA in response provided Mr Durant with copies of documents it held in computerised form, some of which had been redacted so as not to disclose the names of others. It refused his request for access to the unredacted documents. It also refused the whole of his request for information held on manual files on the ground that the information sought was not 'personal' within the definition of 'personal data' in s. 1 of the Data Protection Act 1998 and that, even if it was, it did not constitute 'data' within the separate definition of that word in s. 1(1)(c) in the sense of forming part of a 'relevant filing system'.

The Court was faced with several questions: (1) What is a 'relevant filing system'? (2) Which data is 'personal' data under that Act? (3) Does a data subject have an entitlement to have access to unredacted data under s. 7? and (4) What limits may be placed on access to conjoined and commixed data?

In answering the first two questions the court first divided all the files Mr Durant sought access to into four categories. These were:

(i) a file relating to the systems and controls Barclays Bank was required to maintain and which was subject to control by the FSA. This file was in date order and also contained a few documents relating to part of the appellant's complaint against the Bank, which concerned such systems and controls;

(ii) a file relating to complaints by customers of Barclays Bank to the FSA. The file was sub-divided alphabetically by reference to the complainant's name and contained, behind a divider marked 'Mr Durant', a number of documents relating to his complaint filed in date order;

(iii) a Bank Investigations Group file, relating and organised by reference to issues or cases concerning Barclays Bank, but not necessarily identified by reference to an individual complainant. It contained a sub-file marked 'Mr Durant', which contained documents relating to his complaint. Neither the file nor the sub-file was indexed in any way save by reference to the name of the appellant on the sub-file itself; and

(iv) Company Secretariat papers comprising a sheaf of papers in an unmarked transparent plastic folder held by the FSA's Company Secretariat, relating to the Mr Durant's complaint about the FSA's refusal to disclose to him details and the outcome of its investigation of his complaints against Barclays Bank. This file was not organised by date or any other criterion.

---

[63] [2004] FSR 28.

The Court found:[64]

> **→ Highlight** Relevant Filing Systems (from *Durant v FSA*)
>
> 'A relevant filing system' for the purpose of the Act, is limited to a system:
>
> (1) in which the files forming part of it are structured or referenced in such a way as clearly to indicate at the outset of the search whether specific information capable of amounting to personal data of an individual requesting it under s. 7 is held within the system and, if so, in which file or files it is held; and
>
> (2) which has, as part of its own structure or referencing mechanism, a sufficiently sophisticated and detailed means of readily indicating whether and where in an individual file or files specific criteria or information about the applicant can be readily located.

On this basis it was found that none of the further types of files were 'relevant filing systems' as 'none of the files in question is so structured or indexed as to provide ready access to it ... an ability of staff readily to identify and locate whole files, even those organised chronologically and/or by reference to his and others' names, is not enough.'[65]

This was a rather surprising outcome as it had been thought data held in organised files were covered and as in particular file ii, the Barclay's complaints file, was organised by reference to the complainants' names this seemed to fit the definition of 'relevant filing system' in s. 1 of the Act. What Auld LJ pointed out though was that the Act requires the information to be structured in such a way that 'specific information relating to a particular individual is readily accessible.' In the FSA file Mr Durant's complaint recorded in file ii was not so structured. The data was indexed firstly by reference to Barclays Bank, then by complainant: in effect this was a file about Barclays Bank which mentioned Mr Durant, rather than a file about Mr Durant. Thus, with respect to Mr Durant, it was not 'relevant' to him. This though did not dispense with the question of how to deal with conjoined and commixed data. Although it may be that the files were not 'relevant' they may still contain personal data.

To this end Auld LJ began his analysis of what constitutes personal data with a warning.[66]

> **→ Highlight** Auld LJ's Warning
>
> [The subject access right] is not an automatic key to any information, readily accessible or not, of matters in which he may be named or involved. Nor is to assist him, for example, to obtain discovery of documents that may assist him in litigation or complaints against third parties. As a matter of practicality and given the focus of the Act on ready accessibility of the information—whether from a computerised or comparably sophisticated non-computerised system—it is likely in most cases that only information that names or directly refers to him will qualify.

---

[64] Per Auld LJ at [50].   [65] *ibid* [51].   [66] *ibid* [27].

With this said Auld LJ then went on to analyse what qualifies as 'personal data':[67]

> **→ Highlight** Personal Date (from *Durant v FSA*)
>
> Mere mention of the data subject in a document held by a data controller does not necessarily amount to his personal data … It seems to me that there are two notions that may be of assistance. The first is whether the information is biographical in a significant sense, that is, going beyond the recording of the putative data subject's involvement in a matter or an event that has no personal connotations, a life event in respect of which his privacy could not be said to be compromised. The second is one of focus. The information should have the putative data subject as its focus rather than some other person with whom he may have been involved or some transaction or event in which he may have figured or have had an interest, for example, as in this case, an investigation into some other person's or body's conduct that he may have instigated. In short, it is information that affects his privacy, whether in his personal or family life, business or professional capacity.

This is a vital distinction that may be best thought of in terms of a stage play. There are characters who are central to a stage play, for instance Hamlet in the eponymous Shakespeare tragedy. Then there are characters which support the telling of the story: for instance Ophelia and Laertes. No one would claim the play is about Ophelia or Laertes, but they are essential for the story of Hamlet. So is the case of personal data. Personal data is, in Auld LJ's words, information which has 'the putative data subject as its focus': it is about the lead character not the supporting cast. In the instant case none of the data Mr Durant requested access to was 'personal data'. In each case although he was mentioned and details about him and his complaints were recorded he was not the central character of the files in question.

How then does one know if they are a central character or merely supporting cast in any given file? According to Auld LJ it is a question of 'a continuum of relevance or proximity to the data subject as distinct, say, from transactions or matters in which he may have been involved to a greater or lesser degree.'[68] This means data controllers and perhaps later the Information Commissioner or judges will have to evaluate the degree to which the data subject is the focus of the data in question based upon the biographical focus of the data. Data which is clearly focussed on the data subject will be personal data, even if others are mentioned; data which is clearly focussed on a third party is not, even if it mentions the data subject. Data in between remains somewhat in a grey area to be decided on the facts in a case by case analysis.

The answers to these questions led to the dismissal of Mr Durant's claim to access the further information which had been withheld from him, but what about his claim to have unredacted versions of data already supplied to him? Auld LJ suggested a two

---

[67] *ibid* [28].   [68] *ibid.*

stage approach be taken when considering redaction of data. The first is to ask whether the data redacted 'is necessarily part of the personal data that the data subject has requested'.[69] He defines 'necessarily' as 'Where a data controller cannot comply with the request without disclosing information about another individual who can be identified from the information'. If such information about another is not 'necessarily' part of personal data sought, then 'the data controller, whose primary obligation is to provide information, not documents, can, if he chooses to provide that information in the form of a copy document, simply redact such third party information because it is not a necessary part of the data subject's personal data'.[70] If the data is 'necessarily' part of the data subject's personal data then the second stage is applied. This requires the data controller to balance the interests of the data subjects in question. Should the revealing of personal data about other data subjects appear to be a greater intrusion of privacy, or carry greater risk of harm than the process of redacting does to the original data subject's access request then the data may be redacted. Should there be little risk to other data subjects then the interests of the data subject who made the access request should be protected and unredacted data should be supplied. In Auld LJ's words: 'In short, it all depends on the circumstances whether it would be reasonable to disclose to a data subject the name of another person figuring in his personal data, whether that person is a source, or a recipient or likely recipient of that information, or has a part in the matter the subject of the personal data. Beyond the basic presumption or starting point, I believe that the courts should be wary of attempting to devise any principles of general application one way or the other.'[71]

This left one final question for the court: what discretion do the courts and data controllers have when dealing with subject access requests which may involve conjoined or commixed data? Mr Durant had asked the court to compel the FSA to release to him the data they had retained and redacted under s. 7(9). Although this became a moot point during the analysis applied in answering the prior questions Auld LJ did question when it may be appropriate for a court to so do. His answer was not terribly clear but he did make two points strongly. The first was that the court's discretion under s. 7(9) is general and untrammelled, the second that when dealing with the disclosure of data relating to a third party it may be difficult for a court to order the data be retained if it found it to be reasonable for the data subject to have access to the data. This seems to be a weak support for the view that if the data relating to a third party forms a necessary part of the data relating to the data subject's access request, the court should order the data to be released to the data subject notwithstanding the effect this may have on the third party.

In sum *Durant* is a simple case dealing with complex issues. The case is simple because as noted by another of the judges in the case, Buxton LJ, 'the information sought by

---

[69] *ibid* [65].   [70] *ibid*.

[71] *ibid* [66]. In the instant case the Court found Mr Durant had no right to unredacted copies of the data supplied to him as in most cases it was not 'necessarily part of the personal data that he had requested'. On the two occasions the data redacted did pass the first hurdle of the test it fell down at the second hurdle as 'they were of the name of an FSA employee which, in itself, can have been of little or no legitimate value to Mr Durant and who had understandably withheld his or her consent because Mr Durant had abused him or her over the telephone' (at [67]).

Mr Durant was by no stretch of the imagination a borderline case'.[72] Mr Durant was seeking to use the subject access right found in the Data Protection Act to effect pre-trial discovery in the hope of finding evidence to allow him to raise a further claim against either Barclays Bank or the FSA. This was a clear abuse of the s. 7 procedure. In future there will be more borderline cases which will be much more difficult for judges. The complexity of the case was in the type of data in question: most data is not 'clean' data about a single data subject. Data is processed and reordered regularly. It is commixed and conjoined to create new data and identifying 'a' data subject or 'the' data subject is increasingly difficult. It is less often about Hamlet: a central character surrounded by supporting cast. More often we are dealing with a complex ensemble piece with no clear central role. This will prove continually more complex for both data controllers and the courts.

18.6.2 Correcting and managing data

Following a subject access request the data subject may, should they find data which is inaccurate or out of date, make a number of applications to have the data corrected or if necessary destroyed. By s. 10 the data subject may object to processing likely to cause damage or distress. The damage or distress must be 'substantial' and the harm 'unwarranted'. This is achieved by making an application in writing to the data control- ler. The data controller then must within twenty-one days either reply to the data sub- ject stating that they have stopped processing the data in question or that they intend to do so, or must state reasons why they believe the data subject's request is unjustified either in whole or in part.[73] In the event the data controller refuses to comply with the data subject's request the data subject may apply to the court under s. 10(4) for an order forcing compliance. This, like the s. 7(9) order discussed in *Durant,* is at the discretion of the court. Often s. 10 applications are made by the families of recently deceased relatives to have their names removed from automated lists such as marketing lists. Although strictly speaking in such cases the application does not come from the data subject, data controllers usually accede to such requests. By s. 11, the data subject may specifically apply to prevent processing for direct marketing purposes. Such an appli- cation must be in writing and the data controller must comply with the application within a reasonable period. Direct marketing is defined as 'communication (by what- ever means) of any advertising or marketing material which is directed to particular individuals.'[74] This wide definition includes direct mail, marketing calls, spam email, and spam texts. To assist with the management of s. 11 many direct marketers work with an industry association to allow for blanket opt-out applications. Thus the Tele- phone Preference Service allows individuals to opt-out of marketing calls while the Mail Preference Service performs the same function for direct mail.

Section 12 allows data subjects to object to systems of automated decision making. This is similar in form to the rights awarded under sections ten and eleven. The data sub- ject may write to the data controller requiring that the data controller takes no decision, or allows no decision to be taken on his behalf, purely on the processing by automatic means of personal data. The data controller must, within twenty-one days of receipt

---

[72] *ibid* [80].   [73] DPA 1998, s. 10(3).   [74] DPA 1998, s. 11(3).

of such a notice inform the data subject whether any such decisions were made, and if necessary to make arrangements to make a new decision detailing the steps that will be taken in making the new decision. Again if the data controller unreasonably refuses to comply with the data subject's application the court may at its discretion require the data controller to comply.[75] Requests under s. 12 are also commonly made by data subjects in relation to automated 'credit scoring' systems which may due to their closed set of algorithms produce a result which is unfairly prejudicial to the data subject, such as for instance in cases of military personnel who frequently move address, a factor which impacts negatively on creditworthiness.

Finally, under s. 14 the data subject is given a strong and wide-ranging right to correct or destroy data relating to them. To enforce the right under s. 14 the data subject must apply to the court. The court may then 'order the data controller to rectify, block, erase or destroy those data and any other personal data in respect of which he is the data controller and which contain an expression of opinion which appears to the court to be based on the inaccurate data.' In truth application to the court under s. 14 is very much a last resort which both data subjects and data controllers wish to avoid. In the ten years the Act has been in force s. 14 has only been used on seven occasions. In truth it is in the interests of data controllers to have accurate and up-to-date information: data is only valuable if it is accurate. A simple request to a data controller to delete inaccurate data, or to update details is usually well received and if the data controller does not comply the data subject may enrol the assistance of the Office of the Information Commissioner who may be able to broker a deal. Section 14 is therefore a long-stop provision designed to be used where parties cannot broker a reasonable settlement.

18.7 **State supervision of data controllers**

If the data controller acts unreasonably, either in response to data subject requests or by processing data in breach of the data protection principles, it is the responsibility of the Office of the Information Commissioner in the first instance to take action. Much of the enforcement provisions of the 1998 Act have their root in the old 1984 procedures with Information Notices, Enforcement Notices, and the Information Tribunal central to the new regime.

The Information Commissioner's first line of control is of course the notification procedure. By ss. 17 and 21 it is an offence to process personal data without first notifying the Information Commissioner. Obviously there have to be exemptions to this rule in the information society or everyone would be required to submit for notification as even the simple everyday task of storing a friend's mobile phone number, email, or address in your phone would constitute processing personal data. This is why s. 36 states: 'Personal data processed by an individual only for the purposes of that individual's personal, family or household affairs (including recreational purposes) are exempt from the data protection principles and the provisions of Parts II and III.' In addition to this there are numerous further exceptions which assist in the management of the notification procedure and exempt a number of public interest and public

---

[75] DPA 1998, s. 12(8).

policy procedures. Thus we find in s. 33 an exemption for processing for the purpose of research, history, and statistics, while s. 32 provides an exemption for processing for journalistic, artistic, and literary purposes including 'the special importance of the public interest in freedom of expression [and] publication in the public interest'. Most exemptions though are for processing carried out by public bodies in the discharge of their duties. Thus s. 28 exempts processing for reasons of national security, while s. 29 exempts processing carried out for the detection and prosecution of crime and for the collection of taxation revenues and s. 31 exempts the activities of a number of regulators such as the Financial Services Authority and the Charities Commission. The number and width of exceptions found in Part IV of the Act mean that an extensive proportion of processing may be carried out without notification. This, along with the fact that notification provides little practical information as to how data is being processed, means that the enforcement and educational provisions found in Parts V and VI of the Act remain crucial.

18.7.1 The information commissioner as regulator

The lower level regulatory functions of the Information Commissioner are to be found in Part VI. By s. 52 the Information Commissioner may make codes of practice. These are non-binding guidelines designed to form a template for good practice within an industry sector. The Commissioner has issued a number of such guidelines in industry sectors such as CCTV, health, education, and marketing. In addition a number of general codes cover subjects such as data security, information sharing, and dealing with enquiries. This educational function provides basic guidelines for data controllers, but beyond this the Commissioner retains an important role in the direct investigation and prosecution of breaches of the Act. The regulatory framework is little changed from that seen in the 1984 Act. The Information Commissioner may begin an assessment at any time, but in particular under s. 42 a data subject may request the Commissioner to begin an assessment. Should the Commissioner deem an assessment to be necessary then the primary investigative weapon of the Commissioner is the Information Notice which may be served under s. 43. This requires the data controller to furnish the Commissioner with the information set out in the Information Notice within a time specified in the notice. Failure to comply with the notice is an offence under s. 47. The notice carries a right to appeal to the Information Tribunal under s. 48.[76] In addition to the standard Information Notice, there is a Special Information Notice which may be served under s. 44. This is used where the data controller claims an exemption under s. 32 for data processed in the pursuit of literary, journalistic, or artistic purposes. In effect the rights and responsibilities, including the right to appeal, are the same as for an Information Notice but such notices are used expressly to discover whether the processing being carried out by the data controller qualifies for the exemption given. In exceptional circumstances where either speed is of the essence, or where the Information Commissioner believes that serious abuses of the data protection principles are ongoing, the Commissioner may elect to request a search warrant under Schedule 9. This allows the Commissioner, and

---

[76] On appeal the Tribunal may uphold or overturn the notice. Under s. 49(6) there is a further right of appeal to the High Court/Court of Session on a point of law.

his staff, with the prior agreement of a Circuit Judge, to enter the premises of the data controller and to inspect any documents, materials, or equipment found therein. There are extensive protections surrounding search warrants under the Act and in general they may only be issued if the data controller has previously unreasonably refused entry to the Information Commissioner's staff. In addition to the usual search powers there is additionally the power under Schedule 9(3) to 'seize any documents or other material found there which may be such evidence'. This may be particularly useful in later issuing an enforcement notice or in bringing a prosecution.

Once the Commissioner obtains the necessary information under the Information, or Special Information, Notice, or following an on-site investigation, he will then decide whether further action is necessary. If he decides to press on with further action he may take a number of further actions. If, following the implementation of a Special Information Notice he finds that the processing in question is not exempted by s. 32 he may issue a Determination under s. 45 which details why he believes the processing is not exempt. Following a Determination he may issue an Enforcement Notice under s. 46 which restricts the processing of data until such time as the data controller complies with the requirements of the Act including notification. Alternatively, where the Commissioner is satisfied that 'a data controller has contravened or is contravening any of the data protection principles', he may serve an enforcement notice under s. 40. This is similar to an Information Notice in that it carries a right of appeal under s. 48 and failure to comply is an offence under s. 47, but it is much more wide-ranging in effect. The Commissioner may use an Enforcement Notice to restrict or event prevent processing of some or all data held by the data controller, or he may require to rectification or even destruction of inaccurate or out of date data. In effect an enforcement notice may make any requirements of a data controller to ensure compliance with the Act and the data protection principles. The issue of Enforcement Notices is worryingly common. The Commissioner keeps a record or Enforcement Notices issued and agreed formal undertakings[77] on the ICO website.[78] This data reveals that between March 2007 and March 2009 thirty-two undertakings or notices were agreed/issued. This is an average of 1.3 actions per month and although this may not sound many when one considers this the very tip of the enforcement powers of the Commissioner it demonstrates the level of noncompliance with the Act.[79]

Although the Commissioner's direct powers of enforcement are exhausted by the issuing of an enforcement notice, this does not signal the end of enforcement powers under the Act. By s. 60 the Commissioner, or the Director of Public Prosecutions, may instigate criminal proceedings for any offence under the Act. These includes the s. 21 offence of processing without notification, the s. 47 offence of failing to comply with a notice, the s. 55 offence of unauthorised access to data, the s. 56 offence of abuse of subject access rights, and the new monetary penalty notice provision found in s. 55A.

---

[77] A formal undertaking is where the data controller voluntarily agrees to make changes to their data processes without the need to issue a formal notice following an assessment. If the data controller fails to implement the undertaking a formal notice will then be issued.

[78] At http://www.ico.gov.uk/what_we_cover/data_protection/enforcement.aspx.

[79] Arguably more worrying are the data controllers involved. A large proportion are NHS trusts. Also several police forces and a number of financial organisations including leading high street banks.

These powers are not often used but can produce substantial fines including the recent £5,000 fine awarded against Ian Kerr, the founder of the Consulting Association which illegally stored and sold employees confidential data. Kerr kept a database of information on employees of major construction companies and offered to 'vet' staff before appointments were made. It is believed he operated the business for many years before being prosecuted by the Information Commissioner.

18.8 **Conclusion**

Data management and data processing is a ubiquitous activity in the information society. As Cate demonstrated the unique properties of digital data make it more valuable and therefore more commercialised than analogue data ever was. But with so many decisions automated and so much personal information now held in the form of proxy data the risk of harm to the individual is great. The Data Protection Act is our first line of defence against invasions of data privacy and against unfair and unreasonable data processing.

The Act is, as we have seen, less directive more a series of guidelines for data controllers and data processors. The heart of the Act is in the data protection principles found in Schedule 1 and in the interpretative provisions seen in Schedules 2 and 3. The application of the Act, due to its framework approach can sometimes seem counter-intuitive. To find Mrs Lindqvist responsible for processing data in an unfair fashion for placing some humorous anecdotes on a webpage while holding that the Medical Defence Union acted within the terms of the Act in processing Mr Johnson's data to determine whether to continue to offer cover to a client who had never made a claim on his insurance seems perverse; yet when one thinks of the Directive and Act as frameworks or guides for fair processing these decisions make sense. The MDU had a clear policy which was fair and reasonable; Mrs Lindqvist acted without thought, policy or permission.

There remains though the concern that this framework approach does little to protect the data privacy or individuals. The Act and Directive instead focus on data integrity and data security. This may be seen in the concerns of the Article 29 Working Party with regard to opt-in/opt-out boxes or in the decision of *Durant* where Mr Durant was denied access to data about himself (albeit in that case reasonably). The concern is that data protection laws, designed in the 1990s for an environment where most data was gathered in a traditional form and was merely stored and processed on computer are out of date in an environment where data is gathered from a multiplicity of sources and is processed and transferred automatically and instantly. This is the data environment we find ourselves in now, and this is the focus of the next chapter.

FURTHER READING

Books

P. Carey, *Data Protection: A Practical Guide to UK and EU Law* (2009)

F. H. Cate, Privacy in the Information Age (1997)

C. Kuner, *European Data Protection Law: Corporate Compliance and Regulation* (2007)

Chapters and Articles

D. Garrie & R. Wong, 'The Future of Consumer Web Data: a European/US Perspective' [2007] *IJLIT* 129

A. Warren, 'Right to Privacy? The Protection of Personal Data in UK Public Organisations' (2002) 103 *New Library World* 446

A. Guadamuz, 'Habeas Data vs. the European Data Protection Directive' (2001) 3 *JILT*

19

Data and personal privacy

The digitisation of data effects not only digital information held on a computer or in a relevant filing system. It is also affecting how information is gathered, processed, and interpreted in the real world using 'enhanced surveillance'. Enhanced surveillance can take a number of forms from basic addition of digital storage and transmission facilities to CCTV systems to biometric tracking and threat assessment. It can also use a variety of tools from remote video surveillance tools such as CCTV, to tracking tools such as GSM and GPS tracking and data and identity authentication tools such as biometrics and RFID. By choosing a selection of tools it is possible for governments, or even in some cases private citizens, to track an individual, to monitor his behaviour, and even to target personalised advertising content to the location where that person is. This chapter will examine some of the technologies involved, discuss the challenge they pose to the current legal settlement and ask what, if anything, needs to be done to protect the rights of the individual against the forever developing technology of enhanced surveillance.

19.1 Enhanced CCTV

One of the earliest mass-surveillance tools was Closed Circuit Television, or CCTV. CCTV was developed during the Second World War to remotely monitor rocket tests. It was reportedly first applied as a security and safety tool on a public street in Oleon, NY in 1968. By the early 1970s experiments with CCTV in the UK saw it being used to monitor transport movements and some rail and underground stations. But analogue CCTV was relatively expensive to install and run and required constant monitoring meaning it was generally restricted to areas where either there was a risk of public violence, such as football matches, or where it could be used to monitor traffic or transport movements. According to Newburn & Hayman although the technology for mass CCTV was available in the 1970s 'metropolitan councils ... initially on ideological grounds and later on practical and financial grounds' objected to CCTV installation.[1]

In the 1980s their approach changed. The Government announced the 'Safer Cities' initiative which made government funding available for cities to spend on schemes to

---

[1] T. Newburn & S. Hayman, *Policing, Surveillance and Social Control: CCTV and Police Monitoring of Suspects* (2002), 15.

enhance city centre security.[2] Many smaller towns then followed the lead of the cities by paying for CCTV to be installed from local government funds.[3] By the mid 1990s, around eighty towns and cities had CCTV schemes, but this number is still far short of the over 530 UK towns and cities to have CCTV systems installed by the turn of the millennium.[4]

What prompted this sudden explosion of CCTV in the UK? Newburn & Hayman suggest a number of factors were at work including a shift in policy on the part of local authorities who now embraced CCTV and the savings it could offer; secondly they identify a shift in political ideology of policing led in part by the New York experience of zero tolerance. UK local authorities saw CCTV as an essential part of their new policy on crime prevention, but they also note that 'it was given further impetus as a result of the broadcast of electronic images taken at a Merseyside shopping centre of the "moment" at which 2 year old James Bulger was abducted ... even if CCTV had not saved the toddler, at least it had contributed to the identification of the killers.'[5]

For Newburn and Hayman, who were writing about the adoption of CCTV as a tool of crime prevention and investigation the word 'electronic' in that sentence was probably throwaway, but they had also identified another key driver of CCTV in the late 1990s. Analogue systems were replaced by digital systems which allowed for cheaper cameras which were more durable, smaller, and had a longer operating life. Also images could be stored to HDD rather than analogue videocassettes which allowed for lower operating costs. Digital CCTV could also be more easily enhanced and transmitted and so quickly, Fred Cate's four generic reasons for the growth of digital information and digital information management became true of digital CCTV.[6]

During the late 1990s and into the twenty-first century the installation and use of CCTV as a tool of law enforcement and public safety has been in a constantly upward self-reinforcing cycle in the UK. The more CCTV there is, the more public authorities and private bodies desire to install and use CCTV, until by 2002 the now infamous McCahill and Norris paper estimated that there were around 4,285,000 CCTV cameras installed in the UK.[7] Although their findings have been challenged,[8] estimates of the number of installed CCTV cameras in the UK range vary wildly from 1.5 million to 4.5 million.[9] The figures range so extensively because there is no database of users or licensing system required for CCTV. Whichever figure is correct three things are clear: (1) the number of cameras on UK streets and in shops, petrol stations, and car parks will continue to rise with an estimate suggesting the installed base will double by 2018;[10] (2) the UK has the highest proportion of cameras to citizens in the world with London being the most densely monitored city in the

---

[2] *ibid*,16.   [3] *ibid*.   [4] *ibid*.   [5] *ibid*, 17.

[6] These are discussed above at pp. 36–47.

[7] M. McCahill & C. Norris, 'CCTV in London' *UrbanEye Working Paper No .6*: http://www.urban-eye.net/results/ue_wp6.pdf.

[8] Channel 4 News, *Fact Check: how many CCTV cameras?* 18 June 2008: http://www.channel4.com/news/articles/society/factcheck+how+many+cctv+cameras/2291167.

[9] P. Fry, 'How many cameras are there?' *CCTV User's Group*, 18 June 2009: http://www.cctvusergroup.com/art.php?art=94.

[10] Security Park, *Number of CCTV cameras in the UK expected to double by 2018*, 2 July 2008: http://www.securitypark.co.uk/security_article261721.html.

world with its citizens being estimated to be caught on camera 300 times per day;[11] and (3) more and more cameras and CCTV systems will be enhanced in some way to increase their effectiveness by the use of digital enhancements such as pattern recognition, facial recognition, and fluid dynamics.

19.1.1 Pattern recognition: ANPR

The most common form of enhanced CCTV in use in the UK at the moment is pattern recognition. This is used extensively in transport management systems through the use of the ANPR programme which allows for automatic identification of cars by Automatic Number Plate Recognition.[12] The system is made up of several components. Primarily it relies upon clear and easily read car number plates. This is ensured by The Road Vehicles (Display of Registration Marks) Regulations 2001,[13] which sets out precise regulations for the design and display of number plates. These Regulations are designed to meet the needs of the ANPR system which uses a digital camera to capture an image of the number plate and then specialist software to extract from the image the vehicle number. This is then checked against a database which gives basic information such as the registered keeper of the vehicle, but also advanced information such as whether it has been reported stolen, has been declared to be off the road, or is untaxed or uninsured.

ANPR is used extensively by the police (most traffic patrol cars have an ANPR enabled surveillance camera) as well as by the highways agency. One common use of ANPR in recent years has been in 'weighted-average' speed cameras commonly used over extended stretches of motorways or other primary roads where road works are in place. One camera captures an image of the vehicle entering the controlled area and records its entry time, another captures it leaving the controlled area and the exit time. These times are then used to calculate an average speed for the vehicle over the fixed distance: if this average speed is in excess of the allowed limit a fine will automatically be sent to the registered keeper of the vehicle. The most widespread use of ANPR in the UK is though to police the London Congestion Charge zone.[14] This functions through the use of a fixed 'ring' of ANPR enabled cameras which capture the number plate of each vehicle entering the zone, supplemented by mobile cameras within the zone. The system then checks these plates against a list of exempt plates (such as for buses or taxis or zero emission vehicles), if the plate is not exempted it is placed on the 'chargeable register'. The vehicle owner has until midnight to pay his/her congestion charge fee: after midnight the congestion charge system checks the chargeable register for that day against the payment register. Any number plates on the chargeable register

---

[11] B. O'Neill, 'Watching you watching me', *New Statesman*, 2 October 2006: http://www.newstatesman.com/200610020022; BBC News, *The Statistics of CCTV*, 20 July 2009: http://news.bbc.co.uk/1/hi/uk/8159141.stm; S. Stecklow, J. Singer & A. Patrick, 'Watch on the Thames', *The Wall Street Journal*, 8 July 2005: http://online.wsj.com/public/article/SB112077340647880052-mG vd5MGVX8aM_8TMTf6F6nQe9pg_20060707.html.

[12] A detailed description of ANPR technology may be found at: http://www.cctv-information.co.uk/i/An_Introduction_to_ANPR.   [13] SI 2001/561.

[14] For details of the London Congestion Charge scheme see: http://www.tfl.gov.uk/roadusers/congestioncharging/.

not found on the payment register then generate a penalty charge notice which, following a manual check to ensure the data is accurate, is sent to the registered keeper of the vehicle.

With all ANPR systems a large amount of personal data is created as images of vehicles (and sometime occupants) are recorded at each camera point in the network. To reduce the potential privacy implications of such a system and to ensure compliance with the Fifth Data Protection principle which requires that 'personal data processed for any purpose or purposes shall not be kept for longer than is necessary for that purpose or those purposes'[15] most systems will automatically discard any images captured once the check is complete. Thus a weighted average speed camera may check thousands of vehicles per hour. Vehicles which do not exceed the speed limit will be immediately deleted from the system, only those vehicles found to be in excess of the limit will be retained (with the relevant images for the purpose of proof), similarly the London Congestion Charge system deletes images from its database once it is established the vehicle is exempt or that the charge payment has been made.

19.1.2 Pattern recognition: biometrics

ANPR is not the only enhanced CCTV system in use in the UK currently. There are a number of systems both in use and in trial which monitor for suspicious movements using pattern recognition systems.

One of the best known was Ipsotek's Intelligent Pedestrian Surveillance system previously used on the London Underground. This system monitors movements and items to try and predict criminal and terrorist activity as well as potential suicides. The system works by comparing the movements and actions of individuals on platforms against pre-programmed normal parameters. Once deviation from those normal parameters is detected the system can alert staff in the control room who may investigate. Although full details of the system are not in the public domain it is believed that for example it can help identify passengers who may be a suicide risk by the different patterns of behaviour a suicidal individual follows to those of a 'normal' passenger. It can also identify unattended baggage and may be able to identify individuals loitering with criminal intent. The system worked to some extent on the underground because of the highly regulated nature of the underground network. From entry at the barriers to exit from the network users are under the management of Transport for London. This is seen in the environment of the tube station with one-way networks and 'entry' and 'exit' tunnels from platforms, from the tube etiquette promoted by TfL and by the nature of the system which sees most people follow a single path from entrance to platform and then get on the first available train. Thus someone who walks against the natural flow of persons *may* be a pickpocket, someone who loiters on the platform *may* be considering suicide while someone who abandons a bag *may* be a terrorist. The system cannot tell someone *is* a pickpocket, terrorist, or suicide risk, it merely alerts staff who are trained to make judgements based on the situation. The Ipsotek system unfortunately proved to be not as reliable as had been hoped and was abandoned

---

[15] DPA 1998, Sch. 1.

in 2005; however a second-generation system offering greater functionality, initially trialled in the New York subway, is now in use in London.[16]

Systems such as the Intelligent Pedestrian Surveillance system are less effective out-with the controlled environment of the underground network. On the streets people often meander through crowds in an undirected manner; they often loiter and items are frequently discarded. Further whereas tube stations have staff on hand to investigate suspicious activity on the street the police may be some distance away. This does not mean enhanced CCTV is of no use on the high street or other public place. A number of systems are being trialled in the UK and overseas including 'The Bug' an intelligent camera system trialled in Luton, Chester, and Exeter which can measure a reported 50 behaviour traits that indicate whether somebody is acting or loitering in a suspicious manner and can then automatically track that individual over an extended distance by CCTV,[17] and 'MEDUSA' a system developed at Loughborough University which may allow computers to tell if someone is carrying a concealed weapon by mapping the movements and their gait.[18] The possibility of tracking someone's unique walking style or 'gait' has even raised the possibility of tracking an individual seamlessly across a city using a sequence of CCTV cameras.[19] In addition to these biometric and pattern recognition systems many CCTV systems today allow for an older technology: facial recognition.

Facial recognition is a well established CCTV enhancement. It has been in development and use since the 1990s and has been deployed in several high profile situations. Possibly the highest-profile application of facial recognition technology was its use at Super Bowl XXXV held in January 2001 in Tampa Bay, Florida. A system was installed, at the request of local law enforcement, by Identix, a pioneer in facial recognition technology. The system took a photograph of every person entering the stadium as they passed through the turnstiles and compared them to an undisclosed database which is presumed to be the Tampa Police database of wanted persons. The system led to nineteen arrests being made at the event but later the police were forced to admit that some of those arrested proved to be false alarms, while no one flagged by the system was anything more than a petty criminal such as a ticket tout.[20] This reflects early problems with the reliability of facial recognition technology which was quite unreliable. As with any algorithmic facial recognition can produce four outcomes: Positive, Negative, False Positive, and False Negative.

The programmer is looking to maximise the 'correct' or actual returns while minimising the 'false' or negative returns to the left of the vertical axis. A false positive leads to someone being detained after being falsely tagged by the system as being a person of interest, while a false negative allows someone who should have been detained to pass unhindered. The result most sought by enhanced security systems is the true positive

[16] G. Evans, *Visionary Technology*, 13 February 2008: http://www.railway-technology.com/features/feature1611/.

[17] T. Kelly, 'The intelligent CCTV system that can weed out the villains', *Daily Mail*, 15 April 2007: http://www.dailymail.co.uk/news/article-448748/The-intelligent-CCTV-weed-villains.html.

[18] D. Bradley, 'Stars of CCTV Spotted Carrying Guns' *Science Base*, 14 April 2006: http://www.sciencebase.com/science-blog/cctv-gun-crime.html.

[19] University of Southampton, *Walk this Way*: http://www.soton.ac.uk/research/southampton-stories/medhealthlife/walk_this_way.html.

[20] American Civil Liberties Union, *Q&A on Face-Recognition*: http://www.aclu.org/privacy/spying/14875res20030902.html.

Figure 19.1 Potential outcomes of algorithmic tests

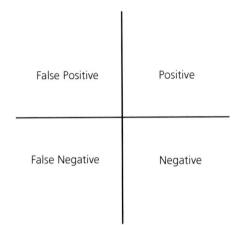

where a person of interest is apprehended. The problem is that achieving accuracy with facial recognition software is extremely complex. Human faces change all the time and environmental conditions such as lighting can have a dramatic effect. A 2003 study found that at that time the three leading facial recognition systems had a maximum accuracy rate of around 90%.[21] This meant that of the 65,000 attending the game that day potentially 6,500 were wrongly categorised by the system. Assuming an even spread of false positives and negatives there were potentially 3,250 other persons of interest in the stadium which the system missed. Although this is in fact highly unlikely it is almost certainly the case that more than nineteen persons of interest were missed by the system meaning it failed more than it succeeded.

Since 2001 the technology employed in facial recognition software has improved greatly. The 2006 Face Recognition Grand Challenge showed accuracy rates were approaching 99%, the minimum necessary for widespread application.[22] The technology continues to improve through the application of high-definition cameras and high resolution scans with the most accurate systems now able to distinguish between identical twins.[23] But environmental factors continue to affect the accuracy of facial recognition technology with one researcher noting that 'face recognition has been getting pretty good at full frontal faces and 20 degrees off, but as soon as you go towards profile, there've been problems'.[24] This is because most facial recognition programs map fixed points on the face seen most clearly in a full frontal image: they include the distance from the bridge of the nose to the eyes, the distance from the bridge of the nose to the ears, and many more calculations using the chin, nose, eyes, ears, and mouth. In profile

---

[21] Talkleft, *Facial Recognition Systems: New Accuracy Study*, 21 March 2003: http://www.talkleft.com/story/2003/03/21/454/98977.

[22] M. Williams, 'Better Face-Recognition Software', *MIT Technology Review*, 30 May 2007: http://www.technologyreview.com/Infotech/18796/?a=f.   [23] *ibid.*

[24] Ralph Gross, quoted in Williams, *ibid.*

these calculations are lost as half of the face is obscured while the fixed distances for the parts of the face visible are obscured by the profile of the face. This does not mean that facial recognition cannot be achieved with a face in profile, just that different measurements are needed.

This problem has limited the commercial application of facial recognition systems. There is though one widespread use of the technology currently in protecting frontiers at border control posts. Border control posts are tightly controlled environments where the individual can be directed to stand directly in front of a camera. This allows for a full-on facial image to be captured and used for identification. This system is in use throughout the EU with cameras installed at passport control posts at several major ports and airports. The system captures an image of the person standing in front of the immigration official. This image is then checked against the data held on the individual's biometric passport (if they have one) to confirm the individual presenting the passport is the authorised holder. This system forms the centrepiece of the Commission's 2008 Communication on entry/exit systems for *bona fide* travellers and electronic travel authentication.[25] Here the Commission states its intention that there should be an automated border control system for EU citizens moving between EU member states.

> **→ Highlight** Automated Border Controls
>
> The introduction of Automated Border Control systems can enable the automated verification of travellers' identity without the intervention of border guards. A machine reads the biometric data contained in the travel documents or stored in a system or database and compares them against the biometrics of the traveller, accelerating border checks by creating automated separate lanes replacing the traditional control booth.
>
> Commission Communication on entry/exit systems Com(2008) Final, 6.

This approach has been criticised by human rights pressure group Privacy International who believe it is a method to covertly track millions of travellers, and who are concerned that the technology is not proven and that the data held on verification databases could be open to abuse.[26]

19.1.3 Regulating CCTV: the code of practice

Despite the challenges that enhanced CCTV offers to individual privacy and liberty there is at the time of writing no specific regulation of enhanced CCTV in the UK. Instead the operation of some CCTV, including usually enhanced CCTV, is regulated by the Data Protection Act. When a CCTV image is recorded, or processed by a computer as part of an enhanced CCTV system it may be classified as personal data under the Act and as a result operators of CCTV systems must comply with the Data Protection Act and

---

[25] Com(2008) Final: http://www.privacyinternational.org/issues/borders/eu/CCE-Entry_Exit.pdf.
[26] See: http://www.privacyinternational.org/article.shtml?cmd[347]=x-347-560378.

Principles.[27] Obviously it is not possible to seek permission of each data subject captured on camera so CCTV should only be used where one of the other conditions precedent for the processing of data is permitted by Schedule 2 of the Act.

Most commonly processing is carried out by police and local authorities in accordance with statutory duties and thus is permissible as being 'necessary for compliance with any legal obligation to which the data controller is subject'. In addition to public sector CCTV though there is a large body of private sector CCTV operated by banks, supermarkets, operators of shopping centres, and transport providers. The operation of such CCTV is usually justified on grounds of public safety and thus is 'necessary in order to protect the vital interests of the data subject'. When CCTV images are recorded and stored then by Principle 7 'appropriate technical and organisational measures [must] be taken against unauthorised or unlawful processing of personal data and against accidental loss or destruction of, or damage to, personal data', while by Principle 5 'personal data processed for any purpose or purposes [should] not be kept for longer than is necessary for that purpose or those purposes' and by Principle 3 'personal data [should] be adequate, relevant and not excessive in relation to the purpose or purposes for which they are processed.' The complexity of treating images of individuals as 'personal data' and complying with the Data Protection Principles in this area are such that the Information Commissioner's Office has issued a CCTV Code of Practice to assist both CCTV operators and members of the public.

The Code of Practice was first issued in 2000 and then revised and reissued in 2008, in part in response to the growing number of enhanced CCTV systems in use. As its name suggests the code is not in itself a set of rules, but is rather guidance on how to comply with the Data Protection Act and the privacy requirements of the Human Rights Act 1998. The code opens by drawing a distinction between the domestic operation of CCTV on private premises and CCTV in public places. By s. 36 of the Data Protection Act 'Personal data processed by an individual only for the purposes of that individual's personal, family or household affairs (including recreational purposes) are exempt from the data protection principles.' This is translated in the Code of Practice as 'The use of cameras for limited household purposes is exempt from the DPA. This applies where an individual uses CCTV to protect their home from burglary, even if the camera overlooks the street or other areas near their home. Images captured for recreational purposes, such as with a mobile phone, digital camera or camcorder, are also exempt.'[28] The Code goes on to explain that all other private uses of CCTV will ordinarily be covered by the Data Protection Act, but that covert surveillance by law enforcement bodies is not, being separately regulated by the Regulation of Investigatory Powers Act 2000.

With this general guidance of applicability done the code goes on to give advice on all aspects of CCTV use. It suggests CCTV should only be used where its application is proportionate to the potential harm it seeks to avoid, noting that 'CCTV can be privacy intrusive,

---

[27] It should be noted that where CCTV is merely passive, that is there is simply observation of the CCTV system but no processing or storing of images takes place the Data Protection Act will not usually apply.

[28] Information Commissioner's Office *CCTV Code of Practice, Revised Edition 2008*, 5: http://www.ico.gov.uk/upload/documents/library/data_protection/detailed_specialist_guides/ico_cctvfinal_2301.pdf.

as it is capable of putting a lot of law-abiding people under surveillance and recording their movements as they go about their day to day activities. You should carefully consider whether to use it; the fact that it is possible, affordable or has public support should not be the primary motivating factor. You should take into account what benefits can be gained, whether better solutions exist, and what effect it may have on individuals.'[29]

Where the aims of the CCTV operator may be achieved without CCTV use it is suggested the alternative should be used. If though CCTV is necessary then it is clearly advised that CCTV cameras should be sited where they are least invasive to the general public and must not 'view areas that are not of interest and are not intended to be the subject of surveillance, such as individuals' private property.'[30] In addition CCTV operators must consider whether it is possible to limit the hours of operation of their CCTV system, and must periodically review its use to ensure that the continued use of CCTV is still necessary. CCTV operators are further exhorted to ensure security and accuracy of images captured and stored is ensured with advice to ensure wireless networks are secure, date and time stamps are accurate, and CCTV control rooms are secure.[31] Finally the Code proposed good practice for the storing and retention of images as well as systems for administering the CCTV system. CCTV operators are advised that access to stored images should be restricted to authorised persons and should be kept in a secure location and that although 'the DPA does not prescribe any specific minimum or maximum retention periods which apply to all systems or footage ... you should not keep images for longer than strictly necessary to meet your own purposes for recording them.'[32] The Code gives some examples of 'strictly necessary' periods:

> **⊛ Examples** Necessary Retention of CCTV Images
>
> 1. A system installed to prevent fraud being carried out at an ATM may need to retain images for several weeks, since a suspicious transaction may not come to light until the victim gets a bank statement.
>
> 2. Images from a town centre system may need to be retained for enough time to allow crimes to come to light, for example, a month. The exact period should be the shortest possible, based on your own experience.
>
> 3. A small system in a pub may only need to retain images for a shorter period of time because incidents will come to light very quickly. However, if a crime has been reported to the police, you should retain the images until the police have time to collect them.

The fair administration of CCTV systems is a major concern of the Code of Practice. It provides that CCTV operators must clearly signpost that CCTV surveillance is in operation. The signs should be clearly visible and should contain the contact details of the CCTV operator and the reasons for which CCTV is being used at that location. The Code notes that signs are particularly important where 'the cameras themselves are very

---

[29] *ibid*, 6.   [30] *ibid*, 9.   [31] *ibid*, 10–11.   [32] *ibid*, 14.

discreet, or in locations where people might not expect to be under surveillance' and 'as a general rule, signs should be more prominent and frequent where it would otherwise be less obvious to people that they are on CCTV.'[33] In particular 'in areas where people have a heightened expectation of privacy, such as changing rooms or toilet areas, cameras should only be used in the most exceptional circumstances where it is necessary to deal with very serious concerns. In these cases, you should make extra effort to ensure that those under surveillance are aware.'[34] Where images are gathered CCTV operators are reminded they have to comply with subject access rights under s. 7 of the Data Protection Act and as such are advised to have a subject access policy to help them comply with such requests.[35] Finally operators of CCTV are advised to carry out periodic Data Protection audits to ensure they remain compliant with the Act.[36]

Although wide-ranging the Code is entirely directive. It merely suggests to CCTV operators how to ensure compliance with the Data Protection Act through good practice: in other words there is no specific UK legislation to regulate the CCTV industry. This has been heavily criticised by commentators who point out that CCTV is unusually intrusive and in form is rather different to other forms of personal data as it 'captures the person' in a way other forms of data cannot.

Lynsey Dubbeld in her paper *Observing bodies: Camera surveillance and the significance of the body*, notes that 'the use of camera surveillance implies an inbuilt asymmetry with respect to the embodiment of observers and the observed. The camera operators are hidden from view: their bodies are beyond scrutiny because in the control room they are physically separated from the observed populations. The observants, on the other hand, are radically exposed: their bodies are revealed through the camera system and put on display on the control room monitors.'[37] Dubbeld notes that data protection laws do little to redress this imbalance: 'Data protection laws have meant to limit the use and storage of personal data in camera systems and redress the imbalance between data processing organisations and data subjects. Nevertheless, the surveilling organisations possess considerably more information on the targets of CCTV than those subjected to the camera gaze (for instance through management information systems keeping track of incidents captured on tape), and more instruments and techniques for data processing (for example through "rogues galleries" printed from electronic sources).'[38]

In his paper Thomas Murphy notes that 'the Act is (necessarily) too generalised to consider the specific nuances of CCTV', this he notes is not in of itself a problem but when combined with the CCTV Code of Practice, which he labels a quasi-judicial intervention, it leads to confusion and 'confusion and uncertainty are not traditionally regarded as characteristics of effective legislation and may instead result in failure to meet actual obligations under the legislation and may dissuade data subjects from exercising their rights.'[39] Because of these problems Murphy believes there is insufficient oversight of CCTV systems and their operators in the UK.[40]

---

[33] *ibid*, 15.   [34] *ibid*, 9.   [35] *ibid*, 15–16.   [36] *ibid*, 8.
[37] L. Dubbeld 'Observing bodies: Camera surveillance and the significance of the body' (2003) 5 *Ethics and Information Technology* 151, 154.   [38] *ibid*.
[39] T. Murphy 'Teeth, But a Questionable Appetite: The Information Commissioner's Code of Practice and the Regulation of CCTV Surveillance' (2007) 21 *IRLCT* 129, 138.   [40] *ibid*.

It is therefore not surprising that CCTV, and in particular the regulatory regime surrounding CCTV, should feature heavily in the 2009 *Report of the House of Lords Constitution Committee on Surveillance: Citizens and the State*.[41] Here their Lordships found that 'there are few restrictions on the use of public area CCTV cameras in the UK'.[42] Of particular concern was that 'as the DPA only governs how information that has been recorded and stored is dealt with, in principle it does not apply to situations where cameras are used for observation only and where no recording is made. As a consequence, local authorities and the police are in principle free to use CCTV cameras for general, unrecorded surveillance.'[43] Noting that recent European moves, in particular the Venice Commission,[44] had proposed that new, strict CCTV regimes were needed to protect the privacy of citizens the Report recommended that 'the Government should propose a statutory regime for the use of CCTV by both the public and private sectors, introduce codes of practice that are legally binding on all CCTV schemes and establish a system of complaints and remedies. This system should be overseen by the Office of Surveillance Commissioners in conjunction with the Information Commissioner's Office.'[45]

The Government responded to the Report on 13 May 2009.[46] In this response the Government noted that it launched a National CCTV Strategy in October 2007 and as part of this strategy 'the Policing Minister indicated the Government's support for the recommendation that there should be a national body to oversee the use and deployment of CCTV. The National CCTV Strategy Programme Board is currently considering what form that body might take.'[47]

This is a polite way of saying the Government intends to take no action to change the current regulatory regime surrounding CCTV systems at this time: however this may soon be a moot issue. Although technologies which make use of pattern tracking and recognition continue to grow and develop, the apparent weaknesses in facial recognition technology seem to already be consigning it to niche applications. The EU biometric passport for Schengen states (i.e. all EU states except the UK and Ireland) which originally contained only a digitised facial image now also contains fingerprint data (the UK is considering adding fingerprint data to UK passports). This, rather than facial recognition, will form the foundation of automated border controls. The problem with facial recognition is that it was an early enhanced technology but the complexity of recognising the human face in real time and in complex environmental conditions has seen the technology overtaken by simple biometrics such as fingerprints, and more recently by complex biomechanical systems such as gait tracking, as

[41] 2009 HL 18: http://www.publications.parliament.uk/pa/ld200809/ldselect/ldconst/18/18.pdf.
[42] *ibid* [213].
[43] *ibid*. It should be noted though that processing of information in an enhanced CCTV system would probably lead to the application of the DPA. If however that data is not retained the application of the Act will be extremely limited.
[44] European Commission for Democracy Through Law (Venice Commission), Opinion on Video Surveillance in Public Places by Public Authorities and the Protection of Human Rights, March 2007: http://www.venice.coe.int/docs/2007/CDL-AD(2007)014-e.asp.
[45] 2009 HL 18, [219].
[46] Secretary of State for Justice, *The Government Response to the House of Lords Select Committee on the Constitution's Report Surveillance: Citizens and the State*, 13 May 2009, Cm 7616: http://www.parliament.uk/documents/upload/GovernmentResponseSurveillance.pdf.   [47] *ibid*, 11.

discussed above. Further cheaper and simpler systems to track and monitor individuals are being developed which rely upon simply tracking items carried by individuals such as mobile phones, passports, or identity cards. At the heart of many of these are two related technologies Near Field Communication (NFC) and Radio Frequency Identification (RFID).

19.2 **RFID tracking**

The already discussed EU biometric passport makes use of RFID technology. This technology allows for developers to build what is known as 'the internet of things', a network in which physical objects can communicate with network systems to integrate the virtual world with the physical world.[48] If you have a UK passport issued after March 2006 it will have a small computer chip surrounded by a length of coiled copper wire on the last page (see Figure 19.2).

This is a Radio Frequency Identifier Chip or RFID. The chip contains a small amount of ROM memory and a simple activation and transmission programme. It needs no power to function meaning it can be miniaturised. When the chip passes a chip reader device radio waves transmitted by the chip reader are captured by the antenna. These radio waves provide enough power to activate the chip. The chip then transmits its data back to the reader.

Initially designed as an asset tracking tool to replace the barcode RFIDs now have a number of applications. At the most basic level they are used by supermarkets and other stores to track stock levels and to function as a basic security device (RFIDs not deactivated at checkouts set off alarms), but they have a number of roles which are more interesting. They are used on a number of near field communication devices such

Figure 19.2 RFID Chip in UK biometric passport

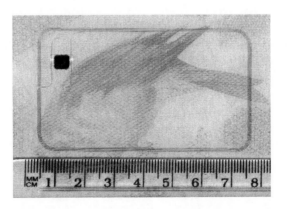

[48] For more on this see L. Yan *et al.* (eds) *The Internet of Things* (2008).

as smart travel cards and contactless payment systems; they can be implanted into pets or commercial farm animals allowing for identification or as part of a pet passport scheme. They have been used track passenger luggage in airports, to track high value casino chips on the casino floor, for timing competitors in races such as the London Marathon, for automated payment systems on toll roads, and for tracking and keeping safe children in amusement parks.

Probably the most controversial use of RFID though is human implantable RFID. The RFID chip can be enclosed in a silicate glass capsule to prevent rejection and then be implanted under the skin. In 1998 Kevin Warwick, Professor of Cybernetics at Reading University, implanted an RFID chip which allowed him to open secure doors and turn on lights and heating with a wave of his arm. In the years that have followed RFID chips have been implanted in humans to contain medical data and records when in hospital and have been implanted in some Alzheimer's sufferers in Florida to assist authorities should they be found unattended in public. It has been reported that in the US where the Verichip human RFID system is approved for human implantation some eighty hospitals have elected to use the implantable VeriMed Patient Identification system as a means of linking patients to electronic health care records.[49] One club owner with clubs in Barcelona and Rotterdam has even offered the system to VIP customers of his clubs allowing them to gain entry to the VIP section of the clubs and to pay for drinks with a wave of their hand.[50]

The potential benefits, but also implications of RFID tags cannot be underestimated. Systems which are being imagined, and developed, which would allow for RFID tags to replace traditional identification techniques in secure environments: thus as already used in travel cards to ensure that only paying customers get access to the travel network an RFID tag could be attached to the staff uniform or name badge of staff in hospitals, airports, stations, and other venues which have public and private areas. The tag could be programmed to automatically allow or deny access to secure areas so that a cleaner gets access to general staff areas and cleaning supplies while a security officer is allowed access to areas such as the CCTV control room. Doors would open automatically allowing easy access and egress.

Other potential benefits include targeted advertising: an RFID tag sewn into the lining of a jacket could be read by advertising screens in tube stations or at bus stops and then display adverts targeted at the user based upon their clothing preferences, such as for items in the Armani sale for the person in the Armani suit and the fall fashion line from Gap for the person in Gap jeans. Some believe RFID tags may even allow for physical cash to be phased out reducing the amount of muggings and personal robberies. An RFID tag either physically embedded below the skin, or fixed in some form of carried device, could identify the user to shops and service providers allowing for immediate electronic funds transfers to take place from their designated bank account or credit (card) account. It is possible that the supermarket of the future will have no cash registers and few staff. You will be able to enter the store, place goods in your trolley (which will display a running total of goods bought), and then simply pay by walking out of

[49] I. Byles, 'Health-care chips could get under your skin', *Physorg*, 12 June 2006: http://www.physorg.com/news69341086.html.
[50] D. Hemment, *Last Night An Arphid Saved My Life*: http://www.drewhemment.com/2006/last_night_an_arphid_saved_my_life.html.

the store: the money being debited automatically from your account. Shoplifting will also become a thing of the past with anyone who tries to take anything out of the store being automatically charged for it: if they don't have enough funds to pay for the transaction the police and store security will be immediately notified.

19.2.1 **Regulating RFID**

Obviously though if such systems are put in place considerable safeguards would be required to protect the privacy of individuals: personalised advertising would possibly not be appreciated by the individual in the expensive-looking suit who is bombarded in public with advertisements for discount retailers while travelling around the city. Equally knowing your every move may be tracked by the authorities is not desirable to most. For these reasons RFID technology has excited a great deal of debate and discourse. In 2003 a joint position statement was issued endorsed by no less than forty-five privacy and human rights groups including the American Civil Liberties Union, the Electronic Frontier Foundation, and Liberty UK.[51] This identified five primary threats to personal privacy from RFID technology.

> **Highlight** The five primary threats to personal privacy from RFID technology
>
>   1. **Hidden placement of tags.** RFID tags can be embedded into/onto objects and documents without the knowledge of the individual who obtains those items. As radio waves travel easily and silently through fabric, plastic, and other materials, it is possible to read RFID tags sewn into clothing or affixed to objects contained in purses, shopping bags, suitcases, and more.
>
>   2. **Unique identifiers for all objects worldwide.** The Electronic Product Code potentially enables every object on earth to have its own unique ID. The use of unique ID numbers could lead to the creation of a global item registration system in which every physical object is identified and linked to its purchaser or owner at the point of sale or transfer.
>
>   3. **Massive data aggregation.** RFID deployment requires the creation of massive databases containing unique tag data. These records could be linked with personal identifying data, especially as computer memory and processing capacities expand.
>
>   4. **Hidden readers.** Tags can be read from a distance, not restricted to line of sight, by readers that can be incorporated invisibly into nearly any environment where human beings or items congregate. RFID readers have already been experimentally embedded into floor tiles, woven into carpeting and floor mats, hidden in doorways, and seamlessly incorporated into retail shelving and counters, making it virtually impossible for a consumer to know when or if he or she was being 'scanned'.
>
>   ➡

---

[51] The statement is available from: http://www.privacyrights.org/ar/RFIDposition.htm.

➡

5. **Individual tracking and profiling.** If personal identity were linked with unique RFID tag numbers, individuals could be profiled and tracked without their knowledge or consent. For example, a tag embedded in a shoe could serve as a de facto identifier for the person wearing it. Even if item-level information remains generic, identifying items people wear or carry could associate them with, for example, particular events like political rallies.

To alleviate these risks the position statement sets out five proposed minimum guidelines for RFID users as well as a number of proposed prohibited uses.

➡ **Highlight** The five proposed minimum guidelines for RFID users

1. RFID users must make public their policies and practices involving the use and maintenance of RFID systems, and there should be no secret databases. There should be no tag-reading in secret.

2. RFID users must give notice of the purposes for which tags and readers are used.

3. The collection of information should be limited to that which is necessary for the purpose at hand.

4. RFID users are responsible for implementation of this technology and the associated data. RFID users should be legally responsible for complying with the principles. An accountability mechanism must be established. There must be entities in both industry and government to whom individuals can complain when these provisions have been violated.

5. There must be security and integrity in transmission, databases, and system access. These should be verified by outside, third-party, publicly disclosed assessment.

The statement then goes on to suggest the following should be prohibited.

➡ **Highlight** The four proposed prohibited activities for RFID users

1. Merchants must be prohibited from forcing or coercing customers into accepting live or dormant RFID tags in the products they buy.

2. There should be no prohibition on individuals to detect RFID tags and readers and disable tags on items in their possession.

3. RFID must not be used to track individuals absent informed and written consent of the data subject. Human tracking is inappropriate, either directly or indirectly, through clothing, consumer goods, or other items.

4. RFID should never be employed in a fashion to eliminate or reduce anonymity. For instance, RFID should not be incorporated into currency.

The position statement is a powerful document. It brings together many of the leading human rights organisations of the US and Europe to agree a common position on this (at that time) fledgling technology. The potential impact of this technology seems to demand close legal scrutiny and regulation, but as we shall see some seven years on from the position statement regulation of this sector remains minimal.

In the UK regulation of RFID technology, like CCTV regulation remains primarily the preserve of the Information Commissioner, with the only direct legal controls on the application of RFID technology being found in the Data Protection Act. With the potential privacy implications of RFID being even greater than CCTV one would expect a robust regulatory regime would be developing around this technology but this seems not to be the case. At the time of writing the primary guidance from the Information Commissioner's Office on the interaction between RFID and the DPA is a seven page document *Data Protection Technical Guidance: Radio Frequency Identification.*[52] This notes that 'There are two ways in which personal data might be processed using RFID. First, personal data may be stored on the tags themselves, or linked to a database containing personal data. Secondly, if tags on individual items can be used to identify the individual associated with the item, they will be personal data.'[53] Rather alarmingly it then goes on to note: 'In other situations, there will be no data protection implications. In most of the current applications of RFID, there are few data protection concerns because the tags do not store or communicate personal data, and are not linked to an identifiable individual.'[54]

While this may be true as the technology stands, there are legitimate personal and data privacy concerns surrounding the use of RFID technology. It may therefore have been expected that the House of Lords Constitution Committee on Surveillance: Citizens and the State would take an interest in RFID technology. Unfortunately their report was rather thin on RFID applications.[55] In fact the Report omitted any systematic examination of RFID instead merely noting that they would make tracking and surveillance easier and cheaper.[56] Indeed Parliament has been rather quiet on the whole issue of regulation of RFID deployment and surveillance until relatively recently. Most Parliamentary discussion has surrounded the benefits of RFID as a system for tracking goods and the UK's status as a leader in the technology. In the few discussions which have taken place surrounding the development of the internet of things and pervasive computing UK Parliamentarians have tended to refer simply to The Privacy and Electronic Communications (EC Directive) Regulations 2003 and the Data Protection Act 1998. A prime example is Lord Sainsbury, Parliamentary Under-Secretary of State, Department of Trade and Industry who in July 2006 in response to the enquiry 'Whether [the Government] will introduce legislation to protect privacy in response to the growth of pervasive computing' stated 'My Lords, there are already in place regulations to protect privacy in the electronic communications field. The Privacy and Electronic Communications (EC Directive) Regulations 2003 and the Data Protection Act 1998 implement the relevant EC directives in this respect. The Government will keep this legislation under review as the use of technology develops over time.'[57]

---

[52] http://www.ico.gov.uk/upload/documents/library/data_protection/detailed_specialist_guides/radio_frequency_indentification_tech_guidance.pdf.   [53] *ibid*, 3.
[54] *ibid.*   [55] Above n. 41 and related text.   [56] *ibid* [51]–[52].
[57] HL Deb, 18 July 2006, c. 1117.

In fact, as we have seen the DPA is of minimal effect in regulating RFID technology, while The Privacy and Electronic Communications Regulations, with their focus on public telecommunications networks provide probably less effective public safeguards than the DPA. The problem is that policymakers do not yet see RFID as a threat to personal privacy. Mostly RFID is used in shops and supply chains to track goods, or in livestock and pets for tracking and identification. The application of RFID technology to track persons, to allow permissions (such as access to secure areas), or to produce personalised advertising seem futuristic, yet already Transport for London's Oyster Card allows for tracking of individuals as was demonstrated in January 2006 when TfL were able to reconstruct the last journey of murdered solicitor Tom ap Rhys Price and then catch his murderer on CCTV the following morning using his stolen Oyster Card at Kensal Green Station, just yards from where the murder occurred.

19.2.2 The EU action plan

While the UK Parliament has avoided debate of RFID technology discussion was taking place at a European level. Since 2006 the EU Commission has had a high level working group looking at RFID technology and the possibility of linking RFID enabled devices to the internet to create the Internet of Things (IoT). Finally in June 2009 the first major report of this group was published: *Internet of Things—An Action Plan for Europe*.[58] As its name suggests this does not outline the form regulation of RFID and NFC should take, but rather outlines a framework for future policy development in this area. The Action Plan opens by dismissing the concept that the development of the IoT should be left to the private sector: 'Simply leaving the development of IoT to the private sector, and possibly to other world regions is not a sensible option in view of the deep societal changes that IoT will bring about. Many of these changes will have to be addressed by European policy-makers and public authorities to ensure that the use of IoT technologies and applications will stimulate economic growth, improve individuals' well-being and address some of today's societal problems.'[59] From this starting point it goes on to identify six policy issues which require the intervention of regulators.

→ Highlight Six Policy Issues for RFID and the Internet of Things

1. Standardisation and technical management
2. Privacy and the protection of personal data
3. Trust, acceptance and security
4. Research, development and innovation
5. International dialogue, common standards and access
6. Waste management

---

[58] COM(2009) 278 final: http://ec.europa.eu/information_society/policy/rfid/documents/commiot2009.pdf.   [59] *ibid*, 4.

The fourth and sixth policy issues deal with narrow issues of funding, support for research and development and planning and will therefore not be discussed further. By contrast, the first and fifth policy issues, standardisation and international standards, are seen as a major issue for states regulators.

They deal with questions such as, who assigns unique identifiers to RFID chips, who sets industry standards for interoperability, and who ensures there is security of transmissions and data? The Commission recommends that the EU plays an active role in international efforts to standardise RFID systems by defining a set of principles which will underlie the IoT and by working with international bodies such as the International Telecommunications Union and the International Standards Organisation to develop 'an "architecture" with a sufficient level of decentralised management, so that public authorities throughout the world can exercise their responsibilities as regards transparency, competition and accountability.'[60] This is a long-term architectural regulatory function which will probably not produce results until 2012 or beyond given the number of actors involved.

More immediately though the Commission has set out specific aims to meet the requirements of personal privacy and data security (policy issues two and three). It has already recommended that 'Member States should ensure that (the RFID) industry, in collaboration with relevant civil society stakeholders, develops a framework for privacy and data protection impact assessments. This framework should be submitted for endorsement to the Article 29 Data Protection Working Party within 12 months from the publication of this Recommendation in the Official Journal of the European Union.'[61] In addition it has recommended that 'Member States should support the Commission in identifying those applications that might raise information security threats with implications for the general public. For such applications, Member States should ensure that operators, together with national competent authorities and civil society organisations, develop new schemes, or apply existing schemes, such as certification or operator self-assessment, in order to demonstrate that an appropriate level of information security and protection of privacy is established in relation to the assessed risks.'[62] In addition to these requirements the Recommendation contains a number of additional recommendations requiring member states to implement a series of transparency provisions including a requirement that operators of RFID technology, like CCTV operators, inform members of the public that they are being surveilled and the reasons for the use of RFID as well as details of what data is recorded and who collects the data.[63] In addition to these Recommendations the Action Plan notes that 'The Commission will launch a debate on the technical and legal aspects of the "right to silence of the chips" ... the idea that individuals should be able to disconnect from their networked environment at any time.'[64]

---

[60] *ibid*, 5.

[61] Recommendation on the implementation of privacy and data protection principles in applications supported by radio-frequency identification, C(2009)3200, Recommendation 4: http://ec.europa.eu/information_society/policy/rfid/documents/recommendationonrfid2009.pdf.

[62] *ibid*, Recommendation 6.   [63] *ibid*, Recommendation 7.   [64] COM(2009) 278 final, 6.

At the time of writing the UK Government is considering how to implement these recommendations. It is likely that the RFID industry will be asked to self-regulate in the first instance as required by Recommendation 4. This is supported by the Department for Business, Innovation and Skills' support for the CASAGRAS project,[65] an industry-led forum to discuss RFID technology and governance. The seventh CASA-GRAS white paper, *Socio-economic components of RFID usage in the Internet of Things*, advocates that regulation of the IoT be a partnership between governments, industry, and civil society groups in a fashion similar to the World Summit on the Information Society, recommending that there is established 'an international Internet of Things Development and Governance Forum [which will] undertake rapid research into the issues for ensuring and agreeing appropriate and effective governance, including the revenue and registration schemes that will be needed and the political framework that will be necessary to facilitate appropriate international collaboration.'[66] This medium-term aim seems to be supported by the UK Government and seems to suggest that public sector actors view the internet of things as being akin to the internet of bits: one best regulated by industry actors in partnership with standards organisations, states regulators, and civil society groups. The danger of this approach though is that as with the internet of bits what is created is under-regulated with concerns such as privacy and data security being relegated behind concerns of interoperability, access, and standards. As we have seen already the internet has for too long allowed data to be gathered or 'scraped' with little state intervention: if the internet of things is similarly under-regulated we may find every aspect of our lives, including where we go, what we wear, and who we meet being recorded and catalogued by private organisations. The development of governance structures in this area is therefore of vital interest to everyone.

19.3 **Data retention and identity**

RFID Tags and Near Field Communication can be added to any device meaning the internet of things and the internet of data begin to merge. One place where this convergence is already taking place is in mobile communications technology. As mobile phones are basically always connected handheld computers the merging of thing and data is already occurring here. In Chapter 22 we will see how augmented reality is allowing users of mobile phones to experience an immersive technology which blends the real and the virtual. By using built in GPS and cameras, smartphones such as the Apple iPhone and the Palm Pre can augment the real world environment. For example a user outside Buckingham Palace could have details of opening times, the history of the palace, information about the Royal Family, or details of the art collection housed inside displayed on her phone screen. Other simple augmented reality

---

[65] CASAGRAS is an acronym for **C**oordination **A**nd **S**upport **A**ction for **G**lobal **R**FID-related **A**ctivities and **S**tandardisation.

[66] CASAGRAS, *Socio-economic components of RFID usage in the Internet of Things*, May 2009, 21. http://www.rfidglobal.eu/userfiles/documents/white%20papers%207.pdf.

apps for the iPhone include Google Latitude which allow users to track their friends using Google maps or Grindr which allows users to find potential dates by tracking and displaying the details of other Grindr users near to the user and allowing them to chat over IM.

These are fledgling technologies and it is likely that in future mobile phones will allow us to be tracked very precisely and may, like RFID tags, transmit data about us to advertisers or businesses. Systems such as Google Latitude work by using the inbuilt GPS in most modern phones and it requires the permission of the user for so-called location services. Where GPS is not installed or is not functioning (say because the user is underground) then cell triangulation tracking (where the signal of the phone is triangulated using local cell towers) may be substituted. These systems are extremely accurate and in future could be linked to systems such as live camera feeds to track a person in real time.

Individuals have no right to track another unless that person has given their permission. In the UK the practice of so-called passive location technology, as used by Google Latitude and a number of other services such as *Trace a Mobile*, *Mobile Locate*, and *Child Locate* is regulated by an industry code of practice.[67] This requires that:

> ### → Highlight Code of Practice on Location Services
>
> 1. Location services must be consent-based and simple for consumers to understand and use with confidence.
> 2. Where practical, in the interests of simplicity, recommended industry standard text should be used for obtaining consents, sending alerts and stopping or suspending services.
> 3. Location services should not be used to undermine customer privacy and, in particular, should not be used for any form of unauthorised surveillance.
> 4. Alert messages should be sent at random to guard against consumers being located without their knowledge.
> 5. Location services should be easy to stop or temporarily suspend.
> 6. Advice on how to use location services and key safety messages should be readily at hand.

Interestingly there is no requirement that the person being tracked is informed each time a request to locate them is made. In 2006 *Guardian* journalist Ben Goldacre wrote a chilling piece entitled *How I stalked my girlfriend*.[68] In it he described how he had set up a location service on his girlfriend's phone when she was busy elsewhere in the house then tracked her for a week using a passive location service without her knowledge.

---

[67] Industry Code of Practice For the use of mobile phone technology to provide passive location services in the UK, 1 October 2006: http://www.mobilebroadbandgroup.com/documents/UKCoP_location_servs_210706v_pub_clean.pdf.

[68] *The Guardian*, 1 February 2006: http://www.guardian.co.uk/technology/2006/feb/01/news.g2.

During this time it appeared his girlfriend never received a random alert message as required by the code of practice.[69] This demonstrates the weakness of the code of practice. As alert messages are random there is no requirement one is sent every time the person is tracked. Further as there is no time requirement attached to alert messages one sent once per annum would meet the requirements of the code of practice. These services tend to be used by employers to track employees but as Ben Goldacre demonstrated it could easily be abused to track family, partners, or just about anyone. It is not impossible to imagine passive location being used to stalk an ex-partner or to track a current partner one suspects of having an affair.

Currently there is no government regulation of this area (absent the Regulation of Investigatory Powers Act) and no intent from government to intervene. It seems that passive location technology is seen as a niche application which has few privacy implications and which is self-regulated. But as the internet of things develops the ability of passive location technology to track individuals and even to track their movements relative to others provides massive opportunities for businesses to map social responses, characteristics of individuals, and to develop marketing strategies aimed at individuals and groups. It may be that regulation of private passive tracking will soon be necessary.

19.3.1 The regulation of investigatory powers act

Of course governments have long had the ability to track mobile phones both passively and actively.[70] Police and law enforcement authorities have the ability to track individuals in real time using either GPS or mobile phone cell triangulation and then to observe that individual using CCTV. They even have the ability to turn on the microphone of a mobile phone remotely to record conversations which the user may be having with others in a bar, house, or office.[71] As their powers of surveillance and data gathering are so extensive legislative controls are necessary to prevent abuse or unwarranted intrusion.

This is primarily achieved through the Regulation of Investigatory Powers Act 2000 (RIPA). By s. 1 it is an offence for any person (either a person involved in an investigation of a law enforcement body or a private person) to intercept any communication in the course of its transmission by means of a private telecommunication system. This covers not only telephone calls but also emails, SMS and MMS messages, and IM messages. It was s. 1 which brought the News of the World royal affairs editor to justice after he was found guilty of 'hacking' the voicemail messages of members of the Prince of Wales' staff in 2006.

---

[69] Mobile phone tracking, girlfriend stalking and the law, *Out-Law News*, 2 February 2006: http://www.out-law.com/page-6601.

[70] Passive tracking occurs when a phone is located or 'pinged' only when requested. Active tracking constantly tracks a phone or other device.

[71] There is no evidence UK authorities have ever used a mobile phone as a remote microphone in this fashion. In theory though it would be legal for UK authorities to do so with an interception warrant issued under s. 7 of the Regulation of Investigatory Powers Act 2000. It does though appear that authorities in the US have done this under a roving wiretap warrant: see D. McCullagh, 'FBI taps cell phone mic as eavesdropping tool', *ZDNet News*, 1 December 2006: http://news.zdnet.com/2100-1035_22-150467.html.

An exception is given in s. 3 where all persons have agreed to the recording of the communication, and by ss. 6–11 lawful law enforcement authorities may seek a warrant to intercept.

Part II of the Act regulates surveillance and is thus directly applicable to passive and active mobile phone tracking. Mobile phone tracking is termed 'direct surveillance' under RIPA, this is: 'surveillance [which is] covert but not intrusive and is undertaken (a) for the purposes of a specific investigation or a specific operation; (b) in such a manner as is likely to result in the obtaining of private information about a person (whether or not one specifically identified for the purposes of the investigation or operation); and (c) otherwise than by way of an immediate response to events or circumstances the nature of which is such that it would not be reasonably practicable for an authorisation under this Part to be sought for the carrying out of the surveillance.'[72] To carry out directed surveillance a public authority must have authorisation under s. 28 which may only be issued by an 'authorised person'.[73] The authorisation may only be issued in the prescribed circumstances,[74] and the authorised person must believe it to be proportionate to the potential harm. The prescribed circumstances found in s. 28 map closely to the exceptions to the right of privacy found in Article 8(2) of the ECHR and herein a vital component of the RIPA procedure becomes clear. In some ways we as citizens of the state have less to fear from state surveillance as we are protected by the Human Rights Act in our dealings with the state and state actors. RIPA was a necessary update to the law on surveillance and interception of communications in the UK given our newly acquired commitment to the ECHR. Private citizens are not directly regulated by the ECHR meaning that there are greater safeguards in place. While your partner may track your movements using your mobile phone and passive location techniques just by a few clicks of the mouse while you are asleep the authorities must carry out an evaluation of proportionality and make a case for directed surveillance to be authorised, which decision is taken by a senior officer or official and which is reviewable by the Office of the Surveillance Commissioners and ultimately by the European Court of Human Rights. That is not to say that the risk of extensive state surveillance using modern active and passive surveillance techniques is to be underestimated.

19.3.2 **Data retention**

As the war on terror continues security forces find themselves constantly stretched. The risk is that at some point their stretched resources mean vital information is being lost. This was illustrated in the immediate aftermath of the 7 July 2005 attacks in London.

---

[72] RIPA, s. 26(2).
[73] The full list of authorised persons may be found in The Regulation of Investigatory Powers (Directed Surveillance and Covert Human Intelligence Sources) Order 2003, SI 2003/3171 and The Regulation of Investigatory Powers (Directed Surveillance and Covert Human Intelligence Sources) (Amendment) Order 2005, SI 2005/1084. Basically for Police forces it is an officer of Superintendent or above, for GCHQ and officer of rank GC8 or above, for Mi5 an officer of rank 3 or above, and for Mi6 (SiS) an officer of grade 6 or above.
[74] These are: it is necessary (a) in the interests of national security; (b) for the purpose of preventing or detecting crime or of preventing disorder; (c) in the interests of the economic well-being of the UK; (d) in the interests of public safety; (e) for the purpose of protecting public health; (f) for the purpose of assessing or collecting any tax, duty, levy or other imposition, contribution or charge payable to a government department; or (g) for any purpose (not falling within paragraphs (a) to (f)) which is specified for the purposes of this subsection by an order made by the Secretary of State.

The attacks were committed by a small group of UK nationals who had obviously been in contact with supporters of terrorism but who had not been under surveillance. What security forces feared was that there were other cells ready to commit further attacks, a fear raised further after the abortive attacks of 21 July 2005. The security forces attempts to piece together the events preceding 7 July were hampered by their lack of available data. They wanted to know who the bombers were talking to, who they were emailing, and what information they were accessing online. To assist with future investigations the UK Government, as Chair of the Council of Europe, suggested new measures be taken to retain private communications data in case it were needed in future by security services or law enforcement bodies. The end result was the Data Retention Directive.[75]

This provided that member states could require telecommunications and internet service providers to retain certain forms of data for a period of not less than six months and not more than two years.[76] The types of data affected were all set out in Article 5.

➡ Highlight Data to be Retained

1. Data necessary to trace and identify the source of a communication: this is data such as the telephone number of the caller; the name and address of the subscriber or registered user; a user ID or an IP address allocated to a user.

2. Data necessary to identify the destination of a communication: this is data such as telephone number(s) dialled; call forwarding data; names and addresses of subscribers; the IP address, email address or user ID of the intended recipient of the communication.

3. Data necessary to identify the date, time and duration of a communication: this is data such as the date and time of the start and end of the communication; the date and time of the log-in and log-off of the Internet access service, together with the IP address allocated by the Internet access service provider or the date and time of the log-in and log-off of the Internet email service or Internet telephony service.

4. Data necessary to identify the type of communication: this is data such as the telephone or internet service used.

5. Data necessary to identify users' communication equipment or what purports to be their equipment: this is data such as the calling and called telephone numbers; the International Mobile Subscriber Identity (IMSI) or the International Mobile Equipment Identity (IMEI) of the called or calling party or the digital subscriber line (DSL) or other end point of the originator of an internet communication.

This data must be retained by the telecommunications or internet service provider for the prescribed time and must be made available to the relevant authorities upon a formal request. The UK implemented the Data Retention Directive in two stages, firstly

---

[75] Directive 2006/24/EC of the European Parliament and of the Council of 15 March 2006 on the retention of data generated or processed in connection with the provision of publicly available electronic communications services or of public communications networks.   [76] Art. 6.

The Data Retention (EC Directive) Regulations 2007 (now revoked),[77] and then subsequently the Data Retention (EC Directive) Regulations 2009.[78] The 2007 Regulations covered only telecommunications data; that is data relating to telephone calls made from fixed line and mobile telephones. They require that telecommunications providers retain session data for voice calls (that is the telephone numbers of the caller and recipient of the call, the date and duration of the call, the telephone service used, the IMSI and the IMEI of the both telephones and for cell phones the cell location in which the call was made and received) for a period of twelve months.[79]

The 2009 Regulations extend and revoke the 2007 Regulations to also cover internet communications. After repeating the requirements of the 2007 Regulations with respect to fixed line and mobile telecommunications, they then go on to require Internet Service Providers and Internet Access Providers to retain the name and address of the subscriber or registered user to whom an Internet Protocol (IP) address, user ID, or telephone number was allocated at the time of the communication; the DSL or dial-up number of the subscriber; the date and time the subscriber logged on and off from the service; email user ID details and the internet service used. Again this must be retained for twelve months.[80]

This is a new form of surveillance. It is not active surveillance, it is not direct surveillance, it is not even passive surveillance in the traditional sense. This is blanket passive surveillance. Everyone across the EU is having sessional data for all their telecommunications transmissions retained for between six and twenty-four months. This is only possible due to the massive storage facilities the information society offers and although in all likelihood this data will never be accessed for the overwhelming majority of citizens it raises questions of proportionality. Is it really proportionate to retain such a massive amount of personal data? Data which if accessed may be used to track where an individual was when she made calls on her mobile phone, record who she called and how long she spoke for. From this data security services may be able to find her on recorded CCTV, as well as the person she spoke to, and track her movements using a mixture of recorded CCTV and sessional data retained by her mobile phone provider. You may think this is not unreasonable given the harm of 7 July 2005 or in Madrid on 11 March 2004 but there is a concern that data retention marks a change in attitude of government and security services. Whereas the RIPA was about safeguarding individual privacy and autonomy the Data Retention Directive and related Regulations demonstrate governments willing to harness the power of the information society to gather extensive personal data and to store such data in massive databases in a form of mass surveillance.[81]

These concerns have further coalesced in the Home Office's Interception Modernisation Programme, a programme at the heart of a recent Home Office Consultation on

---

[77] SI 2007/2199.   [78] SI 2009/859.

[79] SI 2007/2199, regs 4 and 5. In addition reg. 5 requires that where a call is made from an anonymous pre-paid phone the service provider must retain a record of the date and time of the initial activation of the service and the cell ID from which the service was activated.

[80] SI 2009/859. reg.5, Schedule Part III.

[81] See, e.g. C. Walker, 'Data retention in the UK: pragmatic and proportionate, or a step too far?' (2009) 25(4) *Computer Law & Security Review* 325; G. Davies and G. Trigg, 'Being data retentive: a knee jerk reaction?' (2006) 11 *Communications Law* 18.

Protecting the Public in a Changing Communications Environment.[82] Although the Government announced that it 'has no plans to create a centralised database to store all communications data' it also concludes that 'doing nothing is not an option.'[83] As a result it proposes that instead it provides funds to telecommunications providers to allow them to 'not only to collect and store data but to organise it, matching third party data to their own data where it had features in common (for example, where it relates to the same person or to the same communications device)'.[84]

In this way telecommunications providers become data retention and processing agents for the Government, public bodies, and security services. In many cases it will mean public authorities will be able to access all the data they need by making a single request to one telecommunications provider: in real terms it is the contracting out of the government communications database. In their response Liberty note: 'the proposals contained in this consultation are highly intrusive. On its face, the consultation sets out plans for the creation of a number of mini-centralised databases of communications data to be held—but perhaps not controlled—by private companies. What's more, this proposal comes at a time when the distinction between communications data and interception of the content of communications is increasingly blurred ... As a result the proposals are even more intrusive then they first appear. On this basis, we have no choice but to reject these proposals on the basis that they would be incompatible with the right to private life as protected under Article 8 of the Human Rights Act 1998 (HRA).'[85] Meanwhile the Information Commissioner's Office in a hard-hitting response suggests the Government is being disingenuous. In reply to the question which alternative should the Government adopt (1) a centralised database; (2) do nothing; or (3) the preferred decentralised database the ICO notes: 'The consultation states that if the single store solution is rejected, then the remaining two options are the only other options available. The ICO would suggest that there is at least one further viable option available to the Government which has not been detailed in the consultation and which has been discussed briefly above ... Has the Government considered bringing forward legislation that would allow specified public authorities to request that this further communications data be collected only in relation to specified individuals, and possibly their associates, who have come to the attention of those authorities by other means? ... Such a targeted use of communications data could also simplify the day to day operational judgments of proportionality and necessity where applied to access such data, as these factors would have already have been assessed when the decision to start collecting such data was made.'[86]

---

[82] Home Office, *Protecting the Public in a Changing Communications Environment*, Cm 7586, April 2009.   [83] *ibid*, [3.2].   [84] *ibid*.

[85] Liberty's response to the Home Office consultation: 'Protecting the Public in a Changing Communications Environment', 3–4: http://www.liberty-human-rights.org.uk/pdfs/policy-09/liberty-s-communications-data-consultation-response.pdf.

[86] Information Commissioner's response to 'Protecting the Public in a Changing Communication Environment', [4.3]–[4.5]: http://www.ico.gov.uk/upload/documents/library/data_protection/detailed_specialist_guides/ico_response_home_office_consultation_20090715.pdf.

Whatever decision the Home Office ultimately makes it seems that the current government is seeking to ever increase the availability of personal data to public authorities and to the security services. There are several additional examples one could give of how they seek to harness the power of the information society to observe and track the activities of citizens but one final project deserves special attention. In 2005 the Government announced its intention to introduce a national identity card scheme for the purpose of 'creating safe and secure communities, and fostering a culture of respect.'[87] The Bill introduced became the Identity Cards Act 2006. This mandates the creation of a 'National Identity Register'.[88] The register is to contain the full name; gender; date of birth, place of birth, and if applicable date of death; external identifying characteristics and any previous names or pseudonyms by which an individual capable of entry is known.[89]

Entry on the register is not compulsory, or at least doesn't appear to be. By s. 2(1) 'An entry must be made in the Register for every individual who (a) is entitled to be entered in it; and (b) applies to be entered in it.' But if one examines s. 2(4) we find that 'an entry for an individual may be made in the Register (whether or not he has applied to be, or is entitled to be, entered in it) if (a) information capable of being recorded in an entry for him is otherwise available to be recorded; and (b) the Secretary of State considers that the addition of the entry to the Register would be consistent with the statutory purposes.' Thus the Secretary of State may compulsorily add individuals to the Register even if they have not applied to be so entered. This though will probably be a little used power as from 2011 (as policy currently stands) an application for a UK passport will also contain a 'voluntary' application to be added to the Register. The register will in this case be given your fingerprint data as an 'external identifying characteristic' and this data will be added to your ID card. Although currently the legislation does not require individuals to carry an ID card it would be easy to change this in future. Further if, as reported, the ID card contains an RFID chip, police (and other public officers) would be able to read your ID card from a distance allowing for a surveillance society of people and things.

At the time of writing it is hard to tell whether the UK National Identity Register and allied ID card will ever come into being given the extensive delays to date and the possibility of a change of government in 2010. What is clear is that should it come into effect, this, allied with data retention provisions would give the Government an unparalleled ability to monitor and supervise its people. This cannot be a good thing as government is based upon trust, and government must work for the people. The step from the information society to the surveillance society is short but the effects are potentially colossal.

19.4 **Conclusions**

The power of the information society is that it sets us free. We no longer need to travel to the local shops to buy goods or obtain services. We can have a tailored, personalised service based upon our previous actions and decisions and we can communicate more

---

[87] Queen's Speech 17 May 2005. http://www.number10.gov.uk/Page7488.   [88] s. 1.
[89] s. 1(7).

freely and more easily than ever before. There is though a price to be paid for this freedom. As the previous chapter and this one have shown the warning of Wendell Phillips that 'Eternal vigilance is the price of liberty' is probably of greater truth today than at any point in the last two hundred years. The very digital technology which sets us free also allows for perfect control and observation. CCTV, once a passive 'eye in the sky', can now enforce regulations such as the London Congestion Charge Zone regulations without the intervention of a human operator. New generations of CCTV will perhaps allow for the active surveillance of individuals across cities or even entire states. Facial and biometric recognition systems will take over from guards at borders with travel from France to the UK being allowed (or denied) at a press of the finger.[90] RFID has the potential to radically change our world allowing everything from smartcard enabled travel to the potential for security systems based on embedded chips (either embedded in clothes or even people) to a cashless society. Some of this may sound like science fiction but researchers are working on making it science fact. The problem is that this technology may not be making us freer. As suggested at points throughout this chapter and made clear in the final section it has the ability to control us much more tightly than even George Orwell imagined in his classic dystopia *1984*. The law cannot keep pace with technological development; it always lags some months or years behind. The internet of things is coming; we will become part of the network. What is not clear is whether this will give us greater or less freedom.

FURTHER READING

Books

L. Yan et al. (eds), *The Internet of Things* (2008)

V. Matyá et al. (eds), *The Future of Identity in the Information Society* (2009)

T. Newburn and S. Hayman, *Policing, CCTV and Social Control: Police Surveillance of Suspects in Custody* (2001)

Chapters and Articles

T. Murphy, 'Teeth, But a Questionable Appetite: The Information Commissioner's Code of Practice and the Regulation of CCTV Surveillance' (2007) 21 *IRLCT* 129

C. Walker, 'Data Retention in the UK: Pragmatic and Proportionate, or a Step Too Far?' (2009) 25(4) *Computer Law & Security Review* 325

L. Dubbeld 'Observing Bodies: Camera Surveillance and the Significance of the Body' (2003) 5 *Ethics and Information Technology* 151

---

[90] Of course human border guards will have oversight of the system.

PART VII

Future challenges for information law

Society continues to change apace. New technologies offer new opportunities and new challenges. Is the law ready for them?

20 **The digital public sphere**

    20.1 E-government

    20.2 The digital divide

    20.3 The democratic divide

    20.4 Conclusion

21 **Virtual environments**

    21.1 Virtual worlds, virtual people

    21.2 The virtual gods

    21.3 The game versus the law

    21.4 Conclusion: when worlds collide

22 **What way next?**

    22.1 Future developments

    22.2 Web 3.0

    22.3 Law 2.0

The digital public sphere

The Information Society provides unparalleled opportunities for social inclusion, individual empowerment, and the development of a truly dynamic and inclusive democratic space. Through these it offers our best opportunity to date of enshrining German sociologist and philosopher Jürgen Habermas's model of the public sphere within our society. The public sphere is a key component of democracy in the modern communications society. It was first defined by Habermas in his 1962 book *The Structural Transformation of the Public Sphere: An Inquiry into a Category of Bourgeois Society* as 'a place where everything became visible to all' through discourse between citizens.[1] This initial description being rather cryptic Habermas has continued to evolve his definition over the years with the classically accepted definition of the public sphere today being found in his 1996 text *Between Facts and Norms* as 'a network for communicating information and points of view (i.e., opinions expressing affirmative or negative attitudes); the streams of communication are, in the process, filtered and synthesized in such a way that they coalesce into bundles of topically specified public opinions.'[2] Habermas's use of language, as one would expect of probably the leading contemporary expert on the philosophy of communications and language, is extremely precise. This sometimes makes a simple understanding of his concepts extremely difficult. A rather simpler description of the public sphere is therefore offered by Gerard Hauser of the University of Colorado. It is 'a discursive space in which individuals and groups congregate to discuss matters of mutual interest and, where possible, to reach a common judgment'.[3]

The public sphere is seen as the mediating influence between two other spheres. The first is the private sphere (or in Habermas's language 'the private realm') which is the space the citizen has free from the influences of government and public authorities: it is the place where family is found, usually the home. Martin Heidegger, who taught Jürgen Habermas, believed it was the only place where the citizen could truly be himself. At the other end of the scale is the sphere of public authority. This may be equated to a regulatory or control sphere. Here continuous state activity forms permanent relationships between the various offices of state and the key private bodies such as

[1] J. Habermas, *The Structural Transformation of the Public Sphere: An Inquiry into a Category of Bourgeois Society* (1962, trans. T. Berger, 1989), 4.
[2] J. Habermas, *Between Facts and Norms: Contributions to a Discourse Theory of Law and Democracy* (1996, trans. W. Rehq, 1998), 360.
[3] G. Hauser, 'Vernacular Dialogue and the Rhetoricality of Public Opinion' 65(2) *Communication Monographs* 83 (1998), 86.

stock exchanges and media organisations. Private individuals who have no role in the sphere of public authority sphere are excluded from public authority because they have no office.[4]

The problem Habermas identified was that without a functional public sphere to bridge the divide between the private realm and the sphere of public authority government was likely to become a bourgeois space with democratic failings. The solution was to be found in places where public discourse could take place to bridge the divide: for Habermas this was typified by the seventeenth century coffee houses of London where discourse and political unrest could brew.[5] Habermas believes the ideal type of public sphere is characterised by an ideal speech situation. He develops this in his 1983 text *Moral Consequences and Communicative Action*[6] where he sets out three 'universals' for ideal speech.[7]

→ Highlight Habermas's Three 'Universals' for Ideal Speech

1. Any and every subject capable of speech and [social] action may take part in discourses.

2. Any participant may problematize an assertion. Any participant may introduce any assertion into discourse. Any participant may express his [or her] position, wishes and needs.

3. No participant may be hindered through coercion internal or external to the speech situation, in perceiving his [or her] established rights.

Nowadays it is often assumed that with a liberal media, full enfranchisement for the adult population, protected free expression, and an apparently healthy public appetite for political discourse the public sphere plays an active role within the democratic framework of modern society. But examined closely the types of political discourse found in even the most liberal of western democracies offer fewer opportunities for the unrestricted trading in political opinion imagined by Habermas as being the model of a true public sphere. Even within the free democracies of Western Europe, North America, or Australasia there are natural barriers to discourse. We see that opportunities for the proletariat to engage with the bourgeois are limited and controlled, with political hustings and meetings dominated by party activists or media organisations, while public monitoring tends to chill certain forms of public discourse,[8] while legal controls chill others.[9]

---

[4] See M. Durham & D. Kellner, *Media and Cultural Studies* (2006), 75.

[5] Habermas, above n. 1, Ch. 8.

[6] J. Habermas, *Moral Consequences and Communicative Action* (1983, trans. C. Lenhardt & S. Nichilsen, 1990).

[7] See J. Braaten, *Habermas's Critical Theory of Society* (1991), 44.

[8] Far right political parties such as the British National Party or the Dutch PVV tend to score better on secret ballots than predicted in opinion polls. This is because fewer people to admit to voting for such parties than actually do in secret.   [9] See Ch. 6.

The internet seems to offer an alternative form of public sphere, one where political discourse may more freely be exchanged between the proletariat and the bourgeois, and one where thanks to the pseudonymity offered speech is less susceptible to chilling effects. This attractive prospect has encouraged many academics to discuss the 'virtual public sphere' as an extension of Habermas's original public sphere.[10] In a debate which mirrors the wider regulatory debate between cyberlibertarians and cyberpaternalists others argue that the design of cyberspace may restrict participation in the online environment.[11] Thus, as with many other online freedoms we find that participation in the virtual public sphere rests on a knife edge as many of the threats discussed earlier in this book: threats to freedom of expression and discourse,[12] access,[13] and privacy[14] risk a lack of public confidence in the security of the virtual public sphere and in the freedom to take part in unfettered democratic discourse offered by the information society. This is not to say that the contribution the information society makes to the public sphere is to be ignored, or even undervalued. It affects our understanding of several areas of online activity which will be examined together in this chapter with the aim of taking a collective overview of how the information society is challenging the rule of law with regard to the regulation of political speech and content; and how the power of the network may be harnessed to assist with the dissemination of both political speech and public speech. It opens with a discussion of that most mundane of areas, of political speech communications between a government and its people.

20.1 **E-government**

The information society gives governments a unique opportunity to interact with their citizens. Tools for the distribution of information though government portals (web 1.0 government) have now been supplemented and even surpassed by interactive web 2.0 tools which allow citizens to search for jobs, claim benefits, enter and pay tax returns, make planning applications and objections, and to obtain health and travel advice and support, among others.

For governments the benefits are clear: the direct costs associated with the operation of public services are reduced as the numbers of benefit offices, job centres, and local tax offices may be reduced as central (online) services pick up the bulk of initial contact enquiries. In addition it allows for the provision of 24/7 support, impossible when one is dealing with local offices and impractical when using telephone call centres. It also allows for the implementation of open government initiatives as documents, including policy documents, consultation documents, reports of committees, and legal documents

---

[10] See, e.g. Z. Papacharissi, 'The Virtual Sphere: the Internet as a Public Sphere' (2002) 4 *New Media Society* 9; S. Vaidhyanathan, 'The Anarchist in the Coffee House: A Brief Consideration of Local Culture, the Free Culture Movement, and Prospects for a Global Public Sphere' 70 *Law and Contemporary Problems* 205 (2007); J. Slevin, *The Internet and Society* (2000).

[11] See, e.g. R. Diebert, J. Palfrey, R. Rohozinski & J. Zittrain, *Access Denied* (2008); J. Zittrain, *The Future of the Internet and How to Stop It* (2008).   [12] See Chs 6 and 7.

[13] Discussed in Ch. 3 and again in this chapter.   [14] See Chs 18 and 19.

including Acts of Parliament and Statutory Instruments, may be placed in online depositories allowing citizens to access these at any time and at minimal cost. These activities are more than just cost saving measures. As the American jurist Henry Perritt has demonstrated open government is central to the rule of law, civil society, and democracy.[15]

Perritt in particular believes that in the information society governments have a duty to distribute material in digital form as opposed to paper form for as he argues 'almost all business enterprises and intermediaries such as lawyers, the press, and interest groups use computer technology as their basic way of processing information. When information is available only on paper, it imposes additional burdens on them to translate it into electronic form.'[16] He goes on to demonstrate an additional benefit in having material available online: 'moreover, even individuals who do not use computer technology can benefit enormously from having public information available in electronic form, especially when it is available on the Internet. When such information is available to the Internet, a variety of electronic safety nets can function to help individuals obtain access to public information. These include not only public libraries but also a rich variety of intermediaries which can add specialised information value such as finding aids, pointers to other related information, and tags when the basic content is already available on the Internet. Regardless of whether custodial public institutions add value to the basic information they possess, they should make the basic content available on the Internet so that others can add value to it.'[17]

20.1.1 **UK e-government**

Perritt clearly demonstrates why the 'digital public sphere' is at the centre of democratic discourse in the information society. The UK Government has been at the forefront of developments in this field with a plan for a coordinated e-government strategy since the creation of the office of the e-envoy within the Cabinet Office in 1998.

The e-envoy's first task was to design a coordinated e-government policy for the UK and in April 2000 the office of the e-envoy brought forward their first major report *e-government: A strategic Framework for Public Services in the Information Age.*[18] The strategy document attempted to tie together four strategic aims of the UK Government: (1) to allow citizen choice in access to government services; (2) to make government and its services more available; (3) to afford greater social inclusion; and (4) to use information more efficiently.[19] To achieve these outcomes the government set itself the target that by 2005 all government services were to be electronically accessible, unless it was impossible for operational or security reasons.

Although a highly ambitious target, electronic access was given a wide definition to include communication by email and where appropriate mediated access though the use of a call centre or similar intermediary. At the heart of the report were the creation

---

[15] See H. H. Perritt Jr, 'Open Government' (1997) 14 *Government Information Quarterly* 397.
[16] *ibid*, 400.   [17] *ibid*.
[18] Cabinet Office: IT Unit, *e-government: A strategic Framework for Public Services in the Information Age*, April 2000: http://archive.cabinetoffice.gov.uk/e-envoy/resources-pdfs/$file/Strategy.pdf.
[19] *ibid*, [3].

of three internet portal services which could be used by citizens to access information relating to a wide variety of central or local government services: these portals are the Direct Gov portal *.direct.gov.uk/*, the rather less well known Local Government information portal *.info4local.gov.uk/* and Business Link portal *.businesslink.gov.uk.*

The portals were designed to provide a central access point for all citizens, businesses as well as individuals, to government services. Their design and construction were set out in a subsequent report of the Cabinet Office, *e.gov: Electronic Government Services for the 21st Century*.[20] Here the Prime Minister set out the government's ambitions:

> Electronic service delivery will be a key source of innovation. We can use new digital channels to deliver better quality services to the citizen—available 24 hours each day, faster, more convenient and more personalised. By doing so, we will also stimulate the market for e-commerce, by encouraging the widespread adoption of these new technologies and creating new business opportunities.
>
> I am determined that we should capitalise on these opportunities and that by 2005 at the latest, all government services will be online. Equally important is that by the same time, everyone should have access to the Internet, so that the whole of society can benefit.[21]

To deliver on these promises the government set aside £1bn for the creation of the electronic delivery service as set out in the report with a further £4m ring fenced to develop and build upon the original project.[22] The electronic delivery service or EDS was designed to make use of multiple access points including access by PC, by mobile phone, and by dedicated portals in libraries, job centres, and other public buildings.[23] The aim of the new EDS programme was to refocus government onto the citizens by recasting them as the 'citizen-customer' and borrowing from the private sector. In casting citizens as 'citizen-customers' the government identified four roles government plays for citizens and collected their EDS system around these roles. These are set out in Table 20.1.

The delivery of these services has seen an innovative mix of strategies, some more successful than others. Personalised services are the easiest to operate as the driver behind these is the citizen himself. There are a vast number of citizen-oriented personal services available in the UK including NHS Direct, Jobcentre Plus and Pathways to Work, and HM Revenue & Customs' Self-assessment Online Service. These sites and many more are organised by the Government's primary citizen information portal: Direct Gov.[24]

Direct Gov can perform a number of functions including matching services and pulling together services but it is probably most commonly used as a personalised gateway to government information. The site is organised around ten 'life experiences': (1) Education and Learning; (2) Home & Community; (3) Money, Tax and Benefits; (4) Travel and Transport; (5) Crime, Justice and the Law; (6) Motoring; (7) Employment; (8) Health and Well-being; (9) Leisure and Recreation; and (10) Rights and Responsibilities.

---

[20] Cabinet Office: Performance and Innovation Unit, *e-government: A strategic Framework for Public Services in the Information Age*, September 2000: http://www.idt.unisg.ch/org/idt/ceegov.nsf/0/0c05f1ab1e62510cc1256c8c0051965a/$FILE/e-gov.pdf.

[21] *ibid*, Foreword by the Rt.Hon. Tony Blair MP.   [22] *ibid*, [2.7].   [23] *ibid*, [3.2].

[24] Direct Gov went live in April 2004.

Table 20.1 Four categories of public service

Type of service	Function	Examples
Matching	Matching up citizens with specific services and other citizens relevant to them at a particular time and in a certain area.	Use the population's health records to identify trends and statistical correlations. This could then apply to individuals to give advice on how to prevent illnesses and conditions they might be more likely to get.
Personalising	Services that are formulated for the needs of a single individual and no one else. The individual or the service provider can shape them.	Inform citizens as they travel of the up-to-the-second integrated transport information relevant to their time and place. This could, for instance, help the citizen choose between different modes of transport. This can be delivered through a mobile phone.
Pulling together	Services that bring together in one place information on and services relevant to an issue or group of citizens.	A tax proposal service that draws together all relevant information on the citizen (from banks and insurance companies) then completes that citizen's tax assessment form and presents it to the citizen as a proposal, requesting signature.
Democratising	Typically services that allow citizens to express views.	Enable citizens to vote for their constituency MP from anywhere in the country, or abroad, through the Internet. The tally is instantly counted by computer, allowing a longer time period in which citizens can vote.

From egov: Electronic Government Services for the 21st Century at para. 4.9 and Table 4.2.

This is supplemented by sections relating to six 'audience groups' (1) Parents; (2) Disabled People; (3) Over 50s; (4) Britons living abroad; (5) Carers; and (6) Young People. Each of these 'experiences' or 'audiences' has a separate gateway which may be accessed from the home page and which is tailored to their needs. Many individual pages may be accessed from several different portals: thus by entering either via the 'Young People' gateway or the 'Motoring' gateway one may find their way to the necessary section of the DVLA website to apply for a provisional driving license.

Direct Gov tends to provide information in one of three forms:

(1) General information and advice: usually non-interactive websites containing government advice and information such as Foreign Office travel advice or the address for a local job centre;

(2) Personalised information or advice: interactive services such as NHS Direct's online health and symptoms checker. These interactive sites ask citizens to fill in questionnaires or respond to prompts to produce a personalised service; or

(3) Fully interactive services: these are sites which allow citizens to take advantage of government services or meet obligations to the state online. These include HM Revenue and Customs Self-assessment Online Service as well as the DVLA's license renewal service or Job Centre Plus's job search facility.

Even fully interactive services though merely reflect a digitisation of a previously extant relationship between citizen and state with the Direct Gov portal replacing traditional communications methods such as public advertising campaigns, mail, and telephone.

In comparison, the matching function offers us a glimpse into how e-government can produce a new experience for the citizen. The 'Parents' gateway allows access to the online admissions procedures used by local authorities to allocate places at primary and secondary schools. This procedure is much more than the digitisation of a previous relationship between state and citizen as the electronic admissions gateway allows parents a number of options previously not available including applying for schools places in neighbouring authorities. A similar scheme under the 'Health' gateway allows patients to choose healthcare from at least four alternative NHS hospitals if they are referred for specialist care, again these hospitals may be under the control of different NHS trusts to their local Primary Care Trust. At the time of writing this book, though, possibly the best example of matching services has recently arisen.

In July 2009 in response to the H1N1 Swine Flu pandemic the government launched the National Pandemic Flu Service (NPFS), available as an online and telephone service. The service was designed to give primary advice and care to patients in England and Wales who developed flu like symptoms. Information drawn from the site and the call centre were used to correlate information on incidences of swine flu, locations of 'hotspots', and ongoing advice to citizens. By visiting the NPFS site concerned citizens would receive advice such as 'estimates [suggest] there were 110,000 new cases of swine flu in England last week. This is only slightly up from 100,000 the previous week. This suggests that the rate of infection has started to slow. This may be down to the start of the school holidays and the launch of the National Pandemic Flu Service. There is no sign that the virus is becoming more severe or developing resistance to antivirals. The small number of deaths has mainly been in older children and adults with underlying risk factors. There has been a decrease in the estimated number of cases in five to fourteen year olds. Estimated cases have continued to increase in other age-groups and in the North.'[25]

This gives the populous up-to-date information in a way which would have been almost impossible in the pre-e-government era. In addition the site carried advice on how to reduce risk factors and how to diagnose flu and receive treatment. This information was only available in this form because of the power of the e-government portal, it is the archetypal 'matching' service described nine years earlier in *e.gov: Electronic Government Services for the 21st Century*: 'use the population's health records to identify trends and statistical correlations ... applied to individuals to give advice on how to prevent illnesses and conditions they might be more likely to get.'

By 2009 therefore the UK had a stable e-government platform offering matched and personalised services. Experiments with democratic and 'pulled' services were less successful. E-voting has become relatively commonplace since 2000 and the UK has experimented with e-voting at several levels including text voting and internet voting. The management of e-voting trials was placed with The Electoral Commission who

---

[25] Taken from http://www.direct.gov.uk/en/Swineflu/DG_177831 on Tuesday 4 August 2009.

operated a pilot scheme from 2002 to 2007. During that time they conducted e-voting pilots in local government and European elections in Rushmoor, Sheffield, Shrewsbury and Atcham, South Buckinghamshire, and Swindon. The largest trial was in local and European elections in Sheffield in 2003 when 174,000 citizens were given the opportunity to vote using the internet, kiosks, and mobile phones. Although the Sheffield trial initially appeared to be successful with 40% of voters choosing to use an electronic voting channel the trial revealed some potential problems with e-voting. [26] The biggest problem was security. In their final report on the e-voting pilot scheme in 2007 the Electoral Commission reported that 'there was an unnecessary high level of risk associated with all pilots and the testing, security and quality assurance adopted was insufficient. There was a general lack of transparency around the technology and its use.'[27] Additionally the Commission noted there were high costs for little increase in democratic participation: 'The additional costs for e-voting varied from approximately £600,000 to £1,100,000. The cost per registered elector also varied widely, from approximately £1.80 in Sheffield to £27 in Shrewsbury & Atcham. *The cost per e-voter was extremely high, varying from about £100 to £600.*'[28] This cost may have been acceptable for a large upturn in voter turnout but the report found that 'the majority of those who voted electronically are likely to have voted anyway via another channel',[29] while figures available publicly reveal that in the Sheffield trial there was only a 5.2% increase in voter turnout.[30]

As a result the Commission recommended that:

No further e-voting pilots are undertaken until the following three elements are in place:

(1) There must be a comprehensive electoral modernisation framework covering the role of e-voting, including a clear vision, strategy and effective planning. The strategy must outline how the important issues of transparency and public trust will be addressed and should outline the process by which a more cost-effective deployment of the technology can be achieved.

(2) A central process must be implemented to ensure that tested and approved e-voting solutions can be selected by local authorities. This could be achieved either through an accreditation and certification process or through a more robust procurement framework than is currently in place. This process must be used to enforce the required levels of security and transparency.

(3) Sufficient time must be allocated for planning e-voting pilots. This should be approximately six months between the time the supplier contract is awarded and the elections.[31]

The government has to date taken no steps to restart e-voting trials and with the recent announcement of Lord Bach that 'the Government currently have no plans to extend

---

[26] See E-voting: The people's choice, *Computer Weekly* 28 April 2005: http://www.computerweekly.com/Articles/2005/04/28/209588/e-voting-the-peoples-choice.htm.

[27] The Electoral Commission, *Electronic Voting*, August 2007, 3: http://www.electoralcommission.org.uk/__data/assets/electoral_commission_pdf_file/0008/13220/Electronicvotingsummarypaper_27194-20114__E__N__S__W__.pdf.   [28] *ibid*, 6 (emphasis added).

[29] *ibid*, 5.   [30] See n. 25.   [31] Electoral Commission, above n. 27, 10.

the use of e-voting to mainstream elections'[32] it would appear unlikely that progress on the democratising function of e-government will be felt anytime soon.

Little progress has been made also with regard to designing 'pulling' services. Individual citizen concerns about data privacy and data protection, married to concerns about data security which arose following the government data scandals of 2007,[33] meant that little was achieved in the first phase of implementation which saw the creation of Direct Gov and the e-voting trials. We have recently though moved into the second phase of e-government provision within the UK through the adoption of the Transformational Government Implementation Plan.

20.1.2 The ministerial declaration and transformational government

Although the UK could claim to have stolen a march on other governments with its early declarations of e-government services and the design of the Direct Gov portal by 2004, governments throughout the EU were all designing their own e-government systems by the early years of the new millennium. As a result a series of European-wide initiatives were developed. Prime among these is the *Ministerial Declaration on eGovernment* agreed at the Lisbon eGovernment conference of 2007.[34] The Declaration agrees on four 'priority policy actions' and a number of subsidiary actions. The 'priority' actions are: (1) Cross-border interoperability; (2) Reduction of administrative burdens; (3) Inclusive eGovernment; and (4) Transparency and democratic engagement.

Cross-border interoperability requires member states to develop a pan-European approach to the delivery of certain key projects. The key concern here is that by developing non-interoperable systems of e-government member states may undermine the functioning of the single market. This is of particular concern in e-procurement projects: where governments solicit the supply of goods of services for public projects through the e-government portal. The concern at the European level is that as different governments adopt different e-procurement systems the internal market for the supply of public sector goods and services becomes fractured. Because of this risk the Declaration requires governments of member states to 'identify the areas in which Member States would cooperate and determine, with the European Commission, the appropriate *modus operandi* to define, develop, implement and monitor broad cross-border interoperability.'[35] This requirement is more than just an instruction to governments. It is backed by legal requirements put in place in the Services Directive of 2006.[36] By Article 8(1) 'Member States shall ensure that all procedures and formalities relating to access to a service activity and to the exercise thereof may be easily completed, at a distance and by electronic means, through the relevant point of single contact and with the relevant competent authorities.' A 'service' is defined by

[32] House of Lords *Hansard* 21 July 2009, col.WA.322: http://www.publications.parliament.uk/pa/ld200809/ldhansrd/text/90721w0005.htm.   [33] Discussed above at p. 463.
[34] Ministerial Declaration agreed at the fourth Ministerial eGovernment Conference, Lisbon 19 September 2007: http://ec.europa.eu/information_society/activities/egovernment/docs/lisbon_2007/ministerial_declaration_180907.pdf.   [35] *ibid*, 3.
[36] Directive 2006/123/EC of the European Parliament and of the Council of 12 December 2006 on services in the internal market, OJ L 376/36 (2006).

Article 4 as 'any self-employed economic activity, normally provided for remuneration.' Thus e-procurement procedures must be designed in such a manner as to allow equality of access from any point within the EU. The Directive must be given effect by member states by 28 December 2009. At the time of writing the UK Government is checking primary legislation to ensure compliance and has prepared draft regulations to meet the requirements of the Directive. On a practical level technical compliance forms part of the Transformational Government Implementation Plan discussed below.

Reduction of administrative burdens requires member states to use 'eGovernment as a lever to contribute to the achievement of the objective of reducing administrative burdens for citizens and businesses in Europe, by [making] use of the possibilities for re-use of information with due respect to the legal frameworks, in particular data protection legislation and [paying] special attention to small and medium enterprises (SMEs) as priority beneficiaries of burden reduction and streamlined public services.'[37] The aim here is to pass on at least some of the transactional savings governments make by introducing e-government systems to citizens and small businesses. The aim is to improve competitiveness of small and medium sized enterprises while reducing the administrative burden for citizens. Inclusive e-government requires member states to ensure that all citizens benefit from e-government services by ensuring that services are equally available and accessible to all citizens. This may require member states to take action to translate content into languages other than the official language of the state or to take steps to reduce the effects of digital exclusion and digital divide (discussed below) by making services accessible through terminals and kiosks in public buildings such as libraries, job centres, or community centres. Finally the requirement of transparency and democratic engagement asks member states to take action to 'Explore new ways of public participation and increased transparency enabled by innovative ICT technologies for democratic engagement and transparency.'[38] This includes experiments in e-voting as the UK have trialled but also access to parliamentary reports and debates as well as draft and current legislation. The UK excels in these forms of transparency through sites such as *parliament.uk* which provides access to Parliamentary Reports, Bills, Hansard, and video and audio footage of Debates and Committee Hearings as well as giving advice on how to visit Parliament and *statutelaw.gov.uk*, the Statute Law Database, which provides free access to updated versions of Acts and Regulations.

Despite the success of the first phase of e-government in the UK the government is already deep into the second stage of e-government delivery. This project, started in 2005, aims to surpass the UK Government's obligations under the Lisbon Declaration. It began with the publication of a strategy document entitled *Transformational Government: Enabled by Technology*.[39] The strategy document centred the delivery of government services on three key values:

---

[37] Ministerial Declaration, above n 34, 3.   [38] *ibid*, 4.
[39] Cabinet Office *Transformational Government: Enabled by Technology*, November 2005: http://www.cabinetoffice.gov.uk/media/141734/transgov-strategy.pdf.

(1) Services enabled by IT must be designed around the citizen or business, not the provider, and provided through modern, co-ordinated delivery channels. This will improve the customer experience, achieve better policy outcomes, reduce paperwork burdens and improve efficiency by reducing duplication and routine processing, leveraging delivery capacity and streamlining processes.

(2) Government must move to a shared services culture—in the front-office, in the back-office, in information and in infrastructure—and release efficiencies by standardisation, simplification and sharing.

(3) There must be broadening and deepening of government's professionalism in terms of the planning, delivery, management, skills and governance of IT enabled change. This will result in more successful outcomes; fewer costly delivery failures; and increased confidence by citizens and politicians in the delivery of change by the public services.[40]

The aim of this strategy document was to both meet and exceed the requirements of the Lisbon Declaration and to drive e-government in the UK into areas it had been unsuccessful in meeting in the five years that had passed since the original e-government strategy had been designed in 2000. Thus the document noted that through gateways such as Direct Gov the government had met its earlier targets with 'over 96% of government services "e-enabled" by the end of 2005, with over half of households internet enabled at home and broadband available to almost all homes and businesses. There are also 6000 UK Online centres in place, providing internet access and free assistance to those who do not wish to go online at home.'[41] But failings had to be admitted, mostly surrounding information security, data protection, and the ability of government to provide 'pulled' services:

• There are new information assurance risks: terrorists, organised criminals and hackers threaten information and services, and theft of identity and of personal data is of increasing concern to individuals and businesses.

• Sophisticated, holistic policy solutions, such as those set out in the government's election manifesto, rely upon effective and pervasive technology systems across government and beyond—for instance to support offender management through offender profiling and managed rehabilitation plans and to deliver patient choice in the health service.

• Public use of the internet and telephone continues to rise. As people experience excellent services in parts of the private and public sector, so their expectations of public services rise across the board.[42]

As a result the government set out their agenda for delivering in these areas where e-government had been less successful in the UK. In particular the document focuses on the need for 'a new shared services approach'. This will 'release efficiencies across the system and support delivery more focussed on customer needs [by] providing public service organisations with the opportunity to reduce waste and inefficiency by re-using assets and sharing investments with others.'[43] The government states that they aim to focus upon a number of areas where shared services are appropriate including the

---

[40] *ibid*, [21].   [41] *ibid*, [18].   [42] *ibid*, [19].   [43] *ibid*, [39].

creation of a common infrastructure which should assist in meeting the first (and perhaps the second) of the Lisbon priorities; the creation of a data sharing strategy, which will help implement 'pulled' services and information assurance which is designed to give consumer confidence in systems which share information. This major project is designed to extend beyond 2011 with a three stage delivery process. Phase one is complete. This saw the creation of the Transformational Government Implementation Plan as well as spending reviews and background tasks such as employing key staff to deliver the proposals.

We are now in phase two which is scheduled to take until 2011. This is to implement the proposals found in the Transformational Government Implementation Plan.[44] The plan seeks to give effect to the strategy document. It sets up a common infrastructure board tasked with providing advice and management on the implementation of a common e-government infrastructure. To date they have developed the common infrastructure roadmap which has led to the development of the not yet implemented Public Sector Network (PSN). When complete, which should be by late 2011, PSN will provide a government private intranet for all public sector services in the UK with gateways (most likely though the existing Direct Gov and Business Link gateways) to the internet to allow citizens and business partners to access permitted public sections on the network. PSN is designed to be used by all government departments and agencies in England, the devolved governments and assemblies of Scotland, Wales and Northern Ireland, all local authorities, and some international bodies.[45] It is designed to improve the government's ability to respond to changes in the way government provides services to the citizen, increase opportunities for public sector organisations to collaborate more efficiently, provide a more cost-effective procedure for the procurement of products and services, reduce the cost of service management, improve the ability of public sector organisations to provide services and information, provide secure, flexible, and reliable access to information, and provide faster, more efficient public service provision to the citizen.[46]

PSN is though only part of phase two implementation of the e-government project. The aim overall is to create a fully integrated e-government service. This also includes sharing information between departments to allow for integrated public services built on a 'pulled' delivery system. This vision is fleshed out in a further report the *Information Sharing Vision Statement*.[47] This explains that the government seeks to share information between public sector departments and services within the framework of what is permissible under the Data Protection Act. Their vision, as they explain, 'is to ensure that information will be shared to expand opportunities for the most disadvantaged, fight crime and provide better public services for citizens and business, and in other instances where it is in the public interest.'[48] This is illustrated by an example of how shared information may create 'pulled' resources.

---

[44] Cabinet Office, *Transformational Government: Transformational Government Implementation Plan*, 2006: http://www.cabinetoffice.gov.uk/media/141737/transgovt.pdf.

[45] *ibid*, 48.   [46] *ibid*.

[47] Department for Constitutional Affairs, *Information Sharing Vision Statement*, September 2006: http://www.foi.gov.uk/sharing/information-sharing.pdf.   [48] *ibid*, [8].

> **✱ Example** Creating 'Pulled' Resources
>
> The Department of Work and Pensions is developing an approach that will automatically gather information to help identify entitlement to Council Tax Benefit amongst customers claiming Pension Credit. This proposed process will be much simpler, easier and quicker for the customer as they will not need to provide the same information separately for Council Tax Benefit. The Pension Service will gather information for Council Tax Benefit from customers when they claim Pension Credit. For those customers who receive Pension Credit, the relevant local authority will be notified of the decision and will be passed relevant Council Tax Benefit supplementary information. The local authority will then check for council tax liability and verify any relevant additional information before making an assessment and award of Council Tax Benefit.

The government believes the pooling of information in this way will reduce administrative overheads, provide benefits to citizens, and will protect against fraud. They are confident citizens have little to fear as the Data Protection Act protects individual privacy and prevents abuse of personal data.[49]

Once these separate strands of the Transformational Government Implementation Plan come together sometime in late 2011 the UK Government is confident of offering one of the best and most inclusive e-government systems in Europe, if not the world. They seek to fulfil the four original aims of the e.gov report in 2000 providing personalised and matched services to citizens and small and medium sized enterprises through the Direct Gov and Business Link portals. Pulled services may be online soon after 2011 if the data sharing proposals are fully implemented and while the short lived experiment with e-voting may indicate that we are not quite ready for full digital democracy the success of sites such as the Statute Law Database, the Parliament website, and the official government website (*number10.gov.uk/*)[50] suggest that the UK's e-democracy programme is despite the failings of e-voting in rather fine fettle. The UK also stands on the verge of meeting all the Lisbon priorities. PSN will offer the necessary stability to offer cross-border interoperability, while both PSN and information sharing will assist in the reduction of administrative overheads for both government and citizen. The UK therefore stands ready to meet the challenge of the next phase of e-government. Or does it? Arguably one challenge that remains is the third Lisbon priority, that of Inclusive eGovernment. This requires the government to overcome what is commonly known as 'the Digital Divide'.

[49] *ibid*, [21].
[50] The Number 10 website offers a unique form of digital democracy by allowing citizens to petition the Prime Minister directly. Perhaps unsurprisingly this experiment with direct digital democracy produces that most depressing of knee-jerk responses with the most popular petition by far being for the Prime Minister to resign.

20.2 **The digital divide**

A major problem of the digital public sphere is engaging participants in the discourse necessary for good democratic interaction. This means bridging the digital divide. The digital divide is an often misused term to describe the distinction those who have internet access and those who do not. As Daniel Paré points out the danger of this approach is to become 'techno-centric' by focusing on the technology rather than the social skills one must possess to gain the full benefit of digital access and the social implications of lacking these skills.[51] This is a common view held among sociologists which leads to a much finer classification of the digital divide in sociological texts than is commonly found in legal textbooks. Probably the most complete classification is to be found in Pippa Norris's book *Digital Divide: Civic Engagement, Information Poverty, and the Internet Worldwide.*[52] In this she identifies three distinct aspects of the digital divide.[53]

→ Highlight Norris's Three Aspects of the Digital Divide

The *global divide* refers to the divergence of Internet access between industrialised and developing societies. The *social divide* concerns the gap between information rich and poor in each nation. And lastly within the online community, the *democratic divide* signifies the difference between those who do, and do not, use the panoply of digital resources to engage, mobilise and participate in public life.

This distinction is both important and valuable for studies of the digital divide and for discussions of the digital public sphere. Here we see that access to computers and computer networks is only part of the divide that prevents individuals for playing a full role in the digital public sphere.

20.2.1 **The global divide**

In using Norris's classification we see a distinction between the global divide which is the divide commentators most commonly mean when they discuss 'the digital divide' and the social and democratic divides which are more relevant to the digital public sphere. The global divide refers to the international sphere of the digital divide.

In its first incarnation it was the divide between nations and regions with stable internet access and those without. As Norris explained by the year 2000 the internet had available over two billion pages of data which was accessible by about 400 million users: in other words about 7% of the global population.[54] This divide was the focus of

---

[51] D. Paré 'The Digital Divide: Why the "The" is Misleading?' in M. Klang & A. Murray (eds), *Human Rights in the Digital Age* (2005).
[52] (2002).　　[53] *ibid*, 4.　　[54] *ibid*, 3–4.

most academic study and international cooperation. Norris explains that a number of major international organisations became involved in the movement to alleviate the global digital divide including the United Nations, UNESCO, the OECD, and the G8 grouping of leading industrial nations.[55] These organisations have spearheaded a decade of innovation and investment which has reduced the global divide significantly. The success of programmes such as the One Laptop Per Child initiative as well as the development of satellite and wireless mobile access in Africa meant that by the end of 2008 the global internet population had grown significantly to 1.59 billion users or 23.8% of the global population.

Although these figures demonstrate there is still work to be done progress is clearly being made. In particular the data shows that while North America, Europe, and Australasia have experienced an average growth rate of 193% over these eight years, developing nations have driven the growth in the internet population with the average growth rate across Asia, the Middle East, Latin America and the Caribbean, and Africa being 933%.[56] The statistics also show there is still work to be done to close the global digital divide as internet penetration within North America, Europe, and Australasia is at 61.2% as against 19% in Asia, the Middle East, Latin America and the Caribbean, and Africa.[57] Additionally the figures do not take account of the type of internet access available to users. OECD data reveals that the top thirty countries for broadband penetration in 2008 (whether calculated by numbers of subscribers or by ratio of the population) were all located in Europe, North America, or Australasia with the exceptions of Japan and South Korea.[58] This tells us that the speed of access outside the traditional centres of internet content production and distribution remains relatively slow making full use of internet facilities such as video-on-demand and music streaming and file sharing more difficult.

20.2.2 **The social divide**

The global digital divide remains a current issue, but to solve a problem as vast as this requires global action and consensus and the continued investment of significant resources. This is an issue of global politics, international investment and aid: not a subject for textbooks of law. By comparison the issues caused by the social divide and the democratic divide are mostly of local effect and require the involvement of local and regional governmental solutions often partnered with educational initiatives: in other words questions of democracy, accountability and regulatory control and intervention, clearly subjects which should be at the heart of any book hoping to contextualise legal challenges and developments within their social framework.

The social divide, unlike the global divide, focuses upon the access divide within individual countries or societies. It thus focuses on degrees of penetration and access

---

[55] *ibid*, 5–7.
[56] Source: Internet World Statistics: Usage and Population Statistics: http://www.internetworld-stats.com/stats.htm.   [57] *ibid*.
[58] Source: OECD Broadband Portal: http://www.oecd.org/document/54/0,3343,en_2649_34225_38690102_1_1_1_1,00.html.

within a single nation. As Norris explains even the US which has the highest level of penetration and access worldwide suffers a social divide: a '1998 survey found that affluent households (with income of $75,000 and above) were twenty times as likely to have Internet access as those at the lowest income levels, and more than nine times as likely to have computer access.'[59] This stratifies society, and therefore undermines the development of a digital public sphere as instead of providing a common sphere connecting the private sphere and the sphere of public of public authority the digital sphere becomes a habitat only for the bourgeois. This reinforces the sphere of public authority and excises the proletariat. It is therefore essential that governments take action to reduce the social divide if the digital public sphere is to function.

The UK Government has taken considerable steps to attempt to reduce the social divide through programmes and policies such as the ambitious Becta Home Access Scheme announced in 2008 by the Prime Minister. This is designed to ensure every schoolchild in the UK is afforded broadband-enabled internet access at home by 2011 though a £300m government investment.[60] Raw data also suggests that the UK is closing the social divide with the Office of National Statistics reporting that 'in 2008, 16 million households in Great Britain (65%) had Internet access. This is an increase of just over 1 million households (7%) over the last year and 5 million households (46%) since 2002 ... 56% of all UK households had a broadband connection in 2008, up from 51% in 2007.'[61] Despite this apparent success the data also reveals work still to be done: 'adults under 70 years of age who had a degree or equivalent qualification were most likely to have access to the internet in their home, at 93%. Those individuals who had no formal qualifications, were least likely to have an Internet connection in their home at 56%.'[62]

To overcome the problem of social exclusion at the heart of the social divide governments must do more than simply provide schemes such as the Becta Home Access Scheme. Although an excellent scheme this pays qualifying applicants a grant of between £100–£700 to spend on approved home computer equipment within three months of the date of the award. Any unspent portion of the award is reclaimed and the equipment must come from a pre-approved supplier. At the end of the three months the recipient of the award may possess a brand new computer and twelve months' internet access but there is no ongoing financial support which means at the end of the initial twelve month period the user has to take on the cost of their broadband account, as well as paying for any upgrades or repairs. If we are truly to close the social divide therefore the long-term solution is to be found in lowering the costs of basic hardware, software, and internet access costs: this usually means a regulatory intervention.

Again the UK seems to have been successful in reducing the costs of getting online. Competition in both the hardware and access markets has seen the cost of getting online

---

[59] Norris, above n. 52, 10.

[60] Department of Children, Schools and Families, *Broadening Horizons—England to 'Lead the World' in Computer Access for Young People*, 23 September 2008: http://www.dcsf.gov.uk/pns/DisplayPN.cgi?pn_id=2008_0208. The announcement followed on the publication of the *Report of the Prime Minister's Taskforce on Home Access to Technology*, July 2008: http://about.becta.org.uk/content_files/corporate/resources/news/2008/september/home_access_report.pdf.

[61] Source: National Statistics Omnibus Survey; Northern Ireland Omnibus Survey: http://www.statistics.gov.uk/CCI/nugget.asp?ID=8.   [62] *ibid.*

fall dramatically in the last ten years. In 1999 a standard desktop computer would cost around £999. A similar machine now may be purchased for under £400. Laptops have fallen in price even further from around £1,199 in 1999 to under £300 in 2009 or in many cases being offered for free if the customer signs a mobile broadband contract. The price of internet access has also fallen dramatically. In 1999 most users used dial-up internet access but the cost of an unlimited account at 56.6Kbps speed was likely to be in the region of £30 per month. By 2009 fast broadband access at 8Mbps was available at less that £7.50 per month. Obviously these reductions have been primarily driven by market forces but the UK and the EU have taken steps to ensure the market functions correctly, and it is thanks to these interventions that the social divide is closing.

20.2.3 **The social divide: opening competition in products and services**

The need for intervention in the telecommunications sector to ensure level competition in first dial-up and later the broadband internet access market has been recognised for some time. As early as 1993 the European Union began to examine how to break up the natural monopoly control former state telecoms companies exercised over the so-called 'local loop': the final physical connection, usually a copper wire, which connects the customer to their local telephone exchange.

As most local connections had been made in the days of state telecoms monopolies the companies which inherited the local loop upon privatisation, such as BT in the UK, could exert so called 'gatekeeper control' over possible competitors, preventing competition for subsidiary services such as ADSL internet access. This meant that unless this monopoly could be broken up the only way new entrants into the telecommunications/internet access market could compete with incumbents was to build their own networks at some considerable cost. Recognising that incumbent telecommunications companies held a distinct market advantage over competitors, an advantage most had gained through much earlier public investment in building the telecoms network, the EU took steps to break the incumbent monopoly by instigating a process known as local loop unbundling (LLU). This reached fruition in December 2000 with the promulgation of the Regulation on Unbundled Access to the Local Loop.[63] This provided that 'Notified operators shall publish from 31 December 2000, and keep updated, a reference offer for unbundled access to their local loops and related facilities. The offer shall be sufficiently unbundled so that the beneficiary does not have to pay for network elements or facilities which are not necessary for the supply of its services, and shall contain a description of the components of the offer, associated terms and conditions, including charges.'[64] In effect this means that telecoms companies put on notice (usually ex-state privatised operators) were required to allow competitors access to the local loop to offer competing services, and were required to provide differing levels of access depending upon the use the competing company wished to make of the local loop. Thus an internet access provider could seek data only access negating the need for them to pay the full cost of voice+data access.

---

[63] Reg. 2887/2000, OJ L 336/4 (2000).   [64] Art. 3(1).

To ensure that incumbents did not overcharge for access the Regulation gave states regulators the power to oversee the market, and if necessary to impose reductions in pricing.[65] In the UK the power to supervise LLU was given to Oftel Ofcom. They have supervised the unbundling of the UK local loop since 2000 and in that time have seen nearly six million lines become open to unbundling.[66] They have also closely monitored costs with the most recent 'sustainable competition prices' set by Ofcom for BT Openreach in May 2009 setting the wholesale price of a complete unbundle (voice+data) at £86.40 per annum while a partial unbundle (data services only) is set at £15.60 per annum.[67] These controlled prices allow for active competition in both the telecommunications and internet access market. In particular the low price of data only unbundling makes it possible for companies to offer broadband access for as little as £7.50 per month. This in the long term will prove to be much more important for the narrowing of the social divide than projects such as the Becta Home Access Scheme, as the ongoing costs of running a computer can prove to be as great a barrier to entry as the initial outlay.

Internet access costs are not the only costs which affect the ability of the less wealthy to get online. One of the major initial and ongoing costs of running a computer is the cost of essential software such as the operating system. Like the telecommunications sector it was quickly recognised that a monopoly provider of such software had emerged with Microsoft supplying up to 95% of operating software for Intel-chipped personal computers.[68] This was felt to be harmful to consumers in two ways: (1) by reducing choice and competition in both the operating system market and so-called downstream markets for applications software such as office software, media players, and internet browsers; and (2) by causing consumers to overpay for a product they had no choice but to buy as it came pre-installed on their new PCs.

This led competition authorities on both sides of the Atlantic to take action against Microsoft. In 1998 the US Department of Justice filed a number of anti-trust actions against Microsoft. The focus of the US action was on Microsoft bundling its Internet Explorer Web Browser with its Windows operating system. This it was widely assumed was to commercially undercut the market for competing browser Netscape Navigator which at that time was the market leader. Microsoft argued it was due to developments in both programs which meant they interoperated with each other.

Eventually after three years of litigation which included a finding of fact before the District Court for the District of Columbia[69] an agreement between the US Department

---

[65] Art. 4.

[66] Source: Office of the Telecommunications Adjudicator, *Key Performance Indicators*, July 2009: http://www.offta.org.uk/charts.htm#throughput.

[67] Ofcom, *Ofcom Confirms New Wholesale Prices for Openreach*, 22 May 2009: http://www.ofcom.org.uk/media/news/2009/05/nr_20090522.

[68] Microsoft's enduring high market shares were highlighted by the US District Court for the District of Columbia. Referring to operating systems for Intel-compatible PCs, it held that: '[e]very year for the last decade, Microsoft's share of the market for Intel-compatible PC operating systems has stood above ninety percent. For the last couple of years the figure has been at least ninety-five percent, and analysts project that the share will climb even higher over the next few years.' See Findings of Fact of 5 November 1999, US District Court for the District of Columbia, *US of America v Microsoft Corporation*, Civil Action No. 98-1232 and 1232 (TPJ), at para. 35.

[69] *US of America v Microsoft Corporation*, Civil Action No. 98-1232 (TPJ), Finding of Facts, 5 November 1999: http://www.usdoj.gov/atr/cases/f3800/msjudge.pdf.

of Justice and Microsoft was brokered. Under the terms of the deal Microsoft would make public its applications programming interface (this is the interface between the operating system and the applications software) and agree not to penalise any original equipment manufacturers who installed any product which competed with Microsoft products in the 'installed build' of their machines (i.e. the software which is bundled on a new computer).[70] This has had little impact on the operating system market with Microsoft still reported to control 95% of that market but it has freed up the market for internet browsers. In January 2002 Microsoft controlled 86.8% of the browser market, but by July 2009 this had fallen to 39.4%. In that time Microsoft lost their position as market leader to Mozilla who control 47.9% of the market with their Firefox browser.[71]

A similar competition action was launched in Europe. The focus of the European case was also bundling but here the focus was on the bundling of the Windows Media Player multimedia player and on the charges Microsoft required in royalty payments to gain access to Microsoft's Windows operating system when producing Windows compatible software. This case has been ongoing in various forms for sixteen years at the time of writing, and is not yet complete. It has led to fines totalling €1.67bn for a number of infractions of EU competition law. The two largest single fines were an initial fine of €497m levied in the initial Commission Decision of 23 March 2004 which also required Microsoft to divulge the server information to competitors within 120 days and to produce a version of Windows without Windows Media Player within 90 days,[72] and a subsequent fine for non-compliance of €899m levied on 27 February 2008.[73] Although the case continues with Microsoft appealing against the level of the fines imposed and the Commission extending the scope of its investigation to look at Microsoft's bundling of Internet Explorer with Windows software. The result of all this may appear minimal. Microsoft makes available in Europe a version of Windows which does not come bundled with Windows Media Player, although few equipment manufacturers choose to install it, and they have reduced the royalties payable for access to Windows interfacing from 5.95% of revenue to 0.4%.

How though does all this affect the social divide? Well, as with the US anti-trust investigation it has had an effect wider than simply Microsoft's market share of the operating system market which has remained stable. It has led Microsoft to announce its Office software will support open document format.[74] This allows individuals who need to work on documents created on MS Office software at school, university, or in the workplace to use a cheaper alternative at home such as Sun Microsystem's Star Office, or even free alternatives such as Open Office or Google Docs. This has led to greater competition forcing discounting from Microsoft. In 2000 the standard edition of MS Office 2000 cost £340 plus VAT, in 2009 the same software may be bought by the home user

---

[70] *US of America v Microsoft Corporation*, Civil Action No. 98-1232 (CKK), Final Judgement, 12 November 2002: http://www.usdoj.gov/atr/cases/f200400/200457.pdf.

[71] All data from: *Browser Statistics Month by Month*: http://www.w3schools.com/browsers/browsers_stats.asp.

[72] *Commission of the EU v Microsoft Corporation*, Commission Decision of 24.03.2004 relating to a proceeding under Article 82 of the EC Treaty (Case COMP/C-3/37.792 Microsoft).

[73] *Commission of the EU v Microsoft Corporation*, Commission Decision of 27.02.2008 fixing the definitive amount of the periodic penalty payment imposed on Microsoft Corporation by Decision C(2005)4420 final.

[74] Microsoft Corporation, *Microsoft Expands List of Formats Supported in Microsoft Office*, 21 May 2008: http://www.microsoft.com/Presspass/press/2008/may08/05-21ExpandedFormatsPR.mspx.

under a home and student license first introduced in 2003 for only £68 including VAT. Similarly the cost of the Windows operating system has been reduced from £129 (upgrade price for Windows 2000) to £70 (Windows 7 home premium edition). These reductions in price contribute to cheaper home computing allowing for a narrowing of the social divide. These actions should therefore be seen as more than simply competition law actions: by increasing competition they have reduced prices of both original equipment and upgrades. This allows for greater uptake of home computing among the less financially wealthy sectors of society which make up the plebiscite. By closing the social divide the digital public sphere has life breathed into it.

The social divide remains a real barrier to entry to the digital public sphere and regulators must continue to act to close the divide. Fortunately strong competition in all sectors from chip production to internet access continues to lower the cost of running a computer. As seen in the Office of National Statistics data this is helping to close the divide but there remains one additional problem. When citizens go online do they engage in democratic discourse? This is the question posed by the democratic divide: the divide between those who use the internet for political discourse and civic engagement and those who do not. To answer this question we must return to look at the blogosphere and social networking.

20.3 **The democratic divide**

The democratic divide may be the most difficult of the three divides to bridge in the pursuit of the digital public sphere. Although cyber-optimists believe the internet offers the best opportunity to date for citizens to engage in direct democracy though a number of channels ranging from the creation of online interest groups, through to direct engagement with politicians in online fora and Q&A sessions and ultimately to online voting and referenda, there is a group of cyber-pessimists who believe that 'digital technology [is] a Pandora's box unleashing new inequalities of power and wealth, reinforcing deeper divisions between the information rich and poor, the tuned-in and the tuned-out, the activists and the disengaged. This account stresses that the global and social divides already discussed mean that Internet politics will disproportionately benefit the elite.'[75]

The truth is probably somewhere between the two. While, as we have seen, experiments with electronic voting have had only limited success in the UK, the growth of direct engagement between politicians and citizens demonstrated in such varied outposts as the 10 Downing Street Twitter feed, the Conservative Party's *WebCameron* video blogging service, and the rise of politically motivated Facebook groups such as *Free Gary MacKinnon* and *Liberal Drinks UK*.[76] How then can lawyers and lawmakers support the development of the digital public sphere by closing the democratic divide? The key is to engage a wide range of politically inactive or politically indolent groups and individuals, while protecting the democratic values of our society. This to date has meant

[75] Norris, above n. 52, 13.
[76] For further discussion on Facebook as a political tool see D. Wills & S. Reeves, 'Facebook as a Political Weapon: Information in Social Networks' (2009) 4 *British Politics* 265.

engaging with two new forms of political discourse unique to the digital public sphere, the blogosphere and social networking.

20.3.1 **The democratic divide and the blogosphere**

The blogosphere supported the first generation of direct digital democracy. The blogosphere has a healthy mix of citizen journalists and professional journalists and lobbyists. They range from widely read professionals such as *Guido Fawkes* and *Ian Dale's Diary* to lesser known bloggers such as *Power to the People* and *Kerron Cross*. They also range from generic political blogs such as those mentioned to special interest, or single issue blogs such as *NightJack* (a blog written by a police constable on frontline policing and discussed below); *Mental Nurse* (a similar blog written by a group of nurses working in mental health in the NHS); and *Nearly Legal* (which looks at housing law issues). Additionally there are a variety of forms of blog, ranging from the traditional written blog, to vlogs (video blogs often hosted on sites such a YouTube) to micro-blogs (as pioneered by Twitter). Each fulfils a different role in the digital public sphere. Blogs are places of discourse and often follow the Socratic method of discourse where an original viewpoint will be challenged by a counter-viewpoint in the comments that readers leave: a dialogue between the original poster and the commentator often follows developing ideas and concepts. Vlogs are usually more didactic. The blogger makes a recorded speech which is designed to be viewed. Although sites such as YouTube and Metacafe do offer feedback on posted videos these are not designed to offer the Socratic experience of a blog.[77] Finally micro-blogging is about immediacy and networking. The value of a micro-blog is that it can very quickly reach a large audience due to 'push' technology which sends your update directly to your followers. It is highly interactive and may be seen as Socratic, but the limitations of micro-blogging (Twitter limits tweets to 140 characters) mean that meaningful discourse is extremely difficult. It may be best to think of micro-blogging as more of a 'pub conversation'.

The blogosphere brings incredible vibrancy to the digital public sphere but with this vibrancy comes risks. As was discussed in Chapter 6 the power and freedom of expression afforded by the digital public sphere must be balanced with responsibility on the part of the participants. The public sphere is a place of discourse not discord. To return to Hauser's definition it is 'a discursive space in which individuals and groups congregate to discuss matters of mutual interest *and, where possible, to reach a common judgment.'*[78]

The risk of the blogosphere is unchecked and irresponsible speech which causes a cacophony rather than discussion. This danger arises for, as discussed in Chapter 6, there is no filtering mechanism between writing content and publishing content. With traditional media the publication process ensured all discourse was filtered through intermediary editors and publishers, and where necessary legal advice would be taken before publication took place. This initial filter ensured only reasonable expression

---

[77] A hybrid blog will embed video footage into a more traditional blog. This may be done using traditional blog hosting sites such as Blogger and Wordpress. These hybrids can offer the immediacy of a vlog with the exchange of ideas seen on a blog.

[78] Hauser, above n. 3 (emphasis added).

entered the public sphere. There were of course risks that the sphere was controlled by a few publishers and press barons (who were part of the sphere of public authority) and for this reason many see the development digital public sphere as a positive development.[79] Others though caution against inherent risks found in the blogosphere. Most famously US law professor Cass Sunstein suggested in his book *Republic.com* the nature of the internet was to isolate individuals behind filters and screens rather than to provide for community building and democratic discourse.[80] Sunstein suggested that while a well functioning system of deliberative democracy requires a certain degree of information so that citizens can engage in monitoring and deliberative tasks,[81] the ability to filter information offered by digital technologies interferes with the flow of this information in two ways. The first is that the user may simply choose not to receive some of this information by using filters to ensure they only receive information of interest to them, this is the creation of the so-called Daily Me, a personalised news service which only carries news of interest to the reader.[82] As such there is no homogeneity of information across the macro community of users of the internet making truly deliberative democratic discourse impossible. Further Sunstein recognised that with the advent of internet communications it becomes easier to locate likeminded individuals whatever one's shared interests may be. This creates in Sunstein's words 'fringe communities that have a common ideology but are dispersed geographically'.[83] In turn this leads to community fragmentation.

Sunstein's argument raises the spectre of fragmentation within the public sphere rather than discourse. This occurs when either two groups never engage: such as when right wing bloggers only discuss items of interest within their community with each other and fail to engage for example with left wing bloggers (a process called disengagement), or when groups simply 'talk past each other' with competing but unengaged discussions (non-engagement). We can see each in action with some examples:

✳ Example Disengagement

Aisha is a right wing political blogger. She operates the blog *Pitt's Younger Place*. She is also a member of a group of right wing bloggers called *Churchill's Inner Circle*. Blair, who is also a member of *Churchill's Inner Circle* breaks the news on his blog that a senior Labour cabinet member is having an affair with a businessman who has received extensive financial support from the Government for his new factory. Several other sources including mainstream media and left wing bloggers state this is not true. Aisha though does not read any of these and simply recounts the details of Blair's original blog entry in her blog.

---

[79] See Papacharissi, above n. 10; M. Poster, 'Cyberdemocracy, the Internet and the Public Sphere' in D. Porter (ed.), *Internet Culture* (1997).
[80] C. Sunstein, *Republic.com* (2001).   [81] *ibid*, 174.
[82] This was an idea first advanced by Nicholas Negroponte in *Being Digital* (1995) at 152–154, and developed extensively by Sunstein in *Republic.com*.
[83] *Republic.com* at 58.

> ⊛ **Example** Non-engagement
>
> A further story breaks. This time it is Aisha who breaks the story that a Labour party donor
> has avoided the payment of tax duties in the UK by moving his operations overseas. Charlene
> operates a left wing blog *Atlee's World View*. She writes that the donor's business interests
> moved overseas due to a government initiative to assist developing nations and that no tax
> is avoided. Aisha then writes a further story that the donor has been avoiding tax for several
> years. Charlene writes a further story that the donor's business remains domiciled in the UK for
> tax purposes. Neither acknowledges the other point of view despite several mainstream media
> outlets carrying out extensive investigative reports which reveal there is an element of truth in
> both positions.

There is much the law may do to assist in the development of the digital public
sphere, and to reduce the risk of non-engagement and disengagement. Firstly it is
important that bloggers are aware of their duties and responsibilities to their fellow
citizens. This means it is essential that bloggers should not feel immune to the
controls which restrict free expression in society for the good of society as a whole.
Bloggers are keen to invoke the protection of Article 10 of the European Convention
on Human Rights as given effect by s. 1 of the Human Rights Act 1998. In full Article
10 states:

> 1. Everyone has the right to freedom of expression. This right shall include freedom to hold
> opinions and to receive and impart information and ideas without interference by public
> authority and regardless of frontiers. This article shall not prevent States from requiring the
> licensing of broadcasting, television or cinema enterprises.
>
> 2. The exercise of these freedoms, since it carries with it duties and responsibilities, may be
> subject to such formalities, conditions, restrictions or penalties as are prescribed by law and are
> necessary in a democratic society, in the interests of national security, territorial integrity or
> public safety, for the prevention of disorder or crime, for the protection of health or morals, for
> the protection of the reputation or the rights of others, for preventing the disclosure of
> information received in confidence, or for maintaining the authority and impartiality of the
> judiciary.

The key is Article 10(2) which strictly limits the freedom offered in Article 10(1). This
has long been recognised and accepted by media outlets, with in particular the law of
defamation controlling the greater excesses of the media. Thus, as was extensively discussed in Chapter 7, individuals who make comments of an untrue and harmful nature
about another person risk an action in defamation. The problem with the application
of the law of defamation in the digital public sphere is the reactive nature of legal rules.
Whereas in traditional mainstream media the publisher would control content through
pre-publication procedures, meaning that the harm caused by defamatory content is
limited, the temptation for online bloggers is to publish whatever is most likely to draw
the largest audience to their site whatever the effect is on other citizens. This temptation is driven by the profit model for online publishing which rewards bloggers for

drawing a larger audience, and by the rewards afforded to internet celebrities such as Perez Hilton. Buoyed by these potential rewards, and feeling secure in the privacy of their own study, and protected by pseudonymity, bloggers are more likely to defame or invade privacy than mainstream journalists.[84] This has led Professor Daniel Solove to note that:

> When we envision a blogger, who do we see? I bet for many of us [we imagine Professor Eugene Volkh of the Volkh Conspiracy blog]. We see blogging as something that enhances the freedom of the little guy, providing new ways for people to engage in expression and self-development. But the average blogger isn't Eugene, and the average blog isn't anything close to scholarship. According to one estimate, over fifty percent of blogs are written by children and teenagers under age nineteen. About twenty percent of teens with Internet access have a blog. The most common blogger is a teenage girl. Many blogs are more akin to diaries than news articles, op-ed columns, or scholarship. And that's why there's a problem. From the dawn of time, people have engaged in gossip. According to one study, about two-thirds of all conversations involve gossip. As Keith Devlin notes, 'What people talk about is mostly other people.' Before the advent of modern communications technology, gossip would remain within an individual's social circle—the group of people with whom that person associates. We live amid a number of social circles, such as our colleagues at work, various groups we belong to, and different circles of friends. We share information within these circles. It is often rare for gossip to leap from one social circle to another—because people in one social circle will often not know or care about a person in a completely different circle. But when gossip goes online, it transforms from forgettable whispers within small local groups to a permanent and widespread record that can be pulled up instantly in a Google search. Gossip can more readily jump the boundaries of various social circles, because all it takes is for the gossip to come to the attention of a popular blog, where it can quickly become the buzz of the blogosphere and spread far and wide throughout cyberspace.[85]

Thus Solove believes that blogs mostly do not drive the digital public sphere. Is there anything the law can do to rebalance the contribution of blogs to the digital public sphere? Solove believes that bloggers must be made responsible for their actions by recognising limitations in the right to free speech where the blogger invades the privacy of another or potentially defames them.[86] This of course reflects the position already held in UK law, which, to an American observer such as Solove, offers extensive protection against both defamation[87] and invasion of privacy.[88] The truth is that the legal system already has in place the necessary tools to encourage the cultivation of greater discourse in the public sphere. The problem is that bloggers, on the whole, like file sharers, seem to view the rules on defamation and invasions of privacy as outdated and not applicable to them. This is one of the challenges the law will face in the next ten years: how to recast speech as being a right with substantial responsibility. It is a particular problem as

---

[84] See B. Malloy, 'Anonymous Blogging and Defamation: Balancing Interests of the Internet' 84 *Washington University Law Review* 1187 (2006); D. J. Solove, 'A Tale of Two Bloggers: Free Speech and Privacy in the Blogosphere' 84 *Washington University Law Review* 1195 (2006); D. J. Solove, *The Future of Reputation: Gossip, Rumor, and Privacy on the Internet* (2008).

[85] Solove, 'A Tale of Two Bloggers', *ibid*, 1196–1197.   [86] *ibid*, 1199.

[87] See, e.g. *Loutchansky v Times Newspapers Ltd* [2002] 2 WLR 640; *Applause Store Productions Ltd & Anor v. Raphael* [2008] EWHC 1781 (QB).

[88] See *Mosley v News Group Newspapers Ltd* [2008] EWHC 1777 (QB).

our culture has become obsessed with gossip and celebrity and a shortcut to celebrity and reward in the information society is seen to be to be a controversial figure.[89]

20.3.2 Anonymity and free speech

Not all bloggers act in an irresponsible manner. Sometimes blogs really do shine through as works of genuine quality and in these cases it may be the role of the law to protect the blogger rather than to seek to curb their expression; a prime example being blogs written by whistleblowers and 'employee insiders'.

A whistleblower is an individual who alleges misconduct, deceit, or illegality within an organisation. Whistleblowers are often employees of the organisation in question and as such they place themselves at risk of disciplinary action up to and including dismissal. For this reason the law protects actions defined as 'disclosures in the public interest'. The relevant protection is to be found in the Public Interest Disclosure Act 1998, which added a new Part IVA to the Employment Rights Act 1996. This provides a very narrow defence that only protects 'qualifying disclosures', which are 'disclosures of information which the worker reasonably believes tend to show one or more of the following matters is either happening now, took place in the past, or is likely to happen in the future: (a) a criminal offence; (b) the breach of a legal obligation; (c) a miscarriage of justice; (d) a danger to the health or safety of any individual; (e) damage to the environment; or (f) deliberate covering up of information tending to show any of the above five matters.'[90]

In the event if the disclosure is a 'qualifying disclosure' it may generally only be disclosed to a closed list of recipients. These are the employee's employer or some other person responsible for the activity, the employee's legal advisor, a minister of state, or a prescribed regulator.[91] Only when exceptional circumstances arise will the employee be protected if she makes a general public disclosure. Firstly, the worker must: (a) make the disclosure in good faith; (b) reasonably believe that the information, and any allegation contained in it, is substantially true; and (c) not act for personal gain. In addition, one or more of the following conditions must be met: (a) the worker reasonably believed that she would be subjected to a detriment by her employer if disclosure were to be made to the employer or to a prescribed person; (b) in the absence of an appropriate prescribed person, the worker reasonably believed that disclosure to the employer would result in the destruction or concealment of information about the wrongdoing; or (c) the worker had previously disclosed substantially the same information to her employer or to a prescribed person.[92]

---

[89] For instance Solove discusses the case of Jessica Cutler. Cutler wrote a blog called *The Washingtonienne*, where she chronicled her life working for a US Senator. People didn't read her blog for her thoughts on Congress though; they read it for her explicit posts about sex with a number of different men. When her blog was linked to by the very popular political gossip blog *Wonkette*, Jessica gained instant celebrity. Her blog was discussed in *The Washington Post*, *The New York Times*, and on CNN. She posed for *Playboy* and landed a book deal with a $300,000 advance. Cutler's rise to fame is similar to Belle De Jour whose blog *Diary of a London Call Girl* has led to her publishing five books based on her life as a call girl and has seen her portrayed by Billie Piper in an ITV2 drama.

[90] Employment Rights Act 1996, s. 43B.   [91] Employment Rights Act 1996, ss. 43C–F.
[92] Employment Rights Act 1996, s. 43G.

It is clear that the narrow protections afforded by the Public Interest Disclosure Act will not protect a whistle-blogger who writes a blog detailing the day to day failings of his or her employer, even if their employer is a public sector employer. The truth of this situation came to light in the recent case of *Author of a Blog v Times Newspapers Ltd.*[93] The blog in question was the Orwell Prize[94] winning blog *NightJack*, written by a detective in an English northern police force. *NightJack* clearly at points revealed information which could be protected by the Public Interest Disclosure Act, such as this entry describing the making of an arrest which revealed criminal activity in the force: 'Lee takes his watch and wallet as trophies. Stamps on Mike's head more for the sake of completeness than anything, I mean, that's just what you do, you stamp the head when they are down. Everyone does that. It's soft not to.'[95] In May 2009 journalists from News International identified the author of the *NightJack* blog. They informed the police service and sought to publish his identity. The author sought an injunction against publication of his identity or information which would lead to his identity being revealed. As his actions were not covered by the Public Interest Disclosure Act the claimant sought to rely upon the common law of confidence and privacy as well as his rights under Article 8 of the ECHR. Interestingly though the primary argument put forward by counsel for the claimant is a public sphere argument:

> Mr Tomlinson's primary argument was simply that the claimant wished to remain anonymous and has taken steps to preserve his anonymity accordingly. He says that the defendant is fully aware of the claimant's wish and that, in the circumstances, there is no justification for 'unmasking' him, as he is entitled to keep his identity as the author of the blog private and confidential. Indeed, it is submitted as a general proposition that 'there is a public interest in preserving the anonymity of bloggers.'[96]

Eady J, however, did not believe it was in the public interest to extend privacy in this fashion:

> Hitherto, in those cases which have come before the courts where the claimant relied successfully upon the recently developed cause of action, in the absence of any pre-existing relationship of confidence, the information in question has been of a strictly personal nature concerning, for example, sexual relationships, mental or physical health, financial affairs, or the claimant's family or domestic arrangements. I am not aware of a case in which, as here, there is a significant public element in the information sought to be restricted. I have in mind, of course, that what the claimant seeks to withhold from scrutiny is the identity of the person communicating to the public through his blog. Those who wish to hold forth to the public by this means often take steps to disguise their authorship, but it is in my judgment a significantly further step to argue, if others are able to deduce their identity, that they should be restrained by law from revealing it ... I consider that the claimant fails at stage one, because blogging is essentially a public rather than a private activity.[97]

[93] [2009] EWHC 1358 (QB).
[94] The Orwell Prize is the pre-eminent British prize for political writing.
[95] M. Hughes, 'Online and under cover: Gritty and addictive NightJack blog gives insider's view of modern-day policing', *The Independent* 21 May 2009: http://www.independent.co.uk/news/uk/crime/online-and-under-cover-gritty-and-addictive-nightjack-blog-gives-insiders-view-of-modernday-policing-1688483.html.
[96] [2009] EWHC 1358, [5].   [97] *ibid*, [9], [11].

Eady J did go on specifically to examine whether the political nature of the *NightJack* blog may afford some further protection to the claimant under Article 10 of the ECHR. Perversely he found the political nature of the communication actually reduced the author's right to free expression for as a serving police officer 'the discharge of public duties requires [him] to stand aside from the cut and thrust of such debate'.[98] Ultimately Eady J refused the application allowing *The Times* to publish the identity of the author of the blog, noting: 'it is necessary for me to have in mind the provisions of s. 12 of the Human Rights Act 1998, since the injunction sought would restrain *The Times* from exercising its right of freedom of expression.'[99]

Following the publication of the identity of the author of the blog the *NightJack* blog has been deleted subsequent to disciplinary action taken by Lancashire Police against a detective constable with the force. Although Eady J may have been legally correct the decision has been criticised by many as being morally wrong.[100] *The Times* published a minor news story while a prize winning blog was closed down. Although Eady J was undoubtedly right to hold that *The Times* had broken no confidence and had a right to free expression the decision undoubtedly diminished discourse within the digital public sphere. Further with the decision in *Author of a Blog* demonstrating a lack of legal protection for whistle-bloggers how many others will be discouraged from being forthright and critical of their employers, and how long before journalists, or even other bloggers, unmask other leading whistle-bloggers such as Inspector Gadget, Mental Nurse, and Frank Chalk? This is a future challenge for the legal system. We must decide whether Eady J's decision in *Author of a Blog* is the right one for the digital public sphere. Which is more harmful: pseudonymous blogs written by teachers, police officers, MP's researchers, and NHS staff, or the chilling effect of decisions such as *Author of a Blog*? Only when we can clearly answer that question will the law be able to move forward.

20.3.3 **The democratic divide and social networking**

Social networking sites function very differently to blogs. Whereas the intent of blogs is usually to produce a publicly accessible commentary with the intent that it should contribute to public discourse, in effect a private version of a public media document such as a newspaper, a social networking site is designed to produce communities which mostly congregate around shared experiences, interests, or offline connections. In other words a social networking site is designed to facilitate discourse within groups with shared interests. In many ways this is inimical to the digital public sphere as it risks reinforcing the micro-community values represented by those groups over the shared macro values of the community: in other words it risks Sunsteinien community fragmentation.[101] Like single issue blogs though Social Networking sites can provide a catalyst for campaigning but unlike single issue blogs they can very quickly reach a large

---

[98] *ibid*, [24].   [99] *ibid*, [32].
[100] See, e.g. S. Richmond 'Naming Nightjack: The Times was right legally but wrong morally', *Telegraph.co.uk* 17 June 2009: http://blogs.telegraph.co.uk/technology/shanerichmond/10080637/naming_nightjack_the_times_was_right_legally_but_wrong_morally/.
[101] Discussed above at pp. 59–60.

community. For instance the 'Free Gary MacKinnon' Facebook group had 9,341 members on 28 October 2009. Other wider political groupings can draw much higher membership with the group '1,000,000 United Against the BNP' boasting 691,344 members on the same date. Thus it is clear social networking sites can play an important role in organising groups of individuals around a common theme: an important part of organised political discourse.

What role can the law play in ensuring social networking tools fulfil their potential? The key distinction between social networking sites and blogs is that whereas blogs can be hosted anywhere, a social networking site is naturally hubbed, this means that social networking sites work by drawing people around a hub site such as MySpace, Bebo, Facebook, and LinkedIn. These are all privately owned corporations,[102] meaning that content on these sites may be censored by their operators. There have already been complaints that MySpace censors content. Online activist group MoveOn claims that among other things MySpace have censored an advert by political activist group Common Cause which urged people to send letters to the Federal Communications Commission opposing media consolidation. In the advert Rupert Murdoch was pictured as the symbol of big media. Also they claim MySpace censored a discussion forum on MySpace censorship and in December 2005 attempted to 'wall off' YouTube video content.[103]

The problem was perceived as so great that one of MySpace's original founders Brad Greenspan raised an anti-trust action against MySpace arguing that their policy of blocking links to competing social networking sites, including his vidiLife video hosting site, was a breach of their dominant position. The action failed with Judge A. Howard Matz of the District Court for the Central District of California finding that 'to exit MySpace and visit vidiLife.com presents [little] hassle. Similarly, MySpace users who have placed links on the MySpace site to content on their vidiLife pages can easily place that content directly onto their MySpace site.'[104]

The MySpace case may be seen as a niche decision. It was disposed of before trial and it was raised as an anti-trust action, not a First Amendment case. It does indicate though underlying unease about the way the major social networking sites operate. Further it is likely in future that the leading social networking sites such as MySpace, Facebook, and Bebo will become more interventionist in managing content on their sites. This is because of two pressures. The first is the rise in social networking defamation cases such as *Applause Store*[105] and recent cases such as *Finkel v Facebook*[106] which are attempting to

[102] MySpace is owned by Fox Interactive Media, part of NewsCorp; Bebo is owned by AOL; Facebook is currently an independent corporation as is LinkedIn.

[103] See http://www.civic.moveon.org/pdf/myspace/. See additionally http://www.commonblog. com/story/2007/1/10/103219/774 (on the Common Cause campaign); http://www.censorspace. com/?p=18 (on the discussion board issue) and http://www.nytimes.com/2006/01/02/business/ media/02myspace.html?ex=1293858000&en=bcfedb364352a464&ei=5090&partner=rssuserland &emc=rss (on the walling off of YouTube Video).

[104] *LiveUniverse, Inc. v MySpace, Inc.* Case No. CV 06-6994 AHM (RZx) (CD Cal. June 4, 2007), 24: http://www.cacd.uscourts.gov/CACD/RecentPubOp.nsf/bb61c530eab0911c882567cf005ac6f9/ d856b7ca613a5b36882572fe0051065c/$FILE/CV06-6994AHM.pdf.

[105] *Applause Store Productions Ltd & Anor v Raphael* [2008] EWHC 1781 (QB). Discussed in depth at pp. 162–164.

[106] 102578-09 (N.Y. Supreme Ct. Complaint filed Feb. 24, 2009): http://www.citmedialaw.org/ sites/citmedialaw.org/files/2009-02-16-Finkel%20Complaint.pdf.

hold social networking sites liable as distributors of defamatory content. The second is the danger of Spam in social networking sites. With large captive audiences spammers are attacking social networking sites. This has led to automated Spam filters being enabled on most social networking sites. These are often triggered if a large number of messages or friends requests are sent in a short period of time. The problem with these automated systems came to light in the so called *Blackadder One* case. This involved a Canadian trade unionist Derek Blackadder. Blackadder is an experienced campaigner on behalf of workers' rights around the world. He decided to use Facebook for union organising and campaigns. As a result he would set up a number of campaign pages and then request his many thousands of friends to sign up for each campaign. Unfortunately his messages breached Facebook rules on maximum mailing sizes designed to prevent Spam. His account was therefore suspended. In response a group 'Free the Blackadder One' was created and Facebook relented and reinstated his account. Since this original case there have been many reports of political speech being affected in this fashion.[107] This is not deliberate censorship on the part of the social networking site, merely the impact of harmful unsolicited commercial speech affecting the ability of individuals to communicate in a democratic fashion.

Social networking sites will therefore raise different challenges to blogs in the next 5–10 years. Issues surrounding privacy and pseudonymity are less likely to feature as most people use their true identity or an identifiable proxy on a social networking site. The major issues instead will focus on the social responsibility of both users and operators of such sites. Users, like bloggers, must be aware that with the ability to address large groups comes responsibility. Therefore a rise in defamation actions similar to the *Applause Store* case seems likely. Also it is likely the operators of social networking sites will be called upon to take more proactive action to reduce threats of harassment and bullying,[108] as well as Spam. The challenge for the law is to develop a strategy which allows for the maximisation of the free exchange of ideas and content while protecting the more vulnerable. This will be a major challenge.

20.4 **Conclusion**

This chapter has covered a lot of ground. This reflects the complexity of the challenge facing lawyers and lawmakers in this most vital of subjects to anyone who contributes to the digital public sphere. There seems little doubt that the digital public sphere is unlikely to meet all of the characteristics of Jürgen Habermas's ideal model of the public sphere. Like all prior forms of communication it has inherent flaws which mean that a number of participants are excluded from participation in the discourse that takes place in the digital public sphere either because they lack the means to access the sphere or they lack the skills to participate. Even when participants benefit from all the necessary

---

[107] See, e.g. M. Kirkpatrick, 'Facebook censoring user messaging: spam prevention or un-accountable control of conversation?' *ReadWriteWeb* 21 May 2008: http://www.readwriteweb.com/archives/facebook_censoring_user_messages.php.
[108] See J. Kiss 'Social networking sites sign EU pact to fix cyber-bullying', *The Guardian* 19 February 2009: http://www.guardian.co.uk/media/pda/2009/feb/19/socialnetworking-myspace.

advantages to allow them to fully participate we find that then they fail to engage with one another, or even that they fail to engage at all preferring gossip and rumour to democratic discourse. Lawyers and lawmakers cannot make individuals participate, and it would be undesirable and detrimental for them to do so. Remember Habermas in his ideal public sphere requires that 'any participant may introduce any assertion into discourse'. In other words it is not for us to decide what speech is valid. A discussion of the love life of a celebrity or sports personality is as valid as a discussion of fiscal policy.

What lawyers and lawmakers must do is to allow participants to participate in the digital public sphere. This is a major challenge information law will face in the next ten years. As we have seen in this chapter it involves engagement with two distinct issues. The first is civic engagement between the state and its citizens. The UK Government has already invested heavily in this arena but further challenges will continue to require to be met. In particular the implementation of phase two of the e-government project with its focus on data sharing has already caused concern from civil liberties organisations in the UK. The government may be required to take further steps to demonstrate sufficient data security measures are in place. Further, despite its successes to date, the government still needs to overcome issues of engagement, in particular with younger citizens. As turnout at elections remains low the government may have to revisit questions of e-voting within the next five to ten years including questions of data security and allied costs. The second issue is deliberative discourse between citizens. The digital public sphere offers unparalleled opportunities for individuals to communicate with others across greater distances and in greater numbers than at any previous point in human history. This is a great opportunity. But an unregulated digital public sphere risks being taken over by forms of speech we traditionally view as harmful: defamation, unsolicited commercial communications, and harassment. We must ensure that while the power of the individual to contribute to the digital public sphere is properly supported, action is taken to protect the interests of individuals to engage in discourse securely, privately if desired, and without the interference of harmful speech. Striking this balance may prove to be the greatest challenge for law in the information society in the next ten years.

FURTHER READING

Books

J. Habermas, *Between Facts and Norms: Contributions to a Discourse Theory of Law and Democracy* (1996)

P. Norris, *Digital Divide: Civic Engagement, Information Poverty, and the Internet Worldwide* (2002)

D. J. Solove, *The Future of Reputation: Gossip, Rumor, and Privacy on the Internet* (2008)

R. Diebert et al., *Access Denied* (2008)

Chapters and Articles

Z. Papacharissi, 'The Virtual Sphere: The Internet as a Public Sphere' (2002) 4 *New Media Society* 9

H. H. Perritt Jr, 'Open Government' (1997) 14 *Government Information Quarterly* 397

D. Wills & S. Reeves, 'Facebook as a Political Weapon: Information in Social Networks' (2009) 4 *British Politics* 265

S. Vaidhyanathan, 'The Anarchist in the Coffee House: A Brief Consideration of Local Culture, the Free Culture Movement, and Prospects for a Global Public Sphere' 70 *Law and Contemporary Problems* 205 (2007)

Virtual environments

Throughout this book we have talked of cyberspace as if it were a singular place. This is necessary when one is discussing macro issues such as justice and civil liberties, democracy, community standards, and legal certainty. In truth though as we all know the internet is not a single place but an interconnected variety of communities with a variety of values and with separate community regulations for each. In *The Regulation of Cyberspace*, Murray defines the two types of communities as 'macro communities' and 'micro communities'. 'Macro communities are broad communities which impact extensively on an individual's day-to-day life. Such communities often have rigid community standards or norms which are designed, and enforced, to ensure that the values of the community are upheld. Micro communities are narrow communities focussed on a particular aspect of an individual's life; usually part of their social life.'[1] Examples of each (from real space) would be citizenship of a particular state, or residence of a particular city (macro community) and membership of a private club or society, such as a gym or sports club (micro community). Murray believes that due to the nature of cyberspace macro community recognition is limited to common controls and overarching values such as netiquette or code controls such as Cleanfeed.[2] The internet is the perfect place for the creation of ever more finely-grained micro communities. As discussed in chapter six communities in cyberspace can form around activities of interest to a tiny proportion of society, so while *The Marmite Forum* which brings together fans of a particular yeast extract may appeal to about 50% of UK society (if you believe the advertising campaign) others such as *Worms Direct,* a forum on worm farming and *Looner Fetish,* a forum for individuals with a sexual fetish about balloons are certainly forums created around minority interests.

Among the largest micro communities are online gaming communities. *World of Warcraft*, the largest online gaming community, boasts over 11.5 million subscribers.[3] A number of other major games sites including *Second Life, Everquest, Entropia Universe,* and *Ultima Online* boast large subscription bases also, with Second Life claiming in particular to have over 15 million registered accounts, although more accurate usage statistics show it has a core of about 1.4 million users who log in regularly.[4] What is

[1] A. Murray, *The Regulation of Cyberspace: Control in the Online Environment* (2007), 129.
[2] *ibid* 141–144.
[3] Source: Blizzard Entertainment: http://eu.blizzard.com/en/press/081223.html.
[4] Source: Linden Labs, Second Life Economic Statistics for 13 August 2009: http://www.secondlife.com/statistics/economy-data.php.

more interesting about most of these gaming communities is not their size but the fact that many of them, including *Second Life, Entropia Universe,* and *World of Warcraft* offer the opportunity to trade or earn rewards which may be exchanged for real world cash: in other words these games have real-cash economies, and where financial rewards are available the problems of the real world are usually not far behind, leaving these communities liable to fraud, theft, extortion, money laundering, and trading in illegal and immoral items. Also more mundane issues of ownership and title arise. As a result we are beginning to see legal interventions in these virtual environments.

21.1 **Virtual worlds, virtual people**

The majority of well known online gaming communities, and indeed nearly all of them which offer the opportunity to earn real world rewards, are of a sub-genre known as Massively Multiplayer Online Role Playing Games or MMORPGs.[5] They have some characteristics in common: as their name suggests in each players 'role play' that is they take on the persona of an in-game character or avatar and play through the game in the form of their character. They are all also 'constant worlds': this means the game plays 24/7 whether or not the player is logged in. Thus MMORPGs are like real life: when you go to sleep the world doesn't stop. They also mostly share characteristics of progression and reward for achievements as well as a high reliance on social interaction and often teamwork. After that, however, they vary greatly in genre.

World of Warcraft is a fantasy questing game, sometimes called a 'Dungeons & Dragons' game. This genre is among the most popular type of MMORPG and players can usually play as any one of a variety of characters such as humans, wizards, or elves and gain reward through winning battles, finding treasure, and trading items and sometimes if allowed by the game's rules skills, potions, or spells. There are a number of variations on questing games including ones set in World War II, in science fiction environments, and in ancient civilizations, such as ancient Egypt. *Second Life* is a real-world simulator, or at very least a re-imagination of the real world. Here players may take human or non-human form (in *Second Life* your avatar can be anything you choose) but the gameplay is more focussed on everyday life: buying and selling land, items, and commodities and socialising. There are elements of questing but the majority of second life residents are using it either as an economic or social tool rather than as a games experience. Some people even use second life to gain employment with virtual employers while others set up virtual businesses. In many ways real-world simulators allow people to vicariously live a life they may have hoped to live in real life: with fantastic properties, designer clothes, and sports cars, while they speculate on land and currency, all at a fraction of the cost of the real world equivalent.

The opportunity to make real money from playing MMORPGs has attracted a number of entrepreneurs in recent years. Most famous among them is probably Ailin Graef who became famous as the first US$ millionaire through trading in *Second Life.* Her business is in property development and although she started out by buying and

[5] Aspects of MMORPGs have been discussed previously in Ch. 5.

developing small plots of land and then renting out the property she developed, she now heads a staff of more than 80 full-time developers and artists based in Hubei, China. Although stories like Graef's are rare there are a number of businesses which make regular profits from MMORPGs including businesses specialised to MMORPGs such as avatar designers, property designers, and land developers, as well as virtual equivalents of real world businesses offering services such as legal advice and financial advice or selling virtual (or even real) goods.[6] Some traders, as in the real world, trade in the black market with sales of counterfeit virtual goods such as Gucci sunglasses, Ferrari cars, and Nike trainers being commonplace despite none of these businesses having a presence in *Second Life*. Others specialise in earning rewards, in particular in quest games such as *World of Warcraft* and *Everquest*. By employing teams of highly skilled players these 'gold farmers' collect rewards from playing and search for treasure. They then sell this on to other players on a secondary market. It is not only gold that these businesses specialise in. They will, for a fee, tailor a player's avatar by building up their skill level or will help a player by taking their avatar though a particularly perilous part of their adventure. They will also collect items such as potions, spells, and magical weapons to sell on and will even sell complete accounts on the secondary market. Most gold farming takes place in China and surrounding territories and in December 2008 it was reported that the global value of the business was in excess of $1bn, employing over 400,000 people.[7] Unfortunately the number of gold farms opening in China undermined the market for in-game currencies in some games environments and even affected exchange rates for real world currencies, leading the Chinese government to ban the conversion of virtual money into real money for the purpose of buying actual goods and services.[8]

Even gold farming is not among the worst excesses of MMORPGs though. Further problems with virtual environments include 'griefing', which is basically antisocial behaviour including attacking other players, damaging property of other players, causing system crashes, or abusing other players; pornography and (virtual) prostitution and probably most worryingly age play and virtual child abuse.[9] We cannot just think of MMORPGs as games therefore as the activities of players/residents may be extremely antisocial, harmful to real world business interests, real world property, and may even be illegal. The question then is who should regulate these environments?

[6] For instance IBM uses its second-life based IBM Business Center to showcase new products and services to potential customers, while Kraft foods uses its second life superstore to discuss new products, give customer support and nutritional advice. Some residents of second life sell real goods by opening Amazon affiliate stores in Second Life. See A. Gonsalves, 'Second Life residents build stores around Amazon.com', *Information Week*, 8 November 2006: http://www.informationweek.com/news/internet/ebusiness/showArticle.jhtml?articleID=193600812.

[7] R. Heeks, 'Current Analysis and Future Research Agenda on "Gold Farming": Real-World Production in Developing Countries for the Virtual Economies of Online Game', *University of Manchester, Development Informatics Working Paper Series, No. 32*, December 2008: http://www.sed.manchester.ac.uk/idpm/research/publications/wp/di/documents/di_wp32.pdf.

[8] People's Republic of China, Ministry of Commerce, *China bars use of virtual money for trading in real goods*, 29 June 2009: http://english.mofcom.gov.cn/aarticle/newsrelease/commonnews/2009 06/20090606364208.html.   [9] Age play is discussed above at pp. 377–379.

21.2 **The virtual gods**

Unlike the wider internet, virtual environments have natural rulers. Games environments are, despite their appearances, tightly controlled environments. The larger gaming environments, which have more players, a more solid economy, and therefore the possibility of profit are all controlled by the operators of the games environment: for *World of Warcraft* this is Blizzard Entertainment, a California-based company; for *Second Life* it is Linden Lab, also based in California; while for *Entropia Universe* it is MindArk, a Swedish-based company. Like all software developers they utilise end-user license agreements (EULAs) to manage their software distribution and installation, and via this they extend control into their game environment. For example Linden Lab has a number of policies for *Second Life* on issues such as community standards; 'the goals of the Community Standards are simple: treat each other with respect and without harassment, adhere to local standards as indicated by simulator ratings, and refrain from any hate activity which slurs a real-world individual or real-world community. The Community Standards sets out six behaviors, the "Big Six", that will result in suspension or, with repeated violations, expulsion from the Second Life Community'[10] and rules for regulating in-game copyright infringement: 'Linden Lab will respond to allegations of copyright violations in accordance with the Digital Millennium Copyright Act'.[11]

Gaming environments are not therefore uncontrolled environments; they are similar to real-world sporting environments where players must comply with the rules of the game or risk suspension or expulsion from the gaming arena. Thus we may conceptualise in-game rules for *World of Warcraft* or *Second Life* promulgated by the game controllers, Blizzard Entertainment and Linden Lab, as being akin to in-game rules promulgated in association football by FIFA or UEFA, or in tennis by the International Tennis Federation. What is important about applying this conceptualisation is that is makes clear that players in online virtual environments are subject to distinctive layers of regulation. While the in-game rules are recognised by the wider community as controlling the sporting element of the game, the participants remain subject to external legal rules when the sporting element of the competition is abandoned. Thus, to take an example from the sport of boxing, while the normal rules of assault are willingly suspended in favour of the sporting competition between fighters, should one competitor begin to violently assault the other he may expect to be investigated by the police and may find himself subject to charges. Thus the 'rules of the game' will only be followed where they find acceptance within society at large. This was demonstrated most clearly in the aftermath of the infamous 1987 'Old Firm' derby between the Glasgow football giants Rangers and Celtic.

---

[10] The six are: (1) Intolerance; (2) Harassment; (3) Assault; (4) Disclosure of private data; (5) Setting up Adult Regions, Groups & Listings; and (6) Disturbing the Peace (Griefing). See http://www.secondlife.com/corporate/cs.php
[11] See http://www.secondlife.com/corporate/dmca.php.

Case Study Old Firm Violence

Following an on-field incident which saw a number of players involved in violent conduct which risked spreading to the crowd the referee sent off two players, Rangers goalkeeper and England international Chris Woods and Celtic forward and Scotland international Frank McAvennie. A number of other players were cautioned including Rangers captain and England international Terry Butcher and Rangers midfielder and England international Graham Roberts.

Following an investigation into the incident by Strathclyde police the four players were charged with breach of the peace. Two, Butcher and Woods, were found guilty while McAvennie was found not guilty and Roberts was found not proven. Butcher was fined £250 and Woods £500. Both appealed and the verdicts were upheld.

The fines may have been relatively small but it meant that Butcher and Woods had received a criminal record for an on-field incident. Since then a number of charges have been brought around the globe for incidents that occurred during a sporting event. In 2004 Canadian ice hockey player Todd Bertuzzi received a conditional discharge and probation after pleading guilty to an assault on fellow player Steven Moore during an NHL game. In a similar charge Boston Bruins player Marty McSorley was found guilty of assault with a weapon in a provincial court in British Columbia after attacking Donald Brashear of the Vancouver Canucks in 2000. Probably the worst example of criminal on-field activity to date though is from the sport of rugby and the nation of South Africa. In 2006 two players playing for Delicious Rugby Club were charged with murder after opponent Riaan Loots was kicked to death during a match. Eventually one player, Ben Zimri, was convicted of culpable homicide in the Worcester Regional Court. The murder charge being reduced to culpable homicide, as the court found that Loots's death was caused by negligence on Zimri's part rather than intent to kill.[12]

We may learn a lot from sporting cases such as *Butcher* when dealing with virtual gaming environments. They demonstrate a social contract between the legal system and the administrators of sporting and gaming environments. The administrators are given free reign over the 'rules of the game', while lawmakers, and law enforcement authorities, retain their oversight function to ensure that the wider rules of the community are not disregarded by the players of the game. We can see a similar pattern already emerging with virtual gaming environments.

21.3 The game versus the law

As already stated the in-game activity of some players may be antisocial, bordering on the illegal. When does the law intervene and when are game rules applied? There are a number of reported virtual crimes including virtual assault and

---

[12] See http://www.rugby365.com/all_news/sa/news/1726682.htm.

murder,[13] virtual rape,[14] virtual child abuse,[15] virtual theft,[16] virtual copyright infringement,[17] and virtual fraud.[18] Some of these issues are clearly of interest to the wider community, while others may best be regulated by the rules of the game.

Strangely it tends to be what may, at first glance, seem to be the more extreme forms of criminality that are left to the operators of the games to regulate. These are virtual crimes against the person such as assault, murder, or rape. The truth is that although murder, assault, and rape are among the more serious offences in the real world, due to the harm they do to the individual, in gaming communities where avatars may be instantly healed or resurrected these actions may be seen as part of the game rather than criminal activity. In *World of Warcraft* for example you may attack or even kill another player as part of your quest. The issue of virtual harm to the person (avatar?) tends to arise more in real life simulations as the social context of these games is closer to real world society and players often expect the social norms of the real world to apply. Thus while a player in *World of Warcraft* would expect that combat including possibly a fight to the death to obtain gold or potions is socially normative for that community, a player in *Second Life* would expect the community to act against the aberrant action of another player who attacked him while he was standing in line at the bank and robbed him of his Linden Dollars.

This is reflected in the in-game rules for these different types of virtual environments. Under the *Second Life* Community Standards any player who commits assault, that is: 'shooting, pushing, or shoving another Resident in a Safe Area or creating or using scripted objects which singularly or persistently target another Resident in a manner which prevents their enjoyment of Second Life' may have his or her account suspended or even terminated. There is no equivalent in *World of Warcraft* although the harassment policy does say players may be disciplined for speech which refers to 'clear and masked language which refers to extreme and/or violent sexual acts or extremely violent real life actions'.

To date there have been no cases of law enforcement authorities being asked to investigate a murder in a virtual environment, however crimes against the person have been reported to real world authorities. In 2007 a Belgian citizen of *Second Life* reported a virtual rape to the authorities. Although no criminal action was taken the Brussels public

---

[13] The definition particularly of virtual murder is difficult as often characters will be resurrected after 'death'. For instance the player guide to *Second Life* states: 'When your avatar is in an area that allows damage to occur, a heart is shown at the top of your screen with the percentage of health. When this reached 0%, you will be teleported to your home location. So the "death" isn't a permanent one, you don't lose any inventory and can return to the damage enabled region.' Similarly *World of Warcraft* and *Entropia Universe* allow resurrection.

[14] R. Lynn, 'Virtual Rape Is Traumatic, but Is It a Crime?' *Wired*, 5 April 2007. Available from: http://www.wired.com/culture/lifestyle/commentary/sexdrive/2007/05/sexdrive_0504.

[15] See 'Age Play', Ch. 14, pp. 377–379.

[16] See CNN, *Online gamer in China wins virtual theft suit*, 20 December 2003: http://www.cnn.com/2003/TECH/fun.games/12/19/china.gamer.reut/.

[17] *Eros LLC v Simon et al*. Case: 1:07-cv-04447-SLT-JMA (DC ED NY): 3 December 2007: http://www.citmedialaw.org/sites/citmedialaw.org/files/2008-01-03-Judgment%20by%20Consent%20as%20to%20Simon.pdf.

[18] D. Talbot, 'The Fleecing of the Avatars', *MIT Technology Review*, January/February 2008: http://www.technologyreview.com/Infotech/19844/.

prosecutor asked patrol detectives of the Federal Computer Crime Unit to investigate the incident.[19] Around the same time German and UK authorities began an investigation of age play (a virtual form of child abuse) but again seem to have concluded that this was a matter for in-game controllers rather than public authorities.[20]

Avatars it seems are not legally protected, at least not yet. Instead control over the interactions of individual players, or citizens, is ceded to the game controllers. Thus Linden Lab has an extensive Community Standard statement which bans assault, harassment (including griefing), and adult content (except in designated adult areas). In particular age play is clearly banned,[21] as is virtual assault and sexual assault, including rape.[22] By comparison whereas avatars are viewed as part of the in-game culture, possessions and other forms of property are viewed as having a value outside of the in-game culture due to their independent economic value. For this reason law enforcement authorities and the courts have become involved in a number of disputes over virtual property, copyright infringement, and trade mark infringement.

21.3.1 Virtual property disputes

In several cases disputes over virtual property have led to real life violence. In such cases the authorities always take action. Most famously several disputes in China have led to violent attacks on players, the most dramatic of which is probably the case of Qiu Chengwei. It was widely reported in 2005 that Mr Qiu stabbed a fellow gamer, Zhu Caoyuan, in the chest, killing him when he found out he had sold a virtual sword he had loaned to Mr Zhu. Mr Qiu was eventually sentenced to a suspended death sentence (life imprisonment) for the murder.[23] More recently Dutch authorities brought charges against a fifteen year old and a fourteen year old who forced a thirteen year old to transfer a mask, an amulet, and some credits (virtual cash) to their account in the game *RuneScape*. From reports of the case on 6 September 2007 the two older boys attacked the victim kicking him and threatening him with a knife until he transferred the virtual goods and the credit. The attackers were convicted of 'violent theft' and sentenced to 200 hours community service (for the fifteen year old) and 160 hours' community service (for the fourteen year old). What is interesting is that they were found guilty not of assault but aggravated theft. Unlike the Qiu Chengwei case, which had been prosecuted as a standard murder case the Dutch authorities did not just charge the boys with common assault. The way the court dealt with the transfer of the virtual property in this case makes it a watershed decision. The court is reported to have said in a summary of

[19] A. Webber, 'Belgian police patrols Second Life to prevent rape', *Second Life Insider*, 21 April 2007: http://www.secondlifeinsider.com/2007/04/21/belgian-police-patrols-second-life-to-prevent-rape/.
[20] Above, p. 378.
[21] 'Linden Lab further clarify ageplay policy', *The Metaverse Journal*, 14 November 2007: http://www.metaversejournal.com/2007/11/14/linden-lab-further-clarify-ageplay-policy/.
[22] Linden Lab, *Second Life Community Standards*, Harassment and Assault policies: http://www.secondlife.com/corporate/cs.php.
[23] BBC News, *Chinese gamer sentenced to life*, 8 June 2005: http://news.bbc.co.uk/1/hi/technology/4072704.stm.

its ruling that 'these virtual goods are goods (under Dutch law), so this is theft'.[24] This is the first time a court in Europe has made such a statement, but it may be expected that courts in the Netherlands and elsewhere in Europe may soon be asked frequently to rule on the nature of virtual property.

There have been several cases worldwide which have dealt with virtual property as being akin to physical property even without the element of real world harm seen in the Qiu Chengwei and Dutch *RuneScape* cases. In China reported cases include the case of Li Hongchen who spent two years, and 10,000 Yuan playing *Hongyue*, (Red Moon), before weapons he had accumulated were stolen by a hacker in February 2003. Mr Li asked the company behind the game, Beijing Arctic Ice Technology, to identify the player who stole his virtual property, but it declined, saying it could not give out a player's private details. The police said they could not help so Mr Li took his case to court. The company argued that the value of the virtual property only existed in the game and was 'just piles of data to our operating companies', but the Beijing's Chaoyang District People's Court ruled that the firm should restore Mr Li's lost items, finding the company liable because of loopholes in the server programs that made it easy for hackers to break in.[25] In a further case in 2005 an online gamer in Chengdu found his 'currency' and 'equipment' in the online computer game *The Legend of Mir* abruptly disappeared. The gamer, Mr Zhao, appears to be a gold farmer as it is reported that 'he hired a person to test the game around the clock for three months and paid him 1,500 Yuan (US$181) each month'.[26] It is reported that Mr Zhao complained to the Consumers' Association of Sichuan Province. According to Law of the People's Republic of China on Protection of Consumer Rights and Interests, Article 44 'Business operators shall, if the commodities or services they supply have caused damage to the properties of consumers, bear civil liabilities by repair, remanufacture, replacement, return of goods, make-up for the short commodity, return of payment for goods and services, or compensation for losses and so on as demanded by consumers. If consumers and business operators have otherwise agreed upon, such agreements shall be fulfilled.' The Consumers' Association judged that Mr Zhao's rights should be so protected and the operators of the game should compensate Mr Zhao. It is not known though how much compensation was paid to Mr Zhao.[27]

The courts in the US have also become involved in misappropriated virtual property. Although there have to date been no cases such as the Dutch *RuneScape* case where criminal charges have been brought for the 'theft' of virtual goods there have been several civil cases in the US for misappropriation of virtual goods. The best known of these, is *Bragg v Linden & Rosedale*.[28] In this case the plaintiff Marc Bragg, a Pennsylvania attorney and *Second Life* land developer known as Marc Woebegone, won a settlement from *Second Life* operator Linden Lab after Bragg's account was terminated for improper

---

[24] New Zealand Herald, *Teens convicted for virtual theft in RuneScape heist*, 22 October 2008: http://www.nzherald.co.nz/games/news/article.cfm?c_id=38&objectid=10538822.

[25] CNN, *Online gamer in China wins virtual theft suit*: http://www.cnn.com/2003/TECH/fun.games/12/19/china.gamer.reut/.

[26] S. Xuan, *Virtual Property in Greater China*: http://www.hg.org/article.asp?id=5538.

[27] *ibid*.

[28] Case 2:06-cv-04925-ER (ED Pa) 30 May 2007: http://www.nylawyer.com/adgifs/decisions/101507robreno.pdf.

conduct in relation to land auctions.[29] Although this was in nature a contract dispute over the terms of the *Second Life* EULA the court appeared to be swayed by the evidence laid before it by Mr Bragg that the defendants had promoted *Second Life's* unique properties of land ownership and preservation of property rights.[30] Following the Bragg case there have been a number of cases involving *Second Life* property rights raised in the US. The sister cases of *Eros LLC v Simon et al.*[31] and *Eros LLC v Leatherwood et al.*[32] are *Second Life* copyright and trade mark infringement cases.[33] In both cases Eros, the copyright and trade mark holder, received a quick settlement for the virtual infringement of their rights. Cases which have followed, and been settled (unfortunately none have gone to a full hearing) include *Minsky v Linden Research*,[34] a trade mark infringement case raised over the trade mark 'SLART' owned by the plaintiff and being used for an art gallery in *Second Life*,[35] and *Taser International v Linden Research*,[36] a trade mark claim raised against Linden for allowing users to use 'Taser-style' devices in *Second Life*.[37]

It is clear therefore that virtual property disputes may lead to the intervention of real world courts but this is only the beginning of where courts may be asked to go in future. Already lawmakers have intervened in in-game gambling with Linden Lab announcing in July 2007 that gambling would be outlawed in *Second Life* as 'while Linden Lab does not offer an online gambling service, Linden Lab and *Second Life* Residents must comply with state and federal laws applicable to regulated online gambling, even when both operators and players of the games reside outside of the US. And, because there are a variety of conflicting gambling regulations around the world we have chosen to restrict gambling in Second Life as described in a revised policy.'[38] More recently tax authorities have begun to question how they may tax the profits of virtual businesses which can be quite substantial. It is reported that the Swedish authorities wish to tax the profits of online transactions but as yet have not found a system to do so,[39] while a number of tax authorities, including the UK's HMRC, benefit from an agreement from Linden Lab to gather VAT on user accounts and registrations of land within *Second Life*.[40] This though does not ingather tax on profits made through transactions between

---

[29] The full story of this case is recounted above at pp. 99–100.

[30] *Bragg v Linden*, above n. 28, 3–5.

[31] Case: 1:07-cv-04447-SLT-JMA (DC ED NY): 3 December 2007: http://www.citmedialaw.org/sites/citmedialaw.org/files/2008-01-03-Judgment%20by%20Consent%20as%20to%20Simon.pdf.

[32] Case: 8:2007-cv-01158 (DC MD Fla.): 19 March 2008: http://media.tbo.com/pdf/032108erossettlement.pdf.

[33] The full story of these cases is recounted above at p. 100.

[34] Case No. 1:08-CV-819 (DC ND NY): 22 January 2009: http://www.3dinternetlaw.com/Trademark/Trademark/Minsky_files/Order%20Dismissing%20Action%20by%20Settlement.pdf.

[35] In this case the settlement seems to follow the failure of the plaintiff to prove his case following a defence motion to dismiss on the basis that the plaintiff had failed to establish confusion or harm. See defence motion to dismiss 21 November 2008: http://www.3dinternetlaw.com/Trademark/Trademark/Minsky_files/Kapor%20and%20Rosedale%20Motion%20to%20Dismiss.pdf.

[36] Case 2:09-cv-00811-ROS (DC AZ) filed 17 April 17 2009.

[37] At the time of writing Taser have withdrawn their claim without prejudice meaning they may relaunch the action in future.

[38] R. Linden, *Wagering In Second Life: New Policy* 25 July 2007: https://blogs.secondlife.com/community/features/blog/2007/07/26/wagering-in-second-life-new-policy.

[39] M. Walpole, *Taxing Virtual Profits*, 2: http://www.taxinstitute.com.au/files/contax/docs/feature_article_sept08.pdf.   [40] *ibid*, 4.

players in *Second Life* and for that reason HMRC has shown an interest in taxing the realisation or real world profits made through the virtual environments. According to one report a spokesperson for the Revenue indicated ' ... that users were free to make transactions, but would be taxed on gains beyond their £9,200 annual capital gains allowance. Residents with established businesses will be subject to stricter scrutiny.'[41] The Revenue's VAT information also makes it clear that electronically supplied services of the type described above are subject to VAT on the supplier at the place of supply.[42] The US IRS is also interested in the topic and this prompted a US Congress Joint Economic Committee Enquiry apprehensive of an IRS decision to simply tax the virtual world on transactions inside the virtual world.[43]

To date the difficulty of assessing taxation due for in-game transactions has kept the tax take from virtual worlds to a minimum with the majority of the taxation collected being in the form of VAT collected by operators such as MindArk and Linden Lab on transactions between players and game operators and in the form of self-assessed declarations of taxable capital gains proffered by individuals. But with only one virtual environment (*Second Life*) reporting an average of 214 players achieved in-world business profits of in excess of US$5,000 in the first six months of 2009 and a further 515 players achieving profits of over US$1,000 per month the potential tax take is significant and growing.[44] Taxation is likely to be the next battleground between the realm of the virtual, or game, world and the real world but it is not likely to be the only one.

21.4 **Conclusion: when worlds collide**

As has already been seen the freedom offered by virtual worlds brings the opportunity for players to engage in activities not possible in the real world. These activities offer the opportunity for real profit thanks to currency exchanges, such as the ones operated by *Second Life* and *Entropia Universe* or via secondary markets such as *IgSale.com* which deal in *World of Warcraft* gold. Unfortunately the ability to profit has seen these environments shift subtly away from being pure gaming environments to being fora for criminality. They are in form games environments but in effect they are a part of the real world. Responsibility for controlling the actions of players is, like in sporting environments, split between the games controllers and real world law enforcement bodies. To date these interactions have been kept at a minimum but should the value of in-game economies continue to rise there will no doubt be further interaction as these worlds, virtual and real, collide.

[41] Virtual Worlds News, *UK Looks to Tax Second Life Transactions*, 5 August 2007: http://www.virtualworldsnews.com/2007/08/uk-looks-to-tax.html.

[42] See *VAT Information Sheet 04/03: Electronically supplied services: a guide to interpretation.* Specifically included is the example of 'Accessing automated online games which are dependent on the Internet, or other similar electronic networks, where players are remote from one another.'

[43] Press Release Joint Economic Committee of the Congress of the US, *Virtual Economies Need Clarification, Not More Taxes*, 17 October 2006.

[44] See http://www.secondlife.com/statistics/economy-data.php.

What will this mean for lawyers and lawmakers? As we have already seen there have been a few interactions predicated upon attacks on the person (or avatar) including at least one claim for rape and others for child abuse. It appears though that as these are purely in-game activities the courts and law enforcement authorities will trust the games controllers to manage such activity within their games environment. Thus primary control in such situations may be found in community standards with the primary sanctions being in-game (suspension or termination of account). Where harm occurs in the real world (as in the Dutch *RuneScape* case) then, obviously real world authorities will intervene. Where the harm which occurs online is financial the courts, it appears are more willing to intervene. This reflects the long history of the courts in protecting intangible properties. Thus in the *RuneScape* case the District Court in Leeuwarden was willing to find not only assault but also theft had occurred. Similarly cases in China and the US have extended some form of intervention of the courts where virtual property has been misappropriated. As for the law in the UK, the Theft Act 1968 suggests that the misappropriation of virtual goods would be theft in English Law. By s. 1(1) it is an offence to 'dishonestly appropriate property belonging to another with the intention of permanently depriving the other of it'. Property is described in s. 4(1) as 'includ[ing] money and all other property, real or personal, including things in action and other intangible property.' This would seem to cover the situation where in-game property or money was misappropriated by another player. Equally it is clear that trade mark or copyright disputes such as those seen in the US in *Eros* and *Minsky* would be covered by the appropriate provisions of the Copyright, Designs and Patents Act 1988 and the Trade Marks Act 1994.

These though are only the issues seen in courts to date, what about the future? It is already clear that one of the major issues real world lawmakers want to address is taxation of in-game profits. It may be assumed this will be a key issue in the next five to ten years, but there are other key issues which will no doubt arise. One relates to concerns about money laundering in virtual environments. In 2007 the Fraud Advisory Panel warned that there was a risk of money laundering via virtual cash economies.[45] Currently virtual environments are not subject to money laundering regulations but it seems only a matter of time until governments turn their attention to cash transactions in these environments especially as it is now possible to draw virtual cash such as Project Entropia Dollars and Linden Dollars from ATMs thanks to tie up deals between real world banks and the games controllers of online environments. There are also more outlandish claims, which lawmakers may be unable to ignore, such as claims that virtual terrorist training and recruiting camps have been set up in virtual environments such as *Second Life*.[46] These more outlandish examples of virtual criminality are probably most suitable for direct control from the games controllers, perhaps with the encouragement of law enforcement authorities, as occurred with gambling and age play previously.

It is more likely that the courts will be called in to deal with more mundane matters such as is having an affair in *Second Life* grounds for divorce as adultery? Indeed it was

---

[45] Fraud Advisory Panel, *Government Should Extend Legislation into Virtual World*, 1 May 2007: http://www.fraudadvisorypanel.org/newsite/PDFs/pressreleases/Government%20Should%20Extend%20Legislation%20into%20Virtual%20World%20010507.pdf.

[46] N. O'Brien, 'Spies watch rise of virtual terrorists', *The Australian*, 31 July 2007: http://www.news.com.au/story/0,23599,22163811-2,00.html.

reported in November 2008 that one British couple had divorced after the wife had found the husband was having an affair in *Second Life*, although in that case unreasonable behaviour, not adultery, was listed as the ground for divorce.[47] There is a further question which arises: when someone divorces in real life what claim do they have to financial assets held by their partner's avatar? This question remains currently unresolved but as the value of property portfolios and other assets held by *Second Life* characters increase it seems only a matter of time before a divorce case calls for them to be treated as assets of the marriage. The terms of service in all major virtual worlds do not currently deal with this directly, and in any event it seems a family court would override contractual agreements in determining the value of the marital property. More confusingly a person may marry in some virtual environments. It is possible therefore to have a real life partner and a *Second Life* partner who are different people. *Second Life* sees this as a purely administrative arrangement allowing marriages to be dissolved at the click of a button with each party retaining the property held in their account. It is open to question whether a real world court would entertain a claim based either in contract law, or in unjust enrichment, should one party profit at the expense of the other by 'ending the marriage'. Finally there remains the issue of death and probate. While your *Second Life* avatar may go on forever you won't. What happens when you die? According to Linden Lab's terms of service a *Second Life* account may be bequeathed as part of the player's estate,[48] though not all games controllers extend the same benefit to the deceased.

As people are always marrying, divorcing, and dying, and as people are likely to continue not to plan ahead for these events, these are likely to join copyright infringement, trade mark infringement, and basic virtual theft as the focus of a number of cases at the virtual/real world interface in the next five to ten years. That being said, most people will continue to treat online virtual environments such as *World of Warcraft* and *Second Life* as purely an escapist, gaming experience where the rules of the game are set out by the controller of that environment. It should therefore be assumed that real world cases involving disputes over virtual property or activities in virtual environments will remain relatively rare.

FURTHER READING

Books

A. Sparrow, *The Law of Virtual Worlds and Internet Social Networks* (2009)

J. M. Balkin and B. S. Noveck (eds), *The State of Play: Law, Games, and Virtual Worlds* (2006)

T.L. Taylor, *Play Between Worlds: Exploring Online Game Culture* (2006)

[47] S. Morris, 'Second Life affair leads to real life divorce', *The Guardian*, 13 November 2008: http://www.guardian.co.uk/technology/2008/nov/13/second-life-divorce.
[48] Para. 2.4 of Linden Lab/Second Life terms of service says: 'You may not transfer your Account to any third party without the prior written consent of Linden Lab; notwithstanding the foregoing, Linden Lab will not unreasonably withhold consent to the transfer of an Account in good standing by operation of valid written will to a single natural person, provided that proper notice and documentation are delivered as requested by Linden Lab.'

Chapters and Articles

M. Risch, 'Virtual Rule of Law' 112 *West Virginia Law Review* 1 (2009)

B. Keupink, 'Virtual Criminal Law in Boundless New Environments' (2007) 6 *International Journal of Technology Transfer and Commercialisation* 160

B. Camp, 'The Play's the Thing: A Theory of Taxing Virtual Worlds' 59 *Hastings Law Journal* 1 (2007)

What way next?

To draw together the many themes discussed in this book is challenging. This book has attempted to contextualise the interface between law and technology as we move from the physical society to a digital society. This has involved discussion of digital and virtual property, even virtual societies. It has led us to examine the value of information, including free expression, data privacy, and data protection. It has also led us into the dark side of digital technology with examination of harmful content, digital crime, and even cyberterrorism, yet this chapter is the most difficult of all to write for almost as each chapter in this book was being written it was already on the way to being out of date.

This is because of the pace of change driven by technological advances in the information society. We have gone from computers that filled rooms to computers held in the palm of your hand within forty years. Information stored on reams of punch cards can now fit on a single memory card the size of a fingernail, and processing power increases exponentially so that a computer that costs £300 today has more processing power than the famous Cray 1 supercomputer of the 1970s which cost at least $5m. The speed of development in computer and information technology is driven by a rule known as Moore's Law, named in honour of Intel co-founder Gordon Moore who first set out his principle of computing processing power in his 1965 paper *Cramming More Components onto Integrated Circuits*.[1] Moore's Law, which states: 'the number of transistors that can be placed inexpensively on an integrated circuit has increased exponentially, doubling approximately every two years' has remained true since its introduction and is often credited with advances in data storage, data processing and speed of data access.

Although there is no doubting the veracity of Moore's Law, which is driven by intense competition in the micro-circuit sector, it doesn't fully explain why so many technologies, and services, are driven forward with the same speed in the information society, so everything from storage capacity on HDD and memory cards to internet access speeds, to number of pixels in a digital camera are being driven forward at the same pace. Why is this? It is my belief that it is because Moore's Law is not the driver of change and development but the means of measuring it. The driver of change in the information society was and remains the discovery of the bit.

---

[1] G. E. Moore, 'Cramming More Components onto Integrated Circuits' 38(8) *Electronics*, April 9, 1965.

Much as the discovery of subatomic particles revitalised physics throughout the twentieth century with the new discipline of quantum physics making the most incredible breakthroughs,[2] the discovery of the common building block for storing, transmitting, and processing information has driven the information society forward on all fronts. This common driver of change allows designers of hardware and software, telecommunications engineers, designers of consumer digital goods, and service providers such as telecommunications companies and data processing companies to build a 'virtuous circle' where each feeds off the developments and breakthroughs of the others to allow products and services to develop with lightening speed.[3] This means that information technology, and the information society, is moving forward more quickly than the law, and textbooks, can keep up with. The ambitious aim of this chapter is to gaze into the crystal ball: an exercise in futurology which may assist the reader in staying one step ahead of developments in technology and the challenges these will surely bring to lawyers and lawmakers.

22.1 **Future developments**

22.1.1 **Greater connectivity, greater control**

Exercises in futurology are often exercises in futility. That accepted, if we are to glance into the future of information technology law we need to identify what may prove to be the key characteristics of future technology design. Commentators seem to be split as to how future technologies will affect our society.

Some suggest that as technologies get more complicated and carry out many more functions we will seek refuge in tied devices that specialise in carrying out the tasks we ask of them.[4] For them the future is centred upon consumer devices such as the iPhone, the TiVo video recorder, and the Microsoft xBox. These devices are so-called 'closed boxes' meaning the software supplied with them is proprietary and cannot be studied or copied except within the very strict limits allowed by ss. 50A–50C of the Copyright Designs and Patents Act 1988. For these commentators the natural progression of devices is that each successive generation of consumer devices becomes more powerful and contains more functions but at a cost of freedom.

---

[2] It took only 36 years for physics to progress from Ernest Rutherford's discovery of the atomic nucleus in 1909 to J. Robert Oppenheimer's successful testing of the first atomic bomb, 'Trinity' in Los Alamos, New Mexico.

[3] An example of a virtuous circle would be in the delivery of entertainment products. Firstly a software development: data compression, allowed for the development of compressed sound files (MP3s). This led to an ability to trade MP3s across the improved network speeds of 56.6KBpS. This led hardware manufacturers to design an MP3 player. In turn one manufacturer (Apple) developed an 'online shop'. Increased demand for downloads from the shop led to faster network connection speeds being required (Broadband), this allowed for video to be downloaded. Apple (and others) then designed higher capacity multimedia players. This allowed TV and Movies to be sold via the online shop. This called for more capacity in storage and a better interface. Consumers started to demand access wherever they went to wireless capability was added eventually the MP3 player converged with the mobile phone as the iPhone/smartphone. Next no doubt will come fully functional tablet devices connected to the mobile phone network.

[4] See, e.g. J. Zittrain, *The Future of the Internet and How to Stop It* (2008).

> **Case Study** Home Video Recording
>
> The first generation home video recording devices was the VCR which had no copy controls and allowed for transfer from TV to video and from video to video.
>
> The second generation was the VCR with macrovision. This prevented copying from pre-recorded videos with macrovision protection.
>
> The third generation was DVD-R. This allowed not only for macrovision but also for digital TPMs to be used to prevent copying.
>
> The fourth generation is PVRs (hard disc recorders such as Sky+ and TiVo). These have a variety of controls; some designed for consumer benefits, others for the benefit of the manufacturer or TV broadcaster. Thus Sky+ has a comprehensive parental control system which prevents playback of programmes rated '15' or '18' before the watershed times. Also parents can set controls for all content or varieties of content. There is also an advanced copy control mechanism called CGMS-A (copy generation management system—A) which allows Sky to encode all broadcasts with a copy activation code of either '00' copying allowed; '10' one time only copy; or '11' no copying allowed.

The effects of Sky's CGMS-A system were keenly felt by Sky+ subscribers in late 2008 when a glitch with Sky's broadcast signal caused all material stored to the HDD to be encoded '11' for a period meaning users could not archive programmes by copying them to DVD.[5] Although in this case it was a technical glitch that had caused the problem it served to demonstrate how these latest generation PVRs give control over recordings not to the user in the way a VCR, or even a third-generation DVD did, but retains an element of control to the provider. This leads Jonathan Zittrain to title closed boxes which retain a connection to their supplier 'tethered appliances'. Tethered appliances are devices, such as Sky+ but also including everyday devices such as the Mp3/Mp4 players, mobile phones, games systems, Sat Navs, and eBook Readers, which 'offer a more consistent and focussed user experience at the expense of flexibility and innovation'.[6] For Zittrain, and others, believe that the driving force for social change in the next ten years will be technologically-driven unless consumers mobilise against the technology industry.[7]

If this view is correct then the future direction of IT Law will be move further towards protecting individual rights as tethered technology intervenes more into our private actions. Examples from current technology which illustrate the need for law to intervene include Apple's refusal to license a number of third-party applications for 'App Store' listing: the only effective way of installing third party applications on an iPhone or iPod Touch. To date Apple has refused a number of applications including *NetShare*,

---

[5] G. Cole, 'Sky+ glitch sparks fears over TV archiving', *The Guardian*, 4 December 2008: http://www.guardian.co.uk/technology/2008/dec/04/television-sky-programme-backups.

[6] Zittrain, above n. 4, 59.

[7] See further L. Lessig, *Code Version 2.0*, (2006), 323–324; L. Lessig, *Free Culture: How Big Media Uses Technology and the Law to Lock Down Culture and Control Creativity* (2005), 139–161; J. Cannataci, 'Lex Personalitatis and Technology-driven Law' (2008) 5:1 *SCRIPTed* 1: http://www.law.ed.ac.uk/ahrc/script-ed/vol5-1/editorial.asp.

an application that would allow the iPhone to act as a wireless hotspot for other devices, and a number of applications which involve more mature content such as *Hottest Girls; Ninja Words*, and *BeautyMeter* as well as books with mature themes such as David Carnoy's *Life Music*. The former would seem to invite the application of competition law while the latter, although clearly legal, invites questions about free expression in the tethered environment. Future developments with products such as PVRs, games systems, and eBook readers will no doubt raise further questions about the form and limits of copyright and in particular about the limits technological devices such as content management systems may rightfully impose of fair dealing. This view of the future of the information society thus envisages greater concentration of control in the hands of the hardware, software, and telecommunications companies, with law as the tool of the consumer. In this design rather disappointingly law is reactive and passive.

22.1.2 **Greater connectivity, greater freedom**

There is another model of the future. This sees the empowering nature of technological developments as the main driver of social change.[8] For this school of thought, although it may be true that Apple rules the iPhone environment, the opportunities offered by smartphones and similar technological developments set users free rather than controlling their actions. Yes it is true that if you buy an iPhone you accept the rule of Apple. Yes Apple say which network operator(s) you may use your iPhone on and yes Apple control what applications you may add to your iPhone through iTunes. But this is a conscious trade off by the consumer. They choose to buy an iPhone. If they do not like Apple's fine grained control over the aftermarket for their product they may choose an alternative, whether that be another Smartphone such as the HTC Magic or the Blackberry Bold or a simpler traditional handset such as a Motorola L6.

The point for these commentators is that the end user has a choice. She may choose to buy the tied Apple device with all the controls this brings or she may choose a more traditional handset which brings her more freedom. This is therefore a market decision: the buyer trades the freedom from control a simple handset offers for the functionality of a Smartphone handset. The key for commentators who believe that technological advances offer greater freedom is that without the advances in technology afforded by devices such as the iPhone the consumer does not have this choice. Advances in technology offer greater choice to the consumer: this allows the consumer to decide how much control they are willing to cede to device manufacturers in return for greater functionality.

This approach assumes that society drives technological advances rather than technological advances driving changes in society. Some new technologies make massive breakthroughs despite their design and marketing being undertaken by niche suppliers. Think of the success of the Blackberry handset manufactured by unfashionable Canadian company Research in Motion or the dual cyclone vacuum cleaner manufactured in

---

[8] See, e.g. R. Heilbroner, 'Do Machines Make History?' in M. Smith & L. Marx, *Does Technology Drive History?: The Dilemma of Technological Determinism* (1994); G. Ropohl, 'A Critique of Technological Determinism' in P. Durban & F. Rapp, *Philosophy and Technology* (1983); L. Winner, 'Do Artefacts Have Politics?' in L. Winner, *The Whale and the Reactor: a Search for Limits in an Age of High Technology* (1986).

the first instance by start-up company Dyson. These products broke through because people wanted what they offered: for one email on the move and for the other the end to constantly buying new vacuum bags and losing power while vacuuming. Now think of technology designed at massive cost by leading corporations which have failed as there was no market for them. Sony has probably the most unenviable history of failed platforms with Betamax, Minidisc, Laserdisc, and Universal Media Disk (UMD) all failing to find success in the market. Sony must be relieved that Blu-ray eventually won the format war with HD-DVD. Why though so many failures from such a successful company? At each turn their technology was the best or most convenient but Sony's desire to retain proprietary control of the format led to competitors producing cheaper and more convenient alternatives. The reason Blu-ray broke the mould is that Sony, learning from their previous mistakes, agreed to share Blu-ray technology with competitors. Sony is not the only leading company who has invested heavily in technology which has failed to find a market. Failures such as Motorola's Iridium satellite communications system and Apple's Newton handheld PDA demonstrate that the largest and most successful of electronics companies can misjudge the market.

If it is the case that society determines whether or not a new technology succeeds in the marketplace then this changes our assumptions for modelling legal responses to technological developments. This suggests new technologies will not, as of themselves, restrict or control the rights and choices of individuals. The law does not need therefore to react to threats posed by new technologies; instead the law must ensure consumers have the market information they need to assess whether or not to invest in a new product or service. This means the role of the law switches from being reactive to proactive. The role of the law is to ensure the market functions by allowing customers to exchange information and to allow them access to new products and services whosoever markets them.[9]

22.1.3 Developing technologies and legal responses

Whichever approach is correct we will soon see major upheaval in the information society as developments drive us towards the next evolution of the World Wide Web, web 3.0. Web 3.0 is almost certain to impact hugely on all corners of society as it will be both driven by the promise of what the new technology can offer and by the desire of users to make use of that potential. The web is in many ways the ultimate 'killer application': everyone wants access to it and in a variety of formats (home computer, mobile phone, PDA or smart device such as the Amazon Kindle, games system, etc.); it is free (excepting access charges) and is of limitless potential.

Web 3.0 will change our interaction with information in all forms, and in particular will change how we locate and access data. If you are of the techno-deterministic school you will believe that the law will be called upon to respond to changes in the way data is gathered, stored, and accessed, with the major challenges being data privacy, data security, and freedom of expression. If you are a follower of the socially-mediated school then you will believe the major challenges will be in ensuring quality of access to data, e-government and the digital divide, and data security and privacy.

---

[9] A. Murray, *The Regulation of Cyberspace: Control in the Online Environment* (2007), Ch. 6.

Whichever approach you favour the outcome is the same when web 3.0 is released it will unsettle the established legal settlement in the same way that web 2.0 unsettled copyright law, defamation, and freedom of expression. The law must evolve to reflect how *both* society and technology evolve, for the truth is that neither the techno-deterministic school nor the socially-mediated school are completely correct. The information society is rooted in connections between people enabled by, and mediated by, digital technology. The area of law which deals with this is similarly rooted in both technology and society. To predict the future of information technology law we must therefore begin by predicting how technology will enable social changes in the next five to ten years.

22.2 **Web 3.0**

The first issue that lawyers will have to deal with is the technology of web 3.0. This is because web 3.0 is a rather more radical departure than the change from web 1.0 to web 2.0. While the development of web 2.0 was evolutionary: a democratising process that gave more power to the user, web 3.0 has to potential to be revolutionary.[10] There are many descriptions of web 3.0[11] and the technology which will drive it but most people begin their search to define it by referring to the creator of web 1.0, Sir Tim Berners-Lee. In 1999 Berners-Lee described what he termed 'the semantic web'. It was 'a Web [in which computers] become capable of analyzing all the data on the Web—the content, links, and transactions between people and computers. [Although] yet to emerge, when it does, the day-to-day mechanisms of trade, bureaucracy and our daily lives will be handled by machines talking to machines. The "intelligent agents" people have touted for ages will finally materialize.'[12] Web 3.0 is slightly different to the semantic web, but as Berners-Lee has explained more recently he sees the semantic web as a cornerstone of web 3.0 which is a more complex software controlled network than the one we are accustomed to today.[13] What will this mean to the user? While much of the discussion of web 3.0 and the semantic web is still at an early stage and is mired in the technical language of software developers,[14] the applications of the semantic web are already becoming apparent to the user.

One is so-called 'augmented reality' (AR) already available in a rudimentary form on some Smartphones. AR uses a number of tools including GPS positioning, embedded markers, and photo image processing to add to user's experience of an event or a place. For instance the Wikitude AR travel guide for the Google Android operating system

---

[10] I say 'has the potential to be' because of the variety of web 3.0 definitions. Some such as Berners-Lee's (below) are truly revolutionary others are more conservative.

[11] See, e.g. R. McManus 'Eric Schmidt defines web 3.0', *ReadWriteWeb* 7 August 2007: http://www.readwriteweb.com/archives/eric_schmidt_defines_web_30.php; S. Baker, 'Web 3.0', *Business Week* 24 October 2006: http://www.businessweek.com/the_thread/blogspotting/archives/2006/10/web_30.html.

[12] T. Berners-Lee & M. Fischetti, *Weaving the Web: The Original Design and Ultimate Destiny of the World Wide Web by its Inventor* (2000).

[13] V. Shannon, 'A "more revolutionary" Web', *International Herald Tribune* 23 May 2006: http://www.iht.com/articles/2006/05/23/business/web.php.

[14] See e.g. O. Lasilla & J. Hendler, 'Embracing "Web 3.0"' (2007) *IEEE Internet Computing* 90; J. Cardoso, 'The Semantic Web Vision: Where are we?' (2007) *IEEE Intelligent Systems* 22.

allows the user to access web data on landmarks in their surroundings. The user points their phone at a landmark of interest, such as Edinburgh Castle, and enables the phone's camera function. The phone will then overlay on the screen data about Edinburgh Castle such as opening times, cost of entry etc. and offer a link to the Wikitude entry on Edinburgh Castle as well as mapping it on Google Maps.

AR is likely to become much more immersive in future as technology allows for augmented advertising on billboards and bus shelters and RFID technology allows for the development of the 'internet of things' as all manner of devices are fitted with RFID chips which may pass data on to enabled devices such as mobile phones, laptops, or even smart clothing or jewellery. It is even possible that AR can be reversed where instead of the user interrogating a tag for information on anything from a tourist site to a new movie the user is interrogated for the purpose of targeted advertising. Thus the businessman in the Alexander McQueen (RFID tagged) suit on his journey into work will, in passing the advertising screens adjacent to the tube escalators, receive an advert for the new season Dior Homme range, while the cleaner three steps behind him wearing his (similarly tagged) Levi Jeans receives an advertisement for GAP Denim. This is still AR but in reverse to the way we usually think of it. The user receives personalised information rather than asking for it.

AR is though only one aspect of web 3.0. Another is the creation of a personalised web experience based on your needs and previous records.

> **★ Example** web 3.0
>
> Sarah is going out for the night. She wants to go to see a movie and then for some dinner afterwards at a restaurant near to the movie theatre. She turns to her laptop and types in to her semantic search assistant 'I want to see a funny movie and then eat at a good restaurant. What are my options?' Unlike web 2.0 search engines a web 3.0 search assistant can understand a complex request such as this and produce complex results.
>
> Sarah will get a limited number of personalised recommendations with a selection of movies showing in her local cinema and suitable restaurants nearby. These can be displayed as single pages showing the name of the movie recommended, where it is showing, when it is show-ing, reviews, the trailer, and a map of the cinema location. Alongside this information will be similar information for the restaurant: reviews, menus, location, opening times etc. Sarah's personalised search assistant can even remember preferences such as 'I don't like Mexican food' and filter out inappropriate restaurants.
>
> Then with a single click Sarah can both book tickets for the movie and reserve a table at the restaurant. Her laptop will ensure all the details are sent to her Smartphone wirelessly including an e-ticket for the cinema so Sarah does not have to queue on her arrival.

If that all sounds like science fiction you may be surprised to know the technology which allows this to happen is already being tested in universities. Your web 3.0 search assistant will have artificial intelligence which allows it to learn your preferences and then deliver to you what you want or need. It will be able to prepare a personalised newspaper, Negroponte's *Daily Me* become real,[15] drawn from stories reported worldwide and collated on a news service such as *Google News*. Your assistant will be able to learn from your reading habits if you are interested in banking regulation, tennis, or celebrity gossip and deliver to you news only of interest to you. In addition all your devices and accounts will work in harmony so if you book flights and a hotel to attend a conference in Rome your calendar will automatically block this time out, your email account will set up an out of office reply, your bank account will be informed of your travel plans, thus avoiding the embarrassment of your card being refused overseas, and your calls will be automatically forwarded to your mobile (assuming these are all things you want).

It is clear from these examples that there are three defining features of web 3.0. Two are user experience features while the third is a technical feature.

→ Highlight Web 3.0 Features

1. User immersion in the digital environment via augmented reality and the 'internet of things'. The human-machine interface changes from being via a screen to natural interaction.

2. Personalised services via your semantic assistant. The idea of 'static' web pages is replaced with dynamic services tailored to the user.

3. Artificial intelligence allows your devices and accounts to learn your preferences and to 'mix and mash' available data to provide tailored results.

From the lawyer's point of view the key attribute of web 3.0 is the last of these three features. The creation of the semantic web involves intelligent agents which will make decisions on our behalf.[16] This changes the nature of the interaction between human and machine: we need to ask is the machine now an actor in any transaction or does it remain simply a carrier of information?[17] This is likely to be the key issue for information technology lawyers in the next ten years.

22.3 **Law 2.0**

It is my belief that the role of the cyber lawyer and the design of the network he is seeking to control are symbiotically linked. We can trace developments in cyberlaw theory as being in parallel with technological developments. The internet has a long history

---

[15] An idea first advanced by Nicholas Negroponte in *Being Digital* (1995), 152–154, and developed extensively by Sunstein in *Republic.com*.

[16] In truth this is not new. Intelligent agents already filter content. Cleanfeed, discussed in Ch. 14, filters for obscene content, while Google Safesearch routinely filters Google search returns to remove obscene and offensive content. The difference with web 3.0 is both the scale of such systems and with their ability to learn, a key cornerstone of intelligence.

[17] See B. Latour, *Reassembling the Social: An Introduction to Actor-Network-Theory* (2005); G. Teubner, 'Rights of Non-humans? Electronic Agents and Animals as New Actors in Politics and Law' (2006) 33 *Journal of Law and Society* 497.

which may be traced back as far as 1969 but the discipline of cyberlaw remained undeveloped until the 1990s. This is because there was no need for the separate discipline of cyberlaw before the release of web 1.0 as the internet was mainly used by a select group of researchers and was self-regulated. Research into information technology law in the 1970s and 1980s was focussed on the computer itself with books on databanks and data processing being the expected output of the researcher into law and computers, as the subject was then known.[18]

The release of web 1.0 was heralded as the beginning of serious research in, and the practice of, cyberlaw. As discussed in chapter four the first stage of this process was the development of the cyberlibertarian movement which responded to the apparent freedom of cyberspace with claims of an unregulable space freed from the constraints of real world regulation by its lack of internal borders and its virtual border with 'real space'. This corresponds to the early network environment which was seen as lawless, a digital equivalent of the old 'wild west' where individuals made claims for valuable land (cybersquatting) and regulation came from within the community only (Town Hall Democracy).[19]

The cyberpaternalist movement quickly appeared in opposition to this idealised view of self-regulation and local democracy.[20] The rise of cyberpaternalism may be mapped on to the rise of regulatory intervention in cyberspace. New initiatives such as the UNCITRAL Model Law on Electronic Commerce;[21] the intervention of the courts in early cybersquatting cases such as *Princeton Review v Stanley H. Kaplan Educational Center Ltd*;[22] and early attempts at legislative intervention such as the Communications Decency Act of 1996,[23] had demonstrated that legal initiatives could affect actions in 'sovereign cyberspace'. Thus as with cyberlibertarianism, cyberpaternalism's roots may be found in the environment it is seeking to study. Even cyberpaternalism's techno-centric approach to law and the information society may be traced to the preponderant use of technological solutions at this period in time. Thus the Digital Millenium Copyright Act focuses legal protection on technical protection measures, while the Telecommunications Act of 1996 required for the installation of the so-called V-chip (a chip used to control minor access to violent or explicit content) in all TV sets sold in the US. Cyberpaternalism and cyberlibertarianism may therefore be seen as reflecting two stages of regulatory development seen in web 1.0. They cannot, unfortunately, claim to be at the forefront of developments as a study of the timelines shows that they formed as explanations of pre-existing structures of control within the larger environment of cyberspace.

---

[18] See, e.g. A. Westin & M. Baker, *Databanks in a Free Society: Computers, Record Keeping and Privacy* (1972).

[19] See S. Biegal, 'New Directions in Cyberlaw' *Los Angeles Daily Journal* 29 November 1996: http://www.gseis.ucla.edu/iclp/nov96.html; H. H. Perritt Jr, 'Cyberspace Self-Government: Town-Hall Democracy or Rediscovered Royalism?' 12 *Berkeley Technology Law Journal* 413 (1997); J. P. Barlow, *A Declaration of Independence for Cyberspace*, 8 February 1996: http://homes.eff.org/~barlow/Declaration-Final.html; D. Johnson and D. Post, 'Law and Borders—The Rise of Law in Cyberspace', 48 *Stanford Law Review* 1367 (1996).

[20] J. Reidenberg, 'Lex Informatica: The Formation of Information Policy Rules Through Technology' (1998) 76 *Texas Law Review* 553; L. Lessig, *Code and Other Laws of Cyberspace* (1999).

[21] Discussed in Ch. 16.

[22] 94 Civ. 1604 (MGC) (S.D.N.Y., filed March 9, 1994). Discussed in Ch. 12.

[23] Discussed in Ch. 14.

The arrival of web.2.0 obviously changed this settlement and as a result one would expect a change in the views of commentators on cyberlaw and regulation. As has been extensively discussed throughout this book web 2.0 was an evolutionary development which saw interactivity brought to the fore of the user experience with democratisation of the internet being seen as the key social contribution of web 2.0. We therefore should have seen the development of a new parallel theory of cyberlaw: law 2.0 if you will. This was not the case. Instead we saw a further incremental development of cyberlaw theory: law 1.5, rather than law 2.0. Law 1.5 manifested itself in the development of network communitarianism. Here commentators focussed on the power of the network to connect individuals and their ability as a community to influence and to accept or reject regulatory interventions.[24] Again the school of thought follows the environmental developments. Now instead of the direct delivery of content seen in web 1.0 and reflected by Lawrence Lessig's model of external modalities pressing down on a pathetic dot, network communitarianism reflects the divergent network of user-generated content and social networking found in web 2.0 by focussing on concepts such as Andrew Murray's active dot matrix.

It is clear there that since the development of the web in late 1990 at each stage of development in the environment of cyberspace there has been a corresponding development in cyberlaw theory. With this in mind we can finally predict what is likely to be the next development in cyberlaw theory. With web 3.0 the focus switches from users to intelligent network agents. Web 3.0 will in some ways see a retreat to the values of web 1.0 with users seeking assistance from the network designers to make sense of the massive amounts of information now available online. But to retain the values of web 2.0 we seek not to return to delivered content but to extend the feeling of personalisation and control that web 2.0 brings. For lawyers and lawmakers though the key aspect of web 3.0 is the intelligent agents designed to manage the information flow. A malevolent programmer could use these to censor content, to gather personal information, to observe patterns of behaviour or even, due to the interaction between the virtual and the physical environment predicted by augmented reality, to track the physical whereabouts of individuals.

The legal issues raised by web 3.0 are therefore substantially the same as those seen in both web 1.0 and web 2.0: privacy, freedom of expression, censorship, democratic discourse, property rights, and commercial interests. The difference is where the locus of power is to be found. Whereas web 1.0 was about passive consumerism and web 2.0 was about user democracy web 3.0 will be about personalisation and user selectivity, **BUT** that personalisation will be done by the user in concert with their device settings: in other words our semantic search assistant will have the power to tailor our web 3.0 experience.

The next school of cyberlaw is therefore likely to focus on the role machines will play as intelligent agents in the network. Law 2.0 will, like web 3.0, be an evolutionary development on what we conceive of as cyberlaw today. The early building blocks of law 2.0 may already be seen in the work of Gunther Teubner.[25] It is likely to ask questions such as how may electronic agents control individuals? Who is responsible for the actions

---

[24] See discussion in Ch. 4 and A. Murray, *The Regulation of Cyberspace: Control in the Online Environment*, Ch. 8.   [25] Above n. 17.

of electronic agents? Is it ethical to use electronic agents to control certain forms of expression? How may users protect their rights to personal and data privacy when they rely heavily on electronic agents? And how do we prevent abuse (including criminal abuse) of the network of electronic agents that form the backbone of web 3.0?

A central question for both philosophers and lawyers will be does an over-reliance on technology potentially lead to injustice? Too often today individuals suffer unjustly because of poorly programmed computer systems which can make all forms of unjust decisions from denying them access to housing or to financial benefits through to denying them access to an overseas state.[26] It is this social injustice that forms the basis of the *Little Britain* comedy sketch 'computer says no' and it brings with it the spectre of a Kafkaesque situation where someone is denied access to a just decision for reasons beyond their comprehension and which they cannot challenge because perversely the computer is entrusted as the arbiter in such decisions. This is likely to be a major focus of law 2.0. When intelligent agents begin making decisions based upon learned behaviour they exceed just the programmed parameters: they are likely to make errors and these errors are likely to cause harm. Thus law 2.0 is going to be the most philosophical enquiry into law. It is going to require us to discuss identity, decision making, fairness, and justice against a backdrop of computer aided decision making.

There is no reason to suspect web 3.0 will be anything less than a positive revolution in the way we interact with technology. Already early experiments with augmented reality are producing exciting outcomes while we all already benefit from some of the early fruits of the network of things through such tools as contactless payment systems, interactive mobile maps, and car tracking and remote disabling systems used to prevent theft of high value vehicles. Unfortunately no-one turns to lawyers when everything is going well. Lawyers tend to become involved when systems fail, when individuals suffer injustice, or when harm has occurred. Much of law 2.0 will be about anticipating these potential harms and about identifying and delineating lines of responsibility, in particular with regard to non-human actors, which aside from animals in tort cases, are a whole new category of actors on the legal stage. My advice for anyone hoping to practice law 2.0 is therefore read Franz Kafka's *The Trial* and Arthur C. Clarke's *2001: A Space Odyssey*. Neither, I hope, are a vision of our future, but both raise questions of control, morality, and justice which will be at the centre of both web 3.0 and law 2.0.

▎FURTHER READING

Books

J. Zittrain, *The Future of the Internet: And How to Stop it* (2008)

L. Winner, *The Whale and the Reactor: a Search for Limits in an Age of High Technology* (1986)

---

[26] See J. Bing, 'Code, Access and Control' in M. Klang & A. Murray (eds) *Human Rights in the Digital Age* (2005).

B. Latour, *Reassembling the Social: An Introduction to Actor-Network-Theory* (2005)

T. Berners-Lee & M. Fischetti, *Weaving the Web: The Original Design and Ultimate Destiny of the World Wide Web by its Inventor* (2000)

Chapters and Articles

J. Bing 'Code, Access and Control' in M. Klang & A. Murray (eds), *Human Rights in the Digital Age* (2005)

J. Cannataci, 'Lex Personalitatis and Technology-driven Law' (2008) 5:1 SCRIPTed 1

G. Teubner, 'Rights of Non-humans? Electronic Agents and Animals as New Actors in Politics and Law' (2006) 33 *Journal of Law and Society* 497

INDEX

A

absolute privilege
defences to defamation claims, 141
abstraction
computer associates three-step test, 200
abuse of process
defamation, and, 149
abusive registration
domain names
ICANN Uniform Dispute Resolution
Policy, 309
Nominet Dispute Resolution Service, 314
acceptance, offer and
electronic contracts, 416–20
active inducement principle
peer-to-peer networks, 245
actor network theory (ANT)
network communitarianism, and, 66–7
advance fee
fraud, 389
advanced electronic signatures
ecommerce, 429, 430–4
adware
digital trespass, 95–6
age play
pornography, and, 377–9
aggregation of information
copyright, 230–3
digitisation, and, 38–9
RFID technology and privacy, 509
ALOHANET
internet, development of, 19, 20
anonymity
democratic digital divide, and, 549–51
ANPR
see **automatic number plate recognition**
ARPANET
internet, development of, 18–19
assets, virtual
disputes over, 562–5
generally, 96–7
misappropriation of, 99–101
taxation of, 566
theft, 566
valuation of, 567
virtual theft, 97–8
asymmetric PKE encryption
ecommerce, 432
asymmetric PKE signatures
ecommerce, 433
atoms
bits, and

generally, 9–10
music, 10–11
social interaction, 11–12
attribution
creative commons licences, 262–3
Australia
regulation of cyberspace, 73
automatic number plate recognition (ANPR)
enhanced CCTV, 498–9

B

bandwidth
ISP regulatory measures
capping, 73
shaping, 73
theft, 403–5
Barendt, Eric
freedom of expression, and, 120
Barlow, John Perry
declaration of independence for cyberspace, 56
disintermediation, and, 40
bills of exchange
historical payment methods, 437–8
binary notation
use of, 7–8
biometrics
enhanced CCTV and pattern
recognition, 499–502
bits
atoms, and
generally, 9–10
music, 10–11
social interaction, 11–12
binary notation, 7–8
digitisation process, 7
introduction, 3–6
legal challenges, 13–15
meaning, 5
protection of information, 15
rivalrous and non-rivalrous goods, 12–13
Von Neumann architecture, 6
Black Baron
computer misuse, 344–5
blocking
ISP regulatory measures, 73
blogging
defamation, 164–5
democratic digital divide, and, 545–9
online political speech, 123–4
border controls
enhanced CCTV, 502

Borland functionality test
copyright infringement, 202
branding
domain names, 297
trade marks, and, 289–91

C

caching
copyright, and, 228–33
card not present
fraud, 390
Cate, Professor Fred
characteristics of digital information, 464
data growth, reasons for, 37
CCTV, enhanced
privacy, and
border controls, 502
code of practice, 502–7
generally, 496–8
pattern recognition (automatic number
plate recognition), 498–9
pattern recognition (biometrics), 499–502
retention of images, 504
child abuse images
generally, 369–71
possession of, 374
China
regulation of cyberspace, 73–4
virtual theft, 97–8
civil liberties
denial of service, 349
commercial speech
cyber-speech
First Amendment, and, 127
information society, and, 128–9
spam regulation in Europe, 129–31
spam regulation in US, 131–33
comparison
computer associates three-step
test, 200
computer associates
three-step test, 200
computer misuse
denial of service
civil liberties, and, 349
law reform, 347–8
scope of offence, 346–7
unauthorised impairment, 348
virtual sit-ins, 349–50
generally, 327–30
hacking
employee hackers, 332–7
external hackers, 337–40
generally, 330–2
hacking tools, supply of, 350–2
McKinnon case, 340–2

mailbombing, 345–6
supply of devices, 350–2
viruses
Black Baron, 344–5
legal history, 342–4
Mad Hacker, 343–4
unauthorised modification, 342
web defacement, 345–6
confidential information
digital property rights, 88–9
connectivity
future developments
control, 570–2
freedom, 572–3
consumer protection
electronic contracts, 423–4
content filtering
ISP regulatory measures, 73
content identification
ISP regulatory measures, 73
contract terms
electronic contracts
consumer protection, 423–4
enforcement, 423–4
express terms, 421
generally, 420–1
implied terms, 422
incorporation by reference, 421–2
contributory infringement
peer-to-peer networks, 240
convergence
author's royalties, 45–6
multi-purpose devices, 44–5
multiple file copies, 46–7
copyright
aggregation, 230–3
caching, 228–33
conclusions, 265
creative commons, 261–4
database rights, and
Database Directive, 271–3
generally, 268–9
listings cases, 269–71
digital environment, 222–3
digital property, and, 87–8
Digital Rights Management, and, 43–4
generally, 173–5
infringement
literal copying, 191–6
non-literal copying, 196–209
permitted acts, 209–12
linking, 223–8
meaning, 87
peer-to-peer networks
A&M Records v Napster, 236–41
early cases, 234–6
generally, 233–4

litigation outside US, 246–50
Pirate Bay Case, 250–4
post-*Napster*, 241–6
Sweden v Neij, 250–4
technical measure to prevent, 254–8
volume litigation, 258–9
public domain, information and, 260–4
software
obtaining protection, 186–9
scope of protection, 189–91
copyright infringement
literal copying
introduction, 191
offline piracy, 192–3
online piracy, 193–6
look and feel infringement
after *Navitaire*, 207–9
Computer Associates v Altai, 199–201
introduction, 197–9
Lotus v Borland, 201–2
Navitaire v easyJet, 205–7
UK courts, 202–5
non-literal copying
generally, 196–7
look and feel infringement, 197–209
permitted acts, 209–12
creative commons
copyright, 261–4
establishment of, 181
credit cards
electronic payments, 441
crime
bandwidth theft, 403–5
child abuse images
generally, 369–71
possession of, 374
computer misuse
denial of service, 346–50
generally, 327–30
hacking, 330–42
hacking tools, supply of, 350–2
mailbombing, 345–6
viruses, 342–5
web defacement, 345–6
conclusions, 408
Convention on Cybercrime, 405–8
cyberstalking, 297–8
cyberterrorism, 398–403
fraud
card not present fraud, 390
escrow fraud, 392
419 advance fee fraud, 389
generally, 388–92
identity fraud, 392–4
overpayment fraud, 392
phishing, 393
Russian scam, 389

generally, 387
grooming, 395–7
harassment, 397–8
identity theft, 392–4
obscenity
cross-border issues, 48–50
Hicklin principle, 355–6
historical development, 353–5
Obscene Publications Acts, 356–7
pornography
age play, 377–9
child abuse images, 369–71
conclusions, 386
cross-border issues, 48–50
extreme pornography, 379–83
First Amendment, 364
global standard, 361–3
historical development, 353–4
introduction, 357
Miller standard, 362
policing pseudo images in UK, 371–4
policing pseudo images
internationally, 375–7
possession of child abuse images, 374
possession of extreme pornography, 380
private regulation, 383–5
Reno decision, 367–9
UK standard, 358–61
US statutory interventions, 363–7
Virgin Killer, 384
cross-border speech
freedom of expression, 114–16
cybercrime
see also **crime**
Convention on, 405–8
cyberlaw
future developments, 576–9
cyber-liberalism
cross-border issues, 47–8
cyberlibertarianism
regulation of digital environment, 56–60
cyberpaternalism
regulation of digital environment, 60–2
cyber-speech
commercial speech
First Amendment, and, 127
information society, and, 128–9
spam regulation in Europe, 129–31
spam regulation in US, 131–33
conclusion, 133
freedom of expression
approached compared, 112
cross-border speech, 114–16
European approach, 111–12
First Amendment approach, 110–11
legal difficulties, 118–19
Yahoo! cases, 113–14, 116–17

cyber-speech (*Cont.*)
  hate speech
    generally, 124–5
    inter-state speech, 126–7
    society, and, 125–6
  introduction, 103–4
  political speech
    economics and the media, 120–1
    generally, 119–20
    online speech, 122–4
  world wide web
    generally, 104–5
    internet fora, 105–6
    law and society, 107
    personal websites, 106
    web 2.0, 107–10
cybersquatting
  domain names, and, 303–5
cyberstalking
  offences, 297–8
cyberterrorism
  offences, 398–403
Cyphermint
  e-money, 443–4

D

data
  meaning, 468
  sensitive personal data, 469
data controllers
  generally, 473
  state supervision of, 491–4
data growth
  reasons for, 37
data processing
  meaning, 472
data processors
  role of, 473
data protection
  Cate's characteristics of digital
      information, 464
  conclusion, 494
  correcting data, 490–1
  data controllers
    generally, 473
    state supervision of, 491–4
  data processors, 473
  Data Protection Act 1984, 466–7
  Data Protection Act 1998, 465–6
  Data Protection Directive, 467–8
  Data Protection Registrar, 473
  data subjects
    data subject rights, 484
    generally, 473
    subject access, 485–90
  data users, 473

  forms of data, 468–70
  Information Commissioner, 473–4, 492–4
  introduction, 463
  managing data, 490–1
  personal data
    conditions for processing, 479–84
    digitisation of, 464–5
  principles, 474–8
  processing data, 470–3, 475–8
  relevant filing system, 487
  subject access, 485–90
  use of data, 470–3
Data Protection Registrar
  role of, 473
data retention
  privacy, and, 517–21
data subjects
  data subject rights, 484
  generally, 473
  subject access, 485–90
data users
  change of terminology, 473
database right
  copyright, and
    Database Directive, 271–3
    generally, 268–9
    listings cases, 269–71
  generally, 179–80
  sui generis right
    after *BHB*, 284–6
    *British Horseracing Board Ltd v William
        Hill*, 279–84
    Database Directive, 274–6
    Fixtures Marketing cases, 276–9
databases
  database right
    copyright, and, 268–73
    generally, 179–80
    sui generis right, 274–86
  information society, and, 286–7
  introduction, 267
  meaning, 277
  spin-off databases, protection of, 278
  substantial investment, meaning of, 278
  substantial part, meaning of, 283
de facto software patents
  European Patent Convention, under, 217–8
debt substitution
  electronic payments, 440
defamation
  abuse of process, and, 149
  conclusion, 165–6
  intermediary liability
    generally, 152–3
    ISP publisher liability in UK, 156–60
    ISPs as publishers, 153–4
    safe harbour, 155–6

introduction, 135–6
publication and republication
   Dow Jones v Gutnick, 142–5
   Dow Jones v Jameel, 148—9
   generally, 141–2
   King v Lewis, 147–8
   Loutchansky v Times Newspapers, 145–7
   Ministry of Justice consultation paper, 151–2
   online defamation post-*Jameel*, 150–1
tort
   defences, 140–1
   generally, 136
   jurisdiction, 138–40
   publication, 137–8
   statements, 137
user-generated content
   blogosphere libel, 164–5
   Facebook libel, 162–4
   generally, 160–2
democratic digital divide
anonymity, 549–51
blogosphere, and, 545–9
free speech, 549–51
generally, 544–5
social networking, 551–3
denial of service
civil liberties, and, 349
law reform, 347–8
scope of offence, 346–7
unauthorised impairment, 348
virtual sit-ins, 349–50
Digicash
e-money, 442–4
digital divide
democratic divide
   anonymity, 549–51
   blogosphere, and, 545–9
   free speech, 549–51
   generally, 544–5
   social networking, 551–3
global divide, 538–9
Norris, Pippa, 538
social divide
   generally, 539–41
   opening competition, 541–4
digital environment
copyright, and, 222–3
regulation of
   conclusions, 80–1
   cyberlibertarianism, 56–60
   cyberpaternalism, 60–2
   introduction, 55
   Lawrence Lessig's modalities, 62–6
   network communitarianism, 66–70
regulators
   private regulators, 70–3
   states, 73–80

supranational regulation
   generally, 73–5
   Internet Governance Forum (IGF), 78–80
   World Summit on the Information Society
     (WSIS), 75–8
digital ownership
conclusions, 101
digital property
   concept, 84–5
   confidential information, 88–9
   information as, 85–6
   intellectual property rights, 86–8
digital trespass
   adware, 95–6
   generally, 89–90
   indexing, 91–2
   Intel v Hamidi, 92
   scraping, 91–2
   servers, to, 90–1
   spyware, 95–6
   UK law, 92–5
introduction, 83–4
virtual property
   generally, 96–7
   misappropriation of, 99–101
   virtual theft, 97–8
digital property
concept, 84–5
confidential information, 88–9
information as, 85–6
intellectual property rights, 86–8
digital public sphere
conclusion, 553–4
digital divide
   democratic divide, 544–53
   global divide, 538–9
   Norris, Pippa, 538
   social divide, 539–44
e-government
   generally, 527–33
   Public Service Network, 536–7
   pulled resources, 537
   transformational government, 533–6
Habermas's universals for ideal speech, 526
scope of, 525–7
Digital Rights Management (DRM)
information management, 43–4
network communitarianism, and, 69–70
digital trespass
adware, 95–6
generally, 89–90
indexing, 91–2
Intel v Hamidi, 92
scraping, 91–2
servers, to, 90–1
spyware, 95–6
UK law, 92–5

Digital Watermarking
information management, 43
digitisation
bits, and, 7
convergence
author's royalties, 45–6
multi-purpose devices, 44–5
multiple file copies, 46–7
cross-border issues
cyber-liberalism, 47–8
pornography, 48–50
information, of
aggregation, 38–9
collection, 38–9
data growth, reasons for, 37
Digital Rights Management,
and, 43–4
disintermediation, 39–42
exploitation, 38–9
information management, 43–4
management, need for effective, 36
intellectual property rights,
and, 180–1
law, and, 50
personal data, 464–5
society, and, 35–6
disengagement
democratic digital divide, 546
disintermediation
digitisation, and, 39–42
dispute resolution
domain names
cybersquatting, 303–5
early disputes in UK, 301–3
early disputes in US, 298–301
ICANN Uniform Dispute Resolution
Policy, 307–12
Nominet Dispute Resolution
Service, 312–16
Phones4U, 305–7
distribution
disintermediation, 39–42
domain names
brand values, 297
disputes concerning
cybersquatting, 303–5
early disputes in UK, 301–3
early disputes in US, 298–301
ICANN Uniform Dispute Resolution
Policy, 307–12
Nominet Dispute Resolution
Service, 312–16
Phones4U, 305–7
sale of, 296
second level domains, 295–6
sex.com, 296–8
uniform resource locator, properties
of, 294–5

E

ecommerce
electronic contracts
conclusion, 434–5
contract terms, 420–4
contracting informally, 413–16
electronic signatures, 427–34
formal contracts, 424–7
introduction, 413
regulating offer and acceptance, 416–20
electronic payments
alternative payment systems, 440–1
conclusion, 457–8
early e-money, 441–4
Electronic Money Directive, 444–52
history of payment methods, 436–8
token payments, 439–40
taxation, and
Ottawa Framework general
principles, 454
place of sale, 452–3
sales tax, 453–5
VAT on Ecommerce Directive, 455–7
e-government
generally, 527–33
Public Service Network, 536–7
pulled resources, 537
transformational government, 533–6
Electoral Commission
online political speech, 122
electronic contracts
conclusion, 434–5
contract terms
consumer protection, 423–4
enforcement, 423–4
express terms, 421
generally, 420–1
implied terms, 422
incorporation by reference, 421–2
electronic signatures
advanced, 429, 430–4
asymmetric PKE encryption, 432
asymmetric PKE signatures, 433
formalising, 429–30
generally, 427–9
primary function, 428
standard, 429
symmetric encryption, 431
formal contracts, 424–7
informal contracts
contract formation, 414–6
generally, 413–4
introduction, 413
regulating offer and acceptance
communicating acceptance, 418–20
Electronic Commerce
Directive, 416–8

electronic payments
  bills of exchange, 437–8
  conclusion, 457–8
  credit cards, 441
  debt substitution, 440
  early e-money
    consumer reluctance, 444
    Cyphermint, 443–4
    Digicash, 442–4
    Mondex, 442
    novation, 441
    Peppercoin, 443
  Electronic Money Directive
    e-money issuers, 444–8
    review of, 448–52
  fund transfers, 441
  history of payment methods, 436–8
  liquidity, functions of, 440
  money, functions of, 439
  token payments, 439–40
Electronic Product Code
  RFID technology and privacy, 509
electronic signatures
  advanced, 429, 430–4
  asymmetric PKE encryption, 432
  asymmetric PKE signatures, 433
  formalising, 429–30
  generally, 427–9
  primary function, 428
  standard, 429
  symmetric encryption, 431
e-money
  consumer reluctance, 444
  Cyphermint, 443–4
  Digicash, 442–4
  Electronic Money Directive
    e-money issuers, 444–8
    review of, 448–52
  Mondex, 442
  novation, 441
  Peppercoin, 443
employees
  hacking, and, 332–7
encryption
  electronic signatures
    asymmetric PKE encryption, 432
    symmetric encryption, 431
end-to-end architecture
  internet, development of, 26
enforcement
  electronic contracts, 423–4
enhanced CCTV
  privacy, and
    code of practice, 502–7
    generally, 496–8
    pattern recognition (automatic number
      plate recognition), 498–9
    pattern recognition (biometrics), 499–502

environments, virtual
  conclusion, 565–7
  game versus law, 560–2
  generally, 556–7
  virtual assets
    taxation of, 566
    theft of, 566
    valuation of, 567
  virtual gods, 559–60
  virtual people, 557–8
  virtual property
    disputes over, 562–5
    generally, 96–7
    misappropriation of, 99–101
    virtual theft, 97–8
  virtual worlds, 557–8
  when worlds collide, 565–7
escrow fraud
  offences, 392
European Digital Library
  public domain, information in, 260
European Patent Convention
  software protection, 217–18
exploitation of information
  digitisation, and, 38–9
express terms
  electronic contracts, 421

F

Facebook
  defamation, 162–4
fair comment
  defences to defamation claims, 140
Fanning, Shawn party analogy
  peer-to-peer networks, 237
file sharing (peer-to-peer networks)
  copyright, and
    A&M Records v Napster, 236–41
    early cases, 234–6
    generally, 233–4
    litigation outside US, 246–50
    Pirate Bay Case, 250–4
    post-*Napster*, 241–6
    Sweden v Neij, 250–4
    technical measure to prevent, 254–8
    volume litigation, 258–9
filtration
  computer associates three-step
    test, 200
First Amendment to US Constitution
  cyber-speech
    commercial speech, 127
    freedom of expression, 110—11
  pornography, 364
  text of, 110
first sale right
  exhaustion of, 191

forums
 cyber-speech, and, 105–6
fraud
 card not present fraud, 390
 escrow fraud, 392
 419 advance fee fraud, 389
 generally, 388–92
 identity fraud, 392–4
 overpayment fraud, 392
 phishing, 393
 Russian scam, 389
freedom of expression
 approached compared, 112
 cross-border speech, 114–16
 European approach, 111–12
 First Amendment approach, 110–11
 legal difficulties, 118–19
 Yahoo! cases, 113–14, 116–17
freedom of speech
 democratic digital divide,
  and, 549–51
Fry, Stephen
 web 2.0 definition, 108
fund transfers
 electronic payments, 441
future developments
 connectivity
  control, 570–2
  freedom, 572–3
 cyberlaw, 576–9
 legal responses to developing
  technologies, 573–4
 web 3.0, 574–6

G

gods, virtual
 regulation of, 559–60
Google
 cache facility, 228–33
 information exploitation,
  and, 38
grooming
 offences, 395–8

H

Habermas, J.
 universals for ideal speech, 526
hacking
 employee hackers, 332–7
 external hackers, 337–40
 generally, 330–2
 hacking tools, supply of, 350–2
 McKinnon case, 340–2
harassment
 offences, 397–8

hate speech
 generally, 124–5
 inter-state speech, 126–7
 society, and, 125–6
hidden readers
 RFID technology and privacy, 509
hidden tags
 RFID technology and privacy, 509
higher level protocols
 hypertext transfer protocol (HTTP), 32
 real-time transfer protocol (RTP), 31
 simple mail transfer protocol (SMTP), 31
 stratification, use of, 30–1
 voice over the internet protocol (VoIP), 31
 world wide web (WWW), 32–4
hosts
 communications over the internet, 23
hyperlinking
 copyright, and, 223–8
hypertext transfer protocol (HTTP)
 development of worldwide web, 32

I

IBCOS test
 copyright infringement, 204
ICANN
 see **Internet Corporation for Assigned
  Names and Numbers**
identity fraud
 offences, 392–4
IGF
 see **Internet Governance Forum**
identity theft
 offences, 392–4
immigration controls
 enhanced CCTV, 502
implied terms
 electronic contracts, 422
incorporation by reference
 electronic contracts, 421–2
indexing
 digital trespass, 91–2
Information Commissioner
 data protection, 473–4, 492–4
informational paradox
 nature of information, 14
infringement of copyright
 literal copying
  introduction, 191
  offline piracy, 192–3
  online piracy, 193–6
 look and feel infringement
  after *Navitaire*, 207–9
  Computer Associates v Altai, 199–201
  introduction, 197–9
  Lotus v Borland, 201–2

Navitaire v easyJet, 205–7
  UK courts, 202–5
non-literal copying
  generally, 196–7
  look and feel infringement, 197–209
  permitted acts, 209–12
Intel v Hamidi
  digital trespass, 92
intellectual property rights
  copyright
    aggregation, 230–3
    caching, 228–33
    conclusions, 265
    databases, and, 268–73
    digital environment, 222–3
    digital property, and, 87–8
    Digital Rights Management, and, 43–4
    generally, 173–5
    linking, 223–8
    meaning, 87
    peer-to-peer networks, 233–59
    public domain, information
      and, 260–4
    software, 186–91
  copyright infringement
    literal copying, 191–6
    non-literal copying, 196–209
    permitted acts, 209–12
  databases
    copyright, and, 268–73
    database right, 179–80, 274–86
    information society, and, 286–7
    introduction, 267
  digital property, 86–8
  digitisation, and, 180–1
  introduction, 171–3
  MacCormick's legal properties, 290
  patents
    digital property, and, 86–7
    generally, 175–7
    meaning, 86
    software, 212–20
  software
    conclusions, 220–1
    copyright, 186–91
    copyright infringement, 191–212
    history, 183–6
    patents, 212–20
    trade marks, 177–9
interface message processors (IMPs)
  internet, development of, 18
intermediary liability
  defamation
    generally, 152–3
    ISP publisher liability in UK, 156–60
    ISPs as publishers, 153–4
    safe harbour, 155–6

internet
  functionality
    end-to-end architecture, 26
    hosts, 23
    internet protocol version 4 (IPv4), 24
    internet protocol version 6 (IPv6), 24
    internet service providers, 25
    IP address, 24
    net neutrality, 27–30
    network access points, 25
    network service providers, 25
    packets, 24
    recipients, 23
    sending TCP/IP communications, 23–6
    wireless local area networks, 25
    wireless wide area networks, 25
  higher level protocols
    hypertext transfer protocol (HTTP), 32
    real-time transfer protocol (RTP), 31
    simple mail transfer protocol (SMTP), 31
    stratification, use of, 30–31
    voice over the internet protocol (VoIP), 31
    world wide web (WWW), 32–34
  history
    ALOHANET, 20
    ARPANET, 18–19
    building the internet, 19–22
    interface message processors (IMPs), 18
    internet protocols, ground rules for, 21
    introduction, 17–18
    network control protocols (NCPs), 21
    open architecture network, 20
    SATNET, 20
    transmission control protocol/internet
      protocol (TCP/IP), 22
    transmission control protocols (TCPs), 22
Internet Assigned Numbers Authority
  (IANA)
  domain name management, 76
Internet Corporation for Assigned Names and
  Numbers (ICANN)
  domain name management, 76
  Uniform Dispute Resolution Policy (UDRP)
    abusive registration, 309
    background, 307–9
    criticisms, 311–12
    defences, 310
    ICANN's responsibilities, 308
    mandatory nature, 309–10
    prerequisites for a claim, 310
    procedure, 310–11
    statistics, 311
Internet Governance Forum (IGF)
  mandate, 78
  supranational regulation, 78–80
internet protocols
  ground rules for, 21

internet protocols (*Cont.*)
  higher level protocols
    hypertext transfer protocol (HTTP), 32
    real-time transfer protocol (RTP), 31
    simple mail transfer protocol (SMTP), 31
    stratification, use of, 30–1
    voice over the internet protocol (VoIP), 31
    world wide web (WWW), 32–4
  IP addresses, 24
  transmission control protocol/internet protocol
      (TCP/IP), 22
  version 4 (IPv4), 24
  version 6 (IPv6), 24
internet service providers
  intermediary liability
    ISPs as publishers, 153–4
    publisher liability in UK, 156–60
  internet, development of, 25
  regulation of cyberspace, 70–3
Internet Watch Foundation (IWF)
  regulation of cyberspace, 70–3

J

John of Utynam's patent
  patent history, 175
jurisdiction
  defamation, 138–40

L

layering
  higher level protocols, 30–1
Lessig, Lawrence
  intellectual property rights and
      digitisation, 181
  modalities of regulation, 62–6
licences
  creative commons, 262–4
linking, web
  copyright, 223–8
liquidity
  functions of, 440
literal copying
  copyright infringement
    introduction, 191
    offline piracy, 192–3
    online piracy, 193–6
location services
  code of practice, 515
  privacy, and, 514–5
look and feel infringement
  after *Navitaire*, 207–9
  Computer Associates v Altai, 199–201
  introduction, 197–9
  Lotus v Borland, 201–2
  Navitaire v easyJet, 205–7
  UK courts, 202–5

M

MacCormick, Neil
  properties of intellectual property rights, 290
Macrossan test
  patent protection for computer software, 219
Mad Hacker
  computer misuse, 343–4
mailbombing
  computer misuse, 345–6
**massively multiplayer online role playing
  games (MMORPGs)**
  see **virtual environments**
Meiklejohn, Alexander
  freedom of expression, and, 119
mere conduit
  defences to defamation claims, 158
Miller standard
  obscenity, and, 362
misappropriation
  virtual property, 99–101
Mondex
  e-money, 442
money
  see also **electronic payments, e-money**
  functions of, 439
Murray, Andrew
  network communitarianism, 66–70
music
  digitisation, and, 10–11
  Lawrence Lessig's modalities of regulation,
      and, 62–6

N

Napster
  disintermediation, and, 41–2
Negroponte, Nicholas
  internet forums, 105–6
net neutrality
  internet, development of, 27–30
network access points
  internet, development of, 25
network communitarianism
  regulation of digital environment, 66–70
network control protocols (NCPs)
  internet, development of, 21
network service providers
  internet, development of, 25
networks
  see also **internet**
  introduction, 16–17
Nominet Dispute Resolution Service
  abusive registration, 314
  appeals, 315–16
  burden of proof, 313–14
  defences, 314

establishment of, 312–13
procedure, 313
review of, 316
Ryanair, 314–15
non-engagement
democratic digital divide, 546
non-literal copying
copyright infringement
generally, 196–7
look and feel infringement, 197–209
non-rivalrous goods
meaning, 12–13
Norris, Pippa
digital divide, 538
novation
e-money, 441
**number plate recognition, automatic
(ANPR)**
enhanced CCTV, 498–9

O

obscenity
cross-border issues, 48–50
Hicklin principle, 355–6
historical development, 353–5
Obscene Publications Acts, 356–7
Ofcom
regulation of cyberspace, and, 73
offences
bandwidth theft, 403–5
child abuse images
generally, 369–71
possession of, 374
computer misuse
denial of service, 346–50
generally, 327–30
hacking tools, supply of, 350–2
hacking, 330–42
mailbombing, 345–6
viruses, 342–5
web defacement, 345–6
conclusions, 408
Convention on Cybercrime, 405–8
cyberstalking, 297–8
cyberterrorism, 398–403
fraud
card not present fraud, 390
escrow fraud, 392
419 advance fee fraud, 389
generally, 388–92
identity fraud, 392–4
overpayment fraud, 392
phishing, 393
Russian scam, 389
generally, 387
grooming, 395–7

harassment, 397–8
identity theft, 392–4
obscenity
cross-border issues, 48–50
Hicklin principle, 355–6
historical development, 353–5
Obscene Publications Acts, 356–7
pornography
age play, 377–9
child abuse images, 369–71
conclusions, 386
cross-border issues, 48–50
extreme pornography, 379–83
First Amendment, 364
global standard, 361–3
historical development, 353–4
introduction, 357
Miller standard, 362
policing pseudo images in UK, 371–4
policing pseudo images internationally,
375–7
possession of child abuse images, 374
possession of extreme pornography,
380
private regulation, 383–5
Reno decision, 367–9
UK standard, 358–61
US statutory interventions, 363–7
Virgin Killer, 384
offer and acceptance
electronic contracts, 416–20
online gaming
virtual property
generally, 96–7
misappropriation of, 99–101
virtual theft, 97–8
open architecture network
internet, development of, 20
O'Reilly, Tim
web 2.0 definition, 108
overpayments
fraud, 392

P

packets
communications over the internet, 24
parliamentary privilege
defences to defamation claims, 141
passports
radio frequency identifier chips, 507
patentability
test for, 176
patents
digital property, and, 86–7
generally, 175–7
meaning, 86

patents (*Cont.*)
  software
    Aerotel Ltd v Telco and Macrossan's
      application, 218–20
    computer-related inventions
      (VICOM), 214–15
    European Patent Convention, 217–18
    introduction, 212–14
    State Street Bank, effect of, 215–16
pattern recognition
  enhanced CCTV
    automatic number plate recognition, 498–9
    biometrics, 499–502
peer-to-peer networks
  copyright, and
    A&M Records v Napster, 236–41
    early cases, 234–6
    generally, 233–4
    litigation outside US, 246–50
    Pirate Bay Case, 250–4
    post-*Napster*, 241–6
    Sweden v Neij, 250–4
    technical measure to prevent, 254–8
    volume litigation, 258–9
people, virtual
  regulation of, 557–8
Peppercoin
  e-money, 443
permitted acts
  copyright infringement, 209–12
personal data
  see also **data protection**
  conditions for processing, 479–84
  digitisation of, 464–5
  processing of, 474–5
  sensitive personal data
    meaning, 469
    processing, 483–4
phishing
  fraud, 393
Phorm
  information exploitation, and, 38
piracy
  offline, 192–3
  online, 193–6
PKE encryption, asymmetric
  ecommerce, 432
PKE signatures, asymmetric
  ecommerce, 433
political speech
  economics and the media, 120–1
  generally, 119–20
  online speech, 122–4
pornography
  age play, 377–9
  child abuse images
    generally, 369–71
    possession of, 374

  conclusions, 386
  cross-border issues, 48–50
  extreme pornography, 379–83
  First Amendment, 364
  global standard, 361–3
  historical development, 353–4
  introduction, 357
  Miller standard, 362
  policing pseudo images
    internationally, 375–7
    UK, 371–4
  possession
    child abuse images, 374
    extreme pornography, 380
  private regulation, 383–5
  Reno decision, 367–9
  UK standard, 358–61
  US statutory interventions, 363–7
  Virgin Killer, 384
port blocking
  ISP regulatory measures, 73
possession
  child abuse images, 374
  extreme pornography, 380
privacy
  data protection
    Cate's characteristics of digital
      information, 464
    conclusion, 494
    correcting data, 490–1
    data controllers, 473
    data controllers, state supervision of, 491–4
    data processors, 473
    Data Protection Act 1984, 466–7
    Data Protection Act 1998, 465–6
    Data Protection Directive, 467–8
    Data Protection Registrar, 473
    data subject, 473
    data subject rights, 484
    data user, 473
    forms of data, 468–70
    Information Commissioner, 473–4, 492–4
    introduction, 463
    managing data, 490–1
    personal data, conditions for
      processing, 479–84
    personal data, digitisation of, 464–5
    principles, 474–8
    processing data, 470–3, 475–8
    subject access, 485–90
    use of data, 470–3
  data retention, 517–21
  enhanced CCTV
    code of practice, 502–7
    generally, 496–8
    pattern recognition (automatic number
      plate recognition), 498–9
    pattern recognition (biometrics), 499–502

location services, 514–5
radio frequency identifier chip (RFID) tracking
    EU action plan, 512–14
    regulation of, 509–12
    use of, 507–9
Regulation of Investigatory Powers Act, 516–7
profiling
RFID technology and privacy, 510
property, virtual
disputes over, 562–5
generally, 96–7
misappropriation of, 99–101
taxation of, 566
theft, 566
valuation of, 567
virtual theft, 97–8
protocol blocking
ISP regulatory measures, 73
pseudo images, policing
internationally, 375–7
UK, 371–4
public domain
copyright, and, 260–4
public interest
defences to defamation claims, 140
Public Service Network (PSN)
e-government, and, 536–7
publication
defamation
    Dow Jones v Gutnick, 142–5
    Dow Jones v Jameel, 148—9
    generally, 141–2
    King v Lewis, 147–8
    Loutchansky v Times Newspapers, 145–7
    Ministry of Justice consultation paper, 151–2
    online defamation post-*Jameel*, 150–1
pulled resources
e-government, and, 537

Q

qualified privilege
defences to defamation claims, 141

R

radio frequency identifier chip (RFID) tracking
EU action plan, 512–14
minimum guidelines, 510
policy issues, 512
prohibited activities, 510
regulation of, 509–12
threats to privacy, 509–10
use of, 507–9
real-time transfer protocol (RTP)
use of, 31

recipients
communications over the internet, 23
registered trade marks
see also **trade marks**
use of, 291–2
registration, abusive
domain names
    ICANN Uniform Dispute Resolution
        Policy, 309
    Nominet Dispute Resolution Service, 314
regulation of digital environment
conclusions, 80–1
cyberlibertarianism, 56–60
cyberpaternalism, 60–2
introduction, 55
Lawrence Lessig's modalities, 62–6
network communitarianism, 66–70
regulators
    private regulators, 70–3
    states, 73–80
supranational regulation
    generally, 73–5
    Internet Governance Forum (IGF), 78–80
    World Summit on the Information Society
        (WSIS), 75–8
regulators
private regulators, 70–3
states, 73–80
relevant filing system
data protection, and, 487
republication
defamation
    Dow Jones v Gutnick, 142–5
    Dow Jones v Jameel, 148–9
    generally, 141–2
    King v Lewis, 147–8
    Loutchansky v Times Newspapers, 145–7
    Ministry of Justice consultation
        paper, 151–2
    online defamation post-*Jameel*, 150–1
RFID tracking
see **radio frequency identifier chip (RFID)**
    tracking
Richardson, John
copyright infringement test, 204
rivalrous goods
meaning, 12–13
royalties
digital convergence, and, 45–6
Russian scam
fraud, 389

S

safe harbour
intermediary liability, 155–6
SATNET
internet, development of, 20

Saudi Arabia
regulation of cyberspace, 74–5
scraping
digital trespass, 91–2
search engines
intermediary liability, 159–60
trade marks, and, 320–2
secondary markets
trade marks, and, 317–20
sensitive personal data
meaning, 469
processing, 483–4
servers
trespass to, 90–1
Shaw's principle
freedom of expression, 118
signatures, electronic
advanced, 429, 430–4
asymmetric PKE encryption, 432
asymmetric PKE signatures, 433
formalising, 429–30
generally, 427–9
primary function, 428
standard, 429
symmetric encryption, 431
simple mail transfer protocol (SMTP)
use of, 31
sit-ins, virtual
denial of service, 349–50
site blocking
ISP regulatory measures, 73
social digital divide
generally, 539–41
opening competition, 541–4
social interaction
digitisation, and, 11–12
social networking
democratic digital divide, and, 551–3
web 2.0, and, 108–10
social responsibility
freedom of expression, and
approached compared, 112
cross-border speech, 114–16
European approach, 111–12
First Amendment approach, 110–11
legal difficulties, 118–19
Yahoo! cases, 113–14, 116–17
social systems theory (SST)
network communitarianism, and, 66–7
software
conclusions, 220–1
copyright
obtaining protection, 186–9
scope of protection, 189–91
copyright infringement, 191–212
history, 183–6
patents

Aerotel Ltd v Telco and Macrossan's
application, 218–20
computer-related inventions
(VICOM), 214–15
European Patent Convention, 217–18
introduction, 212–14
State Street Bank, effect of, 215–16
space shifting
peer-to-peer networks, 235–6, 239
spam regulation
direct marketing, 129
Europe, 129–31
statistics, 128
US, 131–33
spyware
digital trespass, 95–6
states
regulation of digital environment
generally, 73–5
Internet Governance Forum (IGF), 78–80
World Summit on the Information Society
(WSIS), 75–8
stratification
higher level protocols, 30–1
subject access
data protection, 485–90
supply of devices
computer misuse, 350–2
supranational regulation
generally, 73–5
Internet Governance Forum (IGF), 78–80
World Summit on the Information Society
(WSIS), 75–8

T

taxation
ecommerce
Ottawa framework general
principles, 454
place of sale, 452–3
sales tax, 453–5
VAT on Ecommerce Directive, 455–7
virtual assets, 566
terrorism
see **cyber-terrorism**
theft
bandwidth, 403–5
identities, 392–4
virtual property, 97–8, 566
token
electronic payments, 439–40
trade marks
branding, and, 289–91
characteristics, 293–4
conclusions, 322
domain name disputes

cybersquatting, 303–5
early disputes in UK, 301–3
early disputes in US, 298–301
ICANN Uniform Dispute Resolution
    Policy, 307–12
Nominet Dispute Resolution Service,
    312–16
Phones4U, 305–7
domain names
    brand values, 297
    sale of, 296
    second level domains, 295–6
    sex.com, 296–8
    uniform resource locator, properties
        of, 294–5
generally, 177–9
global business environment, and
    registered trade marks, 291–2
    trade mark characteristics, 293–4
    unregistered trade marks, 292–3
ICANN Uniform Dispute Resolution Policy
    abusive registration, 309
    background, 307–9
    criticisms, 311–12
    defences, 310
    ICANN's responsibilities, 308
    mandatory nature, 309–10
    prerequisites for a claim, 310
    procedure, 310–11
    statistics, 311
Nominet Dispute Resolution Service
    abusive registration, 314
    appeals, 315–16
    burden of proof, 313–14
    defences, 314
    establishment of, 312–13
    procedure, 313
    review of, 316
    Ryanair, 314–15
registered trade marks, 291–2
search engines, 320–2
secondary markets, 317–20
unregistered trade marks, 292–3
transmission control protocols (TCPs)
generally, 22
TCP/IP
    communications using, 23–6
    meaning, 22
trespass, digital
adware, 95–6
generally, 89–90
indexing, 91–2
Intel v Hamidi, 92
scraping, 91–2
servers, to, 90–1
spyware, 95–6
UK law, 92–5

U
unauthorised impairment
denial of service, 348
unauthorised modification
computer misuse, 342
**Uniform Dispute Resolution Policy (ICANN
    UDRP)**
abusive registration, 309
background, 307–9
criticisms, 311–12
defences, 310
ICANN's responsibilities, 308
mandatory nature, 309–10
prerequisites for a claim, 310
procedure, 310–11
statistics, 311
uniform resource locator (URL)
properties of, 294–5
unique identifiers
RFID technology and privacy, 509
unregistered trade marks
see also **trade marks**
use of, 292–3
user-generated content
defamation
    blogosphere libel, 164–5
    generally, 160–2
    Facebook libel, 162–4
unsolicited mail, regulation of
direct marketing, 129
Europe, 129–31
statistics, 128
US, 131–33

V
VAT
ecommerce
    Ottawa framework general
        principles, 454
    place of sale, 452–3
    sales tax, 453–5
    VAT on Ecommerce Directive, 455–7
veritas
defences to defamation claims, 140
Virgin Killer
pornography, and, 384
regulation of cyberspace, and, 72, 80–1
virtual assets
disputes over, 562–5
generally, 96–7
misappropriation of, 99–101
taxation of, 566
theft, 566
valuation of, 567
virtual theft, 97–8

virtual environments
  conclusion, 565–7
  game versus law, 560–2
  generally, 556–7
  virtual assets
    taxation of, 566
    theft of, 566
    valuation of, 567
  virtual gods, 559–60
  virtual people, 557–8
  virtual property
    disputes over, 562–5
    generally, 96–7
    misappropriation of, 99–101
    virtual theft, 97–8
  virtual worlds, 557–8
  when worlds collide, 565–7
virtual gods
  regulation of, 559–60
virtual people
  regulation of, 557–8
virtual property
  disputes over, 562–5
  generally, 96–7
  misappropriation of, 99–101
  taxation of, 566
  theft, 566
  valuation of, 567
  virtual theft, 97–8
virtual sit-ins
  denial of service, 349–50
virtual worlds
  regulation of, 557–8
viruses
  Black Baron, 344–5
  legal history, 342–4
  Mad Hacker, 343–4
  unauthorised modification, 342
**voice over the internet protocol
(VoIP)**
  use of, 31
Von Neumann architecture
  meaning, 6

W

web defacement
  computer misuse, 345–6
web linking
  copyright, and, 223–8
web 2.0
  definition, 108
web 3.0
  future developments, 574–6
wireless local area networks
  internet, development of, 25
wireless wide area networks
  internet, development of, 25
**World Summit on the Information
Society (WSIS)**
  supranational regulation, 75–8
world wide web (WWW)
  cyber-speech
    generally, 104–5
    internet fora, 105–6
    law and society, 107
    personal websites, 106
    web 2.0, 107–10
  development of, 32–4
**Working Group on Internet
Governance (WGIG)**
  role of, 77–8